# FISH  NUTRITION

# CONTRIBUTORS

Laurence M. Ashley

Roger E. Burrows

L. M. Dickie

L. Friedman

Pietro Ghittino

John E. Halver

W. H. Hastings

D. J. Lee

Edwin T. Mertz

Arthur M. Phillips, Jr.

S. I. Shibko

R. O. Sinnhuber

S. F. Snieszko

H. L. Tarr

# FISH NUTRITION

*Edited by* **JOHN E. HALVER**

*Western Fish Nutrition Laboratory*
*Bureau of Sport Fisheries and Wildlife*
*U. S. Department of the Interior*
*Cook, Washington*

ACADEMIC PRESS          1972
New York   San Francisco   London
*A Subsidiary of Harcourt Brace Jovanovich, Publishers*

ACADEMIC PRESS, INC.
111 Fifth Avenue, New York, New York 10003

*United Kingdom Edition published by*
ACADEMIC PRESS, INC. (LONDON) LTD.
24/28 Oval Road, London NW1

LIBRARY OF CONGRESS CATALOG CARD NUMBER: 68-8432

PRINTED IN THE UNITED STATES OF AMERICA

# CONTENTS

## 3 The Protein and Amino Acid Needs

EDWIN T. MERTZ

## 4 Lipid Requirements

D. J. LEE AND R. O. SINNHUBER

## 5 Nonnutrient Components of the Diet

L. FRIEDMAN AND S. I. SHIBKO

## 10   Nutritional Pathology

LAURENCE M. ASHLEY

## 11   The Diet and General Fish Husbandry

PIETRO GHITTINO

## Appendix

# LIST OF CONTRIBUTORS

Numbers in parentheses indicate the pages on which the authors' contributions begin.

LAURENCE M. ASHLEY (439), Western Fish Nutrition Laboratory, Bureau of Sport Fisheries and Wildlife, U. S. Department of the Interior, Cook, Washington

ROGER E. BURROWS* (375), Salmon-Cultural Laboratory, Bureau of Sport Fisheries and Wildlife, U. S. Department of Interior, Longview, Washington

L. M. DICKIE (327), Marine Ecology Laboratory, Bedford Institute of Oceanography, Fishery Research Board of Canada, Dartmouth, Nova Scotia

L. FRIEDMAN† (181), Department of Nutrition and Food Science, Massachusetts Institute of Technology, Cambridge, Massachusetts

PIETRO GHITTINO (539), Instituto Zooprofilattico, Sperimentale del Piemonte e della Liguria, Via Bologna, Torino, Italy

JOHN E. HALVER (29), Western Fish Nutrition Laboratory, Bureau of Sport Fisheries and Wildlife, U. S. Department of the Interior, Cook, Washington

* Present address: 2842 Magnolia St., Longview, Washington.
† Present address: Division of Toxicology, Food and Drug Administration, Washington, D. C.

W. H. HASTINGS (327), Fish Farming Experimental Station, Bureau of Sport Fisheries and Wildlife, U. S. Department of the Interior, Stuttgart, Arkansas

D. J. LEE (145), Department of Food Science and Technology, Oregon State University, Corvallis, Oregon

EDWIN T. MERTZ (105), Department of Biochemistry, Purdue University, Lafayette, Indiana

ARTHUR M. PHILLIPS, JR.,* (1), Eastern Fish Nutrition Laboratory, Bureau of Sport Fisheries and Wildlife, U. S. Department of the Interior, Cortland, New York

S. I. SHIBKO† (181), Department of Nutrition and Food Science, Massachusetts Institute of Technology, Cambridge, Massachusetts

R. O. SINNHUBER (145), Department of Food Science and Technology, Oregon State University, Corvallis, Oregon

S. F. SNIESZKO (403), Eastern Fish Disease Laboratory, Bureau of Sport Fisheries and Wildlife, Kearneysville, West Virginia

H. L. TARR†† (255), Vancouver Laboratory, Fisheries Research Board of Canada, Vancouver, Canada

* Present address: 12 Melvin Avenue, Cortland, New York.
† Present address: Division of Toxicology, Food and Drug Administration, Washington, D. C.
†† Present address: 4160 Marine Drive, West Vancouver, B.C., Canada.

# PREFACE

This treatise is comprised of chapters submitted by recognized experts in the several subject matters developed. The contributions present the current state of knowledge of basic and applied nutritional requirements of fishes. The material is often fragmentary, which reflects the scattered research efforts by the small number of fishery scientists available in the scientific community. Often the discussion must, of necessity, follow analogy from nutrition and metabolism studies with other animals. All too often the sequence of the discussion of a metabolic pathway is interrupted by the lack of research data. This is evident in the paucity of information on lipid nutrition and metabolism, and in the function of amino acids in pathways for protein metabolism in animals which utilize nearly half their diet as protein for efficient rapid growth.

Much of the material in this book concerns nutrition and metabolism of nutrients in salmonids simply because more work has been completed with these fishes. Recently however, fish have been recognized as important agricultural animals by the International Union of Nutritional Sciences. Considerable effort has been expended on basic nutrient requirements of cyprinids. New experimental laboratories have been built to study the nutrition of eels, and also of other fishes, prawns, and shellfish reared in brackish or seawater. More effort in scientific fish husbandry will undoubtedly occur as need and knowledge grow.

This treatise was not designed to present an exhaustive review of all information available in the general field of applied fish nutrition, but of some information on classes of nutrients and requirements for several types and classes of fishes. Thus, the student of fish nutrition may obtain a general review in perspective of similarities and differences on what is generally known about nutrient requirements of fishes, and will develop a concept of the similarities and differences which exist between requirements of different types of fishes and the established nutrient requirements of many agricultural animals.

This treatise was made possible by the special efforts and close cooperation of senior scientists who had many other responsibilities besides compiling a manuscript. Special thanks are due to Dr. C. B. Croston, who carefully reviewed all the manuscripts submitted, and assembled the Subject Index. Sincere appreciation is expressed for the long, patient understanding of my wife Jane and my family during the time this treatise was in preparation.

JOHN E. HALVER

# 1

# CALORIE AND ENERGY REQUIREMENT

*Arthur M. Phillips, Jr.*

1

## I. Introduction

### A. Definition

Classically, energy is defined as the capacity to do work and is required for all phases of body metabolism. The amount of energy required depends upon body activity; there is no time during life that energy is not needed. The minimum energy required is that necessary for the mere maintenance of life. Energy comes from the food that is eaten.

Two kinds of energy result from food catabolism, free ($\Delta F$) and heat ($\Delta H$) energy. Free energy is used for work, while heat energy is useful only for temperature control. In terms of work, heat energy is wasted.

### B. Measurement

Food energy is expressed in terms of calories. A large or kilogram calorie, abbreviated kcal (the one usually used in nutrition), is the amount of heat required to increase the temperature of 1 kg of water one degree centigrade. The gram calorie, abbreviated gcal, is the amount of heat necessary to raise the temperature of 1 gm of water one degree centigrade and is a smaller unit that is useful when dealing with low energy levels.

Since both free and heat energy may be expressed as heat, the calorie confounds them. This confounding does not limit usage because calories are used as comparative values.

## C. Source

The ultimate source of energy comes from food catabolism (destructive metabolism). The immediate source of energy is adenosine triphosphate (ATP). Adenosine diphosphate (ADP) traps energy that is formed during catabolism, forming ATP. The high energy bonds of ADP offer a means for energy storage so the body may receive a free flow of energy as required. This energy release has been likened to that from a storage battery (Maynard, 1962).

Both ADP and ATP have been isolated from fish tissue, indicating an energy cycle in these cold-blooded animals similar to that of the warm-blooded animals.

## II. Energy Requirement of Fish

### A. Total Energy

Schaeperclaus (1933) showed that the total energy required varies with the species and from the work of Lindstedt (1904) calculated that tench require 10 gcal per square decimeter of body surface per hour at 15°C; carp 25 gcal; and rainbow trout 60 gcal. These are in agreement with the ascending magnitude of values reported by other workers for the oxygen consumed and the respiratory rates of these fish species (Belding, 1929; M'Gonigle, 1932; Schaeperclaus, 1933).

Phillips and Brockway (1959) found that the energy requirement of brook, brown, and rainbow trout (*Salvelinus fontinalis, Salmo trutta*, and *Salmo irideus*) was similar. These workers reported that 2100 kcal were required to produce a pound of trout (4600 kcal/kg) after feeding high-calorie diets (excess of 700 kcal per pound or 1540/kg of food); 1200 kcal were required (2600 per kilogram) after feeding moderate calorie diets (all-meat diets containing 450 kcal per pound or 990/kg of food); and 900 kcal were required (2000 per kilogram) after feeding relatively low calorie diets (natural foods containing 336 kcal per pound or 640 kcal/kg of food). The energy required to produce a pound (kilogram) of trout varied with the diet but was relatively independent of water temperature. These requirements did not change with changes in water temperature, since as the water temperature increased additional calories were supplied by increased food allowance and the pounds of fish produced increased accordingly. With a decrease in water temperature, there was less fish growth and the lower levels of food provided reduced caloric intake.

Since this initial work Phillips and Hammer (1965), by altering the caloric ratio and diet composition, reduced the calories required to about 1800 per pound of fish produced (3960/kg) when feeding high calorie diets. Tiemeier *et al.* (1965) determined that 1700 kcal were required to produce a pound of channel catfish (*Ictalurus punctatus*) (3740/km) and calculations based upon the data of Fowler *et al.* (1966) provided a value of 1850 kcal to produce a pound of chinook salmon (*Oncorhynchus tshawytscha*) (4070 kcal/km). Thus, all three fish species have a similar caloric requirement under hatchery production conditions.

## B. Growth Energy

The estimation of the energy requirement for tissue production is not a simple calculation. Winberg (1960) has presented an excellent summary of fish metabolism and developed equations useful for estimating growth requirements. Winberg pointed out that calculations of growth energy requirements, from empirical data, for one species of fish are not necessarily applicable to other species. Precise methods for these estimations are not available, although attempts have been made to equate the known factors.

Winberg believes that the material in the yolk of the egg represents food composition close to optimal for the embryo. In chicks, at the end of embryonic development, 67% of the energy formerly in the yolk is present in the chick body. This probably represents near maximum utilization. Such efficiency would not be approached in older animals because body activity increases and the many disturbing factors of the environment play a vital role in calorie utilization. Calories used by the embryo for growth must now be used for activities necessary for survival such as search for food, protection from predators, and adjustment to environmental changes.

Ivlev (1939) (quoted by Winberg 1960) found in studies with the sac fry of sheatfish (*Silurus glanis*, that 65.7% of the calories in the yolk were present in the bodies of the fish at the time of complete yolk absorption. This is near the level reported for chicks and probably represents maximum utilization of energy for growth by these fish, if the yolk food is accepted as near optimal. If such efficiency were to be duplicated by growing fish fed hatchery diets or natural foods, the food composition would need to be near optimal and all body activities kept to a minimum. The normal activity of feeding fish decreases the efficiency of the utilization of even an optimal food. Sac fry are not subjected to these interferences and their efficiency of food utilization is greater in comparison to active swimming fish that must hunt for and feed upon an external food supply.

Winberg (1960), quoting the values of Rubner (1942), stated that between 14 and 33% of the calories consumed by pike (*Esox lucius*) were deposited in the body tissues. The actual amount deposited was dependent upon fish size and, starting with pike weighing 70 gm, the amount deposited first increased and then decreased as the fish grew.

Phillips and Brockway (1959), based upon empirical data, recovered approximately 30% of the calories fed in the tissues of the bodies of brook trout. These experiments were conducted on small (1.0–20.0 gm), rapidly growing brook trout over a 20-week experimental period. Subsequent studies have verified these results and the value has been a useful approximation for forecasting results from feeding different hatchery foods to trout.

Gerking (1952) reported that longear sunfish (*Lepomis megalotis*) weighing 10 gm utilized 33% of absorbed protein for growth. Longear sunfish weighing 105 gm utilized only 5% of their consumed protein for growth. The remaining protein was utilized for other purposes (energy?). He called the less efficient protein utilization with size increase a phenomenon of "aging."

Schaeperclaus (1933) calculated that the ratio between demands for growth and demands for sustenance in young rainbow trout depended upon their weight and varied from a ratio of 1:1.5 to 1:3.2. Schaeperclaus believes that these values would be average for most pond fish. From the data of Phillips and Brockway (1959), brook trout fall within this range (1:2.3).

Diet composition is of prime importance in maintaining maximum efficiency of the utilization of food calories for tissue production. The first prerequisite is a nutritionally complete diet with the proper ratios between the caloric sources.

From this discussion, it is readily seen that there is no one single value that can be given for the energy required for fish growth.

## C. MAINTENANCE ENERGY

By inference, the calories required for maintenance of the fish's body is the difference between that consumed and that deposited in the fish's body. By this method Phillips and Brockway (1959) arrived at the conclusion that 70% of the food calories is used by brook trout for maintenance purposes. Since this value was determined by difference, there are inherent errors. The usefulness of this value is limited because after feeding other diets with different ingredient ratios to various sizes of trout, similar results might not be found. The value of 70% for maintenance is not unreasonable, however, in view of nutrition studies upon other animals and is reasonably close to values calculated from the data of Brown (1957).

The energy required for maintenance metabolism varies with fish size, fish species, and environmental activity. This additional energy may be supplied by increased caloric intake.

## III. Factors Altering the Energy Requirements of Fish

A. Fish Species

Metabolism is a chemical action and therefore increases in rate with temperature. The metabolic rate of warm-water fish is greater than that of cold-water fish. In their normal habitats the energy requirement of warm-water fish is greater than that of equally active cold-water fish.

Recently Dean and Goodnight (1964) have shown that fish have an optimum temperature range that may be interpreted as providing the most desirable metabolic rate (and therefore optimal energy requirements) for the species. They found that black bass (*Micropterus salmoides*), a warm-water fish, fatigued more quickly (measured by changes in blood and tissue chemistry) in cold (5°C) than in warm water (20°C), but the crappie (*Pomoxis annularis*), a cold-water species, fatigued more quickly in the warm than in the cold water. The bluegill sunfish (*Lepomis macrochirus*), with a wider ecological temperature range, resisted fatigue at both temperatures.

Differences in metabolic rates and therefore in energy requirement may be estimated by the respiratory rate and oxygen consumption of fish. Belding (1929) reported that brook trout have a higher respiratory rate than carp (*Cyprinus carpio*), and it is presumed that brook trout have a higher metabolic rate and therefore higher energy requirement, than carp.

M'Gonigle (1932) concluded that at the same water temperature, brown trout consumed more oxygen per unit body weight than carp, thus illustrating a higher metabolic rate, and therefore a greater energy requirement. Schaeperclaus (1933) has shown a similar difference between trout, carp, and European tench (*Tinca tinca*).

Based upon oxygen consumption, Beamish (1964) found the energy requirement differed between five species of fish. Moss and Scott (1961) found that, under similar conditions, the standard metabolic rate of bluegill sunfish was lower than either large-mouth bass or channel catfish.

A sluggish fish, such as the carp, has a lower metabolic rate (and therefore a lower energy requirement) than do active fish, such as the pike.

Growth rate is a measure of energy requirement. Tunison and McCay (1938) reported no difference between the growth rates of brook, brown, rainbow, or lake trout (*Cristivomer namaycush*) and therefore under the conditions of their experiment [constant water temperature of 47°F (8.3°C) and a similar diet] it may be concluded that the energy requirements were similar for the four trout species. Other studies have shown a wide variation in growth rates between different fish species held under similar conditions (Cooper, 1935). The energy requirement of these species differ as widely as their growth rates.

## B. Water Temperature

For all practical purposes the body temperature of fish is similar to that of the water. As the water temperature increases or decreases, so does the metabolic rate of the fish and, therefore, the energy requirements. This increase (or decrease) may not be optimum for metabolism.

Sumner and Lanhan (1942) found that fish of the same species consumed more oxygen at a higher than a lower temperature. This increased oxygen intake indicates an increased metabolic rate and therefore an increased energy requirement. Brett (1965) found that at a water temperature of 24°C the basal metabolic rate of salmon (*Oncorhynchus*) was six times higher than at 5°C.

Fry (1947) has shown that when given the opportunity of living in an environment with a temperature gradient, goldfish (*Carassius auratus*) will remain in one temperature zone, by choice, most of the time.

Rozin and Mayer (1961), in an amazing experiment with goldfish, found that after a training period, the fish pressed a lever to cause a drop in the water temperature when it became too warm. The fish maintained their environment usually between 33.5° and 36°C.

These two experiments (Fry, 1947; Rozin and Mayer, 1961) show that goldfish will control their body temperature through the environmental temperature when possible and bring their metabolic rates to a seemingly optimum level thereby standardizing their energy requirements.

Changes in environmental temperatures change the energy requirements as shown by increased or decreased growth rates, respiratory rates, and oxygen consumptions. That the fish will fatigue more quickly when in abnormal temperatures (Dean and Goodnight, 1964) and will select their environmental temperature when allowed (Fry, 1947; Rozin and Mayer, 1961) indicates that some of these energy changes associated with environmental temperature may be undesirable in terms of optimal metabolism.

TABLE I

COMPARISON OF WEIGHTS OF BROOK TROUT STARVED IN WATER AT TEMPERATURES OF 8.2° AND 14.4°C

| Time (weeks) | Actual weight of fish held in water at 8.2°C (gm) | Weight of fish held in water at 14.4°C | | Difference |
| --- | --- | --- | --- | --- |
| | | Actual (gm) | Estimated (gm) | |
| 0 | 2.31 | 2.31 | — | — |
| 4 | 1.96 | 1.77 | 1.75 | +0.02 |
| 8 | 1.90 | 1.74 | 1.65 | +0.09 |
| 12 | 1.85 | 1.60 | 1.57 | +0.03 |

According to Sumner (1929) the metabolic rate of warm-blooded animals increases 10% for each degree centigrade rise in body temperature. In agreement with this, Schaeperclaus (1933) reported that for fish a rise of 10 degrees in water temperature nearly doubles the rate of metabolic activities until the optimum is reached.

Phillips *et al.* (1960) found a similar effect during starvation studies with brook trout. Table I illustrates data from these experiments. The trout were starved in water at 14.4° and 8.2°C, a difference of 6.2°C. If Sumner's relationship applies, the metabolic rate of fish held in the warmer water should be 62% greater than of those held in the colder water. If weight losses are valid estimates of metabolic rates, the fish starved in the warmer water should differ in weight from those starved in the colder water by 62%.

The estimated and actual weights of the starved fish for the three intervals are in reasonable agreement (Table I) and, for all practical purposes, the metabolism of the trout's body did indeed increase 10% for each degree centigrade rise in body temperature.

## C. FISH SIZE

Smaller fish have a higher metabolic rate than larger fish. This is indicated by the reduction in the growth rate of trout, held under constant environmental conditions and fed without diet changes as the fish grew larger. At the Cortland laboratory, brook trout averaging 1.0 gm in weight and held in 8.3°C water gain approximately 100% per month, but the rate is reduced to about 35% after the fish reach an average weight of 20 gm. Schaeperclaus (1933) estimated the energy requirement of a 12 gm carp as 24.48 kcal/kg of weight per 24 hours versus a requirement of only 7.97 kcal/kg of weight per 24 hours for carp 600 gm in weight. The larger fish have proportionally less body surface and therefore, according to Schaeperclaus, a lower energy requirement. There is apparently less loss of energy (heat) to the water with the proportionally less body surface of the larger fish.

## D. FISH AGE

In general, the caloric requirement of an animal decreases with age. It would presumably be so with fish. However, since fish continue to grow throughout their life-span, such a reduction would be less drastic than with other animals. The decreased caloric requirement would be more accurately associated with reduced growth rates than with age alone. In fish the age factor is completely confounded with growth and it is difficult to measure the effect of aging alone.

## E. TYPE OF FEEDER

Although there is little direct evidence, it may be speculated that the food consumed by fish affects their metabolic rates. Carnivorous fish are expected to have a relatively high metabolic rate because they consume high levels of protein which is, in part, utilized for energy. Protein catabolism increases the energy requirement because of the necessity of ridding the body of toxic nitrogenous waste products.

Herbivorous fish are expected to have a lower metabolic rate since they feed largely on plant products which contain high levels of carbohydrate that are used, along with fat, for energy. There is no large volume of toxic nitrogenous products to eliminate and less energy is required.

Omnivorous fish are intermediate in their energy requirement, somewhat less than carnivores and somewhat more than herbivores. These fish utilize some protein for energy (and therefore have nitrogenous catabolic products to eliminate) as well as carbohydrate and fat. Differences between carnivorous and omnivorous fish are illustrated in part by the higher respiratory rates and greater oxygen consumption of brook trout (a carnivore) in comparison with the lower rates and consumption of carp (an omnivore) (Belding, 1929; M'Gonigle, 1932).

## F. PHYSIOLOGICAL ACTIVITY

Energy requirements change with obvious changes in physiological activity such as the formation of reproductive products and spawning activity. The increase in energy requirement is caused by the loss of calories to the body by their deposition in the egg and by the energy required for the formation of the products themselves. The increased energy for spawning activity is obvious.

There are other physiological changes that apparently alter the energy requirement of fish that are not obvious or well defined. These changes may be described as metabolic cycles and represent those that occur with the seasons, but are not necessarily associated with water temperature or fish size. Schaeperclaus (1933) noted increased periodic metabolic changes associated with spawning and decreased seasonal changes in metabolism that he designated as "habitual winter rest." Neither spawning nor "habitual winter rest" were correlated with temperature by Schaeperclaus. Spawning activity in fish is a phototropic response (Pickford and Atz, 1957). There could also be a phototropic response associated with reduced metabolic activity. Scarcity of food in the winter months in temperate climates could explain the possible presence of a mechanism triggered by seasonal light changes to reduce food need during the winter months by reduced metabolic activity. Chepik (1964) supports this theory by his observation that the protein and carbohydrate digestive activity of carp intestines varies with the season and is highest in the spring and summer and lowest in the fall and winter.

Shell (1961) found seasonal changes in the blood chemistry of smallmouth black bass that he associated with cyclic changes in metabolism and offered possible explanations of the causes of metabolic cycles for the many changes in blood components that he observed over a 1-year period.

The Cortland workers have postulated the presence of metabolic cycles (Phillips *et al.*, 1960) and have observed seasonal changes in the pyridoxine requirement of fish that are not associated with fish size or water temperature (Phillips and Livingston 1966).

Brown (1946) reported that under constant light and temperature conditions in England, maximum growth of brown trout occurred in February, gradually fell off until August, and then markedly decreased to a minimum in October and November. Environmental conditions were constant in these experiments with a water temperature of 11.5°C, constant flow the year around, and light 12 hours per day. The diet was not changed and the fish were fed all they would eat. These experiments indicate a cyclic change in the energy requirement of fish through changes in growth rates. The changes were not controlled by temperature, light cycles, or fish size.

Swift (1961) demonstrated growth rate cycles in brown trout and found both hatchery and wild yearlings have a high growth rate in the spring and fall and a low growth rate in the winter and summer. His data indicate that water temperature was the main influencing factor and maximum growth was achieved at 12°C. Reduced growth at the higher temperatures in summer were thought to be due to the inadequacy of the fish's respiratory system at the higher temperature. Phototropism does not appear to be a factor in Swift's observations. However, the cycles he describes, physiological in nature, represent changes in energy requirements of the fish.

The possibility of metabolic cycles are important in considering the establishment of energy requirements for fish. Much work needs to be done in this phase of fish metabolism.

## G. Light Exposure

Phillips *et al.* (1958) found that trout exposed to continuous light over a 20-week period grew at reduced rates and postulated that additional energy was expended because of increased activity when the fish were exposed to continual light. Qasim (1955) believed that fish need a rest period ("sleep") and provided evidence that fish grew faster if maintained in 16–17 hours of darkness than when in continuous light. Brown (1946) reported that at a constant temperature of 11.5°C, the specific growth rates of brown trout were significantly lower when exposed to 12–18 hours of standard light per day than when exposed to only 6 hours of light. Rest periods induced by darkness reduces the energy required for maintenance and offer an explanation for the observed increased growth rates following periods of reduced light exposure.

However, Pyle (1969) found that brook trout grown under continuous light of constant intensity increased their length at a constant rate per 2-week period over at least 15 months. Fish held under either constant darkness or simulated natural light cycles grew at a reduced rate starting in late October that lasted for 16 weeks. Light cycles were completely eliminated for the fish exposed to either constant light or constant darkness in Pyle's experiments. In the earlier work of Phillips *et al.* (1958) the fish received daily changes in light intensity (and therefore were exposed to light cycles) because they were exposed to natural light during the day and artificial light at night. Continual light of constant intensity did increase the total yearly growth of brook trout.

## H. Environmental Factors

Increased water flow, necessitating active opposition to the current for position maintenance, increases the energy requirement of the fish. Over a period of time, brook trout in a stream have a higher energy requirement than the same species residing in a lake.

### I. Water Chemistry

Belding (1929) has shown that environmental toxins decrease the respiratory rate of trout, suckers (family Catostomidae), carp, and goldfish. After exposure to lethal doses of hydrogen sulfide, the respiratory rate initially rose, then decreased until death of the fish. Belding also showed that as the dissolved oxygen decreased, the respiratory rate of the fish increased until the oxygen was too low to support life. The respiratory rate decreased from this point to death. These changes in respiratory rates indicate changes in energy requirement.

A reduced oxygen content of the water, increasing the respiratory rate, increases the fish's energy requirement.

Phillips *et al.* (1957) and Podoliak (1965) demonstrated that transfering brook and brown trout from hard to soft waters increased the metabolic rate of the fish to actively oppose loss of ions to the environment. This net increase in metabolism reflects an increase in energy requirement. Such an effect was earlier described by Krogh (1939).

Organic pollution increases the metabolic rate (as measured by the respiratory rate) with the net result of temporarily increasing the energy requirement of the fish. The products of fish metabolism may be considered organic pollution as they accumulate in the environment.

### J. Fish Activity

An increase in fish activity increases the energy requirement, as measured by increased respiratory rates. Increased activity may result from increased water flow, physical handling, feeding, or responses to the environment.

Schaeperclaus (1933) illustrated the effect of excitement on metabolic rate by mentioning that tench tripled their oxygen consumption immediately after transfer from a pond to a barrel. Brett (1965) reported that the energy requirement of sockeye salmon (*Oncorhynchus nerka*) (measured by oxygen consumption) increased in a manner similar to a compound interest curve as the swimming speed of the fish increased. Brett and Sutherland (1965) showed an increased rate of oxygen consumption (energy requirement) of pumpkinseed (*Lepomis gibbosus*) with increased swimming speed. Beamish (1964) found that at comparable swimming speeds and under comparable conditions the endurance was greatest for winter flounder and was followed by cod (*Gadus*), redfish (*Sebastodes*), longhorn sculpin (*Cottus*), ocean trout (*Hexagrammos*), and sea raven (*Hemitripterus*). Under similar conditions the energy available for work varied between species.

## K. Diet Composition

The ratios of food groups in a diet alters the energy requirement of the animal. A diet that contains a higher percentage of protein, resulting in the utilization of protein for energy, increases the metabolic rate of the animal's body (Section III, E). Diets containing a high percentage of minerals increase the energy requirement because the absorbed excess minerals must be eliminated and the elimination process increases the energy requirement. Both the level and ratio of the food groups alter the metabolic rate and therefore the energy requirement of the fish.

Smith (1967) found that the metabolizable energy for rainbow trout (energy available to the body for energy purposes) varied with diet composition. It was highest in all-protein diets and lowest in diets containing $\alpha$-cellulose or corn starch. There was little difference between diets containing glucose, dextrin, or cooked corn starch as calorie sources.

He reported a more positive nitrogen balance in fish fed diets that contained easily digested carbohydrates, indicating less usage of protein for energy and more usage for growth. Under this condition the total energy requirement of the fish is reduced because there is a minimum level of products of protein catabolism to be eliminated (Section III, E).

## L. Starvation

Phillips *et al.* (1953) found that in addition to changes in metabolic rate during starvation that were associated with changes in body weight (Section III, B), there were other changes measured by blood chemistry and ammonia excretion. After 48 hours the blood glucose remained at a constant level of approximately 40 mg/100 ml of blood, indicating that the fish were in a state of conservation metabolism. The blood glucose remained at this level for a considerable period and then gradually dropped as starvation continued. Starvation also reduced the elimination of ammonia. These changes reflect the reductions in energy expended during periods of starvation.

## IV. The Energy Value of Foods For Fish

## A. The Calorie Value of Food Groups

The average caloric value of the food groups was established many years ago as 5.65 kcal/gm of protein; 9.45/gm of fat; and 4.0/gm of carbohydrate. These are total calories and not all are available to the body. Based upon average digestibility of the food groups by human beings (and correcting protein for the calories present as nitrogen and unavailable for energy) the caloric values were reduced to 4/gm of protein, 9/gm of fat, and 4/gm of carbohydrate. Although originally established for human beings, it is these values that have been largely used to estimate the caloric content of foods for all animals. For precise studies, values should be established for the species under consideration.

## B. CALORIES IN FISH FOOD

Schaeperclaus (1933) estimated the total and the usable caloric content of natural and hatchery fish foods. The usable calories were estimated by adjusting the total calories for digestibility of the food groups by fish.

Darlington (1956), Ostanenya and Serger (1964), and Geng (1925) have estimated the caloric values of natural fish foods using the standard calorie values. Since they did not adjust for digestibility their caloric values represent the total present and not necessarily those available for fish.

Phillips and Brockway (1959) described a method for calculating the caloric value of trout diets taking into account the digestibility of the food groups by these fish.

These authors used the following values for digestibility of the energy food groups by trout:

> Protein, 90% digested (from Tunison *et al.*, 1942; Wood, 1952)
> Fat, 85% digested (from McCay and Tunison, 1935)
> Carbohydrate, 40% digested (starch) (from Phillips *et al.*, 1948)

The digestive value for protein is used for both plant and animal products (fresh or dried) since neither Tunison *et al.* (1942), nor Wood (1952) were able to show significant differences between the digestibility by fish of the proteins of these groups of foods. The value for fat is a compromise value between that of hard and soft fats and the levels of these two types of fats usually found in trout diets. The digestive value for carbohydrate is based upon the assumption that most of the carbohydrate in trout diets is present as raw starch. Foods that contain a higher level of the simple or compound sugars or partially digested starches (dextrins) would have a higher value for the digestibility of the carbohydrate.

To determine the calorie values of trout diets, the digestibility of the food groups was taken into consideration in the following manner:

5.65 (total kcal/gm protein) − 1.3 (kcal as nitrogen and unavailable for energy) × 0.90 (percentage protein digested) = 3.9 kcal available to trout/ gm of food protein                                                                                                    (1)

9.45 (total kcal/gm fat) × 0.85 (percentage fat digested) = 8.0 kcal available to trout/gm of food fat                                                                                                    (2)

4.10 (total kcal/gm carbohydrate) × 0.40 (percentage carbohydrate digested as starch) = 1.6 kcal available to trout/gm of food carbohydrate as starch                                                                                                    (3)

If either simple or compound carbohydrates are present in the diet a higher value for digestibility is required to estimate the caloric value of carbohydrates for trout. For example, if glucose is present (99% absorbed, Phillips *et al.*, 1948) the caloric value per gram of carbohydrate would be:

$$4.10 \times 0.99 = 4.0 \text{ kcal/gm of glucose} \tag{4}$$

Or if sucrose is present (78% absorbed, Phillips *et al.*, 1948) the caloric value per gram of carbohydrate would be:

$$4.10 \times 0.78 = 3.2 \text{ kcal/gm of sucrose} \tag{5}$$

The digestibility and absorption of several carbohydrates by trout has been described by Phillips *et al.* (1948) and combinations of these values may be used to establish the calories available as carbohydrate to trout if the diet contains a mixture of carbohydrate sources.

## V. Food Sources For Calories

### A. PROTEIN

Proteins are readily usable sources of calories for trout and a high degree of digestion and absorption is expected from most proteins used in trout diets. Whether protein calories are used for catabolic or anabolic purposes is dependent upon the availability of other calorie sources (fats and limited carbohydrate) to spare the protein for tissue production, and upon the quality of the protein for the fish. Protein of poor quality is burned for energy or deposited as fat.

### B. CARBOHYDRATES

According to Phillips *et al.* (1948) trout utilize only limited levels of carbohydrates. They established the allowable dietary level as 12% digestible carbohydrate and found that higher levels resulted in an accumulation of glycogen in the liver of the fish, eventually causing death of the trout. They believed that trout are physiologically unable to handle high dietary levels of carbohydrates and carbohydrates are only limited sources of energy.

Buhler and Halver (1961) reported that salmon can utilize relatively high levels of carbohydrate without physiological upsets and concluded that dietary imbalances were partially responsible for the results of Phillips *et al.* (1948) with trout. There were increases in liver glycogen in the salmon with increases in dietary carbohydrate, but these increases apparently were not considered as possible harmful effects. Later, Phillips *et al.* (1966) found that maltose was utilized for energy by trout and this carbohydrate had a sparing action on protein. However, when fed at levels as low as 6% there was an increase in both the liver size and glycogen content. The long-time effect of these liver changes have not been determined. There may be a species difference in carbohydrate utilization between trout and salmon.

Schaeperclaus (1933) concluded (from data of Knauthe, 1901) that carp utilize 30–90% of their dietary carbohydrate at temperatures from 19° to 20°C. Differences were not recognized between the various types of food carbohydrates.

## C. Fats

Fat calories are used by fish to spare the protein for protein purposes. This has been shown experimentally for brook and brown trout by Phillips *et al.* (1964, 1965) and for salmon by Combs *et al.* (1962) and Fowler *et al.* (1966). McCay and Tunison (1935) showed that brook trout utilized fats that were liquid at 8.3°C more efficiently than fats that were solid at this temperature. Schaeperclaus (1933) reported that fat calories are readily available to carp and from the data of Knauthe (1901) he concluded that between 84 and 96% of the food fat was utilized by these fish at a temperature of 19° to 20°C.

## VI. Estimation of Caloric Needs of Fish

### A. Schaeperclaus Method

Schaeperclaus (1933) estimated the calories required for fish production based upon body surface, water temperature, and the caloric need per hour (Section II, A). His calculations are as follows for a 100 gm rainbow trout held in water at a temperature of 15°C:

$$\text{Body surface} = 10 \times \text{body weight}^{2/3} \tag{6}$$

or

$$\text{Body surface} = 10 \times 100^{2/3} = 2.154 \text{ square decimeters} \tag{7}$$

According to Schaeperclaus the caloric needs of rainbow trout are 60 gcal per hour per square decimeter (Section II, A). Therefore:

$$60 \text{ gcal per hour} \times 24 = 1440 \text{ gcal per day per square decimeter or } 1.44 \text{ kcal} \tag{8}$$
$$\text{per day per square decimeter}$$

$$2.154 \text{ square decimeters (body surface 100 gm rainbow trout)} \times 1.44 \text{ (kcal}$$
$$\text{required per square decimeter per day by rainbow trout)} = 3.1 \text{ kcal re-} \tag{9}$$
$$\text{quired by the 100 gm rainbow trout per day}$$

## B. CORTLAND METHOD

The values described in Section II,A, developed by Phillips and Brockway (1959), are used to estimate the amount of food required to provide the necessary calories for flesh production. Since most hatchery diets are in excess of 700 kcal per pound (1540 kcal/kg) the value of 1800 kcal to produce a pound of fish is used (3960 kcal/km). Assuming a pelleted fish food, containing 1200 kcal per pound (2640 kcal/kg), the food required for production is:

$$\frac{1880 \text{ (kcal required per pound fish produced)}}{1200 \text{ (kcal per pound of diet)}} = 1.5 \text{ pounds of food per pound} \quad (10)$$

of fish produced (3.3 kg of food per kilogram of fish produced)

## C. BROWN'S METHOD

Brown (1957) developed an equation for determining the "net efficiency" of food. Brown defined net efficiency as a measure of the utilization of available food for growth (food eaten–maintenance requirement). Brown's equation is:

Net efficiency

$$= \frac{\text{Weight increase of fish}}{\text{Weight of food eaten } - \text{ weight food required for maintenance}} \quad (11)$$

To make this equation workable the maintenance requirement must be known. Through a series of experiments Brown determined the maintenance requirement of 50 gm brown trout and showed that as the water temperature increased, so did the energy requirement.

The net efficiency may be compared to gross efficiency for a measure of the utilization of the food for specific flesh production. Gross efficiency is the standard conversion of food into flesh obtained by dividing the food fed by the gain in weight of the fish.

## D. WINBERG'S METHOD

Winberg (1960) developed an equation for total energy used by the body which he describes as a "balanced equation."

Physiological useful energy = energy of weight increase        (12)

+ energy of metabolism

Since Winberg believed that 80% of the food is utilized the equation becomes:

0.8 (energy of the ration) = energy of weight increase        (13)

+ energy of metabolism

This is a balanced equation for the energy turnover in the body. Throughout his work Winberg separates the energy deposited in the body and that required for maintenance. The latter he refers to as metabolic energy, which is the energy of catabolism lost to the body for flesh production.

Winberg (1960) developed the equation to:

$$\text{Energy of the ration} = \frac{1}{.80} \text{ (energy of metabolism} \tag{14}$$

$$+ \text{ energy of weight increase)}$$

or

$$\text{Energy of ration} = 1.25 \text{ (energy of metabolism} \tag{15}$$

$$+ \text{ energy of weight increase)}$$

These relationships are useful in considering the utilization of calories within the fish's body.

Ivlev (1961) redescribed the "balanced equation" of Winberg (1960) in the following generalized form:

$$0.8 \, Q = (p - p_0) + T \tag{16}$$

in which 0.8 is a correction for incompleteness of utilization of consumed food (efficiency assumed 80%); $Q$, the total quantity of food; $p_0$, initial weight of fish; $p$, final weight of fish for the period; $T$, food expenditure for metabolism (energy or catabolism in this case).

Ivlev developed methods for determining the food used for growth and maintenance. The known caloric content of foods are utilized to convert the data to estimate the total calories for production.

## E. Winberg's Expenditure Equation

Winberg (1960) derived the following equation to express the expenditure of energy for metabolism (catabolism) over a 24-hour period:

Expenditure for metabolism per day (as percentage of weight)

$$= \frac{\text{(consumption of } O_2 \text{ as ml/gm wet weight/hour)} \times 240}{\text{content of dry substance in percentage}} \tag{17}$$

Winberg states that this equation is permissible if 1 ml of oxygen consumed corresponds to 1 mg of dry weight. From the size of the metabolic rate (milliliter oxygen consumed per gram of wet weight per hour) the expenditures for metabolism per day as a percentage of the dry substance can be obtained. Under these assumptions Eq. (13) can be rewritten as follows:

$$0.8 \text{ (dry substance of ration)} = \text{increase fish weight dry basis} \qquad (18)$$
$$+ \text{ expenditure of the dry substance for metabolism}$$

Equation (18) is possible if it can be assumed that the caloric equivalent of the dry substance of the fish's body and of its food are the same.

## VII. Dietary Calories and the Production of Fish

### A. PRODUCTION OF TROUT

Table II lists the calories required to produce a kilogram of trout fed different diets. The table illustrates the fallacy of using the conversion

TABLE II

TOTAL CALORIES REQUIRED TO PRODUCE OF TROUT FED DIFFERENT DIETS[a]

| Composition of diet fed (%) | Number of observations | Average total percentage gain | Average total conversion | Total calories per kilogram of diet | Calories fed per kilogram of fish produced |
|---|---|---|---|---|---|
| Brook trout, water temperature 8.3°C | | | | | |
| Pork spleen 50 Dry meal 50[b] | 13 | 1854 | 2.9 | 1588 | 4605 |
| Pork spleen 49 Beef liver 49 Salt 2[c] | 10 | 1717 | 2.9 | 913 | 2648 |
| Natural food 100[d] | 2 | 335 | 2.7 | 740 | 1998 |
| Brown trout, water temperature varied with season (8.3° to 15.6°C) | | | | | |
| All dry diet (pelleted food)[e] | 2 | 950 | 1.75 | 2759 | 4828 |

[a] From Phillips and Brockway, 1959.

[b] Average weight fish at start 0.5 to 0.8 gm. Dry meal composed of equal parts of cottonseed meal, wheat middlings, dried skim milk, and fish meal, and 4 parts of salt. Twenty-week experimental period.

[c] Average weight of fish at start 0.5 to 0.8 gm. Twenty-week experimental period.

[d] Average weight of fish at start 0.058 gm. Five-week experimental period. Fish fed living brine shrimp.

[e] Average weight of fish at start 12 gm. Fed Cortland pellet composed of all dry ingredients as described by Phillips *et al.* (1953). Experimental period of 1 year.

of food into flesh as a measure of total efficiency. Pelleted fish foods (Table II) are the most efficient in terms of food conversion (1.75). In terms of calories, however, this food is the least efficient. There is no difference between the food conversion of the remaining three diets but the difference between their calorie efficiencies is highly significant Natural foods are the most efficient, mixture of spleen and dry meal mixtures the least efficient, and all-meat diets are intermediate.

Phillips and Brockway (1959) concluded that approximately 4620 kcal were required per kilogram of fish produced after feeding high-calorie diets (diets containing in excess of 1540 kcal/kg). Table III shows the observed and calculated values for the food conversions of several of these high-calorie diets. There is no significant difference between the calculated and observed values and these calculations add validity to this method of estimating caloric requirements for production. However, recent experiments (Phillips *et al.*, 1964) have shown that the conversion rates of improved pelleted foods have been lower and the food efficiencies

TABLE III

CALCULATED AND OBSERVED CONVERSIONS OF HIGH-CALORIE DIETS[a] INTO FLESH ASSUMING 4620 CALORIES ARE REQUIRED PER KILOGRAM OF FISH PRODUCED[b]

| Diet composition (%) | Kilograms of food per kilogram of fish produced | |
|---|---|---|
| | Calculated | Observed |
| Pork spleen 50<br>Dry meal 50 | 2.9 | 2.9 |
| Pork spleen 30<br>Beef liver 20<br>Dry meal 50 | 2.8 | 2.7 |
| Beef spleen 32<br>Beef liver 16<br>Dry meal 52 | 2.8 | 2.9 |
| All dry diet 100 | 1.66 | 1.75 |
| All dry diet 5 days, meat 2 days weekly | 2.2 | 2.1 |
| All dry diet 6 days, meat 1 day weekly | 1.9 | 2.0 |

[a] Containing excess 1540 calories/kg.
[b] From Phillips and Brockway, 1959.

TABLE IV

RESULTS FROM FEEDING IMPROVED ALL DRY PELLETS AS COMPLETE FOOD FOR
BROWN TROUT OVER AN 18-MONTH PERIOD[a]

| Pellet number | Average weight of fish at end (gm)[b] | Total percentage gain | Total conversion | Calories per kilogram of pellet | Calories required per kilogram of fish produced |
|---|---|---|---|---|---|
| 4 | 266 | 2884 | 1.87 | 1925 | 3600 |
| 5 | 263 | 2849 | 1.71 | 2253 | 3850 |
| 6 | 319 | 3489 | 1.56 | 2605 | 4060 |

[a] Data calculated from Phillips and Hammer, 1965.
[b] Average weight at start 8.9 gm.

have increased. It is apparent that a more accurate value for these improved pelleted foods is 1800 kcal per pound of fish produced (3960 kcal/kg). Undoubtedly this value will be further decreased as diets and feeding methods are improved. The ultimate goal is to reach the efficiency of natural foods (Table II).

Table IV lists the results after feeding of improved pelleted foods (Phillips and Hammer, 1965). The calories required to produce a kilogram of fish approach those found after feeding either all-meat hatchery diets or natural foods (Table II).

## B. PRODUCTION OF SALMON

Combs *et al.* (1962), using the method of Phillips and Brockway (1959) for estimating the caloric content of salmon diets, found that at a 20% level of protein in the diet as fed, increasing the caloric content of the diet with peanut oil to 1650 kcal/kg increased protein deposition and protein utilization. Increasing the level to 2000 kcal/kg did not further increase protein utilization or deposition. These results demonstrate a sparing action of the peanut oil on the protein.

Fowler and McCormick (1964) reported that supplemental energy calories provided as fat resulted in a sparing action on the protein and vitamin requirements of salmon. They found that as the fish grew the energy requirement of salmon increased in proportion to the protein requirement.

The calorie content of these diets was lower than those fed to trout by the Cortland workers.

## VIII. Calorie Ratios in Fish Diets

### A. TROUT DIETS

Most artificial hatchery diets (as fed) contain approximately 70% of their calories as protein which is similar to natural foods (as eaten) that have approximately 72% of their calories as protein (Phillips and Brockway, 1959 and calculated from Phillips *et al.*, 1954, and from Wood *et al.*, 1957) and to all-meat diets (as fed) that contain about 78% of their calories as protein. Both natural foods and all-meat diets are more efficient producers of fish flesh than meat–meal mixtures or all-dry trout diets (Table IV).

In general, an increase in the protein level of a diet necessitates an increase in the caloric level to provide energy for the metabolizing of the additional protein. The high-energy diets fed to hatchery trout (all-dry diets and meat–dry meal mixtures, that contain 2600 and 1600 kcal/kg respectively) also contain relatively high protein levels (approximately 27 and 43% protein, respectively).

There is a limit beyond which the animal body cannot use all of the protein for protein purposes because maximum growth is reached. The

TABLE V

SUMMARY OF THE EFFECT OF PROTEIN AND CALORIE LEVELS UPON THE GROWTH EFFICIENCY OF BROWN TROUT OVER A 20-WEEK EXPERIMENTAL PERIOD[a]

| Diet number[b] | Calories per kilogram of diet | Percentage protein in the diet | Percentage of the calories as protein | Average weight of the fish at end in grams[c] | Total percentage gain | Total conversion | Calories required per kilogram of fish produced |
|---|---|---|---|---|---|---|---|
| 1 | 1485 | 26.9 | 70 | 22.8 | 1100 | 3.0 | 4455 |
| 1a | 979 | 18.2 | 72 | 13.4 | 602 | 4.1 | 4014 |
| 1b | 1483 | 18.2 | 48 | 25.5 | 1242 | 2.9 | 4301 |

[a] Calculated from Phillips *et al.*, 1965.

[b] Diet composition: The base of each diet was composed of 25% each of beef spleen and beef liver, 3% carboxymethyl-cellulose, and 2% salt. The dry meal used was composed of 33.3 parts of wheat middlings, 35.6 parts of fish meal, and 31.1 parts of distiller's solubles. Diet No. 1, The base diet plus 45% of the dry meal; diet No. 1a, The base diet plus 12.5% cellulose flour, 10% water, and 22.5% of the dry meal; diet No. 1b, The base diet plus 9.25% cellulose flour, 7% water, 22.5% of the dry meal, and 6.25% corn oil.

[c] Weight at start, 1.90 gm.

excess protein is stored as fat or used for energy. These are uneconomical diets. It is essential to reach a balance between calories and protein that will provide maximum protein for protein purposes but not supply an excess that will be wasted as stored fat or used for energy. Other calorie sources should supply energy (fats and/or carbohydrates) and spare the protein for protein purposes.

Experiments have shown (Table V) that it is possible to reduce the protein content of high calorie–high protein trout diets, providing the calorie level is maintained with fat. In recent studies at the Cortland laboratory it was possible to reduce the protein level of a meat–meal mixture from 27 to 18% without loss of trout growth if the calorie content was maintained with corn oil at levels isocaloric with the original mixture (Phillips *et al.*, 1965). In these diets the percentage of the calories as protein was lowered from 70 in the original diet to 48% in the isocaloric-reduced protein diets (Table V). The supplemental fat spared the protein for protein purposes.

In these experiments, although there was an increase in protein synthesis in the bodies of fish fed the low protein-high calorie diets, there was also an increase in deposited body fat. Either a portion of the dietary protein could not be utilized for protein purposes because it was of unsuitable quality or there was a surplus of total calories. For maximum utilization the calorie sources must be suitable for fish growth and in the proper ratio.

## B. Salmon Diets

Fowler and McCormick (1964) reported that a protein calorie to energy calorie ratio of 1:1 appeared optimum at a 20% dietary protein level. As the fish grew this ratio changed to 1:1.35, indicating a higher energy requirement for the larger salmon. Body analyses showed that during this time of apparent increased energy requirement, the body fat decreased but the percentage of body protein remained essentially the same.

Comparing these results with those of trout, the values obtained from feeding trout the low protein-high calorie diet (Table V, No. 1b) were similar to salmon. The diet with 48% of its calories as protein was the most efficient. Expressed in terms of Fowler and McCormick the protein to calorie ratio was 1:1.4, similar to that of the larger salmon (1:1.35).

## C. Other Fish Species

There has been little work done upon the calorie ratios of the diets of other species of fish. This represents a void in the nutritional knowledge of fishes and offers a field for future study.

## IX. Methods for Determining the Amount of Food to Feed

### A BASIS FOR FEEDING LEVELS

Although there are a number of systems for establishing the amount of food to feed fish, essentially all of them are based upon the total metabolism and the effect different factors have on metabolic rates It is appropriate that a brief description of the different methods, and the basis for their calculations should be included in this discussion since all have the common goal of providing the calories and materials necessary for growth. Almost all of the work has been done with trout and salmon.

### B. FISH WEIGHT

The original trout feeding tables of Deuel *et al.* (1937) established the amount to feed in relation to fish size and weight. Since that time Burrows *et al.* (1951) have provided similar tables for salmon and a number of commercial feed manufacturers have tables available that suggest levels for their foods in terms of fish weight (See Appendix.)

### C. FISH LENGTH

Haskell (1959) developed a unique equation for determining trout feeding levels based upon fish length. Haskell believes that trout increase in length at a constant rate and that the body form of hatchery trout remains reasonably constant at least the first 1.5 years of their hatchery life. With the acceptance of these two premises, Haskell derived his feeding equation as follows:

$$\text{Daily percentage gain in weight} = \frac{3}{L} \times \Delta L \times 100 \tag{19}$$

in which $L$ = length in inches; $\Delta L$ = daily increase in length in inches; $3$ = a constant derived from the weight–length equation ($W = KL^3$)

Percentage to feed of body weight daily

$$= \frac{200 \times \text{conversion} \times \text{percentage gain in weight}}{200 \times 1 \text{ day}} \tag{20}$$

This above simplified to:

Percentage to feed of body weight daily $\qquad\qquad$ (21)
$$= \text{conversion} \times \text{daily percentage gain in weight}$$

Combining Eqs. (19) and (21):

$$\text{Percentage to feed of body weight daily} = \frac{3 \times \text{conversion}}{L} \times \Delta L \times 100 \tag{22}$$

To use this equation it is necessary to know the conversion rate of food into flesh, either from hatchery records or calculated from the caloric content of the diet (Section VI, B), and the rate of increase in fish length per day. This latter value is obtained from tables using the number of fish per unit at the start and end of a period (Haskell, 1959). A new length increase determination is necessary for each water temperature.

Since Haskell's method is based upon food conversion and growth rate (increase in length), fish size and diet calorie levels are confounded and automatically taken into consideration. No additional calculations are necessary.

Butterbaugh and Willoughby (1967) refined Haskell's method by establishing feeding guides and hatchery constants that greatly simplified the application of Haskell's equation at all salmonid hatcheries including those with variable water temperatures.

## D. GROWTH RATE

If the growth rate (percentage) and the food conversion are known, the amount to feed trout can be determined from the following equation of Deuel *et al.* (1952):

$$\text{Percentage to feed} = \frac{2 \times \text{conversion} \times \text{percentage gain} \times 100}{(200 + \text{percentage gain}) \text{ No. of days}} \tag{23}$$

in which the percentage gain is expressed as a whole number (representing the pounds gained per 100 pounds of fish).

From any periodic percentage gain, the daily percentage gain may be obtained from the table of Deuel *et al.* (1952). After establishing the daily percentage gain the number of days in Eq. (23) becomes one and the daily food allowance may be calculated. This equation also confounds fish size and caloric content of the diet. No further calculations are necessary.

## E. NEW YORK STATE METHODS

Freeman *et al.* (1967) described three methods used by New York fish hatcheries to establish feeding levels. The first method is based upon an expected percentage gain in fish weight and an expected food conversion, both obtained from past hatchery records. The amount to feed is calculated by multiplying the estimated gain in pounds (established from the percentage gain) by the food conversion. The second method is based upon the monthly gain in length in inches and the gain in pounds of fish represented by the length increase (obtained from tables). The amount to feed is calculated by multiplying the expected pounds gained by a conversion rate estimated from the caloric content of the diet and the calories required to produce a pound of fish. The third method is a nomograph that directly establishes the percentage to feed through a relationship with a known percentage gain in fish weight and a conversion of food into flesh. All three methods are simplified techniques that have proved useful and accurate for hatchery management.

### F. CALORIC CONTENT OF THE DIET

Fish fed high-calorie diets require less food than do those fed low calorie diets. If feeding tables are used (Deuel *et al.*, 1952 or others) adjustments are made to account for difference in caloric content of the diets. The tables of Deuel *et al.* (1952) apply to trout foods containing approximately 700 kcal per pound (1540 kcal/kg). Those foods containing more or less calories are fed at lower or higher levels. (See Appendix.)

### G. WATER TEMPERATURE

Most feeding tables are based upon fish size and water temperature, and the amount fed is governed by these factors, both of which alter the metabolic rate and therefore the energy requirement of the fish. If the equation of Haskell (Section IX,C) is used, a new trout length increase is calculated for each water temperature since the metabolic rate changes with increases or decreases of water temperature and the energy requirements are altered. Butterbaugh and Willoughby's modification of Haskell's method provides for a hatchery constant that takes into account the water temperature of the hatchery. In the method of Deuel *et al.* (Section IX,D) the inclusion of both the gain and the conversion rate in the equation confounds changes in metabolism caused by temperature (reflected in growth rate) and automatically takes them into account. All three methods described by Freeman *et al.* (Section IX, E) automatically confound temperature and no special considerations are necessary.

### H. WATER FLOW

Although fish must expend more energy to maintain themselves in increased flows of water, present feeding methods do not allow for adjustment to changes in these conditions. Experiments in New York State Hatcheries (Phillips *et al.*, 1959) did not show changes in energy expenditures as measured by levels of body fat in fish exposed to periodic increased water flow, sufficient to cause an active opposition to the increased current for position maintenance. If water flow is a factor in the energy requirement of fish it probably is not of sufficient magnitude in most hatchery operations to cause concern for changes in the caloric intake of the fish.

## References*

Beamish, F. W. H. (1964). *Can. J. Zool.* **42**, 177.
Belding, D. L. (1929). *Trans. Amer. Fish. Soc.* **59**, 238.
Brett, J. R. (1965). *J. Fish. Res. B. Can.* **22**, 1491.
Brett, J. R., and Sutherland, D. B. (1965). *J. Fish. Res. B. Can.* **22**, 405.
Brown, M. E. (1946). *J. Exp. Biol.* **22**, 130.
Brown, M. E. (1957). "The Physiology of Fishes," Academic Press, New York.
Buhler, D. R., and Halver, J. E. (1961). *J. Nutr.* **74**, 307.
Burrows, R. E., Robinson, L. A., and Palmer, D. D. (1951). *U.S. Fish and Wild. Ser. Spec. Sci. Rep. Fish* **59**.
Butterbaugh, G. L., and Willoughby, H. (1967). *Progr. Fish. Cult.* **29**, 210.
Chepik, L. (1964). *Chem. Abstr.* **61**, 13667e.
Combs, B. D., Heinemann, W. W., Burrows, R. E., Thomas, A. E., and Fowler, L. G. (1962). *U.S. Fish Wild. Ser. Spec. Sci. Rpt. Fish* **432**.
Cooper, G. P. (1935). *Trans. Amer. Fish. Soc.* **65**, 132.
Darlington, W. W. (1956). Thesis. University of Oklahoma Agricultural and Mechanical College, Stillwater, Oklahoma.
Dean, J. M., and Goodnight, C. J. (1964). *Physiol. Zool.* **37**, 280.
Deuel, C. R., Haskell, D. C. and Tunison, A. V. (1937). "The New York State Fish Hatchery Feeding Chart." State of New York Conser. Dept., Albany, New York.
Deuel, C. R., Haskell, D. C., Brockway, D. R., and Kingsbury, O. R. (1952). *Fish. Res. Bull.* **3**.
Fowler, L. G., and McCormick, J. H., Jr. (1964). *U.S. Fish Wildl. Ser. Spec. Sci. Rep. Fish.* **480**.
Fowler, L. G., McCormick, J. H., Jr., and Thomas, A. E. (1966). *Bur. Sport Fish. and Wild., U.S. Dept. of Interior, Tech. pap. 6.*
Freeman, R. I., Haskell, D. C., Longacre, D. L., and Stiles, E. W. (1967). *Prog. Fish Cult.* **29**, 194.
Fry, E. E. J. (1947). *Publ. Ontario Fish. Res. Lab.* **55**, 5.
Geng, H. (1925). *Z. Fisch. Hilfswiss.* **23**, 156.
Gerking, S. D. (1952). *Physiol. Zool.* **25**, 358.
Haskell, D. C. (1959). *N. Y. Fish Game J.* **6**, 204.
Ivlev, V. S. (1961). *Fish. Res. Bd. Can. Transl. Ser.* **371**.
Knauthe, K. (1901). "Die Karpfenzucht," Neudamn.
Krogh, A. (1939). "Osmotic Regulation in Aquatic Animals." Cambridge University Press, London.
Lindstedt, P. (1904). *Z. Fisch. Hilfswiss.* **14**, 143.
McCay, C. M., and Tunison, A. V. (1935). *Rept. Exp. Work Cortland Hatchery Year 1934. State N. Y. Conserv. Dept. Albany, New York.*
Maynard, L. A. (1962). "Animal Nutrition." McGraw-Hill, New York.
M'Gonigle, R. H. (1932). *Trans. Amer. Fish. Soc.* **62**, 119.

* References designated as *Fish. Res. Bull.* are published by the New York State Conservation Department, Albany, New York.

Moss, D. D., and Scott, D. C. (1961). *Trans. Amer. Fish. Soc.* **90,** 377.

Ostanenya, A. P., and Serger, A. I. (1964). *Biol. Abstr.* **45,** 67465.

Phillips, A. M., Jr. and Brockway, D. R. (1959). *Prog. Fish. Cult.*, **21,** 3.

Phillips, A. M., Jr., and Hammer, G. L., (1965). *Fish. Res. Bull.* **28,** 23.

Phillips, A. M., Jr., and Livingston, D. L. (1966). *Fish. Res. Bull.* **29.**

Phillips, A. M., Jr., Tunison, A. V., and Brockway, D. R. (1948). *Fish. Res. Bull.* **11.**

Phillips, A. M., Jr., Lovelace, F. E., Brockway, D. R., and Balzer, G. C., Jr. (1953). *Fish. Res. Bull.* **16.**

Phillips, A. M., Jr., Lovelace, F. E., Brockway, D. R. and Balzer, G. C., Jr. (1954). *Fish. Res. Bull* **17.**

Phillips, A. M., Jr., Podoliak, H. A., Brockway, D. R. and Balzer, G. C., Jr. (1957). *Fish Res. Bull.* **20.**

Phillips, A. M., Jr., Podoliak, H. A., Brockway, D. R., and Vaughn, R. R. (1958). *Fish. Res. Bull.* **21.**

Phillips, A. M., Jr., Podoliak, H. A., Dumas, R. F., and Thoesen R. W. (1959). *Fish. Res. Bull.* **22.**

Phillips, A. M., Jr., Podoliak, H. A., Livingston, D. L., Dumas, R. F., and Thoesen, R. W. (1960). *Fish. Res. Bull.* **23.**

Phillips, A. M., Jr., Podoliak, H. A., Poston, H. A., Livingston, D. L., Booke, H. E., Pyle, E. A., and Hammer, G. L. (1964). *Fish. Res. Bull.* **27.**

Phillips, A. M., Jr., Livingston, D. L., and Poston, H. A. (1965). *Fish. Res. Bull.* **28,** 28.

Phillips, A. M., Jr., Livingston, D. L., and Poston, H. A., (1966). *Fish. Res. Bull.* **29,** 6.

Pickford, G. E., and Atz, J. W. (1957). "The Physiology of the Pituitary Gland of Fishes." New York Zoological Society, New York.

Podoliak, H. A. (1965). *Fish. Res. Bull.* **28,** 71.

Pyle, E. A. (1969). *Fish. Res. Bull.* **31,** 13.

Qasim, S. Z. (1955). *Nature* (London) **175,** 217.

Rozin, P. N., and Mayer, J. (1961). *Science* **134,** 942.

Rubner, M. (1942). *Biochemistry.* **148,** 222.

Schäperclaus, W. (1933). *U.S. Fish. Wildl. Ser. Fish. Leafl.* **311.**

Shell, E. W. (1961). *U.S. Fish Wildl. Ser. Sci. Res. Rep.* **57.**

Smith, R. R. (1967). Thesis. Utah State University, Logan, Utah.

Sumner, J. B. (1929). "Textbook of Biological Chemistry." MacMillan, New York.

Sumner, J. B., and Lanhan, V. N. (1942). *Biol. Bull.* **42,** 313.

Swift, D. R. (1961). *J. Exp. Biol.* **38,** 595.

Tiemeier, O. W., Deyoe, C. W., and Wearden, S. (1965). *Trans. Kansas Acad Sci.,* **68,** 180.

Tunison, A. V., and McCay, C. M. (1938). *Cortland Hatchery Rep.* **6,** *N. Y. Conserv. Dep., Albany, N. Y.*

Tunison, A. V., Phillips, A. M., Jr., Brockway, D. R., Dorr, A. L., and Mitchell, C. R. (1942). *Fish. Res. Bull.* **1.**

Winberg, G. G. (1960). *Fish. Res. Bd. Can., Transl. Ser.* **194.**

Wood, E. M. (1952). Thesis. Cornell University Graduate School, Ithaca, New York.

Wood, E. M., Yasutake, W. T., Woodall, A. N., and Halver, J. E. (1957). *J. Nutr.* **61,** 479.

# 2

## THE VITAMINS

*John E. Halver*

## I. Historical Introduction

### A. PIONEERS AND CONCEPTS

Diet deficiency diseases have been recognized in man and in animals for several hundred years. Vedder (1912), who worked on beriberi, traced recognition of this disease by the Chinese to as early as 2697 *B.C.*; but it was Eijkman and Grijns (Williams, 1961) at the end of the nineteenth century who showed how polyneuritis could be reduced by addition of rice husks or pericarp to the diet, and Vorderman (Williams, 1961) who correlated fowl polyneuritis with human beriberi. Casimir Funk (1912) isolated the water-soluble antiberiberi compound in partially purified state and in a paper on etiology of deficiency diseases published in 1912 used the term "vitamine" for the first time. He reviewed the literature on beriberi, pellagra, and scurvy with the view that all were deficiency diseases (Funk, 1922).

Scurvy was also an ancient disease and the first treatise on description and experimental cure was published by Lind in 1753 who showed that oranges, lemons, or apple cider contained a scurvy preventive factor. Then, 150 years later, Holst and Frölich (1907) produced a deficiency disease similar to scurvy in guinea pigs; 25 years later King and Waugh (1932) and Waugh and King (1932) identified vitamin C as ascorbic acid.

A similar scientific history applies to the description of pellagra in peasants in Spain by Casal in 1735 (Harris, 1919). A long delay followed before Spencer, in 1916, and Chittenden and Underhill, in 1917, produced black tongue in dogs as a deficiency disease similar to pellagra. Twenty more years elapsed before Elvehjem and co-workers (1937, 1938) cured black tongue with nicotinic acid; the new vitamin was immediately applied to the treatment of pellagra by Fouts *et al.* (1937), by Smith *et al.* (1937), and finally shown to be effective by Nakao and Greenberg (1958).

Fish have been confined and fed for several thousand years. Mosaic walls in ruins of ancient Greece and Rome depict fish being fed in impoundments.

Whenever intensive fish culture was employed with more purified, artificial diets many of the fish became anemic and died. McCay and Dilley (1927), at Cornell, worked industriously to identify the antianemic factor H which was present in fresh meat and which was necessary in the diet when trout were held more than 10–12 weeks on the best purified diets then available for animal nutrition studies. Twenty years elapsed, however, before this water-soluble factor was identified as a combination of vitamin $B_{12}$ and folic acid.

One of the first reports of a specific vitamin deficiency in fish was in 1941 when Schneberger at the Thunder River Hatchery in Wisconsin reported that paralysis in rainbow trout (*Salmo gairdneri*) which were fed carp (*Cyprinus carpio*) could be cured by injecting crystalline thiamine into individual fish or by feeding dried brewer's yeast. Fish diet disease was reported by Louis Wolf (1942) to be due to thiaminase present in fresh fish tissue which would hydrolyze thiamine in the commercial meat–meal mixtures fed to fish in the hatchery. That same year Tunison *et al.* (1942) measured levels of thiamine, riboflavin, and nicotinic acid in the liver, pyloric caeca, kidney, and muscle in order to establish base lines for experiments to measure requirements of trout for these vitamins. Dietary gill disease was also reported during this decade and could be reduced by incorporating fresh liver or dried yeast in the diet (Wolf, 1945). McCay and Tunison (1934) observed scoliosis and lordosis in brook trout (*Salvelinus fontinalis*) fed Formalin-preserved meat, but the symptoms took nearly 1 year to develop and were not correlated with the recently identified vitamin C. Many of the fish disease reports of the 1940's inferred that dietary deficiencies may have caused or augmented the symptoms observed when a specific pathogen and Koch's postulates could not be followed for a specific disease episode.

## B. Avitaminosis

Typical avitaminosis symptoms of Chastek-type paralysis, cataracts, convulsions, scoliosis, anemia, slime patch disease, clubbed gills, poor growth, anorexia, and increasing mortality were reported wherever fish were concentrated and intensive fish cultural practices were used. As diets became manufactured more from agricultural products, anemia and diet disease symptoms became more common but specific cause and effect relationships were often difficult to define.

## C. Hypervitaminosis

Hypervitaminosis D and A were reported when seal and whale liver were used as one of the fresh meat components in salmon diets (Burrows *et al.*,

1952). An analogy was drawn between symptoms observed in fish and those reported for other experimental animals, but no good experimental diets were available with positive experimental control over the particular vitamin that investigators wished to study.

## D. TEST DIETS AND CONDITIONS

Barbara McLaren, working with Conrad Elvehjem, and others at Wisconsin, developed a vitamin test diet containing crystalline vitamins, casein, dextrin, and oils with crab meal or dried liver as the source of the antianemic factor (McLaren et al., 1947b). These pioneer fish nutritionists were able to report tentative qualitative, then quantitative requirements of rainbow trout for thiamine, riboflavin, pyridoxine, pantothenic acid, inositol, biotin, folic acid, choline, and niacin (McLaren et al., 1947a). These values were based on fish growth response and food conversion. This test diet did furnish some control over many vitamins but assays revealed low levels of several of the water-soluble vitamins present in the dietary components; and when the diet excluded dried liver or crab meal, fish became anemic and died (McLaren et al., 1946). Xanthopterin was once thought to be the fish antianemic factor because young chinook salmon (*Oncorhynchus tshawytscha*) showed improvement in hematology when this material was injected (Simmons and Norris, 1941). Tunison et al. (1943) reported that riboflavin, pyridoxine, and pantothenic acid would improve anemic brook trout and could be part of McCay's factor H. Three years later, in 1946, Phillips et al. (1946), working in the same laboratory, could not repeat the response with these three vitamins even when folic acid was added to the vitamin mixture. These workers could, however, cure the anemia when dehydrated liver powder was added. Norris and Halver tested xanthopterin again in 1949 at the University of Washington and injected this material alone and in combination with folic acid and vitamin $B_{12}$ into young anemic chinook salmon. A measurable response was obtained from xanthopterin and more from folic acid, but the most dramatic stimulation of erythropoiesis was obtained when folic acid and vitamin $B_{12}$ were injected in combination of one part vitamin $B_{12}$ to one-hundred parts folic acid (Halver, 1969). That winter Louis Wolf (1951) developed a test diet for rainbow trout which contained commercial casein, gelatin, potato starch, hydrogenated cottonseed oil, $\alpha$-cellulose flour, minerals, cod liver oil, and crystalline vitamins. The diet was used successfully to induce several vitamin deficiency syndromes by deleting one vitamin at a time from the vitamin supplement and feeding the resultant diets to trout (Wolf, 1951). During the summer of 1951 this crude test diet was improved by changing to vitamin-free casein, purified gelatin, white dextrin for potato starch, corn oil for Crisco, and a simplified mineral mix (Halver, 1953a). Chinook salmon fingerlings grew as well on this diet as on Wolf's test diet (Halver, 1953a, 1957). Later this original, complete vitamin test diet was improved by lowering the protein content and used for short-term feeding studies with coho salmon (*O. kisutch*) and sockeye salmon (*O. nerka*) (Halver, 1966) and for long-term feeding studies for at least three reproductive cycles with rainbow trout in 8°, 10°, 15°, and 17°C water systems (Halver, 1970; Halver and Coates, 1957). The tool had been forged to test for specific qualitative and quantitative vitamin requirements of salmonids (Table I). Applications of the diet to salmon, trout, and other species were rapid and produced dramatic results. Specific deficiency

TABLE I

WATER-SOLUBLE VITAMIN TEST DIET H-440[a]

| Complete test diet (gm) | | Vitamin mix (mg) | | Mineral mix (mg) | |
|---|---|---|---|---|---|
| Vitamin-free casein | 38 | Thiamine·HCl | 5 | USP XII No. 2 | plus |
| Gelatin | 12 | Riboflavin | 20 | $AlCl_3$ | 15 |
| Corn oil | 6 | Pyridoxine·HCl | 5 | $ZnSO_4$ | 300 |
| Cod liver oil | 3 | Choline chloride | 500 | CuCl | 10 |
| White dextrin | 28 | Nicotinic acid | 75 | $MnSO_4$ | 80 |
| α-Cellulose mixture[b] | 9 | Calcium pantothenate | 50 | KI | 15 |
| α-Cellulose 8 | | Inositol | 200 | $CoCl_2$ | 100 |
| Vitamins 1 | | Biotin | 0.5 | per 100 gm of salt mixture | |
| | 9 | Folic acid | 1.5 | | |
| Mineral mix | 4 | L-Ascorbic acid | 100 | | |
| Water | 200 | Vitamin $B_{12}$[d] | 0.01 | | |
| Total diet as fed | 300 | Menadione (K) | 4 | | |
| | | α-Tocopherol[c] acetate (E) | 40 | | |

[a] Diet preparation: Dissolve gelatin in cold water. Heat with stirring on water bath to 80°C. Remove from heat. Add with stirring—dextrin, casein, minerals, oils, and vitamins as temperature decreases. Mix well to 40°C. Pour into containers; move to refrigerator to harden. Remove from trays and store in sealed containers in refrigerator until used. Consistency of diet adjusted by amount of water in final mix and length and strength of beating.

[b] Delete 2 parts α-cellulose and add 2 parts CMC for preliminary feeding.

[c] Dissolve α-tocopherol in oil mix.

[d] Add vitamin $B_{12}$ in water during final mixing.

syndromes occurred whenever one of the required vitamins was deleted from the vitamin mix and fish were fed for adequate test periods. Eleven water-soluble vitamins were soon identified as required for salmon and trout (Halver, 1957; Coates and Halver, 1958; Kitamura *et al.*, 1967). Qualitative water-soluble vitamin requirements were also identified for catfish (*Ictalurus punctatus*) (Dupree, 1966), carp (Ogino, 1967a,b), yellow-tail (*Seriola quinqueradiata*) (Sakaguchi *et al.*, 1969), and eel (*Anguilla japonica*) (Hashimoto *et al.*, 1970).

## II. The Water-Soluble Vitamins

Water-soluble vitamins include eight well-recognized members of the vitamin B complex, the water-soluble essential nutritional factors choline, inositol, ascorbic acid, and the less-defined vitamin activity for fish of *p*-aminobenzoic acid, lipoic acid, citrin, and undefined growth factors. The first eight are required in small amounts in the dietary but play major roles in growth, physiology, and metabolism. The essential nutritional factors choline, inositol, and ascorbic acid are required in appreciable levels in the diet and sometimes are not referred to as vitamins but as major dietary nutrients. The last group of growth factors are less well defined for fish and more research is needed to determine the exact role of these components in cell physiology and metabolism in fish tissues. All are included in this portion of the discussion on water-soluble vitamins. The American Institute of Nutrition names for the B complex vitamins will be used although the order of presentation will suggest the more classical, historical identification of the B vitamin complex. Chemical structure, characteristics, and analogs will be presented to assist the reader in identifying the particular compound discussed in the text. Since fish nutritionists are concerned with the specific role and function of the vitamins in physiology and metabolism, chemical formulas (1) will be followed by (2) discussion of real or potential positive function; (3) the deficiency syndrome observed in fish and other animals; (4) a listing of requirements when known for different types of fishes; (5) sources of these essential nutrients; (6) antimetabolites which can interfere or inactivate the required vitamins; and finally (7) methods for clinical assessment of nutritional status. Since several forms for many of the particular vitamins exist, the term "vitamers" may be used with the understanding that this terminology applies to the group of compounds of that particular vitamin activity.

## A. THIAMINE

Experimental beriberi was produced in fowl by Eijkman in Java in 1886 (Williams, 1961). The antiberiberi factor was crystallized by Funk in 1911 and named "vitamine" (Funk, 1912). Thiamine was isolated from rice polishings by Jansen and Donath in 1926 and was synthesized by Williams and co-workers in 1936 (Williams and Cline, 1936; Cline *et al.*, 1937). The first reported use in fish was by Schneberger in 1941 who injected crystalline thiamine to cure "diet disease" in rainbow trout (Schneberger, 1941).

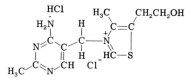

FIG. 1. Thiamine hydrochloride.

### 1. *Chemical Structural Characteristics*

Thiamine hydrochloride is a water-soluble, colorless, monoclinic, crystalline compound with empirical formula $C_{12}H_{18}ON_4SCl_2$ and structure shown in Fig. 1. It is comparatively stable to dry heat but is rapidly broken down in neutral or alkaline solutions and is split by sulfites into constituent pyrimidine and thiazole moieties. It has a characteristic yeastlike odor. The pyrimidine ring is relatively stable, but the thiazole ring is easily opened by hydrolysis. Several derivatives are stable to heat and appear to be more completely soluble in weak alkaline solutions than thiamine itself and still show biological activity in animals. These derivatives include thiamine propyl disulfide, benzoylthiamine disulfide, dibenzoylthiamine, and benzoylthiamine monophosphate. Undoubtedly, new, more stable compounds will be synthesized in the future for dietary ingredients. Both thiamine hydrochloride and thiamine mononitrate have been successfully used as the active vitamin in test diets for fish nutrition studies.

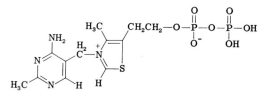

FIG. 2. Cocarboxylase or thiamine pyrophosphate.

## 2. *Positive Function*

Thiamine is part of the coenzyme cocarboxylase illustrated in Fig. 2 which participates in the oxidative decarboxylation of $\alpha$-keto acids, especially pyruvic acid, eventually releasing carbon dioxide. Thiamine is an antagonist to acetylcholine. Jansen (1954) has pointed out that pyruvic acid stands at the crossroads of carbohydrate intermediary metabolism and is the end point in the anaerobic process before decarboxylation and oxida-

TABLE II

Vitamin Deficiency Syndromes

| Vitamin | Symptoms in salmon, trout, carp, catfish[a] |
|---|---|
| Thiamine | Poor appetite, muscle atrophy, convulsions, instability and loss of equilibrium, edema, poor growth |
| Riboflavin | Corneal vascularization, cloudy lens, hemorrhagic eyes—photophobia, dim vision, incoordination, abnormal pigmentation of iris, striated constrictions of abdominal wall, dark coloration, poor appetite, anemia, poor growth |
| Pyridoxine | Nervous disorders, epileptiform fits, hyperirritability, ataxia, anemia, loss of appetite, edema of peritoneal cavity, colorless serous fluid, rapid postmortem rigor mortis, rapid and gasping breathing, flexing of opercles |
| Pantothenic acid | Clubbed gills, prostration, loss of appetite, necrosis and scarring, cellular atrophy, gill exudate, sluggishness, poor growth |
| Inositol | Poor growth, distended stomach, increased gastric emptying time, skin lesions |
| Biotin | Loss of appetite, lesions in colon, coloration, muscle atrophy, spastic convulsions, fragmentation of erythrocytes, skin lesions, poor growth |
| Folic acid | Poor growth, lethargy, fragility of caudal fin, dark coloration, macrocytic anemia |
| Choline | Poor growth, poor food conversion, hemorrhagic kidney and intestine |
| Nicotinic acid | Loss of appetite, lesions in colon, jerky or difficult motion, weakness, edema of stomach and colon, muscle spasms while resting, poor growth |
| Vitamin $B_{12}$ | Poor appetite, low hemoglobin, fragmentation of erythrocytes, macrocytic anemia |
| Ascorbic acid | Scoliosis, lordosis, impaired collagen formation, altered cartilage, eye lesions, hemorrhagic skin, liver, kidney, intestine, and muscle |
| p-Aminobenzoic acid | No abnormal indication in growth appetite, mortality |

[a] See Table I, Chapter 10, for comparative clinical pathology in other animals.

tive reactions begin the reverse process. He assumes that the exact type of reaction depends upon the protein of the apoenzyme to which thiamine pyrophosphate is combined. An interrelation between thiamine and lipoic acid has been reported (Reed, 1959), although little of this work has been confirmed in fish. Thiamine pyrophosphate, a coenzyme for the trans-ketolase system, is part of the direct oxidative pathway of glucose metabolism occurring in the cytoplasm of cells (Handler, 1958). Brin (1963) has used this as a method of estimating status in experimental animals including salmon and trout.

Thiamine is essential for good appetite, normal digestion, growth, and fertility. It is needed for normal function of nervous tissue and the requirement is determined by the caloric density of the diet (Krampitz, 1969).

### 3. Deficiency Syndrome

Deficiency signs in salmonids involve impaired carbohydrate metabolism, nervous disorders, poor appetite, poor growth, and increased sensitivity to shock by physical blow to container or from light flashes (Schneberger, 1941; Wolf, 1942; McLaren et al., 1947a; Halver, 1953a,b; Halver, 1957; Coates and Halver, 1958). A trunk-winding symptom in eels has been reported together with hemorrhage at the base of the fins (Hashimoto et al., 1970). Skin congestion and subcutaneous hemorrhage occurs in carp fed thiamine-deficient diets (Aoe et al., 1969). Typical symptoms observed in salmonids, carp, and catfish are listed in Table II. Thiamine deficiency has also been reported in marine flatfish started on clam neck diets stored long enough for the thiaminase present to hydrolyze the thiamine in the ration (Shelbourne, 1970). Typical nervous paralysis occurred with rapid mortality from physical shock.

### 4. Requirements

Thiamine requirements for trout and salmon were determined by feeding diets containing different amounts of thiamine for periods long enough for the vitamin deficiency syndrome to appear. At the end of the experimental test period, storage of the vitamin in the liver was measured. Differences in growth response and food conversion were calculated (McLaren et al., 1947a).

Requirements of rainbow trout for thiamine were determined by Phillips and co-workers at the fish nutrition laboratory in Cortland, New York (Phillips et al., 1946). These requirements were determined by assaying meat–meal mixtures for thiamine content, feeding these rations to groups of young fish until positive growth differences were observed, and finally assaying the liver of the test fish for thiamine content. Requirements listed in Table III for chinook and silver salmon were determined by feeding duplicate lots of initial feeding fry the thiamine-deficient test diet derived from Table I to which increments of thiamine hydrochloride were added. Two different year classes of fish were fed five different vitamin levels for 12 weeks in 15°C water. At the end of the experimental period, twenty-five livers from each duplicate lot on each diet treatment were assayed microbiologically for thiamine content. The minimum dietary intake which produced maximum liver thiamine content was selected as that diet treatment which would satisfy the vitamin requirement for that species. Similar techniques were used for the other vitamin requirements listed in Table III.

The requirements for carp were estimated by feeding different levels of thiamine in a modified test diet noting growth performance, food conversion, and measuring thiamine content in hepatic pancreas (Aoe *et al.*, 1967b). Some considerations must be placed upon the dietary ingredients in the ration. The National Research Council estimates thiamine requirement for mammals at about 0.5 mg/1000 cal in the diet. The requirement for carnivorous fish does not seem much different; however, the requirement for omnivores or herbivorous fish like the carp may explain the apparent increased requirement reported. The fat content of the diet may affect not only caloric intake but also the thiamine requirement because cocarboxylase participates in the oxidation of fat through $\alpha$-ketoglutarate. Therefore, fish on a high fat diet and low thiamine intake might take longer to develop deficiencies, or, conversely, when test diets containing more dietary fat were used to assess thiamine requirement, erroneous low levels of the apparent requirement might be obtained. Fish are poikilothermic and the protein requirement varies with size and water temperature (DeLong *et al.*, 1958a). Therefore, thiamine requirements were calculated using a standard test diet in a standard test condition with standard temperature of 10°C for salmon, 15°C for trout, 25°C for catfish, and 30°C for carp.

### 5. *Sources and Protection*

Common sources for thiamine are in plant seeds, dried peas, beans, soybeans, cereal bran, and dried yeast. Fresh glandular tissue is also a good source for thiamine and other members of the B vitamin water-soluble complex, but is seldom used in modern commercial fish diets.

Thiamine can be easily lost by holding wet diet ingredients too long in storage or by preparing the diet under slightly alkaline conditions or in the presence of sulfide. Since thiamine is relatively stable to dry heat, dry pellet rations will retain the vitamin through the pelleting process and

TABLE III

VITAMIN REQUIREMENTS FOR GROWTH[a]

| Vitamin (mg/kg dry diet) | Rainbow trout | Brook trout | Brown trout | Chinook salmon | Coho salmon | Carp | Eel | Goldfish | Yellowtail | Channel catfish |
|---|---|---|---|---|---|---|---|---|---|---|
| Thiamine | 10–12 | 10–12 | 10–12 | 10–15 | 10–15 | R[b] | R | R | R | R |
| Riboflavin | 20–30 | 20–30 | 20–30 | 20–25 | 20–25 | 7–10 | | | R | R |
| Pyridoxine | 10–15 | 10–15 | 10–15 | 15–20 | 15–20 | 5–10 | | | R | R |
| Pantothenate | 40–50 | 40–50 | 40–50 | 40–50 | 40–50 | 30–40 | | R | R | R |
| Niacin | 120–150 | 120–150 | 120–150 | 150–200 | 150–200 | 30–50 | | | | R |
| Folacin | 6–10 | 6–10 | 6–10 | 6–10 | 6–10 | ? | | | | R |
| Cyanocobalamin | R | R | R | 0.015–0.02 | 0.015–0.02 | ? | | | | R |
| *myo*-Inositol | 200–300 | R | R | 300–400 | 300–400 | 200–300 | | | | R |
| Choline | R | R | R | 600–800 | 600–800 | 1500–2000 | | | | R |
| Biotin | 1–1.2 | 1–1.2 | 1.5–2 | 1–1.5 | 1–1.5 | 1–1.2 | R | | R | R |
| Ascorbate | 100–150 | R | R | 100–150 | 50–80 | R | | R | R | R |
| Vitamin A | 2000–2500 | R | R | R | R | 1000–2000 | | R | R | R |
| Vitamin E[c] | R | R | R | 40–50 | R | 80–100 | | | R | R |
| Vitamin K | R | R | R | R | R | | R | | | R |

[a] Fish fed at reference temperature with diets at about protein requirement.

[b] R = required.

[c] Requirement directly affected by amount and type of unsaturated fat fed.

subsequently during dry-sealed storage. Wet or frozen diets pose a different problem because moisture content allows increased chemical reaction and subsequent increased danger for biological hydrolysis and thus destruction of the thiamine moiety. Obviously, wet or moist diet preparations containing any fresh fish or shellfish tissue must be used immediately or suffer loss of thiamine through thiaminase hydrolysis (Deutsch and Ott, 1942; Agren, 1945).

### 6. *Antimetabolites and Inactivation*

Acetylcholine is an antagonist to thiamine and pyrithiamine. Oxythiamine and normal butylthiamine are specific antimetabolites (West *et al.*, 1966). Several thiaminases occur which destroy thiamine. These rupture the thiazole ring at the sulfur bond making the residue inactive. Freshwater fish tissues have high thiaminase activity as do tissues from clams, shrimp, and mussels. Thiaminases have also been found in beans and mustard seed and in several microorganisms (Goldsmith, 1964). Thiaminase activity is low in most saltwater fish tissues, however, and the enzyme is inactivated by heating or prolonged pasteurization. Thiamine present in fresh Torula yeast is relatively unavailable to fish, but the yeast becomes an excellent thiamine source after rupturing the cells by steam treatment or by dehydration.

### 7. *Clinical Assessment*

Clinical assessment for thiamine status in fish may be made by measuring erythrocyte transketolase activity in rainbow trout and silver salmon using the method of Brin (1963). Levels of thiamine can also be assessed by microbiological assay of liver tissue from representative samples of the fish population. As an example, typical saturated levels for thiamine activity in sea salmon range from 15–20 $\mu$g of thiamine/gm of wet liver tissue. Fingerling chinook or coho salmon reared in 10° or 15°C water on test diets containing the listed amount or more of thiamine hydrochloride, assayed at 8–10 $\mu$g of thiamine/gm of wet liver. These liver storage levels and normal erythrocyte transketolase activity in the absence of any deficiency sign, coupled with good growth and good food conversion, will indicate an adequate thiamine intake for that fish population.

## B. RIBOFLAVIN

Growth-promoting yellow-green pigments were isolated in 1879. Emmett and McKim showed two "B" vitamins present (Emmett and McKim, 1917). Vitamin G deficiency was described by Goldberger and Lillie (1926). A rat assay for vitamin $B_2$ was designed by Bourquin and Sherman (1931),

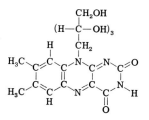

FIG. 3. Riboflavin.

and crystalline riboflavin was isolated by Kuhn *et al.* (1933). Lactoflavin, hepatoflavin, and ovoflavin were shown to be identical with the pure riboflavin synthesized by Kuhn *et al.* (1933) and Karrer *et al.* (1935). Riboflavin was postulated as one part of factor H for fish by Tunison *et al.* in 1943. Riboflavin deficiency in trout was first described by McLaren *et al.* (1947a) and in salmon by Halver in 1951.

### 1. *Chemical Structure, Characteristics, and Analogs*

Riboflavin is a yellow-brown crystalline pigment with chemical formula $C_{17}H_{20}N_4O_6$ and the structural formula shown in Fig. 3. The material is slightly soluble in water with yellow-green fluorescence and is very soluble in alkali. It is insoluble in most fat solvents except alcohol. It is stable to oxidizing agents in strong mineral acids and in neutral aqueous solution and in dry form is heat stable. It is irreversibly decomposed on irradiation with ultraviolet rays or visible light breaking down to lumiflavin. Riboflavin phosphate is the chemically active group of Warburg's "yellow" enzyme.

### 2. *Positive Functions*

Riboflavin functions in the tissues in form of flavin adenine dinucleotide (FAD) or as flavin mononucleotide (FMN). Free riboflavin has been isolated in urine, plasma, and in the retina of the eye. The flavoproteins function as enzymes of tissue respiration and are involved in hydrogen transport to catalyze the oxidation of reduced pyridine nucleotides (NADH and NADPH). Thus, these function as coenzymes for many oxidases and reductases such as cytochrome *c* reductase, D- and L-amino acid oxidases, xanthine and aldehyde oxidase, succinic dehydrogenase, glucose oxidase, and fumaric dehydrogenase. Riboflavin is involved with pyridoxine in the conversion of tryptophan to nicotinic acid and is most important in respiration of poorly vascularized tissues such as the cornea of the eye. Riboflavin is involved in the retinal pigment during light adaptation and lack of it causes impaired vision and photophobia in experimental animals including fish.

### 3. *Deficiency Syndrome*

A summary of deficiency signs in fish is included in Table II. Riboflavin tissue storage is exhausted in young salmonids after 10–12 weeks on ribo-flavin-deficient diets in 10°–15°C water systems. Poor appetite and poor diet efficiency are the first signs followed by photophobia, mono- or bi-lateral cataracts, corneal vascularization, eye hemorrhage, incoordination, and general anemia. Dark pigmentation coupled with striated constrictions of abdominal wall in salmon have been noted. Skin atrophy has been reported for some fish species and abnormal pigmentation of both skin and iris has been noted (Aoe *et al.*, 1967b; Halver, 1953a,b). Replacement of riboflavin in the dietary reduces the symptoms except when cataracts have developed and protein crystal structure of the lens of the eye has been lost (Halver, 1957). This irreversible condition will continue in monolateral cataracts throughout the life of the fish, whereas bilateral cataracts largely result in eventual starvation and death of the afflicted animal. The first specific signs have consistently appeared in and about the eye of salmonids, carp (Aoe *et al.*, 1967b), and catfish (Dupree, 1966).

### 4. *Requirements*

The requirements of fish for riboflavin under experimental conditions in 10°–15°C water supplies are listed in Table III. These values have been determined for trout by assaying riboflavin content in meat–meal mixtures with microbiological assay techniques, feeding these diets to fish until growth differences were observed, and then assaying for maximum liver storage of the vitamin. Values for the trout are slightly lower than those reported for salmon which were fed the test diet containing different increments of crystalline riboflavin, measuring growth response for 10 weeks, and then assaying the livers to determine the diet treatment which would induce maximum liver storage. The requirements may vary depending upon the balance of other dietary ingredients, caloric density, and environmental conditions under which the fish is raised. The requirement listed under these standard test conditions described should furnish a tentative requirement which will satisfy biological demands for normal growth, health, and physiological function. Most of these requirement studies have been made on very young fish, often initial feeding fry, with the logical assumption that the vitamin requirement of these young fish would be more than that of larger fish having advanced metabolic enzyme systems with ability to synthesize at least some of the requirement for these vitamins.

## 5. *Sources and Protection*

Riboflavin is widely distributed in plants and in animal glandular tissues. Milk, liver, kidney, heart, yeast, germinated grains, peanuts, soybeans, and eggs are rich sources. Protection of finely ground raw materials and mixing processes from sunlight or intense artificial light is necessary to minimize loss of the vitamin by conversion to lumiflavin. Fortunately, the pH conditions for most diet preparations with ingredients commonly used in either dry or wet fish rations involve a relatively stable environment for retention of riboflavin activity during diet preparation. As long as the ingredients and the stored rations are protected from light in dark bags or in tight containers, most of the riboflavin activity will be carried from the raw materials into the food fed.

## 6. *Antimetabolites and Inactivation*

Galactoflavin is an antagonist to riboflavin and inhibits growth of rats when the diet contains this compound. Flavin monosulfate inhibits D-amino acid oxidase and appears to act as a competitor and inhibitor of riboflavin for growth of *Lactobacillus casei*. When the ribose group in the molecule is replaced by other groups, analogs have been formed which either have some activity or become antimetabolites. The hydroxyethyl analog is an antagonist for riboflavin function in both rats and bacteria and also shows antifungal activity (West *et al.*, 1966).

## 7. *Clinical Assessment*

Liver tissue of actively feeding sea salmon has between 6–8 $\mu$g of riboflavin/gm of wet tissue. In a freshwater environment, young feeding fish fed test diets in 15°C water systems showed liver storage of 3.5–4.0 $\mu$g/gm. Some estimate of riboflavin content of the diet may be obtained from microbiological assay since this vitamin is relatively stable, and one can calculate approximate dietary intake from levels present in the food supply. Riboflavin content of blood plasma does not change significantly in riboflavin deficiency in other experimental animals. However, the erythrocyte riboflavin content has been reported as around 10 $\mu$g/100 ml blood for man on low riboflavin intake and approximately twice that level on high intake (Bessey *et al.*, 1956). Urinary excretion of riboflavin has been used clinically with 200 $\mu$g in 24 hours suggesting adequate intake and less than 100 $\mu$g indicating low intake. Excretion of 50 $\mu$g or less daily is strong indication of extended dietary deficiency. Several studies indicate excretion of less than 200 $\mu$g of riboflavin/gm of creatinine would be indicative of deficiency (Goldsmith, 1964). Specific clinical tests for riboflavin content in biological tissues of fish need to be developed to assist in assessing adequate dietary status of this important required vitamin.

## C. Pyridoxine

A new factor which would cure dermatitis in rats was reported by György (1935). The active material was isolated in 1938 by several groups and pyridoxine was synthesized by Harris and Folkers (1939). Tunison *et al.* listed the first quantitative requirements for fish in 1944. Pyridoxine deficiency in trout was reported by McLaren *et al.* (1947a) and in salmon by Halver (1953a,b).

### 1. *Chemical Structure, Characteristics, and Analogs*

The vitamers $B_6$ consist of pyridoxine, pyridoxal, pyridoxamine, and several other derivatives which have biological activity or can be converted into the most biologically active form of pyridoxal. The stable pyridoxine hydrochloride form has a chemical formula of $C_8H_{11}O_3N_7HCl$ and the structural formulas for the three common forms of vitamin $B_6$ are shown in Fig. 4. Pyridoxine hydrochloride is readily soluble in water and is heat stable in either acid or alkaline solution. Pyridoxal phosphate acts as the coenzyme in a number of systems and pyridoxic acid, deoxypyridoxine, and methoxypyridoxine are closely related compounds with varying degrees of activity. Pyridoxine is sensitive to ultraviolet light in neutral or alkaline solutions. Pyridoxamine and pyridoxal in dilute solutions are labile compounds which are rapidly destroyed by exposure to air, heat, or light (Chow, 1964). Therefore, most vitamin supplementation is in the form of pyridoxine hydrochloride and analysis for pyridoxine activity by microbiological assay of diet ingredients probably measures pyridoxal phosphate and other intermediates as well.

### 2. *Positive Functions*

Pyridoxal phosphate is the coenzyme, codecarboxylase, for decarboxylation of amino acids. It is also involved in the transaminase systems and twenty-two different transaminases in animal tissues have been shown to require a distinct enzyme with pyridoxal phosphate as the coenzyme

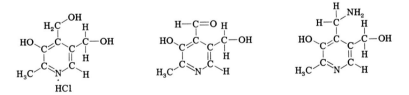

Fig. 4. Pyridoxine. Three common forms used are (*left to right*) pyridoxine hydrochloride, pyridoxal, and pyridoxamine.

(Cammarata and Cohen, 1950). Pyridoxal phosphate has been shown to be the coenzyme for decarboxylation of 5-hydroxytryptophan with the consequential production of 5-hydroxytryptamine or serotonin (Weissbach *et al.*, 1959). Pyridoxal phosphate is also required for assisting desulfhydrase in converting cysteine to pyruvic acid. Porphyrin synthesis is also involved and pyridoxal phosphate is the cofactor for synthesis of $\gamma$-aminolevulinic acid. Many neuro hormones require pyridoxal phosphate as a coenzyme in their synthesis and it is involved and is essential for tryptophan utilization and metabolism of glutamic acid, lysine, methionine, histidine, cysteine, and alanine. Pyridoxine is also involved in fat metabolism especially of the essential fatty acids. It is involved in synthesis of messenger RNA which generates transfer of information at the site of polypeptide synthesis (Montjar *et al.*, 1965). The vitamers $B_6$ play a most important role in protein metabolism and, as a result, carnivorous fish have stringent requirements for pyridoxine in the diet and stores are rapidly exhausted.

### 3. *Deficiency Syndrome*

Signs of pyridoxine deficiency in fish are listed in Table II. Since salmonids, ictalurids, and very young cyprinids are carnivorous, with protein requirements for young animals between 40–50% of the ration, pyridoxine stores are rapidly exhausted when fish are held on pyridoxine-deficient rations. Acute deficiency signs occur in salmon after 14–21 days on a diet devoid of pyridoxine and the entire population when fed 50% or more protein diet dies in 28 days in 12°–15°C water. Since pyridoxine is involved in brain metabolism and in the homeostasis of serotonin, epileptic-type fits occur. Also, general nervous disorders, hyperirritability, and alteration in control of melanophore contraction occurs. Postmortem rigor mortis occurs very rapidly. Rapid and gasping breathing with flexing of the opercles is a common observation and edema in the peritoneal cavity with colorless serus fluid occurs in some fish on some experimental treatments (Halver, 1953a, 1957; Coates and Halver, 1958). Salmon, trout, carp, and yellowtail exhibit premortem rigor a few hours before death and, when the deficiency has progressed this far, recovery is very unlikely unless fish are injected with pyridoxal phosphate. Handling the animals generally induces more damage than vitamin administration corrects. Recovery of those fish still feeding is equally rapid and dramatic upon administration of pyridoxine hydrochloride in the diet. Deficiency signs disappear within a day or two after the pyridoxine is replaced in the ration. Erythrocyte transaminase activity and plasma transaminase activity reflect the deficiency state.

4. *Requirements*

Pyridoxine requirements for trout, salmon, carp, and yellowtail are listed in Table III. Trout requirements were obtained from analysis of meat–meal mixtures, growth response, and assay for maximum liver storage. Salmon requirements were assessed by feeding different increments of crystalline pyridoxine hydrochloride added to the vitamin test diet, measuring growth response, and maximum liver storage. Trout requirements appear less than that of salmon but the salmon on experiment were smaller fish and may have reflected the higher protein requirement for that size of animal and water temperature.

5. *Sources and Protection*

Good sources of vitamers $B_6$ activity are yeast, cereal brans, cereal grains, cereal germ, egg yolk, liver, and glandular tissues. Pyridoxine compounds in phosphorylated form present in agricultural products are fairly stable but are labile to ultraviolet radiation. Dietary ingredients in open pans should be protected from exposure to sunlight. Some pyridoxal phosphate will be lost on exposure to air. Free forms of pyridoxal and pyridoxamine are rapidly destroyed by air, light, and heat when in a moist form such as in preparation of moist diets. Pyridoxine hydrochloride supplementation is most desirable for preparation of custom or commercial fish diets because of the tremendous role pyridoxine plays to maintain normal protein metabolism during growth of carnivorous fish.

6. *Antimetabolites and Inactivation*

Antagonists may compete for reaction sites of the apoenzyme or may react with pyridoxal phosphate to form inactive compounds. Deoxypyridoxine is a potent $B_6$ antagonist because of competition for apoenzyme sites but is a useful agent to accelerate $B_6$ deficiency in experimental animals (Martin *et al.*, 1948). This same compound inhibits tyrosine decarboxylase (Beiler and Martin, 1947). Methoxypyridoxine is another antagonist and toxopyrimidine (2-methyl-4-amino-5-hydroxymethylpyrimidine) produces liver damage in rats, inhibits glutamic acid decarboxylase, and causes convulsions (Nishizawa *et al.*, 1958). Isonicotinic acid hydrazide used for the treatment of tuberculosis is chemically related to pyridoxine and acts as a $B_6$ antagonist. Specific pyridoxal-5-phosphate antagonists were reviewed by Chow (1964).

7. *Clinical Assessment*

Plasma and erythrocyte transaminase activity has been shown to reflect pyridoxine status of the animal. High tryptophan load in the diet increases the vitamin $B_6$ requirement and misleads plasma transaminase activity measurements (Chow, 1964). Liver storage measured by microbiological assay was at 5–6 $\mu$g of $B_6$ activity/gm of fresh sea salmon liver; whereas, fingerling salmon fed on 50% protein diet in freshwater had 2–3 $\mu$g/gm of wet tissue. Assay of diet for the vitamers $B_6$ by microbiological methods gives a more true representation of total $B_6$ activity including intermediates than is obtained in specific chemical determinations. A fluorescent lactone of pyridoxic acid can be prepared from urine of man by heating with strong acids, but this simple fluorometric analysis needs to be tested for fish metabolic wastes because of altered pathways for elimination of nitrogenous compounds by these aquatic animals.

### D. PANTOTHENIC ACID

A chick dermatitis was cured by Elvehjem and Koehn in 1935 by a factor containing $\beta$-alanine. The rat requirement for this factor was determined by Lepkovsky in 1936 and the active material was isolated and used by Jukes (1939) and by Woolley *et al.* (1939). Pantothenic acid was synthesized by Stiller *et al.* (1940). Pantothenol was shown to be the active factor by Pfaltz in 1943 (Hein, 1964). Phillips *et al.* observed clubbed gills in trout fed pantothenic acid-deficient diets in 1945. Rucker *et al.* (1952) observed that salmon fed low pantothenic acid diets developed clubbed gills.

### 1. *Chemical Structure, Characteristics, and Analogs*

Pantothenic acid may be considered as a dihydroxydimethylbutyric acid bonded to $\beta$-alanine. The chemical formula is $C_9H_{17}O_5N$ and the structural formula for 2,4-dihydroxy-3,3-dimethylbutyryl-$\beta$-alanine is shown in Fig. 5. The free acid is a yellow, viscous oil and therefore the compound generally used in fish nutrition is the calcium salt. This salt is a white crystalline powder readily soluble in water, mild acid, and almost insoluble in fat solvents. It is stable to oxidizing and reducing agents and to autoclaving, but is labile to dry heat, hot alkali, or hot acid. Pantothenol has almost as much activity as pantothenic acid for growth of chicks. Pantothenic acid acetate, benzoate, and diphosphate esters are biologically

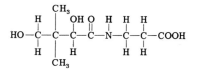

FIG. 5. Pantothenic acid.

active for animals but not for lactic acid bacteria. The optical isomer L-pantothenic acid appears physiologically inert. Some organisms may utilize a portion of the molecule. Bacteria appeared to require only the dihydroxydimethylbutyric acid, and some yeasts utilize only β-alanine. Animals, however, need the entire pantothenic acid molecule or its reduced alcohol form to satisfy the vitamin requirements (Chow, 1964).

## 2. *Positive Functions*

Pantothenic acid is part of acetyl coenzyme A which occurs in many enzymatic processes involving 2-carbon compounds. It has been shown to be required by all animal species studied and by many microorganisms (Chow, 1964; West *et al.*, 1966). The acetyl coenzyme A system is involved in the acetylation of aromatic amines and choline; condensation reactions for synthesis of acetate, fatty acids, and citrate; the oxidation of pyruvate and acetaldehyde; and is essential for the development of the central nervous system. The 2-carbon fragment called "active acetate," or acetyl coenzyme A, is an essential intermediate in metabolism. It is involved in most acylation reactions in the body including acyl groups other than acetate such as succinate, benzoate, propionate, and butyrate. Pantothenic acid is involved in adrenal function and for the production of cholesterol. Coenzyme A is also involved in many other steps of intermediate metabolism of carbohydrates, fats, and proteins. It is obviously a key nutrient for normal physiology and metabolism of a growing fish.

## 3. *Deficiency Syndromes*

Deficiency signs for pantothenic acid are summarized in Table II. Under standard test conditions with deficient diet fed in 10°–15°C water systems, salmon and trout exhaust pantothenic acid stores in from 8–12 weeks. Fish stop feeding and microscopic or hand lens examination of gill filament show proliferation of epithelial surface plus swelling and clubbing together of the filaments and lamellae. The surface of the gills is often covered with an exudate. Fish become prostrate or sluggish. The opercles are distended and the animals appear to have a "mumpy" appearance when viewed from above (Phillips *et al.*, 1945; Rucker *et al.*, 1952). Necrosis, scarring, and cellular atrophy of the tender gill elements occur and anemia develops after long deficiency (Halver, 1953a,b, 1957). Dietary gill disease has been adequately described and correlated with pantothenic acid deficiency (Fig. 6). The same type of symptom has been observed in salmon, trout, eel, carp (Ogino, 1967b; Steffens, 1969), and catfish (Dupree, 1966). After replacement of pantothenic acid in the diet, recovery is rapid for those fish still feeding and the typical clubbed gill disappears clinically after about 4

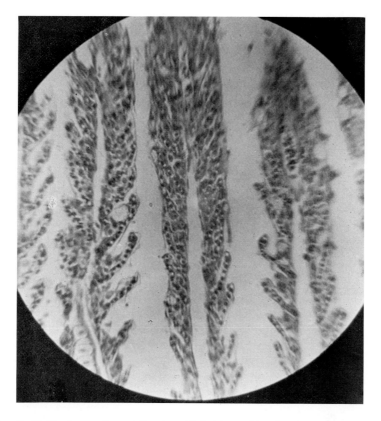

Fig. 6. Clubbed gills of pantothenic acid-deficient chinook salmon. (From Halver, 1953a.)

weeks on the recovery diet; however, evidence of necrosis and scarring are retained as the gill filaments and lamellae repair.

### 4. *Requirements*

Dietary requirements for salmon, trout, and other fish are listed in Table III. Trout values were determined by using the Wisconsin technique for maximum growth response or by using the Cortland technique of assaying diet ingredients, measuring growth response and assaying for maximum liver storage for the different diet treatments. Salmon values were determined by using test diets supplemented with increments of calcium pantothenate, measuring growth response, and assaying for maximum liver storage.

## 5. *Sources and Protection*

Good sources for pantothenic acid are cereal bran, yeast, liver, kidney, heart, spleen, and lung. Fish flesh is a relatively rich source, although the content is only about 20% of pantothenic acid found in animal glandular tissue. Royal jelly probably contains the greatest amount and must have some role in the transformation of bee larva into queen bees as it contains over 500 $\mu$g of pantothenol/gm dry weight (Pearson and Burgin, 1941). Pantothenic acid in the sodium or calcium salt form is relatively stable and can be incorporated into either moist or dry fish diets. Some loss is incurred during autoclaving and excessive heat should therefore be minimized during diet preparations. Since the free acid is labile to heat and also to acid and alkali, some loss can be expected during warm, moist, diet preparation or during warm, moist storage. Certain cereal brans may have pantothenic acid bound in a form unavailable to fishes because of the low digestibility coefficients and should be used sparingly as the pantothenic acid source for the diet. During pasteurization some loss may occur during preparation of wet fish or animal glandular tissue in the moist diet formulas.

## 6. *Antimetabolites and Inactivation*

Since pantothenic acid affects the respiration of many types of cells, compounds like 6-mercaptopurine, 2,6-diaminopurine, and 8-azaguanine, which inhibit growth of tumors are antagonistic to pantothenic acid (Chow, 1964). Pantoyltaurine is an antimetabolite of pantothenic acid and has been used to accelerate deficiency syndromes in experimental animals (Winterbottom *et al.*, 1947). Many derivatives of this compound have been prepared and have been used for this purpose. Winterbottom *et al.* (1947) reported methyl $\omega$-pantothenic acid is also an antagonist which interferes with the formation of acetyl coenzyme A and accelerates deficiency syndrome symptoms in animals. This compound inhibits sulfanilamide acetylation in pigeon liver homogenates but did not prevent citric formation (Dietrich and Shapiro, 1956). Pantothenic acid itself can be used to overcome inhibitory effects of these antagonists. It has been shown to reverse the blocking with 6-mercaptopurine of nuclear mitosis in animals. High pantothenic acid or coenzyme A intake is effective. The migratory urge of salmon can be inhibited by providing high levels of calcium pantothenate in the diet, but this effect is only transitory and salmon reverted to migratory urge after about 3 weeks of high pantothenic acid dietary intake (Burrows *et al.*, 1951).

## 7. *Clinical Assessment*

Assay of pantothenic acid content in the diet may be misleading unless care is exercised in proper hydrolysis of the raw materials being assayed.

Pantothenic acid is only slowly liberated by normal hydrolytic procedures and inadequate hydrolysis will result in low values. Complete hydrolysis with enzyme preparations will liberate all of pantothenic acid from biologically active material of glandular tissues, fish flesh, yeast, and bran. Coenzyme A is present in cells of most biological material which must be hydrolyzed adequately to liberate pantothenic acid, pantotheine, phosphopantothenic acid, phosphopantotheine, and bound coenzyme A (Brown, 1959). Liver storage for actively feeding sea salmon shows pantothenic acid content of 18–20 μg/gm of fresh tissue. Young chinook and coho salmon fingerlings reared in freshwater at 12°–15°C showed maximum liver storage at about 14–16 μg of pantothenic acid/gm of fresh liver tissue. Load tests and acetylation reactions of sulfanilamide have been used in man and other experimental animals but have not yet been extended for assessment of pantothenic acid status in fish.

### E. Niacin

Nicotinic acid was synthesized by Huber and Weidel in 1873 (Hein, 1964) but was left on the shelf as an organic compound unrelated to the severe pellagra afflictions occurring throughout the world at that time. Sixty years later Warburg and Christian (1935) showed it to be present in coenzymes I and II, and 2 years thereafter Elvehjem et al. (1937) cured "black tongue" in dogs with the vitamin. Niacin was postulated to be part of factor H for fish in 1937 (Tunison et al., 1943) but deficiency symptoms were not adequately described until reported in trout by McLaren et al. (1947a).

### 1. Chemical Structure, Characteristics, and Analogs

Niacin or nicotinic acid is pyridine-3-carboxylic acid with chemical formula $C_6H_5O_2N$ and the structural formula shown in Fig. 7. Niacin is the preferred nomenclature rather than nicotinic acid, the original name of the material synthesized in 1873 by Hubert and Euler. Nicotinic acid amide or niacinamide is the common form in which the vitamin is physiologically active. Niacin is a white, crystalline solid, soluble in water and alcohol and more soluble in alkali. It is stable in the dry state and may be autoclaved for short periods without destruction. It is also stable to heat

Fig. 7. Niacin. Nicotinic acid on left and niacinamide on right.

in mineral acids and alkali. Niacin is both a carboxylic acid and an amine and forms quaternary ammonium compounds because of its basic nature. Acidic characteristics include salt formation with alkali and reactional heavy metal salts. Niacin can be esterified easily, then converted to amides. Niacinamide is a crystalline powder with formula $C_6H_6N_2O$ and is soluble in water and ethanol and the dry material is stable up to about 60°C. In aqueous solutions it is stable for short periods of autoclaving. It is the form of the vitamin normally found in niacinamide adenine dinucleotide (coenzyme I or NAD), and in niacinamide adenine dinucleotide phosphate (NADP). Niacin, niacinamide, NAD, and several derivatives of NAD and NADP have biological activity.

### 2. *Positive Functions*

The major function of niacin in NAD and NADP is the removal of hydrogen from substrates and the transfer of hydrogen or electrons to another coenzyme in the hydrogen transport series. Most of these enzyme systems function by alternating between the oxidized and reduced state of the coenzymes NAD-NADH and NADP-NADPH. These oxidation-reduction reactions are anaerobic, as, for example, when pyruvate acts as the hydrogen acceptor and lactate is formed. The second type of oxidation-reduction reaction is coupled to electron transport with subsequent oxidation of reduced NADH or NADPH, and these are anaerobic reactions which function in respiration. Both NAD and NADP are involved in synthesis of high energy phosphate bonds which furnish energy for certain steps in glycolysis, in pyruvate metabolism, and in pentose synthesis. Niacin is also involved in lipid metabolism, amino acid and protein metabolism, and in photosynthesis. An interrelationship between thiamine and niacin exists since both vitamins are involved in coenzyme systems of carbohydrate metabolism in energy generating systems of intermediary metabolism where food material is oxidized to furnish heat for physiological functions, to maintain homeostasis, for body temperature in homeotherms, or to generate high energy phosphate bonds for subsequent physiological reactions of the living organism. A good review of niacin biochemistry has been presented by Goldsmith (1964).

### 3. *Deficiency Syndrome*

The deficiency signs in fish are listed in Table II. Stores of niacin are more slowly exhausted under experimental conditions than some of the other vitamins resulting in less defined and more slowly developing symptoms. Elvehjem cured black tongue in dogs by administration of niacin in 1937 (Elvehjem *et al.*, 1937) and a history of pellagralike symptoms in primates of ancient record was elegantly described by Casal over 200 years ago (Harris, 1919). Niacin deficiencies in fish were experimentally induced in the late 1940's and early 1950's by using basal diets which had low niacin content. Loss of appetite and poor food conversion were the first signs noted. Then fish turned dark and went off feed. Upon continued exposure to the deficient regimen, lesions in the colon appeared, erratic motion was observed, edema of the stomach and colon appeared and muscle spasms occurred while fish were apparently resting (McLaren *et al.*, 1947a; Wolf, 1951; Halver, 1953a,b, 1957). A predisposition to sunburn in fish confined in the open in shallow ponds or raceways was described (DeLong *et al.*, 1958b). Carp showed a congestion of the skin with subcutaneous hemorrhages (Aoe *et al.*, 1967a). Common symptoms of niacin deficiency in most fish studied were muscular weakness and spasms, coupled with poor growth and poor food conversion.

### 4. *Requirements*

Niacin requirements in young fish experimentally tested are listed in Table III. Brook and brown trout requirements were calculated by feeding meat–meal mixtures which were assayed for niacin content and then noting growth response and calculating point of maximum liver storage at the end of the experimental period. Rainbow trout and salmon requirements were determined by feeding test diets containing different increments of niacin, measuring growth, and point of maximum liver storage at the end of the experimental period. Salmon requirements appear to be approximately twice those of trout and may reflect differences in metabolism or imbalance of nutrients in the test diets. In homeotherms on a balanced test ration the niacin requirement is generally estimated to be about ten times that of the thiamine requirement. These rations generally contain considerable carbohydrate material to furnish energy to maintain body temperature. In fish the requirement appears to be twenty to thirty times that of the thiamine needs determined for the same test conditions and test rations. This difference may be due to low carbohydrate content of young fish diets and the higher protein content of these rations. A well-established conversion of tryptophan to niacin has been reported by Nishizuka and Hayaishi (1963) for mammalian liver. This conversion may account for the slow development of the niacin-deficiency syndrome in fish. However, after 10–14 weeks on diets devoid of niacin, deficiency symptoms did occur in several species of fish. The symptoms were reduced by replacement of niacin in the ration even when high protein diets containing an excess of tryptophan were fed. Therefore, if conversion of tryptophan to niacin does satisfy part of the niacin requirements for normal growth and physiological function in fish in 10°–15°C water environments, an additional amount of niacin is required for maximum liver storage. However, too much niacin inhibits growth (Poston, 1969a).

### 5. Sources and Protection

Niacin is found in most animal and plant tissues. Rich sources are yeast, liver, kidney, heart, legumes, and green vegetables. Wheat contains more niacin than corn and the vitamin is also found in milk and egg products. The vitamin is very stable since it is generally found in coenzyme form in raw materials. Niacin added to the diet as a supplement remains relatively unaltered during diet manufacture, processing, and storage.

### 6. Antimetabolites and Inactivation

Pyridine-3-sulfonic acid and 3-acetylpyridine are compounds structurally related to niacin and are antimetabolites for this vitamin in animals and in microorganisms. Additional niacin can overcome the antimetabolite effect. A niacin-deficiency symptom in rats may be induced by 6-amino niacinamide. The symptom is reversed by addition of ten times more niacinamide than antimetabolite (Goldsmith, 1964). Thioacetamide has been reported to inhibit niacin function in fish and thus cause predisposition to sunburn and skin lesions.

### 7. Clinical Assessment

Liver storage levels of actively feeding sea salmon show 70–80 $\mu$g of niacin/gm of wet liver tissue. About half of this amount is present in fingerling salmon raised in 12°–15°C water environments and fed test rations containing 40–50% protein and niacin supplements of 500–750 mg/kg dry diet. Urinary metabolites of niacin have been measured in other animals on standard niacin load in test rations containing a standard tryptophan load. The technique is well developed to measure the $N^1$-methyl derivative in mammalian urine (Handley and Bond, 1948). These data have not been reported for fish but metabolism chambers are available for collecting branchial and urinary wastes from large fish intubated with different diet material.

### F. BIOTIN

Egg white "injury" in rats was described by Bateman (1916) and by Boas (1927). Neural disturbances from this "injury" were reported by Findlay and Stern in 1929, and the active material was called "coenzyme R" by Allison et al. (1933) and "vitamin H" by György in 1939. Biotin was isolated by Kogl and Tonnis (1936) and the functions were defined for the active material by György in 1940. Biotin was synthesized by du Vigneaud (1942) and by Harris *et al.* (1943). Biotin was once thought to be part of factor H for fish. Blue slime patch disease in trout due to biotin deficiency was reported by Phillips *et al.* (1945) and by McLaren *et al.* (1947a).

### 1. *Chemical Structure, Characteristics and Analogs*

*d*-Biotin, hexahydro-2-oxo-1-thieno-3,4-imidazole-4-valeric acid, has the chemical formula $C_{10}H_{16}O_3N_2S$ and the structural formula shown in Fig. 8. It is a monocarboxylic acid slightly soluble in water and alcohol and insoluble in fat solvents. Salts of the acid are soluble in water. Aqueous solutions or the dry material are stable at 100°C and to light. The vitamin is destroyed by acids and alkalis and by oxidizing agents such as peroxides or permanganate. Biocytin is a bound form of biotin isolated from yeast, plant, and animal tissues (Wright *et al.*, 1954). Other bound forms of the vitamin can generally be liberated by peptic digestion. Oxybiotin has partial vitamin activity but oxybiotin sulfonic acid and other analogs are antimetabolites inhibiting the growth of bacteria. This inhibition can be overcome by additional biotin and therefore must be due to inhibition of incorporation of the biotin into coenzymes (West *et al.*, 1966). Avidin, a protein found in raw egg white, binds biotin and makes it unavailable to fish and other animals. This binding is irreversible in raw material but heating to denature the protein makes the bound biotin available again to the fish. Biocytin or ε-biotinyl lysine (the epsilon amino group of lysine and the carboxyl of biotin being combined in a peptide bond) is hydrolyzed by the enzyme biotinase making the protein-bound biotin available.

### 2. *Positive Functions*

Biotin is required in several specific carboxylation and decarboxylation reactions reviewed by Lardy and Peanasky (1953), Vagelos (1964), and Knappe (1970). Biotin is part of the coenzyme of several carboxylating enzymes fixing $CO_2$ such as propionyl coenzyme A in formation of propionic acid. Carboxylase fixation of $CO_2$ to form methylmalonyl coenzyme A is involved in the carboxylation and decarboxylation of tricarboxylic acids.

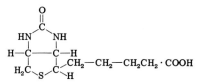

FIG. 8. Biotin.

Biotin is also involved in purine synthesis and is the coenzyme of malonyl coenzyme A involved in elongation of fatty acids (Waite and Wakil, 1966). It is involved in general lipid synthesis in animals and in the deamination and biosynthesis of citrulline. It is involved in the conversion of unsaturated fatty acids to the stable *cis* form in synthesis of biologically active fatty acids.

### 3. *Deficiency Syndrome*

Some signs of biotin deficiency in salmonids are skin disorders, muscle atrophy, lesions in the colon, loss of appetite, and spastic convulsions. Hematology discloses fragmentation of erythrocytes. Poor growth is a common symptom and has been reported for salmonids (McLaren *et al.*, 1947a; Phillips *et al.*, 1949; Wolf, 1951; Halver, 1953a,b, 1957), common carp (Ogino *et al.*, 1970b), goldfish (*Carassius auratus*) (Tomiyama and Ohba, 1967), and eel (Nose, 1970). Blue slime patch disease in brook trout deficient in biotin appears typical for this species and is described in detail by Phillips *et al.* (1949). Fish reared in 10°–15°C water exhaust biotin stores in 8–12 weeks and the first signs are anorexia, poor food conversion, and general listlessness before the more acute deficiency symptoms become detectable.

### 4. *Requirements*

The biotin requirements for young salmon, trout, carp, goldfish, and eel raised under experimental conditions appear to be about the same. Brown trout appear to require nearly twice as much biotin in the diet as do brook or rainbow trout (Phillips *et al.*, 1949). Requirements are listed in Table III and were determined for trout by feeding different meat–meal mixtures containing various levels of biotin and assaying for liver storage. The requirements for salmon were determined by feeding test diets with different increments of biotin added. The requirements for carp were likewise determined by the use of test diets and added biotin.

### 5. *Sources and Protection*

Rich sources of biotin are liver, kidney, yeast, milk products, and egg yolks. Nut meats contain good supplies of biotin isotels. The diet should be protected from strong oxidizing agents or conditions which promote oxidation of ingredients. Raw egg white should not be incorporated into moist fish diets. Cooking will inactivate the avidin which irreversibly binds biotin.

## 6. *Antimetabolites and Inactivation*

Raw egg white has already been discussed which irreversibly binds biotin and makes it unavailable to young fish. Many biotin homologs with different side chain lengths inhibit the growth of bacteria. Oxybiotin sulfonic acid inhibits biotin and generates deficiency symptoms. Oxybiotin can form derivatives which compete for biotin sites during formation of coenzymes. Oxybiotin, a chemically synthesized compound, has about the same biological activity as the natural *d*-biotin.

## 7. *Clinical Assessment*

Measurement of urinary excretion of biotin in animals does not prove a good clinical method since biotin is synthesized by several organisms in the gut. In fish, this technique needs to be explored and may well be valuable as a clinical tool since the gastrointestinal tract of many freshwater fish contains only small quantities of bacteria. Biotin is one of the most expensive vitamins to add to fish rations. Actively feeding sea salmon have liver biotin concentrations of 10–12 $\mu$g/gm of wet liver tissue. The concentrations in the liver of young salmon fingerlings fed test diets containing an excess of biotin in freshwater were between 6–8 $\mu$g of the vitamin/gm of tissue. Fish with these levels of biotin in the liver should probably be in sound biotin nutritional status.

### G. Folic Acid (Folacin)

A megaloblastic anemia was induced in monkeys by McCarrison in 1921 (Hein, 1964). An active extract was isolated and used to cure anemia by Day *et al.* (1938) and vitamin M and vitamin $B_c$ were reported by Stokstad (1943). Folic acid was synthesized by Pfiffner *et al.* in 1946 and was soon used in fish diets to try to cure purified diet anemia. Tunison *et al.* (1943), Phillips *et al.* (1947), and McLaren *et al.* (1947a), all worked with folic acid as the antianemic factor in 1945–1947. Halver and Norris tested it in salmon in 1949 and Wolf incorporated it into his test diets for trout in 1950 (Wolf, 1951).

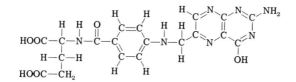

Fig. 9. Folic acid.

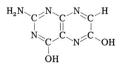

Fɪɢ. 10. Xanthopterin.

## 1. *Chemical Structure, Characteristics, and Analogs*

Folic acid, pteroylglutamic acid, or folacin has the chemical formula $C_{19}H_{19}N_7O_6$ and the structural formula shown in Fig. 9. Folic acid crystallizes into yellow spear-shaped leaflets which are soluble in water and dilute alcohol. It can be precipitated with heavy metal salts. In acid it is easily destroyed by heat and deteriorates when exposed to sunlight, or during prolonged storage. Several analogs have biological activity including pteroic acid, rhizopterin, folinic acid, xanthopterin and several formyl-tetrahydropteroylglutamic acid derivatives. These have closely allied ring structures and many have been isolated as derivatives in various animal or microbiological preparations. One simple form, xanthopterin, present

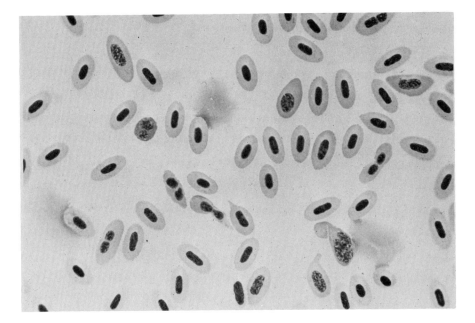

Fɪɢ. 11. Blood smear of folic acid-deficient coho salmon. Note senile cells and divided nucleus of erythrocytes.

in the pigments of insects is shown in Fig. 10 and is of special interest because of early work with this compound as the antianemic factor H for fish (Simmons and Norris, 1941).

## 2. *Positive Functions*

Folic acid is required for normal blood cell formation and is involved as a coenzyme in one-carbon transfer mechanisms (Huennekens *et al.* 1957, 1958; Nakao and Greenberg, 1958). In the presence of ascorbic acid, folic acid is transformed into the active 5-formyl-5,6,7,8-tetrahydropteroyl-glutamic acid. Folic acid is involved in many one-carbon metabolism systems such as serine and glycine interconversion, methionine-homocysteine synthesis, histidine synthesis, and pyrimidine synthesis (Hartman and Buchanan, 1959). Several coenzyme forms of the active vitamin have been isolated. A good general discussion can be found in West *et al.* (1966). Folic acid is involved in the conversion of megaloblastic bone marrow to nomaloblastic type. It has a role in blood glucose regulation and improves cell membrane function and hatchability of eggs.

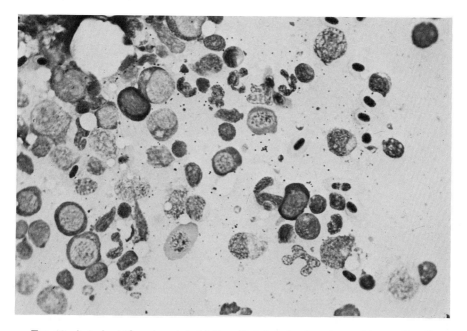

FIG. 12. Anterior kidney imprint of folic acid-deficient coho salmon. Note senile cells, divided nucleus, and absence of immature or proforms of erythrocytes.

### 3. *Deficiency Syndrome*

Macrocytic normochromic anemia occurs in several experimental animals, including fish, fed diets devoid of the vitamers folacin (Aoe *et al.*, 1967c; Smith, 1968; Smith and Halver, 1969). Increasing numbers of senile cells are observed as the deficiency progresses until only a few old and degenerating cells are found in the blood of deficient fish. Anterior kidney imprints disclose only adult cells and no proforms present. Figures 11 and 12 show blood smears from deficient coho salmon and kidney imprints from these same fish. In comparison Fig. 13 shows a blood smear of fish 28 days after folic acid was replaced in the ration and Fig. 14 shows an anterior kidney imprint with many immature cells and proforms present. Other signs observed have been poor growth, anorexia, general anemia. lethargy, fragile fins, dark skin pigmentation, and infarction of spleen.

### 4. *Requirements*

Folic acid requirements based on feeding meat–meal mixtures or test diets plus crystalline compounds, measuring growth response, and food conversion, observing for anemia, and finding maximum liver storage of the vitamin are listed in Table II. The requirement seems to be about the

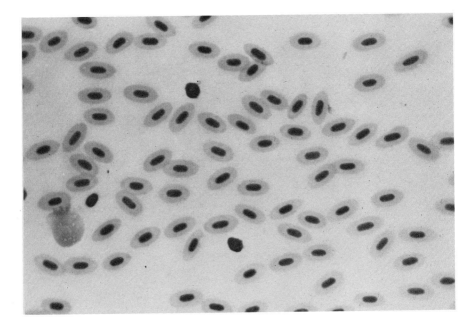

Fᴵɢ. 13. Blood smear from normal coho salmon. Note variety of erythrocyte types including immature forms present.

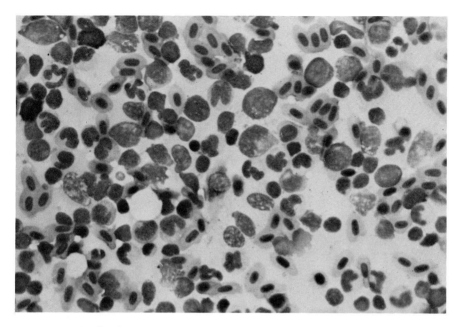

Fig. 14. Head kidney imprint of normal coho salmon. Note variety of cells present and proforms of erythrocytes during different stages of development.

same for trout and salmon. Marginal macrocytic anemias occur in fish fed diets containing marginal amounts of folacin. Individual fish ingesting adequate amounts of the vitamin have low variation in total erythrocyte counts.

### 5. Sources and Protection

Yeast, green vegetables, liver, kidney, glandular tissue, fish tissue, and fish viscera are good sources of folic acid. Insects contain xanthopterin which has folic acid activity and the same nuclear structure as folic acid. At one time the yellow pigment of xanthopterin was identified as the fish antianemic factor H, but subsequent experiments showed only partial activity and that folic acid itself was a much more potent antimacrocytic anemia factor. Probably, insects do contribute toward the folacin requirement of wild fish, but in scientific fish husbandry other agricultural or industrial products form more reliable sources. Activity is lost during extended storage and when material is exposed to sunlight. Therefore, dry diet materials should be carefully protected during manufacture and moist diet rations should be carefully preserved. Both types of fish diets should be fed soon after manufacture to assure original folic acid activity.

### 6. *Antimetabolites and Inactivation*

One antagonist for folacin is 4-aminopteroylglutamic acid or aminopterin. This material, when incorporated in the diet of guinea pigs and rats, induces anemia and leucopenia and has been used to treat leukemia in man (Chow, 1964). Amethopterin (4-amino-$N^{10}$-methylpteroylglutamic acid) also can be used to induce deficiency by suppressing 4-amino coenzymes with resultant poor purine, pyrimidine, and nucleic acid production. Likewise amethopterin inhibits nucleic acid synthesis and macrocytic anemia eventually occurs.

### 7. *Clinical Assessment*

Hematology is used as a simple clinical tool to assess hemopoiesis in fish. Anterior kidney imprints easily disclose normal distribution of immature cells and proforms undergoing reticulosis. Actively feeding sea salmon and young salmon fingerlings fed diets rich in folacin show liver storage of 3–4 $\mu$g of folic acid/gm of wet tissue. Microbiological assay is preferred for assessment of total vitamers for folacin in dietary raw materials because the total biological activity it measures includes all the various coenzyme forms and folic acid analogs. Assessment of the dietary level of the vitamers folacin and intake of fish fed is important for intensive cold water fish husbandry. In pond culture techniques where the dietary is supplementary in nature and fish eat aquatic and terrestrial insects, algae, and other food, folic acid in the supplement is not as critical as when the animal must depend entirely upon the supplement. Since folic acid is labile in storage, excessive amounts are generally added during feed manufacture in anticipation of improper or long-term storage. However, prudent fish husbandry dictates rapid use of manufactured rations with minimum storage and/or additional supplementation with folic acid. Routine periodic hematology of the fish assures proper nutritional status for maximum production and sound health. The author has noted in several series of experiments that when fish diseases occur through inadvertent contamination of the water supply, those groups of fish partially or completely deficient in folic acid were the first lots to show acute disease symptoms. Therefore, folic acid must also play an important role in resistance to disease. Experiments testing this hypothesis should yield important dividends to improve fish husbandry.

### H. VITAMIN $B_{12}$

The antipernicious anemia factor was isolated and crystallized nearly simultaneously by Rickes *et al.* (1948) and by Smith (1948). A tentative chemical formula for the active APF (animal protein factor) was established by Todd and co-workers in 1955 (Hein, 1964). One milligram of vitamin $B_{12}$ was made available by Dr. Major of Merck and Co. to test antianemic action in salmon in the late fall of 1949, and Halver and Norris injected anemic salmon with crystalline $B_{12}$ alone and in combination with folic acid and xanthopterin. Positive hemopoiesis occurred within a few days after vitamin $B_{12}$ plus folic acid was injected, and the salmon showed rapid recovery from the anemia. Wolf in 1950 added both vitamin $B_{12}$ and folic acid to supply factor H in his trout test diet.

## 1. *Chemical Structure, Characteristics, and Analogs*

Vitamin $B_{12}$ or cyanocobalamin has the approximate molecular weight of 1500 with the chemical formula of about $C_{63}H_{88}O_{14}PCo$ depending on state of hydration (Smith, 1960). The approximate structural formula is shown in Fig. 15. The molecule has a planar group and a nucleotide group lying nearly at right angles to one another (Chow, 1964). Cyanocobalamin is a red crystalline compound which was isolated almost simultaneously

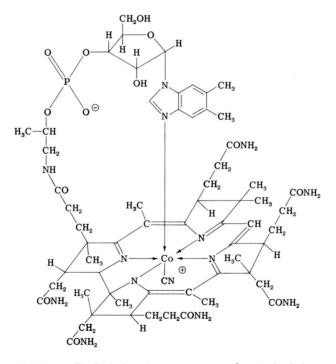

Fig. 15. Vitamin $B_{12}$ depicting planar structure and central cobalt atom.

by investigators in England and in the United States. This cobalt-containing vitamin has a net charge of one and has a cyano group linked to the central cobalt molecule which can be replaced with various other small groups forming hydroxocobalamin, nitrocobalamin, thiocyanocobalamin, and chlorocobalamin. The crystalline material or aqueous solution of vitamin $B_{12}$ is stable to mild heat in neutral solution, but is rapidly destroyed by heating in dilute acid or alkali. Crude concentrates are more unstable and rapidly lose activity. The compound is similar to the porphyrins in spatial configuration with a central cobalt atom linked to four reduced pyrrole rings which form a large macro ring (Hein, 1964). Several other vitamers $B_{12}$ have been isolated with good biological activity for animals or bacteria (Chow, 1964).

### 2. *Positive Functions*

Cyanocobalamin is involved with folic acid in hemopoiesis. It is required for growth by many microorganisms and is a growth factor for many animals (Hunter *et al.*, 1949; Hartman *et al.*, 1949; Ott *et al.*, 1948; Johnson and Neumann, 1949). The animal protein factor present in fish meal and other animal meals was not correlated with fish antianemic factor H until crystalline vitamin $B_{12}$ was injected into anemic chinook salmon fingerlings in 1949 and positive hemopoiesis was observed (Halver, 1953a, 1969). A coenzyme incorporating vitamin $B_{12}$ is involved in the reversible isomerization of methylmalonyl coenzyme A to succinyl coenzyme A and in the isomerization of methylaspartate to glutamate. Cyanocobalamin is involved in the coenzyme for the methylation of homocystine to form methionine. It is also involved in several other one-carbon metabolism reactions and in the synthesis of labile methyl compounds. One vitamin $B_{12}$ containing coenzyme acts in methylation of the purine ring during thymine synthesis. Vitamin $B_{12}$ is also involved in cholesterol metabolism, in purine and pyrimidine biosynthesis, and in the metabolism of glycols (Chow, 1964).

### 3. *Deficiency Syndrome*

Deficiency signs in young pigs, chicks, and rats show abnormal blood elements, poor growth, porphorin whiskers, scaly feet, and pernicious anemia (West *et al.*, 1966). An intrinsic factor is necessary for good absorption of the vitamin from the gut. This factor is a low molecular weight mucoprotein which normally occurs in gastric juice, and especially in hog gut mucosa (Abeles and Lee, 1961; Landboe-Christensen and Plum, 1948). Pernicious anemia which results without gastric intrinsic factor or vitamin $B_{12}$ is characterized by abnormal hematology. This same picture occurs in blood smears in fish deficient in vitamin $B_{12}$. Erythrocytes are fragmented with many aberrant forms present. Hemoglobin determination is erratic between fish and erythrocyte counts have a range extending from frank anemia to a near normal blood pattern. Cyanocobalamin stores in fish tissues are slowly exhausted and only after 12–16 weeks on test do the symptoms appear in deficient salmon populations. Poor appetite, poor growth, poor food conversion, and some dark pigmentation can be observed before frank anemia is detected (Halver, 1957). Chinook or coho salmon reared on diets devoid of vitamin $B_{12}$ but with adequate sources of folic acid show typical microcytic hypochromic anemia with fragmented erythrocytes and many immature forms present in both blood smears and in erythrocyte counting chambers.

### 4. *Requirements*

Difficulties in assaying for the vitamers $B_{12}$ in diets, the long induction period for anemias to develop, and the preparation and assay problems for assessment of liver storage have limited quantitative requirement determinations to only young chinook salmon fingerlings raised on stringently controlled test diets in special water systems of low microorganism count. The figure listed in Table III is the best tentative requirement which could be calculated from the crystalline vitamin $B_{12}$ intake observed, the absence of microcytic pernicious anemia, normal hematology at the end of the 16-week feeding period, and maximum liver storage of vitamers $B_{12}$ determined by *Lactobacillus leichmannii* microbiological assay.

### 5. *Sources and Protection*

Rich sources of animal protein factor or vitamers $B_{12}$ are found in fish meal, fish viscera, liver, kidney, glandular tissues, and slaughter house waste meat. Since vitamin $B_{12}$ is labile on storage, and in mild acid solution is easily destroyed by heating, care must be exercised in diet preparation containing flesh or meat scraps poorly stored with low pH and which are subsequently pasteurized or sterilized. Likewise, storage conditions should be cold and of short duration before diet is used to assure maximum retention of vitamin $B_{12}$ activity in the diet when consumed.

### 6. *Antimetabolites and Inactivation*

Hydroxocobalamin, chlorocobalamin, nitrocobalamin, and other derivatives of the cyanide radical attached to the cobalt atom in vitamin $B_{12}$ have varying degrees of activity, but mild *in vitro* treatment with cyanide converts these analogs back into cyanocobalamin (Kaczka *et al.*, 1950). The vitamin $B_{12}$ coenzymes are very unstable in light, and exposure to direct sunlight for a few minutes results in complete decomposition of the coenzyme. Also, dilute acid solutions increase sensitivity, and purine-containing analogs of $B_{12}$ coenzymes are very labile in dilute acid solution (Chow, 1964). Therefore, $B_{12}$ preparations for experimental work should be carefully preserved in acotinic glass, in neutral solutions, until time for use in the experiment. Likewise, moist diet preparations should be protected from light and maintained at neutral rather than in acid or alkali pH ranges to preserve as much vitamin $B_{12}$ activity as possible.

### 7. *Clinical Assessment*

Generalized anemia with fragmentation of erythrocytes and extremely varying hemoglobin erythrocyte counts indicate suspect $B_{12}$ deficiency. Prompt response in individual fish is obtained by injecting $B_{12}$ alone or in combination with folic acid in the ratio 1 part vitamin $B_{12}$ to 100 parts folic acid. Hematology in fish and vitamin $B_{12}$ deficiency is characterized by these varied blood cell types whereas folic acid deficiency shows only senile cells, some with pyknotic nuclei, characteristic of macrocytic normochromic anemia. Therefore, characterization of the anemia is critical to separate symptoms of one antianemic factor from the other. Combination of the two vitamins is McCay's fish antianemic factor H.

### I. Ascorbic Acid

Experimental work to cure scurvy with fruit juice was described by Lind in 1753 (Stewart and Guthrie, 1953), but nearly 200 years elapsed before the exact chemical compound responsible for reducing the symptoms was defined. Vitamin C was named by Drummond (1920). L-Glucuronic acid was isolated by Szent-György in 1928. Crystalline vitamin C was isolated and demonstrated to be the antiscorbutic vitamin by King and Waugh (1932, Waugh and King, 1932), was named "ascorbic acid" by Szent-György and Haworth (1933), and L-dihydroascorbic acid was synthesized by Reichstein *et al.* (1933) in that same year. McCay and Tunison reported scoliosis in brook trout fed Formalin-preserved meat in 1934 and McLaren *et al.* (1947a) observed hemorrhages in trout fed rations low in ascorbic acid. Nearly 20 years then elapsed before Kitamura *et al.* (1965) demonstrated a critical need for trout for vitamin C, and 4 years later the need for L-ascorbic acid was demonstrated in salmon by Halver *et al.* (1969). Fish were thus only recently added to the list of animals requiring L-ascorbic acid in the diet.

### 1. *Chemical Structure, Characteristics, and Analogs*

Ascorbic acid and its inactive analog dehydroascorbic acid have the formula $C_6H_6O_6$ and the structural formulas shown in simple form in Fig. 16. The reduced or active form is a white, odorless, crystalline compound,

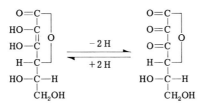

F<small>IG</small>. 16. Vitamin C. L-Ascorbic acid on left and oxidized form or dehydroascorbic acid on right.

soluble in water but insoluble in fat solvents. Dihydroascorbic acid is easily and rapidly oxidized to dehydroascorbic acid which is much less active biologically than the reduced form. Ascorbic acid readily forms salts and is labile to free oxygen. Reduced ascorbic acid is very stable in acid solution because of the preservation of the lactone ring, but in alkaline solution hydrolysis occurs rapidly and vitamin activity is lost. Copper and heavy metal ions enhance oxidation; and while reduction back from the oxidized to the reduced form can be accomplished in the laboratory, this reaction does not proceed readily in the body. Vitamin C is very heat labile and prone to atmospheric oxidation, especially in the presence of copper, iron, or several other metallic catalysts. The reduced form is the most biologically active form but several derivatives or salts may be formed which have varying degrees of ascorbate activity (Woodruff, 1964; WHO, 1970).

### 2. *Positive Functions*

L-Ascorbic acid acts as a biological reducing agent for hydrogen transport. It is involved in many enzyme systems for hydroxylation, i.e., hydroxylation of tryptophan, tyrosine, or proline. It is involved in detoxification of aromatic drugs and also acts in the production of adrenal steroids (WHO, 1970). Ascorbic acid is necessary for the formation of collagen and normal cartilage as well as normal tooth formation, bone formation, bone repair, and wound healing (Knox and Goswami, 1961; Gould, 1960). Ascorbic acid plays a role synergistically with vitamin E for the maintenance of intracellular antioxidants and free radical traps. The conversion of folic acid to folanic acid requires vitamin C for the active coenzyme form (Wolbach and Home, 1926; Woodruff, 1964). Ascorbic acid is involved in the formation of chondroitin sulfate fractions and intercellular ground substance, and is capable of forming sulfate derivatives with very stable chemical characteristics (West *et al.*, 1966). Intubated labeled ascorbic acid is rapidly mobilized and fixed in deficient fish in areas of rapid collagen synthesis and becomes concentrated in the thick collagen of the skin and in cartilagenous bones. Also pituitary and adrenal glands of the anterior

TABLE IV

GROWTH AND TISSUE ASCORBATE[a]

| C diet treatment | Trout | | | Salmon | | |
|---|---|---|---|---|---|---|
| | Av wt at 24 weeks | Ascorbate concentrate[b] | | Av wt at 24 weeks | Ascorbate concentrate[b] | |
| | | Blood | Kidney | | Blood | Kidney |
| mg/100 gm | gm | $\mu$g/gm | $\mu$g/gm | gm | $\mu$g/gm | $\mu$g/gm |
| 0 | 2.4 | —[c] | —[c] | 5.0 | 22.3 ± 2.2 | 89 |
| 5 | 9.6 | 34.4 ± 2.9 | 125 | 6.0 | 30.5 ± 1.2 | 132 |
| 10 | 10.6 | 34.6 ± 1.3 | 137 | 5.7 | 35.8 ± 1.6 | 265 |
| 20 | 10.1 | 38.8 ± 3.3 | 132 | 6.1 | 34.2 ± 2.3 | 183 |
| 40 | 10.2 | 46.8 ± 6.2 | 162 | 6.3 | 33.7 ± 2.0 | 225 |
| 100 | 10.8 | 51.0 ± 4.6 | 247 | 6.0 | 37.8 ± 2.3 | 321 |

[a] From Halver et al., 1969.
[b] Average of five samples for blood (±S.D.) and two for head kidney tissue.
[c] No fish available for assay.

kidney of partially deficient fish concentrate intubated vitamin C. Ascorbic acid is also involved in maturation of erythrocytes for maintenance of normal blood hematology (Johnson et al., 1971).

### 3. Deficiency Syndrome

Scurvy with impaired collagen formation perifollicular hemorrhages, loose teeth and poor osteoid formation, anemia, and edema have been reported in other animals (WHO, 1970). Deficiency signs in fish are generally related to impaired collagen formation. Fish soon show hyperplasia of collagen and cartilage, then scoliosis, lordosis, internal hemorrhage, resorbed opercles and abnormal support cartilage in gill, spine, and fins with hyperplasia of jaw and snout (Halver et al., 1969). The same symptoms have been observed in trout, salmon, yellowtail, carp, guppies (*Poecilia reticulata*), and char (Kitamura et al., 1965; Poston, 1967). Histologically, hypertrophy of the adrenal tissue and hemorrhages at the bases of fins have been observed in coho salmon. Deficiency signs cease to develop and new growth becomes normal upon replacement of ascorbic acid in the ration. An anemia eventually develops in extremely deficient fish and extreme scoliosis and lordosis do not repair but are walled off with new growth around the afflicted areas of the spine when ascorbic acid is added to the deficient ration (Kitamura et al., 1965).

### 4. Requirements

Rainbow trout have been most studied with a variety of test diets and different ascorbic acid intake. These fish have a varied requirement depending upon the criteria used to measure the need. Reasonable blood and anterior kidney storage levels were obtained with an intake of about

100 mg of vitamin C/kg of dry ration in 10°, 12°, or 15°C water systems. When wound repair experiments were initiated, however, or when fish were exposed to other stress, then the requirements doubled or tripled. When severe abdominal or intramuscular wounds were inflicted, young fish needed at least 500 mg of active ascorbate for tissue repair comparable with control fish receiving 1 gm or more of ascorbate in the diet/kg of dry diet. Coho salmon appear to need about half of these requirements for adequate tissue levels and for maximum severe wound repair rates (Halver *et al.*, 1969). This phenomenon is illustrated in Table IV showing growth response and tissue repair for rainbow trout and coho salmon and in Fig. 17–21 showing wound repair rates in typical fish fed 50, 100, 200, 400, or 1000 mg of reduced ascorbic acid/kg of diet 3 weeks after wounds were inflicted. The requirement for ascorbic acid must therefore be related to the stress, to the growth rate, to the size of the animal, and to the other nutrients present in the diet. A compromise value of about 200 mg of ascorbic acid/kg diet for trout and salmon raised in freshwater systems be-

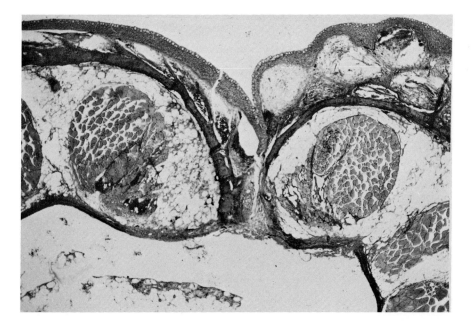

Fig. 17

Figs. 17–21. Typical sections through abdominal tissue wounds showing repair after 3 weeks in rainbow trout fed: Fig. 17, 50 mg; Fig. 18, 100 mg; Fig. 19, 200 mg; Fig. 20, 400 mg; Fig. 21, 1000 mg of L-ascorbic acid/kg of diet, respectively. Rate of wound repair was directly related to vitamin C content of the diet.

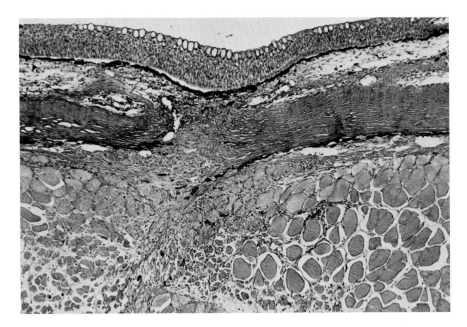

Fig. 18.

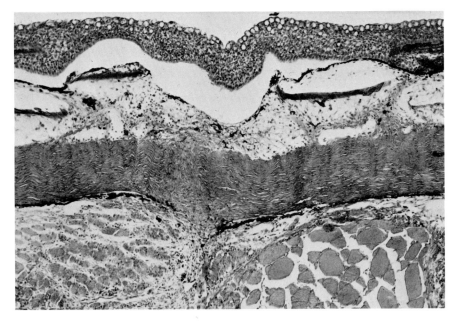

Fig. 19.

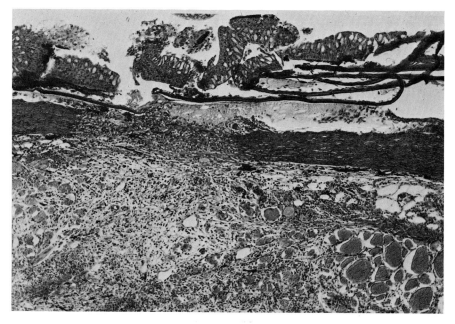

Fig. 20.

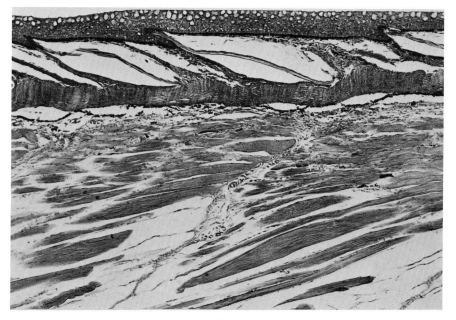

Fig. 21.

tween 10°–15°C would ensure reasonable tissue storage levels and furnish some excess for mild stress conditions and for ascorbic acid loss from the diet through oxidation during feed preparation and subsequent storage before the food is fed. Large carp can synthesize some ascorbate and the requirement for this species may be dependent on size of fish and environment in which reared (Ikeda and Sato, 1964).

### 5. *Sources and Protection*

Ascorbic acid is widely distributed in nature with citrus fruits, cabbage, liver, and kidney tissue good sources for the vitamin. Probably, synthetic industrial material should be considered for addition to the ration, however, to assure adequate intake of this important vitamin for normal growth, tissue repair, and sound physiological function of fish. Fresh insects and fish tissues contain reasonable amounts of the vitamin, and certain dried fruits like lingonberries and cranberries, which have a high benzoic acid to protect vitamin C content, are exotic but rich sources of the vitamin. The food must be protected from aerobic oxidation and any moist feed must be carefully protected from oxidizing agents, air, and from copper, iron, and other metals which catalyze the oxidation of ascorbic acid into the biologically inactive form. Fish food should be kept sealed or frozen, and used rapidly to prevent loss of active ascorbic acid until such time as more heat and oxidation stable analogs become available for dietary use.

### 6. *Antimetabolites and Inactivation*

D-Ascorbic acid, the optical isomer of the active form, has no activity and competes for sites of several enzyme reactions. 6-Deoxy-L-ascorbic acid has very low activity and L-glucoascorbic acid very little activity. These can be expected to be involved in chemical reaction because of the close similarity to the parent compound. Low tryptophan content in the diet appears to increase the demand for ascorbic acid (West *et al.*, 1966). This other nutrient is certainly not an antimetabolite of the oxidation reduction or hydrogen transport vitamin but may increase the demand for vitamin C during detoxification and elimination of unneeded amino acid. Dehydroascorbic acid has very low activity and yet is similar enough to be involved in some metabolism reactions. As mentioned above, L-dihydroascorbic acid is extremely labile to oxidation and especially so in the presence of copper, iron, or several other metals which catalyze atmospheric oxidation into the biologically inactive form.

### 7. *Clinical Assessment*

Ascorbic acid status for experimental animals is normally attempted by tissue ascorbate analysis. Most of the assays previously used measure total ascorbate and not biologically active dihydroascorbic acid (Woodruff, 1964). Thus these are consequently fraught with errors and misconception of true vitamin C status. In fish tissues, blood and liver do not adequately reflect the ascorbic acid intake and status, but assay of the anterior kidney which contains adrenal tissue is a fairly representative tissue storage site for the vitamin. Stress rapidly reduces the ascorbic acid content of this tissue with concurrent production of adrenal steroids (Wedemeyer, 1969). Conversely, dietary intake is reflected up to the point of four- or fivefold storage from deficient levels and only massive dietary intake appears to elevate tissue storage further (Halver *et al.*, 1969). Examination of fragile support cartilage in the gill filaments under low magnification will detect early hypovitaminosis C before clinically acute symptoms become noticeable. However, the best tissue for routine clinical analysis to assess vitamin C status in trout and salmon appears to be the anterior kidney with samples selected from the junction of the two wings forward, tissues then blotted free of blood with filter paper, and then assay of total ascorbate by one of the improved quick methods to determine total ascorbate in this typical storage area for vitamin C in fish (Halver *et al.*, 1969).

## J. INOSITOL

Muscle "sugar" was discovered by Scherer in 1850 and was characterized by Maquenne in 1887 (Scherer, 1850; Maquenne, 1900). Woolley showed it to be an alopecia preventing factor for mice (1940), and the stereo configuration of the active factor, myo-inositol, was proved by Posternak (1936) and by Dangschat (1942). McLaren *et al.* (1947a) observed poor growth and poor food passage in inositol-deficient trout, and these symptoms were confirmed in salmon by Halver (1953a,b) and in carp by Aoe and Masuda (1967).

### 1. *Chemical Structure, Characteristics, and Analogs*

Seven optically inactive and two optically active isomers of hexahydroxycyclohexane can exist. One of the optically active forms, *meso*-inositol

Fig. 22. Inositol, depicting *myo*-inositol form of the vitamin.

or *myo*-inositol, has the biological activity. The chemical formula is $C_6H_{12}O_6$ and the structural formula with the hydroxyl groups in positions 1, 2, 3, 5, in one plane, and 4, 6, in the other plane, is shown in Fig. 22. *myo*- or *meso*-Inositol is a white crystalline powder soluble in water and insoluble in alcohol and ether. The material can be synthesized but is easily isolated from biological material in free or combined forms (Anderson and Wallis, 1948; Weidlein, 1954). The mixed calcium–magnesium salt of the hexophosphate is phytin. Isomers have little biological activity but will compete in chemical reactions.

### 2. *Positive Functions*

*myo*-Inositol is a structural component in living tissues. It has lipotropic action preventing accumulation of cholesterol in one type of fatty liver disease and is involved with choline for homeostasis of normal lipid metabolism (West *et al.*, 1966). It is a growth-promoting substance for microorganisms and prevents an alopecia in mice (Woolley, 1940). It is an emergency carbohydrate source in muscle and is a major structural component in the phospholipid structures in animal tissues (Stetten and Stetten, 1946). The primary function appears to be to serve as a structural element with the six hydroxy groups available for esterification or for acid salt formation to form an integral portion of cell membranes. The stereo configuration of these cell membrane elements probably plays a major role in cell membrane permeability to various ions and molecules (West *et al.*, 1966).

### 3. *Deficiency Syndrome*

Poor growth, increased gastric emptying time, edema, dark color, and distended stomachs are symptoms observed in salmon, trout, carp, and catfish held for long periods on inositol-deficient test rations (Halver, 1970). A spectacle eye condition described for rats (Woolley, 1940) has not been observed under the experimental conditions used in fish studies. The major deficiency sign is inefficiency in digestion and food utilization and concomitant poor growth leading to a population of fish with distended abdomens.

### 4. *Requirements*

Inositol needs have been measured in only two species of salmon and carp and the requirement is high for maximum growth and maximum liver storage. Whether liver storage is accurate criteria to determine requirements is debatable since inositol intake was compared with maximum growth rate and diet conversion to develop a tentative requirement for young fish for this "muscle" sugar.

## 5. *Sources and Protection*

*myo*-Inositol occurs ubiquitously in large amounts wherever biological tissue is found. Wheat germ, dried peas, and beans are rich sources. Brain, heart, and glandular tissues are very good sources for biologically active inositol. Citrus fruit pulp and dried yeast also contain inositol. The compound is stable so normal diet preparation and storage technique should assure adequate intake for young growing fish.

## 6. *Antimetabolites and Inactivation*

Seven optically inactive and one optically active but biologically inactive stereo isomers occur. Since inositol is synthesized in the biologically active form by many microorganisms in the gut, only chemically synthesized inactive isomers added to diets would appear in sufficient amounts to interfere with the metabolism of inositol for growth and normal physiological function. Because of the spatial configuration of the biologically active form and the need to fit these forms into tissue stereobiochemical structure, biologically inactive forms do not compete for critical sites in metabolism. However, the active *cis-trans* isomer does compete and introduces errors in the structural configuration of essential components. Methyl derivatives and mono-, di-, and triphosphoric acid esters occur naturally. Salts of the hexaphosphate or phytin make the bound inositol partially unavailable to the animal (Weidlein, 1954; West *et al.*, 1966).

## 7. *Clinical Assessment*

Tissue analysis for inositol status of the animal has not been successfully employed in animal nutrition except for measurement of free inositol in seminal plasma in animal sires (Hartree, 1957). Bull plasma contained over 500 mg% of the material in healthy animals in good breeding status. The seminal plasma of bulls, rabbits, rams, and stallions ran lower in exhausted animals and during recovery back to good breeding status. The exact explanation for the presence of these very high quantities of free inositol has not been adequately explained. Assessment in fish has been based on lack of deficiency signs coupled with the most efficient food conversion. Actively feeding sea salmon show 1–1.5 mg of inositol/gm of fresh liver tissue and young fingerlings raised in freshwater at 10°–15°C had 600–700 $\mu$g/gm of liver tissue. An alternate, better assessment may be based on a standard muscle section or whole carcass analysis for free or for bound inositol. Projection of inositol intake from normal fish diet ingredients should indicate an excess of this particular vitamin.

K. CHOLINE

Methylation as a basic metabolic process was postulated by Hofmeister (1894). Methyl transfer was shown *in vivo* by Thompson (1917) and the interrelationships between choline, methionine, and homocystine were shown by du Vigneaud in 1939–1942 (Rosenberg, 1945). Trout fed low choline rations developed hemorrhagic kidneys according to McLaren *et al.* (1947a) and salmon showed an aversion to food in choline-deficient diet experiments of Halver (1953a,b).

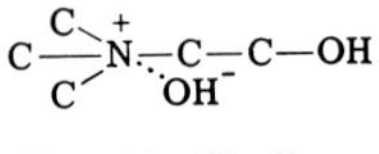

$$C \overset{\displaystyle C}{\underset{\displaystyle C}{\diagdown}} \overset{+}{N} \underset{\overset{..}{\phantom{.}} OH^-}{-} C-C-OH$$

FIG. 23. Choline.

### 1. *Chemical Structure, Characteristics, and Analogs*

Choline has the chemical formula $C_5H_{15}NO_2$. It readily forms salts with a structural formula shown in Fig. 23. Choline is a very strong organic base and forms many derivatives widely distributed in animal and vegetable tissue. One derivative, acetylcholine, is involved in transmission of nerve impulses across synapses. Choline is very hygroscopic, very soluble in water, and is stable to heat in acid solutions but decomposes in alkaline solutions. Choline reacts with many chemical compounds since it is a strong base.

### 2. *Positive Functions*

Choline acts as a methyl donor for methylation of tissue intermediates. It is a lipotropic and antihemorrhagic factor preventing the development of fatty livers. It is involved in synthesis of phospholipids and in fat transport. Acetylcholine transmits the excitatory state across the ganglionic synapses and neuromuscular junctions (Griffith and Nye, 1954; West *et al.*, 1966). Choline is essential for growth and good food conversion in fish.

### 3. *Deficiency Syndrome*

Deficiency signs involve poor growth and poor food conversion with impaired fat metabolism. Hemorrhagic kidneys and intestines have been reported in trout (McLaren *et al.*, 1947a) and increased gastric emptying time has been observed in salmon (Halver, 1957, 1970). Symptoms observed in other animals are shown in Table I, Chapter 10.

### 4. *Requirements*

The requirements for salmon are listed in Table III. The requirements listed for salmon were determined by feeding increments of choline in test diets to young fish in a carefully controlled environmental system, observing growth response, and assessing requirement by maximum growth and food conversion at the minimum intake which would promote maximum liver storage of choline. At the end of the 12-week experimental period, both chinook salmon and coho salmon appear to require about the same dietary intake of choline. The requirement of carp was reported to be about 100 mg/kg body weight/day (Ogino *et al.*, 1970a) to prevent fatty liver development in young fish.

### 5. *Sources and Protection*

Rich sources of choline are wheat germ, soybean and other bean meals, brain, and heart tissue. Choline hydrochloride, a common supplementary form used in fish diet preparations, reacts with $\alpha$-tocopherol and vitamin K preparations—probably inactivating these vitamins when mixed into diet preparations. Therefore, choline should be added in a water carrier and the fat-soluble vitamins added to an oil carrier to prevent reaction when in direct contact in high concentrations with this strong base.

### 6. *Clinical Assessment*

Choline status of fish can be estimated from assay of choline content of the dietary ingredients and the absence of deficiency signs. Maximum liver storage may not be the best criteria to determine choline nutritional status but has been used to assess the tentative requirement listed for two species of salmon.

### L. *p*-AMINOBENZOIC ACID

### 1. *Chemical Structure, Characteristics, and Analogs*

*p*-Aminobenzoic acid has the chemical formula $C_8H_7O_2N$ and the structural formula shown in Fig. 24. This compound is a substituted benzoic acid and isomers with the amino group in the *ortho*, *meta*, or *para* positions occur. Various derivatives of the carboxyl group can be made. *p*-Aminobenzoic acid is a white crystalline powder which is water soluble and heat and light stable in aqueous and mild alkaline solution (West *et al.*, 1966).

FIG. 24. *p*-Aminobenzoic acid.

## 2. *Positive Functions*

*p*-Aminobenzoic acid is a growth-promoting vitamin for microorganisms and large intake has been shown to counteract the antimetabolite effect of sulfonamides in bacterial culture (Wagner and Folkers, 1964). No positive function or deficiency signs have been observed in fish and no requirements have been determined for this compound except for microorganisms. The vitamin status of *p*-aminobenzoic acid is probably confined to microorganisms where it is utilized in the synthesis of folacin compounds. A common antimetabolite of *p*-aminobenzoic acid is sulfonilamide and other sulfa compounds which are toxic to microorganisms forming the basis for sulfa therapy for bacterial infection.

### M. Lipoic Acid

#### 1. *Chemical Structure, Characteristics, and Analogs*

Lipoic acid has the chemical formula $C_8H_{13}O_2S_2$ and the structural formula shown in Fig. 25. Lipoic acid is both fat soluble and water soluble. Several derivatives of the carboxylic acid group have been identified.

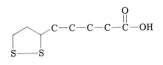

Fig. 25. Lipoic acid.

#### 2. *Positive Functions*

Lipoic acid functions as a coenzyme in $\alpha$-ketoacid decarboxylation. It was discovered independently in several laboratories during the period 1945–1950 and shown to be an essential component of multienzyme units. Its functions have been reviewed by Wagner and Folkers (1964). It is an extremely active biological catalyst. It has been called the pyruvate oxidation or pyruvate decarboxylation factor as it is involved in pyruvate oxidative decarboxylation. The multienzyme unit also includes thiamine pyrophosphate, coenzyme A, and flavin adenine dinucleotide. Therefore, it is closely associated with thiamine in many oxidative decarboxylations of $\alpha$-ketoacids. Glandular tissues are good sources of vitamers lipoic acid. No requirements have been determined for fish.

### III. The Fat-Soluble Vitamins

The fat-soluble vitamins A, D, E, and K each occur in different chemical forms having physiological activity. Isotels for these vitamers are well known but only one or two of the more common and well-recognized forms can be included for discussion. The fat-soluble vitamins differ also from the water-soluble vitamins in accumulative action. Little evidence has been recorded for hypervitaminosis with the water-soluble vitamins since these compounds are rapidly metabolized and excreted when intake exceeds liver or tissue storage capacity, but hypervitaminosis is a common occurrence in fish and other animals when large quantities of any one of the fat-soluble vitamins are ingested. Sometimes these hypervitaminosis symptoms mimic hypovitaminosis signs, as in the case of the vitamers A and D. The toxicity symptoms observed when excess vitamin E or K is ingested are more discrete. Fish rations often include large quantities of fish meal or fish viscera and are often enriched with fish oils to increase caloric density of the ration. In these cases, excessive intake of the fat-soluble vitamins is often encountered.

## A. The Vitamers A

A fat-soluble rat growth-promoting factor was described by Hopkins (1912) and by Osborne and Mendel in the early 1900's (1914). McCollum and Simmonds (1917) cured eye disease, xerophthalmia, with this material. The chemical structure of vitamin A and its relationship to $\beta$-carotene was shown by Von Euler *et al.* (1928). The active vitamin A was synthesized by Fuson and Christ (1936) and by Kuhn and Morris (1937). The interrelationships between retinene and retinene$_2$ corresponding to vitamers $A_1$ and $A_2$ were defined by Morton *et al.* (1947), by Koehn (1948), and by Olson (1961, 1964). Fish oil was shown to be a rich source of vitamers A and to contain vitamin $A_1$ and neovitamin A in a 2:1 ratio. No need for vitamin A in fish was reported until Halver observed xerophthalmia and cataracts in fish fed vitamin A-deficient diets in 1958 and Higashi *et al.* (1960) reported vitamin A had a growth-promoting effect in eels. Hypervitaminosis A was reported to occur in salmon by Burrows *et al.* (1952) and in trout by Poston *et al.* (1966).

### 1. Chemical Structure, Characteristics, and Analogs

Vitamin $A_1$ (retinol) has the chemical formula $C_{20}H_{29}OH$ and vitamin $A_2$ (retinol$_2$) has the formula $C_{20}H_{27}OH$. The structural formula for these fat-soluble alcohols is shown in Fig. 26. The relationship of the vitamin A alcohols to natural occurring $\beta$-carotene containing two symmetrical betaionone rings is shown in Fig. 27. Retinene, the aldehyde form of vitamin A, has been isolated from the retina of dark adapted eyes and is involved in vision in dim light. Retinoic acid, which is the oxidized form of vitamin A alcohol, has been shown to have some vitamin A activity. Olson

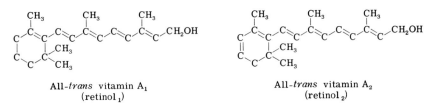

All-*trans* vitamin A₁
(retinol₁)

All-*trans* vitamin A₂
(retinol₂)

Fig. 26. Vitamers A₁ and A₂.

(1964) has reviewed biosynthesis and metabolism of carotinoids and vitamers A. Vitamin A₁ is found in saltwater fishes whereas vitamin A₂ is more abundant in freshwater fishes. Braekkan *et al.* (1969) has shown interconversion of one form to the other in living fish tissues. Fish oils contain vitamin A as free alcohols or esters. Vitamin A alcohol occurs as a light colored viscous oil which is heat labile and subject to air oxidation. β-Carotene occurs as an orange, crystalline compound which is more stable to heat and oxidation. The vitamers A are water insoluble but are soluble in fat and organic solvent (Dam and Søndergaard, 1964).

## 2. *Positive Functions*

Vitamin A is essential in maintaining epithelial cells. McCollum and Davis (1913) and Osborne and Mendel (1914) first showed that cod liver

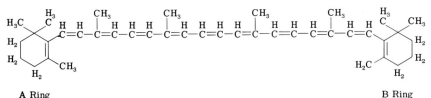

A Ring                                                                        B Ring

β-Carotene

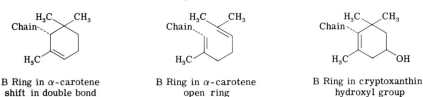

B Ring in α-carotene
shift in double bond

B Ring in α-carotene
open ring

B Ring in cryptoxanthin
hydroxyl group

Fig. 27. β-Carotene above and altered B-ring structures in α-carotene, γ-carotene, and cryptoxanthin. (From West *et al.*, 1966.)

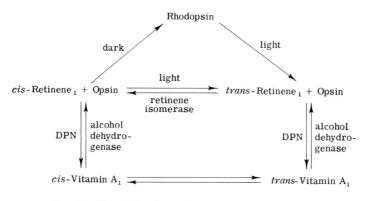

FIG. 28. The rhodopsin cycle. (From West *et al.*, 1966.)

oil contained a substance which promoted growth; and in 1917, McCollum and Simmonds soon showed that the substance would prevent xerophthalmia in rats. Many changes in organ epithelial, including the respiratory tract, tongue and tissues of the mouth, the eye, liver, and kidney, have been described by Wolbach and Bessey (1942) and by Follis (1958). Atrophy of the epithelium and formation of stratified keratinizing tissue occurs. Vitamin A is a stimulus for new cell growth and aids in maintaining resistance to infection. It increases longevity under various conditions of senility in mammals. Vitamin A and retinene are essential for normal vision (Dam and Søndergaard, 1964; West *et al.*, 1966). The interrelationships of *cis*- and *trans*-vitamin A in the rhodopsin cycle are shown in Fig. 28.

### 3. *The Syndrome of Deficiency or Excess*

Hypovitaminosis A is characterized by poor growth, poor vision, keratinization of epithelial tissue, xerophthalmia, night blindness, hemorrhage in the anterior chamber of the eye, hemorrhage at the base of the fins, and abnormal bone formation (Dam and Søndergaard, 1964; West *et al.*, 1966; Aoe *et al.*, 1968; Kitamura *et al.*, 1967). Nerve degeneration has been reported in pigs, chickens, rats, rabbits, and ducks but only occasionally observed in fish after long periods of deficiency. Hypervitaminosis A has been described in fish (Burrows *et al.*, 1952; Halver, 1970; Poston *et al.*, 1966) and in other animals and involved enlargement of liver and spleen, abnormal growth, skin lesions, epithelial keratinization, hyperplasia of head cartilage, and abnormal bone formation resulting in ankylosis and fusion of vertebrae. Hypervitaminosis A is reflected in very high liver oil vitamin A content and elevated serum alkaline phosphatase. Removal of excess vitamin A from the diet promotes rapid recovery.

## 4. *Requirements*

Dietary requirements for vitamin A alcohol are listed in Table III. Jones *et al.* (1966) has shown a requirement for growth in fish held in light, but not in darkness, and Dupree has reported similar problems in determining requirements in catfish. Therefore, the requirement for maximum growth and reproduction is related to exposure to light and reflects observations in other animals that near normal growth will occur at very low vitamin A intake in protected environments where fish are not exposed to stress, infection, and ultraviolet radiation.

## 5. *Sources and Protection*

Table V indicates levels of vitamin A in several fish liver oils. Cod liver oil is one typical standard reference oil, which contains relatively small amounts of vitamin A, whereas black sea bass, swordfish, or ling cod oils contain 100-fold more. Whale liver oil contains kitol which has little or no biological activity until heated above 200°C (Embree and Shantz, 1943). Then one molecule of biologically active vitamin A is generated per molecule of whale kitol. This biologically inactive kitol may be deposited in the whale as a defense mechanism against hypervitaminosis A during excessive vitamin A intake. A possibility of hypervitaminosis A occurs when tuna, shark, or ling cod viscera are used in preparation of moist diets. Synthetic

TABLE V

Vitamin A Content of Fish Oils[a]

| Common name | Vitamin A IU/gm | |
| --- | --- | --- |
| | Range | Average |
| Soupfin shark (male) | 45,000–200,000 | 120,000 |
| Halibut | 40,000–160,000 | 87,000 |
| Sablefish | 50,000–190,000 | 90,000 |
| Ling cod | 40,000–550,000 | 175,000 |
| Albacore tuna | 10,000–60,000 | 25,000 |
| Bonito | 15,000–60,000 | 35,000 |
| Swordfish | 20,000–400,000 | 250,000 |
| Black sea bass | 100,000–1,000,000 | 300,000 |
| Cod | 1,000–6,000 | 2,000 |
| Herring[b] | 50–300 | 90 |

[a] Adapted from Butler (1946).
[b] Figures for oil from entire body.

vitamin A preparations, such as vitamin A palmitate, are available and are often used to supplement rations low in fish meal, fish viscera, or carotenes. Some fish species seem able to utilize $\beta$-carotene as a vitamin A source (Morton and Creed, 1939), whereas others are unable to split the $\beta$-carotene molecule and vitamin A must be added to the diet in the retinol, retinene, or retinoic acid form (Neilands, 1947; Poston, 1969b).

### 6. *Clinical Assessment*

Vitamin A status can best be assessed by absence of deficiency signs and assay of liver oil for vitamin A content. Assay for blood or plasma vitamin A levels in other animals has not shown vitamin A status. The simple Carr-Price vitamin A determination in liver oil indicates storage and the information can be used to give the vitamin A status of fish.

### B. The Vitamers D

Rickets was induced with test diets by Hopkins (1906) and Mellanby (1919) cured the disease in dogs by adding cod liver oil to the ration. Steenbock and Black (1924) showed ultraviolet light was involved in antirachitic function, and provitamin D was identified as ergosterol by Windaus and Hess (1927) and by Rosenheim and Webster (1927). Crystalline vitamin D was isolated by Angus *et al.* (1931) and activated 7-dehydrocholesterol was isolated by Windaus *et al.* (1936). One early report by Jewell *et al.* (1933) on fish diet tests mentioned the need of catfish and goldfish for vitamin D (cod liver oil) in the diet, but the test diets used probably were deficient in other vitamins or growth factors which the crude cod liver oil furnished. Hypervitaminosis D has been shown to elevate alkaline phosphatase in trout and salmon.

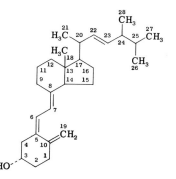

Fig. 29. Vitamin D₂. (From Beaton and McHenry, 1964).

### 1. *Chemical Structure, Characteristics, and Analogs*

Several biologically active forms of vitamin D occur and the chemical structure of one, vitamin $D_2$ or ergocalciferol, with the chemical formula $C_{28}H_{44}O$, is shown in Fig. 29. Vitamin $D_3$ or activated 7-dehydrocholesterol has the chemical formula $C_{27}H_{44}O$ and contains a more simplified, unsaturated 8-carbon side chain. Vitamin $D_3$ (cholecalciferol) is formed in most animal tissue by rupture of one of the ring bonds of 7-dehydrocholesterol when exposed in the skin to ultraviolet radiation. Cholecalciferol is a white, crystalline compound soluble in fat and organic solvents and is stable to heat and oxidation in mild alkali or acid solution (Dam and Søndergaard, 1964). Several derivatives from substitution in the rings or of functional groups in the side chain are isomers of the precursors or isotels of the vitamin and have variable biological activity in different animals. These have not been tested for maintaining homeostasis of calcium and phosphate in fish. The conversion of ergosterol to vitamin $D_2$ and several side compounds is shown in Fig. 30.

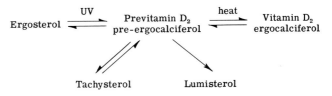

FIG. 30. Conversion of ergosterol to vitamin $D_2$. (From West *et al.*, 1966.)

### 2. *Positive Functions*

Vitamin D is essential for maintaining homeostasis of calcium and inorganic phosphate. Vitamin D is involved in alkaline phosphatase activity, promotes intestinal absorption of calcium, and influences the action of parathyroid hormone on bone (Dam and Søndergaard, 1964; West *et al.*, 1966). Lovelace and Podoliak (1952) have shown that fish may sequester calcium from water through the gill membrane; thus the major function of vitamin D for other animals may not be necessary to satisfy calcium requirements for fish.

### 3. *Syndrome of Deficiency or Excess*

Hypovitaminosis D for fish has not been described. Rickets and abnormal bone formation described in detail for animals has not been observed in fish fed low vitamin D diets. However, little work has been done under carefully controlled conditions with young growing fish and only alteration in alkaline phosphatase activity has been reported on different vitamin D diet intakes. Hypervitaminosis D, however, has been reported. Poston (1969b) has shown that brook trout fed large doses of vitamin D show impaired growth, lethargy, and dark coloration. High intake of vitamin D mobilizes phosphorus and calcium from the bone and tissues and may result in fragile bones, poor growth, and poor appetite related to the nausea described in man afflicted with hypervitaminosis D (Dam and Søndergaard, 1964; West *et al.*, 1966).Arterial and kidney lesions reported for rats (Gillman and Gilbert, 1956) and dogs (Herzfeld *et al.*, 1956) have not been described histologically for fish and hypercalcemia in blood plasma has not been described for fish on high vitamin D diets. This area needs to be explored because of the potential for hypervitaminosis D in fish fed diets containing various fish viscera which might contain large amounts of the vitamers D. Tuna liver oil may contain, for example, 100 to 1000 times as much active vitamin D as cod liver oil.

### 4. *Requirements*

No requirements of fish for vitamin D have been described to date but little work has been done in this area using highly purified diets and controlled experiments with young growing fish. Likewise, no demonstration of synthesis of vitamers D in fish reared on diets devoid of vitamin D or vitamin D precursors has been reported. Therefore, actual requirement of vitamin D for maintenance of homeostasis of calcium–phosphorus levels in the young growing animal has not been adequately investigated and the true requirements of vitamin D in young fish have not been defined.

### 5. *Sources and Protection*

Vitamin D requirements of many animals can be met by exposure to sunlight of the skin where cholesterol derivatives are activated by ring structure rupture. This subject is well reviewed by Dam and Søndergaard (1964) and by Wagner and Folkers (1964). Since the vitamin is fat soluble and accumulates in lipid stores, fish liver oil is a rich source of the material. Content varies tremendously in liver oil, however, with values of about 25 IU/gm present in soup fin shark liver oil and over 200,000 IU/gm in albacore tuna liver oil (West *et al.*, 1966). Cod liver oil contains from 100–500 IU/gm and animal liver contains some vitamin D. One international unit (IU) is equal to 0.025 $\mu$g of crystalline vitamin $D_3$.

### 6. *Clinical Assessment*

Absorption maxima in the ultraviolet region can be used to detect provitamins D in the nonsaponifiable fraction of oils. Concentrated preparations of vitamin D can be assayed by the Carr-Price antimony trichloride reaction when assay is necessary to determine biologically active materials in liver oil of fish on different treatments. The chick assay may not apply to fish liver storage levels because the biologically active form for fish has not been determined. Therefore, clinical assessment for hypervitaminosis A must rely on crude methods for determination of pro and active vitamin D in liver oil samples by the Carr-Price reaction or by measuring absorption in the UV spectrum.

## C. The Vitamers E

The existence of an antisterility vitamin was postulated by Evans and Bishop (1922). This factor was named "vitamin E" by Sure (1924). The active tocopherol was isolated, characterized, and synthesized by Karrer *et al.* (1938).

### 1. *Chemical Structure, Characteristics, and Analogs*

The vitamers E are compounds known as tocopherols and are derivatives of tocol which has a saturated side chain or of tocotrienol which contains three unsaturated carbon–carbon bonds in the side chain. One of the most important tocopherols, α-tocopherol (5,7,8-trimethyltocol), has the chemical formula $C_{29}H_{50}O_2$ and the structural formula shown in Fig. 31. Eight naturally occurring tocopherol derivatives have been isolated and all belong to the D series. Synthetic α-tocopherol is a racemic DL-α-tocopherol mixture (Dam and Søndergaard, 1964; West *et al.*, 1966). The derivatives of tocol or of tocotrienol are named alpha, beta, gamma, delta, epsilon, eta, zeta₁, and zeta₂-tocopherol as shown in Table VI. The pure tocopherols are fat-soluble oils which are capable of esterification to form crystalline compounds. The tocopherols are stable to heat and acids in the absence of oxygen but are rapidly oxidized in the presence of nascent oxygen, peroxides, or other oxidizing agents (Dam and Søndergaard, 1964). The tocopherols are sensitive to ultraviolet light and are excellent antioxidants in the free form, whereas the tocopherol esters are poor *in vitro* antioxidants. The esters are more stable and are commonly used as dietary supplements— anticipating hydrolysis in the gut and absorption of the free alcohol to act

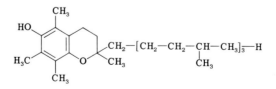

Fig. 31. α-Tocopherol (5,7,8-trimethyltocol). (From Beaton and McHenry, 1964.)

TABLE VI

THE TOCOPHEROLS

| | |
|---|---|
| $\alpha$-Tocopherol (alpha) | 5,7,8-trimethyltocol |
| $\beta$-Tocopherol (beta) | 5,8-dimethyltocol |
| $\gamma$-Tocopherol (gamma) | 7,8-dimethyltocol |
| $\zeta_2$-Tocopherol (zeta$_2$) | 5,7-dimethyltocol |
| $\eta$-Tocopherol (eta) | 7-methyltocol |
| $\delta$-Tocopherol (delta) | 8-methyltocol |
| $\epsilon$-Tocopherol (epsilon) | 5,8-dimethyltocotrienol |
| $\zeta_1$-Tocopherol (zeta$_1$) | 5,7,8-trimethyltocotrienol |

as an active intra- and intercellular antioxidant. Ethyl derivatives on the aromatic ring are also active. Oxidation products of $\alpha$-tocopherol can be reduced with hydrosulfite to $\alpha$-tocopherylhydroquinone or, in the presence of ascorbic acid, to $\alpha$-tocopherol (Dam and Søndergaard, 1964; Vit. E Sym., 1962). The oxidation-reduction of the tocopherylquinones is indicated in Fig. 32.

2. *Positive Functions*

The tocopherols act as inter- and intracellular antioxidants to maintain homeostasis of labile metabolites in the cell and tissue plasma. As physiological antioxidants, these usually protect oxidizable vitamins and labile unsaturated fatty acids. Vitamers E are involved in encephalomalacia in chicks (Pappenheimer and Goettsch, 1931), erythrocyte hemolysis in several animals (György and Rose, 1948; Horwitt *et al.*, 1963; Woodall *et al.*, 1964), and steatitis in mink, pigs, and farm animals (Dam and Søndergaard, 1964). The tocopherols prevent exudative diathesis in chicks,

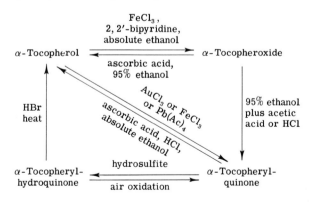

FIG. 32. Oxidation reduction of $\alpha$-tocopherol. (From Beaton and McHenry, 1964.)

white muscle disease in lambs and calves, and dietary liver necrosis in rats. Vitamers E are involved with selenium and with vitamin C for normal reproductive activity and are involved in prevention of nutritional muscular dystrophy in the chick, the yellowtail (Sakaguchi and Hamaguchi, 1969), and carp (Hashimoto *et al.*, 1966). The tocopherols act as free radical traps to stop the chain reaction during peroxide formation and stabilize unsaturated carbon bonds of polyunsaturated fatty acids and other long-chain labile compounds (Dam and Granados, 1945; Dam *et al.*, 1952; Tappel and Zalkin, 1960). Vitamin E in its antioxidant capacity is involved in the maintenance of normal permeability of capillaries and heart muscle. It was first shown to be involved in prevention of sterility and fetal resorption in rats. It may likewise be involved in embryo membrane permeability and hatchability of fish eggs.

### 3. *Syndrome of Deficiency or Excess*

Deficiency signs in fish are listed in Table II. One of the first signs for fish fed normal amounts of polyunsaturated fatty acids is erythrocyte fragility closely followed by anemia, ascites, xerophthalmia, poor growth, poor food conversion, epicarditis, and ceroid deposits in spleen and liver. Muscle dystrophy and xerophthalmia have been described in yellowtail and carp (Sakaguchi and Hamaguchi, 1969; Hashimoto *et al.*, 1966). Several nonspecific cell degenerative conditions have been described in several species of fish fed large quantities of polyunsaturated fatty acids with inadequate tocopherol in the ration. Hypervitaminosis E involves poor growth, toxic liver reaction, and death (Watanabe *et al.*, 1970; Poston, 1971).

### 4. *Requirements*

Requirements of fish for vitamin E are shown in Table III. The exact requirement of the fish for α-tocopherol, the vitamin E form used in these test diet experiments, may depend upon the amount and type of polyunsaturated fatty acids in the oil components of the ration (Woodall *et al.*, 1964; Watanabe *et al.*, 1970). Polyunsaturated labile fish oils may invoke an increased requirement for intracellular antioxidants (Hashimoto *et al.*, 1966). Also, the amount of tocopherol needed as a supplement to the ration will depend upon the form of the vitamer used, the method of diet preparation, and the storage conditions under which the rations are held before feeding. The physiological requirements of the species tested are listed and were determined with carefully protected test diets prepared immediately before feeding and containing relatively low amounts of polyunsaturated fatty acids.

## 5. *Sources and Protection*

Wheat germ oil, soybean oil, and corn oil are rich sources of tocopherols. Synthetic $\alpha$-tocopherol in esterified acetate or phosphate form is commonly used as a diet supplement. These esters are much more stable than the free form which is rapidly lost by air oxidation or in the presence of labile compounds like the polyunsaturated fish oils. Wheat, corn, or bean oils are very stable and when incorporated into the diet tend to stabilize as well the labile fatty acids present. An interrelationship between vitamins E, C, and A is involved in the protection of the labile vitamin A molecule (Dam and Granados, 1945; Dam *et al.*, 1952). Therefore, it is essential to prepare, store, and feed fish rations containing quantities of labile fish oils (Sinnhuber, 1969; Stansby, 1967) in the minimum time to prevent loss of tocopherol content and subsequent rapid destruction of vitamins E, C, and A. Addition of *in vitro* antioxidants such as BHA (butyl hydroxyanisole) and BHT (butyl hydroxytoluene) tends to protect fats and other labile compounds in the ration from oxidation, but these antioxidants have little vitamin E activity as the physiological intracellular antioxidant for the growing fish.

## 6. *Clinical Assessment*

The erythrocyte fragility test indicates physiological state of the fish (Woodall *et al.*, 1964). Absence of histologically detectable ceroid in liver and spleen from representative samples in the population is a good clue on presence of adequate amounts of physiological antioxidants in the fish (Wood and Yasutake, 1956). A barbituric acid test for oxidation of components in the ration or a peroxide number test for peroxidation of diet components has not been applied to fish tissues as a clinical tool for assessment of nutrition state except when liver oils become saturated with very labile polyunsaturated fatty acids such as when feeding squid or saury oils (Hashimoto *et al.*, 1966; Watanabe *et al.*, 1970). These assays are good indicators of state of potential oxidation and oxidized state of the finished ration, but the absence of deficiency signs and normal erythrocyte fragility are better clinical tests. Analysis for tocopherol is difficult and time-consuming and only applicable under critical research experiment situations.

## D. THE VITAMERS K

The name of vitamin K (for "koagulation") was proposed by Dam (1935). Dam *et al.* (1939) and McKee *et al.* (1939) isolated the vitamin from alfalfa and from fish meal in 1939 and it was synthesized in the Almquist (Almquist and Klose, 1939), Doisey (McKee *et al.*, 1939), and Fieser (1939) laboratories later that year.

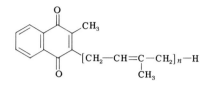

Fɪɢ. 33. Vitamin $K_2$ series; $n$ may equal 6, 7 or 9 isoprene units. (From Beaton and McHenry, 1964.)

### 1. Chemical Structure, Characteristics, and Analogs

Vitamin $K_1$ is 2-methyl-3-phytyl-1,4-naphthoquinone with chemical formula $C_{31}H_{46}O_2$ and structural formula shown in Fig. 33. The vitamers $K_2$ contain 6, 7, or 9 isoprene units in the side chain which varies from 30–45 carbon atoms. Many isotels on vitamin K have been identified in animal tissues, plant tissues, and microorganisms. The structure of phthiocol, 2-methylhydroxy-3-1,4-naphthoquinone, and menadione ($K_3$), 2-methyl-1,4-naphthoquinone, are shown in Fig. 34. These are fat-soluble, fairly stable compounds but as methylnaphthoquinones are labile to oxidation and exposure to ultraviolet radiation. Menadione is very reactive and is subject in aqueous media to chemical interaction and the formation of compounds and complexes which may interfere with physiological activity (Dam and Søndergaard, 1964).

### 2. Positive Functions

Vitamin K is involved in the synthesis of messenger RNA involved in synthesis of blood clotting proteins—prothrombin, plasma, thromboplastic, proconvertin, and at least one other factor. A simplified scheme of blood coagulation is shown in Fig. 35. Substituted forms of vitamin K are strongly bacteriostatic and may serve as an alternate defense mechanism for bacterial infections. Vitamin K is involved with vitamins A and E and ascorbic acid for homeostasis of physiologically active vitamins A and E (Dam and Søndergaard, 1964). Vitamin K may be involved in coenzyme

Fɪɢ. 34. Active naphthoquinones. Phthiocol is shown on the left and menadione pictured on the right. (From West *et al.*, 1966.)

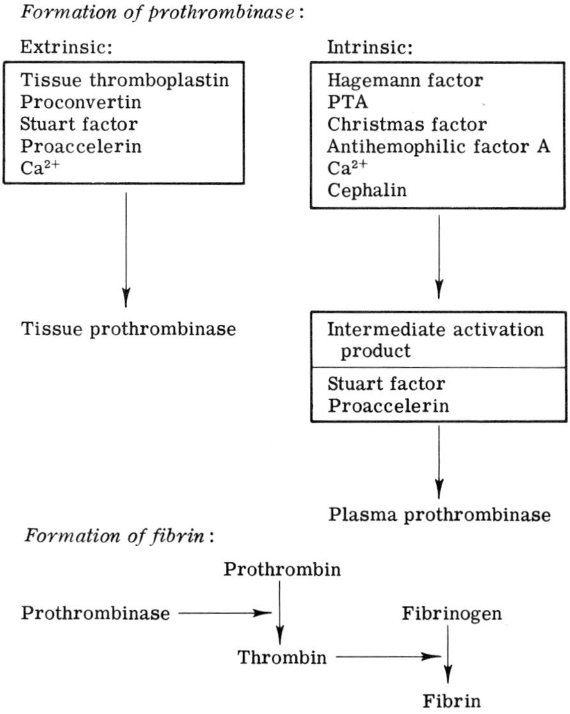

*Formation of prothrombinase*:

Extrinsic:

| |
|---|
| Tissue thromboplastin |
| Proconvertin |
| Stuart factor |
| Proaccelerin |
| $Ca^{2+}$ |

Intrinsic:

| |
|---|
| Hagemann factor |
| PTA |
| Christmas factor |
| Antihemophilic factor A |
| $Ca^{2+}$ |
| Cephalin |

Tissue prothrombinase

| |
|---|
| Intermediate activation product |
| Stuart factor |
| Proaccelerin |

Plasma prothrombinase

*Formation of fibrin*:

Prothrombin

Prothrombinase ⟶

Fibrinogen

Thrombin ⟶

Fibrin

Fig. 35. Blood coagulation. A simplified version of processes involved in blood coagulation—both extrinsic and intrinsic factors are involved in the production of prothrombinase to initiate hydrolysis of prothrombin to activate the clotting action. (From Beaton and McHenry, 1964.)

Q-type compounds which function between flavo proteins and cytochromes in electron transport mechanisms (West *et al.*, 1966). The primary role of vitamin K is to maintain a fast normal blood clotting rate which is so important to fish living in a water environment.

### 3. *Syndrome of Deficiency or Excess*

A summary of the deficiency signs is listed in Table III. Prothrombin time in salmon fed diets devoid of vitamers K was increased three to five times and, during prolonged deficiency states, anemia and hemorrhagic areas appeared in the gills, eyes, and vascular tissues. Increased blood clotting time has also been reported for other fish reared on diets with low vitamin K content. Interrelationships with other vitamins have not been documented in fish experiments and the primary deficiency signs remain as slow as blood clotting and hemorrhage, severe anemia, or death in wounded fish. Hemorrhagic areas often appear in fragile tissues such as the gills.

## 4. Requirements

Tests for qualitative requirements of fish for vitamin K have been completed (Phillips *et al.*, 1963). The deficiency signs occur in from 10–14 weeks on test when good diets are used with positive control of the vitamin K content. Quantitative requirement studies have not been completed and are needed to define the vitamin K requirement of rapidly growing young fish, especially those held in high population density under intensive fish husbandry techniques.

## 5. Sources and Protection

Vitamin K sources are green, leafy vegetables. Alfalfa leaves are one of the best components for vitamers K. Low levels are found in soybeans and animal liver (Isler and Wiss, 1959). Synthetic menadione is a good supplement for adequate vitamin K intake. Vitamin K content of ground alfalfa is fairly stable but the synthetic material should be protected from exposure to ultraviolet light and to excessive oxidizing or reducing conditions. The use of dry rapidly cured alfalfa is essential to minimize formation of the physiological antagonist, dicumarol. The diet should be kept dry, prepared with minimum exposure to air oxidation, and fed as soon as practicable after manufacture to minimize vitamin K loss through storage, interreaction, and oxidative destruction.

## 6. Antimetabolites and Inactivation

Dicumarol, 3,3'-methylenebis (4-hydroxycoumarin), and warfarin are shown in Fig. 36. Dicumarol was isolated from spoiled sweet clover hay and shown to prevent the normal function of vitamin K in maintenance of normal blood clotting times (Link, 1959). Early work was with cattle and hogs but was soon extended to rats, other experimental animals, and man. Dicumarol is an anticoagulant and has been used to prevent thrombosis in animals and man. It is not an antimetabolite competing for vitamin K sites but plays another role in preventing normal blood clotting. Vitamin K counteracts the dicumarol effect and results are quantitative with intake,

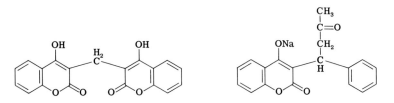

Fig. 36. Dicumarol and warfarin. Note the similarity of the first half of the molecular structure. (From West *et al.*, 1966.)

allowing dicumarol to be administered to adjust the blood clotting time in special situations according to the vitamin K status of the animal, and then counteracting the dicumarol effect by administration of more vitamin K (Mushett and Seeler, 1947). Another anticoagulant, warfarin, is a common rat poison which has five to ten times the anticoagulant activity of dicumarol (Shapiro and Ciferri, 1957). Warfarin effect can be reversed also by administration of vitamin K. Both compounds are general antagonists to vitamin K.

### 7. *Clinical Assessment*

Vitamin K status of fish is determined by determining the blood clotting time. Chemical methods for determination of menadione to assess content of active metabolite after storage can use the 2,4-dinitrophenylhydrazone derivative and measure the content spectrophotometrically. The standard Dam and Søndergaard chick assay (1953) will measure total biologically active vitamers K in dietary raw materials but this type of technique has not been applied to vitamin K activity in the liver or tissues of young growing fish.

## IV. Other Unknown Factors

### A. More Animal Protein Factors

Each year more forms of animal protein factor (vitamins $B_{12}$, $B_{13}$, etc.) have been either isolated or postulated as being present in meat, fish, yeast or other biological materials used as diet components for experimental animals. Whether these factors are specific vitamins or a particular form which increases utilization or function of one of the other vitamins or one of the other major nutrient components in the ration, has not been defined. Whenever purified test rations are used to rear fish under controlled experimental conditions, these rations contain all the known demonstrated nutrients; but these fish populations fail to grow as well as those fed moist diets consisting of fish tissue, glandular tissue, animal tissue, dextrinized starch, and fish oils. Generally, about 10% difference in growth is observed between the best purified diets and practical moist or dry rations. These growth response differences are most common when protein is used as the major dietary component and may be due to increased activation of proteolytic enzymes with concomitant orderly hydrolysis and absorption of amino acids at or near the rate used for tissue protein synthesis in the growing animals. The fish meal or animal protein components may contain as yet unisolated and undefined new animal protein factors.

## B. Citrovorum Factor

Szent-György and Rusznyák (1936) reported "vitamin P" in pepper, citrus fruit, and paprika which improved capillary fragility in guinea pigs on a flavin-free diet containing adequate ascorbic acid (Zacho, 1939). Some capillary hemorrhage and a characteristic wrist stiffness developed in guinea pigs and was remedied by material present in the rinds of citrus fruits (Bourne, 1943). Vitamin P activity is found in rutin isolated from buckwheat and in esculin from chestnuts. Structural formulas for these are shown in Fig. 37. Other citrovorum factors are concentrated in citrus fruit pulp and rind but requirements for fish have not been demonstrated.

## C. Factors in Cell Permeability

Unknown factors exist which influence osmoregulation and cell membrane permeability. These may be especially important in fish during transition from freshwater to a saltwater environment where the water flow through exposed tissues is reversed and the kidneys alternatively excrete much dilute urine or become quiescent, depending upon the external environment of the fish. An interrelationship between vitamin E, ascorbic acid, vitamin K, and vitamin A in respiration has been mentioned but the exact role of these and other factors such as selenium, zinc, copper, and sodium chloride has not been defined. Both pituitary function and thyroid function are associated during smoltification with rapid development of gill secretory cells which maintain salt and water balance in the new hypertonic environment. Much work needs to be done in this area and fish may be important experimental animals to study cell permeability because of the unique environmental demands on these animals for survival.

## D. Coenzyme Activation Factors

Interrelationships between thiamine, zinc, cocarboxylase activity, trace amounts of copper, several oxidation–reduction systems, iodine, iodinated

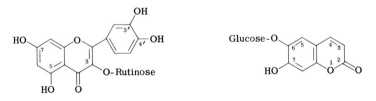

Fig. 37. Vitamers P. Rutin is shown on the left and esculin on the right. These compounds may have vitaminlike activity in certain animals, alone or in conjunction with other vitamin factors. (From West *et al.*, 1966.)

amino acids, and metabolic rate should be mentioned. These are examples which show the interrelationship in the viable animal system of vitamins, coenzymes, and mineral ions. Part of the structural stereo configuration of several proteins like insulin, for example, is determined in part by the zinc present. Another example is the planar structure of vitamin $B_{12}$ relative to the central cobalt atom. Most of the water-soluble vitamins act as coenzymes for enzyme functions which often require trace amounts of certain mineral ions for activation. This is another area where fish could be used as study animals and model systems to develop comparative biochemistry experiments to define the general nature of certain basic biological processes in cell physiology and intermediary metabolism.

## V. Anemias and Hemapoiesis

Several types of nutritional anemias occur which may be due to several nutritional deficiencies. Unfortunately, most anemias are multiple deficiencies of essential nutrients and the fish clinician must carefully observe characteristics of the anemia involved to obtain clues as to the nutritional cause.

### A. MEGALOBLASTIC ANEMIAS

Deficiencies in folic acid, ascorbic acid, and iron can cause megaloblastic anemia with characteristic macrocytic, senile erythrocytes in the circulating blood. An adequate description of folic acid, macrocytic, normochromic anemia has been reported by Smith and forms a reference for the cytology of this type hematology (Smith, 1968; Smith and Halver, 1969). Feeding folic acid, xanthopterin, increasing the ascorbic acid content, and assuring adequate ferrous ion intake will result in rapid recovery with anterior kidney imprints and blood smears showing rapid regeneration of the pro forms of the erythrocytes. Many immature forms will be seen within a few days after administration of the missing nutrients.

### B. PERNICIOUS ANEMIAS

The more common type of anemia encountered in fish is similar to the pernicious anemias described in other experimental animals. This disease can be caused by inadequate intake of vitamin $B_{12}$ which is necessary for the conversion of 5-methyltetrahydrofolate back into the active folic acid pool. The net result is the decreased synthesis of deoxyribonucleic acid which is necessary for the synthesis and development of new red blood cell pro forms. A hog mucosa factor improves absorption of vitamin $B_{12}$

severalfold and adequate $B_{12}$ is necessary for proper folic acid function in the synthesis and maturation of pro erythrocyte forms. Little is known about the role of gastric mucosa factor for the absorption of vitamin $B_{12}$ in fish tissues, but it is important and may determine adequate absorption of dietary vitamin $B_{12}$ in rats, in other experimental animals, and in man.

The clinical characteristic of pernicious anemias is the presence of distorted blood cells and cellular debris in the plasma. Inadequate amounts of vitamin E to maintain blood cell membrane integrity also result in a pernicious type of anemia with many abnormal blood cells present. This is also commonly seen when diets rich in polyunsaturated fatty acids but with inadequate *in vitro* antioxidants and inadequate vitamin E content are fed for 12–20 weeks to salmonids. Locker burned food generally means oxidized, polymerized fatty acids, ceroid in the liver and spleen, and little if any active tocopherols left in the ration (Wood and Yasutake, 1956). Pernicious-type anemia is one of the first symptoms observed in fish fed these storage-oxidized products. This can be differentiated from animal protein factors anemia by failure to respond to either vitamin $B_{12}$ or to a water-soluble vitamin supplement. Other pernicious-type anemias can occur from deficiencies of biotin, pantothenic acid, and niacin. The history of fish nutrition is replete with many vitamin combinations which were reported to have factor H activity (McCay and Dilley, 1927). Anemias resulting from these are general destructive anemias not due to any one particular cause but a general breakdown in nucleic acid synthesis and subsequent protein synthesis with resultant hematology and cytology indicative of pernicious anemia.

## C. Hemapoiesis

The most convenient tool for the fish nutritionist to assess clinical status is hematology. The first general sign of abnormal hematology is impaired hemapoiesis. The fish clinician must realize that many factors are involved including vitamins, minerals, amino acids, antagonist hormones, and physiological stimulations. Folic acid, vitamin $B_{12}$, and ascorbic acid nutritional state are obvious determinants. Also, limiting trace minerals like iron and copper and limiting amino acids in the diet result in abnormal growth by interfering with the rate of protein structure. Fish erythrocytes are enucleated and need proper nucleic acid synthesis for normal erythropoiesis. Erythropoiesis-inhibiting agents such as dicumarol, warfarin, or phenylhydrazine should be considered. Finally, pituitary and adrenal hormones which stimulate protein synthesis, and thyroid hormones which regulate metabolic activity and protein synthesis, play dominant roles in blood cell formation. Repeated extraction of quantities of blood for clinical experiments through indwelling cannula will stimulate erythropoiesis which will be reflected in blood cytology and in anterior kidney imprints (Ashley and Smith, 1963). The tremendous physiological change involved in transition of anadromous fish from a hypo- to a hypertonic environment appears to increase sensitivity to hemorrhage and probably also has effects on normal hemapoiesis (Zaugg and McLain, 1969; Zaugg, 1970).

## References*

Abeles, R. H., and Lee, H. A. (1961). *J. Biol. Chem.* **236,** 2347.

Agren, G. (1945). *Acta Physiol. Scand.* **9,** 221–233.

Allison, F. E., Hoover, S. R., and Burk, D. (1933). *Science* **78,** 217.

Almquist, H. J., and Klose, A. A. (1939). *J. Amer. Chem. Soc.* **61,** 2557.

Anderson, R. C., and Wallis, E. S. (1948). *J. Amer. Chem. Soc.* **70,** 2931.

Angus, T. C., Askew, F. A., Bourdillon, R. B., Bruce, H. M., Callow, R. K., Fishmann, C., Philpot, J. St. L., and Webster, T. A. (1931). *Proc. Roy. Soc. (London)* **13108,** 340.

Aoe, H., and Masuda, I. (1967). *Bull. Jap. Soc. Sci. Fish.* **33,** 674–680.

Aoe, H., Masuda, I. and Takada, T. (1967a). *Bull. Jap. Soc. Sci. Fish.* **33,** 681–685.

Aoe, H., Masuda, I., Saito, T., and Komo, A. (1967b). *Bull. Jap. Soc. Sci. Fish.* **33,** 355–360, 970–974.

Aoe, H., Masuda, I., Saito, T., and Takada, T. (1967c). *Bull. Jap. Soc. Sci. Fish* **33,** 1068–1071.

Aoe, H., Masuda, I., Mimura, T., Saito, T., and Komo, A. (1968). *Bull. Jap. Soc. Sci. Fish.* **34,** 959–964.

Aoe, H., Masuda, I., Mimura, T., Saito, T., Komo, A., and Kitamura, S. (1969). *Bull. Jap. Soc. Sci. Fish.* **35,** 459–465.

Ashley, L. M., and Smith, C. E. (1963). *Progr. Fish. Cult.* **25,** 93.

Bateman, W. G. (1916). *J. Biol. Chem.* **26,** 263.

Beaton, G. H., and McHenry, E. W. (1964). *Nutrition* **2,** 20.

Beiler, J. M., and Martin, G. J. (1947). *J. Biol. Chem.* **169,** 345.

Bessey, O. A., Horwitt, M. K., and Love, R. H. (1956). *J. Nutr.* **58,** 367.

Boas, M. (1927). *Biochem. J.* **21,** 712.

Bourne, G. H. (1943). *Nature (London)* **152,** 659.

Bourquin, A., and Sherman, H. C. (1931). *J. Amer. Chem. Soc.* **53,** 3501.

Braekkan, O. R., Ingebrigsten, O., and Myklestad, H. (1969). *Int. Z. Vitaminforsch.* **39,** 123–130.

Brin, M. (1963). *Amer. J. Clin. Nutr.* **12,** 107.

Brown, G. M. (1959). *J. Biol. Chem.* **234,** 379.

Burrows, R. E., Robinson, L. A., and Palmer, D. D. (1951). *U.S. Fish Wildl. Ser., Spec. Sci. Rep.* **59,** 1.

Burrows, R. E., Palmer, D. D., Newman, H. W., and Azevedo, R. (1952). *U.S. Fish Wildl. Ser., Spec., Sci. Rep.* **86,** 1.

Butler, C. (1946). *Com. Fish. Rev.* **8,** 12.

Cammarata, P. S., and Cohen, P. P. (1950). *J. Biol. Chem.* **187,** 439.

* References designated as *Fish. Res. Bull.* are published by the New York State Conservation Department, Albany, New York.

Casal, D. G. (1762). "Historia natural y medica de el Principado de Asturias." Madrid, 327-260. Cited by H. F. Harris (1919). "Pellagra." Macmillan, New York.

Chittenden, R. H., and Underhill, F. P. (1917). *Amer. J. Physiol.* **44**, 13.

Chow, B. F. (1964). *In* "Nutrition" (G. H. Beaton and E. W. McHenry, eds.), Vol. II, pp. 208, 219, 241, 242. Academic Press, New York.

Cline, J. K., Williams, R. R., Ruehle, A. E., and Waterman, R. E. (1937). *J. Amer. Chem. Soc.* **59**, 530.

Coates, J. A., and Halver, J. E. (1958). *U.S. Fish Wildl. Ser., Spec. Sci. Rep.* **281**, 1.

Dam, H. (1935). *Biochem. J.* **29**, 1273.

Dam, H., and Granados, H. (1945). *Acta Physiol. Scand.* **10**, 162.

Dam, H., and Søndergaard, E. (1953). *Acta Pharmacol. Toxicol.* **9**, 131.

Dam, H., and Søndergaard, E. (1964). *In* "Nutrition" (G. H. Beaton and E. W. McHenry, eds.), Vol. II, pp. 1, 60. Academic Press, New York.

Dam, H., Geiger, A., Glavind, J., Karrer, P., Karrer, W., Rothschild, E. E., and Salomon, H. (1939). *Helv. Chim. Acta* **22**, 310.

Dam, H., Prange, I., and Søndergaard, E. (1952). *Acta Pharmacol. Toxicol.* **8**, 1.

Dangschat, G. (1942). *Naturwissenschaften* **31**, 146.

Day, P. L., Langston, W. C., and Shakers, C. F. (1938). *Proc. Soc. Exp. Biol. Med.* **38**, 860.

DeLong, D. C., Halver, J. E., and Mertz, E. T. (1958a). *J. Nutr.* **65**, 589.

DeLong, D. C., Halver, J. E., and Yasutake, W. T. (1958b). *Progr. Fish. Cult.* **20**, 111.

Deutsch, H. F., and Ott, G. L. (1942). *Proc. Soc. Exp. Biol. Med.* **51**, 119–122

Dietrich, L. S., and Shapiro, D. M. (1956). *Proc. Soc. Exp. Biol. Med.* **93**, 191.

Drummond, J. C. (1920). *Biochem. J.* **14**, 660.

Dupree, H. K. (1966). *U.S Dep. Interior Bur. Sport Fish. Wildl. Tech. Pap.* **7**, 1.

du Vigneaud, V. (1942). *Science* **96**, 455.

Eijkman, C. Cited by Williams, R. R. (1961). "Toward the Conquest of Beriberi," p. 36. Harvard Univ. Press, Cambridge, Massachusetts.

Elvehjem, C. A., Madden, R. J., Strong, S. M., and Woolley, D. W. (1937). *J. Amer. Chem. Soc.* **59**, 1767.

Elvehjem, C. A., Madden, R. J., Strong, S. M., and Woolley, D. W. (1938). *J. Biol. Chem.* **123**, 137.

Embree, N. D., and Shantz, E. M. (1943). *J. Amer. Chem. Soc.* **65**, 910.

Emmett, A. D., and McKim, L. H. (1917). *J. Biol. Chem.* **32**, 409.

Evans, H. M., and Bishop, K. S. (1922). *J. Metab. Res.* **1**, 319.

Fieser, L. F. (1939). *J. Amer. Chem. Soc.* **61**, 2559.

Findlay, and Stern. Cited by Hein, R. E. (1964). "Nutritional Data," p. 37. H. J. Heinz, Pittsburg, Pennsylvania.

Follis, R. H., Jr. (1958). "Deficiency Disease." Thomas, Springfield, Illinois.

Fouts, P. J., Helmer, O. H., Lepkovsky, S., and Jukes, T. H. (1937). *Proc. Soc. Exp. Biol. Med.* **37**, 405.

Funk, C. (1912). *J. State Med.* **20**, 341.

Funk, C. (1922). "The Vitamins." Williams & Wilkins, Baltimore, Maryland.

Fuson, R. E., and Christ, R. E. (1936). *Science* **84**, 294.

Gillman, J., and Gilbert, C. (1956). *Exp. Med. Surg.* **14**, 136.

Goldberger, J., and Lillie, R. D. (1926). *U.S. Public Health Rep.* **41**, 1025.

Goldsmith, G. A. (1964). *In* "Nutrition" (G. H. Beaton and E. W. McHenry, eds.), Vol. II, pp. 109, 149, 161. Academic Press, New York.

Gould, B. S. (1960). *Vitamins Hormones* **18**, 89.

Griffith, W. H., and Nye, J. F. (1954). *In* "The Vitamins" (W. H. Sebrell, Jr., and R. S. Harris, eds.), p. 15. Academic Press, New York.

Grijns, G. Cited by Williams, R. R. (1961). "Toward the Conquest of Beriberi," p. 42. Harvard Univ. Press, Cambridge, Massachusetts.

György, P. (1931). *Z. Arzl. Fortbildung* **28,** 377.

György, P. (1935). *Z. Vitaminforsch* **4,** 223.

György, P., and Rose, C. S. (1948). *Science* **108,** 716.

György, P., Rose, C. S., Hofman, K., Melville, D. B., and du Vigneaud, V. (1940). *Science* **92,** 609.

Halver, J. E. (1953a). Ph.D. Thesis, Univ. of Washington, Seattle, Washington.

Halver, J. E. (1953b). *Trans. Amer. Fish. Soc.* **83,** 254.

Halver, J. E. (1957). *J. Nutr.* **62,** 225.

Halver, J. E. (1966). *European Inland Fisheries Advisory Commission* 66, SC II-3.

Halver, J. E. (1969). *In* "Fish in Research" (O. W. Neuhaus and J. E. Halver, eds.), p. 209. Academic Press, New York.

Halver, J. E. (1970). *In* "Marine Aquaculture" (W. J. McNeil, ed.), p. 75. Oregon State Univ. Press, Corvallis, Oregon.

Halver, J. E., and Coates, J. A. (1957). *Progr. Fish. Cult.* **19,** 112.

Halver, J. E., Ashley, L. M., and Smith, R. R. (1969). *Trans. Amer. Fish. Soc.* **98,** 762.

Handler, P. (1958). *Fed. Proc.* **17,** 31.

Handley, J. M., and Bond, H. W. (1948). *J. Biol. Chem.* **173,** 513.

Harris, H. F. (1919). *In* "Pellegra." Macmillan, New York.

Harris, S. A., and Folkers, K. (1939). *J. Amer. Chem. Soc.* **61,** 1245.

Harris, S. A., Wolf, D. E., Mozingo, R., and Folkers, K. (1943). *Science* **97,** 447.

Hartman, A. M., Dryden L. P., and Cary, C. A. (1949). *Arch. Biochem. Biophys.* **23,** 165.

Hartman, S. H., and Buchanan, J. M. (1959). *Ann. Rev. Biochem.* **28,** 365.

Hartree, E. F. (1957). *Biochem. J.* **66,** 131.

Hashimoto, Y., Okaichi, T., Watanabe, T., Furukawa, A., and Umezu, T. (1966). *Bull. Jap. Soc. Sci. Fish.* **32,** 64–69.

Hashimoto, Y., Arai, S., and Nose, T. (1970). *Bull. Jap. Soc. Sci. Fish.* **36,** 791–797.

Hein, R. E. (1964). "Nutritional Data," pp. 33 and 44. H. J. Heinz, Pittsburg, Pennsylvania.

Herzfeld, E., Loudon, M., and Zweymuller, E. (1956). *Z. Ges. Exp. Med.* **127,** 272.

Higashi, H., Hirao, S., Yamada, J., Kikuchi, R., Noguchi, H., and Izuka, M. (1960). *Bull. Tokai Reg. Fish. Res. Lab.* **27,** 61–66.

Hofmeister, F. (1894). *Arch. Exp. Pathol. Pharmakol.* **33,** 198.

Holst, A., and Frölich, T. (1907). *J. Hyg.* **7,** 634.

Hopkins, F. G. (1906). *Analyst* **31,** 385.

Hopkins, F. G. (1912). *J. Physiol. (London)* **44,** 425.

Horwitt, M. K., Century B., and Zeman, A. A. (1963). *Amer. J. Clin. Nutr.* **12,** 99.

Huennekens, F. M., Hatefi, Y., and Kay, L. D. (1957). *J. Biol. Chem.* **224,** 435.

Huennekens, F. M., Osborn, M. J., and Whiteley, H. R. (1958). *Science* **128,** 120.

Hunter, S. H., Provasoli, L., Stokstad, E. L. R., Hofman, C. E., Belt, M., Franklin, A. L., and Jukes, T. H. (1949). *Proc. Soc. Exp. Biol. Med.* **70,** 118.

Ikeda, S., and Sato, M. (1964). *Bull. Jap. Soc. Sci. Fish.* **30,** 365.

Isler, O., and Wiss, O. (1959). *Vitamins Hormones* **17,** 53.

Jansen, B. C. P. (1954). *In* "The Vitamins" (W. H. Sebrell and R. L. Harris, eds.,) p. 425. Academic Press, New York.

Jansen, B. C. P., and Donath, W. F. (1927). *Meded. Dienst. Volksgezondheid. Ned.-Indië* **16,** 186.

Jewell, M. E., Schneberger, E., and Ross, J. A. (1933). *Trans. Amer. Fish. Soc.* **63,** 338.

Johnson, B. C., and Neumann, A. L. (1949). *J. Biol. Chem.* **178,** 1001.
Johnson, C. L., Hammer, D. C., Halver, J. E., and Baker, E. M. (1971). *Fed. Proc.* **30** (2), abst. 1822.
Jones, J. H., Bullard, E. B., and Rodriquez, A. (1966). *Fed. Proc.* **25,** 234.
Jukes, T. H. (1939). *J. Amer. Chem. Soc.* **61,** 975.
Kaczka, E. A., Wolf, D. E., Kuehl, F. A., Jr., and Folkers, K. (1950). *Science* **112,** 354.
Karrer, P., Schopp, K., and Benz, F. (1935). *Helv. Chim. Acta* **18,** 426.
Karrer, P., Fritzsche, H., Ringier, B. H., and Salomon, H. (1938). *Helv. Chim. Acta* **21,** 810.
King, C. G., and Waugh, W. A. (1932). *Science* **75,** 357.
Kitamura, S., Ohara, S., Suwa, T., and Nakagawa, K. (1965). *Bull. Jap. Soc. Sci. Fish.* **31,** 818–826.
Kitamura, S., Suwa, T., Ohara, S., and Nakagawa, K. (1967). *Bull. Jap. Soc. Sci. Fish.* **33,** 1126.
Knappe, J. (1970). *Ann. Rev. Biochem.* **39,** 757.
Knox, W. E., and Goswami, M. N. D. (1961). *Advan. Clin. Chem.* **4,** 122.
Koehn, C. J. (1948). *Arch. Biochem. Biophys.* **17,** 337.
Kogl, F., and Tonnis, B. (1936). *Z. Physiol. Chem.* **242,** 43.
Krampitz, L. O. (1969). *Ann. Rev. Biochem.* **38,** 213.
Kuhn, R., and Morris, C. J. O. R. (1937). *Ber.* **70,** 853.
Kuhn, R., György, P., and Wagner, J. T. (1933). *Ber. Deut. Chem. Ges.* **66,** 576.
Landboe-Christensen, E., and Plum, C. M. (1948). *Amer. J. Med. Sci.* **215,** 17.
Lardy, H. A., and Peanasky, R. (1953). *Physiol. Rev.* **33,** 560.
Lind, J. "A Treatise of the Scurvy." A. Millar, London, 1753. Republished by C. P. Stewart and D. Guthrie (1953). (eds), "Lind's Treatise on Scurvy." Univ. Press, Edinburgh, 1953.
Link, K. P. (1959). *Circulation* **19,** 97.
Lovelace, F. E., and Podoliak, H. A. (1952). *Progr. Fish. Cult.* **14,** 154.
McCarrison, (1921). Cited by Hein, R. E. (1964). "Nutritional Data," p. 40. H. J. Heinz, Pittsburg, Pennsylvania.
McCay, C. M., and Dilley, W. E. (1927). *Trans. Amer. Fish. Soc.* **57,** 250.
McCay, C. M., and Tunison, A. V. (1934). *Fish. Res. Bull. No.* **5,** 18.
McCollum, E. V., and Davis, M. (1913). *J. Biol. Chem.* **15,** 167.
McCollum, E. V., and Simmonds, N. (1917). *J. Biol. Chem.* **32,** 181.
McKee, R. W., Binkley, S. B., MacCorquadale, D. W., Thayer, S. A., and Doisy, E. A. (1939). *J. Amer. Chem. Soc.* **61,** 1295.
McLaren, B. A., Herman, E. F. and Elvehjem, C. A. (1946). *Arch. Biochem. Biophys.* **10,** 433.
McLaren, B. A., Keller, E., O'Donnell, D. J., and Elvehjem, C. A. (1947a). *Arch. Biochem. Biophys.* **15,** 169.
McLaren, B. A., Keller, E., O'Donnell, D. J., and Elvehjem, C. A. (1947b). *Arch. Biochem. Biophys.* **15,** 179.
Maquenne, L. (1900). "Les Sucres et leurs Principaus Dérivés," p. 190. Carrie et Nand, Paris.
Martin, G. J., Avakian, S., and Moss, J. (1948). *J. Biol. Chem.* **174,** 495.
Mellanby, E. (1919). *Lancet* **1,** 407.
Montjar, M., Axelrod, A. E., and Trakatellis, A. C. (1965). *J. Nutr.* **85,** 45–51.
Morton, R. A., and Creed, R. H. (1939). *Biochem. J.* **33,** 318.
Morton, R. A., Salah, M. K., and Stubbs, A. L. (1947). *Nature (London)* **159,** 744.

Mushett, C. W., and Seeler, A. O. (1947). *J. Pharmacol. Exp. Therap.* **91**, 84.

Nakao, A., and Greenberg, D. M. (1958). *J. Biol. Chem.* **230**, 603.

Neilands, J. B. (1947). *Biochem. Biophys.* **13**, 415.

Nishizawa, Y., Kodama, T., and Kooka, T. (1958). *J. Vitaminol. (Osaka)* **4**, 63.

Nishizuka, Y., and Hayaishi, O. (1963). *J. Biol. Chem.* **238**, PC 483.

Nose, T. (1970). Personal communication.

Ogino, C. (1967a). *Bull. Jap. Soc. Sci. Fish.* **31**, 546.

Ogino, C. (1967b). *Bull. Jap. Soc. Sci. Fish.* **33**, 351.

Ogino, C., Ando, K., Watanabe, T., and Iida, Z. (1970a). *Bull. Jap. Soc. Sci. Fish.* **36**, 1140–1146.

Ogino, C., Watanabe, T., Kakino, J., Iwanaga, N., and Mizuno, M. (1970b). *Bull. Jap. Soc. Sci. Fish.* **36**, 734–40.

Olson, J. A. (1961). *Amer. J. Clin. Nutr.* **9**, 1.

Olson, J. A. (1964). *J. Lipid Res.* **5**, 281.

Osborne, T. B., and Mendel, L. B. (1914). *J. Biol. Chem.* **17**, 401.

Ott, W. H., Rickes, E. L., and Wood, T. R. (1948). *J. Biol. Chem.* **174**, 1047.

Pappenheimer, A. M., and Goettsch, M. (1931). *J. Exp. Med.* **53**, 11.

Pearson, P. B., and Burgin, C. J. (1941). *Proc. Soc. Exp. Biol. Med.* **48**, 415.

Pfaltz, Cited by Hein, R. E. (1964). "Nutritional Data," p. 38. H. J. Heinz, Pittsburg, Pennsylvania.

Pfiffner, J. J., Calkins, D. G., Bloom, E. S., and O'Dell, B. L. (1946). *J. Amer. Chem. Soc.* **68**, 1392.

Phillips, A. M., Tunison, A. V., Shaffer, H. B., White, G. K., Sullivan, M. W., Vincent, C., Brockway, D. R., and McCay, C. M. (1945). *Fish. Res. Bull. No.* **8**, 1.

Phillips, A. M., Jr., Brockway, D. R., Rodgers, E. O., Sullivan, M. W., Cook, B., and Chipman, J. R. (1946). *Fish. Res. Bull. No.* **9**, 11, 21.

Phillips, A. M., Brockway, D. R., Rodgers, E. O., Robertson, R. L., Goodsell, H., Thompson, J. A., and Willoughby, H. (1947). *Fish. Res. Bull. No.* **10**, 35.

Phillips, A. M., Jr., Brockway, D. R., Bryant, M., Rodgers, E. O., and Maxwell, J. M. (1949). *Fish. Res. Bull. No.* **13**, 1.

Phillips, A. M., Jr., Podoliak, H. A., Poston, H. A., and Livingston, D. L. (1963). *Fish. Res. Bull. No.* **26**, 15.

Posternak, T. (1936). *Helv. Chim. Acta* **19**, 1333.

Poston, H. A. (1967). *Fish. Res. Bull. No.* **30**, 46.

Poston, H. A. (1969a). *Fish. Res. Bull. No.* **31**, 9.

Poston, H. A. (1969b). *Fish. Res. Bull. No.* **32**, 41, 48.

Poston, H. A. (1971). *Fish. Res. Bull. No.* **33**, 9.

Poston, H. A., Livingston, D. L., Pyle, E. A. and Phillips, A. M., Jr. (1966). *Fish. Res. Bull. No.* **29**, 20.

Reed, L. J. (1959). "Biological Function of Lipoic Acid in Organic Sulfur Compounds." Pergamon, New York.

Reichstein, T., Grüssner, A., and Oppenauer, R. (1933). *Helv. Chim. Acta* **16**, 1019.

Rickes, E. L., Brink, N. G., Koniuszy, F. R., Wood, T. R., and Folkers, K. (1948). *Science* **107**, 396.

Rosenberg, H. R. (1945). "Chemistry and Physiology of the Vitamins," p. 543. Interscience, New York.

Rosenheim, O., and Webster, T. A. (1927). *Lancet* **1**, 306.

Rucker, R. R., Johnson, H. E., and Kaydas, G. M. (1952). *Progr. Fish. Cult.* **14**, 10.

Sakaguchi, H., and Hamaguchi, A. (1969). *Bull. Jap. Soc. Sci. Fish.* **35**, 1207–1214.

Sakaguchi, H., Takeda, F., and Tange, K. (1969). *Bull. Jap. Soc. Sci. Fish.* **35**, 1201–1206.

Scherer, J. (1850). *Justus Liebigs Ann. Chem.* **73**, 322.

Schneberger, E. (1941). *Progr. Fish. Cult.* **56**, 14.

Shapiro, S., and Ciferri, F. E. (1957). *J. Amer. Med. Ass.* **165**, 1377.

Shelbourne, J. E. (1970). *In* "Marine Aquaculture" (W. J. McNeil, ed.), pp. 15–36. Oregon State Univ. Press, Corvallis, Oregon.

Simmons, R. W., and Norris, E. R. (1941). *J. Biol. Chem.* **140**, 679.

Sinnhuber, R. O. (1969). *In* "Fish in Research" (O. W. Neuhaus and J. E. Halver, eds.), p. 245. Academic Press, New York.

Smith, C. E. (1968). *J. Fish. Res. Bd. Can.* **25**, 151–156.

Smith, C. E., and Halver, J. E. (1969). *J. Fish. Res. Bd. Can.* **26**, 111.

Smith, D. T., Ruffin, J. M., and Smith, S. G. (1937). *J. Amer. Med. Ass.* **109**, 2054.

Smith, E. L. (1948). *Nature (London)* **161**, 638.

Smith, E. L. (1960). "Vitamin $B_{12}$." Methuen, London.

Spencer, T. N. (1916). *Amer. J. Vet. Med.* **11**, 325.

Stansby, M. E. (1967). "Fish Oils." Avi, Westport, Connecticut.

Steenbock, H., and Black, A. (1924). *J. Biol. Chem.* **61**, 405.

Steffens, W. (1969). *Deut. Fisch. Atg.* **16**, 129–135.

Stetten, M. R., and Stetten, D. W. Jr. (1946). *J. Biol. Chem.* **164**, 85.

Stiller, E. T., Harris, S. A., Finkelstein, J., Keresztesy, J. C., and Folkers, K. (1940). *J. Amer. Chem. Soc.* **62**, 1785.

Stokstad, E. L. R. (1943). *J. Biol. Chem.* **149**, 573.

Sure, B. (1924). *J. Biol. Chem.* **58**, 693.

Szent-György, A. (1928). *Biochem. J.* **22**, 1387.

Szent-György, A., and Haworth, W. N. (1933). *Nature (London)* **131**, 23.

Szent-György, A., and Rusznyák, I. (1936). *Nature (London)* **138**, 27.

Tappel, A. L., and Zalkin, H. (1960). *Nature (London)* **185**, 35.

Thompson, W. H. (1917). *J. Physiol. (London)* **51**, 347.

Tomiyama, T., and Ohba, N. (1967). *Bull. Jap. Soc. Sci. Fish.* **33**, 448–452.

Tunison, A. V., Brockway, D. R., Maxwell, J. M., Dorr, A. L., and McCay, C. M. (1942). *Fish. Res. Bull. No.* **4**, 52.

Tunison, A. V., Brockway, D. A., Shaffer, H. B., Maxwell, J. M., McCay, C. M., Palm, C. E., and Webster, D. A. (1943). *Fish. Res. Bull. No.* **5**, 26.

Vagelos, P. R. (1964). *Ann. Rev. Biochem.* **33**, 139.

Vedder, E. B. (1912). *Philippine J. Sci.* B**7**, 415.

Von Euler, B., Euler, H., and Hellström, H. (1928). *Biochem. Z.* **203**, 370.

Vorderman, A. G. (1898). *Geneesk. Tijdschr. Ned. Indië* **38**, 47. Cited by Williams, R. R. (1961). "Toward the Conquest of Beriberi," p. 42. Harvard Univ. Press, Cambridge, Massachusetts.

Wagner, A. F., and Folkers, K. (1964). *Vitamins Coenzymes* **278**, 330.

Waite, M., and Wakil, S. J. (1966). *J. Biol. Chem.* **241**, 1909.

Warburg, O., and Christian, W. (1935). *Biochem. Z.* **275**, 464.

Watanabe, T., Takashima, F., Ogino, C., and Hibiya, T. (1970). *Bull. Jap. Soc. Sci. Fish.* **36**, 972.

Waugh, W. A., and King, C. G. (1932). *J. Biol. Chem.* **97**, 325.

Wedemeyer, G. (1969). *Comp. Biochem. Physiol.* **29**, 1247.

Weidlein, E. R., Jr. (1954). *In* "The Vitamins" (W. H. Sebrell, Jr., and R. S. Harris, eds.), Vol. 2, p. 339. Academic Press, New York.

Weissbach, H., Toohey, J., and Barker, H. A. (1959). *Proc. Nat. Acad. Sci. U.S.* **45,** 521.

West, E. S., Todd, W. R., Mason, H. S. and Van Bruggen, J. T. (1966). "Textbook of Biochemistry," 734, 749, 760, 765, 778, 787, 798, 810, 816, 820, 823, 959, 1185, 1252. Macmillan Co., New York.

WHO (1970). *Tech. Rep. Ser.* **452,** 25.

Williams, R. R. (1961). *In* "Toward the Conquest of Berberi," pp. 36, 42. Harvard Univ. Press, Cambridge, Massachusetts.

Williams, R. R., and Cline, J. K. (1936). *J. Amer. Chem. Soc.* **58,** 1504.

Windaus, A., and Hess, A. (1927). *Nachr. Ges. Wiss. Göttingen Kl.* **111,** 175.

Windaus, A., Schenck F. and Verder, F. (1936). *Z. Physiol. Chem.* **241,** 100.

Winterbottom, R., Clapp, J. W., Miller, W. H., English, J. P., and Roblin, R. O. (1947). *J. Amer. Chem. Soc.* **69,** 1393.

Wolbach, S. B., and Bessey, O. A. (1942). *Physiol. Rev.* **22,** 233.

Wolbach, S. B., and Home, P. R. (1926). *Arch. Pathol.* **1,** 1.

Wolf, L. E. (1942). *Fish. Res. Bull. No.* **2,** 1.

Wolf, L. E. (1945). *Fish. Res. Bull. No.* **7,** 1.

Wolf, L. E. (1951). *Progr. Fish. Cult.* **13,** 17.

Wood, E. M., and Yasutake, W. T. (1956). *Amer. J. Pathol.* **32,** 591.

Woodall, A. N., Ashley, L. M., Halver, J. E., Olcott, H. S., and Van der Veen, J. (1964). *J. Nutr.* **84,** 125.

Woodruff, C. W. (1964). *In* "Nutrition" (G. H. Beaton and E. W. McHenry, eds.), Vol. II, p. 265. Academic Press, New York.

Woolley, D. W. (1940). *Science* **92,** 384.

Woolley, D. W., Waisman, H. A., and Elvehjem, C. A. (1939). *J. Amer. Chem. Soc.* **61,** 977.

Wright, L. D., Cresson, E. L., Valiant, J., Wolf, D. E., and Folkers, K. (1954). *J. Amer. Chem. Soc.* **76,** 4163.

Zacho, C. E. (1939). *Acta Pathol. Microbiol. Scand.* **16,** 144.

Zaugg, W. S. (1970). *Trans. Amer. Fish. Soc.* **99,** 811.

Zaugg, W. S., and McLain, L. R. (1969). *In* "Fish in Research" (O. W. Neuhaus and J. E. Halver, eds.), p. 293. Academic Press, New York.

# 3

# THE PROTEIN AND AMINO ACID NEEDS

*Edwin T. Mertz*

## I. Introduction

The first animal whose protein and amino acid needs were clearly revealed under carefully defined conditions was the young albino rat (*Rattus norvegicus*). Using a mixture of purified amino acids commonly found in plant and animal proteins, Rose and his students (Borman *et al.*, 1946; Womack and Rose, 1947) showed that threonine, tryptophan, histidine, leucine, lysine, isoleucine, methionine, valine, and phenylalanine cannot be synthesized by the rat from materials ordinarily available in the diet; arginine can be synthesized but not at a rate commensurate with maximum growth, and glycine, alanine, serine, proline, hydroxyproline, aspartic acid, glutamic acid, cystine, and tyrosine can be synthesized at an adequate rate when one alone is missing from the diet.

The successful demonstration of qualitative amino acid needs paved the way for the determination of quantitative requirements. Using a suitable mixture of purified amino acids at an adequate nitrogen level, Rose and co-workers (1949) varied the level of individual amino acids to find the minimum level associated with maximum growth rate. The sum of the minimum requirements for the ten essential amino acids (arginine included) was only 5.8% of the diet. Growth at about 40% of the maximum rate could be obtained on this mixture as the only source of nitrogen. The ten essential amino acids at the 5.8% level furnish 1.4 gm of total nitrogen. An additional 0.6 gm of nitrogen from diammonium citrate permitted maximum gains on this diet. This extremely efficient combination of essential amino acids and diammonium citrate provides a diet with only 12.5% crude protein (N $\times$ 6.25), and showed that with proper balance and density of essential amino acids, the total protein requirement is reduced.

The classical studies of Rose with the rat have served as models for analogous studies in other species, including fish.

## II. Qualitative Amino Acid Requirements of Chinook Salmon (*Oncorhynchus tshawytscha*)

The amino acid test diets developed by Rose and co-workers were not completely suitable for feeding experiments with fish. The crude protein level seldom exceeded 20% of the diet, as compared to a level of 60–65% in practical fish hatchery diets (Wood *et al.*, 1957), and the bulk of the ration consisted of dextrin or sucrose, which were considered to be poorly tolerated by fish (Phillips *et al.*, 1948; McLaren *et al.*, 1946). Halver (1957a)

TABLE I

AMINO ACID COMPOSITION OF YOLK SAC FRY AND SALMON FINGERLINGS AND OF
EXPERIMENTAL DIETS[a]

| | Microbiological Assays | | | Amino Acid diet mixtures | |
|---|---|---|---|---|---|
| Ingredient | Yolk-sac fry (gm) | Salmon fingerlings (gm) | Casein Gelatin control (gm) | C-G (gm) | YSF (gm) |
| L-Arginine · HCl | 1.41 | 1.36 | 4.44 | 5.00 | 2.50 |
| L-Histidine · HCl · H₂O | 2.07 | 1.80 | 2.13 | 2.50 | 3.00 |
| L-Isoleucine | 4.76 | 5.38 | 4.11 | 4.00 | 6.00 |
| L-Lysine · HCl | 2.09 | 2.07 | 5.05 | 5.00 | 3.00 |
| L-Methionine | 1.23 | 1.30 | 1.91 | 2.00 | 2.00 |
| L-Phenylalanine | 2.69 | 2.64 | 3.84 | 4.00 | 3.00 |
| L-Threonine | 1.00 | 0.95 | 2.47 | 2.50 | 1.50 |
| L-Tryptophan | 0.97 | 1.00 | 0.74 | 1.00 | 1.50 |
| L-Tyrosine | 2.32 | 2.05 | 3.86 | 4.00 | 2.50 |
| L-Valine | 1.10 | 0.91 | 4.29 | 4.00 | 1.50 |
| Glycine | | | 4.70 | 5.00 | 5.00 |
| L-Alanine | | | 3.40 | 3.50 | 5.00 |
| L-Aspartic acid | | | 4.20 | 5.00 | 5.00 |
| L-Cystine | | | 0.20 | 0.50 | 2.50 |
| L-Glutamic acid | | | 13.60 | 8.00 | 10.00 |
| L-Proline | | | 6.08 | 5.00 | 5.00 |
| L-Serine | | | 3.17 | 3.00 | 5.00 |
| Total | 19.64 | 19.46 | 68.19 | 70.00 | 70.00 |
| Amino acid mix | | | | 70 | 70 |
| Vitamin-free casein | | | 55 | — | — |
| Gelatin | | | 15 | — | — |
| Corn oil | | | 5 | 5 | 5 |
| Cod liver oil | | | 2 | 2 | 2 |
| Dextrin, white | | | 6 | 6 | 6 |
| Mineral mix | | | 4 | 4 | 4 |
| Vitamin mix | | | 3 | 3 | 3 |
| α-Cellulose flour | | | 8 | — | — |
| Carboxymethyl cellulose | | | 2 | 10 | 10 |
| Water | | | 300 | 100 | 100 |

[a] From Halver (1957a).

recognized these problems and modified the Rose diet. Starting with a casein–gelatin diet which he had successfully used for determining the vitamin requirements of fingerling salmon (Halver, 1957b), he compared the efficiency of an amino acid pattern based on the casein-gelatin component with one based on the amino acid composition of yolk sac fry and salmon fingerlings (Table I). The casein-gelatin pattern was found to give better growth and feed efficiency, and was therefore adopted as the amino acid test diet. The composition of this diet (diet C–G) is shown in Table I. The major differences between this diet and the Rose diets are the high level of purified L-amino acids (70% of the dry ingredients) with complete absence of D-amino acids, the low level of digestible carbohydrate (6% of the dry ingredients), and the presence of a hydrophilic colloid, carboxymethyl cellulose, which permits the addition of water to the dry ingredients with the formation of a stiff dough.

The first successful feeding test which clearly revealed the qualitative amino acid needs of a fish species was reported by Halver *et al.* (1957) using the amino acid test diet (diet C–G) described above. Tunison *et al.* (1942) and Gerking (1952) had previously reported experiments on measuring nitrogen balance in trout and sunfish, respectively, but appropriate diets for studying amino acid requirements were not developed prior to that of Halver (1957a).

In the feeding experiments reported by Halver *et al.* (1957) a clear-cut classification of essential amino acids for chinook salmon was obtained. Since feed preparation and feeding practices are quite dissimilar for warm-blooded animals and fish, it seems appropriate to describe details of these first amino acid studies in fish.

## A. Preparation of Diets

The amino acid test diet was prepared in a dough mixer equipped with a wire beater. To prepare 200 gm of diet, 70 gm amino acid mixture, 5 gm corn oil, 2 gm cod liver oil, 6 gm white dextrin, 4 gm mineral mixture, and 3 gm α-cellulose flour containing the vitamin supplement were blended in the dry state until a homogeneous mixture was obtained. To these ingredients was added 100 ml of distilled water that had been heated to 80°–90°C. The mass was then stirred until homogeneous and until the soluble components were in solution. With the mixer in motion, 10 gm carboxymethyl cellulose was added slowly and as the diet began to solidify, the speed of the blender was increased to incorporate air into the mixture. The final diet (200 gm) was about the consistency of bread dough. When stored in low form fruit jars in the refrigerator, the firmness increased and the diet could be fed easily through a garlic press without wastage. Only as much diet as needed for 1 week of feeding was prepared and stored at 4°–6°C until used. In the deficient diets, α-cellulose flour replaced on an equal weight basis the amino acid dropped from the basal (amino acid test) diet.

## B. FEEDING PRACTICES

The growth experiments were conducted in screen-covered wood plank troughs that had been sealed with an inert plastic film. The spring water supply (3 gallons/minute/trough) was practically free of fish pathogens and remained at 47° ± 1°F throughout the 10-week feeding period. Two trough sizes were available–18 × 10 × 84 inches and 18× 10 × 60 inches. Approximately 5000 actively feeding chinook salmon fingerlings were transferred from a federal production hatchery to the experimental hatchery, and twenty lots of 200 fish each were hand counted into the troughs. Variation in total weight of fish per trough was small. Throughout the remainder of the feeding tests the entire population of each trough was weighed biweekly by one individual as follows: the entire population was removed in a net, the water allowed to drain from the net for 10 seconds, the fish then dropped into a tared container on a solution balance, weighed to within one gram, and immediately returned to the trough.

Since the salmon had been actively feeding on a production diet in a hatchery raceway (8 × 80 feet), the change to the special diets was great, and the fish were given an adaptation period using a beef liver diet prior to the start of the feeding trial. After 5 days, the fish were feeding actively on the liver diet, on the sixth day the diet was altered to contain one-third complete amino acid test diet, on the seventh day to contain two-thirds, and on the eighth and ninth days, test diet alone. During the adaptation period, dead fish were replaced and at the end of the period an initial experimental weight for the fish in each trough was obtained (374–400 gm).

The fish were fed a slowly sinking diet expelled through a garlic press into the upper portion of the water. Diets were fed as long as the fish accepted them, and feeding ceased as soon as any portion of the diet reached the bottom of the trough. The fish would eat off the bottom but this was avoided as much as possible since leaching of nutrients from the diets must occur. Apparatus common to more than one trough was cleaned and disinfected between troughs to minimize inadvertent transfer of disease organisms or food particles. Fish were fed three times a day, 6 days a week on a rigid schedule (8:00 A.M., 1:00 P.M., and 4:00 P.M,). The fish seemed to consume more in the first two feedings. Troughs were

TABLE II

Average Data for Chinook Salmon on Basal Diet and on Diets Lacking in Dispensable Amino Acids[a]

| Diets | Initial wt. (gm) | Av. wt. 2nd wk. (gm) | Av. wt. 4th wk. (gm) | Av. wt. 6th wk. (gm) | Av. wt. 8th wk. (gm) | Av. wt. 10th wk. (gm) |
|---|---|---|---|---|---|---|
| Basal, lot 1 | 2.00 | 2.26 (0)[b] | 2.48 (0) | 2.78 (0) | 3.10 (1) | 3.42 (2) |
| Basal, lot 2 | 1.87 | 2.13 (0) | 2.44 (1) | 2.70 (0) | 2.99 (1) | 3.29 (2) |
| Alanine-deficient | 1.90 | 2.13 (0) | 2.40 (0) | 2.65 (1) | 2.97 (0) | 3.23 (2) |
| Aspartic acid-deficient | 1.92 | 2.16 (2) | 2.47 (2) | 2.76 (1) | 3.07 (0) | 3.46 (0) |
| Cystine-deficient | 1.90 | 2.14 (1) | 2.45 (0) | 2.73 (0) | 3.03 (2) | 3.28 (1) |
| Glutamic acid-deficient | 1.93 | 2.22 (1) | 2.56 (1) | 2.86 (0) | 3.23 (1) | 3.52 (1) |
| Glycine-deficient | 1.89 | 2.11 (0) | 2.47 (1) | 2.83 (0) | 3.11 (0) | 3.33 (1) |
| Proline-deficient | 1.91 | 2.11 (0) | 2.39 (0) | 2.76 (0) | 3.01 (0) | 3.29 (0) |
| Serine-deficient | 1.94 | 2.18 (0) | 2.49 (0) | 2.83 (0) | 3.13 (0) | 3.44 (4) |
| Tyrosine-deficient | 1.92 | 2.16 (0) | 2.51 (1) | 2.70 (1) | 2.98 (1) | 3.31 (0) |

[a] From Halver *et al.* (1957).
[b] Numbers within parentheses indicate the mortality during the preceding 2-week period.

cleaned partially daily without removing the fish, and were drained, cleaned, and disinfected during the biweekly weighing period.

Table II summarizes the results of feeding the amino acid test diet to two lots of 200 fingerlings. In the table, data are also included for separate lots of fish fed the amino acid test diet lacking in one of the following amino acids: alanine, aspartic acid, cystine, glutamic acid, glycine, proline, serine, or tyrosine. Omission of any one of these amino acids had no effect on growth, and it may be concluded that they can be synthesized by the chinook salmon. In contrast, Table III shows that arginine, histidine, isoleucine, leucine, lysine, methionine, phenylalanine, threonine, tryptophan, and valine are indispensable for growth in this species of fish. On diets deficient in any one of these ten amino acids, curbed intake of food was noted within 10 days after the fish were placed on the deficient diet. The fish tended to swim slowly to the surface, take a piece of food, mouth it, and then expel it. They hovered near the surface when being fed, and ate very little diet.

At the end of the sixth week the deficient fish in each of the ten lots shown in Table III were split into two subgroups by crowding them into one end of the trough and swirling them with a net. A second net was dipped into the swirling fish and approximately one-half were removed. Both groups were hand counted and made equal. Subgroup one was continued on the same amino acid-deficient ration, and subgroup two was placed on the basal diet (Table I) containing all eighteen amino acids. By the seventh day, fish in subgroup two were feeding actively, swimming rapidly to the surface, and even breaking the surface to obtain food. These fish showed an immediate and substantial growth response to the com-

TABLE III

AVERAGE DATA FOR CHINOOK SALMON ON THE VARIOUS DIETS LACKING IN ESSENTIAL AMINO ACIDS[a]

| Diets | Initial wt. (gm) | Av. wt. 2nd wk. (gm) | Av. wt. 4th wk. (gm) | Av. wt. 6th wk. (gm) | Av. wt. 8th wk. (gm) | Av. wt. 10th wk. (gm) |
|---|---|---|---|---|---|---|
| Arginine-deficient | 1.88 | 1.84 (3) | 1.86 (0) | 1.76 (0) | 1.84 (2) | 1.71 (4) |
| Basal | | | | 1.76 | 2.04 (1) | 2.41 (0) |
| Histidine-deficient | 1.88 | 1.99 (3) | 2.03 (0) | 2.01 (0) | 1.91 (0) | 1.80 (2) |
| Basal | | | | 2.01 | 2.35 (0) | 2.74 (1) |
| Isoleucine-deficient | 1.88 | 1.93 (0) | 1.93 (1) | 1.88 (1) | 1.84 (1) | 1.59 (2) |
| Basal | | | | 1.88 | 2.19 (1) | 2.41 (2) |
| Leucine-deficient | 1.91 | 1.86 (0) | 1.90 (2) | 1.68 (8) | 1.63 (1) | 1.42 (1) |
| Basal | | | | 1.68 | 1.86 (0) | 2.11 (0) |
| Lysine-deficient | 1.87 | 1.94 (0) | 1.96 (0) | 1.86 (1) | 1.86 (0) | 1.81 (1) |
| Basal | | | | 1.86 | 2.17 (0) | 2.50 (1) |
| Methionine-deficient | 1.88 | 2.00 (0) | 2.05 (0) | 1.99 (1) | 1.83 (0) | 1.82 (0) |
| Basal | | | | 1.99 | 2.20 (0) | 2.47 (0) |
| Phenylalanine-deficient | 1.96 | 2.11 (1) | 2.09 (0) | 2.07 (0) | 1.96 (0) | 1.87 (0) |
| Basal | | | | 2.07 | 2.38 (1) | 2.71 (0) |
| Threonine-deficient | 1.90 | 1.98 (0) | 1.96 (0) | 1.95 (1) | 1.97 (2) | 1.97 (1) |
| Basal | | | | 1.95 | 2.32 (1) | 2.65 (0) |
| Tryptophan-deficient | 1.92 | 1.93 (0) | 1.96 (1) | 1.94 (1) | 1.86 (1) | 1.77 (3) |
| Basal | | | | 1.94 | 2.36 (1) | 2.49 (0) |
| Valine-deficient | 1.93 | 2.00 (0) | 2.05 (0) | 1.97 (1) | 1.94 (2) | 1.78 (0) |
| Basal | | | | 1.97 | 2.15 (0) | 2.38 (1) |

[a] From Halver *et al.* (1957).

[b] Numbers within parentheses indicate the mortality during the preceding 2 week period.

plete ration. The fish in subgroup one (deficient diet) continued to show a curbed intake of food and a relatively low degree of activity.

Figure 1 compares the growth curve of the fish on the arginine-deficient diet with the average growth curve of the two control lots. Similar results were obtained with the other nine indispensable amino acids. The nine dispensable amino acids gave growth curves similar to that shown for cystine in Fig. 2. Pictures comparing the appearance of typical fish selected from the glutamic acid-, arginine-, and leucine-deficient lots with fish from the control lots are shown in Fig. 3 (top, center, and bottom rows, respectively).

These data show that, unlike the weanling rat (Borman *et al.*, 1946) and the weanling pig (Mertz *et al.*, 1952), young chinook salmon are unable to synthesize arginine; in this respect the salmon resembles the chick (Almquist and Grau, 1944). In contrast to the chick, however, which needs glycine for adequate feathering, glycine can be synthesized at a rate adequate to meet the needs for normal growth. The qualitative amino acid requirements of the young salmon are therefore not exactly the same as those of either the young rat or the chick. This emphasizes the differences which exist between species.

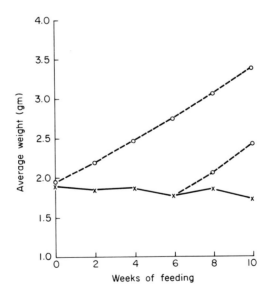

Fig. 1. Growth of arginine-deficient fish. The deficient group was divided after 6 weeks on the deficient diet and the missing amino acid was replaced in one of the two sublots. ×—×, Arginine-deficient diet; ○—○, complete diet.

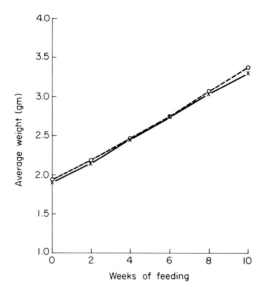

FIG. 2. Growth of cystine-deficient fish. No difference in growth was discernible between cystine-deficient and control lots of salmon. ×—×, cystine-deficient diet; ○—○, complete diet.

## III. Quantitative Amino Acid Requirements of Chinook Salmon

Because of the high cost of the purified L-amino acids used in the amino acid test diet described in the previous section, Halver and co-workers used a modified diet to determine quantitative amino acid requirements of the chinook salmon.

### A. THREONINE REQUIREMENT

DeLong *et al.* (1962) used the basal diets shown in Table IV to determine the threonine requirement at two water temperatures, 8° and 15°C. A mixture of casein, gelatin, and L-amino acids to give a crude protein content (N × 6.25) of 40 gm/100 gm of dry diet was devised. The essential amino acids were supplied in the balance and in the amounts found in 42 gm of whole egg protein in experiment I and in 40 gm of whole egg protein in experiments 2 and 3 (Table IV) except for the variable threonine. Table V summarizes the growth data obtained using 200 fish at each threonine level. The methods of diet preparation and general feeding techniques were the same as those described in the previous section.

FIG. 3.

TABLE IV

BASAL DIET FOR THREONINE STUDIES[a]

|  | Exp. 1 | Exp. 2, 3 |
|---|---|---|
|  | gm/299 gm diet | |
| Casein | 8.00 | 13.30 |
| Gelatin | 2.00 | 3.00 |
| Amino acid mixture[b] | 34.58 | 27.45 |
| White dextrin | 21.42 | 26.05 |
| $\alpha$-Cellulose | 10.00 | 5.00 |
| Corn oil | 5.00 | 5.00 |
| Cod liver oil[c] | 2.00 | 2.00 |
| Minerals[d] | 4.00 | 4.00 |
| CMC[e] | 10.00 | 10.00 |
| Vitamins[d] | 3.00 | 3.00 |
| Water | 100.00 | 100.00 |

[a] From DeLong *et al.* (1962).

[b] Individual amino acids listed in Table 2, DeLong *et al.* (1962).

[c] USP Standard, Nutritional Biochemicals Corp., Cleveland.

[d] Mineral mix and vitamin mix contained the same ingredients as reported previously (Halver and Shanks, 1960).

[e] Carboxymethylcellulose.

Plotting the data in Table V gave growth curves (Figs. 1 and 2; DeLong *et al.*, 1962) which suggest that the threonine requirement of chinook salmon at both 8° and 15°C is approximately 0.9% of the dry diet. Since the diets contained about 40% crude protein, this would correspond to a threonine requirement of 2.25% of the dietary protein. When placed on a protein basis, the threonine requirement of the chinook salmon is somewhat lower than that of other species. Thus, the rat requires 0.5% of threonine at a crude protein level of 16% or 3.1% of the dietary protein (Frost, 1950), the weanling pig requires 0.4% threonine at a crude protein level of 13.2% protein or 3.0% of the dietary protein (Beeson *et al.*, 1953), and the chick requires 0.6% of threonine in a diet containing 20% protein, which is 3.0% of the dietary protein (Block and Weiss, 1956).

FIG. 3. Amino acid-deficient and control chinook salmon. Top row, glutamic acid-deficient (first 3) and control fish; center row, arginine-deficient (first 3) and control fish; bottom row, leucine-deficient (first 3) and control fish.

TABLE V

GROWTH DATA FROM THREONINE QUANTITATION STUDIES[a]

| Threonine in diet (%) | Starting average weight (gm) | Final weight (gm) | Individual mortality | Total average gain (gm) |
|---|---|---|---|---|
| Experiment 1 at 15°C | | | | |
| 0.40 | 5.83 | 5.61 | 15 | —0.22 |
| 0.50 | 6.00 | 6.70 | 22 | 0.70 |
| 0.60 | 5.93 | 7.35 | 11 | 1.42 |
| 0.80 | 5.99 | 8.03 | 20 | 2.04 |
| 1.00 | 5.97 | 9.76 | 13 | 3.79 |
| 1.81 | 6.25 | 9.53 | 11 | 3.28 |
| Experiment 2 at 15°C | | | | |
| 0.60 | 1.26 | 3.07 | 6 | 1.81 |
| 0.80 | 1.26 | 3.40 | 7 | 2.14 |
| 0.90 | 1.22 | 3.81 | 4 | 2.59 |
| 1.00 | 1.26 | 3.50 | 6 | 2.24 |
| 1.10 | 1.29 | 3.29 | 7 | 2.10 |
| 1.20 | 1.28 | 3.53 | 4 | 2.25 |
| 1.80 | 1.22 | 3.51 | 2 | 2.29 |
| Experiment 3 at 8°C | | | | |
| 0.60 | 3.02 | 5.39 | 6 | 2.37 |
| 0.70 | 3.12 | 5.88 | 12 | 2.76 |
| 0.80 | 3.06 | 6.19 | 49 | 3.13 |
| 0.90 | 3.09 | 6.43 | 4 | 3.24 |
| 1.00 | 3.05 | 6.36 | 8 | 3.31 |
| 1.10 | 3.00 | 6.38 | 6 | 3.38 |

[a] From DeLong *et al.* (1962).

## B. LYSINE AND METHIONINE REQUIREMENTS

Using the diet of experiment I in Table IV with adequate levels of all essential amino acids except the one under quantitation, Halver *et al.* (1958) found a lysine requirement of approximately 2.0%, and, in later studies (1959), a methionine requirement between 0.5–0.6% of the dry diet in the presence of 1.0% cystine. When these requirement values are expressed as percentage of dietary protein, these agree very well with values obtained for the weanling pig and rat. Thus, the lysine requirement of the chinook salmon is 5.0% of the crude protein, for the weanling pig it is 4.7% (Germann *et al.*, 1958), and for the weanling rat 5.2% (Bressani and Mertz, 1958). The methionine requirement in the presence of adequate cystine is 1.5% of the crude protein (0.6/40) in the chinook salmon, and 1.4% in the weanling pig (0.3/21) (Shelton *et al.*, 1951a).

## C. ISOLEUCINE, LEUCINE, VALINE, AND PHENYLALANINE REQUIREMENTS

Chance *et al.* (1964) reduced the proportion of purified L-amino acids even further in the diet which they designed to study these essential amino acids. Table VI shows the composition of the diet employed. The diet contained casein and gelatin as natural proteins to supply minimal quantities of the amino acids being studied, yet maximal quantities of several other amino acids. Crystalline amino acid supplements complemented the natural protein to give an overall pattern of indispensable amino acids similar to that found in whole egg protein. The dry solids contained 41% of crude protein (N × 6.25). Isonitrogenous and isocaloric diets were maintained by altering glutamic acid and dextrin, respectively,

TABLE VI

EXPERIMENTAL DIET[a,b]

|  | gm/300 gm of diet |
| --- | --- |
| Gelatin | 20.00 |
| Casein | 5.00 |
| Amino acid mixture[c] | 20.22 |
| White dextrin | 35.78 |
| α-Cellulose flour | 7.00 |
| Mineral mixture[d] | 4.00 |
| Vitamins[e] | 1.00 |
| Corn oil | 5.00 |
| Cod liver oil | 2.00 |
| Water | 200.00 |

[a] From Chance *et al.* (1964).

[b] All ingredients except corn oil supplied by Nutritional Biochemicals Corporation, Cleveland.

[c] Amino acid components listed in Table 2, Chance *et al.* (1964).

[d] Same as reported by Nicolaides and Woodall (1962).

[e] Added via α-cellulose: (in mg) thiamine·HCl, 5; riboflavin, 20; pyridoxine·HCl, 5; nicotinic acid, 75; Ca-pantothenate, 50; *i*-inositol, 200; ascorbic acid, 100; biotin, 0.5; folic acid, 1.5. Added via aqueous solution: (in mg) choline·Cl, 500; vitamin $B_{12}$, 0.01. Added via corn oil: (in mg) menadione, 4; α-tocopheryl acetate, 40.

TABLE VII

Growth Data for Leucine[a,b]

| Leucine in dry diet (%) | No. fish[c] | Initial weight (gm) | Gain (%) | Feed/gm gain (gm) |
|---|---|---|---|---|
| 1.00 | 200(0) | 2.44 | 28 | 2.29 |
| 1.20 | 200(1) | 2.44 | 34 | 1.71 |
| 1.40 | 200(2) | 2.48 | 77 | 1.28 |
| 1.60 | 200(0) | 2.48 | 111 | 1.11 |
| 2.10 | 200(4) | 2.52 | 100 | 1.16 |
| 3.10 | 200(1) | 2.58 | 101 | 1.19 |
| Control diet[d] | 200(4) | 2.49 | 91 | 1.22 |

[a] From Chance et al. (1964).

[b] Conducted for 8 weeks during the summer of 1959 with spring run salmon from Eagle Creek National Fish Hatchery, Estacada, Oregon.

[c] Numbers in parentheses indicate mortality.

[d] Contained an indispensable amino acid pattern similar to that of whole egg protein.

TABLE VIII

Growth Data for Isoleucine[a] (Exp. 1)[b]

| Isoleucine in dry diet (%) | No. fish[c] | Initial weight (gm) | Gain (%) | Feed/gm gain (gm) |
|---|---|---|---|---|
| 0.50 | 250(17) | 1.00 | 80 | 2.04 |
| 0.70 | 250(18) | 0.94 | 121 | 1.44 |
| 0.90 | 250(11) | 0.97 | 142 | 1.35 |
| 1.10 | 250(16) | 0.97 | 207 | 1.08 |
| 1.30 | 250(12) | 0.96 | 162 | 1.28 |
| 1.50 | 250(13) | 0.97 | 170 | 1.22 |
| 2.00 | 250(19) | 0.96 | 147 | 1.38 |
| Control diet[d] | 250(17) | 0.98 | 136 | 1.39 |

[a] Experiment conducted during summer of 1959 with fall run salmon from Willard National Fish Hatchery, Cook, Washington.

[b] From Chance et al. (1964).

[c] Numbers in parentheses indicate mortality.

[d] Contained an indispensable amino acid pattern similar to that of whole egg protein.

with the amino acids studied. Gelatin served as the binding agent, replacing carboxymethyl cellulose.

### D. Leucine Requirement

The data in Table VII when plotted (Fig. 1; Chance *et al.*, 1964) showed that the leucine requirement of chinook salmon fingerlings is about 1.6% of the dry diet or 3.9% of the crude protein. On a protein basis this is in good agreement with the leucine requirement of the pig (4–5% for baby pigs according to Eggert *et al.*, 1954) and 4.6% for weanling pigs (Mertz *et al.*, 1955). It is lower than that suggested for the rat, 7% (Rose *et al.*, 1949), and chick, 7% (Bird *et al.*, 1960).

### E. Isoleucine Requirement

Experiments were carried out by Chance *et al.* (1964) to determine the isoleucine requirement at different dietary leucine levels. Results from one experiment (Table VIII) were plotted and suggested a requirement of

TABLE IX

Growth Data for Isoleucine[a] (Exp. 3)[b]

| Isoleucine in dry diet (%) | No. fish[c] | Initial weight (gm) | Gain (%) | Feed/gm gain (gm) |
|---|---|---|---|---|
| 1.50% of leucine in diet | | | | |
| 0.50 | 250(4) | 0.83 | 182 | 1.34 |
| 0.70 | 250(2) | 0.80 | 257 | 1.25 |
| 0.90 | 250(3) | 0.84 | 299 | 1.17 |
| 1.10 | 250(3) | 0.81 | 301 | 1.19 |
| 1.30 | 250(9) | 0.81 | 326 | 1.16 |
| 1.50 | 250(7) | 0.80 | 302 | 1.20 |
| Control diet[d] | 250(1) | 0.78 | 348 | 1.22 |
| 6.00% of leucine in diet | | | | |
| 0.50 | 250(7) | 0.79 | 157 | 1.30 |
| 0.70 | 250(6) | 0.76 | 233 | 1.14 |
| 0.90 | 250(11) | 0.78 | 278 | 1.20 |
| 1.10 | 250(11) | 0.79 | 280 | 1.22 |
| 1.30 | 250(0) | 0.80 | 314 | 1.17 |
| 1.50 | 250(1) | 0.81 | 303 | 1.16 |
| Control diet[d] | 250(1) | 0.78 | 348 | 1.22 |

[a] Conducted for 10 weeks during summer of 1960 with fall run salmon from Willard National Fish Hatchery, Cook, Washington.

[b] From Chance *et al.* (1964).

[c] Numbers in parentheses indicate mortality.

[d] Contained an indispensable amino acid pattern similar to that of whole egg protein.

about 1.0% of the dry diet when the leucine level used was the same as that of the control diet (3.68%). Another experiment was designed to study the isoleucine requirement at two dietary leucine levels. The low level, 1.5%, represented the approximate minimal requirement for leucine, whereas the high level, 6.0%, represented an excess level that decreased growth when fed in conjunction with the minimal requirement level of isoleucine. Results from this experiment (Table IX) when plotted suggest that the minimal isoleucine requirement is about 0.9% of the dry diet with the low leucine level, and somewhat greater than 0.9% with the high leucine level. By plotting isoleucine levels against percentage hematocrits (Fig. 4; Chance *et al.*, 1964), the authors concluded that the minimal isoleucine requirement ranged from 0.9–1.1% of the dry diet depending upon the dietary leucine level. The isoleucine requirement appeared to be about 0.9% of the diet in the presence of 1.5% leucine, and increased about 0.1% with every additional 2.3% of dietary leucine. Expressed as percentage of the crude protein, the isoleucine requirement ranged from 2.2 to 2.7%, or approximately 2.5% of the dietary protein. This requirement is somewhat low when compared with other species. Brinegar *et al.* (1950) reported that the isoleucine requirement was 0.7% of a 22% protein diet or 3.2% of the protein. Becker and co-workers (1957) believe that the requirement of the young pig varies with the level of protein in the diet. At the 13.35% protein level, the requirement was 3.4% of the protein, whereas at the 26.7% protein level the requirement was only 2.4% of the protein. The latter value agrees with the values obtained with salmon.

The requirement of young chicks at the 20% protein level is listed as 0.6% of the diet, or 3.0% of the protein (Bird *et al.*, 1960). Rose *et al.* (1949) obtained a value of about 4.0% of the protein for young white rats on a 12–13% protein diet.

The antagonistic effect of excess leucine on the isoleucine requirement of salmon is in agreement with studies on rats by Harper (1958). He found that the growth-depressing effects of 3.0% leucine added to a 9% casein diet could be eliminated with small supplements of isoleucine. However, Harper was unable to obtain this effect by feeding the same level of leucine in an 18% casein diet. Salmon fingerlings may be more sensitive to amino acid imbalance than rats, particularly since the protein needs of salmon are greater, as will be discussed in a later section.

## F. Effect of Excess Isoleucine on the Growth of Chinook Salmon

To study this relationship, three levels of isoleucine (1.00, 3.00, and 5.00%) were fed to salmon receiving a slightly suboptimal level of leucine

TABLE X

GROWTH DATA FOR ISOLEUCINE: LEUCINE RATIOS[a,b]

| Isoleucine and leucine in dry diet (%) | No. fish[c] | Initial weight (gm) | Gain (%) | Feed/gm gain (gm) |
|---|---|---|---|---|
| 1.00 Isoleucine, 1.25 leucine | 500(0) | 0.69 | 242 | 1.32 |
| 3.00 Isoleucine, 1.25 leucine | 500(13) | 0.69 | 182 | 1.40 |
| 5.00 Isoleucine, 1.25 leucine | 500(16) | 0.69 | 164 | 1.40 |
| Control diet[d] | 500(3) | 0.69 | 272 | 1.31 |

[a] From Chance *et al.* (1964).

[b] Conducted for 10 weeks during summer of 1960 with fall run salmon from Willard National Fish Hatchery, Cook, Washington. Data represent average of 2 replicates.

[c] Numbers in parentheses indicate mortality.

[d] Contained an indispensable amino acid pattern similar to that of whole egg protein.

(1.25%). The 1.00% level of isoleucine with 1.25% of leucine supported a gain slightly less than that of the egg pattern control diet, indicating that the leucine level fed was below the requirement (Table X). However, growth with this treatment was 89% of that of fish fed the basal diet, whereas the 3.00 and 5.00% levels of isoleucine supported growth that was only 67 and 60% of that with the control diet, respectively. Thus, an imbalance of isoleucine with respect to leucine can be as harmful to good growth as the reverse. If the leucine level had been at, or close to, the minimum requirement level of 1.60%, this effect might not have been so profound. It is possible that the leucine requirement may actually be less than 1.60% when a more favorable level of isoleucine is fed simultaneously, such as the minimal requirement level of 1.00% rather than the whole egg pattern level of 3.2%, which was the level present in the diets used to determine the leucine requirement.

Brinegar *et al.* (1950) obtained a growth depression in young pigs fed 2.08% of isoleucine in the diet. This level corresponds to the 3.00% level based on protein used in the salmon experiments. Also, Sauberlich (1961) found that the growth of rats was depressed 50% when a 6% casein control diet was supplemented with 5% of DL-isoleucine; similarly, 5% of L-leucine in the diet depressed growth 55%.

## G. VALINE REQUIREMENT

The data in Table XI were plotted and the curve indicated that the valine requirement of salmon is about 1.3% of the dry diet, which corresponds to 3.2% of the dietary protein. This value is similar to that of

TABLE XI

GROWTH DATA FOR VALINE[a,b]

| Valine in dry diet (%) | No. fish[c] | Initial weight (gm) | Gain (%) | Feed/gm gain (gm) |
|---|---|---|---|---|
| 0.65 | 500(9) | 0.67 | 206 | 1.42 |
| 0.90 | 500(11) | 0.67 | 244 | 1.40 |
| 1.15 | 500(5) | 0.67 | 276 | 1.35 |
| 1.40 | 500(13) | 0.67 | 290 | 1.32 |
| 1.65 | 500(8) | 0.69 | 283 | 1.34 |
| 1.90 | 500(10) | 0.67 | 285 | 1.32 |
| Control diet[d] | 500(3) | 0.69 | 272 | 1.31 |

[a] From Chance *et al.* (1964).

[b] Conducted for 10 weeks during summer of 1960 with fall run chinook salmon from Willard National Fish Hatchery, Cook, Washington. Data represent average of 2 replicates.

[c] Numbers in parentheses indicate mortality.

[d] Contained an indispensable amino acid pattern similar to that of whole egg protein.

TABLE XII

GROWTH DATA FOR PHENYLALANINE[a,b]

| Phenylalanine in dry diet[c] (%) | No. fish[d] | Initial weight (gm) | Gain (%) | Feed/gm gain (gm) |
|---|---|---|---|---|
| 0.96 | 200(3) | 2.60 | 70 | 1.37 |
| 1.50 | 200(31)[e] | 2.60 | 87 | 1.24 |
| 2.00 | 200(2) | 2.62 | 98 | 1.15 |
| 2.50 | 200(4) | 2.62 | 100 | 1.17 |
| 3.00 | 200(3) | 2.62 | 102 | 1.17 |
| 3.50 | 200(4) | 2.72 | 100 | 1.17 |
| Basal diet[f] | 200(4) | 2.49 | 91 | 1.22 |

[a] From Chance *et al.* (1964).

[b] Conducted for 8 weeks during summer of 1959 with spring run salmon from Eagle Creek National Fish Hatchery, Estacada, Oregon.

[c] Includes 0.35% of tyrosine in basal diet.

[d] Numbers in parentheses indicate mortality.

[e] High mortality results from fish jumping from unscreened trough during third week of experiment.

[f] Contained an indispensable amino acid pattern similar to that of whole egg protein.

the weanling pig, which was reported by Jackson *et al.* (1953) to be 3.1% of a corn–amino acid diet. Somewhat higher values were obtained in feeding tests with the chick (4.0% by Bird *et al.*, 1960), and with the rat (5–6% by Rose *et al.*, 1949). Since valine, isoleucine, and leucine are similar in structure, the valine requirement may have been increased by the relatively high levels of isoleucine and leucine (3.20 and 3.68%, respectively) in the egg pattern control diet. Thus, the valine requirement may be lower than 1.3% of the dry diet when a more optimal combination of isoleucine and leucine is fed.

## H. PHENYLALANINE REQUIREMENT

Data presented in Table XII were plotted and suggest a phenylalanine requirement of 1.7% in the presence of 0.4% of tyrosine. If the tyrosine is sparing an equal amount of phenylalanine, then the requirement would be 2.1% in the absence of tyrosine. When expressed as a percentage of the total protein, the combined phenylalanine plus tyrosine requirement is 5.1%. This value is in the range of values obtained with warm-blooded animals. Mertz *et al.* (1954) reported a value of 3.6% in weanling pigs, Rose and Womack (1946) a value of 6–7% in weanling rats, and Bird *et al.* (1960) a value of 7.0% in chicks.

## I. TRYPTOPHAN REQUIREMENT

Diets containing casein and gelatin supplemented with crystalline L-amino acids to simulate whole egg protein at 40% of the ration (Chance *et al.*, 1964) were fed to triplicate lots of chinook salmon fingerlings for 10 weeks (Halver, 1965). Tryptophan increments in the diets were fixed at 0.15, 0.25, 0.35, 0.45, 0.65, and 1.05% of the ration and all treatments were maintained isonitrogenous by adjusting proline added. Almquist-type plots of growth responses indicated a tryptophan requirement between 0.15 and 0.25% of the diet. This corresponds to a tryptophan requirement of approximately 0.5% of the protein, which is lower than the estimated requirement of 1% for the rat (Oesterling and Rose, 1952), 0.75% for the chick (West *et al.*, 1952), and 0.8% for the pig (Shelton *et al.*, 1951b). The same tryptophan requirement (about 0.2%) was found for sockeye salmon (*Oncorhynchus nerka*) and silver salmon (*O. kisutch*) in the studies by Halver (1965). The qualitative requirements of sockeye salmon are discussed in a later section.

## J. ARGININE AND HISTIDINE REQUIREMENTS

Studies with chinook fingerlings (Klein and Halver, 1970) using diets similar to those employed for L-tryptophan quantitation, gave minimum requirement values of 2.4 and 0.7% for arginine and histidine, respectively. Coho (silver) salmon had a minimum requirement of 2.3% for arginine and 0.7% for histidine. This corresponds to an arginine requirement of 6% of the protein, and a histidine requirement of 1.7%. The arginine requirement of salmonids thus resembles that of the chick, which is 6% of the protein (Bird *et al.*, 1960), and is four to six times higher than that of the young rat and young pig (Mertz *et al.*, 1952). The histidine requirement resembles that of the chick (1.7%) (Bird *et al.*, 1960), and lies between that of the pig (1.5%) (Mertz *et al.*, 1955) and the rat (2.1%) (Borman *et al.*, 1946).

## IV. Protein Requirements of Chinook Salmon

Bressani and Mertz (1958) in studies on weanling rats found a linear inverse relationship between the minimum lysine requirement at a particular dietary protein level and the logarithm of the protein level. Thus, the lysine requirement expressed as percentage of dietary protein was 6.7 with their 8% protein diet, 5.2 with the 16% protein diet, and 2.2 with the 40% protein diet. Since the minimum protein requirement for maximum growth was approximately 16%, the lysine requirement value (5.2% of the protein) obtained at this protein level would have the greatest value in the formulation of practical diets of maximum protein efficiency. Comparison of amino acid requirements of different species would be simplified considerably if investigators would include a quantitation of the amino acid at or near the minimum protein requirement level. Lack of such data probably accounts for some of the variations between species discussed in the previous section on amino acid requirements of salmon.

In order to determine the minimum protein requirements of salmon, DeLong *et al.* (1958) formulated diets whose composition is shown in Tables XIII and XIV. The diets contained a mixture of purified L-amino acids, casein, and gelatin with a balance of essential amino acids similar to that in whole egg protein (Table XIII). Other components of the diet (Table XIV) were the same as those used previously by Halver (1957a). Variations in the total crude protein content were obtained by reducing the amount of each of the three nitrogenous components proportionately. As the components were reduced in the diet, these were replaced by an equivalent weight of dextrin. The levels in the first feeding trial were 13, 39, 52, and 65% protein. The second feeding trial consisted of nine protein levels at 5% increments from 25 to 65%. Since these tests were carried out before any information on quantitative amino acid needs of salmon were available, the amino acid pattern of whole egg protein was considered to be the most suitable substitute.

TABLE XIII

Source and Amino Acid Composition of 65% Protein Diet[a]

| Amino acid | Amino acids in 70 gm whole egg protein (gm) | Amino acids supplied by 40 gm casein (gm) | Amino acids supplied by 10 gm gelatin (gm) | Amino acids supplied by cryst. amino acids (%) | Protein supplied by cryst. amino acids (%) |
|---|---|---|---|---|---|
| Arginine | 4.48 | 1.68 | 0.82 | 1.98 | 3.98 |
| Histidine | 1.47 | 1.28 | 0.09 | 0.10 | 0.17 |
| Lysine | 5.04 | 3.40 | 0.50 | 1.14 | 1.37 |
| Phenylalanine | 4.41 | 2.52 | 0.23 | 1.66 | 0.88 |
| Tyrosine | 3.15 | 2.56 | 0.05 | 0.54 | 0.26 |
| Tryptophan | 1.05 | 0.52 | 0.00 | 0.53 | 0.45 |
| Cystine | 1.68 | 0.16 | 0.01 | 1.51 | 1.10 |
| Methionine | 2.87 | 1.40 | 0.08 | 1.39 | 0.82 |
| Threonine | 3.01 | 1.80 | 0.19 | 1.02 | 0.74 |
| Leucine | 6.44 | 4.00 | 0.35 | 2.09 | 1.40 |
| Isoleucine | 5.60 | 3.00 | 0.17 | 2.43 | 1.62 |
| Valine | 5.11 | 3.08 | 0.28 | 1.75 | 1.31 |
| Glycine | | | | 5.06 | 5.90 |
| Total | 44.31 | 25.40 | 2.77 | 21.20 | 20.00 |

[a] From DeLong *et al.* (1958).

TABLE XIV

Components of Diet[a]

| Component | Range (gm) |
|---|---|
| Casein | 8–40 |
| Gelatin | 2–10 |
| Amino acid mix | 4.5–22 |
| Dextrin | 61.5–4 |
| Corn oil | 5 |
| Cod liver oil | 2 |
| Minerals[b] | 4 |
| α-Cellulose + vitamins[b] | 3 |
| Carboxymethyl cellulose | 10 |
| | 100 |
| Water | 100 |
| Total | 200 |

[a] From DeLong *et al.*, (1958).
[b] See Halver (1957b).

The feeding tests were carried out at two water temperatures, 47° and 58°F. Pentalow (1939) had found that consumption of natural foods and growth rates of young brook trout, another salmonid, increased with rising temperature up to 60°F then decreased with rising temperature. Baldwin (1957) confirmed these results but in his studies found the maximum to be 56°F.

The methods of diet preparation and general experimental feeding techniques of DeLong *et al.* (1958) were the same as those described in previous sections. Table XV shows the average individual weight gains obtained in 10 weeks on different protein levels with water temperatures of 47° and 58°F. In the first feeding test at 47°F with protein levels of 13–65%, the fish were small, averaging 1.5 gm at the start. The final weights averaged from 1.95 to 2.34 gm, and the highest average gain of 0.85 gm was observed with the 39% level. A growth depression was observed at the higher levels of crude protein. In the second feeding tests at 47°F, nine levels of crude protein were used, and the hatchery fish available were about three times heavier than those used earlier in the summer, averaging about 5.6 gm. The final individual average weights ranged from 6.0

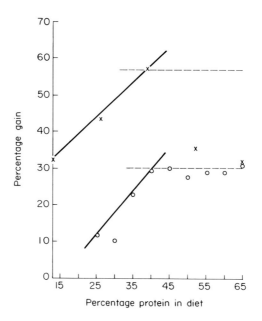

FIG. 4. Protein requirement at 47°F.

to 7.6 gm, and the fish at the 40% protein level made an individual average gain of 1.64 gm. Higher protein levels showed no improvement over
the 40% level and no growth depression was observed. In Fig. 4, the percentage of protein in the diet has been plotted against percentage gain
in body weight for the 10-week period. The upper curve represents the
smaller fish in the first feeding trial. A hypothetical growth plateau representing maximum growth has been projected (dotted line). In the lower
curve are plotted the percentage gains of the larger fish in the second
feeding test. The curves suggest a minimum requirement of 40% crude
protein at a water temperature of 47°F.

Table XV also summarizes the average individual weight gains ob-

TABLE XV

Protein Requirement of Chinook Salmon[a]

| Crude protein (%) | Requirement at 47°F | | | Requirement at 58°F | | |
|---|---|---|---|---|---|---|
| | Av. initial weight (gm) | Av. final weight (gm) | Av. gain (gm) | Av. initial weight (gm) | Av. final weight (gm) | Av. gain (gm) |
| 13 | 1.49 | 1.97 | 0.48 (12)[b] | 2.77 | 3.80 | 1.03 (57)[b] |
| 26 | 1.49 | 2.13 | 0.64 (12) | 2.50 | 4.95 | 2.45 (28) |
| 39 | 1.49 | 2.34 | 0.85  (7) | 2.60 | 6.65 | 4.05 (20) |
| 52 | 1.47 | 1.99 | 0.52 (19) | 2.57 | 7.68 | 5.11 (22) |
| 65 | 1.48 | 1.95 | 0.47 (19) | 2.46 | 8.04 | 5.58 (32) |
| 25 | 5.50 | 6.19 | 0.69  (4) | 5.82 | 8.36 | 2.54 (33) |
| 30 | 5.48 | 6.03 | 0.55  (3) | 5.80 | 8.71 | 2.75  (4) |
| 35 | 5.50 | 6.74 | 1.24  (0) | 5.83 | 8.84 | 3.01  (3) |
| 40 | 5.56 | 7.20 | 1.64  (0) | 5.56 | 9.22 | 3.66  (2) |
| 45 | 5.66 | 7.33 | 1.67  (3) | 5.56 | 8.84 | 3.28  (1) |
| 50 | 5.47 | 6.96 | 1.49  (2) | 6.00 | 10.30 | 4.30  (1) |
| 55 | 5.80 | 7.46 | 1.66  (1) | 5.55 | 10.18 | 4.75  (0) |
| 60 | 5.34 | 6.87 | 1.53  (3) | 5.44 | 9.18 | 4.18  (5) |
| 65 | 5.80 | 7.60 | 1.80  (0) | 5.54 | 10.05 | 4.51 (19) |

[a] From DeLong *et al.* (1958).
[b] Fish mortality is given within parentheses. Two hundred fish in each of first 5 lots
and 150 in each of last 9 lots, at start of experiment.

tained in 10 weeks on different protein levels with a water temperature of 58°F. In the first feeding test with protein levels of 13–65%, the initial individual average weights were about 2.6 gm. The final individual weights ranged from 3.8 to 8.0 gm, and the highest average gain of 5.58 gm was observed at the 65% protein level. In the second feeding test, nine levels of crude protein were used and the fish were heavier, varying from 5.4 to 6.0 gm average individual weight between lots. The final individual average weights per lot ranged from 8.4 to 10.3, and the fish at the 55 and the 65% protein levels made the highest individual average gains, 4.8 and 4.5 gm, respectively.

In Fig. 5, the percentage protein in the diet is plotted against percentage gain in body weight for the 10-week period. Projecting horizontal lines through the highest points and determining the intercept with lines representing the slopes of the rising part of the curves gives a minimum requirement value of approximately 55% protein.

It was concluded by DeLong *et al.* (1958) that the optimum protein level for chinook salmon is dependent upon the water temperature, rising from 40% at 47°F to 55% at 58°F. The protein requirements of fish are thus two to four times higher than that of warm-blooded animals. Bressani and Mertz (1958) found a requirement of not more than 16% (a graph

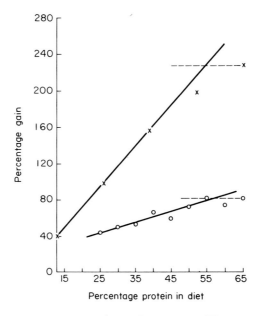

Fig. 5. Protein requirement at 58°F.

plot suggested 14%) for weanling rats fed a corn gluten–purified amino acid diet having the same amino acid pattern as whole egg protein. Beeson *et al.* (1953) stated that weanling pigs weighing 25 pounds required 18% protein when fed a balanced diet of natural feedstuffs, but that this could be reduced to approximately 13% by proper supplementation of ground corn with a mixture of essential amino acids.

There are no reports known to this writer suggesting that the minimum protein requirement of warm-blooded animals varies with the environmental temperature. The chinook salmon is the first animal in which this unusual phenomenon has been demonstrated. Future research will probably demonstrate a similar variation in protein requirements of other poikilothermous animals.

## V. Utilization of Nitrogen Supplements by Chinook Salmon

Studies with rats and pigs have shown that several nitrogen sources can serve as raw materials for the synthesis of the nonessential amino acids. Rose *et al.* (1949) found that ammonium salts and L-glutamic acid were more efficient in rats than urea or glycine. Frost (1950) reported that the ability of the rat to convert essential amino acid nitrogen to nonessential amino acids was not as high as the ability to convert other sources of nitrogen to these compounds. Diammonium citrate in combination with a mixture of the ten essential amino acids permitted an excellent rate of gain (1 pound per day) in weanling pigs (Mertz *et al.*, 1952). A careful study by Birnbaum *et al.* (1957) in rats showed that L-alanine, L-arginine, ammonium L-glutamine, ammonium L-aspartate, and L-proline were all highly efficient sources of nitrogen for the synthesis of the dispensable amino acids when each supplied 62.5% of the nitrogen and the remaining 37.7% was supplied by the ten essential amino acids. Ammonium acetate was more effective than urea or glycine but was only 80% as effective as the compounds listed above. L-Arginine was highly effective even in diets containing combinations of all the nonessential amino acids in addition to the essential amino acids.

DeLong *et al.* (1959) compared the efficiency of L-arginine, glycine, urea, and diammonium citrate as sources of nitrogen in the diet of the chinook salmon. The methods of diet preparation and general feeding techniques were the same as those described in a previous section of this chapter. Table XVI shows the composition of the diets. The basal diet contained 20% of crude protein made up of casein and gelatin supplemented with an amino acid mixture to give the balance of indispensable amino acids found in whole egg protein. Diet 1 (Table XVI) contained 40% of this

TABLE XVI

Composition of Nitrogen Supplement Diets[a]

| Diets | Basal (gm) | 1 (gm) | 2 (gm) | 3 (gm) | 4 (gm) | 5 (gm) |
|---|---|---|---|---|---|---|
| Casein | 28.5 | 60.0 | 28.5 | 28.5 | 28.5 | 28.5 |
| Gelatin | 7.15 | 15.0 | 7.15 | 7.15 | 7.15 | 7.15 |
| Amino acid mixture[b] | 15.68 | 32.9 | 15.68 | 15.68 | 15.68 | 15.68 |
| Dextrin | 138.67 | 82.1 | 107.95 | 94.92 | 120.61 | 72.77 |
| Corn oil | 12.5 | 12.5 | 12.5 | 12.5 | 12.5 | 12.5 |
| Cod liver oil | 5.0 | 5.0 | 5.0 | 5.0 | 5.0 | 5.0 |
| Minerals[c] | 10.0 | 10.0 | 10.0 | 10.0 | 10.0 | 10.0 |
| CMC[d] | 25.0 | 25.0 | 25.0 | 25.0 | 25.0 | 25.0 |
| Vitamins[c] | 7.5 | 7.5 | 7.5 | 7.5 | 7.5 | 7.5 |
| Water | 250.0 | 250.0 | 250.0 | 250.0 | 250.0 | 250.0 |
| Arginine · HCl | | | 30.72 | | | |
| Glycine | | | | 43.75 | | |
| Urea | | | | | 18.08 | |
| Diammonium citrate | | | | | | 65.9 |

[a] From DeLong *et al.* (1959).

[b] The same as in diet used for protein requirement studies (DeLong, Halver and Mertz, 1958). This mixture balances the "essential" amino acid content of casein and gelatin to the balance found in whole egg protein.

[c] Mineral and vitamin mixtures the same as reported previously (Halver, 1957[b]).

[d] Carboxymethyl cellulose.

TABLE XVII

Growth and Mortality of Experimental Fish[a]

| Diet | Av. initial wt. (gm) | Av. final wt. (gm) | Av. gain[b] (gm) |
|---|---|---|---|
| Basal | 3.63 | 4.41 | 0.78 (1) |
| 1 | 3.71 | 5.81 | 2.13 (1) |
| 2 | 3.52 | 5.10 | 1.58 (1) |
| 3 | 3.57 | 4.69 | 1.12 (0) |
| 4 | 3.64 | 4.35 | 0.71 (3) |
| 5 | 3.67 | 3.47 | −0.20 (2) |

[a] From DeLong *et al.* (1959).

[b] Fish mortality within parentheses.

balanced protein. Diets 2–5 contained 20% of the balanced protein and 20% of crude protein (N × 6.25) supplied only as one of the compounds studied: L-arginine·HCl, glycine, urea, or diammonium citrate. Diets 1–5 were isonitrogenous.

The average individual weight gains obtained in 6 weeks are shown in Table XVII. The biweekly weight gains are plotted in Fig. 6. The 20% protein diet (diet 0) was the basal diet, and it can be seen from Fig. 6 that a supplement of an additional 20% of the balanced protein (diet 1) greatly increased growth. Weight gains on the 40% balanced protein diet were 2.7 times the weight gains on the 20% balanced protein diet. Providing the additional crude protein as L-arginine (diet 2, Fig. 6) instead

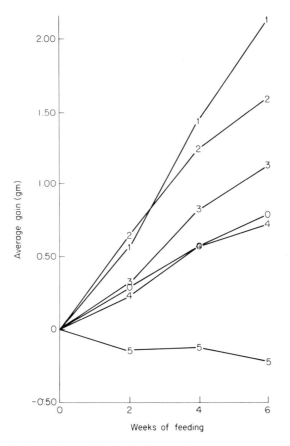

FIG. 6. Growth of experimental fish fed different nitrogen sources. O, 20% protein; 1, 40% protein; 2, 20% + Arg; 3, 20% + Gly; 4, 20% + Urea; 5, 20% + diammonium citrate.

of balanced protein gave an average gain that was two times the basal (diet 0). A 20% crude protein supplement as glycine (diet 3) also showed some stimulation and gave an average gain that was 1.4 times the basal. Urea under the same conditions (diet 4) had no effect, and diammonium citrate (diet 5) caused a weight loss in the fish.

The authors concluded from these studies that chinook salmon are similar to warm-blooded animals with respect to their ability to convert

TABLE XVIII

BASAL RATION[a]

| Constituent | Amount (gm) |
|---|---|
| L-Arginine·HCl | 3.6 |
| L-Histidine·HCl·H$_2$O | 1.8 |
| L-Isoleucine | 2.9 |
| L-Leucine | 4.3 |
| L-Lysine·HCl | 3.6 |
| L-Methionine | 1.4 |
| L-Threonine | 2.9 |
| L-Tryptophan | 0.7 |
| L-Tyrosine | 2.9 |
| L-Valine | 2.9 |
| L-Phenylalanine | 1.8 |
| Glycine | 5.3 |
| L-Alanine | 2.5 |
| L-Aspartic acid | 3.6 |
| L-Cystine | 0.5 |
| L-Glutamic acid | 5.7 |
| L-Proline | 3.6 |
| White dextrin | 25.0 |
| Corn oil | 5.0 |
| Cod liver oil | 2.0 |
| Carboxymethyl cellulose | 10.0 |
| Mineral mix[b] | 4.0 |
| α-Cellulose + vitamins[c] | 4.0 |
| Water | 100 |

[a] From Halver and Shanks (1960).

[b] Mineral mix the same as reported previously (Halver, 1957[b]).

[c] Contains (in mg): thiamine·HCl, 5; riboflavin, 20; pyridoxine·HCl, 5; choline chloride, 500; nicotinic acid, 75; Ca-pantothenate, 50; inositol, 200; biotin, 0.5; folic acid, 1.5; ascorbic acid, 100; menadione, 4; α-tocopheryl acetate, 40; cyanocobalamin, 0.01.

arginine and glycine to nonessential amino acids. However, in contrast to warm-blooded animals, they do not seem able to convert urea or diammonium citrate to these compounds for growth.

## VI. Amino Acid Requirement Studies in Other Fish Species

### A. SOCKEYE SALMON

Halver and Shanks (1960) determined the qualitative amino acid requirements of another species of salmonid, the sockeye salmon (*O. nerka*). The basal ration, shown in Table XVIII, contained approximately 50% purified L-amino acids instead of the 70% level used in the classification studies on chinook salmon. The new level was closer to the minimum

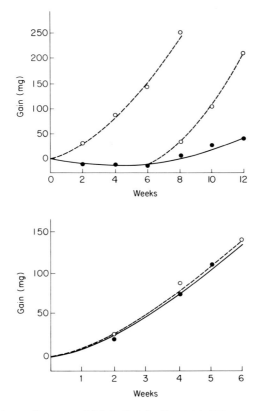

FIG. 7. Typical growth curves of fish in first feeding trial. (A) O—O, Complete diet; ●—●, arginine-deficient diet. (B) O—O, Complete diet; ●—●, tyrosine-deficient diet.

protein requirement found for chinook salmon raised at a water temperature of 8°C. Hydroxyproline and serine were omitted. In these studies feeding trials were conducted in covered 10-gallon glass aquariums supplied with a constant flow of deep well water, heated to 11°C. In the first feeding trial, fish with average initial individual weights of 0.2 gm were used, 200 per aquarium. In the second feeding trial, the average initial individ-

TABLE XIX

AVERAGE DATA FOR SOCKEYE SALMON FED VARIOUS DIETS[a]

| Diets | Initial weight (gm) | Av. weight 6th week (gm) | Av. weight 12th week (gm) |
|---|---|---|---|
| Arginine-deficient | 0.216 | 0.203 | 0.261 |
| Basal | | 0.206 | 0.433 |
| Histidine-deficient | 0.213 | 0.256 | 0.257 |
| Basal | | 0.244 | 0.348 |
| Isoleucine-deficient | 0.216 | 0.248 | 0.272 |
| Basal | | 0.241 | 0.378 |
| Leucine-deficient | 0.200 | 0.201 | 0.225 |
| Basal | | 0.198 | 0.393 |
| Lysine-deficient | 0.220 | 0.238 | 0.254 |
| Basal | | 0.227 | 0.343 |
| Control group 1 | 0.221 | 0.367 | 0.777 |
| Control group 2 | 1.270 | 2.227 | |
| Methionine-deficient | 1.345 | 1.619 | 1.757 |
| Basal | | 1.524 | 2.564 |
| Phenylalanine-deficient | 1.325 | 1.576 | 2.043 |
| Basal | | 1.619 | 2.750 |
| Valine-deficient | 1.220 | 1.446 | 1.446 |
| Basal | | 1.305 | 2.074 |
| Threonine-deficient | 1.285 | 1.425 | 1.385 |
| Basal | | 1.427 | 2.244 |
| Tryptophan-deficient | 1.117 | 1.239 | 1.314 |
| Basal | | 1.467 | 2.279 |
| Cystine-deficient | 1.295 | 2.126 | |
| Glycine-deficient | 1.200 | 1.647 | |
| Alanine-deficient | 0.213 | 0.331[b] | |
| Aspartic-deficient | 0.216 | 0.344[b] | |
| Glutamic-deficient | 0.205 | 0.344[b] | |
| Tyrosine-deficient | 0.204 | 0.322[b] | |
| Proline-deficient | 0.212 | 0.337[b] | |

[a] From Halver and Shanks, (1960).
[b] This group terminated after 5 weeks.

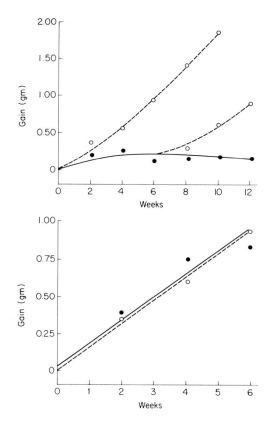

Fig. 8. Typical growth curves of fish in second feeding trial. (A) O—O, Complete diet; ●—●, tryptophan-deficient diet. (B) O—O, Complete diet; ●—●, cystine-deficient diet.

ual weight was about 1.2 gm, so only 100 fish were used in each aquarium. The data in Table XIX show the initial weights in each lot, the average weights at the end of 6 weeks when the deficient groups were divided into two subgroups, and the average weights at the end of 12 weeks when the majority of the groups were terminated. These results show that the sockeye salmon has the same qualitative amino acid requirements as the chinook salmon with the possible exception of glycine, which needs further study. Figures 7 and 8 show typical growth curves for the fish in the first and second feeding trials, respectively.

One interesting condition noted in these studies, but not observed in the studies with chinook salmon, was the development of a specific deficiency syndrome for tryptophan, observed after only 4 weeks of feeding.

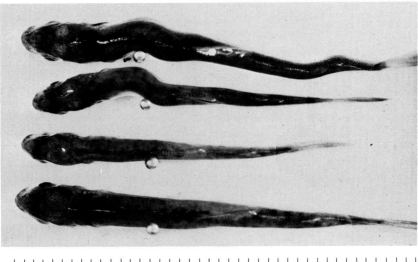

FIG. 9. Deficiency syndrome for tryptophan in salmon. The upper two fish show pronounced scoliosis when tryptophan was deleted from the ration for 21 to 28 days. The condition was reduced in 7 to 14 days after adding tryptophan to the deficient ration, as can be seen in the bottom two fish.

Pronounced scoliosis with some lordosis was noted in about 20% of the population (Fig. 9). This condition continued to develop in the tryptophan-deficient lot until the end of the 12-week feeding period when over 50% of the fish had become deformed. This condition did not produce greater mortality, for only one fish died in the deficient sublot after subdivision of the lot into subgroups at the sixth week. Care was exercised in dividing the affected fish equally between the two sublots to measure response when the missing amino acid was returned to the ration. In every case, the scoliosis and lordosis disappeared within 2 weeks after addition of tryptophan to the ration. In contrast, the tryptophan-deficient sublot continued to develop symptoms until, at the end of the feeding trial, over one-half of the population was affected.

## B. RAINBOW TROUT

Shanks *et al.* (1962) used techniques similar to those described above to determine the qualitative amino acid requirements of a third species of salmonid, the rainbow trout (*Salmo gairdneri*). A requirement similar to that of the chinook salmon was observed. However, like the sockeye salmon, about 25% of the tryptophan deficient-fish developed scoliosis.

## C. Channel Catfish

Dupree and Halver (1970) fed amino acid mixtures similar to those used by Halver and Shanks (1960) for sockeye salmon, to channel catfish (*Ictalurus punctatus*) fingerlings and found that this species requires the same ten amino acids needed by other fish species.

## VII. Protein Requirement Studies in Other Fish Species

Shell and Nail (1962) have studied the protein requirement of channel catfish. Table XX shows the composition of the diets fed. In these diets, casein served as the protein source, and was increased or decreased at the expense of "Alphacel," cellulose filler. Two levels of dextrin, 9.3 and 18.6% were tested. The experimental work was conducted in the Farm Ponds Laboratory of Auburn University, Auburn, Alabama.

Each of forty stainless steel troughs was stocked with twenty-five 6 to 7-inch fish. The fish were fed test diets at a rate of 2.5% of their body weight per day. Every 14–21 days during the test period from June 22

TABLE XX

Diets Used in Channel Catfish Studies

| Ingredients | Acclimation diets | | | | | | | |
|---|---|---|---|---|---|---|---|---|
| | 1 | 2 | 3 | 4 | 5 | 6 | 7 | 8 |
| Casein[a] | 9.3 | 23.3 | 37.2 | 51.2 | 9.3 | 23.3 | 37.2 | 51.2 |
| Dextrin | 9.3 | 9.3 | 9.3 | 9.3 | 18.6 | 18.6 | 18.6 | 18.6 |
| Corn Oil | 8.4 | 8.4 | 8.4 | 8.4 | 8.4 | 8.4 | 8.4 | 8.4 |
| Minerals | 3.7 | 3.7 | 3.7 | 3.7 | 3.7 | 3.7 | 3.7 | 3.7 |
| Alphacel[b] | 62.3 | 48.4 | 34.4 | 20.5 | 53.0 | 39.1 | 25.1 | 11.1 |
| Vitamin mix[c] | 1.9 | 1.9 | 1.9 | 1.9 | 1.9 | 1.9 | 1.9 | 1.9 |
| Agar | 4.7 | 4.7 | 4.7 | 4.7 | 4.7 | 4.7 | 4.7 | 4.7 |
| Actual percentage protein | 6.3 | 15.8 | 25.3 | 34.8 | 6.3 | 15.8 | 25.3 | 34.8 |

[a] The casein used in this experiment was 68.0% protein.
[b] The Alphacel was used as a diet filler.
[c] A vitamin fortification mixture was added at the rate of 20 gm per 1000 gm of diet.

to September 3, 1961, the fish were reweighed and the daily amount of food adjusted to the new weight. Water temperatures are not listed.

Statistical analysis indicated that of the levels tested, a level of 25.3% protein (37.2% casein) produced optimum growth. Growth was obtained on the lowest level or 6.3% protein diet. The authors estimated that the maintenance requirement for channel catfish in this experiment was 0.079 gm of protein per day per 100 gm of fish on the 9.3% carbohydrate diets and 0.029 gm of protein on the 18.6% carbohydrate diets. It was calculated that 0.23 gm of carbohydrate fed per 100 gm of fish would spare 0.05 gm of protein.

A decrease in the growth rates of fish in all troughs was noticed in August, during which time the water temperature was at its highest point. This was attributed to the high water temperature and/or a physiological cycle associated with the growth rate.

It is not possible to compare the protein requirement of 25.3% obtained by Shell and Nail (1962) in 6–7-inch channel catfish with the requirements of 40 and 55% at 47° and 58°F, respectively, obtained by DeLong *et al.* (1958) in chinook salmon. In the latter studies, fingerling fish weighing 1.5–6 gm were fed as much as each would consume, were kept at a constant temperature, and were fed isocaloric diets by varying two ingredients, protein and dextrin. In the studies on catfish, food intake was restricted to a constant percentage of body weight, the temperature apparently was ambient, and the caloric density of the diet varied with protein level. It is interesting to note that the carbohydrate, dextrin, was well tolerated by both salmon and catfish. Phillips *et al.* (1948) reported that the safe level of digestible carbohydrate in fish diets was about 9%. Levels over this could cause "high glycogen" livers which were swollen, glossy in appearance, and pale in color. This value was calculated with a meat diet and corresponds to 33% of the diet as carbohydrate on a dry weight basis. McLaren *et al.* (1946) have shown that the liver damage due to excess carbohydrate could be reduced if 5% liver or a vitamin supplement was added to the diet. In the studies of DeLong *et al.* (1958), levels of carbohydrate as high as 61% did not produce liver damage as described by Phillips *et al.* and McLaren and co-workers. In the studies of Shell and Nail (1962), a level of 18.6% carbohydrate apparently had no harmful effect in catfish, and was shown to have a protein-sparing effect. Dupree and Sneed (1966) found a minimum protein requirement of 40% in fingerling catfish on a casein diet at water temperatures of 69° and 76°F. The diets were nonisocaloric and, therefore, cannot be compared directly with the diets of DeLong *et al.* (1958). Their findings suggest that the catfish fingerling protein requirement is lower than that of the chinook salmon fingerling at high water temperatures.

## VIII. Plasma Amino Acid Levels in Fish

Chance (1962) determined the levels of free amino acids and related compounds in the blood plasma of chinook salmon using an automatic amino acid analyzer based on the ion-exchange method of Moore and Stein. In August, 1960, three chinook salmon actively feeding in the Pacific Ocean and weighing 5, 10, and 20 pounds were placed in a holding tank and taken ashore at Westport, Washington, within 2 hours after being caught. In addition to immediate blood samples, a 24-hour fasting sample was obtained only from the 20-lb fish since the other fish died within 24 hours of captivity. In another study in September, 1960, blood was obtained from five male chinook salmon, averaging 25–35 pounds, about 2 weeks prior to the spawning season. These were caught at the mouth of the Little White Salmon River where it empties into the Columbia River approximately 150 miles upstream from the Pacific Ocean. Plasmas from these fish were pooled into one sample.

Just prior to bleeding, each fish was placed in a small tank of water containing an anesthetic (MS 222—tricaine methanesulfonate, Sandoz Pharmaceuticals, Handover, New Jersey) used to calm or immobilize cold-blooded animals. Immediately following immobilization, the fish was taken from the tank and placed on its back in a V-shaped bleeding trough. Twenty to thirty milliliters of blood were obtained through Nos. 19 and 20 gauge needles via heart puncture with 50-ml syringes previously rinsed in a physiological saline solution. The needles were removed and the blood carefully expelled into plastic centrifuge tubes containing 4–5 mg of heparin (NO-KLOT, Medical Chemical Corporation, Los Angeles, California). A protein-free filtrate was prepared from the plasma by treatment with picric acid according to the method of Stein and Moore (1954).

Table XXI shows that the levels of the free amino acids and related compounds varied with the size of the fish. Comparison of the 5 with the 20 pound actively feeding salmon shows a drop in many plasma amino acids with age. A 24-hour fast also produced a drop in level of several amino acids in the 20-pound specimen. In contrast, the pooled plasma of the spawning males which had been fasting for several weeks and converting carcass tissues to sperm, showed a much different pattern of metabolites. A metabolite of histidine, 1-methyl histidine, increased more than 60-fold, along with marked increases in $\beta$-alanine, cystathionine, taurine, and $\alpha$-amino-$n$-butyric acid.

The high levels of these metabolites in the plasma of the spawning males suggests an unusually active metabolism of histidine, the sulfur-containing amino acids, methionine and cystine, and glutamic acid, which are pre-

TABLE XXI

Amino Acids and Related Compounds in the Blood Plasma of Chinook Salmon[a]

| | Actively Feeding | | | 24-hr Fast | Spawning males |
|---|---|---|---|---|---|
| Compound | 5lb | 10 lb | 20 lb | 20 lb | 25–35 lb |
| Arginine | 63 | 24 | 12 | 3 | 40 |
| Histidine | 19 | 22 | 19 | 18 | 14 |
| Isoleucine | 73 | 22 | 37 | 47 | 22 |
| Leucine | 126 | 38 | 66 | 82 | 33 |
| Lysine | 87 | 38 | 23 | 10 | 83 |
| Methionine | 33 | 9 | 17 | 5.6 | 13 |
| Cystine | 0 | 0 | 2 | 0 | 2 |
| Phenylalanine | 30 | 21 | 19 | 12 | 17 |
| Tyrosine | 40 | 18 | 22 | 13 | 10 |
| Threonine | 58 | 52 | 67 | 17 | 36 |
| Tryptophan | Trace | Trace | 0 | 0.5 | Trace |
| Valine | 119 | 44 | 74 | 90 | 49 |
| Alanine | 159 | 118 | 153 | 54 | 101 |
| Asparagine plus glutamine | 30 | 30 | 12 | 36 | 77 |
| Aspartic Acid | 10 | 2 | 2 | 3 | 4 |
| Glutamic Acid | 24 | 33 | 26 | 18 | 28 |
| Glycine | 40 | 40 | 42 | 35 | 38 |
| Proline | 34 | 12 | 23 | 11 | 14 |
| Serine | 41 | 21 | 18 | 9 | 107 |
| $\beta$-Alanine | 1 | 2 | 1 | 1 | 11 |
| Ammonia | 28 | 23 | 13 | 13 | 13 |
| $\alpha$-Amino-$n$-butyric acid | 4 | 6 | 4 | 4 | 5 |
| $\beta$-Aminoisobutyric acid | Trace | Trace | Trace | Trace | 3 |
| $\gamma$-Amino-$n$-butyric acid | 6 | 2 | 3 | 6 | 17 |
| Carnosine | 0 | 0 | 1 | 0 | Trace |
| Citrulline | 18 | 7 | 9 | 7 | Trace |
| Cystathionine | 4 | 1 | 1 | 1 | 12 |
| Ethanolamine | 0.5 | 3 | 2 | 2 | 1 |
| 1-Methyl Histidine | 2 | 0.7 | 0.7 | 1 | 1 |
| 3-Methyl Histidine | Trace | Trace | 0.3 | 0 | 1 |
| Hydroxylysine | 1 | 0.4 | 0.7 | 0.3 | 2 |
| Hydroxyproline | 8 | 3 | 11 | 0 | 0 |
| Ornithine | 6 | 3 | 2 | 2 | 11 |
| Phosphoethanolamine | 13 | 22 | 23 | 11 | 17 |
| Sarcosine | 4 | Trace | 0.6 | 0 | Trace |
| Taurine | 49 | 91 | 59 | 61 | 338 |
| Urea | 67 | 48 | 87 | 150 | 28 |

[a] Values in micrograms per milliliter.

cursors of 1-methyl histidine, cystathionine and taurine, and $\gamma$-amino-*n*-butyric acid, respectively.

An inspection of the levels of the plasma amino acids in the spawning males shows marked rises (compared with the fasting values obtained on the 20-pound normal salmon) in arginine, lysine, methionine, and serine. Serine is involved in the conversion of methionine to cystine, and arginine, lysine, and histidine are found in large amounts in histones and protamines. Histones and protamines are the major types of proteins found in sperm.

## IX. General Discussion and Conclusions

Since publication 12 years ago of the first successful amino acid test diet for fish, considerable progress has been made in assessing the protein and amino acid needs of the chinook salmon. Studies with this species have led to the development of special types of diets and feeding practices which can be adapted to other species of cold and warm water fishes.

The studies with chinook salmon have served to emphasize certain similarities as well as differences between warm- and cold-blooded animals. The chinook salmon resembles young domestic animals and the young albino rat in its total inability to synthesize nine essential amino acids. It resembles the chick in its total inability to synthesize arginine. Like these species, the salmon can use arginine and, to a lesser extent, glycine, as nitrogen sources for the synthesis of the dispensable amino acids. When the quantitative requirements for the essential amino acids are expressed as a percentage of the dietary protein, there is a striking similarity between the chinook salmon and warm-blooded species.

The chinook salmon differs from young domestic animals and the young albino rat in several respects. The protein requirement is two to three times higher, and varies directly with the water temperature. In addition, the salmon appears to be unable to use urea and diammonium citrate as precursors of dispensable amino acids. Rats, pigs, and even humans can make efficient use of these nitrogen sources.

Thus, in the past decade, major progress has been made in understanding the protein and amino acid needs of fish, but much remains to be done. In the chinook salmon, the methionine-cystine, phenylalanine-tyrosine, and tryptophan-niacin relationships need to be explored. Additional studies should be carried out with the sockeye salmon and other salmonid species, i.e., silver salmon, rainbow trout, etc. as well as other cold and warm water fishes, to determine species differences in protein and amino acid needs. The interesting observation of a special scoliosis syndrome in sockeye salmon and rainbow trout fed a tryptophan-deficient diet should be verified at several niacin levels and ascorbic acid levels in the test diets. The indication that glycine may be synthesized in sockeye salmon at a rate which is insufficient to meet the demands for maximum growth should be explored further. Is it possible that a fish covered with heavy scales needs more glycine just as a chick needs more of this amino acid to make feathers?

Finally, we must always keep in mind the fact that the quantitative needs for amino acids and protein vary with the nature and proportions of natural proteins in the diet. Feeding tests with mixtures of purified amino acids and certain test proteins therefore can serve only as guide lines. Eventually, feeding tests which detect the first, and possibly the second, limiting amino acid in mixtures of natural proteins, must be made in order to find "least cost" formulas.

## References

Almquist, H. J., and Grau, C. R. (1944). *J. Nutr.* **28,** 325.

Baldwin, N. S. (1957). *Trans. Amer. Fish. Soc.* **87,** 323.

Becker, D. E., Jensen, A. H., Terrill, S. W., Smith, I. D., and Norton, H. W. (1957). *J. Animal Sci.* **16,** 26.

Beeson, W. M., Jackson, H. D., and Mertz, E. T. (1953). *J. Animal Sci.* **12,** 870.

Bird, H. R., Almquist, H. J., Clandinin, D. R., Cravens, W. W., Hill, F. W., and McGinnis, J. (1960). "Nutrient Requirements of Poultry," p. 827. National Research Council, National Academy of Sciences, Washington, D. C.

Birnbaum, S. M., Winitz, M., and Greenstein, J. P. (1957). *Arch. Biochem. Biophys.* **72,** 428.

Block, J. R., and Weiss, K. W. (1956). "Amino Acid Handbook. Methods and Results of Protein Analysis." Thomas, Springfield, Illinois.

Borman, A., Wood, T. R., Black, H. C., Anderson, E. G., Oesterling, M. J., Womack, M., and Rose, W. C. (1946). *J. Biol. Chem.* **166,** 585.

Bressani, R., and Mertz, E. T. (1958). *J. Nutr.* **65,** 481.

Brinegar, M. J., Loosli, J. K., Maynard, L. A., and Williams, H. H. (1950). *J. Nutr.* **42,** 619.

Chance, R. E. (1962). Ph. D. Thesis, Purdue University, Lafayette, Indiana.

Chance, R. E., Mertz, E. T., and Halver, J. E. (1964). *J. Nutr.* **83,** 177.

DeLong, D. C., Halver, J. E., and Mertz, E. T. (1958). *J. Nutr.* **65,** 589.

DeLong, D. C., Halver, J. E., and Mertz, E. T. (1959). *J. Nutr.* **68,** 663.

DeLong, D. C., Halver, J. E., and Mertz, E. T. (1962). *J. Nutr.* **76,** 174.

Dupree, H. K., and Sneed, K. E. (1966). *Bur. Sport Fish. Wildl. U.S. Dept. Interior, Tech. Pap. No.* **9.**

Dupree, H. K. and Halver, J. E. (1970). *Trans. Amer. Fish. Soc.* **99,** 90.

Eggert, R. G., Williams, H. H., Scheffy, B. E., Sprague, E. G., Loosli, J. K., and Maynard, L. A. (1954). *J. Nutr.* **53,** 177.

Frost, D. V. (1950). *In* "Protein and Amino Acid Requirements of Mammals" (A. A. Albanese, ed.). Academic Press, New York.

Germann, A. F. O., Mertz, E. T., and Beeson, W. M. (1958). *J. Animal Sci.* **17,** 52.

Gerking, S. D. (1952). *Physiol. Zool.* **25,** 358.

Halver, J. E. (1957a). *J. Nutr.* **62,** 245.

Halver, J. E. (1957b). *J. Nutr.* **62,** 225.

Halver, J. E. (1965). *Fed. Proc.* **24,** 229.

Halver, J. E., and Shanks, W. E. (1960). *J. Nutr.* **72,** 340.

Halver, J. E., DeLong, D. C., and Mertz, E. T. (1957). *J. Nutr.* **63,** 95.

Halver, J. E., DeLong, D. C., and Mertz, E. T. (1958). *Fed. Proc.* **17,** 1873.

Halver, J. E., DeLong, D. C., and Mertz, E. T. (1959). *Fed. Proc.* **18,** 2076.

Harper, A. E. (1958). *Ann. N. Y. Acad. Sci.* **69,** 1025.

Jackson, H. D., Mertz, E. T., and Beeson, W. M. (1953). *J. Nutr.* **51,** 109.

Klein, R. G. and Halver, J. E. (1970). *J. Nutr.* **100,** 1105.

McLaren, B. A., Herman, E. F., and Elvehjem, C. A. (1946). *Arch. Biochem. Biophys.* **10,** 433.

Mertz, E. T., Beeson, W. M., and Jackson, H. D. (1952). *Arch. Biochem. Biophys.* **38,** 121.

Mertz, E. T., Henson, J. N., and Beeson, W. M. (1954). *J. Animal Sci.* **13,** 927.

Mertz, E. T., DeLong, D. C., Thrasher, D. M., and Beeson, W. M. (1955). *J. Animal Sci.* **14,** 1217.

Nicolaides, H., and Woodall, A. N. (1962). *J. Nutr.* **78,** 431.

Oesterling, M. J., and Rose, W. C. (1952). *J. Biol. Chem.* **196,** 33.

Pentalow, F. T. K. (1939). *J. Exp. Biol.* **16,** 446.

Phillips, A. M., Tunison, A. V., and Brockway, D. R. (1948). *N.Y. Cons. Dep. Fish. Res. Bull. No.* **11,** 44 pp.

Rose, W. C., and Womack, M. (1946). *J. Biol. Chem.* **166,** 103.

Rose, W. C., Smith, L. C., Womack, M., and Shane, H. (1949). *J. Biol. Chem.* **181,** 307.

Sauberlich, H. E. (1961). *J. Nutr.* **75,** 61.

Shanks, W. E., Gahimer, G. D., and Halver, J. E. (1962). *Progr. Fish. Cult.* **24,** 68.

Shell, E. W., and Nail, M. L. (1962). M. S. Thesis by M. L. Nail, Auburn University, Auburn, Alabama.

Shelton, D. C., Beeson, W. M., and Mertz, E. T. (1951a). *J. Animal Sci.* **10,** 57.

Shelton, D. C., Beeson, W. M., and Mertz, E. T. (1951b). *J. Animal Sci.* **10,** 73.

Stein, W. H., and Moore, S. (1954). *J. Biol. Chem.* **211,** 915.

Tunison, A. V. Brockway, D. R., Maxwell, J. M., Dorr, A. L., and McCay, C. M. (1942). *N.Y. State Cons. Dep. Cortland Hatchery Rep. No.* **11.**

West, J. W., Carrick, C. W., Hauge, S. M., and Mertz, E. T. (1952). *Poultry Sci.* **31,** 479.

Womack, M., and Rose, W. C. (1947). *J. Biol. Chem.* **171,** 37.

Wood, E. M., Yasutake, W. T., Woodall, A. N., and Halver, J. E. (1957). *J. Nutr.* **61,** 479.

# 4

## LIPID REQUIREMENTS

*D. J. Lee and R. O. Sinnhuber*

## I. Introduction

The use of lipids as a source of energy for animal diets has been recognized for many years. Formulation of high-energy production diets, such as those used by poultry producers, depends heavily on the economical energy provided by fats and oils. In comparison, fish culturists have not used fats as energy sources to the same degree. This can be attributed to a variety of reasons. Until recent years an economical supply of fresh meat, fish scrap, and liver was available and comprised the bulk, if not all, of most fish diets. Differences in the lipid requirement of fish and terrestrial species were often overlooked in early feeding trials and resulted in a poor response to high-energy diets. The introduction of dry pelleted fish feeds dictated that unsaturated oils be kept to a minimum to prevent lipid autoxidation. Probably the most serious faults of many of these low-fat diets are that they force the fish to utilize relatively expensive protein for energy and in many cases do not provide adequate amounts of essential fatty acids.

The following discussion dealing with the nutrition of teleost fishes, describes some of the unique characteristics of fish oils, compares lipid metabolism in fish with that in mammals, and points out some properties of lipids that should be considered when using them in fish diets.

## II. Lipid Composition

### A. FATTY ACIDS

The many compounds that can be grouped under this classification prohibits a detailed discussion of the subject in this text. The authors will confine themselves to the types of acids found in fish lipids and those which have importance in fish nutrition. While both branched-chain fatty acids and ones with unusual chemical moieties in or on the chain are known to exist, the acids discussed here will be the more normal straight-chain compounds containing an even number of carbons and from 0 to 6 double bonds. Conjugated polyenoic acids are found in certain plant oils, but the majority of naturally occurring fatty acids contain a methylene group between *cis* double bonds. Readers interested in fatty acid chemistry and a discussion of known types are referred to Deuel (1951), Hilditch and Williams (1964), and Gunstone (1967). Fatty acids will be described by using the prevalent abbreviation that consists of two numbers separated by a colon. The first number designates the number of carbon atoms and the second designates the number of double bonds in the molecule. Thus 18:2 would describe a fatty acid containing eighteen carbon atoms and two double bonds.

The position of double bonds in the carbon chain are important to both the physical characteristics and nutritional value of an acid. Mead (1961) initiated a widely used classification of fatty acids according to the location of the double bond nearest the terminal methyl group. The four types of fatty acids were named from naturally occurring acids containing the representative structural configuration.

$$CH_3—CH_2—CH = \text{linolenic type}$$

$$CH_3—(CH_2)_4—CH = \text{linoleic type}$$

$$CH_3—(CH_2)_7—CH = \text{oleic type}$$

$$CH_3—(CH_2)_5—CH = \text{palmitoleic type}$$

A common designation for the various types of acids is one in which *omega* ($\omega$) is used to indicate the location of the terminal double bond. Oleic acid would be identified as 18:1, $\omega$9, linolenic as 18:3, $\omega$3, palmitoleic as 16:1, $\omega$7, etc.

Biological systems produce long-chain fatty acids by lengthening the molecule from the carboxyl end so many acids can be included in each classification. Gunstone (1967) reports that these four types account for 59 unsaturated fatty acids with 17 in the linolenic ($\omega$3) group, 21 in the $\omega$6 group, 12 in the $\omega$9 group, and 9 with the $\omega$7 configuration.

The characteristic properties of fish lipids arise from the high content of long-chain polyenoic acids, most of which belong to the linolenic ($\omega$3) group. The relative amount of fatty acids in fish oils varies widely with species, age, sex, and temperature, and is influenced greatly by diet. Literature values for the fatty acid composition of striped mullet (*Mugil cephalus*), coho salmon (*Oncorhynchus kisutch*), guppy (*Lebistes reticulatus*), and capelin (*Mallotus villosus*) are presented in Table I not only to illustrate differences between species, but how environment influences values within a species.

Two samples of mullet collected from the same area were both analyzed by the same laboratory (Gruger *et al.*, 1964). As can be seen by the data presented in Table I, considerable differences in fatty acid composition of body oils were found to exist between fish caught in December and those taken in July. The oil from fish taken in the winter contained 13.4% docosahexaenoic acid as compared to 3.2% in fish captured in July. The summer caught fish contained higher percentages of 20:5, 16:2, 16:1, and 14:0. No information was given by the authors about differences in sexual development, age, or diet of the two samples that might explain the observed differences. It should be noted that the mullet contained high levels of a 15-carbon acid. According to Sen and Schlenk (1964) mullet contains high levels of odd carbon fatty acids, which have been found to make up as much as 25% of the total acids.

TABLE I

Comparison of the Fatty Acid Composition of Various Fish Species under Different Environmental Conditions[a]

| Fatty acid | Striped mullet | | Coho salmon | | Guppy | Capelin | | Cod flesh | Cod liver |
|---|---|---|---|---|---|---|---|---|---|
| | Sample 1[b] | Sample 2[b] | Sample 1[c] | Sample 2[b] | Sample 1[d] | Sample 1[e] | Sample 2[e] | Sample 1[b] | Sample 1[f] |
| 14:0 | 4.6 | 7.5 | 4.6 | 3.7 | 3.7 | 8.6 | 8.8 | 1.8 | 3.5 |
| 15:0 | 6.3 | 4.5 | 0.5 | 0.5 | + | — | — | 0.5 | 0.5 |
| 16:0 | 17.3 | 13.9 | 14.7 | 10.2 | 22.5 | 13.3 | 12.0 | 33.4 | 10.4 |
| 16:1 | 11.0 | 15.5 | 9.0 | 6.7 | 14.1 | 16.5 | 14.9 | 2.4 | 12.2 |
| 16:2 | 3.8 | 6.0 | 1.4 | 1.2 | + | — | — | 0.6 | 0.4 |
| 17:0 | 0.8 | 1.0 | — | 0.9 | — | — | — | 0.9 | 0.1 |
| 18:0 | 5.0 | 5.1 | 6.1 | 4.7 | 7.7 | 1.6 | 1.8 | 4.0 | 1.2 |
| 18:1 | 8.4 | 9.1 | 19.3 | 18.6 | 25.7 | 10.7 | 9.0 | 11.8 | 19.6 |
| 18:2 | 3.2 | 2.2 | 11.7 | 1.2 | 8.0 | — | — | 1.2 | 0.8 |
| 18:3 | 1.4 | 1.0 | 1.0 | 0.6 | 1.7 | — | — | 0.8 | 0.2 |
| 18:4 | 3.0 | 3.1 | 4.3 | 2.1 | 1.3 | — | — | 1.2 | 0.7 |
| 19:0 | 1.5 | 1.6 | — | 1.8 | — | — | — | — | — |
| 20:1 | 0.7 | 0.6 | 3.0 | 8.4 | 3.6 | 17.2 | 21.5 | 1.6 | 14.6 |
| 20:4 | 2.6 | 3.6 | 3.8 | 0.9 | 2.7 | — | — | 3.2 | 1.7 |
| 20:5 | 7.5 | 11.8 | — | 12.0 | 0.7 | 8.6 | 5.8 | 12.4 | 5.0 |
| 22:1 | 0.7 | — | 0.5 | 5.5 | — | 14.2 | 18.5 | 0.7 | 13.3 |
| 22:5 | 3.9 | 3.2 | 1.8 | 2.9 | 0.6 | 0.9 | 0.5 | 0.6 | 2.0 |
| 22:6 | 13.4 | 3.2 | 7.4 | 13.8 | 4.0 | 4.8 | 3.6 | 21.9 | 10.5 |

[a] —, Indicates no value given; +, indicates a trace was found. Some trace fatty acids were not listed for simplification.

[b] Gruger et al. (1964), sample 1 was caught in December; sample 2 in July.

[c] Saddler et al. (1966), immature salmon fed tubificid worms.

[d] Knipprath and Mead (1966), guppies fed a commercial trout chow.

[e] Ackman et al. (1963), sample 1 were females; sample 2 were males.

[f] Ackman and Burgher (1964).

The differences in the fatty acid composition of coho salmon when determined by separate laboratories can be largely explained by the environment of the fish prior to sampling and to differences in procedure. Saddler *et al.* (1966) analyzed the entire body of immature coho fingerlings fed tubificid worms for 2 to 6 weeks before sampling. Gruger *et al.* (1964) analyzed the muscle (steaks) from adult coho taken from a marine environment. The most striking difference is the higher content of ω6 acids in the young salmon with a larger percentage of 18:2, ω6 and lower levels of 20:5, ω3, 22:5, ω3, and 22:6, ω3 than in the ocean caught fish.

The analysis of whole body capelin oils was included in Table I to show how sex can be a factor in determing the fatty acid composition of fish oils. Ackman *et al.* (1963) found females to contain an oil with a higher iodine value than the males (144 compared to 125). This higher degree of unsaturation was due to higher levels of 20:5, 22:5, and 22:6 in the oil of females. Since the fish were captured at or immediately prior to spawning, it was thought that the increase in pentaenoic and hexaenoic acids was due to the presence of mature eggs, which are known to be rich in highly unsaturated fatty acids. Gruger *et al.* (1964) found the oil from pink salmon eggs to contain 41% pentaenoic and hexaenoic acids as compared to 35% in muscle oils. The most notable difference was the increase in 20:5, ω3 from 13 to 21%. In some species, however, egg oil apparently does not contain higher levels of long-chain polyunsaturated fatty acids than muscle. Ackman and Burgher (1964) found Atlantic cod roe oil to be higher in 16:1 and 18:1 than flesh lipids, but to contain a lower percentage of 22:6. Differences in the amount of phospholipids in these oils could possibly account for this variation.

The relative percentages of fatty acids in an oil are influenced markedly by the tissue or organ from which the lipid was obtained. This should be considered, along with the presence of eggs in mature females, when analyzing data. The fatty acid compositions for cod body oil and cod liver oil indicate that liver lipids contain less 20:5, 22:5, and 22:6 (17%) than body oil (35%). In this species, liver lipids were found to contain 59% monoethenoid acids (16:1, 18:1, 20:1, and 22:1). In contrast, these acids made up only 16% of the total in oils extracted from the flesh. However, the fat content of a particular tissue should not be overlooked when total amount of a certain acid is being considered.

The effect of temperature on the fatty acid composition of fish is somewhat difficult to clearly define because of possible indirect influences. In a natural environment, changes in the lipids of the food chain may be reflected in the body lipids of fish. Lewis (1962) found plankton taken from cold waters had fatty acids that were of shorter chain length with a greater degree of unsaturation than those from a warmer environment. Farkas and Herodek (1964) reported that freshwater planktonic crustacea contained greater amounts of polyenoic acids as water temperature decreased. In an experiment in which the diet was controlled, Reiser *et al.* (1963) found no influence on the interconversion or deposition of polyenoic fatty acids in mullet (*Mugil cephalus*) and goldfish (*Carassius auratus*) with a temperature difference of 10°C (13° and 23°C). In contrast, Knipprath and Mead (1965, 1966, 1968) found that mosquito fish (*Gambusia affinis*), guppy (*Libistes reticulatus*), goldfish (*Carassius auratus*), and rainbow trout (*Salmo gairdneri*) contained a more highly unsaturated fat when held at low temperatures. Species differences were observed and it was noted that while a cold environment caused the trout to accumulate docosahexaenoic acid the total amount of long-chain polyenoic acids decreased in the goldfish. Overall unsaturation in this species was obtained by a slight increase in 16:1, a slight decrease in 16:0 and 18:0, and a large increase in 18:1.

## B. TRIGLYCERIDES

Only minute amounts of the fatty acids found in animal tissues exist as free acids. They are normally component parts of larger, more complex molecules of various types. One of the major lipid components in which they are found is the triglyceride, which consists of three fatty acids attached by ester linkages to a glycerol molecule. The nature of the fatty acids is the primary factor in determining the physical properties of triglycerides, thus, fish lipids with a high content of polyenoic acids are liquid at room temperature. Because of the many possible combinations of acids on the glycerol molecule, fish oils, with as many as forty or more fatty acids, are extremely complex mixtures.

Recent developments in methodology (Brockerhoff, 1965) have enabled workers to investigate the position of fatty acids in triglycerides to determine if a nonrandom distribution exists. Evidence presented by Brockerhoff *et al.* (1963), Brockerhoff and Hoyle (1963), and Litchfield (1968) indicate that eicosapentaenoic and docosahexaenoic acids are preferentially bound to the 2-carbon of glycerol in several species of marine fishes. Subsequent work by Brockerhoff *et al.* (1968) showed this was also true in four species of freshwater fish, burbot (*Lota lota*), sheepshead (*Aplodinotus grunniens*), speckled trout (*Salvelinus fontinalis*), and goldfish (*Carassius auratus*). In contrast, mammals, including marine species, preferentially incorporate these acids into the 3 position and linoleic acid on the 2-carbon (Brockerhoff *et al.*, 1967, 1968; Litchfield, 1968).

The distribution of fatty acids, in general, follows the scheme delineated by the above workers, but exceptions are known to exist. In some cases, differences are found in the positional distribution of fatty acids in depot fat and that of triglycerides from the liver. Brockerhoff and Hoyle (1963) observed that triglycerides from harbor seal liver contained a high concentration of 22:6, ω3, on the 2-carbon in contrast to blubber triglyceride and that the 18:2 in lard was not preferentially bound in the 2-position. Amphibians exhibit a distribution pattern similar to mammals. In contrast, the herring gull (*Larus argentatus*), the grey gull (*Larus marinus*), and the cormorant (*Phalacrocorax auritus*) show a nearly random positioning of triglyceride fatty acids (Brockerhoff *et al.*, 1968).

The significance of a certain fatty acid distribution pattern to particular species is unknown but recent investigations suggest that the fatty acid pattern found in fish oils may reflect that in the diet. Brockerhoff *et al.* (1964b) found phytoplankton and zooplankton taken from the north Atlantic to have the polyenoic $C_{20}$ and $C_{22}$ acids preferentially bound to the 2-carbon in the same manner as found in fish. Subsequent work (Brockerhoff and Hoyle, 1965) showed that the pancreatic lipase of the skate hydrolyzed triglycerides at the 1- and 3-positions in the same manner as the mammalian enzyme. This would indicate that the resulting monoglyceride could be incorporated into the tissue of animals in the food chain intact. This would explain the high percentage of long-chain polyenoic acids found attached to the 2-carbon in triglycerides of fishes. Mammals apparently change the 2-carbon configuration of the triglyceride because as previously mentioned in these species the polyenoic acids are preferentially esterified in the 3-position.

Closely related to the triglycerides are the mono- and diglycerides, but as they are normally found in only trace amounts in natural lipids they will not be discussed here. The structures of some glycerol esters are shown below.

$$
\begin{array}{ccc}
\mathrm{CH_2O-CO-R} & \mathrm{CH_2O-CO-R} & \mathrm{CH_2OH} \\
\mathrm{R-CO-OCH} & \mathrm{HOCH} & \mathrm{R-CO-OCH} \\
\mathrm{CH_2O-CO-R} & \mathrm{CH_2O-CO-R} & \mathrm{CH_2OH} \\
\text{Triglyceride} & \text{1, 3-Diglyceride} & \text{2-Monoglyceride}
\end{array}
$$

## C. PHOSPHOLIPIDS

Several types of lipids contain a phosphate moiety and are included in this general classification, but the most commonly occurring class of phospholipids found in animal tissue are the phosphoglycerides. The compounds have a basic structural unit of phosphorylated glycerol, glycerophosphoric acid. The two phosphoglycerides of primary interest in the area of nutrition are phosphatidylcholine (PC) and phosphatidylethanolamine (PE). These two compounds are the major phospholipids of both terrestrial and aquatic animal species.

$$
\begin{array}{c}
\mathrm{CH_2OH} \\
| \\
\mathrm{HOCH} \\
| \\
\mathrm{CH_2OPO_3H_2}
\end{array}
\qquad\qquad
\begin{array}{c}
\mathrm{CH_2O-CO-R} \\
| \\
\mathrm{R-CO-OCH} \\
| \\
\mathrm{CH_2OPO_3H_2}
\end{array}
$$

Glycerophos-
phoric acid
　　　　　　　　　
Phosphatidic
acid

$$
\begin{array}{c}
\mathrm{CH_2O-CO-R} \\
| \\
\mathrm{R-CO-OCH} \\
| \\
\mathrm{CH_2OPO_3H-CH_2CH_2\overset{+}{N}(CH_3)_3OH^-}
\end{array}
\qquad
\begin{array}{c}
\mathrm{CH_2O-CO-R} \\
| \\
\mathrm{R-CO-OCH} \\
| \\
\mathrm{CH_2OPO_3H-CH_2CH_2NH_2}
\end{array}
$$

Phosphatidylcholine (PC)
　　　　　　　　　
Phosphatidyl-
ethanolamine (PE)

Other phosphoglycerides that have been reported in fish lipids are phosphatidylserine (PS) and phosphatidylinositide (Silk and DeKoning, 1964). Sphingomyelins were also found by these workers and these important constituents of brain and nervous tissue are undoubtedly important in the physiological and biochemical functions of fish. Little work has been reported on the types of sphingolipids present in fishes but presumably they would be similar in structure to the ones isolated from mammalian tissue.

$$
\mathrm{CH_3(CH_2)_{12}-CH-\underset{\underset{\displaystyle OH}{|}}{CH}-\underset{\underset{\displaystyle NH-COR}{|}}{CH}-CH_2O\overset{\overset{\displaystyle O}{\|}}{\underset{\underset{\displaystyle O^-}{|}}{P}}O-CH_2-CH_2\overset{+}{N}(CH_3)_3}
$$

Sphingomyelin

In a study of menhaden muscle, Froines *et al.* (1965) found phospholipids to make up 0.45 to 0.55% of the wet tissue weight and 15% of the total lipids. Phosphatidylcholine accounted for 63% of the phospholipids, phosphatidylethanolamine, and phosphatidylserine together, 17%, and sphingomyelin, 3%.

Investigations by several workers have shown that phospholipids from fish tissue contain higher levels of polyenoic fatty acids, particularly 22:6, ω3, than are found in the neutral lipids. Froines *et al.* (1965) noted that in addition to the glycerophosphatide fatty acids containing three times the level of 22:6 as neutral lipids, cephalin (phosphatidylethanolamine and phosphatidylserine combined) contained more short-chain fatty acids, twelve carbons or less, and more stearic acid than either the phosphatidylcholine or neutral lipid fractions. The lecithin from menhaden muscle they examined contained a high percentage of 16:0 (40%) in its fatty acid content.

Brockerhoff *et al.* (1963) and Menzel and Olcott (1964) both found that in a variety of fishes and crustaceans the positional distribution of fatty acids in the glycerophosphatides is the same as that in triglycerides. The preferential esterification of long-chain polyenoic acids in the 2-position of phosphatidylcholine and phosphatidylethanolamine is not unique for fishes. Brockerhoff *et al.* (1967) fed mackerel to mink and rats and determined that 20:5, ω3, 22:5, ω3 and 22:6, ω3 were preferentially bound in the 2-position of liver PC and PE in the same manner as 18:2, ω6, and 20:4, ω6. The fish diet had little influence on the fatty acid composition of the 1-position with an increase in 16:0 being the most noticeable effect. As the fatty acid composition of phospholipids is somewhat less influenced by diet than that of triglycerides, a comparison of phospholipid acids might be helpful in distinguishing species differences.

## D. STEROIDS

Levels of cholesterol and related steroids in fish lipids have not been studied in as much detail as the fatty acids. This is probably due, in part, to the fact that they do not lend themselves to analysis by gas–liquid chromatography which is used extensively for fatty acid quantification.

The cholesterol content of salmonid fishes is apparently dependent on the stage of sexual development of the sample. Idler and Tsuyuki (1958) found the levels of plasma cholesterol in migrating sockeye salmon to drop during travel to the spawning area, however, the flesh of these fish showed an increase in cholesterol concentration during the spawning migration (Idler and Bitners, 1958). When the loss of body protein and lipid was considered, male fish showed a gain of 12% in total cholesterol and females a 13% loss.

In work at our laboratory (Putnam, 1970) with rainbow trout, it has been found that there is a marked sex difference in serum cholesterol levels. Young fish (6 months) had variable individual differences but no distinction between immature males and females was found. Sexually precocial males of the same age exhibited greatly elevated serum cholesterol levels, 344 mg/100 ml of serum as compared to an average of 237 for normal fish. Two-year-old fish showed this same sex difference with mature males averaging 453 mg cholesterol/100 ml of serum and ripe females 256 mg. This relationship of cholesterol levels and sexual development may not exist in other species, but it does indicate the variability of tissue cholesterol levels that can occur within a given species.

E. OTHER LIPIDS

There are several naturally occurring lipid components, especially in fish and marine mammals, which do not fall into any of the four major classes we have discussed previously. Little is known of the biochemical and physiological significance of these various compounds, but certain species contain large amounts of one or more of them.

Waxes are found in a number of fishes and consist of aliphatic fatty acids esterified to alcohols other than glycerol, usually straight-chain, mono-hydric compounds containing between 12 to 20 carbons. In a recent review, Malins (1967) cites publications in which waxes are reported to comprise the major component of depot fat in eight species of fish and three marine mammals. Nevenzel and co-workers (1965) analyzed the gempylid fish (or ratfish) (*Ruvettus pretiosus*) and found muscle lipids to contain 91.5% waxes and the liver, 3.9%. Oleic acid made up 77% of the fatty acids from the wax esters while a 16-carbon, saturated alcohol (chimyl alcohol) and an 18-carbon compound with one double bond (selachyl alcohol) accounted for 58 and 29%, respectively, of the total alcohols.

Plasmologens are compounds very closely resembling triglycerides and phosphoglycerides in structure. The distinguishing characteristic of this group of compounds is that an alkyl group is bound to glycerol with an ether linkage, and in many cases contains a double bond in the 1-position. Acid hydrolysis of these vinyl ethers results in the cleavage of an aldehyde from the glycerol moiety. Most of the aldehydes are hexadecanal, octode-canal, and octadec-9-enal. Readers who are interested in pursuing the chemistry of plasmologens further are referred to Gunstone (1967).

This ether-containing group of lipids is widespread in lipids of marine fish and mammals and in certain species a high percentage of glyceryl ethers have been found in the nonsaponifiable fractions. Malins *et al.* (1965)

$$
\begin{array}{cc}
& CH_2\!-\!O\!-\!R \\
R\!-\!CO\!-\!O\dot{C}H & \\
& CH_2O\!-\!CO\!-\!R
\end{array}
\qquad\qquad
\begin{array}{cc}
& CH_2\!-\!O\!-\!R \\
HO\!-\!\dot{C}H & \\
& CH_2OH
\end{array}
$$

|                              |                              |
|:----------------------------:|:----------------------------:|
| Diacylated                   | Glyceryl ether               |
| glycerol ether               | (component following         |
|                              | alkaline hydrolysis of       |
|                              | diacylated glycerol ether)   |

$$
\begin{array}{cc}
& CH_2\!-\!O\!-\!R \\
R\!-\!CO\!-\!O\dot{C}H & \\
& CH_2OPO_3X
\end{array}
$$

Phosphorylated                    X = any of groups discussed in
glycerol ether                        phospholipids section

isolated the diacylglyceryl ethers from dogfish (*Squalus acanthias*) and found the material from flesh to contain a high percentage of polyenoic $C_{20}$ and $C_{22}$ acids. In contrast, ethers from the liver contained very little of these acids and a high percentage of $C_{20}$ and $C_{22}$ monoenoic acids. Seventy percent of the aldehydes released from the glycerol was madeup of hexadecanal and octadec-9-enal. Hanahan and Thompson (1963) found glyceryl ether phospholipids in the lipids of several terrestrial animal species and presumably they are also present in aquatic species.

Cerebrosides, sulfatides, and gangliosides are lipids found in brain and nervous tissue which closely resemble sphingomyelin but contain no phosphorus and yield long-chain bases, fatty acids, and carbohydrates when completely hydrolyzed. They have been found in marine fish (Silk and DeKoning, 1964), but little is known about their structure or physiological role.

## III. Lipid Metabolism

### A. Fatty Acids

In recent years, there has been a rapid accumulation of knowledge concerning both the catabolism and biosynthesis of fatty acids in animal tissue. While most of the work has dealt with mammalian tissues, especially the rat, certain reactions and synthetic pathways are apparently basic to all species studied. In view of this, it seems likely that these same schemes are basically true in fish. A brief summary of these biochemical pathways follows. Recommended references for readers who wish to pursue this area in more detail are reviews by Masoro (1968), Harper (1967), Mead (1968), and Lynen (1967). Mead and Kayama (1967) recently reviewed lipid metabolism in fish.

### B. *de Novo* Synthesis of Fatty Acids

Acetate, or more strictly speaking acetyl-CoA, is the primary precursor for the biosynthesis of fatty acids by animal tissue. Two biochemical pathways are involved in fatty acid synthesis, the mitochondrial system that seems to be primarily involved in chain elongation, and the extramitochondrial system that primarily produces palmitate. The extramitochondrial system is quite active in the incorporation of acetyl-CoA into palmitate and is found in the soluble portion of tissue homogenates. A scheme for the extramitochondrial system is shown in Fig. 1 (Harper, 1967), and, as can be seen, biotin and $CO_2$ are essential requirements for this pathway. The acyl group remains attached to the acyl carrier protein during the series of reactions leading to palmitate.

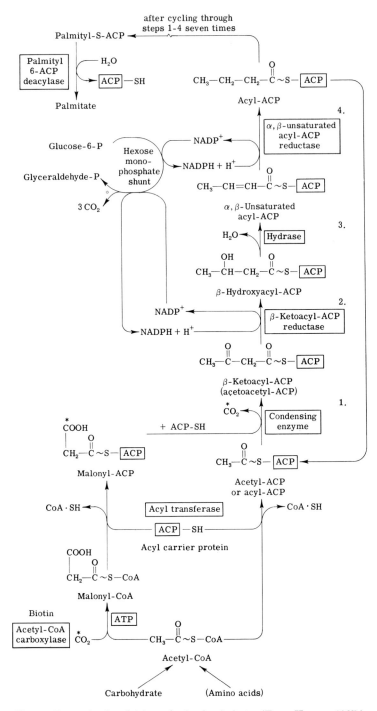

FIG. 1. Extramitochondrial synthesis of palmitate. (From Harper, 1967.)

The mitochondrial system is not as well understood as the extramito-chondrial scheme, but apparently the same enzymes that catalyze $\beta$-oxidation are involved. One exception is that the reduction of $\alpha,\beta$-unsaturated acyl-CoA is catalyzed by the NADPH requiring enoyl-CoA reductase (Wakil, 1961). Evidence indicates that this pathway is primarily used for elongation of fatty acids, i.e., palmitate to stearate. A scheme showing the steps involved in chain elongation is presented in Fig. 2. Fatty acids containing 20 and 22 carbons are obtained by repeating the sequence of reactions. Carnitine ($\beta$-hydroxy-$\gamma$-trimethyl ammonium butyrate) was found to stimulate the oxidation of fatty acids (Fritz and Yue, 1963) and is believed to be a carrier of acyl units across the mitochondrial membrane. Figure 3 shows some of the relationships that exist between the two fatty acid synthesizing systems. In addition to the reactions diagramed, it is

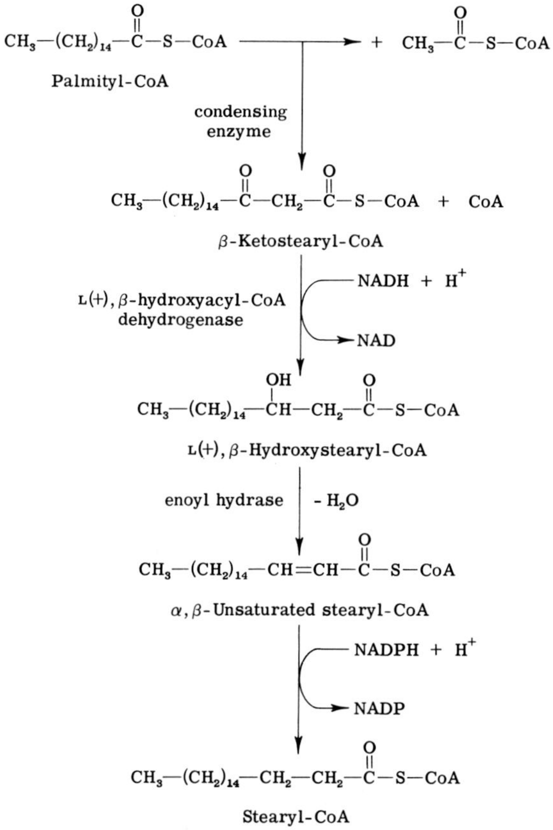

FIG. 2. Mitochondrial system of chain elongation.

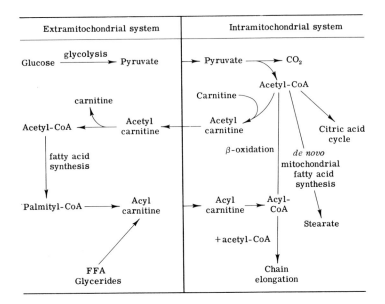

FIG. 3. Relationship of intra- and extramitochondrial systems.

known that acetyl-CoA can be synthesized from glutamate via the tri-carboxylic cycle:

$$\text{Glutamate} \xrightarrow{-\text{NH}_3} \alpha\text{-ketoglutarate} \longrightarrow \text{citrate} \tag{1}$$

$$\text{Citrate} \longrightarrow \text{acetyl-CoA} + \text{oxalacetate} \tag{2}$$

The relative importance of the various pathways in fatty acid synthesis is disputed by workers in this field, but it has been shown that citrate contributes significantly to the amount of acetyl-CoA formed in tissues (Srere, 1965).

The two fatty acid synthesizing pathways discussed previously have saturated acids as their end products. Another system involved in the production of long-chain unsaturated fatty acids is found in the microsomes. This system elongates the carbon chain by reacting malonyl-CoA with a long-chain acyl-CoA. The desaturase system that converts stearic and palmitic to oleic and palmitoleic is known to require $O_2$ and NADPH or NADH. This system also forms double bonds in conjunction with carbon chain elongation so that polyenoic acids with 20 and 22 carbons are produced. Details of work with the microsomal system can be found in reports by Nugteren (1965), Elovson (1965), Klenk (1965), and Wakil (1964). A summary of the reactions occurring in the microsomal system that result in polyenoic acids is presented in Fig. 4.

## C. Dietary Fatty Acids

Virtually all the fatty acids present in animal and fish feeds are esterified to glycerol in the form of triglycerides and phospholipids. The mechanism by which fish digest and absorb fats has not been thoroughly examined, but the limited number of investigations that have been conducted indicate it is similar to the one found in mammals. Mammalian digestion and absorption of fats has been reviewed by Senior (1964) and Isselbacher (1965). Fat absorption in the carp was found to be slower, but in many respects similar to that in the rat, in experiments conducted by Tsuchiya and Kayama (1958) and Kayama and Tsuchiya (1959). Recently, Brockerhoff and Hoyle (1965) demonstrated that pancreatic lipase from the skate had hydrolytic activity specific for the α-position in the same manner as the mammalian enzyme. The findings of the above workers indicate that fat digestion is similar in fish and mammals. The triglycerides are cleaved into free fatty acids, glycerol, and monoglycerides. In an experiment with cod, lobster, and trout, Brockerhoff *et al.* (1964a) fed tri-

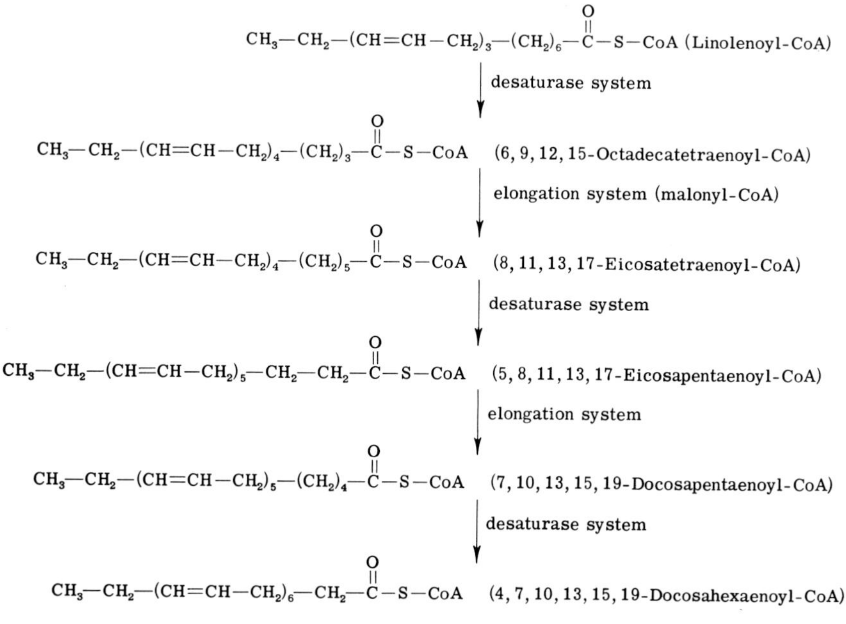

$$CH_3-CH_2-(CH=CH-CH_2)_3-(CH_2)_6-\overset{\overset{\text{O}}{\|}}{C}-S-CoA \text{ (Linolenoyl-CoA)}$$

desaturase system

$$CH_3-CH_2-(CH=CH-CH_2)_4-(CH_2)_3-\overset{\overset{\text{O}}{\|}}{C}-S-CoA \quad (6,9,12,15\text{-Octadecatetraenoyl-CoA})$$

elongation system (malonyl-CoA)

$$CH_3-CH_2-(CH=CH-CH_2)_4-(CH_2)_5-\overset{\overset{\text{O}}{\|}}{C}-S-CoA \quad (8,11,13,17\text{-Eicosatetraenoyl-CoA})$$

desaturase system

$$CH_3-CH_2-(CH=CH-CH_2)_5-CH_2-CH_2-\overset{\overset{\text{O}}{\|}}{C}-S-CoA \quad (5,8,11,13,17\text{-Eicosapentaenoyl-CoA})$$

elongation system

$$CH_3-CH_2-(CH=CH-CH_2)_5-(CH_2)_4-\overset{\overset{\text{O}}{\|}}{C}-S-CoA \quad (7,10,13,15,19\text{-Docosapentaenoyl-CoA})$$

desaturase system

$$CH_3-CH_2-(CH=CH-CH_2)_6-CH_2-\overset{\overset{\text{O}}{\|}}{C}-S-CoA \quad (4,7,10,13,15,19\text{-Docosahexaenoyl-CoA})$$

Fig. 4. Microsomal unsaturation and chain elongation.

glycerides containing palmitate-$^{14}$C in the 2-position and found 50–80% of the acid was retained in this position in triglycerides isolated from the fish.

After absorption into the body tissues, a fatty acid can be oxidized as a source of energy, converted to a different acid by elongation and unsaturation, or incorporated intact into a triglyceride or phospholipid. The biochemistry of these various pathways is fairly well understood in mammalian systems but much work remains to be done to determine the similarities and differences that occur in fish.

The oxidation of fatty acids has been reviewed in detail (Green and Wakil, 1960; Masoro, 1968; Harper, 1967) and only a summary will be presented here. Figure 5 presents the $\beta$-oxidation mechanism as it is understood to exist in mammalian and avian species.

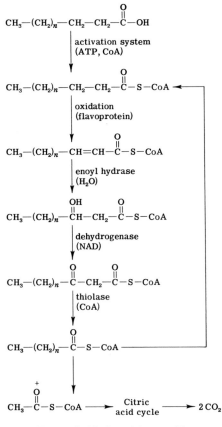

FIG. 5. Oxidation of fatty acid.

Because of the high intake of fat and the low ingestion of carbohydrate by many species of fish, it would seem likely that $\beta$-oxidation of fatty acids would constitute a major energy source. The relative amounts of energy derived from the various biochemical pathways by fish remains to be determined, but the findings of some workers suggest that the described oxidation mechanism is also present in fish. Brown and Tappel (1959) found mitochondria from carp liver required the same cofactors for fatty acid oxidation as did those from rat liver. A basic difference between fish and mammals that would apparently affect fat metabolism is that in certain species, the liver is a primary site for lipid storage. The body of the fish also contains two distinct types of muscle tissue. Braekkan (1956) found that aerobic oxidation of fat was the chief energy source for the red muscle. The dark muscle of rainbow trout (Bilinski, 1963) and sockeye salmon, *O. nerka* (Jonas and Bilinski, 1964), were found to produce $CO_2$ from fatty acids at a rate several times that of white muscle. In the sockeye salmon, the kidney exhibited the fastest oxidation rate of all tissue tested. Lateral line muscle (dark) oxidized acetate at a rate nearly equal to that of the liver in the adult salmon. In other work, Bilinski and Jonas (1964) demonstrated that a particulate fraction (presumably a mitochondrial preparation) required the same cofactors for the oxidation of fatty acids as those from the liver and in addition coenzyme A. In view of these findings, it seems likely that the same relationship exists between the white and dark muscles of fish as is found in birds, where the dark flight muscles are well developed for aerobic oxidation.

The conversion of ingested fatty acids to longer chain lengths and more highly unsaturated types has been found to occur in fish by several workers. Mead *et al.* (1960) and Kayama *et al.* (1963) conclusively showed with tracer studies that tetraenoic, pentaenoic, and hexaenoic acids were formed from linoleate and linolenate. Apparently this was accomplished with the same biochemical mechanism as found in mammalian tissue.

The conversion of the three major types of fatty acids, $\omega 3$, $\omega 6$, and $\omega 9$ to longer chain polyunsaturates is influenced by the relative amounts of each in the diet. The influence of one type acid on the conversion rate of the other types has been ascribed to competitive inhibition for active enzyme sites by a number of workers. Mohrhauer and Holman (1963b) found the addition of linolenate (18:3, $\omega 3$) to the diet of rats increased the amount of linoleate and decreased the amount of arachidonic acid (20:4, $\omega 6$) in the body tissue. Linoleate (18:2, $\omega 6$) sharply decreased the amount of 20:3, $\omega 9$, a metabolic product of oleate, when fed to rats previously receiving a linoleate-free diet. From this study they concluded that the affinity for enzyme sites is directed by the terminal end of the carbon chain with ω9 having the least affinity and ω3 the most. Holman (1964) points out that competition for enzyme sites could occur at any of the elongation and dehydrogenation steps involved in polyunsaturate formation. Lowry and Tinsley (1966) reported that high oleic/linoleic acid ratios interfered with 18:2, ω6 conversion to 20:4, ω6 in rats. They also observed a sex difference, in that the conversion of linoleic to arachidonic was not inhibited to as great a degree in females as in males. This is consistent with the fact that males are more sensitive to essential fatty acid deficiency than females (Anisfeld et al., 1951). The same type of interaction between fatty acids occurs in avian species. Marco et al. (1961) and Machlin (1962) reported that dietary 18:3, ω3 increased the amount of linoleate and decreased arachidonic levels in the liver of chickens.

Conclusive evidence that this inhibitory relationship between the fatty acid types exists in fish has not been obtained. However, the variety of species it does occur in strongly suggests that it is also present in aquatic animals. The interrelationship between fatty acids has practical significance as high levels of nonessential acids, such as oleic, could precipitate a deficiency condition. This type of situation could occur in fish held under hatchery conditions and fed diets composed of vegetable and animal products with little or no marine oils.

Fish are like mammals in that they cannot synthesize acids containing the ω3 or ω6 configuration. Mead et al. (1960) observed that no linoleic acid was synthesized from acetate-1-$^{14}$C given to Tilapia mossambica, although labeled arachidonic acid was formed by elongation and desaturation of the 18:2, ω6 acid. Nicolaides and Woodall (1962) found chinook salmon to show poor growth when on a fat-free diet. The addition of 3% trilinolein or linolenic acid greatly improved growth and indicated that fish require a dietary source of certain essential fatty acids. Castell et al. (1972a) found 20:3, ω9 to accumulate in rainbow trout tissue in the same manner as in fat-deficient rats when the fish were held on a fat-free diet. The nutritional implications of this inability to biosynthesize required acids will be discussed later.

Almost all fatty acids in the tissues of animals, including fish, are found esterified in triglycerides, phospholipids, waxes, etc. Very little work has been done to elucidate the biochemical reactions involved in the esterification of fatty acids in fish. Considerable knowledge has been accumulated concerning triglyceride and phospholipid formation in mammalian and microbial species and it is assumed that the same basic pathways exist in fish. A scheme of the reactions occurring in the biosynthesis of triglycerides and phosphoglycerides in mammalian systems is given in Fig. 6. Masoro (1968) and Harper (1967) cover this subject in detail.

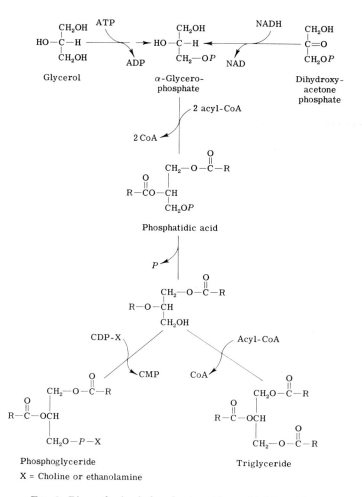

Fig. 6. Biosynthesis of phosphoglycerides and triglycerides.

In this discussion of the similarities and differences in lipid metabolism of fish and mammals, one is immediately aware of the lack of information concerning the fishes. It is hoped that knowledge concerning fish will soon be on an equal status with that for other species.

### D. STEROID BIOSYNTHESIS

The biochemical mechanisms involved in the formation of cholesterol by fish tissues are virtually unknown. The work that has been published on this subject has been recently reviewed by Idler (1969). The few investigations conducted in this area indicate that steroid biosynthesis in fish is quite similar to that in mammals. Siperstein (1966) and Putnam (1970) both found that trout liver slices converted acetate-$C^{14}$ to labeled cholesterol and that dietary cholesterol lowered the rate at which the synthesis occurred. Thus, cholesterol synthesis in rainbow trout seems to be under the same feedback control as in mammals (Siperstein and Fagan, 1964; Linn, 1967; Dietschy and Siperstein, 1965). The change in cholesterol levels during sexual maturity of trout mentioned previously would suggest that its conversion to steroid hormones could be an important part of steroid metabolism. The conversion of cholesterol to 11-deoxycorticosterone via pregnenolone and progesterone was shown to occur in dogfish (*Squalus acanthias*) semen (Simpson et al., 1964a). The same workers also found testis of these species to contain $17\alpha$-hydroxylase and $20\beta$-hydroxy steroid dehydrogenase (Simpson et al. 1964b).

Putnam (1970) found 0.5% cholesterol added to a semipurified casein-gelatin diet significantly increased the serum cholesterol levels of young rainbow trout after a 2-week period. This study indicates that dietary level of cholesterol influences its tissue concentration. The effect of other dietary ingredients, such as saturated fats and refined sugars, on cholesterol levels in fish tissues is not known.

## IV.  Lipid Requirements of Fish

The economical value of trout and salmon has resulted in the bulk of basic nutritional studies being made with these species. Only limited information is available regarding the requirements of other fishes, therefore, the following discussion will, of necessity primarily deal with the salmonids. Some of the early attempts to develop purified diets for trout are described by McCay et al. (1927) and McLaren et al. (1946, 1947).

In relatively recent years, the unfavorable economics and shortage of horse meat, liver, and meat scraps made the formulation of fish diets from other materials a necessity. Fish culturists and fish food manufacturers were then confronted with the problem of how much fat could be added to a diet and the type of fat that could be used by fish. Fats and oils have traditionally been thought of primarily as sources of energy and until recent years this has been the primary concern of workers in the development of fish diets. It is now known that the factors important in evaluating a dietary lipid include: (1) digestibility; (2) the presence of any toxic materials in a particular oil; (3) the degree of oxidation present, or the possibility of autoxidation, in the case of unsaturated oils; (4) the content of fatty acids essential for the particular species of interest; and (5) level of fat the animal can tolerate.

## A. Digestibility

The digestibility of fats is known to be related to the degree of unsaturation, or melting point. It was soon found that fish did poorly on diets containing appreciable levels of tallow or other hard animal fats (Phillips *et al.*, 1963) and these have been little used in trout diets. This might be expected when the short digestive tract of the trout is considered. Moderately soft fats can be utilized, however, as Phillips *et al.* (1964) found brown trout could utilize hydrogenated cottonseed oil and Dupree (1969) reported solid corn oil had a greater protein sparing action than liquid corn oil when fed to channel catfish. The iodine value of the dietary lipids was not given by either worker. Dupree (1969) noted that beef tallow was apparently not absorbed readily by the fish although it did cause a decrease in the iodine number of fish body lipids.

The need for more work on the digestibility of fats by various species of fish is quite evident. An area that has not been adequately explored is the effect of feeding both a solid fat and an unsaturated oil. From the standpoint of formulating practical rations with the use of the most economical lipid sources available, this information would be quite valuable.

## B. The Presence of Toxic Substances

Naturally occurring oils often contain trace amounts of unusual compounds, either fatty acids or others that can have deleterious effects on fish. In this instance, the residual oil in meals should be considered as well as extracted and refined lipids.

The availability of cottonseed products has prompted the use of cottonseed meal, and, in some cases, cottonseed oil in many practical trout rations. The undesirable effects of cottonseed meal or unrefined oil when fed to poultry has been recognized for years (Phelps *et al.*, 1965). Work at our laboratory has shown this is also true with rainbow trout. Two compounds present in cottonseed products that have undesirable biological activity are the cyclopropenoid fatty acids, sterculic and malvalic. These unique acids occur in varying amounts from a trace to 1.5% of the cottonseed oil. Sinnhuber *et al.* (1968) found cyclopropenoid fatty acids to reduce the growth rate of trout when fed at 220 ppm and to greatly enhance the incidence and growth rate of aflatoxin $B_1$-induced tumors. Roehm *et al.* (1970) found that feeding 20 ppm of methyl sterculate for 7 days in a purified test diet caused a shift in the fatty acid composition (higher 18:0/

18:1 and 16:0/16:1 ratios) of trout livers. Livers from fish fed the cyclo-propenoid were pale in color and showed large depositions of glycogen. Liver and muscle triglycerides from fish fed sterculate 9 weeks also contained lower levels of 22:6, $\omega$3 than the controls, which indicates an inhibition with the elongation and desaturation of long-chain polyenoic acid synthesis. The inhibitory action of cyclopropenoid fatty acids on the desaturase system in the conversion of stearic to oleic has been well documented in mammalian and avian species (Raju and Reiser, 1967; Johnson *et al.*, 1967, 1969). The effect of these compounds in other species of fish is not known, but Reiser *et al.* (1963) noted that cottonseed oil fed at 30% of the diet produced an increase in the stearic acid content of the body tissue of one fundulus, *Fundulus grandis*.

Gossypol is another toxic lipid-soluble component of cottonseed that must be considered when the meal is fed. Methods for "degossypolizing" meal are commonly used today and have proved successful in the feeding of poultry, but more work is needed to determine its effects on fish. This is especially true in formulating diets that will be fed over an extended period of time, such as those used for rearing and holding brood stock. Recent work at this laboratory (Roehm *et al.*, 1967) showed that trout accumulate gossypol (fed as gossypol acetate in a purified diet) in body tissues to quite high levels and have difficulty in eliminating it when placed on a gossypol-free diet. Deposits of a material believed to be gossypol were found to accumulate in the livers of fish fed this cottonseed pigment.

The results of the feeding trials mentioned above clearly show the importance of minor constituents of lipids in considering them as energy sources in fish diets. This is true not only of the extracted oil but also of residual oil and lipid-soluble compounds that might be present in oilseed meals.

## C. Autoxidation of Dietary Lipids

Fats and oils containing unsaturated fatty acids are known to be quite susceptible to autoxidation when exposed to atmospheric oxygen. Unsaturated lipids included in a diet often oxidize quite rapidly because of the catalytic action of the heavy metals and blood pigments which are normally present. The difficulty in preventing oxidation has kept the amounts of oils in dry pelleted diets to quite low levels. Oxidized lipids not only form toxic compounds themselves, but react with protein and lower its nutritional value. Vitamins are also destroyed by oxidizing lipids, probably both by chemically reacting with the hydroperoxides and carbonyls formed during autoxidation and by increased chemical reactivity brought about by the rise in temperature often accompanying this event.

This situation is most likely to occur in fish meal manufacture or during storage of pellets.

The destruction of other dietary essentials makes it somewhat difficult to determine the physiological effects of oxidized lipids per se, but Fowler and Banks (1969) described symptoms occurring in chinook salmon fingerlings when rancid fish meals were fed. These included dark coloration, anemia, lethargy, brown-yellow pigmented livers, abnormal kidneys, and some gill clubbing. Histological examination of the liver showed fatty degenerative lesions and inflammatory and necrotic foci. Kidney abnormalities were primarily a reduction of hematopoietic tissue and fatty infiltration. The addition of $\alpha$-tocopherol to the diets protected the fish from the effects of the rancid fish meal. Watanabe and Hashimoto (1968) also reported that $\alpha$-tocopherol reduced the toxicity symptoms of oxidized oil. They found reduced severity of toxicity when carp fed 20% oxidized saury oil received $\alpha$-tocopherol. The ability of vitamin E to prevent the deleterious effects of rancid diets and the similarity of the described symptoms and those reported by Woodall *et al.* (1964) for tocopherol-deficient fish would seem to indicate a vitamin deficiency. If the oxidation of the stored diets destroyed the $\alpha$-tocopherol originally present, this situation could arise. The toxicity of oxidized oils per se in rainbow trout was studied by Sinnhuber *et al.* (1968). Young trout were held for 20 months on a diet containing 5% salmon oil oxidized to give a peroxide value of 220–240. Adequate $\alpha$-tocopherol was added to the test diet and no ill effects were observed and good growth was obtained. This would indicate either that no toxic compounds were present in the oxidized oil, or, if present, that they had no deleterious effect in the presence of tocopherol. It should be kept in mind, however, that regardless of the exact nature of the deleterious effects seen when rancid diets low in vitamin E are fed, lipid oxidation in practical diets is a serious problem. Care should be taken not to use rancid fats and prepared diets should be protected to prevent further oxidation.

## D. ESSENTIAL FATTY ACIDS

The first conclusive evidence that animals require certain polyunsaturated fatty acids in their diet was presented by Burr and Burr (1929, 1930). They reported that rats fed a fat-free diet grew slowly and developed dermatitis. The addition of linoleic acid (18:2, $\omega$6) prevented these symptoms from occurring and cured them in deficient animals. Recent reviews by Holman (1968), Holman (1970), and Alfin-Slater and Aftergood (1968) cite evidence for the requirement of $\omega$6 acids by all mammalian and avian species investigated. The growth rate of fat-deficient rats is stimulated by linolenic acid (18:3, ω3), but not to the same extent as when ω6 acids are administered (Mohrhauer and Holman, 1963a). Reproductive failure, another essential fatty acid deficiency symptom, was prevented by linoleate and archidonate but not by linolenate (Quackenbush *et al.*, 1942). Deficiency symptoms that require ω6 fatty acids for prevention or cure are dermatitis, resorbtion of young in females, testicular degeneration in males, and the development of kidney lesions. The bulk of this work has been done with rats and mice. Other indications of fatty acid deficiencies are red blood cell fragility (Watson, 1963) in rats, and abnormal mitochondria in rats (Johnson, 1963) and mice (Wilson and LeDuc, 1963). An increase in tissue levels of a trienoic acid (20:3, ω9) and a decrease in tetraenoic acids was seen by Rieckehoff *et al.* (1949) in deficient rats and has since been found by a number of workers. The accumulation of 20:3, ω9 is one of the earliest deficiency symptoms to appear in rats fed a fat-free diet.

Very few investigations have been made to determine the response of fish to fat-free diets and the ability of different fatty acids to prevent or cure deficiency symptoms. Evidence obtained from this limited number of experiments indicate that certain species of fish have different essential fatty acid requirements than mammals although much work remains to be done in this area.

Chinook salmon held on a purified test diet that lacked added lipid were observed to have a slow growth rate and abnormal coloration (Nicolaides and Woodall, 1962). Recovery diets that contained trilinolein or linolenic acid improved growth while triolein had little effect. Only trilinolein restored the normal greenish-black coloration. The authors concluded that linoleic acid was required for complete recovery while linolenic acid only improved growth in a manner analagous to its action in rats.

Higashi *et al.* (1966) reported severe symptoms developing in rainbow trout held on a fat-free diet for 3 months. The fish developed a hardened and discolored condition in the posterior body region and a severe degeneration and erosion of the posterior fin. In extreme cases, terminals of the spinal column were exposed. Recovery was obtained when ethyl linoleate, ethyl linolenate, or a fraction from squid oil, containing highly unsaturated fatty acids, were fed. The ability of both linoleic and linolenic acids to cure skin disorders in rainbow trout but not in chinook salmon is puzzling and leaves unanswered the question of whether ω3 or ω6 acids, or both, can cure this symptom. Differences in experimental conditions, such as exposure to sunlight and water temperature, might account for the deficiency symptoms observed by the two groups.

Lee *et al.* (1967) found ω3 fatty acids to be essential for the growth of rainbow trout. Fish fed a purified casein–dextrin test diet, containing 10% corn oil, had a sharp increase in mortality and the growth rate decreased markedly during the fourth month. The corn oil-fed trout were divided into five groups and fed one of the following test diets; corn oil, 10%; salmon oil, 5%, corn oil, 5%, salmon oil, 1%, corn oil, 9%; soybean oil, 10%; 2.16% methyl linolenate concentrate (supplied 1% 18:3, ω3), and corn oil, 7.84%. The fish received the test diets for 12 weeks and when the feeding trial was terminated fish body lipids were analyzed for fatty acid composition, as were the lipids. Growth data is presented in Table II along with the fatty acids in the test diets.

The addition of ω3 acids, even in very low levels, significantly improved growth and reduced mortality. The 1.2% 18:3, ω3 present in the corn oil, equivalent to 0.12% of the diet, apparently was not able to meet the re-

TABLE II

EFFECT OF DIET LIPID COMPOSITION ON GROWTH AND MORTALITY OF RAINBOW TROUT[a]

| Fatty acid | 10% C.O. | 5% S.O. 5% C.O. | 1% S.O. 9% C.O. | 10% S.B.O. | 1% 18:3 9% C.O. |
|---|---|---|---|---|---|
| 14:0 | Trace | 2.41 | 0.48 | | Trace |
| 16:0 | 11.74 | 14.68 | 11.34 | 11.40 | 11.98 |
| 16:1ω7 | | 4.91 | 0.98 | | |
| 16:2? | | 0.54 | 0.10 | | |
| 18:0 | 2.11 | 2.87 | 2.25 | 3.70 | 2.69 |
| 18:1ω9 | 28.10 | 29.40 | 28.27 | 22.41 | 30.21 |
| 18:2ω6 | 56.86 | 30.53 | 51.72 | 55.60 | 53.99 |
| 18:3ω3 | 1.18 | 1.24 | 1.19 | 7.30 | 10.71 |
| 20:1ω9 | Trace | 2.66 | 0.53 | | Trace |
| 20:4ω6 | | 0.30 | Trace | | |
| 22:1 | | 1.74 | 0.34 | | |
| Unknown | | 0.62 | 0.12 | | |
| 20:5ω3 | | 3.07 | 0.61 | | |
| 22:5ω3 | | 1.12 | 0.22 | | |
| 22:6ω3 | | 2.41 | 0.48 | | |
| 12-Week gain (gm) | 4.2 | 13.9 | 7.9 | 9.2 | 8.4 |
| Feed/gain | 1.22 | 0.77 | 1.02 | 0.77 | 0.92 |
| Mortality (%) | 25 | 5 | 6 | 4 | 2 |

[a] C.O., corn oil; S.O., salmon oil; S.B.O., soybean oil; 1% 18:3, ω3 supplied by 2.16% methyl linolenate concentrate + 7.84 % corn oil. Some minor components omitted for clarity.

quirements for this acid. Competitive inhibition between linoleic and
linolenic acid metabolism, as mentioned in Section III, might have been a
factor in fatty acid utilization. In addition, ω3 acids eliminated a peculiar
reaction to stress that was observed in the corn oil-fed fish. Any stimulus
such as handling during weighing or being exposed suddenly to light would
cause a large number of the trout to exhibit a violent swimming motion,
with little forward movement. This was immediately followed by a comatose condition in which the fish would float motionless in the water, with
spasms occurring in the side muscles in many cases. Most of the fish would
regain equilibrium after 1 to 5 minutes, but death would occasionally
occur. The physiological cause of this condition is unknown but its relationship with fatty acids makes abnormal development of nerve tissue an
attractive postulation.

TABLE III

PERCENTAGE COMPOSITION OF FATTY ACIDS FROM PHOSPHOLIPIDS OF FISH ON
THE TEST DIETS[a]

| Fatty acid | Diet | | | |
|---|---|---|---|---|
| | 10% C.O. | 5% S.O. 5% C.O. | 10% S.B.O. | 1% 18:3 9% C.O. |
| 14:0 | 1.05 | 1.30 | 1.10 | 1.51 |
| 15:0 | Trace | 0.19 | — | Trace |
| 16:0 | 24.73 | 23.82 | 16.99 | 18.15 |
| 16:1, ω7 | 2.19 | 3.97 | 2.81 | 3.02 |
| 17:0 | Trace | 0.19 | — | Trace |
| 16:2 ? | Trace | 0.31 | — | Trace |
| 18:0 | 5.80 | 5.26 | 7.43 | 6.51 |
| 18:1, ω9 | 16.55 | 19.25 | 22.14 | 17.93 |
| 18:2, ω6 | 17.76 | 11.63 | 20.52 | 16.05 |
| 18:3, ω6 | 1.58 | 0.56 | 0.35 | Trace |
| 18:3, ω3 | — | — | 1.49 | 2.86 |
| 20:1, ω9 | 0.58[b] | 1.44[b] | 0.69 | 1.15 |
| 18:4, ω3 | 0.17 | 0.34 | — | 1.29 |
| 20:2 ? | 0.79 | 0.81 | 1.75 | 1.67 |
| 20:3, ω6 | 4.22 | 2.71 | 4.50 | 3.74 |
| 20:4, ω6 | 8.97 | 4.48 | 4.76 | 5.69 |
| 20:5, ω3 | — | 1.40 | 1.50 | Trace |
| 22:4, ω6 | 0.98 | 1.13 | Trace | Trace |
| 22:5, ω6 | 11.22 | 3.27 | 8.72 | 7.05 |
| 22:6, ω3 | 3.14 | 17.15 | 5.69 | 8.04 |

[a] From Lee *et al.* (1967).
[b] Includes 18:3.

TABLE IV

PERCENTAGE COMPOSITION OF FATTY ACIDS FROM NEUTRAL LIPIDS OF FISH ON THE TEST DIETS[a]

| Fatty acid | Diet | | | |
|---|---|---|---|---|
| | 10% C.O. | 5% S.O. 5% C.O. | 10% S.B.O. | 1% 18:3 9% C.O. |
| 14:0 | 0.10 | 2.54 | 1.38 | 1.26 |
| 15:0 | 0.11 | 0.24 | — | Trace |
| 16:0 | 15.61 | 17.14 | 15.91 | 14.17 |
| 16:1, ω7 | 2.43 | 5.60 | 3.06 | 3.68 |
| 17:0 | 0.10 | 0.21 | — | Trace |
| 16:2 ? | 0.20 | 0.37 | — | 0.16 |
| 18:0 | 3.34 | 3.69 | 6.61 | 5.24 |
| 18:1, ω9 | 28.81 | 35.28 | 29.61 | 30.76 |
| 18:2, ω6 | 38.04 | 22.85 | 32.81 | 28.79 |
| 18:3, ω6 | 5.31 | 1.11 | 2.67 | 2.72 |
| 18:3, ω3 | — | — | 2.01 | 2.41 |
| 20:1, ω9 | 0.94[b] | 4.53[b] | 0.99 | 1.05 |
| 18:4, ω3 | 0.56 | 0.66 | 0.30 | 0.95 |
| 20:2 ? | 0.87 | 0.93 | 1.45 | 1.44 |
| 20:3, ω6 | 1.78 | 0.95 | 1.75 | 2.07 |
| 20:4, ω6 | 1.29 | 2.40 | 0.75 | 1.26 |
| 20:5, ω3 | — | Trace | 0.36 | 1.14 |
| 22:4, ω6 | Trace | Trace | Trace | Trace |
| 22:5, ω6 | 0.51 | Trace | 0.36 | — |
| 22:6, ω3 | — | 1.45 | Trace | — |

[a] From Lee *et al.* (1967).
[b] Includes 18:3.

Fatty acid compositions of fish fed the test diets (Tables III, IV) indicate that ω3 acids in the fish are metabolized and incorporated into phospholipids in the same manner as ω6 acids in mammals. Both 18:2, ω6 and 18:3, ω3 acids were converted to long-chain polyunsaturated acids but 22:6, ω3 was preferred over 20:4, ω6 for phospholipid synthesis. The addition of 1% methyl linolenate to the diet resulted in an increase of 22:6, ω3 in the phospholipids over the corn oil control (3.1–8.01%) and a decrease in 22:5, ω6 and 20:4, ω6 levels, 11.2 and 9.0% to 7.0 and 5.7%, respectively. These differences were even greater when 5% salmon oil, containing 20:5, ω3, 22:5, ω3, and 22:6, ω3 was fed.

In a subsequent study at this laboratory Castell *et al.* (1972a,b,c) fed rainbow trout fry a solvent-extracted purified diet which contained 2%

TABLE V

DIETARY LEVELS OF LIPIDS IN EXPERIMENTAL DIETS

| | % Fatty acid (ethyl ester) | | |
|---|---|---|---|
| Diet no. | Laurate | Linoleate | Linolenate |
| 7 | 2.0 | 0 | 0 |
| 8 | 1.9 | 0 | 0.1 |
| 9 | 1.5 | 0 | 0.5 |
| 10 | 1.0 | 0 | 1.0 |
| 11 | 0 | 0 | 2.0 |
| 12 | 1.0 | 0.1 | 0.9 |
| 13 | 1.0 | 0.3 | 0.7 |
| 14 | 1.0 | 0.5 | 0.5 |
| 15 | 1.0 | 0.7 | 0.3 |
| 16 | 1.0 | 1.0 | 0 |

ethyl laurate as the sole lipid source. After the fish were fed this diet for 1 month, from the time they started to feed, they were divided into groups that received one of the following dietary lipids (Table V).

The fish fed the 2% laurate had a high mortality rate, exhibited the peculiar shock reaction to stress described earlier for corn oil-fed fish, and developed erosion of the fins similar to the condition described by Higashi *et al.* (1966). Livers from these fish were enlarged, very fatty (12%), and were a pale yellowish color. Growth was very slow (see Fig. 7) for the laurate-fed fish.

Addition of linoleate (18:2, ω6) to the diet improved growth (Fig. 8) and the fin condition was not observed. The unusual response to stress was the most severe and appeared earlier in the fish getting only 18:2, ω6 than in the laurate-fed group which indicated that the ω6 acid was enhancing deficiency symptoms. After 14 weeks on the test, fish fed only 18:2, ω6 had slightly enlarged fatty livers, although the condition was not as pronounced as in the laurate-fed group. Muscle tissue had a high water content and many fish developed abnormal hearts.

Fish fed linolenate showed the best growth (Fig. 8), feed conversion (Fig. 9), and had the lowest mortality. Increasing the dietary level of linolenate from 0.1 to 1% apparently caused a logarithmic response in growth rate (Fig. 10).

Mitochondrial swelling was increased in the laurate-fed fish when compared to those fed linolenate. This symptom of essential fatty acid deficiency was only partially alleviated in fish receiving linoleate. The respiration rate (oxygen uptake) of liver homogenates was the greatest for fish not receiving the unsaturated acids. The values for fish fed 18:2, ω6 were intermediate between those of fish fed 18:3, ω3 and those receiving only 12:0.

The feeding studies discussed show a definite requirement for ω3-type fatty acids by the rainbow trout, and indicate that ω6 acids, in contrast with mammalian species, are not required. Regardless of the absolute requirement, ω3-type acids are recommended for trout diets.

The role of ω3 fatty acids as a dietary essential has not been investigated with other fish species, but indirect evidence suggests an important role. Several investigators have noted that ω3 acids, particularly 20:5, ω3 and 22:6, ω3, are metabolized in and incorporated into fish tissue in the same manner that 18:2, ω6, and especially 20:4, ω6, are in mammalian systems. Brockerhoff and Hoyle (1963) found the positional location of polyenoic ω3 acids in fish lipids was similar to the 20:4, ω6 distribution in mammals and suggested an important role for them. The very low level of ω6 acids found in fish, especially certain marine species, suggests a different role for ω3 acids in fish than in mammals. Richardson and Tappel (1962) re-

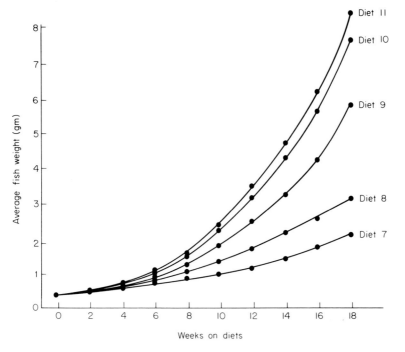

Fig. 7. Growth of fish fed diets containing different amounts of linolenic acid (0–2.0%).

ported liver mitochondrial lipids in white catfish (*Cattus albus*) to contain 6.9, 13.5, 1.2, and 11.3% of 20:4, 20:5, 22:5, and 22:6, respectively. Rat liver mitochondrial lipids contained these acids at levels of 23.4, 0.0, 0.0, and 4.0%, respectively. In a survey of the fatty acid composition of heart and liver mitochondrial lipids, Richardson *et al.* (1962) found the ω6:ω3 ratio for fish was 0.1, marine birds 0.6, seal 0.8, rat liver 205, beef liver 500, and chicken liver 9. The extent to which diet determined these ratios is unknown, although it obviously had a strong influence. The extremely low level of ω6 acids in fish mitochondria, however, would suggest an active role for the ω3 type.

Chinook salmon fingerlings were reported by Fowler and Banks (1967) to show better growth and protein deposition when fed soybean oil in a practical diet than when peanut oil, corn oil, cottonseed oil, or safflower oil were used. The principle difference in the fatty acid composition of soybean oil and the others fed, is the higher content of linolenic acid, 7 to 10% as compared to 1.5% or less. It would seem the increased growth was due to the added ω3 acids. This finding confirms our work with rainbow trout fed soybean oil (Lee *et al.*, 1967).

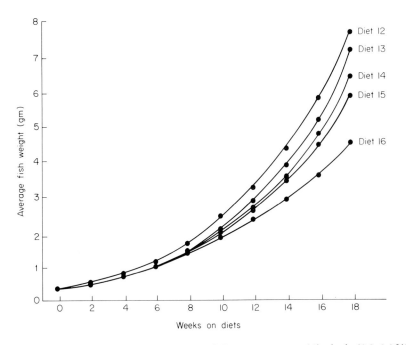

FIG. 8. Growth of fish fed diets containing different amounts of linolenic (0.3–0.9%) and linoleic (0.1–1.0%).

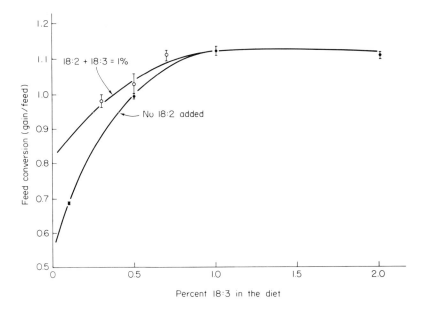

Fig. 9. Influence of 18:3, ω3 and a combination of 18:2 + 18:3 on the feed conversion of young trout. (From Castell *et al.*, 1972c.)

## E. Level of Dietary Lipids

No definite level of dietary lipid can be given for fish diets without considering factors such as the type of fat, and protein content of the diet. The species of fish is of primary importance and little work has been done to determine species differences. Sinnhuber (1969) cited commercial fish diets as having a fat content of 5.9 to 14.2%, most of which was vegetable oils. Higashi *et al.* (1964) found rainbow trout fed a practical diet of fish meal, soybean meal, wheat meal, and beef liver grew well with as much as 25% added marine oil. Fat content of fish tissue increased as the oil content of the diet was increased, but no ill effects were noted.

The amount and type of lipids present in the natural food of a particular species should be considered when designing pilot feeding trials to establish dietary lipid levels. Possible changes in utilization of dietary fat with age is a consideration that remains to be investigated as does its role in reproduction. Eggs from essential fatty acid-deficient hens are known to have poor hatchability, and it seems likely that a similar situation would occur with fish.

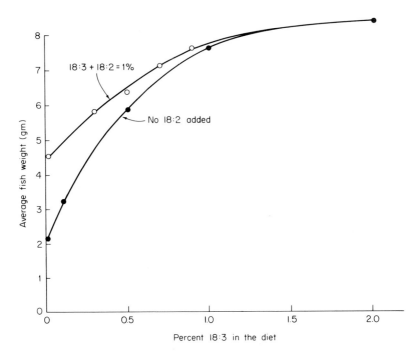

Fig. 10. Stimulatory effect of dietary linolenic acid with and without linoleic acid on the growth rate of young trout. (From Castell *et al.*, 1972c.)

## V.   Conclusion

As noted in preceding sections, there is a paucity of knowledge concerning the role of lipids in fish nutrition. The composition of fish oils, particularly marine species, has been studied extensively and their components are well documented. However, the question as to the type and amount of lipid required by fish to meet their requirements has received little attention. In most cases, knowledge pertaining to the nutritional requirements of mammalian species were applied to fishes with little regard to possible basic differences.

The discovery that rainbow trout require a dietary source of ω3-type fatty acids has enormous practical significance. Many of the trout feeds available today are comprised chiefly of vegetable products with little regard for supplying linolenic-type fatty acids. The question of whether this requirement is universal for teleost fishes remains to be answered.

The biochemical mechanisms involved in the metabolism of lipids by fish are only partially understood, and have been studied in very few species. Most of the present day working knowledge concerning lipid metabolism comes indirectly from feeding trials and from the interpolation of knowledge gained from experiments with mammalian species.

Salmon and trout have had the most attention in the United States in regard to their nutritional requirements. With the advent of predicted aquaculture enterprises in the near future the need for knowing the basic nutritional requirements for many species will be felt. This will especially be true as competition for feed ingredients forces fish culturists to utilize the most economically favorable components. This situation has already occurred in the case of vegetable products largely replacing meat and liver in trout diets.

It is hoped that this contribution will both aid those working in the field of fish nutrition and stimulate an awareness of the need for basic nutrition research.

## References*

Ackman, R. G., and Burgher, R. D. (1964). *J. Fish. Res. Bd. Can.* **21**, 367.
Ackman, R. G., Jangaard, P. M., Burgher, R. D., Hughes, M. L., and MacCallum, W. A. (1963). *J. Fish. Res. Bd. Can.* **20**, 591.
Alfin-Slater, R. B., and Aftergood, L. (1968). *Physiol. Rev.* **48**, 758.
Anisfeld, L., Greenberg, S. M., and Deuel, H. J., Jr. (1951). *J. Nutr.* **45**, 599.
Bilinski, E. (1963). *Can. J. Biochem. Physiol.* **41**, 107.
Bilinski, E., and Jonas, R. E. E. (1964). *Can. J. Biochem.* **42**, 345.
Braekkan, O. R. (1956). *Nature (London)* **178**, 747.
Brockerhoff, H. (1965). *J. Lipid Res.* **6**, 10.
Brockerhoff, H., and Hoyle, R. J. (1963). *Arch. Biochem. Biophys.* **102**, 452.
Brockerhoff, H., and Hoyle, R. J. (1965). *Biochim. Biophys. Acta* **98**, 435.
Brockerhoff, H., Ackman, R. G., and Hoyle, R. J. (1963). *Arch. Biochem. Biophys.* **100**, 9.
Brockerhoff, H., Hoyle, R. J., and Ronald, K. (1964a). *J. Biol. Chem.* **239**, 735.
Brockerhoff, H., Yurkowski, M., Hoyle, R. J., and Ackman, R. G. (1964b). *J. Fish. Res. Bd. Can.* **21**, 1379.
Brockerhoff, H., Hoyle, R. J., and Hwang, P. C. (1967). *Biochim. Biophys. Acta* **144**, 541.
Brockerhoff, H., Hoyle, R. J., Hwang, P. C., and Litchfield, C. (1968). *Lipids* **3**, 24.
Brown, W. D., and Tappel, A. L. (1959). *Arch. Biochem. Biophys.* **85**, 149.
Burr, G. O., and Burr, M. M. (1929). *J. Biol. Chem.* **82**, 345.
Burr, G. O., and Burr, M. M. (1930). *J. Biol. Chem.* **86**, 587.
Castell, J. D., Lee, D. J. and Sinnhuber, R. O. (1972a). *J. Nutr.* **102**, 93.
Castell, J. D., Sinnhuber, R. O., Lee, D. J. and Wales, J. H. (1972a). *J. Nutr.* **102**, 87.
Castell, J. D., Sinnhuber, R. O., Wales, J. H. and Lee, D. J. (1972a). *J. Nutr.* **102**, 77.
Deuel, H. J., Jr. (1951). *In* "The Lipids," Vol. I, 982 pp. Wiley (Interscience), New York.
Dietschy, J. M., and Siperstein, M. D. (1965). *J. Clin. Invest.* **44**, 1311.

* References designated as *Fish. Res. Bull.* are published by the New York State Conservation Department, Albany, New York.

Dupree, H. K. (1969). *U.S. Dep. Interior, Fish Wildl. Serv. Tech. Pap. No.* **27**.

Elovson, J. (1965). *Biochim. Biophys. Acta* **106**, 291.

Farkas, T., and Herodek, S. (1964). *J. Lipid Res.* **5**, 369.

Fowler, L. G., and Banks, J. L. (1967). *U.S. Bur. Sport Fish. Wildl. Tech. Bull.* **13**, 3.

Fowler, L. G., and Banks, J. L. (1969). *U.S. Bur. Sport Fish. Wildl. Tech. Pap. No.* **26**, 3.

Fritz, I. B., and Yue, K. T. H. (1963). *J. Lipid Res.* **4**, 279.

Froines, J. R., Shuster, C. Y., and Olcott, H. S. (1965). *J. Amer. Oil Chem. Soc.* **42**, 887.

Green, D. E., and Wakil, S. J. (1960). *In* "Lipid Metabolism" (K. Bloch, ed.). Wiley, New York.

Gruger, E. H., Jr., Nelson, R. W., and Stansby, M. E. (1964). *J. Amer. Oil. Chem. Soc.* **41**, 662.

Gunstone, F. D. (1967). "An Introduction to the Chemistry and Biochemistry of Fatty Acids and Their Glycerides," 209 pp. Richard Clay (The Chaucer Press) Ltd., Bungay, Suffolk.

Hanahan, D. J., and Thompson, G. A. Jr. (1963). *Annu. Rev. Biochem.* **32**, 215–240.

Harper, H. A. (1967). "Review of Physiological Chemistry," 11th Ed., 522 pp. Lange Medical Publ. Los Altos, California.

Higashi, H., Kaneko, T., Ishii, S., Masuda, I. and Sugihashi, T. (1964). *Bull. Jap. Soc. Sci. Fish.* **30**, 778.

Higashi, H., Kaneko, T., Ishii, S., Ushiyama, M., and Sugihashi, T. (1966). *J. Vitaminol.* **12**, 74.

Hilditch, T. P., and Williams, P. N. (1964). "The Chemical Constitution of Natural Fats," 4th Ed. Wiley, New York.

Holman, R. T. (1964). *Fed. Proc.* **23**, 1062.

Holman, R. T. (1968). *In* "Progress in the Chemistry of Fats and Other Lipids" (R. T. Holman, ed.), Vol. IX, pp. 275–348. Pergamon, New York.

Holman, R. T. (1970). *In* "Progress in the Chemistry of Fats and Other Lipids." (R. T. Holman, ed.), vol. IX, pp. 611–682. Pergamon, New York.

Idler, D. R. (1969). *In* "Fish in Research" (O. W. Neuhaus, and J. E. Halver, eds.), p. 121. Academic Press, New York.

Idler, D. R., and Bitners, I. (1958). *Can. J. Biochem. Physiol.* **36**, 793.

Idler, D. R., and Tsuyuki, H. (1958). *Can. J. Biochem. Physiol.* **36**, 783.

Isselbacher, K. J. (1965). *Fed. Proc.* **24**, 16.

Johnson, A. R., Pearson, J. A., Shenstone, F. S., and Fogarty, A. C. (1967). *Nature (London)* **214**, 1244.

Johnson, A. R., Fogarty, A. C., Pearson, J. A., Shenstone, F. S., and Bersten, A. M. (1969). *Lipids* **4**, 265.

Johnson, R. M. (1963). *Exp. Cell Res.* **32**, 118.

Jonas, R. E. E., and Bilinski, E. (1964). *J. Fish. Res. Bd. Can.* **21**, 653.

Kayama, M., and Tsuchiya, Y. (1959). *Tohoku J. Agr. Res.* **10**, 229.

Kayama, M., Tsuchiya, Y., Nevenzel, J. C., Fulco, A., and Mead, J. F. (1963). *J. Amer. Oil. Chem. Soc.* **40**, 499.

Klenk, E. (1965). *J. Amer. Oil. Chem. Soc.* **42**, 580.

Knipprath, W. G., and Mead, J. F. (1965). *Fish. Ind. Res.* **3**, 23.

Knipprath, W. G., and Mead, J. F. (1966). *Lipids* **1**, 113.

Knipprath, W. G., and Mead, J. F. (1968). *Lipids* **3**, 121.

Lee, D. J., Roehm, J. N., Yu, T. C., and Sinnhuber, R. O. (1967). *J. Nutr.* **92**, 93.

Lewis, R. W. (1962). *Comp. Biochem. Physiol.* **6**, 75.

Linn, T. C. (1967). *J. Biol. Chem.* **242**, 990.

Litchfield, C. (1968). *Lipids* **3,** 417.

Lowry, R. R., and Tinsley, I. J. (1966). *J. Nutr.* **88,** 26.

Lynen, F. (1967). *Biochemistry* **102,** 13.

McCay, C. M., Bing, F. C., and Dilley, W. E. (1927). *Trans. Amer. Fish. Soc.* **57,** 240.

Machlin, L. J. (1962). *Nature (London)* **194,** 868.

McLaren, B. A., Herman, E. F., and Elvehjem, C. A. (1946). *Arch. Biochem. Biophys.* **10,** 433.

McLaren, B. A., Keller, E., O'Donnell, D. J., and Elvehjem, C. A. (1947). *Arch. Biochem. Biophys.* **15,** 179.

Malins, D. C. (1967). *In* "Fish Oils" (M. E. Stansby, ed.), p. 31. Avi Publ., Westport, Connecticut.

Malins, D. C., Wekell, J. C., and Houle, C. R. (1965). *J. Lipid Res.* **6,** 100.

Marco, G. J., Machlin, L. J., Emery, E., and Gordon, R. S. (1961). *Arch. Biochem. Biophys.* **94,** 115.

Masoro, E. J. (1968). *In* "Physiological Chemistry of Lipids in Mammals," p. 304. Saunders, Philadelphia, Pennsylvania.

Mead, J. F. (1961). *Fed. Proc.* **20,** 952.

Mead, J. F. (1968). *In* "Progress in The Chemistry of Fats and Other Lipids" (R. T. Holman, ed.), Vol. IX, p. 161. Pergamon, New York.

Mead, J. F., and Kayama, M. (1967). *In* "Fish Oils" (M. E. Stansby, ed.), p. 289. Avi Publ., Westport, Connecticut.

Mead, J. F., Kayama, M., and Reiser, R. (1960). *J. Amer. Oil Chem. Soc.* **37,** 438.

Menzel, D. B., and Olcott, H. S. (1964). *Biochim. Biophys. Acta* **84,** 133.

Mohrhauer, H., and Holman, R. T. (1963a). *J. Lipid Res.* **4,** 151.

Mohrhauer, H., and Holman, R. T. (1963b). *J. Nutr.* **81,** 67.

Nevenzel, J. C., Rodegker, W., and Mead, J. F. (1965). *Biochemistry* **4,** 1589.

Nicolaides, N., and Woodall, A. N. (1962). *J. Nutr.* **78,** 431.

Nugteren, D. H. (1965). *Biochim. Biophys. Acta* **106,** 280.

Phelps, R. A., Shenstone, F. S., Kemmerer, A. R., and Evans, R. J. (1965). *Poultry Sci.* **44,** 358.

Phillips, A. M., Jr., Tunison, A. V., and Balzer, G. C. (1963). *U.S. Dep. Interior Fish Wildl. Circ.* **159,** 1.

Phillips, A. M., Jr., Livingston, D. L., and Poston, H. A. (1964). *Fish. Res. Bull.,* **28.**

Putnam, G. B., (1970). Personal Communication.

Quackenbush, F. W., Kummerow, F. A., and Steenbock, H. (1942). *J. Nutr.* **24,** 213.

Raju, P. K., and Reiser, R. (1967). *J. Biol. Chem.* **242,** 379.

Reiser, R., Stevenson, B., Kayama, M., Choudhury, R. B. R., and Hood, D. W. (1963). *J. Amer. Oil Chem. Soc.* **40,** 507.

Richardson, T., and Tappel, A. L. (1962). *J. Cell Biol.* **13,** 43.

Richardson, T., Tappel, A. L., Smith, L. M., and Houle, C. R. (1962). *J. Lipid Res.* **3,** 344.

Rieckehoff, I. G., Holman, R. T., and Burr, G. O. (1949). *Arch. Biochem. Biophys.* **20,** 331.

Roehm, J. N., Lee, D. J., and Sinnhuber, R. O. (1967). *J. Nutr.* **92,** 425.

Roehm, J. N., Lee, D. J., Wales, J. H., Polityka, S. D., and Sinnhuber, R. O. (1970). *Lipids* **5,** 80–84.

Saddler, J. B., Lowry, R. R., Krueger, H. M., and Tinsley, I. J. (1966). *J. Amer. Oil Chem. Soc.* **43,** 321.

Sen, N., and Schlenk, H. (1964). *J. Amer. Oil Chem. Soc.* **41,** 241.

Senior, J. R. (1964). *J. Lipid Res.* **5,** 495.

Silk, M. H., and DeKoning, A. J. (1964). *J. Amer. Oil. Chem. Soc.* **41,** 619.

Simpson, T. H., Wright, R. S., and Renfrew, J. (1964a). *J. Endocrinol.* **31,** 11.

Simpson, T. H., Wright, R. S., and Hunt, S. V. (1964b). *J. Endocrinol.* **31,** 29.

Sinnhuber, R. O. (1969). *In* "Fish in Research" (O. W. Neuhaus, and J. E. Halver, eds.), p. 245. Academic Press, New York.

Sinnhuber, R. O., Lee, D. J., Wales, J. H., and Ayres, J. L. (1968). *J. Nat. Cancer Inst.* **41,** 1293.

Siperstein, M. D. (1966). *Proc. 7th Can. Cancer Conf.,* p. 152.

Siperstein, M. D., and Fagan, V. M. (1964). *In* "Advances in Enzyme Regulations" (G. Weber, ed.), Vol. 2, p. 249. Pergamon, New York.

Srere, P. A. (1965). *Nature (London)* **205,** 766.

Tsuchiya, Y., and Kayama, M. (1958). *Tohoku J. Agr. Res.* **9,** 41.

Wakil, S. J. (1961). *J. Lipid Res.* **2,** 1.

Wakil, S. (1964). *In* "Metabolism and Physiological Significance of Lipids" (R. C. Dawson, and D. N. Rhodes, eds.) p 3.. Wiley, New York.

Watanabe, T., and Hashimoto, Y. (1968). *Bull. Jap. Soc. Sci. Fish.* **34,** 1131.

Watson, W. C. (1963). *Brit. J. Hematol.* **9,** 32.

Wilson, J. W., and LeDuc, E. H. (1963). *J. Cell. Biol.* **16,** 281.

Woodall, A. N., Ashley, L. M., Halver, J. E., Olcott, H. S., and van der Veen, J. (1964). *J. Nutr.* **84,** 125.

# 5

## NONNUTRIENT COMPONENTS OF THE DIET*

*L. Friedman and S. I. Shibko*

* Department of Nutrition and Food Science, Massachusetts Institute of Technology, Contribution No. 974.

## I.  Introduction

At the beginning of the twentieth century chemists had attempted to arrive at an understanding of nutritional needs by a more detailed analysis of foodstuffs. The work of the pioneers of modern nutritional research such as F. G. Hopkins, E. V. McCollum, Osborne, and Mendel, and others had demonstrated that nutritional requirements could be determined only by a study of the performance of experimental animals during the controlled feeding of purified diets. The resulting highly selective approach to the chemistry of foodstuffs emphasized the components usually listed in food composition tables. The goal of achieving a complete analytical balance sheet for a foodstuff was set aside and has still not been attained for any one item. Preoccupation with the essential nutritional factors has tended to obscure the fact that food materials are complex mixtures of many components. The science of nutrition, however, must deal with each component of the diet that may be of physiological significance.

Food scientists are aware of many of the nonnutrient components of food because of the influence these have on important characteristics of food products such as odor, flavor, texture, stability, and color. The biological scientist has been influenced in his awareness of the nonnutrient components by the fact that food may be a source of harm as well as benefit, so that those components that have a potential for harm at relatively low levels of intake and are commonly classified as poisons are the substances he thinks of when considering nonnutrient components of food.

From the point of view of nutrition, it is well to remember that every food substance may be classified according to the level of intake as either physiologically inert, physiologically beneficial, or potentially hazardous. Nutritionists are as much concerned with the problems caused by an excess of a food component as with the problems resulting from the deficiency of an essential nutrient. They have in common with all the branches of toxicology a concern with the potential hazards inherent in the intake of substances in excess. The concept of levels of intake, although applied usually to extraneous components, is clearly illustrated by the nutrients themselves. Although it would be difficult to say at what level a nutrient is physiologically inert, there is no question that certain levels of intake are insufficient to maintain normal function. The level of nutrient requirement associated with normal health, that is, with physiological function and benefit, is well understood for most nutrients. For every nutrient there is also a level of intake that constitutes a potential hazard. The margin between the level of function and the level of hazard varies considerably with each nutrient. Everyone is familiar with the example of vitamin A in warm-blooded animals where only a tenfold increase in the usual daily requirement brings it into the range of potential hazard. One may even consider slight excesses of energy intake as constituting a potential hazard in light of the consensus that the most important problem of malnutrition in the United States today is obesity—and this does include fish reared in hatchery environments. It is clear that in the case of energy the margin between the level of caloric intake consistent with normal physiological function and that creating a potential hazard is sometimes very narrow. One may justifiably consider the portion of the daily intake of a nutrient which is in excess of the daily requirement as constituting intake of a nonnutrient material.

The nonnutrient components may be classified according to whether they are present because of the inherent genetic characteristics of the plant or animal from which the foodstuff is derived or are substances arising outside the food itself. The latter substances can be further subdivided as to their origin: (1) whether they have become part of the food as a result of man's activities in agriculture, food processing, storage, packaging, transportation, etc.; or (2) whether they are unwanted contaminants resulting from careless handling, spoilage, or some other uncontrolled or uncontrollable circumstance.

We shall deal with the question of these components in a general way on the assumption that fish are basically similar to all other animal species that have been studied with regard to their nutritional characteristics, recognizing, however, the uniqueness of fish with regard to their watery environment, manner of feeding, and poikilothermic metabolism. Wherever possible, specific examples will be used that are directly applicable to fish. However, examples from animal husbandry and human experience will be given to illustrate the kind of situations that have arisen in the past and to emphasize the importance of an awareness of the presence of nonnutrient components which, when present in excess, may create unusual problems.

Although many nonnutrient components of foods may serve useful purposes physiologically, as, for example, the growth promoters and the therapeutic and prophylactic drugs added to feeds, our concern about knowing of their presence and in what amounts arises from the possibility of excess and the potential hazards derived therefrom. The hazards are of two types: first, the hazard to health and well being of the animal itself; and, second, the effect on the composition of the tissues which will be used as human food. The possibility of concentrating undesirable components and having residues in edible tissues greater than that considered safe for man is an important practical problem.

## II. Genetically Determined Components of Plant and Animal Foodstuffs other than Nutrients

### A. Cellulose, Pentosans, and other Poorly Digestible Carbohydrates

Morrison (1951) has compiled a list of feeding stuffs that are commonly used for the preparation of animal feeds, with details of their composition based on the traditional chemical analysis for moisture, protein, fat, ash, crude fiber, nitrogen-free extract, and also certain minerals. In addition, the digestible nutrients present in these feed ingredients, as determined by feeding experiments with sheep and cattle, are reported. For practical purposes any of the feed ingredients found in this compilation could be used in formula diets for fish. Formerly, animal products constituted the bulk of the materials used in the preparation of fish feeds (Law et al., 1961; Sinnhuber et al., 1961), although plant materials were also added. As our knowledge of the nutrient requirement of fish increases, the feeds formulated for fish husbandry will become more independent of sources of animal protein and consist mainly of ingredients from plant sources. At present, the animal products quite widely used are derived from hogs, oxen, sheep, horses, and fish, such as liver, spleen, heart, lung, tripe and blood, and meat, and bone meal. Plant products used include by-products of milling (e.g., oat hulls, rice bran, alfalfa meal, beet pulp), oilseed meals (e.g., cottonseed, soybean), vegetable oils (e.g., corn oil, peanut oil, safflower oil), and various other products such as yeasts, tomato pomace, carrots, paprika, and distillers residues.

The use of plant products in practical fish diets results in the introduction of varying amounts of fiber and complex carbohydrates. The crude fibers include cellulose, hemicelluloses, pentosans, mannans, and poorly digestible carbohydrates. In addition, certain complex carbohydrates may be present that have an adverse effect on growth. Evaluation of the digestibility of these substances by fish is not possible because few digestibility studies of fiber by fish have been reported. The chemical determination of crude fiber in feeds gives an erroneous estimate of the biological value of the "nonnutritive" residue, because: (1) it has variable composition and digestibility, and (2) the nitrogen-free extract, which has generally been considered to contain highly digestible carbohydrates, contains large amounts of indigestible lignin (Van Soest, 1966). Van Soest (1966) has indicated that in any consideration of the digestibility of plant materials it is important to distinguish between the two categories of vegetable substances: (1) those contained in the plant cell wall, and (2) those contained within the metabolic part of the cell. The plant cell wall consists mainly of hemicellulose, cellulose, pectin, and lignin; the amounts present varying with the age of the tissue. The hemicelluloses, which consist of xylans and other polysaccharides, the cellulose, and the lignin are indigestible unless microbial fermentation exists in the digestive tract. Pectin is easily soluble and digestible and can be considered nutritionally available. The cellular contents contain readily available nutrients such as amino acids, sugars, starch, lipids, and proteins, and other nonprotein nitrogenous substances. Not all the cell protein is digestible; about 5 to 10% is bound within the lignin of the cell wall and is unavailable. Further, considerable loss of protein may occur during commercial processing of the plant material as a result of the nonenzymatic browning reaction. Van Soest (1966) has suggested an analytical scheme for distinguishing the less available parts of the feedstuff which, if carried out in conjunction with digestion trials, should enable fish nutritionists to develop digestibility-predicting equations. In addition, the analytical data would give an indication of the presence of complex polysaccharides that might have adverse effects on the growth of the fish. A detailed study with fish of the digestibility of fiber from various sources has been reported by Bondi *et al.*(1957). A high degree of digestibility was observed in carp with values ranging from 25 to 89% depending on the type of material and the degree of milling. In general, the more finely the grain was milled the greater was the degree of digestibility. Wood *et al.* (1954), who studied the effect of sodium carboxymethyl cellulose (CMC) as a binding agent in the preparation of diets, also observed that the physical state of the feed may be important in determining its digestibility. CMC was shown to be physiologically inert when fed at the 2% level to fish of approximately 500 gm, but when fed to smaller fish at the same level it was shown to have an effect on the rate of growth. However, this effect was not due to the CMC per se, but to its binding effect, which prevented the disintegration of the food and prevented the other nutrients from becoming available. These investigators also studied the use of algin products (Irish moss, Kelgin, and Kelcoloid) as binding agents. Although less efficient binding agents, these substances were reported to be physiologically active. No details of the physiological effects are given, However, algin products have been observed to cause growth depression in other species. Nilson and Schaller (1941) demonstrated a marked growth depression in rats fed more than 5% agar agar or Irish moss.

Shue *et al.* (1962) reported some nutritional studies of complex carbohydrates in which rats fed according to the calorie assay technique of Rice *et al.* (1957) showed a growth depression with agar agar directly related to the level fed. Digestibility data indicated an absorption of 15% of the agar fed. With gum arabic the data indicated absorption of 80%, with a maximum caloric utilization approximately 75% that of sucrose. However, there was a negative regression of weight gain on dose. The possibility that the growth-depressing effect might be due to another component in the gum arabic was not considered. The growth data did not indicate any caloric contribution from cellulose.

Guar meal, a by-product obtained from the seed of guar (*Cyamopis tetragonolobus*) is relatively high in protein but contains a factor deleterious to growing chickens. The effect seems to be related to the gum content of the meal. Additional evidence that naturally occurring gums may have an adverse effect on growth has been reported by Vohra and Kratzer (1964). They found that inclusion of 2% of guar gum, gum tragacanth, or carrageenin, or 4% of pectin in the diet of chickens resulted in a growth inhibition of 25 to 30%. A large percentage of the seeds of species of Leguminosae have shown to contain gum yielding endosperms (Anderson, 1949). Studies on the possible growth-depressing effects of these compounds in fish would be desirable if these foodstuffs are to be used in the diet either as protein sources or as binding materials.

The use of complex indigestible polysaccharides to provide bulk and maintain the tone of the gastrointestinal tract has been favored by some (Davidson and Passmore, 1963). Its value in the feeding of fish is open to question as there seem to be no data on this point.

## B. Toxic Factors Associated with Protein-Rich Seeds

### 1. *Soybeans*

For centuries soybeans have provided a major protein component of the diet of most of the people in the Orient, in spite of the fact that the raw plant material contains several factors that make it undesirable and, for practical purposes, an inedible material. The processes of soaking, cooking, fermentation, etc., that have been developed in various areas of the Orient to deal with these inherent problems are prime examples of the way in which a potentially useful food can be made suitable and safe for consumption. Mickelsen and Yang (1966) have given us a most complete review of the work that has been done with soybeans in connection with the deleterious properties of the raw beans. Although more than 50 years have passed since Osborne and Mendel reported the improved growth-promoting property of cooked versus raw soybeans, a great deal of work is still currently under way, attempting to clarify some of the many problems raised by that observation. Most of these studies have been carried out with chicks, rats, or mice, but few studies appear to have been made with fish.

Studies by Bornstein and Lipstein (1963) showed that chicks fed soybean meal from the time of hatching showed growth depression for the first 8–12 weeks and then appeared to gain weight at a rate equal to that of chicks fed heated soybean meal. When older chicks were fed unheated soybean meal the time required to overcome the inhibitory effect was much shorter. Laying hens were shown to be resistant to the toxic factor in raw soybeans (Fisher *et al.*, 1957). The nutritional value of soybean meal may be improved either by proper heat treatment or supplementation with methionine or cysteine. The heating process has to be very carefully controlled in order to give meal of the highest nutritive value. Much work has gone into development of parameters that might be easily measured and that would correlate well with nutritive value. However, the control of the heating process is still highly empirical. With experience, manufacturers have succeeded in producing meals of high nutritive quality. Overheating, as is the case for many other foodstuffs, leads to rapid deterioration of protein quality. Because only the sulfur amino acids cysteine or methionine are capable of reversing the growth-inhibition effect of raw soybeans, it has been suggested that at least part of the effect of the toxic factors is interference with utilization of these amino acids (Hayward *et al.*, 1936; Hayward and Hafner, 1941).

## 2. *Trypsin Inhibitor*

The trypsin inhibitor is not destroyed by the heat treatments that appear to be satisfactory to overcome the growth-inhibiting factor. The trypsin inhibitor has been isolated from raw soybeans and has been shown to be a crystalline globulin protein. The protein forms a compound with trypsin that results in the inactivation of the enzyme (Kunitz, 1947). The protein is specific in its inhibitory effect on trypsin and does not affect pepsin. The available evidence indicates that the trypsin inhibitor is not responsible for the growth-depressing effects of raw soybeans. Germinating soybeans which are rich in trypsin inhibitor maintain growth rates in rats similar to those obtained with animals maintained on diets containing heated soybean meal (Desikachar and De, 1947). Trypsin inhibitors have also been isolated from raw lima bean, navy bean, and whole wheat flour. In the case of whole wheat flour the trypsin inhibitor activity is only about 1% of that of whole soybean meal and is unlikely to exert any influence on the nutritive value of the flour (Shyamala and Lyman, 1964).

### 3. *Hemagglutinins*

Wada *et al.* (1958) isolated this toxic factor in purified form and showed that it contained a high percentage of glutamine (6–10%). It seems unlikely that the hemagglutinins of soybeans are involved in the growth-depressing effect obtained with the raw meal, since addition of this factor to the diet does not have a direct effect on the growth rate (Wada *et al.*, 1958). In addition, hemagglutinin is readily inactivated by pepsin (Liener, 1958). This suggests that the hemagglutinin fraction is completely removed in the stomach of the animal. Phytohemagglutinins have been isolated from sources such as castor oil seed (*Ricinus*) and the red kidney bean (*Phaseolus vulgaris*). The hemagglutinin preparations appear to contain other toxic factors. In the case of the ricin hemagglutinin, a factor has been separated that has no hemagglutinin activity but is extremely toxic to mice (Ishiguro *et al.*, 1964a,b). Preparations from *Phaseolus vulgaris* have been shown to combine inhibition of proteolytic activity in the pancreas and duodenal mucosa, strong hemagglutination activity, and great toxicity to rats (Tedeschi *et al.*, 1965). In this case it seems likely that the activities were due to different fractions that were incompletely separated.

Another unusual effect of raw soybeans in chicks and rats, the significance of which is still not well understood, is the observation, first by Chernick *et al.* (1948), that a raw soybean ration results in pancreatic enlargement. The response is rapid, and within 72 hours chicks showed maximal enlargement of the pancreas. The size of the pancreas after 6 weeks of feeding was the same as that of chicks after 72 hours of feeding. The return to normal size was equally rapid when the raw soybeans in the rations were replaced with heated beans (Saxena *et al.*, 1963). Although the enlargement of the pancreas produced by raw soybeans appears to be associated with their growth-depressing effect, the addition of methionine to such a ration, which partially overcomes the growth-inhibiting activity, has no effect at all on the size of the pancreas in rats (Haines and Lyman, 1961) and chicks (Chernick *et al.*, 1948).

### 4. *Cottonseed*

*a. Gossypol and Related Pigments.* Cottonseed represents another example of a very good source of protein for man and animals whose utilization for food has been hindered by the presence of several minor toxic components, principally the polyphenolic pigment gossypol 2,2'-bis[8-formyl(1,6,7-trihydro-5-isopropyl-3-methyl naphthyl)]. Gossypol is the principal yellow pigment of cottonseed and causes the oil of cottonseed to become very dark and undesirable unless it is removed. There is a considerable species variation of sensitivity to gossypol. Ruminants appear to be immune after their microflora have been established; rabbits and guinea pigs are particularly sensitive. Rats and poultry show intermediate sensitivity (Altschul *et al.*, 1958). Free gossypol released from the pigment glands combines with the protein of the seed. Lyman *et al.* (1959) have shown that the gossypol reacts with the $\epsilon$-amino groups of lysine in the protein. The bound gossypol is not released by proteolytic enzymes and is relatively nontoxic, and below certain levels presents no practical problems (Altschul *et al.*, 1958). Because of the binding effect, cottonseed that is high in gossypol will show a marked decrease in the biological availability of lysine, and the protein quality may be reduced below acceptable levels. The most common symptom associated with gossypol toxicity is a depressed growth rate and a decreased utilization of feed for body weight gain. Intestinal hemorrhages also appear to be characteristic of gossypol poisoning in rats, mice, guinea pigs, and rabbits (Eagle, 1948). During the past 25 years progress has been made to enable the reduction of free gossypol in cottonseed meal to levels that would permit its successful utilization in poultry and swine feed. This work is still continuing in the effort to make cottonseed safe for human food, and success sufficient to permit its use in all-vegetable mixtures, such as "Incaparina" for the feeding of human children has been achieved (Bressani, 1960). However, not all the questions have been answered, and much work still remains to be done on the practical level and from the point of view of the minor components of the meal. Eagle (1959) showed that when the pigment glands of cottonseed were fed to rats they were much more toxic than would have been expected from their gossypol content. This observation indicated that the pigment gland must contain other toxic substances. Lyman (1964) reported the isolation of a green pigment, gossyverdurin, which is about four times as toxic as gossypol and which gives the same value as gossypol in the analytical method for gossypol. Gossyverdurin, like gossypol, reacts with the $\epsilon$-amino groups of lysine in proteins and even more rapidly than is the case with gossypol. Cottonseed meals containing gossypol have been shown to be nontoxic to brown trout (Wolf, 1952). However, no information was given as to the nature of the gossypol in these preparations, whether it was free or bound, or with respect to the nutritive value of the cottonseed meal fed to these fish. Sinnhuber *et al.* (1965) showed that cottonseed flour, gossypol, and cyclopropene fatty acids were not carcinogenic to trout. No information was given as to other possible toxic effects. In addition to gossypol, cottonseed contains a number of compounds which appear to be formed from it: gossypurpurin, a purple pigment; gossyfulvin, an orange pigment; and gossycaerculin, a blue pigment. All three of these appear to be produced from gossypol during the heating involved in the preparation of the meal. Little is known about the biological activity of these compounds, although gossypurpurin has been reported to be $2\frac{1}{2}$ times less toxic than gossypol (Lyman, 1964).

*b. Cyclopropene Fatty Acids.* Two components in the oil of cottonseed are of interest as they have created problems in the production of hen eggs. Hens fed cottonseed meal containing small amounts of residual oil produce eggs which, on cold storage, are likely to develop abnormal colors in the yolks and whites. This is not due to gossypol which, when present, alters the color of only the yolk of eggs, making it dark. The cyclopropene fatty acids, sterculic and malvalic acid, present in cottonseed oil impart a pink color to egg whites and yolks. Sterculic acid is a 19-carbon fatty acid with a propene ring involving carbons 8 and 9. Malvalic acid is a homolog which contains only 18 carbon atoms. The malvalic acid of cottonseed oil, between 0.7 and 1.5% of the total fatty acid, is about twice that of the sterculic acid, 0.3–0.5%. When present at relatively high levels in the feed, these cyclopropenoids appear to produce undesirable effects, including changes in membrane permeability and/or yolk structure, which lead to egg discoloration, altered fatty acid ratios, increased chick embryo mortality, and retarded development of the reproductive organs (Phelps *et al., 1965*).

### 5. *Linseed Meal*

Linseed meal produces a marked decrease in the growth of chicks, but this effect is lost completely if the meal is first soaked with water or if the pyridoxine content of the diet is increased. The growth-inhibiting substance in linseed meal is destroyed by autoclaving or by incubation of the moistened meal, either with water or 50% ethyl alcohol, whereas dry heat (110°C) has no effect on the compound (Kratzer and Williams, 1948; Kratzer *et al.,* 1954). Kratzer (1946) reported that a 95% alcohol extract of linseed meal showed no growth-inhibiting activity. However, Klosterman *et al.* (1963) found that a 70% aqueous ethanol extract of linseed meal contained most of the growth-inhibiting substance and that the poor growth of the chicks fed this fraction could be overcome by the addition of pyridoxine. This factor has been isolated as a crystalline substance from unheated linseed meal by using a microbiological assay with *Azotobacter vinelandi* to monitor its activity during the purification procedure. It is soluble in water but insoluble in organic solvents and behaves as an amphoteric substance which, on the basis of infrared spectra, appears related to the presence of amino and carboxyl groups. The formula reported for it is $C_{10}H_{18}N_3O_5$. It contains 50% glutamic acid. When this amino acid is removed by acid hydrolysis a compound remains that readily complexes with pyridoxal phosphate. For chicks the pyridoxine antagonist isolated from raw linseed meal is about as potent as deoxypyridoxine. For *Azotobacter* the antagonist is about 1000 times more active than for deoxypyridoxine. This compound is present in linseed meal at a level of 0.002–0.005%.

### 6. *Lathyrism*

Diets containing large amounts of the seeds of certain species of *Lathyrus* and *Vicia* produce a severe disease in man and animals. The disease lathyrism is of two general types: neurolathyrism, which is caused by the seeds of *Lathyrus sativus* and is characterized by degeneration of the fiber tracts of the spinal cord; and osteolathyrism, which is caused by the seeds of *Lathyrus odoratus*, *Lathyrus sylvestris Wagneri*, *Lathyrus latifolius*, and *Vicia sativa* and is characterized by lesions in connective tissue.

L-2,4-Diaminobutyric acid has been identified as the naturally occurring neurotoxin in seeds of *Lathyrus sylvestris Wagneri* and *Lathyrus latifolius* (Ressler, 1964). This compound appears to be present in about 25% of the *Lathyrus* species examined (Bell, 1962). *Lathyrus sativus* and *Vicia sativa* have been shown to contain $\beta$-cyanoalanine as the toxic principle. In seeds and seedlings this compound is mainly present in a bound form being present as the dipeptide glutamyl-$\beta$-cyano-L-alanine. Young seedlings of these plants contain the highest concentration of toxic materials. Different animals show varying degrees of susceptibility to those toxic substances. Both free and bound $\beta$-cyano-L-alanine have been shown to be toxic to chicks when fed or injected. Young rats were susceptible to the toxin when it was injected but not when it was included in the diet (Ressler *et al.*, 1963). The dipeptide appears to be half as toxic as the free $\beta$-cyano-L-alanine.

In experiments with laboratory rats, the common garden sweet pea (*Lathyrus odoratus* L), a species which had not previously been reported toxic was shown to retard growth and produce lameness and skeletal deformity in rats. The compound responsible for the production of the paralysis and skeletal lesions has been identified as $\beta$-($\gamma$-L-glutamyl)-aminopropionitrile (McKay *et al.*, 1954); Schilling and Strong, 1955). Synthetic aminopropionitrile and aminoacetonitrile are capable of producing symptoms and lesions comparable with those produced by the seeds.

Many instances of poisoning of man by *Lathyrus sativus* reported in the older literature remain unexplained. *Lathyrus sativus* poisoning is, at this time, a very important problem in India. It has repeatedly been impossible to produce symptoms in experimental animals with this species. Recently workers in India reported that the seeds of *Lathyrus sativus* contained a compound which is neurotoxic to chicks when administered parenterally. This factor has been identified as $\beta$-$N$-oxalyl-L-$\alpha$,$\beta$-diaminopropionic acid (Rao *et al.*, 1964). At least two other toxic factors are present in 30% alcoholic extracts of *L. sativus*. One is an osteotoxic factor, producing a skeletal abnormality, and the other a factor which has a depressant activity on the central nervous system of monkeys (Annual Report of the Nutrition Research Laboratory, Hyderabad, 1964).

## 7. *Favism*

*Vicia fava*, commonly known as the fava bean, the broad bean, or the horse bean, produces a toxic episode (favism) in susceptible human individuals shortly after exposure either through inhalation of the pollen or by ingestion of raw or partially cooked beans. The susceptible individual suffers from a combination of sensitivity to the fava bean and an inborn metabolic error. The metabolic error consists of a deficiency in glucose-6-phosphate dehydrogenase as well as reduced glutathione stability and lower glutathione levels in the red blood cells (Zinkham *et al.*, 1958; Childs *et al.*, 1958). The nature of the toxic principle is unknown. No reports are available of the occurrence of favism in animals.

## C. Toxic Plants

### 1. *Introduction*

The number of plant and animal species used by man for food is very small compared to the total number of species available to him. This is probably a reflection of the knowledge, gained by painful experience which goes back to the earliest evidences of recorded history, that toxic substances are present in various plants and animals. In addition to the nontoxic plants, man has been able to extend his food supply by learning how to remove or inactivate the toxic components of certain other plants. Noxious weeds were recognized in Biblical times, when sowing of tares was recognized as an unfriendly act, as is dramatized for us in the parable from St. Matthew 13:25, "But while man slept his enemy came and sowed tares among the wheat." This potential problem arises occasionally when the desired crop is contaminated with some of the undesired "thorns and thistles" (Genesis 4:18). For example, wheat contaminated with noxious weeds such as *Senecio* has caused what has been called "bread poisoning" (Tanner and Tanner, 1953). The condition produced in man and animals by plant species containing pyrrolizidine alkaloids has been given the generic name "seneciosis." In animals this worldwide disease has been known for years and has been described in horses, cattle, sheep, goats, pigs, chickens, quail, and pigeons (Garner, 1961). In man it has been known as hepatic venoocclusive disease and has been a particularly troublesome problem among "bush tea" drinkers in Jamaica (Bras *et al.*, 1954). Numerous species of *Crotalaria*, a member of the legume family, have proved poisonous. *Crotalaria spectabilis*, said to be the most toxic of the species, has been used extensively as a cover crop in light soils in the southern United States and has spread and become wild in those areas. The toxic principle is the alkaloid monocrotaline, which produces chronic poisoning for which there is no cure, and death may occur even after intake of the toxin has stopped. Mechanical harvesting equipment recently introduced into the areas where *crotalaria* proliferated did not allow separation of the smaller crotalaria seeds from those of the cultivated crop. As a result, corn, soybeans, etc., were contaminated and presented a serious problem. In chickens crotalaria seeds produced hydropericardium similar to that observed with the chick edema factor (e.g., Section II, D). The degree to which such contamination may occur is illustrated by this item from the annual report of the Food and Drug Administration (1962).

> This last report discussed the seizure of 47 carloads—a total of 2,322 tons–of soybeans contaminated with poisonous crotalaria seeds as a result of the growing of crotalaria plants to improve sandy soils. Only one carload containing 53 tons was located and seized in 1962.

Mickelsen and Yang (1966), in a general discussion of naturally occurring toxicants in foods, point out that most of the research with toxic plants has involved farm animals. These animals often consume large amounts of a particular plant or plant product for long periods. Under such circumstances symptoms of poisoning might develop, whereas lower levels or intermittent intake might produce no noticeable effect. Many of the deleterious effects of toxicants in foods that are beginning to receive more attention by toxicologist, nutritionists, and biochemists have long been problems in veterinary practice. Publications dealing with toxic plants go back to the ancient Greeks, and a recent compilation by Kingsbury (1964), a monograph covering 1715 references dealing only with the poisonous plants of the United States and Canada, is merely an excellent introduction to the literature. Although such plants are of greater interest to pharmacologists who are seeking physiologically active substances, they are of concern to nutritionists also as some of these plants that are not normally used for food may occur in the diet when they contaminate a feed crop. Kingsbury devotes a chapter to the commonly recognized naturally toxic principles which include the following: alkaloids; polypeptides; amines; glycosides, e.g., cyanogenetic (nitrile) glycosides, goitrogenic substances, coumarin glycosides, steroid and triterpenoid glycosides, cardiac glycosides, saponins; oxalates; resins or resinoids; irritant oils; phytotoxins (toxalbumins); mineral poisonings, e.g., selenium, molybdenum, copper, lead, cadmium, fluorine, manganese; nitrogen, e.g., nitrites, nitrates, nitrosos, gaseous oxides of nitrogen; compounds causing photosensitivity, primary photosensitization, and hepatogenic photosensitization.

### 2. Alkaloids

The alkaloids represent most of the toxic nitrogenous materials that occur in plants. Some taxonomic surveys indicate that alkaloids may be present in 5–10% of plant species. They are particularly common in some plant families, e.g., Leguminosae and Amaryllidaceae, and are rare in others. Most alkaloids are very active physiologically although a few produce no reaction. Usually the activity is on the nervous system and they produce no liver damage or other type of lesion. Schoental *et al.* (1954) have shown that the pyrrolizidine alkaloids which cause severe liver damage, are both hepatotoxins and hepatocarcinogens, and probably owe their carcinogenic activity to their ability to act as alkylating agents (Culvenor *et al.*, 1962). Other basic chemical configurations in addition to the pyrrolizidine nucleus that occur in alkaloids are: tropane, pyridine, isoquinoline, indole, quinolizidine, steroid alkaloids including the solanum type and the veratrum type, and polycyclic diterpenes. Although more than 5000 alkaloids have been characterized to some extent and given names, there are still many that are not well known. The poisonous principle of *Astragalus* has been stated to be of an alkaloidal nature (Fraps and Carlysle, 1936). Others are responsible for the nervous disease of horses, sheep, and cattle called "loco." The disease has been of economical importance in the West for a long time and has been studied at length. However, although the syndrome has been associated with alkaloids in the plants responsible for the disease, there is still some doubt as to the identity of the toxic compound.

### 3. Nonprotein Nitrogenous Substances (Amines, Amino Acids, Peptides)

In addition to the alkaloids, the nonprotein nitrogenous substances of plants are widely varied, including nitrates and nitrites, urea and ureides, purines, pyrimidines, nucleosides, nucleotides, and nucleic acids, betaines, porphyrins, amines, and a host of other substances at low concentrations. However, the most abundant organic nitrogenous substances in plant materials are free amino acids, which may account for 70 to 80% of the nonprotein nitrogen. This is discussed by Synge (1963). There are three known cases where the large amounts of unusual amino acids that sometimes occur in the free state are known to be frankly toxic. These are mimosine (I)*, djenkolic acid (II), and hypoglycin A (III). Two of these three are from Leguminosae, a natural family order which is rich in other examples of unusual free amino acids. It is an order of vast economic importance but one which is always giving rise to nutritional problems. Other unusual amino acids whose physiological effects are not well known but which are abundantly present in some plant materials are γ-aminobutyric acid (IV), L-pyrrolidone carboxylic acid (V), β-(3,4-dihydroxyphenyl)-L-alanine, "dopa" (VI), azetidine, 2-carboxylic acid (VII) which occurs in lilies of the valley, 1-aminocyclopropane-1-carboxylic acid (VIII), present in cider and cranberry sauce, (+)S-methyl-L-cysteine sulfoxide (IX),

$$HO\text{---}C=CH$$
$$O=C\qquad N\text{---}CH_2\text{---}CHNH_2\text{---}COOH$$
$$HC=CH$$

Mimosine

(I)

$$HOOC\text{---}CHNH_2\text{---}CH_2\text{---}S\text{---}CH_2\text{---}S\text{---}CH_2\text{---}CHNH_2\text{---}COOH$$

Djenkolic acid

(II)

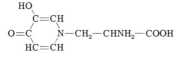

$$H_2C=C\text{---}CH\text{---}CH_2\text{---}CHNH_2\text{---}COOH \qquad HOOC\text{---}CH_2\text{---}CH_2\text{---}CH_2NH_2$$
$$\underset{H_2}{C}$$

Hypoglycin A              γ-Aminobutyric acid

(III)                          (IV)

$$H_2C\text{---}CH_2$$
$$OC\quad\quad$$
$$\underset{H}{N}\quad COOH$$

L-Pyrrolidone
carboxylic acid

(V)

* Figures in parentheses refer to Table I.

isolated from cabbage and turnips (it is an analog of alliin (X), found in garlic), and which is present in cabbage to as much as 4% of the dry matter and probably represented about one-fourth of the organic sulfur compounds present. This substance is the precursor of dimethylsulfide (XI), a major contributor to the familiar odor of cabbage. *S*-Methylcysteine sulfoxide (IX) has been recognized in allium species including onion. It also occurs in some kinds of legumes along with its reduction product, *S*-methylcysteine and the selenium amino acid analog of *S*-methylcysteine has been isolated from *Astragalus bisulcatus* growing on selenium-rich soil.

A few plant species have been shown to contain amines which have pronounced physiological effects, e.g., mistletoe (*Phoradendron flavescens*) contains β-phenylethylamine and tyramine, and *Acacia berlandieri* contains *N*-methyl-β-phenylethylamine (Camp and Lyman, 1956). More

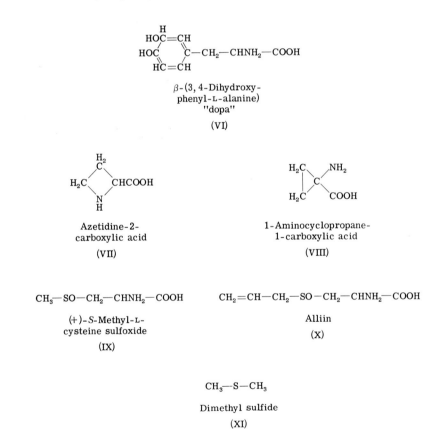

$$\begin{array}{c} H \\ HOC = CH \\ HOC \qquad C-CH_2-CHNH_2-COOH \\ HC = CH \end{array}$$

β-(3, 4-Dihydroxy-
phenyl-L-alanine)
"dopa"

(VI)

Azetidine-2-
carboxylic acid

(VII)

1-Aminocyclopropane-
1-carboxylic acid

(VIII)

$$CH_3 - SO - CH_2 - CHNH_2 - COOH$$

(+)-*S*-Methyl-L-
cysteine sulfoxide

(IX)

$$CH_2 = CH - CH_2 - SO - CH_2 - CHNH_2 - COOH$$

Alliin

(X)

$$CH_3 - S - CH_3$$

Dimethyl sulfide

(XI)

commonly, amines may be present in animal tissues as a result of bacterial decarboxylation of amino acids, e.g., tyramine and histamine.

Waley (1966) has recently reviewed the naturally occurring peptides. Peptides are considered to be compounds containing between two and twenty amino acid residues. Four principal groups of peptides are described: widely occurring peptides, peptides from animal cells, peptides from plant cells, and peptides from bacteria. The widely occurring peptides include such biologically important substances as glutathione, nucleotide peptides, and pteroyl polyglutamates. The well-characterized peptides from animal cells are structural analogs of glutathione and carnosine. In addition, many animal hormones, particularly the pituitary hormones, are peptides. Most of the peptides from plants consist of $\gamma$-glutamyl peptides. It seems unlikely that these substances would have any toxic properties. However, the toxin principle of certain fungi has now been identified as peptides, e.g., phalloidin, the main toxin of *Amanita phalloides*, is a bicyclic heptapeptide. Bacterial peptides form a very large and diverse class. Characteristic structures include the presence of amino acids, unusual amino acids, and rings. Most of the peptides are antibiotics; some are extremely toxic, e.g., actinomycin (*Streptomyces*), and sporidesmolides (*Phthomyces chartarum*).

Virtanen (1962) has pointed out that many of the components isolated from plants are not present in the living, growing plant but are secondary products derived by enzymatic reactions after the plant material has been crushed. For example, the presence of thiocyanate could not be established in intact cabbage although a rampant and profuse formation of thiocyanate was observed when cabbage was crushed. Therefore, animals and man would obtain the thiocyanate when cabbage was used as food, through the enzymatic conversion of the glucobrassicin, a sulfur-containing glucocyanate, to the isothiocyanate, and subsequent decomposition to other products, including free thiocyanate.

In another case, it was observed that only benzoisothiocyanate was obtained from the seeds of *Propaeolum*, whereas mostly benzothiocyanate was formed from the seeds of the related species *Lepidium*. These compounds are derived from the mustard oil glucoside, glucotropaeolin, hydrolysis by the enzyme myrosinase and in the case of *Lepidium*, the isothiocyanate changes to benzothiocyanate by the action of an isomerase and practically only the benzothiocyanate is found. There is a glucoside of rye plants which is transformed enzymatically and the product nonenzymatically to benzoxazolinone. This compound does not have any resemblance to a glucoside derivative, for example, there is no hydroxyl group. A similar glucoside of wheat and corn plants gives rise to a similar compound, 6-methoxybenzoxazolamine. Both of these substances have antifungal properties. Virtanen (1962) has also shown how the substance in onions, L-cysteine-*S*-oxide, is changed both enzymatically and by non-enzymatic reactions to a series of derivatives that are isolated from onions. He points out that,

> When the nutrition of men and animals is involved, the secondary substances are usually the most interesting ones because of their biological activity. When man eats vegetables, for instance, or the cow fodder, the precursors in the plants are decomposed by the influence of plant enzymes and the secondary substances pass into the organism.

On this basis, fresh vegetables, crushed vegetables, and cooked vegetables differ essentially from each other in their minor nonnutrient components (Virtanen, 1962).

In the case of cyanogenetic glycosides, the intact glycoside is not toxic. The violent toxicity of the compound is caused by the cyanide component produced after hydrolysis. Free cyanide is also toxic to the plant tissues. In natural circumstances hydrolysis is brought about by enzymatic action in the plant or in the animal (Moran, 1954). In healthy plants the hydrolytic reaction between enzyme and substrate is blocked in some unknown way. Plants with cyanogenetic potential include flax, lima beans, cherries, apples, vetch seed, corn, and many others. The variation of the cyanogenetic glycoside content in a given wild plant or crop has been explored most thoroughly in the case of sorghum and was shown to depend on such factors as climate, season, amount of rainfall, fertilization, and stage of growth. Hay made from some plants may be dangerous when cut, but may become safe in time, possibly through volatilization of its HCN content.

Saponins are large molecules which form a colloidal solution and produce a nonalkaline, soapy froth or foam when shaken in water. The saponins occur in plants as glycosides and the aglycone portion may be either of a steroid nature or a triterpenoid nature. The physiological reaction, which is believed to account for the toxicity of the saponins, is the destruction of erythrocytes by lysis (Wall *et al.*, 1952).

> Very few toxicological investigations have been made of plants in which toxicity has been attributed to the saponin content. Saponins are not readily absorbed through the uninjured digestive tract. To be toxic, therefore, they must possess or be accompanied in the plant by a substance which possesses irritant properties sufficient to injure the wall of the digestive tract and permit absorption. Saponins by themselves may contribute to gastrointestinal irritation. Administered parenterally some saponins produce marked visceral vasal dilation. (Dollahite *et al.*, 1962)

The plants *Medicago sativa* (alfalfa) and *Medicago lispida* (burr clover), commonly used in animal feeds, contain saponins. Moderate amounts of alfalfa in the diets of chicks have been shown to cause lowered growth rates and this is assumed to be due to the content of saponins (Heywang and Bird, 1954).

Cycad nuts which are used for the preparation of an edible starch contain a toxic glycoside that is readily soluble in water. Methylazoxymethanol is the primary toxic aglycone associated with the glycoside cycasin (Matsumoto and Strong, 1963). Toxic cycad nut meal has been shown to be carcinogenic to rats (Laqueur *et al.*, 1963) and guinea pig (Spatz, 1964). Miller and Miller (1965) have suggested that methylazoxymethanol is metabolized *in vivo* to give the same product as that derived from dimethylnitrosamine and that these products act by alkylating nucleic acids and proteins (Magee and Farber, 1962).

Coumarin glycosides have derivatives of coumarin as an aglycone. The most important of these is the coumarin derivative present in sweet clover (*Melilotus alba*) which, under certain conditions, can polymerize to give rise to dicoumarol. Ingestion of sweet clover containing dicoumarol can reduce blood prothrombin and cause bleeding problems (Stahler and Whitehead, 1941). Scheel (1964) has reviewed the biologically active coumarin compounds associated with food spoilage.

Among the substances known to prevent the thyroid from accumulating inorganic iodide in the normal manner are thiouracil, thiourea, cyanides, and sulfonamides. Two compounds which occur in plants as glycosides have been responsible for losses of stock with symptoms of hypothyroidism. Among the plants containing goitrogenic compounds are chard, kohlrabi, white mustard seed, rape seed or rape meal, black mustard seed, kale, broccoli, cabbage, brussels sprouts, rutabaga, Chinese cabbage, turnip root, soybeans, and flax. The goitrogenic factor in a number of species of *Brassica* was found to be L-5-vinyl-2-thiooxazolidone (Astwood *et al.*, 1949; Nordfeldt *et al.*, 1954).

### 4. *Oxalates*

Many plants contain small amounts of soluble oxalates. A few have enough to be dangerous. Several vegetables which contribute frequently or occasionally to the human diet have been found to contain anhydrous oxalic acid at levels of 10% or greater of the dry weight of the plant. These include spinach, New Zealand spinach, Swiss chard, and beet tops. Oxalate-producing fungi may elevate the oxalate content of some moldy forages to potentially toxic levels (Wilson and Wilson, 1961). Poisoning by oxalate is related to interference with calcium metabolism, but probably of greater importance than the immediate effects of blood cationic imbalance are the consequences of the kidney's reaction to soluble oxalates in the circulation. Moderate amounts are readily excreted but larger concentrations result in precipitation of oxalate crystals in the kidney tubules. In severe cases almost all the tubules are plugged and sometimes cause renal insufficiency. Calculi may also be formed in the urinary tract. Plants which may contain dangerous amounts of soluble oxalates include *Beta vulgaris*, beet or mangels, *Halogeton glomeratus*, halogeton, *Oxalis* spp., sorrel, *Rheum rhaponticum*, rhubarb, *Rumex* spp., sorrel, dock, and *Salsolar kali* var. *tenuifolia*, Russian thistle.

## 5. *Photosensitizers*

When hypersensitivity to light occurs, it is usually associated with the presence of a foreign pigment in the peripheral circulation. The presence of photodynamic pigments in the circulation may be due to certain drugs or genetic and structural diseases and also the ingestion of certain plants. Clare (1955) has reviewed the literature on photosensitization and points out that the photodynamic compounds may be classified according to origin either as (1) primary photosensitizers which are obtained directly from the food unchanged, or as (2) a breakdown product derived from substances that would normally be excreted but are not because of liver dysfunction. Normally the liver eliminates in the bile a number of pigmented breakdown products of digestion. In certain types of liver dysfunction or obstruction of the bile duct these substances, usually pigments, reach the peripheral circulation. One of them, phylloerythrin, a derivative from chlorophyll, has been shown to be photodynamic and to cause photosensitivity. The poisonous principle in hepatogenic photosensitization is the liver toxin contained in the plant, and liver dysfunction is the more important aspect of the disease. Hepatogenic sensitization follows liver damage which results in the inability of the animal to excrete photosensitizing substances that are formed by the breakdown of pigments normally ingested (Brown, 1959).

*Fagopyrum sagittatum*, buckwheat, is a crop grown for food and contains the pigment fagopyrin, a derivative of naphthodianthrone. This pigment is an example of a primary photosensitizer. Cases of photosensitization produced by ingestion of buckwheat vegetation are rare in the western hemisphere.

The liver toxins that have been identified and cause the primary liver lesions include pyrrolizidine alkaloids and the polycyclic triterpenes. However, it seems likely that other unrelated liver toxins may produce these effects. Kingsbury (1964) has listed plants that may cause hepatogenic sensitization. Included in this list are the following plants that may be used in animal feeds: *Brassica napus*, cultivated rape, *Avena sativa*, oats, *Medicago sativa*, alfalfa, *Trifolium* spp., clovers, and *Vicia* spp., vetches.

## 6. *Phytotoxins*

Phytotoxins (sometimes called toxalbumins) are large, complex molecules similar to bacterial toxins and causing somewhat similar reactions. Their antigenic potential does not seem to be the basis of their extreme toxicity. It has been suggested by LeBreton and Moule (1949) that they function *in vivo* as potent proteolytic enzymes and their toxicity is due to breakdown of critical natural proteins and accumulation of ammonia. Phytotoxins are nondialyzable, heat labile, and can be positively identified by precipitin reactions with sera containing known antibodies. Toxic castor bean presscake can be made nontoxic simply by heating. The best known phytotoxin is ricin from castor bean. Recently, Ishiguro *et al.* (1964a,b) succeeded in separating ricin into two components. One of these was highly toxic for mice but gave no evidence of any hemagglutinating or tryptic activity. The molecular weight of this protein was calculated to be 60,000 and its isoelectric point pH 5.9. The other was the hemagglutinating protein which had a molecular weight of 98,000 and had very little, if any, toxic activity when injected into mice.

## 7. *Miscellaneous Poisonous Principles*

*Equisetum* spp., horsetails, *Pteridium aquilinum*, bracken fern, and *Dryopteris filix-mas*, male fern, have been shown to contain a thiaminase which brings about destruction of thiamine in the diet and produces the syndrome of avitaminosis $B_1$ in monogastric animals. Bracken fern also seems to contain a toxic factor for ruminants. Bracken fern poisoning of farm animals has recently been reviewed by Mickelsen and Yang (1966).

Digestive upsets brought about by an excess of a dietary factor normally present in moderate amounts and usually associated with an abrupt change in diet, in particular, overindulgence in a specific foodstuff, have occurred with corn, apples, crucifers, wheat, barley, and other cereal grains (Griffiths, 1963; Preston, 1963).

The alcohol trematol ($C_{16}H_{22}O_3$) which has been found in the closely related, but geographically widely separated species, *Haplopappus hetrophyllus*, rayless goldenrod, and *Eupatorium rugosum*, snakeroot, produce symptoms of poisoning in cattle very slowly so that highly toxic milk may be produced and ingested. It is common for symptoms to appear in a suckling calf before they do in the parent.

It is sometimes difficult to differentiate between normally occurring plant components and those that arise outside the food itself (Friedman, 1964). For our purpose we may agree that, although outside factors may influence the quantitative composition of an organism, those components characteristic of normal development and apparently genetically determined are not adventitious. Those components, however, that vary from practically nothing to relatively large amounts and that depend for their presence on the availability of specific substances in the surrounding soils or waters are foreign. Therefore, although selenium, arsenic, molybdenum, copper, etc., occur in plants, we shall consider those as adventitious components whose presence in physiologically significant amounts depends on other than genetic factors. Kingsbury (1964) points out that the list of species of plants which are definitely known as toxic but for which the toxic principle is unknown is longer than any of the lists given in his book.

## D. PLANT AND ANIMAL PIGMENTS IN COLORATION OF FISH

Just as the presence of certain desirable pigments that will give the desired color to the shanks of chickens is necessary in practical poultry rations, so must one give some attention to the nonnutrient dietary components that are important in the coloration of fish. Two types of factors are important here: (1) hormonal, and (2) chemicals in food (Darr and McCay, 1947). Fish culturists have found that certain foods will produce coloration in trout, e.g., freshwater shrimps, salmon eggs, and salmon oil (Komari, 1940). Astacin ($3,4,3',4'$-tetraketo-$\beta$-carotene) and astaxanthin ($5,5'$-dihydroxy-$4,4'$-diketo-$\beta$-carotene) are two carotenoid pigments derived from shrimp responsible for the coloration of many fish. Goldfish appear to be unable to utilize astaxanthin as the precursor for body color although they can utilize carotene and lutein (Hiro *et al.*, 1963). Several other foodstuffs that have been used in practical diets have been shown to cause pigmentation in trout, e.g., corn gluten, alfalfa meal, and dried hen eggs, all rich sources of xanthophyll, caused yellow pigmentation in brown trout. Summer and Fox (1935) also showed that diets rich in carotene and xanthophyll increased the xanthophyll content of fish. Herring gull eggs are also valuable sources of pigmentation for the coloration of trout. Feeding trials with brook trout fingerlings receiving herring gull eggs showed that coloration appeared as early as 2 weeks after the diet was started and gradually increased in intensity until the trout resembled wild trout (Darr and McCay, 1947). Paprika also seems to be a valuable source for providing utilizable pigments in the diet of fish. Paprika, when incorporated into the diet containing fresh pork spleen, colors trout as well as a diet consisting of 100% gull eggs (Darr and McCay, 1947). Tunison *et al.* (1944) also demonstrated the usefulness of paprika in the diet for coloring trout. Diets containing 2% paprika appeared to be optimal from the standpoint of color produced. Coloration was obtained in 4–6 weeks and this increased with time. A 10% level of paprika in the diet produced brilliant color in the fish and was nontoxic when fed for a period of 24 weeks. However, there does appear to be a species difference in the ability of trout to utilize paprika for coloration. Phillips *et al.* (1945) showed that diets containing paprika caused a marked coloration in brook trout in a short period, whereas brown trout were only slightly colored over a much longer period; rainbow trout showed no coloration.

## E. Fish Toxins and Toxic Algae

Halstead (1965) has reviewed all the knowledge available up to 1964 in the area of marine zootoxicology. As the activities of the various fishing fleets expands into the tropical areas, especially the tropical Pacific areas that are well known for tropical poisonous marine species, the possible use of these fish as sources of protein in feeds for domesticated fish increases. Classifications of fish toxins have been based on poisonings in humans and taxonomic classification of the fish species involved. Banner and Helfrich (1964) have suggested classification of fish poisoning into five major groups based on taxonomic classification of the fishes involved as follows: (1) puffer fish, (2) scombroid fish, (3) clupeoid fish, (4) mullet and submullet, and (5) numerous unrelated fish found in the very limited region of coral reefs in tropical areas (*Ciguatera*). The nature and properties of the toxic substances of puffer fish and scombroid fish have been studied in great detail. The others are less well known. The toxic substance of puffer fish, tetrodotoxin, has been isolated, its chemical structure determined, and its physiological properties studied in great detail (Yudkin, 1944; Mosher *et al.*, 1964; Tsuda *et al.*, 1960).

Scombroid fish toxins are not present in live fish but are caused by the action of bacteria on the flesh of freshly caught fish (Kimata, 1961). The toxin is formed by the action of certain strains of *Proteus morganii* on the histidine in the scombroid fish: tuna, swordfish, and mackerel type fish (Kawabata *et al.*, 1955) with the production of histamine and a possible synergistic agent known as saurine.

Fish causing ciguatera poisoning appeared to be most common in the Pacific and those most commonly involved include snappers (Lutjanidae), groupers (Serranidae), barracuda (Sphyraena), and surgeon fish (Acanthuridae). Studies on the occurrence of ciguatera and the changes in the pattern of toxicity over various periods indicate that the fish become toxic due to factors in their environment (Banner and Helfrich, 1964).

It has been suggested that the ultimate source of toxin may be the blue-green algae (Dawson *et al.*, 1955) which is passed on through the food chain to the larger carnivores. However, investigation of the algae, *Lingbya*, the toxic algae found in the area where ciguatera poisoning is common, has indicated that it is unlikely that toxins from algae and in fish are the same (Banner *et al.*, 1960). At present there is little known about the structure of the ciguatera poisons. However, their physiological action has been studied, and they appear to be powerful cholinesterase inhibitors (Li, 1965). Banner *et al.* (1960) studied the effect of feeding toxic ciguatera fish flesh to fish and other animals. It was found to be toxic to crayfish but had no effect on guppies, swordfish, silversides, or surgeon fish. The same preparation was nontoxic to the various species of mammals tested. However, it should be noted that the toxic factor of toxic ciguatera fish is concentrated mainly in the viscera and only smaller amounts occur in the muscle.

Poisoning is associated with a variety of clupeoid fish and does not appear to be widespread. Nothing is known about the nature of very potent toxin present except that it produces quite different physiological responses than the other toxins.

Mullet and submullet poisoning occurs seasonally (June to August) in limited areas of the Pacific. Nothing is known about the mild toxin present in these species. However, it is possible that this toxin may be derived via the food chain or may be a special substance produced during part of the life cycle of the fish.

Kingsbury (1964) gives a brief but complete summary of the toxic marine and freshwater algae. Halstead (1965) has reviewed the phylum, *Protozoa*, and their relationship to shellfish poisoning. Dinoflagellates are minute, pigmented, flagellated, single-celled organisms which swim in the upper layers of oceanic waters as members of the plankton. Zoologists classify them among the flagellated protozoa because they are motile and may ingest particulate food, whereas, botanists classify them among the algae and treat them as a division of the plant kingdom since they contain photosynthetic pigments.

Among the various species of blue-green algae that may be found in almost any natural body of water certain of these species have the ability to grow very rapidly in great quantity, to "bloom." Certain of the "bloom" forming blue-green algae are toxic. "Blooms" of toxic dinoflagellates are triggered by unknown hydrographic factors which are quite random in time and location and appear to be associated with upwelling of deeper water along the shore. Since the "blooms" are usually composed of mixtures of several species it has been difficult to classify and identify specifically which species are the toxic ones. Because of the varying and changing composition of these natural "blooms" of blue-green algae it has been difficult to extract and identify a toxic principle. However, it is clear that more than one toxic compound is involved. In studies where *Microcystis aeruginosa* were cultured artificially at least four different toxic factors were produced. Three of these were bacterial in origin and unidentified. The fourth, called the fast-death factor, is algal in origin and has been identified as a cyclic polypeptide containing seven amino acids (aspartic acid, glutamic acid, serine, valine, ornithine, alanine, and leucine).

Extensive mortality and morbidity of livestock, pets, wild animals, and human beings has been associated with algal "blooms" in the United States, especially in the northern half and the southern provinces of Canada and in many other countries. Fish are also affected adversely by these toxic algal "blooms." Poisoning does not occur unless a dense "bloom" of toxic organisms has formed and a toxic material has thus been concentrated.

Ingestion of toxic microorganisms by mollusks and other marine animals results in toxic fish and shellfish. Shellfish poisoning is of such serious magnitude that at some times it has threatened the complete shutdown of the shellfish industry from southern California to Alaska and occasionally on the east coast at the Bay of Fundy and the mouth of the St. Lawrence River. The problem has been reviewed most recently by Halstead (1965). Hundreds of cases of severe poisoning and death of human beings and serious poisoning of pets, livestock, and wild animals have been recorded since the first observation of the disease on the west coast in 1798. Intensive study followed an epidemic of poisoning by shellfish on the shores of California in 1927. This poisoning is different from food poisoning caused by spoiled shellfish since a specific toxic substance is present in healthy shellfish. Mussels, clams, scallops, other mollusks, and invertebrates, including crabs, have been found to contain the toxic principle in dangerous amounts. Toxicity of a particular mollusk population depends on the presence, concentration and intrinsic toxicity of a dinoflagellate bloom, selectivity of the species of mollusk, length of time over which the toxin has been concentrated by the mollusk, and speed of excretion of the toxin. Mollusks feed by a rather unselective filtering mechanism and when toxic dinoflagellates are present in abundance they are filtered out of the seawater, digested, and their toxin accumulated in the different tissues of the mollusk in varying concentrations. Some mollusks concentrate it in the viscera, others in the siphon. The white meat of any mollusk is usually lowest in toxicity. Mollusks may contain toxic levels of the poison within a day or so after a "bloom" appears and the rate at which toxicity is lost varies greatly with the type of mollusk. This process is much slower than is accumulation and usually requires up to a month or longer for reduction to decrease below the dangerous level. Mollusks are immune to the toxin but fish are not.

Fish mortality associated with the presence of a conspicuous red dinoflagellate bloom has been reported sporadically along the west coast of Florida from 1844 to the present. Turtles, barnacles, oysters, shrimp, crabs, dolphins, and other animals have been killed in addition to fish. In this case the toxicity was associated with another species of dinoflagellate, *Gymnodinium brevis* (Davis, 1948).

The dinoflagellate responsible for poison accumulation in the Californian mussels and Alaska butter clams is *Gonyaulax catenella*. It has been demonstrated by Burke *et al.* (1960) that the toxin contained in the cell of the dinoflagellate is the same as is found in the toxic shellfish. *Gonyaulax tamarensis* produces the identical toxin. The poison has been isolated and characterized by Schantz (1961). Hypothetical chemical structures based on present knowledge of the chemical properties of the purified shellfish toxin have been suggested and are reported by Halstead (1965). The toxin is similar to curare in its effects and is extremely toxic to warm-blooded animals. The lethal dose for a human being may be contained in less than a one-half dozen clams. The toxin seems to be different from the one produced by *Gymnodinium brevis* that is responsible for the massive fish mortality off the Florida coast. Gymnodinium "blooms" are rapidly toxic to fish and other marine animals. Fish have been observed to die almost immediately after swimming into an area of dinoflagellate concentration.

The yellow-green dinoflagellate *Prymnesium parvum* lives in seawater and in brackish water. When blooms of this organism occur, materials are released that are toxic to fish and other branchiate animals in brackish waters. In countries where fish are cultured in fish ponds, *Prymnesium* causes great damage to the fish breeding industry. The toxin produced affects mammals also. After intoxication the animal exhibits sensory block and motor paralysis with death apparently due to respiratory failure. The future survival and expansion of carp breeding in brackish water areas in Israel largely depends on the successful control of this organism. Shiloh and Rosenburger (1960) have reviewed the studies on toxic principles formed by the *Prymnesium parvum*. Recently Parnas and Abbot (1965) have reported work on the physiological activity and mechanism of action of this toxin. The toxin is different from those reported for other neurotoxins produced by dinoflagellates and some resemblances between the *Prymnesium* toxins and saponins have been pointed out.

The larger seaweeds, particularly brown algae, have been fed to farm animals and commercial supplements made from seaweed have been used beneficially in animal diets, but occasionally specific difficulties have been associated with such seaweed diets (Kingsbury, 1964). For example, a disease in lambs from ewes that have fed heavily on seaweed during pregnancy has been recognized in Iceland (Palsson and Grimsson, 1953). The giant kelp of the Pacific, *Macrocystis pyrifera*, one of the brown algae used in food supplements, also have been shown to contain a moderately toxic principle (Habkosterc *et al.*, 1955).

## F. NATURALLY OCCURRING ANTIBIOTICS IN FOODS

This subject has recently been reviewed in detail by Marth (1966). The use of antibiotics in food preservation has received serious study and consideration and has been approved for certain specific cases like the addition of chlorotetracycline to iced fish. The presence of a large variety of antibiotic substances in foods as they are usually available is not generally recognized and there is little awareness or knowledge of the potential effects of the minor food components. Marth (1966) has reviewed the reports and evidence for the presence of antibiotic substances in onion, garlic, horseradish, banana, sweet potato, cabbage, radish, and a variety of other vegetables such as snap beans, beets, tomatoes, cauliflower, peas, peppers, rhubarb, spinach, brussels sprouts, pea pods, carrots, green beans, tomatoes, celery, okra, chicory, cucumbers, sweet corn, turnip, chard, potato leaves, strawberries, apples, cherries, grapefruit, peaches, pineapple, plums, avocado, and cereals such as rye, wheat, and barley. The value of spices in the preservation of foods has long been realized but specific factors responsible for their inhibitory action against microorganisms have been recognized more recently and include such compounds as $\alpha$-pinene, $\alpha$-terpineol, linalool, geraniol, carvacrol, thymol, isoborneol, salicylaldehyde, anethole, borneol, citral, citronellol, citronellal, limonene, and menthol.

Antimicrobial activity and antifungal activity have been associated with egg white, specifically with the avidin, lysozyme and/or conalbumin fractions. Milk freshly drawn from the normal cow udder contains several substances able to inhibit different organisms. One investigator found milk, whey, and a whey dialyzate able to inhibit *Mycobacterium tuberculosis*. Honey has been used since ancient times to aid in the healing of wounds and several workers have shown that natural unheated honey shows antibacterial activity. Practical application of these observations has been proposed in several instances; for example, the use of the antibiotic from avocados for the preservation of foods has been suggested. The antibiotic from wheat bran has been suggested for use in prevention of brown spots on stored lemon. A pickling solution fortified with antimicrobial substances recovered from iris bulbs, dried sage, and Canadian thistle or bloodroot has been suggested for use in the quick curing of meats. As more knowledge in this area develops and useful practical applications become apparent, it may be expected that many of these minor components will appear in foodstuffs and feeds in larger concentrations than they may occur at the present time. An alertness to the presence of such components in feeds must be maintained in order to ensure that the amount in foods does not exceed the level of benefit and reach into the level of potential hazard.

## III.  Adventitious Components of Foodstuffs (Food Contaminants)

### A.  ACCUMULATION OF SOIL ELEMENTS

For many years, beginning before the Civil War, animals in certain sections of the middle west suffered from a disease called alkali disease or blind staggers according to the symptoms observed. Franke (1934) showed that the disease was related to the consumption of grain grown on certain soils. Many cooperative investigations between the South Dakota Agricultural Experiment Station and several bureaus in the U.S. Department of Agriculture revealed the significance of selenium as a toxic factor in food (Garner, 1961; Yearbook of Agriculture, 1962). Selenium occurs in the soil in both inorganic and organic compounds, not all of which are available to plants. Where selenium poisoning occurs the selenium content of the soil is about 1 to 6 ppm, although values as high as 324 ppm have been reported. The danger to livestock results from the accumulation of selenium by certain plants. Such accumulator plants, also called indicator plants, thrive best on seleniferous soils and commonly contain 2000–6000 ppm of selenium with values as high as 15,000 ppm also reported. The accumulator plants, mainly *Astragalus* spp., in addition to causing selenium poisoning when eaten, also contribute directly to the uptake of Se by other species that do not normally accumulate it. They can take up selenium which seems to be unavailable to ordinary forage plants and convert it to a form which, when returned to the soil by their decomposition, can be absorbed by the forage plants. Cereal grains grown on such areas will contain toxic amounts of selenium. The organic selenium compounds in such toxic grains are about twice as toxic as the inorganic selenides or selenites.

A detailed study of the relationship between selenium content of the soil and numerous species of plants grown in these soils has been made by Williams *et al.* (1941) and Hamilton and Beath (1963a,b, 1964). Selenium in animal feeds should not exceed 5 ppm. Although selenium is now known to be an essential nutrient, at least for cattle and sheep, and some areas selenium deficiency is an important problem, the required level of 0.1 ppm is well below any hazardous level. Selenium in wheat and other food crops is an example of a plant constituent which is difficult to classify. According to our convention, there is no doubt that contents high enough to be toxic represent an unwanted contaminant of a food product.

Although selenium is recognized as an essential element in mammals and chicks and the toxic reactions to excess selenium have been studied in great detail, no information is available as to the necessity or toxicity of inorganic or organically bound selenium to fishes. Because of its probable function as an antioxidant and the high concentration of unsaturated fats in fish, one would expect that the addition of adequate amounts of selenium to the diet of fish should be beneficial.

Schutte (1964) has listed plants that have the ability to accumulate large amounts of certain elements without apparent ill effect to the plant itself. Among the elements which are accumulated are aluminum (Al), boron (B), barium (Ba), copper (Cu), fluorine (F), lithium (Li), manganese (Mn), nickel (Ni), uranium (U), molybdenum (Mo), vanadium (V), and zinc (Zn). Certain plants accumulate nickel, selenium, and zinc in amounts that would be lethal to other plant species, e.g., *Alyssum bertolonii* accumulates nickel in concentrations up to 15,000 ppm, *Astragalus racemosus* accumulates selenium to concentrations of 15,000 ppm, and *Thlaspi calaminae* has been found with 20% zinc oxide in its ash.

Molybdenum is another element that is accumulated by plants, particularly by leguminous plants, on soils rich in this element. Accumulation of molybdenum is promoted by a poorly drained alkaline soil. Ordinarily soils containing more than 5 ppm molybdenum are considered potentially dangerous, although some soils, as in the Everglades, cause trouble at 3 ppm or less. The effect observed in animals depends on the copper content of the soil as well as on the molybdenum content. Abnormally low molybdenum in soils of normal copper content supports forage which promotes copper accumulation in animals and, eventually, development of symptoms of copper poisoning and even death. Abnormally high molybdenum of normal copper content result in forage which depletes the copper reserves of animals over a period of time and results in development of symptoms of copper deficiency. The same effect is observed on soils of moderate molybdenum content but low copper content. Copper and molybdenum are antagonistic in animal nutrition but this effect is influenced by the inorganic sulfate content of the forage and by other factors such as the protein content of the diet. However, in cattle the molybdenosis observed is not exactly equivalent to copper deficiency and is associated selectively with particular kinds of forage which have greater accumulating capacity for molybdenum than others (Kingsbury, 1964).

Numerous studies have shown that under certain environmental conditions a large variety of weeds and crop plants may accumulate high levels of nitrates. Kingsbury (1964) lists forty-seven species of weeds and twenty-one varieties of crop plants in which toxic concentrations of nitrates have been measured. These include corn, wheat, rye, alfalfa, lettuce, barley, carrot, turnip, broccoli and kale, rape, oat hay, beets, mangels, etc. Plants containing more than 1.5% nitrate (as $KNO_3$ dry weight) may prove lethal to livestock. Sublethal poisoning has been caused by ingestion of food containing between 0.5 and 1.5% nitrate. The tendency of various crop plants to accumulate nitrate varies markedly with the content and form of nitrogen in the soil, both before and after fertilization. In addition, the kinds and amounts of other ions present also determine the capacity of the soil to supply nitrates to accumulating plants. Nitrate accumulation is increased by various growth conditions such as drought and decreased light. Nitrate accumulates in vegetative tissues; the grain usually remains safe. The use of the herbicide 2,4-D has been shown to cause an accumulation of toxic quantities of nitrate in certain species of weeds and crop plants (Stahler and Whitehead, 1950). Sugar beet tops, oat hay, corn, sorghum, and pigweed have been shown to be affected. In addition, normally toxic plants such as pigweed, *Amaranthus* spp., ragweed, *Ambroxia* spp., and jimson weed, *Datura stramonium*, which are not normally eaten by cattle, are readily eaten after treatment with 2,4-D. Sheep appeared to be extremely susceptible to high levels of nitrate. The physiological effect and mode of action of nitrate toxicity have been reviewed by Sinclair and Jones (1963). The problem may be specific for ruminant animals following the reduction of nitrate to nitrite by the rumen microorganisms. Under certain circumstances nitrites may be ingested directly. Bacterial denitrification from nitrate to nitrite may occur in haystacks under conditions of unusually high moisture.

## B. SANITATION

The contamination of foodstuffs by microorganisms represents not only a hazard to health because of the potential pathogenic nature of the contaminating organism, but represents also a source of new components added to the food, some of which may be very potent physiologically. That food and feed, particularly when contaminated by filth and insects, can serve as efficient vectors for disease is well known and is one of the first possibilities to be considered when investigation of a new epizootic or epidemic disease is begun. Although control measures have been developed in the last 60 years to deal with the problem of contamination of foods by pathogenic microorganisms, e.g., heat processing of canned food, pasteurization of milk, refrigeration, meat inspection, and examination of foods for filth, they have not altogether served to control the hazard, as is attested to by the continuing incidence of food-borne diseases. In this country staphylococcal infections have long been the major source of food poisonings, whereas in England *Salmonella* contamination provided the greatest reservoir of such incidents. However, salmonellosis, excluding typhoid fever, has become a rather serious problem to the food and feed supply in this country and seems to be increasing (Slocum, 1963). *Salmonella* are common in pigs, poultry, and rodents and are also sometimes found in various wild mammals, birds, and reptiles (Joint WHO/FAO Expert Committee on Zoonoses, 1959). These organisms, which may contaminate foodstuffs, are carried in the intestines in healthy livestock, poultry, and rodents. Foods most commonly contaminated with *Salmonella* include meat and meat products, eggs and egg products, milk and milk products, and fish (Allison, 1963). The appearance, smell, and taste of the food remains unaltered following contamination. The normal ways in which food can become contaminated with this organism have been listed by Dewbery (1959) as follows: (a) intravital infection of animals, (b) failure to pasteurize milk from infected cows, (c) infection of eggs in the oviduct or by contamination of eggs by feces, (d) food contamination in an already contaminated area, (e) use of contaminated egg products, (f) contamination with feces from contaminated rodents, (g) contamination with organisms from flies and other arthropods, and (h) contamination by human excreta. Thatcher (1966) has recently reviewed the food-borne bacterial toxins. He discussed botulism emphasizing the recent problems raised by the recognition in this country of botulinum type E which can produce this very potent toxin at 5°C. This becomes important for so-called semiperishable items or foods in which the storage situation creates anaerobic conditions, either for the whole food batch or for microenvironmental portions. He points out also that, in addition to staphylococcal food poisoning, other bacteria as *Clostridium perfringens* and *Bacillus cereus*, a group of bacteria known as the pathogenic halophiles, represent a particular problem in countries, such as Japan, where uncooked fish is consumed. A prototype of this group is gram-negative pleomorphic rods originally named *Pseudomonas enteritis*. The enteric cocci, *Streptococcus faecalis* and *S. faecium*, have also been reported to be involved in food poisoning as well as *Proteus* and *Escherichia coli*.

## C. Chlorinated Naphthalenes

A new disease of cattle first observed in the early forties was called "X" disease because of its obscure etiology (Garner, 1961). In view of the characteristic tissue changes the term hyperkeratosis is now universally used. The condition has been shown to be caused by the chlorinated naphthalenes and has been reproduced experimentally by administering tri-, penta-, hexa-, and octachloronaphthalene. It appears that the higher the degree of chlorination the greater is the hyperkeratosis-producing property of the compound. These compounds are widely used as components in lubricating oils and in wood preservatives. Outbreaks of hyperkeratosis (one estimate placed the losses up to 1953 in excess of $20 million) have been traced to contamination of feedstuffs where the lubricating oil in the mixing or pelleting machinery has been allowed to contaminate the feed or where, during harvesting, the oil from the farm machinery has contaminated the crop. These compounds are highly toxic to all species and are excreted in the milk of cows. Undoubtedly, after elucidation of the chlorinated naphthalenes-hyperkeratosis relationship there must have been a tendency to ascribe every case of disease to poisoning by these compounds. There is some evidence that even for symptoms of hyperkeratosis there may be occasionally a different etiology. Infestation by toxic species of *Aspergillus* has been implicated in at least two cases by Carll *et al.* (1954).

## D. Chick Edema Factor

In 1957 an epizootic disease caused millions of dollars in losses among broiler flocks throughout a large part of the United States. After successive elimination of all other possibilities the etiological factor was shown to be a toxic substance in the fat of the ration. Autopsy findings revealed hydropericardium, abdominal ascites, subcutaneous edema, swollen liver, swollen and pale kidneys, etc. Laying hens showed a rapid drop in egg production. Hydropericardium, the most common lesion in young birds, was not found in birds of laying age. Guinea pigs, dogs, pigs, rats, and monkeys also showed deleterious effects when fed toxic fat (Friedman, 1962). Highly purified concentrates produce characteristic symptoms in young chicks at dietary levels of 50 ppb. The source of this factor is still unknown. It has been found only in fatty by-products from the production of fatty acids and occurs at sporadic intervals. Its chemistry suggests that it is probably derived in the course of industrial production of chlorinated compounds and may possibly be distributed as a contaminant in some useful agricultural chemical. Cantrell *et al.* (1969) elucidated the structure of one of the components of a purified chick edema concentrate as a hexachlorodibenzo-*p*-dioxin. Tetrachlorodibenzo-*p*-dioxin is probably the most toxic of the family of polychlorodibenzo-*p*-dioxins and has been a troublesome contaminant, although present in ppb, of the herbicide 2,4,5-T.

### E. Minamata Disease

Another example of unintentional food contamination is the so-called "Minamata disease" which was observed among persons living in the vicinity of Minamata Bay in Japan in 1953 (Gerarde, 1964). This is a neurological disease characterized by severe brain and other central nervous system lesions. Some eighty-three cases have been reported, most of which were fatal or involved permanent disability. The toxic agent in these episodes was found to be a mercury-contaminated material coming from the effluent of a large chemical manufacturing plant which emptied into the bay. The toxic substance accumulated in the tissues of fish and shellfish, thereby entering the regular food supply of the Minamata village population. A ban on local fishing was necessary to eliminate the incidence of this disease. (See Addendum.)

## IV. Components Resulting from Technology

### A. Food Additives

Chemicals have played a primary role in the development of the modern food industry which makes possible an adequate diet for city dwellers in our highly developed urbanized culture. The chemicals used in food processing in the United States have been surveyed recently by the Food Protection Committee of the National Academy of Sciences (1965). Every chemical used in food processing, they point out, should serve one or more of these purposes: improve nutritional value, enhance quality or consumer acceptability, improve the keeping quality, make the food more readily available, or facilitate its preparation. The more important classes of substances include: acids, alkalis, buffers and neutralizing agents, bleaching and maturing agents, bread improvers, emulsifying, stabilizing and thickening agents, flavoring materials, food colors, nutrient supplements, preservatives, antioxidants, artificial sweeteners, clarifying agents such as tannins and albumin, sequestering agents such as EDTA and salts, humectants such as glycerine, propylene glycol and sorbitol, glazers and polishers such as waxes and gum benzoin, anticaking agents such as magnesium carbonate and tricalcium phosphate, texture improvers such as calcium chloride, nitrates and nitrites in the curing of meats, a variety of gases such as nitrogen, carbon dioxide, and nitrous oxide in pressure packed containers.

In the case of animal feeds, the major focus is on nutrient demands, and additives are designed to provide essential nutrients that may be missing from common, economical ration ingredients. In addition, various forms of preservatives, mainly antioxidants, and medication which may be classed broadly as growth-promoting substances, and drugs for prophylactic or therapeutic purposes may be added.

Because of the problem of autooxidation of unsaturated fatty acid in the feed and/or the stress that may be placed on an animal fed with a diet rich in unsaturated fatty acids, the addition of a suitable antioxidant may be necessary. Vitamin E ($\alpha$-tocopherol) is probably the most suitable. Commercially produced antioxidants, namely, butylated hydroxytoluene (BHT or 3,5-di-*t*-butyl-4-hydroxytoluene), butylated hydroxyanisole (BHA or 3-*t*-butyl-4-hydroxyanisole), or propyl gallate may also be used. However, BHT and BHA may not be without adverse effects, as high doses of these compounds appear to be capable of producing liver enlargement (Gilbert and Golberg, 1965; Gaunt *et al.*, 1965). The use of antioxidants is limited to animal fats, because at the approved level of use there is no protection of vegetable oil products (Moore and Bickford, 1952). In order to evaluate the necessity of adding antioxidants to the diet, studies should be made of the level of the compounds present in the feed and in the resulting animal tissues. This may be extremely important in fish, because of the high percentage of unsaturated fatty acids present in the tissues.

Nutritional supplements may include vitamins, trace elements, amino acids, and natural sources of pigments such as xanthophylls or carotene. These natural ingredients should not be hazardous if added in the proper amount. However, the amount of nutrient can be increased to potentially dangerous levels, e.g., large excesses of vitamin A or D or essential amino acids (Halver, 1953; Harper, 1956; Allison, 1958).

The most widely used growth-promoting substances are antibiotics such as the chlorotetracyclines, penicillin, bacitracin, and streptomycin (Creek and Schumaier, 1960). Numerous suggestions have been made as to the mode of action of the antibiotic growth promotants. These may be summarized as either an effect on the microflora in the intestinal tract of the animal or an effect on the tissues and organs of the animal (Luckey, 1959). The growth-promoting effect of antibiotics varies with species, age, nutritional status, and environment. Other substances that seem to give growth stimulation in domestic animals when used at low dietary levels include tranquilizing drugs, sulfa drugs, and arsenilic acid and its derivatives (Bird *et al.*, 1949). Arsenilic acid seems to be particularly effective in stimulating the growth of chickens and pigs when used at levels that do not show bacteriostatic activity (Frost and Spouth, 1956). Wagner (1954) studied the effect of antibiotics and arsenilic acid on the growth of rainbow trout fingerlings. Aureomycin, Terramycin, penicillin, Chloromycetin, and arsenilic acid were added singly to the diet at a rate of 10 mg/lb of feed. None of the fish in the group fed antibiotics gained weight as rapidly as the control group. The fish fed aureomycin and penicillin actually lost weight during the first 2 weeks of the diet. Similar failure to stimulate weight increase has been reported by Malikova and Kotova (1964) who studied the effect of addition of biomycin, penicillin, and Terramycin to the diet of salmon, *Salmo salar*, and by Schumacher (1955) who studied the addition of Aureomycin and Aureomycin plus thiamine to the diet of brown trout fingerlings. Snieszko and Wood (1954) studied the effects of sulfonamides on the growth of various species of trout. None of the sulfonamides used had any effect on rainbow trout. Growth of brook trout was retarded but returned to normal when medicated feed was replaced by normal feed.

Another class of substances has been used as growth promoters. These are the hormones, particularly those possessing estrogenic activity, and they have been used for promoting weight increase in meat-producing animals. Diethylstilbestrol is administered to cattle, either orally or as an implant. The general effect of diethylstilbestrol in ruminant species has been summarized by Kastelic (1963). It produces cytological changes in the anterior pituitary which may result in altered production of gonadotrophic hormones, growth hormones, and thyroid-stimulating hormones. The growth effect in different species is quite different, e.g., the primary effect in avians appears to be an enhanced deposition of fat, whereas ruminants exhibit increased protein anabolism and reduced fat deposition (Hinds, 1959). Studies with hydrocortisone have indicated that vertebrates above the level of amphibians show certain responses that are not observed at the level of amphibian and below.

For disease control, many of the same antibiotics and other compounds utilized as growth promotants are used at much higher levels. The substances and the conditions under which they may be used in feeds are described in the Food Additive Regulations of the Food and Drug Administration, Subpart C, Additives Permitted in Feed and Drinking Water of Animals or for the Treatment of Food Producing Animals, Code of Federal Regulations, Section 121.200, etc. (Regulations under the Federal Food, Drug and Cosmetic Act, Code of Federal Regulations, Title 21, Chapter 1, Part 121, Subpart C). Some aspects of the use of antimicrobials (sulfonamides, antibiotics, and nitrofurans) in therapy of bacterial disease has been reviewed by Wolf and Snieszko (1963). The authors pay particular attention to the problem of regulating fish therapy from the point of view of both fish producers and consumers. At that time sulfamerazine was the only drug which could be used as a fish food additive.

## B. Agricultural Chemical Residues

Because of the ever increasing use of chemicals in agriculture, there is a long list varying in nature from simple inorganic and organic substances to extremely complex organic compounds representing a wide range of chemical structures and physiological activities that may occur in foodstuffs as residues. In addition to the direct toxic action of these substances on fishes, there is the problem of possible accumulation in fish flesh which may render the fish unsuitable as food for humans or animals.

The most dramatic use of chemicals in recent years has been the use of organic pesticides and herbicides. The principal chemicals used in this group are organic phosphates, carbamates, and halogenated hydrocarbons. Because of the possible hazards that may arise following misuse of these substances, the F.D.A. has established tolerances for residues of the chemicals in a large variety of food crops. Some examples are given in Table I. The residues relate to the amount of material that may be present following harvest.

The fate of pesticides following administration on plants has been the subject of widespread research. Crafts and Foy (1962) have discussed how both polar and nonpolar pesticides may enter plant tissues. The survival of the pesticide on or in the plant tissue may be affected by many physical and biochemical processes. The pesticide may be removed from the plant

TABLE I

Tolerances in or on Raw Agricultural Commodities[a]

|  | Methoxychlor (ppm) | Heptachlor (ppm) | Parathion (ppm) | Malathion (ppm) | Endrin |
|---|---|---|---|---|---|
| Alfalfa | 100 | 0.1 | 1 | 8 | 0 |
| Clover | 100 | 0.1 | 1 | 8 | 0 |
| Beans | 14 | 0.1 | 1 | 8 | 0 |
| Peanuts | 14 | 0.1 | 1 | — | 0 |
| Wheat |  | 0.1 | 1 | 8 | 0 |
| Sorghum grain |  | 0.1 | — | — | 0 |

[a] Taken from Interagency Coordination in Environmental Hazards (Pesticides) 1963, part 2, p. 764.

by external weathering processes such as rain, wind, or ultraviolet radiation. Pesticides that enter the plant system may be acted upon by a variety of enzymes giving rise to various products which may be more or less toxic than the original material. Koivistoinen *et al.* (1964) have shown that malathion residues on apples and beans disappear rapidly either under field conditions or postharvest conditions. In this case, most of the pesticide must have entered the fruit and been decomposed by the action of enzymes. Animals exposed to chlorinated pesticides tend to accumulate them in the body fat. Marth (1965) has reviewed the literature related to residues and the effects of chlorinated insecticides in biological material. The problem of the potentiation of pesticides by each other which was first noted by Frawley *et al.* (1957) in the case of the two cholinesterase inhibitors EPN (ethyl *p*-nitrophenyl thionobenzenephosphate) and malathion is a matter of continuing concern.

The residues may also be derived from plant growth regulators and herbicides, e.g., maleic hydrazide, which has been used as a herbicide and to control the sprouting of potatoes; and also a large number of chlorophenoxy-type compounds. However, these compounds do not seem to pose a great hazard for mammals because they are fairly quickly metabolized in plants and show a low toxicity in mammals. No information is available as to their effect on fish.

Growth promotants and drugs used in animal feeds are permitted only under conditions of use that will not allow *any* residues of those residues considered to be unsafe for human food. It should be noted parenthetically that many animal products considered legally and by usual practice as inedible and not suitable for human consumption have in the past been devoted for animal feed uses, e.g., animals that have died otherwise than by slaughter, products of rendering plants, etc. One must consider the possibility that animal products to be used for animal feed, and this includes fish food, may sometimes contain fairly large quantities of product derived from such sources. Occasionally these may contain unexpected amounts of hazardous components.

## C. Toxic Substances from Food Processing

Examples where a compound used in the processing of a foodstuff, although leaving no demonstrable residue, did leave an indelible imprint are provided by certain food additives. Mellanby (1946) showed that wheat flour that had been treated with the conditioner and bleach, nitrogen trichloride, or Agene, as it was then called, produced symptoms in dogs which were indistinguishable from canine hysteria, a disease, until then, of unknown etiology. The toxic principle, methionine sulfoximine (Misani and Reiner, 1950) was associated with the protein of the flour and was isolated from treated wheat gluten. It is produced by the action of nitrogen trichloride on methionine. This substance, to which dogs and cats are particularly sensitive, is an antimetabolite to methionine and interferes, among other things, with glutamic acid metabolism in brain tissue (Pace and McDermott, 1952).

Trichloroethylene provides another interesting example of the formation of a toxic derivative by a processing agent. Stockman (1916) established that soybean meal extracted with trichloroethylene was toxic to cattle, producing an aplastic anemia, whereas extraction with other solvents produced a harmless meal. The solvent itself does not produce the toxic syndrome. The active principle is produced by an interaction of the trichloroethylene with the protein of the meal and according to the work of McKinney *et al.* (1959) it is probably the S-dichlorovinyl derivative of L-cysteine and L-glutathione. Extraction of fish meal with 1,2-dichloroethane results in a marked destruction of cysteine and histidine, giving rise to a compound that is metabollically inert (Morrison and Munro, 1965).

The fumigant ethylene oxide is an example of a substance that produces deleterious effects by reacting chemically with food components. In this case, several of the essential nutrients are destroyed, e.g., thiamine, niacin, riboflavin, pyridoxine, folic acid, and probably also histidine and methionine (Hawk and Mickelsen, 1955; Windmueller *et al.*, 1959). However, there is substantial evidence for the safety of methyl bromide as a fumigant. Although methyl bromide can react with histidine residues in proteins, the amount of histidine lost during fumigation is so small that the nutritive value of the wheat is hardly changed (Bridges, 1955; Winteringham *et al.*, 1955). The hazard in these examples is nutritional deficiency rather than specific toxicoses.

Sulfur dioxide gas is also used as a food preserver. It shows low toxicity (615 ppm for rats) but there is ample evidence that sulfur dioxide destroys the thiamine content of foodstuffs (DeEds, 1961). In addition, Miller *et al.* (1955) have shown that the presence of sulfite in the diet may accelerate the development of oxidative rancidity which, in the case of chicks maintained on these diets, resulted in an increase in the occurrence and severity of vitamin E deficiency syndromes.

Other examples of formation of new substances during processing may be drawn from traditional or usual methods of food preparation. In rural areas of Iceland it is customary to preserve mutton and fish by a heavy smoking process. The foods after such treatment have been found to contain significant quantities of 3,4-benzpyrene and to have produced malignant tumors when fed experimentally to rats. Among the human population in Iceland that consumed these foods in substantial quantities over long periods of time gastric carcinoma has been common, being recorded as the cause of death in about 35% of all necropsies (Dungal, 1961). Recently Lijinsky and Shubik (1964) showed that steaks broiled over charcoal in the usual manner showed the presence of fifteen polynuclear hydrocarbons presumably formed by pyrolysis of melting fat dripping onto the hot coals. Most notable among the compounds formed was benz-$\alpha$-pyrene, a known carcinogen.

Another example of formation of unusual compounds during food preparation is represented by the prolonged heating of fats and oils such as in deep fat frying. Firestone *et al.* (1961) have shown that prolonged heating of cooking oil at high temperatures results in the formation of fatty acid monomers and dimers which are unusual in their failure to form urea adducts. These substances are only of slight toxicity acutely (Friedman *et al.* 1961). Probably of greater significance is the finding by Sugai *et al.* (1962) that these nonadducting fatty acids seem to be cocarcinogenic in chronic rat feeding studies. These examples emphasize that we know too little about degradation products that may be formed during processing. This is particularly true of the various residues of antioxidants, preservatives, emulsifiers, pesticides, etc., that are now an inevitable part of the food supply.

## D. Deteriorative Changes

### 1. *Lipid Peroxidation*

The most important change that occurs in foods and feeds resulting in new components is autooxidation of the unsaturated fatty acids. Peroxides, hydroperoxides, epoxides, and isomerized, polymerized, and hydroxylated compounds are formed during oxidation. Rancidification of the fat in the diet is accompanied by the presence of these substances and the incorporation of rancid fat in an animal diet may have marked effects on growth. Rao (1960) has summarized the effects observed when aerated or oxidized fats are included in the diet. The deleterious effects of rancid fats are due, on the one hand, to the deterioration of the vitamin E and vitamin A content and, on the other, to the development of new compounds that have toxic properties. Kaunitz *et al.* (1952) consider it unlikely that the toxic effects are due to the presence of peroxides or breakdown products. They have shown that the peroxide value of the fat reaches a maximum and then declines whereas the toxicity continues to increase. Feeding large amounts of peroxide concentrates to animals did not result in any toxic effects (Kaunitz *et al.*, 1955). Polymer formation may be partly responsible for the toxic action of oxidized fat, as feeding of polymerized fish oils to mice has been shown to produce severe toxic effects (Frahn et al., 1953). However, other workers have concluded that the harmful effects observed in rats are due mainly to the toxicity of peroxide products and that the other products are harmless (Andrews et al., 1960).

In complex biological systems the free radicals formed during the auto-oxidation process react with proteins to give rise to highly polymerized proteins which are quite resistant to digestion and may considerably alter the nutritive value of the feed. These lipoprotein complexes may be similar to the ceroid pigments frequently found in animal tissues. When unsaturated fats oxidized beyond the peroxide stage are fed to rats, deposition of yellow-brown pigments occurs in the adipose tissue (Grenados and Dam, 1950). A similar condition occurred in salmon fed polyunsaturated fatty acids and low $\alpha$-tocopherol (Woodall et al., 1964). Halver (1965) has suggested that the impairment of normal liver function as a result of continuous ingestion of partially oxidized oils without adequate supplies of antioxidants and the concomitant deposition of ceroid pigments in the liver may be one of the vectors in the appearance of liver hepatomas in fish.

### 2. Browning Reaction

Nonenzymatic browning of foodstuffs has proved to be a troublesome problem of practical importance in many food products that are dried or contain relatively low moisture content. The browning occurs when carbonyl groups are available to react with free amino groups. A series of complex compounds that fluoresce and vary from colorless to dark brown are formed. The most striking effect of browning is the decreased nutritive value of the foodstuff, particularly the decrease of protein quality (Friedman and Kline, 1950). This problem has been particularly troublesome in products like dried whole egg. There is no indication that the products of the browning reaction are hazardous except for their nutritional unavailability. The browning reaction is undoubtedly the basis for the development of many flavor components.

### E. Molds and Mold Metabolites

Many commonly consumed foods are produced by microbial fermentations. The lactic acid fermentation is perhaps most frequently used since cheese, cultured milk, sauerkraut, cucumber pickles, green olives, etc., are dependent on it. Molds are used in the ripening of some cheeses and the formation of acetic acid is necessary for the production of vinegar. The processing of soybeans and cassava and other foods which might otherwise be inedible or undesirable depends on some type of fermentation process. Also many sauces and products of that kind are based on the action of microorganisms. Many substances in addition to the ones that are desired are undoubtedly produced in these fermentations. Usually these microbial metabolites are of no consequence but sometimes they may have antibiotic activity or other pertinent physiological action that may become a problem. Undesirable microbial action is a cause of much food spoilage.

Food contamination by secondary mold metabolites is an important problem which has been fully appreciated only during the past 10 years although it has been recognized for generations. Toxicity syndromes arising from contaminated foodstuffs have recently been given the generic name mycotoxicoses and have been the subject of a recent symposium (Wogan, 1965), which has focused attention on the important role that field and storage fungi may play in causing losses among domestic animals and has underscored the great potential of mycotoxins for contamination of human and fish food.

Ergotism is a chronic disease in some countries due to ingestion of grains, especially rye, which have become infested with a fungus *Claviceps purpurea*. Ergotism is still an important problem in veterinary toxicology (Garner, 1961). The active agents causing ergotism have been isolated and characterized and comprise a group of alkaloids, all derivatives of lysergic acid (Rothlin and Bircher, 1952).

In addition to ergot, there has been accumulating in recent years a series of examples where the poisonous agents are extracts of the fungal growths. These have been reviewed by Forgacs and Carll (1962) and a partial list is given in Table II.

An apparently new disease that caused great losses among turkey poults appeared in England in 1960. The causative agent was quickly traced to a feed ingredient, a peanut meal from Brazil. The outbreaks continued into 1961 and shipments of peanut meal from Nigeria, French West Africa, Uganda, Gambia, and India were added to the list of toxic feeds. Ducklings, pigs, and calves were also affected. The toxic agent, extractable by methanol and soluble in chloroform, was demonstrated to be produced by *Aspergillus flavus* Link ex Fries (XVI), a variant of a common storage mold. The toxic peanut meals in England were reported to be carcinogenic in rats, producing liver carcinomas with metastases in approximately 6 months. This observation has been amply confirmed. As little as 75 μg per day of aflatoxin fed for 30 days produced tumors in four out of five rats 10 months later (Wogan, 1966).

The most recent food-associated epizootic disease of obscure etiology is rainbow trout hepatoma. In 1963 the California State Department of

TABLE II

A PARTIAL LIST OF TOXINS OF MOLDS

| Mold | Food infected | Toxin | Reported susceptibility | Symptoms |
|---|---|---|---|---|
| *Sclerotinia sclerotiorum* (XIII)[a] | Celery | 8-Methoxy psoralen | Man, rabbits, mice | Blistering lesions of skin exposed to sunlight (365 m$\mu$) |
| *Fusarium sporotrichioides* | Cereal grain (millet) | Unknown | Man, cat, guinea pig, dog, monkey | "*Alimentary toxic aleukia*"—hemorrhages of skin and mucous membranes. necrotic ulcers in oral and pharyngeal tissues, leukopenia, anemia, fever, bone marrow exhaustion |
| *Sporidesmium bakeri* | Rye grass, Bermuda grass | Sporidesmium ($C_{19}H_{21}O_6$-N[S]Cl) probable | Sheep, cattle, guinea pig, rabbit, mouse | "*Facial eczema in ruminants*"—hyperirritability, lacrimation, nasal discharge. photosensitization, icterus, stenosis and obliteration of bile ducts, cirrhosis |
| *Stachybotrys atra* | Hay, straw, grain | Stable to heat, radiation and destroyed by alkali | Horses, cattle, mice, guinea pig, dogs, man | Stomatitis, inflammation of buccal tissues, thrombocytopenia, prolonged clotting time, fever, leucocytopenia, massive hemorrhages, fatal in 3–4 weeks, dermal inflammation in man |

**Bovine hyperkeratosis moldy corn toxicosis of swine**

| Organism | Substrate | Species | Toxin | Effect |
|---|---|---|---|---|
| *Aspergillus chevalieri* | Hay, grain | Cattle, mice, rabbits | Unknown | Acute, fatal in 4–5 days, chronic hyperkeratosis |
| *A. clavatus* | Pellet feed | Rabbits | Unknown | Dermal toxicity |
| *A. fumigatus* | Fodder | Unknown | Unknown | |
| *A. flavus* | Corn | Swine, mice | Unknown | Anorexia, cachexia, icterus, fatal 1–5 days, profuse hemorrhages in all tissues, mortality 25–50% |
| *P. rubrum* | | | | |

**Yellowsis rice toxicity**

| Organism | Substrate | Species | Toxin | Effect |
|---|---|---|---|---|
| *Penicillium toxicarium* | Cereal grains Rice | Higher vertebrates | Unknown | Ascending paralysis of CNS origin |
| *P. citrinum* (XIV) | Rice | Mice | Citrinin | Acute glomerulonephrosis, liver damage |
| *P. rugulosum* | | Mice, rats | Rugulosin | Fatty degeneration of liver, kidney damage |
| *P. islandicum* (XV) | | Rats | Chloride containing peptide (H$_2$O soluble) Luteoskyrin (pigment, H$_2$O insoluble) | Fatty degeneration of liver, bile duct hyperplasia focal necrosis and hemorrhages of liver, primary malignant hepatomas |
| *A. flavus* Link ex Fries (XVI) | Peanuts, grains | Turkeys, ducks, swine, calves, rats | Aflatoxins | Liver parenchymal cell damage, bile damage, bile duct proliferation, hepatoma |

[a] Roman numerals refer to structural figures.

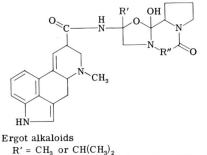

Ergot alkaloids

    R' = CH₃ or CH(CH₃)₂

    R'' = CH₂C₆H₅ or CH(CH₃)₂ or CH₂CH(CH₃)₂

*Claviceps purpurea*

(XII)

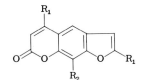

The psoralens

| | R₁ | R₂ |
|---|---|---|
| 8-Methoxypsoralen | H | OCH₃ |
| 4, 5′, 8-Trimethylpsoralen | CH₃ | CH₃ |

*Sclerotinia sclerotiorum*

(XIII)

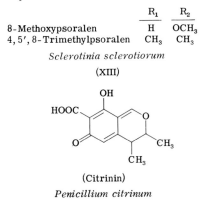

(Citrinin)

*Penicillium citrinum*

(XIV)

Health announced that cottonseed meal was being eliminated as an ingredient of dried fish food in all California hatcheries. Evidence pointed to cottonseed meal or something in the meal as being the causative factor in the high incidence of trout hepatoma in the state fish hatcheries (Wolf and Jackson, 1963). Although it is possible that some other factor may also be operating in the development of trout hepatoma, much evidence has

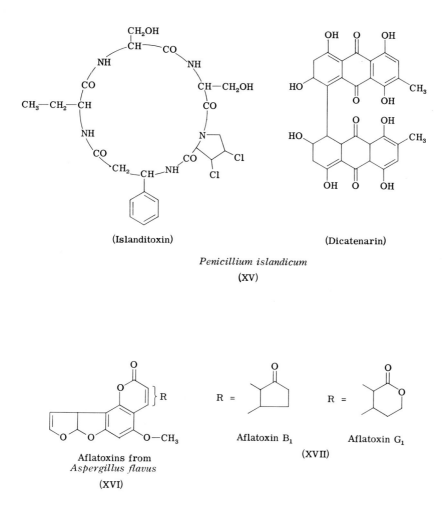

(Islanditoxin)          (Dicatenarin)

*Penicillium islandicum*

(XV)

Aflatoxins from
*Aspergillus flavus*

(XVI)

Aflatoxin B₁          Aflatoxin G₁

(XVII)

been gathered since 1963 to implicate contamination with small amounts of aflatoxin as the probable cause of the rainbow trout hepatoma epidemics (Halver, 1965). This species is exquisitely sensitive. As little as 0.5 ppb aflatoxin $B_1$ (XVII) in the feed will produce a significant incidence of hepatoma (Ashley *et al.*, 1965). Other species of fish may not be so sensitive to aflatoxin. Ashley (1966) has reported that catfish fingerlings fed crude aflatoxin in doses ranging from 0 to 100 mg/kg body weight showed a relatively low level of response, whereas trout fed only 5 mg/kg body weight of the crude aflatoxin died within 3 to 10 days.

Several methods are available for the determination of aflatoxin in seed meals (Nesheim *et al.*, 1964; Pons and Goldblatt, 1965). Chen and Friedman (1966) have reported an assay method that is capable of detecting as few as 0.02 ppb of aflatoxin. It is of interest to note that some samples of cottonseed meal showed no evidence of aflatoxin even at this very low level, indicating that it is possible, despite the hazard of mold contamination, to produce cottonseed meals, at least in the United States, that are, for all practical purposes, free of this contamination.

As the antibiotic and fermentation industries have grown since the second world war, many of the large numbers of microbial metabolites studied have been recognized as highly toxic. The role of fungi as a hazard to food quality, both technologically as well as from the viewpoint of food safety, is being appreciated only recently. Christensen (1957) indicated that some effects of molds, e.g., the lowering or complete destruction of the ability of seeds to germinate, can be observed even in the absence of obvious mold damage or heavy mold contamination. The ubiquity of field and storage fungi, the dependence of modern technology upon harvesting, transport and storage of grains and oilseeds in large bulk, and the increasing knowledge of the destructive and dangerous aspects of mold infestation pose a serious problem for all food industry.

## V. Effect of Toxic Substances Entering Aquatic Environment of Fish

In addition to the potential problems that may arise due to the presence of certain nonnutrient components in practical fish diets, an additional major concern includes the toxic substances that enter the aquatic environment of fishes. These substances may affect the fish directly or indirectly through the various components of the food chain. Further, in the case of extremely low levels of these substances which are not acutely toxic to the fish and other organisms in the environment, the fish will be exposed for as long as they persist. Therefore, it is important to know, first, how long the substances remain in the environment, that is, the rate of biological decay, and second, how fish and other organisms may concentrate these substances and what effect this may have on the well being of the fish and accumulation of undesirable residues that may influence its usefulness as a food.

## A. Toxicity of Metals as Salts

Doudoroff and Katz (1953) have presented an extensive review of literature on the toxicity of industrial wastes and their components to fishes. The toxicity of salts may be due either to the metal ion (particularly the heavy metals) or the anion (chromate or cyanide). Tables showing the lethal limits of metals as salts are given in Jones (1964). In general, the heavy metals Hg, Cu, Zn, and Cd appear to be the most toxic in the species studied. However, the results are concerned with the toxic levels of the salts.

## B. Uptake and Concentration of Metals and Radionuclides

The uptake, concentration, and retention of metals and radionuclides by fish and marine organisms are of practical interest as they may affect the well being of the fish or create a potential hazard when the fish is used as food. The uptake of these compounds may occur by (1) direct uptake and concentration by the fish, and (2) ingestion of these substances through various parts of the food chain, or both.

The concentration of metals by fish in Minamata Bay provides an excellent example of concentration by fish of a metal contaminant from industrial effluents. The concentration in the flesh of fish was high enough to be toxic to man (Gerarde, 1964). The form in which the metal is supplied to the fish is important in determining the organ in which it concentrates. Tsuruga (1963), studying the uptake of $Hg_{203}$ by shellfish which were kept in water to which $Hg_{203}$ had been added in concentration of 0.05 mg/liter, showed that sea mussels concentrated mercury 660 times in 4 days and short-necked clams 180 times in 8 days. If the sea mussels or clams were fed to carp or congo eel, high concentrations of mercury were found in the kidneys, gills, and livers. Only low concentrations were present in muscle tissue. In contrast, fish collected in Minamata Bay where they were exposed to mercury salts in the water had a higher level of mercury in the muscle tissue. Shellfish concentrate arsenic to a high level but apparently the form in which it is available for consumption by man and animals is innocuous (Coulson *et al.*, 1935). The level of lead accumulating in fish muscle may be reaching significant levels due to the large amount of lead entering waters near large cities and near certain coastlines as a result of the large amounts of lead tetraethyl entering the atmosphere from the large consumption of automotive fuels.

The percentage of various radionuclides that occur in seawater at various time intervals following contamination by fission products and their relative concentration in plankton has been determined by Lowman

(1963). Because of the different rates of decay the relative amount found at any given time varies considerably. The isotopes most actively concentrated are $^{90}Zr$, Co isotopes, $^{65}Zn$, $^{55}Fe$ and $^{59}Fe$. Lowman (1963) has listed the principal factors which control the uptake and retention of radionuclides. These are: (1) the amount of radionuclide introduced into the water, (2) chemical and physical characteristics of the radionuclides, (3) chemical and physical forms of nonradioactive materials associated with the radionuclides, (4) the degree to which the radionuclide is adsorbed to the organism, (5) the degree of selective uptake, and (6) biological half-life of the element in the organism.

Numerous reports are available for the uptake, turnover, and transport of various radionuclides in fish. Rosenthal (1963) studied the uptake of $^{45}Ca$, $^{90}Sr$, by guppies (*Lebistes*) from water in which they were swimming. The uptake was linear with time and was also a function of the concentration of the nuclides in the water. The rate of incorporation of the nuclides into the tissues such as muscle, viscera, head, and spine was linear with time, but the distribution of nuclides varied with the nature of tissue and the nuclide involved; $^{45}Ca$ and $^{90}Sr$ were taken up at a similar rate, $^{35}S$ at a slower rate. The rate of turnover of $^{35}S$, $^{45}Ca$, and $^{90}Sr$ was most rapid in the soft visceral tissue and slowest in the spine. Muscle tissue exchanges nuclides at an intermediate rate. Nakatani and Foster (1963) studied the effect of chronic feeding of $^{90}Sr$ and $^{90}Y$ to rainbow trout. Growth depression and significant mortalities occurred in fish fed 0.5 $\mu Ci/gm$ of fish daily for 21 weeks, but other groups receiving low concentrations, 0.05 and 0.005 $\mu Ci/gm$, did not differ from the control fish. At the end of the test period no obvious damage was observed in the low and medium group, but 6 months after treatment the medium group developed leukopenia.

Some studies have been made comparing the uptake of radionuclides from the water and from the diet. Schiffman (1959) studied the uptake of $^{90}Sr$ and $^{90}Y$ from the diet and water by rainbow trout. The concentration of $^{90}Sr$ and $^{90}Y$ in trout was about 1.5 times greater than that in the surrounding water after 3 weeks of exposure. Twenty-one percent of the isotopes administered in a gelatin capsule was retained after 1 day, but after 100 days the level had fallen to 4.4%. When the isotope was incorporated into natural food the retention was only 7%. Under investigational conditions the uptake from environmental water was greater than the uptake through the food chain. However, it should be noted that the true equilibrium of the $^{90}Sr$ in the fish and the water is only reached after a considerable time. Ophel (1963) showed that freshwater fish in a lake accumulated $^{90}Sr$ over a long period, reaching equilibrium after exposure for 4 years. He concluded that true equilibrium is only reached when fish have spent their entire life-span in a contaminated environment and that the resulting concentration factor is much greater than could be predicted from experimental exposure of fish to $^{90}Sr$ for short periods.

Lowman (1963) has studied the uptake of radionuclides at three levels of the food chain. During the first period of 48 hours the radionuclides were taken up at approximately the same ratio that they appeared in the water. After 1 week Co, Zn, and Fe were taken up actively by the plankton in relation to the other radionuclides. Omnivorous fish that fed on plankton almost completely excluded the fission products but on a comparative basis concentrated $^{65}Zn$, $^{55}Fe$, and $^{59}Fe$, but discriminated against the Co isotopes. Carnivorous tunas that feed mainly on omnivorous fishes discriminated in favor of Zn and Mn and against Fe and Co in comparison to the relative amounts of these substances in their feed supply. The relative order of accumulation in fish is probably a reflection of the limited biological demands for these elements. In plankton and algae the problem is different because of surface adsorption which may be the major route of accumulation.

## C. Pesticide Residues and Detergents

Pesticide residues are mainly derived from the waters of areas that have received mass spraying. Most fish show a sharply defined threshold response to pesticide concentration. Cope (1962) has published tables showing the toxicities of some pesticides and fungicides to various species of fish. However, the problem of defining a median tolerance limit is complicated because, in addition to the species of fish, the age of the fish and the water conditions have to be taken into account. Pickering *et al.* (1964) studied the toxicity of eighteen organic phosphorus compounds to fish and found an extremely wide range of toxicity with the 96-hour $TL_m$ values ranging from 0.05–610 ppm. The maximum sensitivity of different species toward a particular compound ranges from four to as high as four-hundred times the minimum. Furthermore, fry from 2–30 days of age were very much more sensitive than adults. Although the problem of acute toxicity can be defined, a major problem arises when subtle long-term effects are considered. A detailed account of the effect of sublethal doses of endrin on fishes has been published by the Fisheries Research Institute, Seattle (1966). The study was designed to determine the effects of long-term exposure to endrin upon the reproduction and development of freshwater fish *Oryzias latipes* (Medaka). Results indicated that parent fish survived in concentrations of 0.05 ppb endrin but produced young that had morphological abnormalites and suffered high mortalites within 2 week of hatching. Studies on the accumulation of DDT in lake trout and the effect on reproduction have been reported by Burdick *et al.* (1964). They found that there is no constant relationship between the DDT content of the spawning trout and that of the fry. However, when the DDT concentration of the egg was 2.95 ppm or more the fry developed a characteristic syndrome and did not survive. In addition to the direct effect of the insecticide on fishes there is the problem of their effect on fish food organisms and other vectors in the food chain. Schoenthal (1963) reported studies on the effect of DDT on cold water fish and fish food organisms. The mortality of trout treated in water containing 1 ppm DDT was shown to be dependent on factors such as temperature, turbidity, and alkalinity of the water. In addition, the mortality rate of trout was greatly increased when fed aquatic insects treated with DDT, whereas feeding with algae that had been exposed to DDT did not increase the mortality. This may be related to the ability of algae to decompose DDT. When DDT is applied to a stream there is a great loss of natural foodstuff, particularly immature insects. This results in a changing of the food habits of the trout and is usually accompanied by reduction of the number of trout in these areas. In addition to contamination of the water, use of insecticides results in large numbers of dead insects contaminated with insecticide falling into the water. Normally fish will eat large numbers of these insects. Hoffman and Suber (1949) studied the effect of feeding DDT-sprayed insects to freshwater fish. The results were not very conclusive. Well fed fish that gorged upon the contaminated insects survived in large numbers even though they were fasted after the feeding. The condition of the fish may be very important in determining their susceptibility to DDT; perhaps as important as the species. It would be of interest to know if fish are able to detoxify some of the commonly used insecticides and also if there is a possibility of developing strains resistant to their toxic action. When Atlantic salmon were exposed to 1 ppm $^{14}$C-labeled DDT it was shown that after 5 minutes exposure there were appreciable amounts of DDT throughout the body. Bioassay showed that an average of about $\frac{2}{3}$ of the absorbed DDT is nontoxic, or at least relatively so, to mosquito larvae. The adsorbed DDT showed little loss of activity (Primdas and Anderson, 1963). Cope (1965) reported attempts that had been made to accustom fish to various pesticides. Juvenile specimens exposed to Telodrin (a chlorinated hydrocarbon) for 5 months at a concentration of 0.01 ppb (concentration of 0.025 ppb was lethal in 10 days) were then exposed to previously determined lethal concentrations of the Dieldrin. Treated fish were found to be just as sensitive as control fish. When the experiment was repeated using endrin as a test compound exposed fishes were found to be more sensitive than control fish. It may be necessary to screen very large numbers of fish to develop resistant strains. However, it should be noted that in some areas fish appear to have developed a high degree of resistance to insecticides. Mosquito fish from water near cotton fields that have had a long history of treatment with chlorinated hydrocarbon pesticides exhibit a marked resistance to DDT (Vinson *et al.*, 1963). As much as 300-fold resistance persists among the first few generations reared in insecticide-free environments (Boyd and Ferguson, 1964). Other species of fish in this area appear to have developed resistance to a variety of insecticides, e.g., delta golden shiners (*Notemigonus crysoleucas*), bluegill sunfish (*Lepomis macrochirus*), and green sunfish (*Lepomis cyanellus*) were shown to be resistant to toxaphene, aldrin, dieldrin, and endrin (Ferguson *et al.*, 1964). It is not known if these fish have developed enzyme systems capable of detoxifying the insecticides, nor are there any reports on the levels of insecticide in the tissues of these fish. Detailed information as to the amount of DDT that has been found in trout in various areas of the United States has been given in the Interagency Coordination in Environmental Hazards (Pesticides, 1964). The greatest concentration was present in bone and fat. Accumulated DDT is not lost from the fish. However, the levels of DDT present were not likely to render the fish unfit for consumption. The problem of accumulation of insecticides may become serious as resistant species are developed which are capable of accumulating large amounts of insecticides.

Oysters have been shown to be particularly sensitive to DDT and under experimental conditions store pesticides present in the water at concentrations as low as 10 ppt. DDT storage in oysters is mainly in the gonads (Butler, 1965). It is not known what effect this has on the viability of gametes and the course of larval development. Because of the extreme sensitivity of oysters to chlorinated hydrocarbons, Butler (1965) has suggested that they could be used to monitor the seasonal pollution in the major shellfish areas.

Linear alkyl sulfonates are toxic to fish under static conditions, the $TL_m$ being about 3 mg/liter and 0.6 mg/liter for the $C_{12}$ and $C_{13}$ homologue, respectively (Swisher *et al.*, 1964). However, these substances are readily biodegradable with the production of nontoxic products and their suitable disposal does not seem to present a problem. Production of tetrapropylene-derived alkyl benzene sulfonates (ABS) which are only slowly and incompletely degraded has been discontinued. The present concentration of ABS in rivers is not considered to be a hazard to fish life (Ohio River Valley Sanitation Commission, Detergent Subcommittee, 1963).

D. Off Flavor

Off flavor is a problem connected with the value of fish as food. Off flavors may be caused either by contamination of the water due to various compounds or by various components of the food chain that contain substances that are absorbed by the fish and give the flesh an undesirable flavor.

Schulze (1961) showed that when phenol was added to the water containing swimming fish, the flavor of the fish was not affected although the phenol was accumulated in certain organs, especially liver and gills. Monochlorphenol imparted a strong flavor to the fish. Petroleum products from outboard motors can have a great effect on the flavor of fish, producing the so-called "harbor taste." A similar taste is produced by less than 1 ppm of kerosene (Interstate Sanitation Commission of New York and New Jersey, 1962). Tainting of fish flesh is detectable at a combined fuel use of 8 gallons/million gallons of water (English *et al.*, 1963) and the daily fuel use of 0.17 gallon/million gallons of water.

The ingestion of certain types of phytoplankton can cause very marked off flavors. The so-called blackberry flavor of Newfoundland cod has been shown to be due to the presence of dimethyl-β-propiothetin (Ackman *et al.*, 1966a) or its decomposition product dimethylsulfide (Sipos and Ackman, 1964) derived from the ingestion of planktonic marine organisms containing these compounds (Ackman *et al.*, 1966b).

## VI.  Summary

It is clear that although the nutrients constitute the major portion of the composition of food materials, that list of nutrients is a small and relatively simple group when compared to the bewildering array of the many various types of substances that are present as components of the materials from which we obtain our nutrients. These other components of our food are usually ignored unless they happen to contribute a very important food characteristic such as taste, odor, color, or texture. They may occur as an inherent component of the basic plant or animal food material or may become part of the food product through some contamination. Inadvertent admixture with unwanted plant and animal materials such as weeds is one of the more simple examples. Other important means of contamination include: enzymatic or chemical changes in plants, deteriorative changes, actions of microorganisms, presence of undesirable physiologically active microbial metabolites, unsanitary surroundings, accumulation of undesirable soil and water components in plants or animals, or toxic industrial waste. Another major source of chemical components in foods is derived from the agricultural and food technology. Many substances used for specific useful purposes in agriculture and in the food industry remain either in the original form or as residues in or on the final product. Such residues are derived from fertilizers, herbicides, plant hormones, pesticides, medicated feeds, from packaging materials or as the result of food processing operations such as dehydration, resulting in a browning reaction, fatty acid derivatives resulting from the reaction of additives with food components such as methionine sulfoximine resulting from the reaction of nitrogen trichloride with the methionine of the plant protein, and last, there is a host of chemicals used as intentional food additives for the achievement of specific results in the manufacture of our food products.

## References

Ackman, R. G., Dale, J., and Hingley, J. (1966a). *J. Fish. Res. Bd. Can.* **23**, 487.
Ackman, R. G., Tocher, C. S., and McLachlan, J. (1966b). *J. Fish. Res. Bd. Can.* **23**, 357.
Allison, J. B. (1958). *Voeding* **19**, 119.
Allison, V. P. (1963). *Roy. Soc. Health J.* **83**, 47.
Altschul, A. M., Lyman, C. M., and Thurber, F. H. (1958). *In* "Processed Plant Protein Foodstuffs" (A. M. Altschul, ed.). Academic Press, New York.
Anderson, E. (1949). *Ind. Eng. Chem.* **41**, 2887.
Andrews, J. S., Griffith, H., Meat, J. F., and Stein, R. A. (1960). *J. Nutr.* **70**, 199.
Annual Report of the Nutrition Research Laboratory, Hyderabad-7 (AB) for the period Oct. 1, 1963 to Sept. 30, 1964, p. 65.
Ashley, L. M. (1966). *Bur. Sport Fish. Wildl. U.S. Rep.* **17**, 28.
Ashley, L. M., Halver, J. E., and Wogan, G. N. (1965). *Fed. Proc.* **24**, 627.
Astwood, E. B., Greer, M. A., and Ettlinger, M. G. (1949). *J. Biol. Chem.* **181**, 121.
Banner, A. H., and Helfrich, P. (1964). *Hawaii Marine Lab. Tech. No.* **3**, 48.
Banner, A. H., Schener, P. J., Sasaki, S., Helfrich, P., and Alender, C. B. (1960). *Ann. N. Y. Acad. Sci.* **90**, 770.
Bell, E. A. (1962). *Nature (London)* **193**, 1078.
Bird, H. R., Groschke, A. C., and Rubin, M. (1949). *J. Nutr.* **37**, 215.
Bondi, A., Spandorf, A., and Calmi, R. (1957). *Bamidgeh.* **9**, 13.
Bornstein, S., and Lipstein, B. (1963). *Poultry Sci.* **42**, 61.
Boyd, C. E., and Ferguson, D. E. (1964). *Mosquito News* **24**, 19.
Bras, G. D., Jellife, B., and Stewart, K. L. (1954). *Arch. Pathol.* **57**, 285.
Bressani, R. (1960). *Biological Studies Proc. Conf. Cottonseed Protein for Animal and and Man, SUROD, UNICEF, NCPA, Nov. 14–16, New Orleans,* Louisiana.
Bridges, R. G. (1955). *J. Sci. Food Agr.* **6**, 261.
Brown, J. M. M. (1959). *J. S. Afr. Vet. Med. Ass.* **30**, 395.
Burdick, G. E., Harris, E. G., Dean, H. J., Walker, T. M., Sken, J., and Colby, D. (1964) *Trans. Amer. Fish Soc.* **93**, 127.
Burke, J. M., Marchisotto, J., McLaughlin, J. J. A., and Provasoli, L. (1960). *Ann. N. Y. Acad. Sci.* **90**, 836.
Butler, P. A. (1965). *U.S. Dep. Interior Fish Wildl. Circ.* **226**, 65.

Camp, B. J., and Lyman, C. M. (1956). *J. Amer. Pharm. Ass.* **45**, 719.

Cantrell, J. S., Webb, N. C., and Mabis, A. J. (1969). *Acta Cryst.* **B25**, 150.

Carll, W. T., Forgacs, J., and Herring, A. S. (1954). *Amer. J. Hyg.* **60**, 15.

Chen, S. C., and Friedman, L. (1966). *J. Ass. Offic. Anal. Chem.* **49**, 28.

Chernick, S. S., Lepkovsky, S., and Chaikoff, I. L. (1948). *Amer. J. Physiol.* **155**, 33.

Childs, B. W., Zinkham, E. A., Browne, E. A., Kimbro, F. L., and Torbert, J. V. (1958). *Bull. Johns Hopkins Hosp.* **102**, 21.

Christensen, C. M. (1957). *Bot. Rev.* **23**, 108.

Clare, N. T. (1955). *Advan. Vet. Sci.* **2**, 182.

College of Fisheries, Fisheries Research Institute, University of Seattle, Washington, Contrib. No. 212 (1966). (1965 Research in Fisheries.)

Cope, O. B. (1962). *U.S. Dep. Interior Circ.* **160**, 81.

Cope, O. B. (1965). *U.S. Dep. Interior Fish Wildl. Circ.* **226**, 51.

Coulson, E. G., Remington, R. E., and Lynch, K. M. (1935). *J. Nutr.* **10**, 255.

Crafts, A. S., and Foy, C. L. (1962). *Res. Rev.* **1**, 112.

Creek, R. D., and Schumaier, A. (1960). *Feedstuffs.*

Culvenor, C. C. J., Dann, A. T., and Dick, A. T. (1962). *Nature (London)* **195**, 570.

Darr, A. L., and McCay, C. M. (1947). *Progr. Fish. Cult.* **9**, 53.

Davidson, S., and Passmore, R. (1963). "Human Nutrition and Dietetics," p. 521. Williams & Wilkins Company, Baltimore, Maryland.

Davis, C. C. (1948). *Bot. Gaz. (Chicago)* **109**, 358.

Dawson, E. Y., Aleem, A. A., and Halstead, B. W. (1955). Allan Hancock Foundation Publ., Univ. Southern Calif. Occ. Paper No. 17.

Daxenbichler, M. E., Van Etten, C. H., Brown, F. S., and Jones, Q. J. (1964). *Agr. Food Chem.* **12**, 127.

DeEds, F. (1961). *Food Technol.* **15**, 28.

Desikachar, H. S. R., and De, S. S. (1947). *Science* **106**, 421.

Dewbery, E. B. (1959). "Food Poisoning," 4th ed. Leonard Hill, London.

Dollahite, J. W., Shaver, P., and Camp, B. J. (1962). *Amer. J. Vet. Res.* **223**, 1261.

Doudoroff, P., and Katz, M. (1953). *Sewage Ind. Wastes* **25**, 802.

Dungal, N. (1961). *J. Amer. Med. Ass.* **178**, 789.

Eagle, E. (1948). *Arch. Biochem. Biophys.* **18**, 271.

Eagle, E. (1959). *Proc. Conf. Chem. Struct. Reactions. Gossypol Non-Gossypol Pigments Cottonseed, New Orleans*, p. 142.

English, J. N., Surber, E. W., and McDermott, G. N. (1963). *J. Water Pollut. Contr. Fed.* **35**, 1121.

Ferguson, D. E., Culley, D. D., Cotton, W. D., and Dodds, R. P. (1964). *Bioscience* **14**, 43.

Firestone, D., Horwitz, W., Friedman, L., and Shue, G. M. (1961). *J. Amer. Oil Chem. Soc.* **38**, 418.

Fisher, H., Johnson, D., Jr., and Ferds, S. (1957). *J. Nutr.* **61**, 611.

Fisheries Research Institute, Seattle (1966). *Annual Report.*

Food and Drug Administration (1962). *Ann. Rep. Dep. Health, Education Welfare*, U.S. Government Printing Office, Washington, D. C., p. 325.

Food Protection Committee of the National Academy of Sciences (1965). Publ. No. 1274. NAS, RNC, Washington, D. C.

Forgacs, J., and Carll, W. T. (1962). *Advan. Vet. Sci.* **7**, 273.

Frahn, H. A., Lembke, A., and von Rappard, G. (1953). *Kiel Milchwirt. Forschungsber.* **5**, 443.

Franke, K. W. (1934). *J. Nutr.* **8**, 597.

Fraps, G. S., and Carlysle, A. (1936). *Texas Agr. Exp. Sta. Bull.*, p. 537.

Frawley, J. P., Hagan, E. C., Fitzhugh, O. G., Fuyat, H. N., and Jones, W. I. (1957). *J. Pharmacol. Exp. Therap.* **119**, 147.

Friedman, L. (1962). *Feedstuffs*, March 17.

Friedman, L. (1964). *Food Technol.* **18**, 49.

Friedman, L., and Kline, O. L. (1950). *J. Nutr.* **40**, 295.

Friedman, L., Horwitz, W., Shue, G. W., and Firestone, D. (1961). *J. Nutr.* **73**, 85.

Frost, D. V., and Spouth, H. C. (1956). *In* "Proceedings of the Symposium on Medicated Feeds" (H. Welch and F. Martin-Ibany, eds.), p. 136. U.S. Food and Drug Administration. Medical Encyclopedia, Inc., New York.

Garner, R. J. (1961). "Veterinary Toxicology," 2nd ed. Williams & Wilkins, Baltimore, Maryland.

Gaunt, I. F., Feuer, G., Fairweather, F. A., and Gilbert, D. (1965). *Food Cosmet. Toxicol.* **3**, 433.

Gerarde, H. W. (1964). *Ann. Rev. Pharmacol.* **4**, 223.

Gilbert, D., and Golberg, L. (1965). *Food Cosmet. Toxicol.* **3**, 417.

Greer, M. A. (1957). *Amer. J. Clin. Nutr.* **5**, 440.

Grenados, H., and Dam, H. (1950). *Acta Pathol. Microbiol. Scand.* **27**, 591.

Griffiths, T. W. (1963). *Vet. Rec.* **75**, 182.

Gyorgy, P., and Tomarelli, R. (1943). *J. Biol. Chem.* **147**, 515.

Habkosterc, I., Fraser, N., and Halstead, B. W. (1955). *J. Wash. Acad. Sci.* **45**, 107.

Haines, P. C., and Lyman, R. L. (1961). *J. Nutr.* **74**, 445.

Halstead, B. W. (1953). *Copeia* **1**, 31.

Halstead, B. W. (1965). "Poisonous and Venemous Marine Animals of the World." U.S. Government Printing Office, Washington, D. C.

Halver, J. E. (1953). *Trans. Amer. Fish. Soc.* **83**, 254–261.

Halver, J. E. (1965). *In* "Mycotoxins in Foodstuffs" (G. N. Wogan, ed.), p. 209. M.I.T. Press, Cambridge, Massachusetts.

Hamilton, J. W., and Beath, O. A. (1963a). *Agron. J.* **55**, 528.

Hamilton, J. W., and Beath, O. A. (1963b). *J. Range Manage.* **16**, 261.

Hamilton, J. W., and Beath, O. A. (1964). *Agr. Food Chem.* **12**, 371.

Harper, A. E. (1956). *Nutr. Rev.* **14**, 225.

Hartley, R. D., Nesbitt, B. F., and O'Kelley (1963). *Nature (London)* **198**, 1056.

Hawk, E. A., and Mickelsen, O. (1955). *Science* **121**, 442.

Hayward, J. W., and Hafner, F. H. (1941). *Poultry Sci.* **20**, 139.

Hayward, J. W., Steenbock, H., and Bohstedt, G. (1936). *J. Nutr.* **12**, 275.

Heywang, B. W., and Bird, H. R. (1954). *Poultry Sci.* **33**, 239.

Hiro, S., Ozawa, S., and Suematsu, Y. (1963). *Bull. J. Soc. Sci. Fish.* **29**, 382.

Hinds, F. C. (1959). Ph.D. Thesis. University of Illinois. Urbana, Illinois, p. 122.

Hoffman, H. C., and Surber, E. W. (1949). *U.S. Dep. Interior Fish Wildl. Serv. Spec. Sci. Rep.* Fish. No. 3.

Interagency Coordination in Environmental Hazards (Pesticides). (1964). 23-7410. U.S. Government Printing Office, Washington, D. C.

Interstate Sanitation Committee, N. Y. and N. J. (1962).

Ishiguro, M., Takahashi, T., Funatsu, G., and Funatsu, K. (1964a). *J. Biochem. (Tokyo)* **55**, 587.

Ishiguro, M., Takahashi, T., Hayishi, K., and Funatsu, M. (1964b). *J. Biochem. (Tokyo)* **56**, 325.

Joint WHO/FAO Expert Committee on Zoonoses (1959). 2nd. Rep., WHO Tech. Rep. Ser. Geneva, 169.

Jones, J. R. E. (1964). "Fish and River Pollution." Butterworths, Washington, D. C.

Kastelic, J. (1963). In "Chemical and Biological Hazards in Food" (J. C. Ayres, A. A. Kraft, H. E. Snyder, and H. W. Walker, eds.), p. 135. Iowa State University Press, Ames, Iowa.

Kaunitz, H., Johnson, R. E., and Slanetz, C. A. (1952). J. Nutr. 46, 151.

Kaunitz, H., Slanetz, C. A., Johnson, R. E., Knight, H. B., Saunders, D. H., and Sivern, D. (1955). Fed. Proc. 14, 408.

Kawabata, T., Ishizaka, K., and Miura, T. (1955). Bull. Japan. Soc. Fish. 21, 335.

Kimata, M. (1961). In "Fish as Food" (G. Borgstrom, ed.), Vol. 1, p .329. Academic Press, New York.

Kingsbury, J. M. (1964). "Poisonous Plants of the United States and Canada." Prentice Hall, Englewood Cliffs, New Jersey.

Klosterman, H. J., Farley, T. M., Parsons, J. L., and Lamoureux, P. (1963). Abst. Amer. Chem. Soc. Meeting, New York, Sept. 9.

Koivistoinen, P., Karinpaa, A., Kononen, M., and Roine, P. (1964). Agr. Food Chem. 12, 551.

Komari, S. (1940). Mitt. Med. Akad. Kioto 29, 795.

Kratzer, F. H. (1946). Poultry Sci. 25, 541.

Kratzer, F. H., and Williams, D. E. (1948). J. Nutr. 36, 297.

Kratzer, F. H., Williams, D. E., Marshall, B., and Davis, P. N. (1954). J. Nutr. 52, 555.

Kunitz, M. (1947). J. Gen. Physiol. 30, 291.

Laqueur, G. L., Mickelsen, O., Whiting, M. G., and Kurland, L. T. (1963). J. Nat. Cancer Inst. 31, 919.

Law, D. K., Sinnhuber, R. O., Yu, T. C., Hublon, W. F., and McKee, T. B. (1961). Res. Brief Fish. Comm. Oregon, p. 64.

LeBreton, E., and Moule, Y. (1949). Bull. Soc. Chem. Biol. 31, 94.

Li, K. M. (1965). Far East. Med. J. 1, 29.

Liener, I. E. (1958). J. Biol. Chem. 233, 401.

Lijinsky, W., and Shubik, P. (1964). Science 145, 53.

Lowman, F. (1963). In "National Symposium on Radioecology" (V. Schultz and A. W. Klement, Jr., eds.), p. 145. Reinhold, New York.

Luckey, T. D. (1959). In "Antibiotics, Their Chemistry and Non-Medical Uses" (H. S. Goldberg, ed.), p. 174. Van Nostrand, New York.

Lyman, C. M. (1964). Proc. Conf. Cottonseed Protein Concentrates, U.S. Dep. Agr. Res. Serv. ARS-72-38, p. 58.

Lyman, C. M., Baliga, B. P., and Slay, M. W. (1959). Arch. Biochem. Biophys. 84, 486.

McKay, G. S., Lalich, J. J., Schilling, E. D., and Strong, F. M. (1954). Arch. Biochem. Biophys. 52, 313.

McKinney, L. L., Picken, J. C., Jr., Weakley, F. B., Eldridge, A. C., Campbell, R. E., Cowan, J. C., and Biesler, H. E. (1959). J. Amer. Chem. Soc. 81, 909.

Magee, P. N., and Farber, E. (1962). Biochem. J. 83, 114.

Malikova, E. M., and Kotova, N. I. (1964). Biol. Abstr. 45.

Marth, E. H. (1965). Res. Rev.

Marth, E. H. (1966). Res. Rev. 12, 65.

Matsumoto, H., and Strong, F. M. (1963). Arch. Biochem. Biophys. 101, 299.

Mellanby, E. (1946). Brit. Med. J. 2, 885.

Mickelsen, O., and Yang, M. G. (1966). Fed. Proc. 25, 104.

Miller, J. A., and Miller, E. C. (1965). *Cancer Res.* **25,** 1292.

Miller, R. F., Small, G., and Norris, L. C. (1955). *J. Nutr.* **55,** 81.

Misani, F., and Reiner, L. (1950). *Arch. Biochem. Biophys.* **27,** 234.

Moore, R. N., and Bickford, W. G. (1952). *J. Amer. Oil Chem. Soc.* **29,** 1.

Moran, E. A. (1954). *Amer. J. Vet. Res.* **15,** 171.

Morrison, A. B., and Munro, I. C. (1965). *Can. J. Biochem. Physiol.* **43,** 33.

Morrison, F. B. (1951). "Feeds and Feeding, A Handbook for the Student and Stock-man," p. 1083. Morrison Publ., Ithaca, New York.

Mosher, H. S., Fuhrman, F. A., Buchwald, H. D., and Fischer, H. G. (1964). *Science* **144,** 1100.

Nakatani, R. E., and Foster, R. F. (1963). *In* "National Symposium on Radioecology" (V. Schultz and A. W. Klement, eds.), p. 359. Reinhold, New York.

Nesheim, S., Banes, D., Stoloff, L., and Campbell, A. D. (1964). *J. Ass. Offic. Agr. Chem.* **47,** 586.

Nilson, H. W., and Schaller, J. W. (1941). *Food Res.* **6,** 641.

Nordfeldt, S., Gellerstedt, N., and Falkner, S. (1954). *Acta Pathol. Microbiol.* **35,** 217.

Ohio River Valley Water Sanitation Commission Detergent Subcommittee. (1963). *J. Amer. Water Works Ass.* **55,** 369.

Ophel, I. L. (1963). *Nucl. Sci. Abstr.* **17,** 1008.

Overby, L. R., and Frost, D. V. (1962). *Toxicol. Appl. Pharmacol.* **4,** 38.

Pace, J., and McDermott, E. E. (1952). *Nature (London)* **169,** 415.

Palsson, P. A., and Grimsson, H. (1953). *Proc. Sco. Exp. Biol. Med.* **83,** 518.

Parnas, A., and Abbott, S. (1965). *Toxicon,* **3,** 133.

Phelps, R. A., Shenstone, F. S., Kemmerer, A. R., and Evans, R. J. (1965). *Poultry Sci.* **44,** 1965.

Phillips, A. M., Tunison, A. V., Shaffer, H. B., White, G. K., Sullivan, M. W., Vincent, C., Brockway, D. R., and McCay, C. M. (1945). *Cortland Hatchery Rep. No.* 14.

Pickering, Q. H., Henderson, C., and Semke, A. E. (1964). *Trans. Amer. Fish. Soc.* **93,** 175.

Pons, W. A., and Goldblatt, L. A. (1965). *J. Amer. Oil Chem. Soc.* **42,** 471.

Preston, T. R. (1963). *Vet. Rec.* **75,** 125.

Primdas, F. H., and Anderson, J. M. (1963). *J. Fish. Res. Bd. Can.* **20,** 827.

Rao, B. Y. (1960). *J. Sci. Ind. Res.* **19A,** 430.

Rao, S. L. N., Adiga, P. R., and Sarms, P. S. (1964). *Biochemistry* **3,** 432.

Report of the Interstate Sanitation Commission of New York, New Jersey and Con-necticut in the Water Pollution Control Activities and the Interstate Air Pollution Program (1962).

Ressler, C. (1964). *Fed. Proc.* **23,** 1350.

Ressler, C., Nigam, S. N., Giza, Y. H., and Nelson, J. (1963). *J. Amer. Chem. Soc.* **85,** 3311.

Rice, E. E., Warner, W. D., Mone, P. E., and Poling, C. E. (1957). *J. Nutr.* **61,** 253.

Roderick, L. M., and Schalk, A. F. (1931). *N. Dakota Agr. Exp. Sta. Bull.* 250.

Rosenthal, H. L. (1963). *Ann. N. Y. Acad. Sci.* **109,** 278.

Rothlin, E., and Bircher, R. (1952). *Progr. Allergy* **3,** 434.

Saxena, H. C., Jensen, L. S., and McGinnis, J. (1963). *J. Nutr.* **80,** 391.

Schantz, E. J. (1961). *J. Med. Pharm. Chem.* **4,** 459.

Scheel, L. D. (1964). *Paper presented 24th Ann. Meeting Inst. Food Technol.*

Schiffman, R. H. (1959). *Hanford Biol. Res. Annu. Rep.* **1958.** *U.S. Atom. Energy. Comm. Rep. HW-59500,* p. 16.

Schilling, E. D., and Strong, F. M. (1955). *J. Amer. Chem. Soc.* **77**, 2843.

Schoental, R., Head, M. A., and Peacock, P. R. (1954). *Brit. J. Cancer* **8**, 458.

Schoenthal, N. D. (1963). *Proc. Mont. Acad. Sci.* **23**, 63.

Schulze, E. (1961). *Intern. Rev. Hydrobiol.* **46**, 419.

Schumacher, R. E. (1955). *Progr. Fish. Cult.* **17**, 123.

Schutte, K. (1964). "The Biology of Trace Elements," p. 158. Lippincott, Philadelphia, Pennsylvania.

Shiloh, M., and Rosenburger, R. F. (1960). *Ann. N. Y. Acad. Sci.* **90**, 866.

Shue, G. M., Douglass, C. D., and Friedman, L. (1962). *Fed. Proc.* **21**, 91.

Shyamala, G., and Lyman, R. L. (1964). *Can. J. Biochem.* **42**, 1829.

Sinclair, K. B., and Jones, D. I. H. (1963). *Rep. Wash. Plant Breeding Sta. 1962*, p. 97.

Sinnhuber, R. O., Law, D. K., Yu, T. C., McKee, T. B., Hublon, W. F., and Wood, J. W. (1961). *Res. Brief Fish Comm. Oregon*, p. 54.

Sinnhuber, R. O., Wales, J. H., Ergebrecht, R. H., Amerd, D. F., Kray, W. D., Ayres, J. L., and Ashton, W. F. (1965). *Fed. Proc.* **24**, 627.

Sipos, J. C., and Ackman, R. G. (1964). *J. Fish. Res. Bd. Can.* **21**, 423.

Slocum, G. G. (1963). *In* "Microbiological Quality of Foods" L. W. Slanetz, C. O. Chichester, A. R. Gaufin, and Z. J. Ordal, eds.), p. 6. Academic Press, New York.

Snieszko, S. F., and Wood, E. M. (1954). *Trans. Amer. Fish. Soc.* **84**, 86.

Spatz, M. (1964). *Fed. Proc.* **23**, 1384.

Stahler, L. M., and Whitehead, E. I. (1941). *J. Biol. Chem.* **138**, 513.

Stahler, L. M., and Whitehead, E. I. (1950). *Science* **112**, 749.

Stockman, S. (1916). *J. Comp. Therap.* **29**, 95.

Sugai, M., Witting, L. A., Tsudiyama, H., and Kummerow, F. A. (1962). *Cancer Res.* **22**, 510.

Summer, F. B., and Fox, D. L. (1935). *Proc. Nat. Acad. Sci.* **21**, 330.

Swisher, R. D., O'Rourke, J. T., and Tomlinson, H. D. (1964). *J. Amer. Oil Chem. Soc.* **41**, 11.

Synge, R. L. M. (1963). *In* "Progress in Nutrition and Allied Sciences" (D. P. Cuthbertson, ed.), p. 31. Oliver and Boyd, London.

Tanner, F. W., and Tanner, F. P. (1953). "Food Borne Infections and Intoxications," 2nd ed., p. 164. Garrard Press, Champaign, Illinois.

Tedeschi, G. G., Petrelli, F., and Amici, D. (1965). *Ital. J. Biochem.* **14**, 237.

Thatcher, F. S. (1966). *Can. Med. Assoc. J.* **94**, 582.

Tsuda, K., Kawamura, M., and Hayatsu, R. (1960). *Chem. Pharm. Bull.* **8**, 257.

Tsuruga, T. (1963). *Nippon Suisan Gakkaishi*, **29**, 303.

Tunison, A. V., Phillips, A. M., Shaffer, H. B., Maxwell, J. M., Brockway, D. R., and McCay, C. M. (1944). *Cortland Hatchery Rep. No. 13.*

Van Soest, P. J. (1966). *J. Ass. Offic. Anal. Chem.* **49**, 547.

Vinson, S. B., Boyd, C. E., and Ferguson, D. E. (1963). *Science* **139**, 217.

Virtanen, A. I. (1962). *Arch. Biochem. Biophys. Suppl.* **1**, 200.

Vohra, P., and Kratzer, F. H. (1964). *Poultry Sci.* **43**, 1164.

Wada, S. M., Pallansh, M. J., and Liener, I. E. (1958). *J. Biol. Chem.* **233**, 395.

Wagner, D. E. (1954). *Progr. Fish. Cult.* **16**, 36.

Waley, S. G. (1966). *Advan. Protein Chem.* **21**, 1.

Wall, M. C., Eddy, C. R., McClennan, M. C., and Klumpp, M. E. (1952). *Anal. Chem.* **24**, 1337.

Williams, K. T., Lakin, H. W., and Byers, H. G. (1941). *U.S. Dep. Agr. Tech. Bull.*, 758.

Wilson, B. J., and Wilson, C. H. (1961). *J. Vet. Res.* **22**, 961.

Windmueller, H. G., Ackerman, C. J., Bakerman, H., and Mickelsen, O. (1959). *J. Biol. Chem.* **234,** 889.

Winteringham, F. P. W., Harrison, A., Bridges, R. G., and Bridges, P. M. (1955). *J. Sci. Food Agr.* **6,** 251.

Wogan, G. N. (1965). "Mycotoxins in Foodstuffs." M.I.T. Press, Cambridge, Massachusetts.

Wogan, G. N. (1966). *Bacteriol. Rev.* **30,** 460.

Wolf, H., and Jackson, E. W. (1963). *Science* **42,** 676.

Wolf, L. E. (1952). *Progr. Fish. Cult.* **14,** 110.

Wolf, S., and Snieszko, S. F. (1963). "Antimicrobials and Chemotherapy," p. 597. Amer. Soc. Microbiol., Ann Arbor, Michigan.

Wood, E. M., Griffin, P. J., and Snieszko, S. F. (1954). *Progr. Fish. Cult.* **16,** 19.

Wood, E. M., Yasutake, W. T., Woodall, A. N., and Halver, J. E. (1958). *J. Nutr.*

Woodall, A. N., Ashley, L. M., Halver, J. E., Olcott, H. S., and Van Der Veen, J. (1964). *J. Nutr.* **61,** 479.

Wootton, J. E., Artman, N. R., and Alexander, J. C. (1962). *J. Ass. Offic. Agr. Chem.* **45,** 739.

Yearbook of Agriculture (1962). *U.S. Dep. Agr. Government Printing Office, Washington,* pp. 37–338, 1100–1101.

Yudkin, W. H. (1944). *Bull. Bingham Oceanogr. Coll.* **9,** 1.

Zinkham, W. H., Lenhard, R. E., Jr., and Childs, B. (1958). *J. Pharm. Exp. Therap.* **122,** 85A.

## Addendum

The prime consideration in preparing the Chapter Nonnutrient Components of the Diet, was a concern for the possible presence of toxic constituents that could be present in prepared diets for fish. Although heavy metals and toxic elements and chemicals may be present in such diets, exposure of fish to this source would be expected to be low, because of regulatory procedures limiting levels of pesticides and other chemicals in foods and feeds.

Since the preparation of this chapter there has developed an increased concern regarding the contamination of the environment with heavy metals and other toxic chemicals and their subsequent entry into the food chain. In the case of the entry of these substances into the aquatic environment, a continuous exposure of the aquatic form of life, with possible entry and accumulation of contaminants in all stages of the food chain will result. A considerable concentration of these toxic materials in animals at the top of the food chain, e.g., predator fish, may take place. The concern is primarily with the effect of chronic exposure of low levels of the contaminants on the well being of the fish, and the concentration of the contaminant in the edible portion of the fish so as to affect the wholesomeness of the fish for human consumption.

Although persistant pesticides enter the environment entirely as a result of man's activity, in the case of trace elements the entry may be as a result of natural geological processes, as well. Bowen (1966) has discussed the problem of water pollution by trace elements, and has attempted to compare the amounts of elements added to rivers and the sea each year by natural and human activities. Based on the rates of mining of the various elements, estimates were made of potential pollution that could occur if the entire industrial production of an element were allowed to enter the aquatic environment. The elements were listed in four classes according to their potential for pollution. Of interest are the group of elements classed as "very high potential pollution." Included in this group are Ag, Au, Cd, Ge, Cu, Hg, Pb, Sb, Sn, Tl, and Zn. The environmental hazards associated with three elements of this group, namely, Hg, Pb, and Cd are presently cause for concern, and these elements as well as other pollutants will be used as a basis for consideration of the problems. Important factors to be considered include: (a) the possible bioconversion of the pollutant to a form that is more toxic and more readily concentrated than the original pollutant, and its subsequent effect on aquatic organisms, and (b) the bioavailability and biotoxicity of the residues in relationship to the wholesomeness of the fish.

## MERCURY

Mercury pollution of the environment can be caused by a number of and toxicologically distinct classes, namely, metallic mercury, inorganic mercury, arylmercurial, alkylmercurials, and alkoxyalkyl mercurials. The toxicity of these compounds administered chronically to mammalian species appears to be directly related to their rate of metabolism to inorganic mercury, as well as their ability to cross the blood brain barrier, and placenta. Chronically, methylmercury is the most toxic of the mercurials. Details of its effects, as well as those of the other mercurials, in mammalian species have been summarized in "Methylmercury in Fish," 1971.

The extreme hazards associated with the concentration of mercury residues in fish have been amply documented in reports of the Minamata and Nigata poisoning episodes (Minamata Disease) (Hazards of Mercury, 1971; Methylmercury in Fish, 1971; Löfroth, 1969). It was established that the poisoning was due to consumption of fish heavily contaminated with an organic form of mercury, which was identified as methylmercury. At that time, because methylmercury was shown to be present in the contaminating effluent in the Minamata episode, the suggestion (Fujiki, cited in Wood *et al.*, 1968) that biological methylation of the mercury had occurred was discounted. However, the subsequent description of the biological methylation of mercury by Wood *et al.* (1968) and Swedish scientists (Jensen and Jernelov, 1969), as well as the information derived from the more recent Swedish and U.S. mercury pollution, indicates that methylation of mercury in sediments on rivers and lakes is a major contributor to the current contamination of aquatic species. All forms of mercury entering the aquatic environment, either as result of man's activities or from natural geological sources, may be converted to methylmercury, which can be concentrated by fish and other aquatic species. The major groups of microorganism that can methylate mercury have not been identified, nor has it been established if methylation may occur by the action of the microorganism on the skin or in the gastrointestinal tract of the fish.

The process of bioaccumulation and biotransformation of mercurials in higher marine organisms is not completely understood. Presumably in fish this can occur via several processes including absorption through the gills or skin, or through components of the food chain. For example, Glooschenko ( 1969 ), has shown that phytoplankton accumulates mercury mainly by surface absorption. Yoshida (1967) showed that *Chlamydomonas angulosa* removed 1.3% of mercuric chloride and 6.5% of a phenylmercuric nitrate from a solution within 48 hours at 26°C. Phytoplankton and algae would thus provide a base for passage of mercury through the food chain. In addition, Korrinja (1952) has suggested that mucus present on the free surfaces of marine organisms may act as an agent collecting mercury as well as other positive polyvalent ions from the aquatic environment.

Although mercury in fish muscle is greater than 90% methylmercury, it is not known to what extent the total exposure of fish to mercury, is in the form of methylmercury. Details of the amount of methylmercury in components of the food chain are lacking, and at present no methodology exists to determine levels of methylmercury in water. However, since the rate of absorption of methylmercury through the gastrointestinal tract of animals is extremely effective compared to that of inorganic mercury (approximately greater than 90 and 2%, respectively), and major differences exist in the distribution and biological half-life of different forms of mercurials in mammalian tissues, it is extremely important to establish the biological half-life and the relative absorption of mercurials in fish. An extremely long biological half-life will result in a situation, where continuous exposure to the contaminant from the environment will result in a continuous increase in residue in the fish. Ohmomo *et al.* (1969) has reported studies on the distribution of [203] Hg labeled methylmercury and phenylmercury in pike, when administered orally in single dose, either in the ionic form or protein bound. The results of these studies provide indirect information on the relative ease of absorption of these mercurials. In the case of phenylmercury approximately 70% of the [203] Hg was present in the digestive organs 3 weeks after the exposure, compared with 30% in the case of methylmercury. No radioactivity was detectable in the brain at that time. High levels of radioactivity were present in the kidney, suggesting a rapid metabolism of the phenylmercury to inorganic mercury, as has been observed in mammalian species. Further, the amount of radioactivity in the flesh of the fish was only 10% of the total body radioactivity compared with approximately 30% in the case of methylmercury. In general, it appears that fish, like mammals, are able to absorb methylmercury more readily than phenylmercury, and that phenylmercury is more rapidly metabolized to inorganic mercury than is methylmercury.

Methylmercury is lost from fish at an extremely slow rate. Miettinen *et al.* (1968) has studied the retention and excretion rate of methylmercury [203]Hg labeled, administered directly into the stomach of fish. The mercury loss was shown to occur in two stages. First a rapid excretion, following a biological half-life of a couple days, slowing down after a couple of weeks. The changes may represent a rapid loss when mercury is being redistributed in the tissues of the fish, followed by an extremely slow loss from established binding sites. For the most part 80–90% of the mercury in fish was shown to follow the slower rate of excretion. The biological half-life of the slower excretion component of methylmercury was 25, 430, 470, and 490 days, respectively for Roach (*Leuciscus rutilus*), Flounder (*Pleuronectes flesus*), Pike (*Esox lucius*), and Perch (*Perca fluviatilis*). The excretion rate for phenylmercury for flounder, perch, and pike was 164, 190, and 157 days, respectively.

Because of the long half-life of methylmercury in fish, environmental contamination will result in a considerable accumulation of methylmercury in fish. It is not known what level of tissue methylmercury will result in fatalities. The highest levels of methylmercury reported in pike are of the order of 8–10 ppm (Stickel, 1971). Fish and shellfish found dead at Minamata had levels of mercury in the range of 9–24 ppm (Löfroth, 1969). Most of the available data on methylmercury residues in fish relates to the level found in edible muscle.

Backstrom (1969) reported on the distribution of [203]Hg labeled mercuric nitrate, phenyl nitrate, and methylmercuric nitrate in a number of species of fish following intramuscular or I. V. injection of the test compound, or in fish maintained in ponds containing these compounds. The species of fish studied included salmon (*Salman salar*), speckled trout (*Salvelinus fontinalis*), pike (*Esox lucius*), pike-perch (*Lucioperca lucioperca*), and perch (*Perca fluviatilis*). The distribution of mercury was studied by whole-body autoradiography techniques. In general, the principal distribution of mercury in fish resembled that observed in birds or mammals, although certain differences were reported. In the case of inorganic mercury, at the longest survival time, the highest concentration of mercury was in kidney, in which it was very unevenly distributed. High concentrations were also present in gills and in the pseudobranch. Distribution of phenylmercury was similar to inorganic mercury, with somewhat higher concentrations appearing in blood, liver, bile, and skeletal muscles. Methylmercury was readily absorbed, and shows important distribution patterns with time. At an early stage there was a marked uptake in brain and spinal cord; later, a high uptake was seen in liver, spleen, kidneys, gills, and pseudobranch and also in blood, myocardium, and pituitary, with lesser amounts in brain and skeletal muscles. This was followed by an increased uptake of mercury in brain and skeletal tissues. In all cases there was a high uptake of mercury in the spleen and gills, as well as the lens of the eye. Mercury (from phenylmercury) was present at a low level in the interstitium of the gonads, but was virtually absent from the germinal cells. Methylmercury given parenterally showed low concentrations in germinal cells and somewhat higher concentrations in gonads. The yolk of fish oocytes did not concentrate any of the mercury compounds used.

Backstrom (1969) discussed the possibility that the mercury in the fish gill prevents the active uptake of sodium which resulted in the inability of the freshwater fish to maintain salt balance with its surroundings. In addition, mercury uptake by the pseudobranch and choroid gland may result in additional disturbances of some regulating mechanisms. The pattern of uptake and concentration of mercury in various tissues reflect types of damage observed in methylmercury poisoned fish. The uptake of mercury in the lens of the fish eye may be associated with the cataracts reported in fish in the Minamata area at the time of the outbreak of Minamata disease. Brain concentration of methylmercury is reflected in the balance disturbances in fish exposed to methylmercury (Hannerz, 1967). The concentration of mercury in gonadal tissue may be associated with a decreased egg production and hatching of young. Kihlstom *et al.* (1971) studied the effect of addition of phenylmercuric acetate to water on the number of eggs laid, and their frequency of hatching in the zebrafish (*Brachydanio nerio* Ham-Buch). The number of eggs decreased in water containing more than 1 ng/gm of phenylmercuric acetate ($ED_{50}$ is 2.2 ng: phenylmercuric acetate/gm water). However, the reproductive capacity of the fish was diminished at even lower concentrations. Water containing 0.2 and 1 ng/gm phenylmercuric acetate caused a significant decrease in the frequency of hatching. It has not been established if this is due to the effect of mercury compounds on mitosis, or its effect on biologically active systems, such as protein hormones involved in egg production and egg laying. The results of this study are particularly significant as the lowest level of phenylmercuric acetate is of the same order as that of mercury present in some freshwater samples (Kihlstrom et al., 1971).

The effect of low tissue concentrations of methylmercury on the well being of the adult fish has not been established. However, Stickel (1971) reported that Johnells had observed that "pike of a population from below a pollution source definitely weighed less at each age than those taken upstream from the source." Other effects such as incoordination and sensory dysfunction have not been studied in detail.

## ARSENIC

Since arsenic is ubiquitous in both freshwater and seawater it is not surprising that all aquatic organisms examined contain a measurable residue of arsenic. Details of the form of arsenic in water and the form in which it is accumulated are lacking. Although it has been established that arsenic can be methylated by strains of *Pseudomonas brevicaule* (Challenger et al., 1933), it is not known if this process has the same significance as in the accumulation of this element by aquatic organisms, as has been established in the case of mercury. Until details of the form of arsenic in aquatic organisms have been established it will be difficult to determine the factors involved in the accumulation and bioconversion of inorganic arsenic. The ability of the aquatic organism to concentrate arsenic is well known.

Junkins (1963) has summarized the available data on accumulation of and residues of arsenic in fish and aquatic organisms. Included in this review are reports that various species of seaweed concentrate arsenic to 200 to 600 the concentration in seawater.

Plankton appear to be efficient concentrators of arsenic (Dupree, 1955; Lawrence, 1957) concentrating sodium arsenite from water approximately 2000 times (from 0.3 to 714 ppm). Since treatment of ponds with arsenite leads to an increase of phosphorus content of the water, it has been suggested that the arsenic may replace phosphorus present in bottom mud and also plankton.

The plankton and algae would provide a rich source of arsenic for marine organisms which may concentrate arsenic through the food chain. However, as in the case of other elements, it is not known if other aquatic species concentrate them directly from the water or through the food chain. Concentration factors for organisms in the marine environment have been reported by Lowman (1970). These include benthic algae (2000), mollusc muscle (650), crustacean muscle (400), fish muscle (700).

Oysters have been reported containing 2 ppm arsenic (Schroeder and Balassa, 1966) and shrimp have been reported containing 42 ppm arsenic (Coulson *et al.*, 1935). Large-mouth black bass (*Huro fluoridana*) have been reported to contain up to 40 ppm arsenic. In general, all marine organisms examined contain arsenic (Schroeder and Balassa, 1966). The fish that were analyzed (mainly ocean species) contained 0.2–15 ppm (wet weight) of arsenic. Whole fat, muscle fat, intestinal fat, and liver fat of marine fish contained 1.8–30.4 ppm arsenic, the highest values being observed in liver lipid. No information is available on the form of arsenic in fish. However, studies on the biotoxicity of arsenic in shellfish indicates that it is not as toxic as arsenite (Coulson *et al.*, 1935), although it seems to be absorbed as well.

EFFECT OF CD ON AQUATIC COMMUNITY AND ACCUMULATION BY AQUATIC SPECIES

If the cadmium pollution in freshwater areas is high enough, then it may completely eliminate normal aquatic life. Cadmium is concentrated by aquatic plants.

The concentration factors are stated to be plankton, 910, brown algae, 890, and freshwater plants, 1620 (Bowen, 1966). Studies with freshwater fish suggest that it is unlikely that there is any marked food chain accumulation of the element.

Lardner and Jernelov (1969) reported that when fish were fed Tubifex (bottom living oligochaete) which had been previously enriched with Cd (up to 20 ppm) the Cd content of the fish did not differ from fish fed Cd-free Tubifex. It was not possible to establish any Cd accumulation in fish through Cd-containing food. However, there was a linear concentration of Cd when fish were exposed to Cd solutions. The biological half-life of Cd in fish was established to be 3–4 weeks. In a study of the Cd enrichment of the sediment of aquariums (up to 400- to 500-fold of water concentration) it was shown that sterilized sediment accumulated more Cd than fresh sediment. It is not known if the sterilized sediment contains more -SH sites for Cd binding than fresh sediment, or if fresh sediment converts Cd to soluble compounds, or exhibits different binding mechanisms. However, accumulation of Cd in fish from Cd-containing water was greatest in tanks containing Cd enriched sludge.

The high levels of Cd observed in fish may be due to direct concentration from seawater. The following range of concentration have been reported for shellfish (Pringle *et al.*, 1968). The concentration factor is based on a seawater concentration of 0.1 ppb.

|              | ppm Wet weight | Concentration factor |
|--------------|----------------|----------------------|
| Clams (soft) | 0.14–0.2       | 1000–2000            |
| Clams (hard) | 0.14–0.49      | 1000–5000            |
| Oysters      | 0.53–1.40      | 5000–14,000          |

In general, the levels of Cd in marine animals are in the range 0.15 to 3 ppm, with the lowest level in the calcareous tissue. In mollusca most of the Cd is accumulated in the viscera. For the species *Pectin*, Cd has been identified in the form of the Cd-Zn protein, metallothionein.

Analysis of tissues of bluegill exposed to Cd for periods up to 90 days, showed that substantial accumulation of Cd occurred in the kidney, liver, gill, and gut, with lesser accumulation in the spleen and no significant accumulation in bone and muscle. The concentrations of Cd in kidney, gut, and spleen varied and were not closely related to cadmium exposure. However, accumulation in liver and gill was related to Cd exposure. Equilibrium was established between concentration of Cd in water and uptake in a period of 30–60 days. The concentration of Cd in the gill is a useful index of acute exposure to Cd. In living bluegills concentration never exceeded 130 $\mu$g/gm gill tissue, death occurring at a minimum concentration of 150 $\mu$g/gm gill tissue. The Cd concentration in liver of bluegill and other fish may be a useful indicator of exposure to Cd. A high concentration of Cd, 300–400 $\mu$g/gm, in liver indicates a past history of exposure, whereas, values less than 75–100 $\mu$g/gm indicates that Cd exposure had been very short or at very low water concentrations (Mount and Stephan, 1967).

A detailed study of the pathological changes observed in the intestinal tract, kidney, and gills of *Fundulus heteroclitus* (common mummichog), after acute exposure to water containing 50 ppm Cd has been reported by Gardner and Yevich (1970). Fish showed damage to the intestinal mucosa, which progressed with time. Kidney damage appeared mainly in proximal tubules. Marked changes occurred in the gill filaments and respiratory lamellae. Examination of circulating blood elements showed rapid and significant changes in the eosinophil-type cells. Specifically, there was a marked increase in the abundance of eosinophils, which corresponded with a marked decrease in the number of eosinophils in the head kidney, suggesting a migration of these cells from the renal hemopoietic site during cadmium poisoning. This change appears to be specific for cadmium and was not observed when fish were acutely exposed to concentrations of other heavy metals (Ag, Cu, Hg, Pb, and Zn).

It is not known if Cd in the aquatic environment can undergo biotransformation into organic forms which may be more readily accumulated by fish than the original Cd pollutant, and also be more toxic as with Hg. The available information on the properties of alkyl and aryl cadmium salts suggests that it is very unlikely that this process could occur. Alkyl or aryl cadmium halides are unknown. The cadmium dialkyls are markedly less stable than those of other metals. Only dimethyl Cd can be kept without decomposition (Sidgwick, 1950).

## LEAD

Detailed information on residues of lead and the concentration factors in fish are generally lacking. The concentration factor for aquatic organisms has been summarized by Lowman (1970). Included in this report were benthic algae (750), phytoplankton (40,000), zooplankton (3000), mollusc (whole animal) 4000, and mollusc muscle (40). Since lead may be poorly absorbed from the gastrointestinal tract if fish resemble mammals in this respect, then the potential for accumulation for lead via the food chain may not be very great.

Lead in water may occur mainly associated with suspended matter (Lazrus, 1970) and the bioavailability of this form of lead in food chains is not clearly understood. Pringle *et al.* (1968) have studied in detail the accumulation of Pb by various species of shellfish in a simulated environmental system. Accumulation depended on environmental concentration of the metal, temperature, species concerned, and physiological activity. Concentration factors reported were oysters 4100, quahaug 5850, and softshell clams 3400. Depletion followed biochemical increases within the animal, and there appeared to be a direct relationship between the uptake rate for a given metal and its depletion for any molluscan species.

Since fish appear to concentrate lead mainly in bone, then levels of Pb in edible fish muscle may not reach significant levels. In a recent FWQA report the concentration factors calculated based on uptake of $^{210}$Pb into tissue was 35 for muscle tissue of ocean fish, 5400 for bone, and 15 for muscle tissue of freshwater fish compared to 1400 for bone and 1050 for clams. Levels of Pb, reported for shellfish range from 0.1–10.20 ppm (Pringle *et al.*, 1968), and for fish 0.24–0.54 ppm (Harley, 1970).

Carpenter (1927) and Jones (1938, 1964) have published data on the effects of acutely toxic levels of lead to various species of fish. Little information is available on the effects of chronic exposure to low levels of lead. Dawson (1935) reported that catfish exposed to levels of Pb in water at 50 ppm for periods of 16–183 days developed blood alterations. A detailed study of hematological and other histopathological effects in tissues of guppies exposed to Pb at concentration of 1–3 ppm, have been reported by Crandall and Goodnight (1963). Jones (1964) has reported behaviorial impairment in *Gasterosteus* exposed to lead nitrate solutions at 1 ppm and *Phoxinus phoxinus* at 0.4 ppm. These levels are well in excess of those occurring in most natural waters in the United States.

## COPPER

Addition of copper salts to the aquatic environment can result in serious ecological changes. In addition to the elimination of some fish through direct toxic action of the copper, reduction in food supply due to the adverse effect of copper on plankton and other components of the food chain may cause a marked decline in fish populations. Derby and Graham (1953) have described such effects in a study of control of aquatic growths in reservoirs by copper sulfate, and secondary effects of such treatment. In this study the use of 0.8 to 1.0 ppm copper sulfate was lethal to suckers, carp, and also paper-shelled mussel (Anadonta), although buffalo fish, black bass, and bluegill were unaffected. Detailed studies have also been reported on the effect of "Copper-Zinc Mining Pollution on the Spawning Migration of Atlantic Salmon" (Saunders and Sprague, 1967; Sprague *et al.*, 1965). These problems were mainly related to pollution from a base metal mine in the northwest Miramichi River, New Brunswick, Canada. In these studies incipient lethal levels (ILL) for young salmon were 48 $\mu$g/liter of copper or 600 $\mu$g/liter zinc in soft water, although mixtures showed modest potentiation. Salmon parr avoided one-tenth of the incipient lethal levels. Because of the pollution many adult Atlantic salmon return prematurely downstream. For example, prior to the pollution occurring, only 1–3% of the salmon returned prematurely downstream, whereas, after the pollution the number rose to 10–22%. During the period of observation there is no indication that the fish are growing accustomed to the pollution.

A study of histological changes in winter flounder to various levels of copper showed that high and medium levels of copper caused fatty metamorphosis in the liver, necrosis of kidney, distinction of the hemopoietic tissue, and gross changes in gill architecture (Baker, 1969). Changes in blood parameters of fish exposed to a sublethal level and toxic chemicals are being studied as one of a number of specific indicators for evaluating the physical condition of the fish and possible long-range effects of the polluting agent. Studies in brook trout exposed to levels of Cu ranging from 3.4 to 32.5 $\mu$g/liter for 337 days showed that blood characteristics were unchanged, except for a measurable decrease in plasma glutamic-oxalacetic transaminase at the highest levels tested. Exposure of brook trout to high concentrations of copper (approx. 70 $\mu$g/liter or 40 $\mu$g/liter) for 6 and 21 days caused a significant increase in erythrocytes, hematocrit, hemoglobin, plasma glutamic-oxalacetic transaminase, and total protein, whereas, plasma chloride and osmolarity decreased (McKim *et al.*, 1970).

PETROCHEMICALS AND OTHER INDUSTRIAL ORGANIC CHEMICALS

Halstead (1970) has reviewed problems associated with pollution of the marine environment with petrochemicals and other industrial organic chemicals. Of concern is the possibility that persistent toxic and carcinogenic pollutants may enter the food chain, and in addition to causing serious effects in the ecosystem, may also become incorporated into marine species that form an important part of man's diet.

The accidental discharge of large amounts of crude petroleum oil introduces into the aquatic environment aromatic, and polycyclic aromatic compounds, as well as saturated hydrocarbons. In addition to the acute toxic effect of the hydrocarbons, additional problems include incorporation of hydrocarbons into marine species, which may pass through the components of the food chain (Blumer and Thomas, 1965; Blumer, 1967). For example, the hydrocarbons of zooplankton have been shown to pass through the digestive tract of the basking shark without fractionation or any structural modification. After absorption they are deposited in the liver. Zitko (1970) has described procedures to determine heavy residual fuel oil in aquatic animals. Samples of flounder from contaminated areas contained levels of 7 ppm of in flesh and 182 ppm in skin. In general, the highest level in organisms studied was present in the gut. Another potential problem relates to the presence of polycyclic hydrocarbons which have been detected in oysters harvested from polluted waters (Callaghan, 1961) at levels up to 1 ppm. An additional problem relating to off-flavor has previously been discussed.

In addition, Halstead (1970) lists other potential carcinogens that may be found in industrial effluents. Included in the list are $\alpha$-naphthylamine, $\beta$-naphthylamine, xenylamine, anthracene and their derivatives, and chloronitrobenzenes, activated carbon from industrial effluent of rubber plants, which have been shown to provide carcinogenic eluates.

Another class of industrial chemicals that have recently been shown to have global distribution, and to have entered the food chain, particularly through the aquatic environment, are the polychlorinated biphenyls

(PCB). These compounds have had wide use as plasticizers, dielectrics, and heat transfer fluid. The PCB's are similar in structure and effects to certain chlorinated hydrocarbons, and until recently because of their properties and ubiquitous distribution, their presence in the environment was confused with that of DDT (Anderson *et al.*, 1969). The more highly chlorinated PCBs are very resistant to degradation by fire and microorganisms (Monsanto Chem. Co., Tech. Bull. PL-306). The present extent of the contamination of the marine food chain in United States (southern California) is indicated by extremely high levels of PCBs in the lipids of thin-shelled eggs of fish eating birds. PCB levels as high as 210–266 ppm were reported (Schmidt *et al.*, 1971). Experimental studies have shown that marine diatoms (*Cylindrotheca dosterium*) can absorb and concentrate PCB (Archlor 1242), to levels of 900 to 1000 times the concentration in seawater (Keil *et al.*, 1971). However, low levels of exposure (0.01 ppm in media) did not affect growth, nucleic acid or chlorophyll production of the diatom. Hansen *et al.* (1971), have studied the uptake and retention of PCB (Arachlor 1254) in two estuarine fishes, juvenile pinfish (*Lagodon rhomboides*) and spot (*Leiostomus xanthurus*). Spot exposed to 1 ppb Arachlor 1254 for 56 days, showed rapid uptake and concentration of the PCB, the maximum level being reached within 24 days. The maximum concentration in the whole spot was $3.7 \times 10^4$ times that in the test medium. The maximum concentration was present in the liver, with lesser amounts in gills, whole fish, heart, brain, and muscle ($7.4 \times 10^3$). Retention studies in exposed fish maintained in PCB-free water showed that after 84 days the relative amount of PCB in whole fish dropped 73%. In another study, Zitko (1971) reported that levels of PCB were present in all samples of fish analyzed (American eel, chain pickerel, Atlantic salmon, herring, mackerel, cod, white hake, plaice, and ocean perch) levels of PCB ranged from 0.02 ppm (hake and cod) to 0.71 ppm (American eel). Since some of the eels were taken from lakes free from industrial pollution, or domestic sewage, both sources of PCB, Zitko (1971) has speculated on the possibility of pollution by aerial fallout of PCBs. In this respect it should be noted that PCB was detected in all samples of rain water obtained over a 12-month period in the United Kingdom (Tarrant and Tatton, 1968). Duke *et al*, (1970), have reported on the effects of Arachlor 1254 on estuarine organisms in sensitive stages of their development. Included in this study were pinfish (*Lagodon rhomboides*), pink shrimp (*Penaeus duorarum*), and oysters (*Crassostrea virginica*), as well as juvenile pink shrimp and blue crabs. A 48-hour exposure to flowing seawater containing 100 ppb PCBs (Arachlor 1254), resulted in 80% mortality of shrimp within 24 hours. Pinfish were not affected at these levels of exposure. During this period shrimp accumulated 3.9 ppm. PCBs in their tissues and pinfish after 48 hours accumulated 17 ppm. Juvenile crabs were not as sensitive as shrimp to PCB. Shrimp died after exposure to 5 ppb of the PCB for varying periods up to 20 days. At day 20 of the test, surviving shrimp had a tissue concentration of 33 ppm PCB. Crabs exposed to flowing seawater containing 5 ppb for 20 days contained 18 to 27 ppm PCB in the whole body. Following 4-week exposure to PCB free water, the average level of PCB in the exposed crabs was 11 ppm. Although PCB are acutely less toxic to fish than organochlorine pesticides (Zitko, 1970), effect of chronic exposure to low levels, particularly on the reproductive process of fish has not been established. In addition, the studies of Duke *et al.* (1970), emphasize the need to study the toxic effects of PCB administered at critical stages of the development of aquatic organisms. Another problem related to the evaluation of the hazard of PCB pollution is the fact that some samples of European PCBs have been shown to contain extremely toxic impurities (Vos *et al.*, 1970). In a study reported by Vos *et al.* (1970), there was a significant difference in toxicity between three commercial PCB preparations. Only two preparations caused high mortality, liver necrosis, and chick edema-like lesions. Detailed analyses of their samples indicated that these two PCB preparations contained polar compounds that were not present in the other PCB preparations. These impurities identified included tetra- and pentachlorodibenzofurans. It is possible that the high toxicity of these PCB samples was due to the dibenzofuran derivatives. At present, work is underway to detect and identify chlorinated dibenzofuran in specimens of wildlife. In this respect, it is of interest that the chick edema factor has been characterized as a family of polychlorodibenzo-*p*-dioxins (Cantrell *et al.*, 1969). The dioxins are extremely toxic and can produce lethal effects on chicks at concentrations of 3 to 5 $\mu$g. It is possible that residues of this highly toxic contaminant may remain in flesh or organs of animals receiving contaminated feed. Studies of polychlorophenols are now focused on the possible presence of polychlorinated benzofurans and polychlorodibenzo-*p*-dioxins.

## Factors Involved in Consideration of Wholesomeness of Fish and Aquatic Foods for Man

In addition to the problem of the effect of the pollutants on the well being of the fish, another problem relates to the concentration of heavy metals and other toxic substances in the edible portion of fish, and its effect on the wholesomeness as a food for man. In order to evaluate the potential hazard of these residues in foods, several types of basic information are required. They include: (1) information on the level of residues in aquatic food, as well as the chemical form of the residue. In addition, information on exposure from other environmental sources, e.g., water, air, and other foods are needed so that an estimate of total exposure to the compound can be made; (2) bioavailability of the chemical form of the residue to determine if this represents a significant route of exposure; (3) detailed information derived from toxicological studies and epidemiological studies to determine acceptable levels of exposure; and (4) detailed information on dietary intake of the contaminated food, so that the levels of residues present in the food and consumption patterns can be related to intake.

Although fish are likely to be contaminated with a number of pollutants, there is no information as to whether or not these would act singly or synergistically. At present evaluation must be made as if the contaminants act singly.

### General References

Toxic Constituents of Plant Foodstuffs (1969). (I.E. Liener, ed.). Academic Press, New York.
Toxicants Occurring Naturally in Food (1966). NAS/NRC, Washington, D. C.

Journals of Specific interest in relation to the pollution of the aquatic environment:

*Bull. Environ. Contam. Toxicol. Environ.*
*Environ. Res.*
*Environ. Sci. Technol.*
*Pollut. Abstr.*

### References

Anderson, D. W., Hickey, J. J., Risenbrough, R. W., Hughes, D. F., and Christansen, R. E. (1969). *Can. Field Natur.* **89,** 89.
Arthur, J. W. and Leonard, E. N. (1970). *J. Fish Res. Bd. Can.* **27,** 1277.
Backstrom, J. (1969). *Acta Pharmacol Toxicol.* **27** (Suppl. 3), 1.
Baker, J. T. P. (1969). *J. Fish Res. Bd. Can.* **26,** 2785.
Blumer, M. (1967). *Science* **156,** 390.
Blumer, M. and Thomas, D. W. (1965). *Science* **148,** 370.
Bowen, H. J. M. (1966). "Trace Elements in Biochemistry." Academic Press, New York.
Callaghan, J. (1961). *Trans. N. Amer. Wildl. Nat. Res. Conf.* **26,** 328.
Cantrell, J. S., Webb, N. C., and Mabis, A. J. (1969). *Acta. Crysto.* (*1969*), **B25,** 150.
Carpenter, K. E. (1927). *Brit. J. Exp. Biol.* **4,** 378.
Coulson, E. J., Remington, R. E., and Lynch, K. M. (1935). *J. Nutr.* **10,** 255.

Challenger, F., Higginbottom, C., and Ellis, L. (1933). *J. Chem. Soc. (London)*, p. 95.
Crandall, C. A. and Goodnight, C. J. (1963). *Trans. Amer. Micropsc. Soc.*, **82**, 59.
Dawson, A. B. (1935). *Biol. Bull.* **68**, 335.
Derby, R. L., and Graham, D. W. (1953). *Proc. Amer. Soc. Civil Eng.* **79**, 203.
Duke, T. W., Lowe, J. F., and Wilson, Jr. (1970). *Bull. Environ. Contam. Toxicol.*, **2**, 171.
Dupree, H. K. (1955). *Proc. S.E. Ass. Gam Fish Comm.*
FWQA (1970). Hazards of Lead in the Environment With Particular Reference to the Aquatic Environment. Federal Water Quality Administration, August, 1970.
Gardner, G. R. and Yevich, P. P. (1970). *J. Fish Res. Bd. Can.* **27**, 2185.
Glooschenko, W. A. (1969). *J. Phycol.* **5**, 224.
Halstead, B. W. (1970). *FAO Tech. Conf. Marine Pollut. and its Effects On Living Resources and Fishing.*
Hannerz, L. (1967). *Rep. Royal Comm. Nat. Resources, Stockholm*, 1967.
Hansen, D. J., Parrish, P. R., Lowe, J. J., Wilson, A. J., Jr. and Wilson, P. D. (1971). *Bull. Environ. Contam. Toxicol.* **6**, 113.
Harley, J. H. (1970). *Environ. Sci. Tech.* **4**, 225.
Hazards of Mercury (1971). *Environ Res.* **4**, 69 pp.
Ikuta, K. (1968). *Bull. Insp. Soc. Sci. Fish.* **34**, 482.
Jensen, S. and Jernelov, A. (1969). *Nature (London)* **223**, 753.
Jones, J. R. E. (1938). *J. Exp. Biol.* **15**, 394.
Jones, J. R. E. (1964). *In* "Fish and River Pollution," Vol. 60, pp. 66–82. Butterworth, London.
Junkins, R. L. (1963). *In* "Radioecology," (V. Schultz and A. W. Kleneal, Jr., eds.) Reinhold, New York.
Keil, J. E., Priester, L. E., and Sandiffer, S. H. (1971). *Bull. Environ. Contam. Toxicol.* **2**, 1971.
Kihlstrom, J. E., Lunberg, C., and Hulth, L. (1971). *Environ. Res.* **4**, 355.
Korrinja, P. (1952). *Res. Biol.* **27**, 266.
Lardner, L. and Jernelov, A. (1969). *Ecol. Res. Comm. Bull. No.* **5**.
Lawrence, J. M. (1957). *Proc. S.E. Ass. Game Fish Comm.*
Lazrus, A. L. (1970). *Advan. Environ. Sci.* **4**, 55.
Lofröth, G. (1969). *Swedish Nat. Sci. Res. Counc. Ecol. Res. Comm. Bull. No.* **4**, 38.
Lowman, F. G. (1970). Accumulation and Redistribution of Radionuclides by Marine Organisms, Bureau of Commercial Fisheries, Unpublished.
McKim, J. M., Christensen, G. M., and Hunt, E. P. (1970). *J. Fish. Res. Bd. Can.* **27**, 1883.
Methylmercury in Fish. (1971) *Nord. Hyg. Tidskr. Suppl.* **4**, 364.
Miettinen, J. K., Tillander, M., Rissaner, K., Miettinen, V., and Mintkinen, E. (1969). *Northern Mercury Symp. Nordfork, Stockholm*, October 10–11.
Monsanto Chemical Company. *Tech. Bull.* PL-306.
Mount, D. I. and Stephan, C. E. (1967). *J. Wildl. Environ.* **31**, 168.
Ohmomo, Y., Miettinen, V., Blankenstein, E., Tillander, M., Rissaner, K., and Miettinen, J. K. (1969). *Fifth Radioactivity in Scandinavia Symp. Helsinki*, May 19–20.
Pringle, B. H., Hissong, D. E., Katz, E. L., and Mulswka (1968). *J. Sanit. Eng. Div. Amer. Soc. Civil Eng.* **94**, 455.
Saunders, R. L. and Sprague, J. B. (1967). *Water Res.*, 419.
Schmidt, T. T., Risebrough, R. W. and Gress, F. (1971). *Bull. Environ. Contam. Tosicol.* **6**, 235.

Schroeder, H. A. and Balassa, J. J. (1966). *J. Chron. Dis.* **19**, 85.

Sidgwick, N. V. (1950). *In* "The Chemical Elements and Their Compounds," Vol. 1. 267. Clarendon Press, Oxford.

Sprague, J. B., Elson, P. F., and Saunders, R. L. (1965). *Int. J. Air Water Pollut.* **9**, 531.

Stickel, W. (1971). *Environ. Res.* **4**, 33.

Tarrant, K. R., and Tatton, O. G. (1968). *Nature (London)* **219**, 725.

Vos, J. G., Koeman, J. H., Van Der Maas, H. L., Ten Noever de Braun, M. C., and de Vos, R. H. (1970). *Fd. Cosmet. Toxicol.* **8**, 625.

Wettenberg, L. (1964). *Lancet* **i,** 498.

Wood, J. M., Kennedy, F. S., and Rosen, C. G. (1968). *Nature (London)* **220**, 173.

Yoshida, T. (1967). *J. Tokyo Univ. Fish.* **53**, 73.

Zitko, V. (1970). *Bull. Environ. Contam. Toxicol.* **5,** 279.

Zitko, V. (1971). *Bull. Environ. Contam. Toxicol.* **6,** 464.

# 6

# ENZYMES AND SYSTEMS OF INTERMEDIARY METABOLISM*

*H. L. A. Tarr*

* Abbreviations used are those officially recognized by the *Journal of Biological Chemistry*. Literature reviewed up to September 1967.

## I. Introduction

In general, the subject of fish biochemistry has been sadly neglected, and the volume of research in this interesting and challenging field is insignificant in comparison with that of mammalian biochemistry. Developments in the latter field have been greatly stimulated because of medical implications and the resultant comparative ease of obtaining financial support for worthy projects. On the other hand, much of the early work on fish biochemistry is owed to pressures created by demands for solving practical problems of the fishing industry. Much of the work was therefore directed to studies of immediate postmortem changes in muscles, such as alterations in proteins or lipids and production of volatile bases or acids or other substances that could be employed as indexes of postmortem spoilage. This created rather narrow zones of interest, and it is only during comparatively recent years that there has been an increasing awareness of the lack of basic knowledge of fish biochemistry, and of the many and varied metabolic processes that occur and the enzymes that mediate these processes.

Several early reviews are available concerning fish biochemistry, but these do not tend to emphasize intermediary metabolism or enzymes. One of the most useful of these was edited by Williams (1951), and certain of the review articles included cover some aspects of intermediary metabolism, particularly those dealing with carotenoids and lipids. Reviews on fish proteins (Geiger, 1948; Hamoir, 1955) did not emphasize enzymes, almost certainly because of the then rather limited knowledge of the field. A review on the biochemistry of fish (Tarr, 1958a) referred only briefly to enzymes and systems concerned with intermediary metabolism.

Another review that appeared at about the same time, and unfortunately in a comparatively obscure publication (Gubmann *et al.*, 1958), gave an excellent account of most of the then known pathways of intermediary metabolism in fishes, marine invertebrates, and mammals. The present review has been restricted to true fishes and is concerned with systems of intermediary metabolism, and, more particularly, with the enzymes that mediate the various reactions. Since the subject of digestion and digestive enzymes of fishes was thoroughly reviewed fairly recently (Barrington, 1957), this subject has been omitted. Likewise, no mention has been made of the enzyme thiaminase, since this has been the subject of several reviews (Harris, 1951; Fujita, 1954; Lee *et al.*, 1955).

## II. Carbohydrate Metabolism

### A. GENERAL OBSERVATIONS

The subject of muscle and liver glycogen concentrations and degradation to lactic and pyruvic acids in fish has been the subject of a large number of publications and several reviews (Black, 1958; Drummond and Black, 1960; Black *et al.*, 1961; Tomlinson and Geiger, 1962). During exercise the muscle glycogen of rainbow trout, *Salmo gairdneri,* falls very rapidly and the lactate and pyruvate levels rise. The recovery to preexercise levels is very slow indeed, taking 8 to over 24 hours in the case of lactate and glycogen, respectively. This suggests that in fish muscle glycogen is used rapidly to supply energy for short bursts of exercise, but not for long sustained efforts as in fish migration. During recent years the subject of carbohydrate metabolism in fish has been the subject of numerous investigations. These have been carried out using either whole live fish, tissue homogenates or slices.

### B. EXPERIMENTS WITH LIVE FISH, TISSUE SLICES OR HOMOGENATES

Ekberg (1958) observed that $Q_{O_2}$ values for gill metabolism of goldfish were higher for fish acclimated at 10°C than for those acclimated at 26°C. The fact that oxygen consumption by gill homogenates of the 10°C acclimated fish was inhibited 53% by iodoacetate, while that of 30°C acclimated fish was inhibited 77% suggested that the tricarboxylic acid cycle is more operative in the 30°C fish. Iodoacetate is a strong inhibitor of glyceraldehyde-3-phosphate dehydrogenase, an important enzyme of glycolysis. He also found a 63% increase in $O_2$ consumption of liver slices of fish acclimated to 10°C over those acclimated to 30°C.

Kanungo and Prosser (1959) showed that liver homogenates from fish acclimated to 20°C had a $Q_{O_2}$ 43% higher than that of warm acclimated (30°C) fish. Since the $Q_{O_2}$ of the liver mitochondria was only 12% higher in the cold acclimated fish, it was suggested that the difference in oxygen consumption of liver and mitochondria was due to the soluble enzymes of the hexosemonophosphate shunt pathway.

Hoskin (1959) studied oxidation of specifically labeled glucose-$^{14}C$ substrates by fish tissues, and more particularly those of the electric eel (*Electrophorus electricus*). Most of his experiments were carried out with tissue slices and he used ratios of $^{14}CO_2$ formed by oxidation of glucose-6-$^{14}C$/glucose-1-$^{14}C$ as criteria of the comparative importance of the glycolytic (Embden-Meyerhof) and pentose phosphate (hexose monophosphate shunt) pathways in glucose metabolism. This criterion he realized is open to a number of criticisms (Wood and Katz, 1958; Katz and Wood, 1960). He concluded that only with the brain tissue of this fish did the ratio approach 1.0, a value which has been assumed to indicate practically exclusive utilization of the Embden-Meyerhof pathway. In heart and ordinary muscle, and even more noticeably in the electric organ, only part of the oxidation proceeded by the Embden-Meyerhof route. In carp tail muscle a very low ratio (0.07) was obtained, indicating a major utilization of the pentose phosphate pathway.

Brown (1960) injected C-1 and C-6-$^{14}C$-labeled glucose intraperitoneally into carp and collected respired $^{14}CO_2$ for a 4-day period, the fish being held at 24°–25°C. His results suggested that there was no important difference when either labeled substrate was employed, and that therefore the pentose phosphate pathway was probably of little importance. In his experiments about 30% of the radioactivity injected appeared as $^{14}CO_2$ in 4 days.

If there were a major utilization of the C-1 of glucose via the pentose phosphate pathway, the loss of this C atom as $^{14}CO_2$ would lessen the amount entering the glycerol molecule in comparison with that if C-6 labeled glucose were used. The results obtained were variable, for in one case the glycerol was more heavily labeled, and in the other less heavily labeled, when C-6 and C-1-labeled glucose was injected. The results could indicate some utilization of the hexose monophosphate pathway. The radioactivity of glutamic acid and alanine from hydrolyzates of the liver protein of injected fish showed no important difference between fish receiving C-1 or C-6-labeled radioactive glucose. If the pentose phosphate pathway were operating to a major extent the specific activities of these amino acids should be much lower with C-1-labeled glucose as substrate since much of the radioactivity would be lost as $^{14}CO_2$.

Additional experiments showed that, while liver homogenates of carp contained both glucose-6-phosphate dehydrogenase and 6-phosphogluconic acid dehydrogenase, these enzymes were present in considerably lower concentrations than those usually occurring in warm-blooded mammals. These results when considered together, all tend to indicate that little of the glucose in these fish was utilized by the pentose phosphate pathway.

Hochachka and Hayes (1962) pointed out that previous work had shown that cold adaptation tended to stimulate, and warm adaptation to diminish, metabolism in fish. They acclimated speckled trout (*Salvelinus fontinalis*) to 4° and 15°C and injected them intraperitoneally with various metabolites. They also studied oxygen consumption of epaxial muscle slices and homogenates and of liver slices under different conditions.

Muscle homogenates of the cold acclimated fish consumed more oxygen at 4°, 10°, and 15°C than did those from warm acclimated fish. On the other hand, at 20°C while those from the latter fish still consumed oxygen, those from the cold acclimated fish were apparently unable to tolerate this temperature and did not consume oxygen. At 4°C the muscle from cold acclimated fish consumed twice as much oxygen as did that from the warm acclimated fish. Inhibition by iodoacetate, a potent inhibitor of the triosephosphate dehydrogenase enzyme of the Embden-Meyerhof glycolytic pathway, was significantly greater in the warm acclimated fish, which was taken to indicate a greater participation of that pathway in these fish.

When $^{14}CO_2$ was injected into fish and liver glycogen was prepared from them 4 to 6 hours later, it was found that in all cases $^{14}C$ accumulated in the C-3 and C-4 atoms of glucose, isolated after hydrolysis of the glycogen, to a much greater extent (over ten times as much) in the warm than in the cold acclimated fish, a finding consistent with a greater participation of the Embden-Meyerhof pathway in the warm acclimated fish. Labeling in carbon atoms 1, 2, 5, and 6 indicated a probable greater participation of the pentose phosphate pathway in the cold acclimated fish. Additional studies showed that muscle and liver tissue preparations from cold acclimated fish incorporated more $^{14}C$ from injected $^{14}CO_2$ into the lipid fraction than did those from warm acclimated fish. Acetate-1-$^{14}C$ yielded less $^{14}CO_2$ but was markedly incorporated into lipid in cold acclimated fish. These data all appear to be consistent with an increased utilization of the pentose phosphate pathway in cold acclimated fish.

Hochachka (1962) demonstrated that intraperitoneally injected gluconate-1-$^{14}$C was not appreciably incorporated into warm acclimated (20°C) *S. fontinalis* liver glycogen, while both C-1 and C-4-labeled glucose were readily incorporated. This result was taken to indicate that gluconate was metabolized via the pentose phosphate pathway. The trace amount of $^{14}$C gluconate which caused slight labeling of glycogen after 14 hours could have occurred by labeling of Embden-Meyerhof pathway intermediates either by $^{14}CO_2$ fixation or by a possible reversion of the 6-phosphogluconate lactonase enzyme system permitting formation of a small amount of 6-phosphogluconic acid.

Thyroxine and 3,5,3′-triiodothyronine, both of which are known to stimulate metabolism of glucose via the Embden-Meyerhof pathway, stimulated $^{14}CO_2$ formation from gluconate-1-$^{14}$C by both whole injected fish and by excised liver tissue, indicating that these hormones probably stimulated operation of the pentose phosphate pathway in these fish.

The first enzymic reaction in the pentose phosphate pathway is that carried out by glucose-6-phosphate dehydrogenase, the product of the reaction being 6-phospho-δ-gluconolactone. Though the *in vitro* reversibility of this system with a yeast enzyme was demonstrated, it was pointed out that formation of glucose-6-phosphate from 6-phospho-δ-gluconolactone is unlikely to occur *in vivo* since the equilibrium is very greatly in favor of lactone formation (Horecker and Smyrniotis, 1953). The second step, hydrolysis of the unstable lactone to yield 6-phosphogluconic acid, is accelerated by a specific lactonase enzyme (Brodie and Lipmann, 1955) and it is doubtful if there is significant reversibility *in vivo*. Thus it might be expected that 6-phosphogluconic acid would almost certainly be metabolized via the pentose phosphate pathway, the C-1 atom yielding $CO_2$ when metabolized by 6-phosphogluconic acid dehydrogenase to yield ribulose-5-phosphate (Horecker *et al.*, 1951). The rate of $^{14}CO_2$ formation from 6-phosphogluconate should give an indication of the comparative importance of the pentose phosphate pathway.

With the above facts in mind the metabolism of $^{14}$C-labeled 6-phosphogluconate and gluconic acid in *S. gairdneri* held at 5°–7°C (cold acclimated) was studied by Tarr (1963). $^{14}CO_2$ was formed 50–75 times as rapidly when glucose-GL (generally labeled)-$^{14}$C was injected intraperitoneally or intramuscularly as when gluconic acid-GL-$^{14}$C was similarly administered. The rate of $^{14}CO_2$ formation was the same when fish were injected with C-1-$^{14}$C, C-6-$^{14}$C or GL$^{14}$C-6-phosphogluconate. Intramuscular or intravenous injection of C-6-$^{14}$C or GL$^{14}$C-6-phosphogluconate, or of GL$^{14}$C-gluconic acid, resulted in labeling of muscle "dextrin," maltose, glucose, glucose-6-phosphate, fructose-6-phosphate, fructose-1, 6-diphosphate, and gluconic acid. On the contrary, maltose, glucose, and the hexose phosphates remained either nonradioactive, or had extremely low specific activities, when fish were injected with 6-phosphogluconate-1-$^{14}$C. These findings are consistent with slow metabolism of 6-phosphogluconate by the pentose phosphate pathway in these cold acclimated fish, and is thus in agreement with findings of other investigations using different methods.

Since gluconic acid of fairly high specific activity was found in muscle of fish injected with labeled 6-phosphogluconate, and radioactive hexose phosphates in muscle of fish injected with labeled gluconic acid, it was assumed that live fish liberated orthophosphate from 6-phosphogluconate and phosphorylated gluconic acid.

MacLeod and his collaborators investigated glycolytic enzymes in the tissues of *S. gairdneri.* Their work was reported briefly by Black *et al.* (1961), but publication of a detailed report was delayed (MacLeod *et al.,* 1963). Tissue homogenates, or supernates of these after centrifugation, were used. The soluble nature of the enzymes studied was evidenced by the fact that clear extracts contained 85 to 90% of the activity of homogenates. While heart muscle converted glucose to lactic acid, skeletal muscle, liver, and kidney were unable to do so unless hexokinase was added. Evidence was obtained indicating that, at least in the homogenates, this discrepancy could be accounted for by a very strong adenosinetriphosphatase that removed adenosine triphosphate required for synthesis of glucose-6-phosphate from glucose. Since it is well known that lactic acid forms very rapidly in skeletal muscle of this fish, the results could also be explained by instability of the hexokinase in the homogenates.

Under conditions designed to inhibit adenosine triphosphatase, and that were optimum for detecting hexokinase activity, skeletal muscle, brain, liver, and kidney were all shown to possess hexokinase, though heart muscle was 60 times as active as skeletal muscle. By recognized techniques the various tissues studied were shown to possess phosphoglucoisomerase, aldolase, phosphofructokinase, glyceraldehyde-3-phosphate dehydrogenase, enolase, phosphoglyceromutase, lactic dehydrogenase, and pyruvic kinase. With the exception of hexokinase and phosphofructokinase, the glycolytic enzymes of the skeletal muscle were 3 to 100 times as active as those of other tissues studied. Diphosphopyridine nucleotide and adenosine diphosphate were cofactors, and iodoacetate and fluoride plus phosphate inhibitors, of fish glycolytic enzyme systems. These and subsequent studies by others (see below) have provided evidence that all the glycolytic enzymes of the classical Embden-Meyerhof pathway are present in fish tissues.

Burt and Stroud (1966) studied 3-carbon atom compounds of the Embden-Meyerhof pathway in cod muscle. Since 1,3-diphosphoglyceric acid is extremely labile, and 2-phosphoglyceric acid is present in very low concentrations, neither compound was studied. Samples of muscle were taken from rested and exhausted cod. 3-Phosphoglyceric acid (10–54 $\mu$moles per 100 gm) was lower in exercised fish and decreased rapidly postmortem. There was an increase (about threefold) in pyruvate in exercised fish, and the concentration fell to about zero within a short time after death. Lactate, which was present in high concentrations, increased during exercise and also during postmortem storage. Moderate amounts of L-$\alpha$-glycerophosphate were formed during exercise and in certain instances there was a postmortem increase; the amounts present were between about 40 and 100 $\mu$moles per 100 gm in most experiments. Dihydroxyacetone phosphate occurred in rather low concentrations (about 10–18 $\mu$moles per 100 gm) and fell to low levels during storage at 0°C, particularly in exercised fish.

Using extracts of skeletal muscle of two species of carp it was shown that 3-phosphoglyceric acid was almost all converted to pyruvic acid under aerobic conditions (Shibata and Yoshimura, 1962). Lactic acid was not formed under the experimental conditions because reduced diphosphopyridine nucleotide was not formed and lactic acid dehydrogenase was consequently inactive.

Boyer (1953) demonstrated that pyruvate kinase, one of the essential enzymes in the glycolytic pathway, is present in muscles of different fish species, and that adenosine triphosphate and potassium ions are necessary for the reaction. Further discussion of activity of enzymes of this pathway are given in Section II, D under postmortem breakdown of glycogen.

## C. Experiments with Isolated Enzyme Preparations

### 1. *Enzymes of the Embden-Meyerhof Pathway*

a. *Glycogen Phosphorylase.* The first study of fish muscle glycogen phosphorylase was reported by Cordier and Cordier (1957). They used muscle of two fish (*Scorpaena porcus* and *Scyllium canicula*) and the eel (*Anguilla vulgaris*). About 1 gm of muscle was homogenized at 0°C with 2 ml of phosphate buffer, pH 7.6, and 2 ml of 0.5 $M$ sodium fluoride solution. Samples were removed and treated with 1.7 ml of 7% trichloracetic acid at zero time and after 15, 30, and 60 minutes at 37°C. The percentage of orthophosphate esterified was used as a measure of formation of glucose-1-phosphate. This method indicated that, while rat muscle esterified 63.8% of the orthophosphate, the fish muscles were considerably less active, esterifying some 20–40% depending on the species.

Ono *et al.* (1957) investigated phosphorylase in the muscle of sea bass

(*Lateolabrax japonicus*). The muscle, excised from the freshly killed fish, was ground and finally homogenized with 5 volumes of 0.2 $M$ barbiturate buffer (pH 6.4) for 30–180 seconds. Enzyme activity was measured by incubating 5 ml of the supernate, after centrifugation, with 1 ml of 1% glycogen solution, and determining increase in reducing sugar and change in concentration of orthophosphate at pH 6.4. The decreases in orthophosphate concentration were by no means as great as those found by Cordier and Cordier (1957) but the enzyme solution used appears to have been less concentrated. Ono and Nagayama (1959) also used decrease in glycogen concentration and increase in total "reducing sugars" as a measure of glycogen phosphorylase activity. However, this method is probably not reliable since glycogen is quite rapidly degraded postmortem to reducing sugars by amylolytic activity in fish muscle.

The above investigators did not apply the more classical assay procedure of Cori in which the amount of inorganic phosphate liberated from glucose 1-phosphate during glycogen synthesis is measured under first-order conditions (Cori *et al.*, 1955). However, Nagayama (1961a), using crude muscle extracts of sea bass found that orthophosphate was liberated from glucose-1-phosphate by such extracts. He also purified the enzyme about twenty-fold by fractionation with ammonium sulfate. Both a and b forms were demonstrated by experiments with adenylic acid. Phosphorylase from sea bass had an optimum temperature of 37°C, while that from rainbow trout was 25°C. Sea bass muscle possessed only $\frac{1}{14}$ of the phosphorylase activity of rabbit muscle (Nagayama, 1961c).

More recently, in the author's laboratory, Yamamoto (1968) obtained a highly purified preparation of glycogen phosphorylase $b$ from the dorsal muscle of rainbow trout by heating a 5000 $g$ supernate at 37°C for 7 minutes, fractionating with ammonium sulfate, and finally eluting the enzyme from a potato starch column using a buffer solution containing 0.4% glycogen. The glycogen– phosphorylase complex thus obtained represented about a 90-fold purification over the 5000 $g$ supernate. The purified enzyme was extremely unstable; about one-half of the total activity being lost in 90 minutes when stored at 0°C. Cysteine (12 m$M$), 2-mercaptoethanol (100 m$M$), sucrose (1.6 $M$), mannitol (0.5 $M$), or Cleland's reagent (6 m$M$) were ineffective when used in attempts to stabilize the enzyme. Purified glycogen phosphorylase $b$ showed maximal activity near pH 6.8, and was not inhibited by cupric, ferric, or mercuric ions, at $0.4 \times 10^{-4}$ $M$ or at $2.0 \times 10^{-4}$ $M$. The $K_m$ for glucose-1-phosphate was about 17 m$M$ when measured in the direction of glycogen synthesis, glucose at 25 m$M$ being a competitive inhibitor in this system. The $K_m$ for 5'-AMP, which was required for the conversion of phosphorylase $b$

to the *a* form, was in the range 0.15–0.40 m$M$, and ATP at 5 m$M$ competitively inhibited this activation process. Of several nucleotides tested, including 5′-GMP, 5′-UMP, 5′-CMP, 5′-TMP, 5′-dAMP, 5′-dGMP, and 5′-dCMP, only 5′-AMP was effective in causing the conversion of phosphorylase *b* to the *a* form. Preliminary studies have clearly indicated the presence in trout muscle of phosphorylase *b* kinase, the enzyme which catalyzes the phosphorylation of phosphorylase *b* by ATP to yield phosphorylase *a*. It was also observed that this conversion of trout muscle phosphorylase *b* to *a* could be effected by purified phosphorylase *b* kinase obtained from rabbit muscle.

*b. Phosphoglucomutase, Phosphoribomutase, and Phosphoglucoisomerase.* Martin and Tarr (1961) studied these three enzymes using preparations obtained from muscle of Pacific lingcod (*Ophiodon elongatus*). Enzyme preparations were made at 0°–3°C. Strictly fresh muscle was blended with 2 volumes of water, the pH being adjusted to 6.0 with 1 $N$ HCl. The supernate that separated on centrifuging at 10,000 $g$ for 10 minutes was saturated with ammonium sulfate at pH 7.0 and the protein precipitate was dialyzed against successive changes of water until it was practically free from ammonium sulfate. The dialyzed solution was flash-heated to 55°C, promptly chilled and centrifuged, the supernate being freeze-dried. Separation of phosphoglucomutase and phosphoribomutase activities from phosphoglucoisomerase was achieved by use of diethylaminoethyl cellulose (DEAE) columns. In a typical experiment, 1.0 ml of the water-soluble extract of a lyophilized preparation (33 mg of protein nitrogen) was absorbed on a 30 × 1.8 (diameter) cm DEAE column equilibrated with 0.01 $M$ tris-HCl buffer and eluted with a gradient of 0.01 $M$ tris into 0.25 $M$ tris, pH 7.0. In general, the main protein "peaks" did not coincide with the fractions containing greatest enzyme activity.

Phosphoglucoisomerase activity appeared in two separate peaks, that emerging first being rather small. This would appear to indicate, as was subsequently shown by Roberts and Tsuyuki (1963), that certain of these fish muscle enzymes exist in multiple forms (see below). Phosphoglucomutase and phosphoribomutase activities were eluted in the same peak and were almost completely separated from phosphoglucoisomerase. They were, however, very unstable being inactivated by freezing and thawing and losing activity rapidly at 0°C. On the other hand, eluates containing phosphoglucoisomerase retained considerable activity after several days at 0°C. On a protein basis the phosphoglucomutase activity of the fraction was about 100 times that of the phosphoribomutase activity. Previous investigators who studied these enzymes from other sources were unable to separate them satisfactorily, and observed that the phosphoglucomutase activity was usually about 100 times that of the phosphoribomutase activity.

The properties of fish muscle phosphoglucomutase were not greatly different from those of the mammalian enzyme. The dephospho enzyme was inactive unless glucose diphosphate was added. Ribose diphosphate and deoxyribose diphosphate could replace glucose diphosphate, but were somewhat less effective. The enzyme required $Mg^{2+}$ ions and cysteine, the optimum concentrations being $1 \times 10^{-3} M$ and $1 \times 10^{-2} M$, respectively. The optimum pH was about 7.5, and at equilibrium the concentrations of glucose-6-phosphate and glucose-1-phosphate were 95 and 5%, respectively.

Phosphoribomutase was inactive unless a diphosphate ester was added, the activating effects of the diphosphates being, ribose diphosphate > deoxyribose diphosphate > glucose diphosphate. This enzyme, however, differed from phosphoglucomutase in that it was strongly inhibited by cysteine in $1 \times 10^{-3} M$ concentration and was almost completely inhibited by $5 \times 10^{-2} M$ $Mg^{2+}$. The pH optimum was about 8.5, and at equilibrium the concentrations of ribose-5-phosphate and ribose-1-phosphate were 85 and 15%, respectively. 8-Hydroxyquinoline enhanced the effectiveness of the diphosphate esters with phosphoribomutase, but depressed it in the case of phosphoglucomutase.

Phosphoglucoisomerase had a wide pH range over which it exhibited marked activity, the optimum being about 9.0. At equilibrium the concentrations of glucose-6-phosphate and fructose-6-phosphate were 38 and 62%, respectively.

Nagayama (1961a) studied phosphoglucomutase of sea bass muscle. Using crude extracts of sea bass he found that the activity varied in different parts of the muscle as follows: caudal > dorsal > ventral. The enzyme acted slowly at 5°–16°C, actively at 25°–45°C, and feebly at 55°C (presumably due to destruction). Much of the activity was lost in muscle held 2 days at 25°C. He also studied phosphoglucoisomerase. The activity was optimum at pH 9.0, was greatest in caudal muscle and, as with phosphoglucomutase, decreased when the muscle was stored (Nagayama, 1961b).

Roberts and Tsuyuki (1963) have recently made use of zone electrophoresis in starch gels to demonstrate the multiple nature of two enzymes of the Embden-Meyerhof pathway in fish muscle. Thus electrophoresis of dilute aqueous extracts of *S. gairdneri* muscle at pH 9.0 showed five different protein zones possessing phosphoglucomutase activity (isozymes). These exhibited marked differences in stability. Thus two were comparatively stable, becoming inactive only after 67 hours at 0°C. The unstable enzymes usually lost most of their activity in 19 hours at 0°C. Tests also revealed that phosphoglucoisomerase exhibited several different "isozymes" (see also Martin and Tarr, 1961), and that there was a strong zone which possessed aldolase activity.

Hashimoto and Handler (1966) purified phosphoglucomutase from shark and flounder muscle by slightly different procedures that involved extraction of tissue with $H_2O$, heating the extract to between 57° and 59°C, precipitation with ammonium sulfate (500 gm/liter), and suspension of the precipitated protein in $H_2O$ to which was added tris buffer (pH 7.5) and $MgCl_2$ to protect the enzyme during a second heating step (0.5–1.0 minutes at 60°C). Further purification resulted on ammonium sulfate fractionation of the supernate from the second heating step, desalting by very rapid passage through a Sephadex G25 column, DEAE-cellulose chromatography and a final ammonium sulfate precipitation. The purifications achieved were 146- and 115-fold for the flounder and shark enzymes, respectively, the corresponding specific activities (micromoles substrate utilized per milligram of protein per minute) being 606 and 630 (similar to that of the rabbit muscle enzyme).

The enzymes were not quite pure by ultracentrifuge analyses and by paper electrophoresis. They were comparatively labile and the molecular weights were about 63,000. Traces of lactic dehydrogenase and phosphofructokinase were present. No "isoenzymes" such as those reported by Roberts and Tsuyuki (1963) were found. However, only paper electrophoresis was carried out using the purified enzyme rather than the more sensitive gel electrophoresis of crude extracts. The pH optima were similar (7.6 and 7.8 for shark and flounder enzymes, respectively). The purified enzymes were rapidly inactivated below pH 5.5. They were stimulated 1.5- to 2-fold by preincubation with histidine or imidazole buffers containing magnesium, but this activation was lower than that found for rabbit muscle phosphoglucomutase. The enzymes possessed -SH groups that reacted with $p$-chloromercuribenzoate, and exhibited a much more marked glucose-1,6-diphosphatase activity than that found for the rabbit enzyme. This effect was traced to phosphorylation of the enzyme by glucose-1,6-diphosphate and spontaneous dephosphorylation of the resulting phosphoenzyme, which does not occur with rabbit phosphoglucomutase. The fish enzymes, unlike the rabbit enzyme, were extremely unstable when held in buffers of low ionic strength. Also, the fish enzymes were irreversibly inactivated below pH 5.0, while the rabbit enzyme is activated by exposure to pH 3.0.

Inactivation of phosphoglumutase by beryllium ions occurs at very low concentrations both with fish and mammalian enzymes. The flounder muscle enzyme is much more radily denatured by urea than is the rabbit enzyme (Hashimoto *et al.*, 1967).

*c. Enolase.* Tsuyuki and Wold (1964) found that eight different species of the genus *Salmo* each possessed three distinct enolase isozymes as revealed by starch gel electrophoresis in dilute borate buffer at pH 8.5. Since the quantitative ratios of the different forms did not alter with changes in extraction procedure (time and temperature) it was concluded that the isozymes were not artifacts created by the method of isolation. Crystalline rabbit muscle enolase gave only a single zone under the same conditions of separation.

More recently, Cory and Wold (1965, 1966) prepared crystalline enolase from *S. gairdneri* muscle by the following procedure. The frozen tissue was blended with 2 parts of 0.05% EDTA, and the supernate was fractionated at about $-5°C$ with acetone, the fraction precipitating between 35 and 46% concentration being retained. This protein was dissolved in 0.05 $M$ imidazole buffer (pH 7.9) containing 0.001 $M$ $MgSO_4$, the acetone was removed, and the protein solution heated 3 minutes at 55°C and chilled rapidly. Ammonium sulfate fractionation was carried out under nitrogen, since at this stage the enzyme is inactivated rapidly in presence of air. The protein fraction precipitating between 0.55 and 0.75 saturation with ammonium sulfate was dissolved in buffer and crystallized under carefully controlled conditions by addition of saturated ammonium sulfate solution.

The recrystallized enzyme had a specific activity (units per gram) of 390 which represented about 16-fold purification and 15% recovery. The molecular weight, as indicated by gel filtration with Sephadex G-100 was about 91,000. Amino acid analyses, based on three moles tryptophan per mole of enzyme, indicated a molecular weight of 91,800. The enzyme contained three moles of free -SH groups and three moles of disulfide, and its activity was accelerated by 0.2–0.3 $M$ KCl. The $K_m$ was $4 \times 10^{-5}$ $M$, the pH optimum 6.9, and it had an absolute requirement for $Mg^{2+}$ (optimum concentration was $1 \times 10^{-3}$ $M$). The enzyme was comparatively stable between pH 7.9 and 11.0 but was very sensitive to acid, the half-life being 2 hours at pH 5.0 and only a few minutes at pH 4.0. It was inactivated by 2 $M$ urea in 1 hour at 25°C. The enzyme occurred in three electrophoretically different forms (isoenzymes), and the ratios of the three forms did not differ during the purification procedure. One striking difference between fish and mammalian or yeast enolases is the ease of irreversible denaturation with the former, while the latter can be reversibly denatured.

*d. Aldolase.* Shibata (1958) prepared carp muscle aldolase by the following method. Aqueous extracts were fractionated by ammonium sulfate. The fraction precipitating between 1.75 and 2.4 $M$ ammonium sulfate concentration was reprecipitated at the same ammonium sulfate concentrations. The preparations were dialyzed against dilute potassium cyanide solution and freeze-dried. Activity was lost slowly by prolonged dialysis against water or by storage for several months. A preparation with lower specific activity was obtained using cold acetone fractionation.

The enzyme appeared to be somewhat less heat stable than rabbit muscle aldolase, and the pH optimum was between 8.3 and 9.4 depending on the buffer system used. The ions $Mg^{2+}$ and $Zn^{2+}$ had no effect at $10^{-5}$ $M$ concentration, but inhibited at $10^{-2}$ $M$. EDTA also had no effect on activity. The enzyme was inhibited by $Hg^{2+}$, $Ag^{2+}$, and cysteine ($5 \times 10^{-3}$ $M$ at pH 8.6). The $K_m$ was $0.45 \times 10^{-3}$ $M$ at pH 7.5–8.6 and $1.0$–$1.45 \times 10^{-3}$ $M$ at pH 9.0. The activity was lower than that of rabbit muscle aldolase, the specific activities being 3.9 and 0.6–2.1 units per gram of muscle for rabbit and carp preparations, respectively.

Kwon and Olcott (1965) purified aldolase from white muscle of frozen yellowfin (*Neothunnus macropterus*) and albacore (*Thunnus germo*). Concentrates of the enzyme were prepared by the method of Taylor (1955) and stored at 0°C in saturated $(NH_4)_2SO_4$ solution. Fractionation with $(NH_4)_2SO_4$ yielded two fractions; 0.50–0.52 saturation with specific activity of 5.41, and 0.52–0.55 with specific activity of 3.70. Refractionation of the pooled fractions gave a preparation with specific activity 7.25 (micromoles fructose diphosphate cleaved per milligram of protein per minute at 30°C and pH 9.0). The yield was 16% of the original aldolase activity and 3% of the total extractable muscle protein. The enzyme had only 60% of the specific activity of rabbit muscle aldolase. In presence of cysteine, which promotes protein aggregation, the enzyme preparation was homogeneous as judged by moving boundary electrophoresis and sedimentation in the analytical ultracentrifuge. The optimum temperature was 42°; the activation energy was $4.2 \times 10^3$ cal, which is one-third of that of rabbit muscle aldolase and one-half that of carp muscle aldolase (Shibata, 1958). The $K_m$ ($2 \times 10^{-3}$ $M$) was similar to the values reported for rabbit and carp enzymes. Borate inhibition was shown to be due to a stoichiometric interaction of the borate with the enzyme molecule and was reversible. In general, the enzyme was less stable than that from rabbit muscle.

*e. D-Glyceraldehyde-3-phosphate Dehydrogenase (Triose Phosphate Dehydrogenase).* Ludovicy-Bungert (1961) prepared D-glyceraldehyde-3-phosphate dehydrogenase from white muscle of mirror carp by the following procedure. The minced muscle was mixed with an equal volume of water, and after 1 hour the aqueous extract was dialyzed 15 hours against double-distilled water. Insoluble denatured protein was removed by centrifuging, and an equal volume of a saturated solution of ammonium sulfate (pH 7.5) was added over a 1-hour period. The pH was adjusted to 8.0 with 15% $NH_4OH$ and the precipitated protein was collected by centrifuging. The precipitate was dissolved in 2 volumes of water and heated briefly at 63°C. The precipitated protein was removed and the soluble fraction dialyzed. The solution was finally fractionated with acetone at $-15°C$, the fraction obtained between 33 and 42% acetone concentration being collected after 15 minutes and dissolved in water and dialyzed. The yield was 0.04% of the whole muscle.

The preparation was homogeneous by moving boundary electrophoresis and in the ultracentrifuge and behaved similarly to mammalian muscle glyceraldehyde-3-phosphate dehydrogenase preparations, but the activity was about three times as high. It was free from aldolase.

An interesting study in comparative biochemistry was carried out with purified crystalline triosephosphate dehydrogenase enzyme preparations from widely different sources including muscle of halibut and sturgeon (Allison and Kaplan, 1964). The sedimentation constants for all preparations (from muscles of rabbit, beef, turkey, chicken, human heart, lobster, halibut, and sturgeon, and from cells of *Escherichia coli* and yeast) were closely similar, indicating a molecular weight of about 120,000. Starch gel electrophoresis carried out at four different pH values indicated a single protein species. However, differences were observed in migration distance and direction (anodic or cathodic). Thus while the sturgeon enzyme behaved like the poultry enzyme, halibut enzyme behaved similarly to beef, horse, and rabbit enzyme in its migration properties. Within the limits of accuracy of the rather exacting analytical technique used, the amino acid composition tended to be similar for triosephosphate dehydrogenase isolated from rather similar muscle (e.g., beef and rabbit muscle). On the other hand, the amino acid compositions of halibut and sturgeon preparations were markedly different from the others. It was suggested that this enzyme in these fish has become quite different during evolution and that the data obtained are consistent with paleontological and anatomical evidence that the sturgeon is a primitive fish which has changed very little from a common ancestor of the bony fishes, whereas the halibut is an advanced species which has undergone marked evolution from such a common ancestor. Immunological data using quantitative complement fixation tests paralleled the results of amino acid analyses. The enzyme from sturgeon, which, unlike the halibut enzyme, had an amino acid composition similar to that of the enzyme from the birds, cross-reacted with antiturkey serum more strongly than did the halibut enzyme. Of particular interest was the finding that the catalytic properties of halibut muscle lactic dehydrogenase resembled those of chicken at 7°C, but were different at 24°C, indicating that the halibut enzyme is geared to function at a lower temperature. It has been shown that crystalline dogfish muscle lactic acid dehydrogenase is much more stable to urea, a natural constituent of dogfish muscle, than is the crystalline bovine or chicken enzyme. These phenomena indicate an adaptation of enzymes to their environment during evolution.

*f. Hexokinase, 6-Phosphogluconic Acid Dehydrogenase, Phosphogluco-isomerase, and Phosphomannoisomerase.* Renold *et al.* (1964) collected pancreatic islets (Brockmann bodies) from the mesentery near the spleen or liver of anesthetized toadfish (*Opsanus tau*). Ten to fifteen islets (2–4 mg each) were homogenized at 0°C with 1 ml of a solution containing 0.15 $M$ KCl and 0.005 $M$ EDTA, buffered to pH 7.5 with a little glycylglycine. A very sensitive assay for hexokinase based on enzymic liberation of radioactive $CO_2$ from 6-phosphogluconic acid, formed enzymically from glucose, was used. This assay, carried out at 22°–25°C was employed since it is specific only for the added glucose, and is not in any way influenced by other sources of glucose such as glycogen.

The islet homogenates of the toadfish possessed marked hexokinase activity, which was absolutely dependent on the presence of ATP. The presence of 6-phosphogluconic acid dehydrogenase was also demonstrated. When fructose-1-[14]C or mannose-1-[14]C were used as substrates the affinity of the enzyme for mannose was the same as for glucose, but was about ten times lower for fructose. Thus the Michaelis constants in different experiments were 1.16 and 1.30 $\times$ $10^{-4}$ $M$ for glucose and 9.88 and 11.0 $\times$ $10^{-4}$ $M$ for fructose. The calculated maximal hexose phosphorylating activity of the homogenates was between 33–45 $\mu$moles/gm nitrogen/minute for glucose, 16–23 for fructose, and only 3 for mannose. The results also indicated that the phosphoglucoisomerase, phosphomannoisomerase, and 6-phosphogluconic acid dehydrogenase activities were present in excess of the hexose phosphorylating enzyme activity.

*g. Lactic Dehydrogenase.* Nagayama (1961d) carried out a limited study of the lactic dehydrogenase of sea bass muscle. This enzyme in the fish muscle extract was rather unstable at 25°C. The amount of lactic acid formed in the muscle postmortem was much lower than that which would be expected if all glycogen is degraded to this compound. Since much of the glycogen in fish muscle is degraded hydrolytically to glucose (see Section II, D) the result is not unexpected.

A very detailed study of crystalline lactic dehydrogenases (LDH) from various sources was carried out by N. O. Kaplan and his associates (Wilson *et al.*, 1964).

Two types of LDH are recognized in animals; heart (H), usually strongly inhibited by pyruvate, and muscle (M) not so inhibited. "Pure" heart and muscle LDH have four identical subunits ($H_4$ and $M_4$ enzymes). "Hybrid" enzymes containing both H and M subunits are found so that five types are recognized.

Wilson *et al.* (1964) crystallized 25 M and H LDH enzymes including those from two bony and one cartilaginous fish. The molecular weights, including LDH from bacteria, were all close to 140,000, so that it was assumed that this was practically unchanged during evolution. The histidine content varied considerably, that of fish and warm-blooded mammals being rather similar. The peptide "finger print" patterns of tryptic hydrolyzates of four classes of vertebrate LDH enzymes (chicken, bullfrog, halibut, and dogfish) differed radically, indicating very diverse amino acid sequences. However, one peptide from the active site give, in all four cases, an identical amino acid sequence. The fish LDH enzymes exhibited temperature stabilities of the same order as those of warm-blooded mammals, namely 50% inactivation at 60° in 20 minutes. The fish $H_4$ LDH enzymes moved more slowly in zone electrophoreses than did those from warm-blooded mammals.

Immunological data using the very sensitive microcomplement fixation technique showed that fish LDH enzymes (and also triosephosphate dehydrogenase) are widely separated from the avian enzymes. Using antisera from rabbits immunized against comparatively pure fish $M_4$ LDH and triosephosphate dehydrogenase, it was shown that, in approximate order of evolution, mackerel, carp, eels, salmon species, pike, sturgeon, lungfish, dogfish, and lamprey enzymes are increasingly removed from halibut and other "flat fishes."

In further studies (Fondy *et al.*, 1965) it was reported that, while mammalian and avian crystalline LDH enzymes have four functionally essential thiol groups per mole of enzyme, halibut $M_4$ does not appear to possess essential thiol groups. The halibut $M_4$ enzyme bound *p*-hydroxymercuribenzoate to 10 moles of nonessential thiol groups before it precipitated. Dogfish $M_4$ LDH possessed essential thiol groups that were protected from *p*-hydroxymercuribenzoate by reduced coenzyme and its acetylpyridine analog.

$M_4$ enzymes which were homogeneous by starch gel electrophoresis, ultracentrifugation, and immunological assay were prepared from halibut, dogfish, and lamprey. These "fish" enzymes had greater turnover numbers than did those from birds and mammals. Certain other interesting differences were reported. Thus the dogfish enzyme formed unusually large crystals and contained one reactive nonessential thiol group per enzyme subunit, whereas similar enzymes from mammals and birds contain four such groups (Pesce *et al.*, 1967).

### 2. Enzymes of the Pentose Phosphate Pathway

It has been noted above (Section II, B) that fish tissues exhibit variable ability to utilize the pentose phosphate pathway of glucose metabolism depending on the conditions under which the fish are held and the tissue involved. Two of the enzymes of this pathway were studied by Tarr (1959). Lingcod (*Ophiodon elongatus*) muscle was blended at pH 6.0 with 2 volumes of water and the suspension centrifuged. The supernate was saturated with ammonium sulfate at pH 7.0 and the protein precipitate collected by filtration at 0°C. The precipitate was dialyzed for 24 hours against several changes of water and the solution was then heated briefly at 55°C, promptly chilled, and precipitated protein removed by centrifuging.

A DEAE column (34 × 1.8 cm) was conditioned with 0.02 $M$ tris-HCl buffer, pH 7.0, and 6 ml of the crude enzyme (236 mg of protein) was placed on the column. It was eluted with a gradient in which 0.25 $M$ tris was run into 0.02 $M$ tris, pH 7.0. The chilled fractions were assayed directly for protein, and for phosphoriboisomerase (PRI) and ribulose-5-phosphate-3'-epimerase (EPIM) enzymes.

Most of the protein (86%) emerged from the column before the enzymes were eluted so that the latter were obtained reasonably free from large amounts of contaminating protein. The fractions containing PRI, which emerged first, were pooled (146 ml); the preparation contained 15 $\mu$g of protein per milliliter. The fractions with EPIM activity were fairly well separated from PRI. The pooled EPIM fractions (156 ml) contained only 5 $\mu$g of protein per milliliter. These preparations were studied with the following results.

PRI was purified about 2000-fold. The specific activity ($\mu$moles of substrate utilized per milligram of enzyme protein per minute at 37°C) of PRI was 20.4 and the optimum pH range was between 7.0 and 8.0, but activity was observed between pH 4 and 11. At equilibrium, about 55–60% of ribose-5'-phosphate and 40–45% of ribulose-5'-phosphate were present. The enzyme was inhibited 28% by 5 × 10⁻⁴ $M$, and 45% by 5 × 10⁻³ $M$ phosphoribonic acid.

The pH optimum of EPIM was similar to that of PRI, and equilibrium was established at about 60% xylulose-5'-phosphate and 40% ribulose-5'-phosphate. The equilibrium in a system containing a mixture of purified

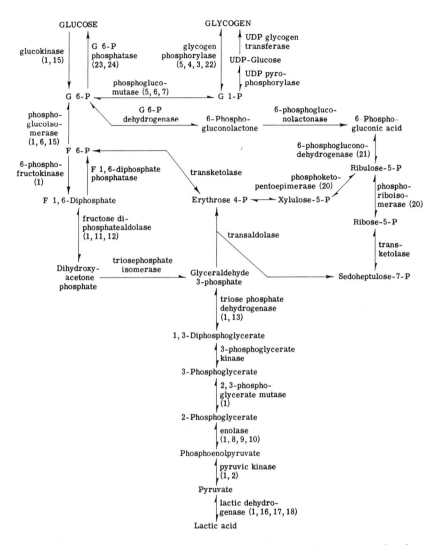

Fig. 1. Occurrence of Enzymes of the Embden-Meyerhof and hexose monophosphate shunt pathways in fish muscles and organs. The figures in parentheses refer to the following references: (1) MacLeod *et al.*, 1963; (2) Boyer, 1953; (3) Cordier and Cordier, 1957; (4) Ono *et al.*, 1957; (5) Nagayama, 1961a; (6) Martin and Tarr, 1961; (7) Roberts and Tsuyuki, 1963; (8) Tsuyuki and Wold, 1964; (9) Hashimoto and Handler, 1966; (10) Cory and Wold, 1965, 1966; (11) Kwon and Olcott, 1965; (12) Shibata, 1958; (13) Ludovicy-Bungert, 1961; (14) Allison and Kaplan, 1964; (15) Renold *et al.*, 1964; (16) Nagayama, 1961d; (17) Wilson *et al.*, 1964; (18) Fondy *et al.*, 1965; (19) Pesce *et al.*, 1967; (20) Tarr, 1959; (21) Brown, 1960; (22) Yamamoto (submitted for publication); (23) Tarr and Leroux, 1962; (24) Ikeda and Shimeno, 1967a,b.

PRI and EPIM was 43.5–46% ribose-5'-phosphate, 29–30.5% ribulose-5'-phosphate, and 29–30.5% xylulose-5'-phosphate. The specific activity was 21.6, and was thus very similar to that obtained with PRI. In general, the properties of these enzymes were rather similar to those isolated from mammalian tissues or other sources.

Other enzymes of this pathway including transaldolase, transketolase, phosphofructoisomerase, and fructokinase do not appear to have been studied in fish tissues.

Figure 1 illustrates the instances where enzymes of the Embden-Meyerhof and hexose monophosphate shunt pathways have been demonstrated in fish tissues.

## D. Postmortem Degradation of Muscle Glycogen

Though it has been known for some time that hexose phosphates (Tarr, 1950) and glucose (Jones, 1958) occur in muscles of live fish the enzymic pathways of degradation of glycogen postmortem are as yet only partially clarified.

Ghankar *et al.* (1956) first reported the occurrence of amylolytic cleavage of glycogen in fish muscle. Nonphosphorolytic degradation of glycogen in fish muscles postmortem was also studied by Andreev (1958). He ground 40 gm of fish muscle to a paste in 2 volumes of $H_2O$ for 30 minutes with toluene and autolyzed the preparation 5–6 hours under toluene. The supernate (50 ml) obtained on centrifugation was dialyzed 24 hours against double-distilled water at 5°–9°C, which served to remove orthophosphate, soluble nucleotides, and their degradation products. The dialyzate was added to 100 ml of water, the precipitated proteins were removed by centrifugation, and the clear supernate (pH 6.7–6.8) was used as an enzyme preparation.

It was found that hydrolysis of starch solutions proceeded in absence of added orthophosphate, and that this hydrolysis was accelerated by 0.44–0.50% NaCl. Nonautolyzed muscle showed insignificant hydrolytic activity. Muscle amylase was obtained from a number of different fish species and exhibited similar properties. The optimum pH for amylase activity in the case of both sea- and freshwater fish was 7.0, and the optimum temperature over a 2-hour period was 37°–42°C. Tail muscle had 1 to 1.5 times the amylase activity of other parts of the muscle. It was concluded that the fish muscle enzyme was of the α-amylase type.

McGeachin and Debnam (1960) studied the distribution of amylase in homogenized tissues of two freshwater fish species, blue-gill and large-mouth black bass. Comparatively high activity was found in liver, bile, stomach, upper intestine, lower intestine, spleen, and ovaries. Serum, gill, heart muscle, kidney, and testes had smaller concentrations. The white muscle tissue had a very low amylase concentration which the authors contrasted with the previous results of Andreev. However, Andreev indicated that high concentrations of amylase are obtained only from autolyzed muscle. Isolated liver cells had a much lower activity than did whole liver tissue.

Andreev (1962) studied fish muscle maltase activity using a dialyzed muscle extract similar to that employed in his work on amylase. These extracts hydrolyzed maltose as determined by the appearance of reducing sugars. Heated extracts were inactive. The maltase was less stable than the amylase. Thus the latter was stable for long periods in salted fish while the former disappeared in 6 days. Muscle maltase was found to be widely spread among different fish species. Since grinding and autolysis stimulated amylase activity, it was suggested that this enzyme may be present in the particulate fraction of the muscle.

Tarr and Leroux (1962), using $^{14}$C-labeled glucose-6-phosphate, showed that only traces of glucose were formed from this substrate when it was added to blended *S. gairdneri* muscle that was held 1 day at 0°C. Ikeda and Shimeno (1967a and b) have now shown that fish muscles possess only a very feeble glucose-6-phosphatase activity. However, $^{14}$C-labeled glycogen has been shown to be quite rapidly degraded to limit dextrin, maltose, and glucose (Tarr and Leroux, 1962), and it is now generally accepted that all, or practically all, glucose found in fish muscle postmortem arises from hydrolytic breakdown of glycogen (Jones, 1962; Tarr, 1964d).

Burt (1966) studied enzymic degradation of added starch using cod muscle extracts, phloridzin being employed to block phosphorylase activity in some experiments and thus to eliminate the Embden-Meyerhof pathway if it was operating. The results were somewhat complicated by certain factors, but it appeared that the hydrolytic route is the main pathway of starch (and glycogen) breakdown postmortem. Optimum hydrolysis of starch was obtained with muscle homogenates that had been autolyzed 3 hours at 37° C, held 18 hours at 0° C and centrifuged. These results suggested that the hydrolytic enzymes might occur in the microsomal fraction or be bound to protein. The hydrolysis was accelerated by NaCl, and the optimum temperature was 52°C. Both maltose and glucose were demonstrated by paper chromatography.

So far none of the above approaches has permitted an accurate assessment of the comparative role of hydrolytic and amylolytic pathways in breakdown of glycogen in fish muscles postmortem. However, these could be quite variable since the hydrolytic route appears to be favored by autolysis.

### III. Tricarboxylic Acid Cycle (TCA) Enzymes

This system accounts for the major portion of the terminal oxidation of important metabolites such as sugars, fats, and amino acids. The end products are carbon dioxide and water. Part of the energy released is stored as high energy level compounds, particularly in the form of adenosine triphosphate. Most of the oxygen used by respiring organisms which possess the TCA cycle is utilized to oxidize various intermediates of this cycle, and, hence, oxygen uptake is a fairly useful measure of the comparative activity of this cycle. It has already been noted above (Section II, B) that tissues from cold acclimated fish tend to take up more oxygen than do those of warm acclimated fish, and this could indicate that the TCA cycle is more active in the cold acclimated fish. Several investigators have studied the TCA cycle in fish, usually with tissue homogenates.

Yamada and Suzuki (1950) noted a postmortem increase in fish muscle citric acid and that this metabolite accumulated upon addition of pyruvate or oxalacetate. This indicated the presence of the condensing enzyme system. Hishida and Nakano (1954) observed that homogenized eggs of *Oryzias latipes* oxidized several TCA intermediates since oxygen uptake was stimulated by citrate, succinate, maleate, glutamate, and pyruvate. With all substrates, except succinate, oxygen uptake was enhanced by adenosine triphosphate. Succinate oxidation by goldfish gill homogenates did not proceed in absence of sulfhydryl compounds (Sexton and Russel, 1955). Lazarow and Cooperstein (1951), studying homogenates of toadfish tissues, showed that succinic dehydrogenase and cytochrome oxidase enzymes were much more active in heart muscle than in liver or kidney tissue. The respiratory enzyme activities of homogenates of carp white muscle, red lateral muscle, liver, and kidney were studied by Unemura (1951a, b, c). Using Thunberg tube technique and malate or succinate as substrates, he showed that red mucle possessed five to eight times more dehydrogenase activity than did white muscle. The dehydrogenase activities of kidney and liver homogenates were not stimulated by malate or succinate. Succinic and cytochrome oxidases were also much more active in red muscle.

Gubmann and Tappel (1962a) were the first investigators to make a really extensive study of enzymes of the TCA cycle in fish tissues. They prepared muscle and liver homogenates and liver mitochondria from *Cyprinidea* (carp or minnows) by accepted methods or slight modifications of these.

Succinic and malic dehydrogenases were shown to occur in the muscle within the range reported by other investigators for fish. However, the

$Q_{O_2}$ values with these substrates were only about one-tenth those reported for rat skeletal muscle.

Both aconitase and fumarase enzyme activities were demonstrated in supernates of liver and muscle homogenates. While the fumarase activities were similar in both tissues, aconitase activity was almost six times higher in liver. With the exception of mammalian liver for which a very high value has been reported in the literature, the fumarase activities of the fish tissues were similar to those reported for mammalian tissues. Isocitric dehydrogenase was also demonstrated in muscle and liver homogenates, the values for muscle being about one-half those found for liver. The levels of activity were lower than those reported for mammalian embryos. Citric acid, in concentrations ranging from 4 to 17 $\mu$g per gram, was found in liver and muscle, and the fact that this compound accumulated when homogenates of these tissues metabolized oxalacetate or pyruvate indicated the presence of condensing enzyme. Liver was more active than muscle in this respect.

Gubmann and Tappel (1962b) also investigated the performance of the TCA cycle in carp liver mitochondria by use of pyruvate and of C-1 and C-2 labeled radioactive DL-alanine. Alanine was utilized by oxidative decarboxylation since, under conditions for oxidative phosphorylation in presence of $\alpha$-ketoglutarate alanine-1-$^{14}$C yielded 50 to 60 times as much $^{14}CO_2$ as did alanine-2-$^{14}$C. Both routes by which pyruvate normally enters the TCA cycle, namely by oxidative decarboxylation and attendant formation of acetyl coenzyme A, and $CO_2$ fixation to form malate and oxalacetate, were demonstrated in the mitochondria. Carp liver mitochondria oxidized pyruvate and alanine without addition of a TCA intermediate (sparker) such as fumarate or malate, and these results were contrasted with the requirement for such primers exhibited by certain mammalian mitochondria. Possibly carp liver mitochondria retain sufficient endogenous substrate to act as primer to sustain oxalacetate for condensation with acetyl coenzyme A.

When carp liver mitochondria were incubated with alanine-2-$^{14}$C, all the intermediates in the TCA cycle became labeled in a manner which indicated a sequential flow of carbon from pyruvate through each intermediate in the cycle. In the normal animal two routes are available for entry of pyruvate into the TCA cycle, namely oxidative decarboxylation to form acetyl coenzyme A and $CO_2$ fixation to form malate and oxalacetate. Carp liver mitochondria, under conditions where oxidative phosphorylation occurred, carried out the latter reaction actively. The authors suggested that their results were best explained by damage to the mitochondria during isolation, so that both intact mitochondria and soluble

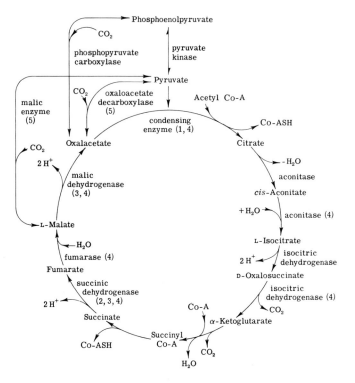

FIG. 2. Occurrence of enzymes of the tricarboxylic acid cycle in fish muscles and organs. The figures in parentheses refer to the following references: (1) Yamada and Suzuki, 1950; (2) Lazarow and Cooperstein, 1951; (3) Unemura, 1951a, b, c; (4) Gubmann and Tappel, 1962a; (5) Gubmann and Tappel, 1962b.

enzymes were acting simultaneously. Figure 2 illustrates the known instances where enzymes or tissue extracts have demonstrated the occurrence of the TCA cycle in fish tissues.

## IV. Oxidative Phosphorylation

By the use of manometric techniques, Gubmann and Tappel (1962a) demonstrated that carp liver mitochondria oxidized a number of substrates with simultaneous consumption of orthophosphate. Substrates utilized included pyruvate, citrate, *cis*-aconitate, isocitrate, $\alpha$-ketoglutarate, succinate, fumarate, malate, oxalacetate, and glutamate. In most cases the P/O ratios were in fairly good agreement with the theoretical values. Dinitrophenol ($1 \times 10^{-4}$ $M$) inhibited uptake of orthophosphate almost completely when $\alpha$-ketoglutarate was the substrate, demonstrating that phosphorylation is coupled with electron transport in the respiratory chain.

In rat liver mitochondria addition of glucose and hexokinase has been reported to enhance substrate oxidation by three to five times. In carp liver mitochondria similar additives caused a much less marked rise in oxygen consumption, indicating much feebler respiratory control, possibly because carp liver mitochondria are less stable than those isolated from mammalian sources.

## V. Electron Transport Systems

Terminal oxidation of metabolites is accomplished by transport of hydrogen and electrons by a chain of reactions involving dehydrogenase enzymes, flavoproteins, and cytochromes. Dehydrogenases may react directly with molecular oxygen (aerobic dehydrogenases) and others are linked to cytochromes, often through pyridine nucleotides such as diphosphopyridine nucleotide (DPN) and triphosphopyridine nucleotide (TPN). Flavoproteins, the prosthetic group of which is flavin adenine dinucleotide (FAD), are also included in such reactions chains.

The presence of certain dehydrogenase enzymes in fish tissues has been referred to above in the discussion of the TCA cycle, and undoubtedly many more exist, though little work appears to have been carried out in this area. Early work (Tarr, 1950) showed that fish muscles contained significant concentrations of nucleotide coenzymes. More recently ion-exchange techniques have enabled investigators to separate the nucleotides and nucleotide coenzymes in fish tissues more accurately. Thus, Murray and Jones (1958) reported that rested Atlantic cod flesh contained 10.7 $\mu$moles of DPN per 100 gm and that this decreased at 0°C to 1.7 $\mu$moles after 6 to 8 days. Later these investigators (Jones and Murray, 1961a, b) reported similar values for DPN in cod muscle, and gave evidence of its postmortem degradation, presumably by a DPNase (pyridine transglycosidase). They also detected small amounts of TPN in the muscles. Tarr and Leroux (1962), working with various species of Pacific ocean fish reported DPN values ranging from zero to 28 $\mu$moles per 100 gm. TPN was present in too small a concentration to assay in most cases, and only in one instance was there sufficient present to identify quantitatively (1.9 $\mu$g per 100 gm).

Matsuura and Hashimoto (1954) showed that red muscle of fish was a much richer source of cytochrome $c$ than ordinary muscle. These investigators (Matsuura and Hashimoto, 1955) also succeeded in obtaining crystalline cytochrome $c$ from heart muscle of tunny (*Thynnus alalunga*) and bonito (*Katsuwonus vagans*). Cytochrome *c* from salmon has been reported to differ from that of beef and chicken in that it contains two, instead of three, histidine residues per mole (Paleus, 1954). Gubmann and Tappel (1962b) have recently presented qualitative evidence, using low-temperature absorbancy spectra technique, for the occurrence of cytochromes $a$, $a_3$, $b$, and $c + c_1$ in carp kidney or liver mitochondria. Moreover, these are spectrally identical with those from rat heart and liver. The ratios of cytochromes $a_3:a:c + c_1$ are approximately unity and the absolute amounts about the same as in rat liver mitochondria.

The presence of cytochrome oxidase in fish tissues has been demonstrated. Thus, Unemura (1951b, c) demonstrated that red muscle of fish possessed greater cytochrome oxidase activity than did that of ordinary muscle, liver, or kidney. The absolute activity of cytochrome oxidase in toadfish tissues (*Opsanus tau*) was only one-third of that found in rat tissues (Lazarow and Cooperstein, 1951).

## VI. Enzymes of Lipid Metabolism

### A. General Observations

Shorland (1962) has recently reviewed the distribution and biosynthesis of fats from the point of view of comparative biochemistry. He pointed out the well-known fact that animal fats are derived either by biosynthesis from nonfatty dietary components (endogenous pathway) or from dietary fats either with or without modification (exogenous pathway). It is now generally accepted that acetate is the precursor of higher fatty acids in animals, the conversion of carbohydrates or proteins to fats involving their prior conversion to acetate. Acetate reacts with coenzyme A in presence of the enzyme β-ketothiolase to form the thioester of coenzyme A and acetic acid, namely acetyl coenzyme A. Through four separate enzymically catalyzed reversible reactions the fatty acid chain is extended by two carbon atoms to yield butyryl coenzyme A. Eight repetitions of this cycle will result in formation of the 18-carbon derivative, stearyl coenzyme A, and so on. These reactions are fully reversible so that fatty acids may be degraded by this cycle with formation of acetyl coenzyme A, which is then able to condense with oxalacetate and thus enter the citric acid cycle. For fatty acid synthesis appropriate concentrations of both reduced diphosphopyridine nucleotide and acetyl coenzyme A must be available. It is generally believed that the complex of enzymes causing oxidative degradation of fatty acids resides in the mitochondria and that cell-free enzyme extracts catalyze their biosynthesis. Biosynthesis of lipids, or phospholipids is presently explained by enzymic synthesis of phosphatidic acids from α-glycerophosphoric acid and acyl coenzyme A. Phosphatidic acids are probably enzymically degraded rapidly to D-1,2-diglycerides, and these may react with long chain coenzyme A fatty acid esters to form triglycerides, or with cytidine diphosphate choline (or other derivative) to form phosphatidylethanolamine (lecithin). Degradation of triglycerides by lipases and of phospholipids by phospholipases may liberate free fatty acids which are available for oxidative degradation.

In recent years considerable progress has been made in tracing the enzymic pathways of fatty acid and lipid metabolism in fish. The incorporation of $^{14}$C-labeled acetate into the lipid fraction of injected fish has already been referred to (Brown, 1960). Farkas *et al.* (1961) injected acetate-1-$^{14}$C into fish and fractionated the fatty acids obtained from the livers. Both saturated and unsaturated fatty acid fractions were radioactive, but the saturated fraction had a specific activity about three or four times as high as the unsaturated fraction. The $C_{18}$, $C_{20}$ and $C_{22}$ unsaturated fatty acids had considerably lower radioactivities than did the $C_{16}$ and $C_{18}$ saturated fatty acids. It was suggested that, while the basic route of enzymic synthesis of fatty acids is identical in mammals and in fishes, the bulk of the $C_{20}$ and $C_{22}$ unsaturated acids arise from the fishes' food. This suggestion is in line with the long-known fact that fish depot lipids are readily modified according to the type of fat consumed. This whole subject was ably reviewed by Lovern (1951). Recently Brenner *et al.* (1961) attributed an unusually large proportion of saturated fatty acids and a lower proportion of unsaturated fatty acids ($C_{20}$, $C_{22}$) in a tropical fish they studied to its diet, which was quite rich in saturated fatty acids. They suggested that the need for "essential fatty acids" in fish nutrition has not been properly established and that it is questionable whether fish can synthesize those that are essential for mammals.

Mead *et al.* (1960) injected acetate-1-$^{14}$C into *Tilapia mossambica* and concluded that essential fatty acids are probably derived from dietary fatty acids such as linoleic and are not synthesized from acetate. Klenk and Kremer (1960) incubated liver slices from different fish with acetate-1-$^{14}$C and found that the labeling occurred predominantly on the carboxyl end of the fatty acids, little or no radioactivity occurring in the middle or methyl end carbons. They concluded that in fish $C_{20}$ and $C_{22}$ polyenoic fatty acids are derived from exogenous precursors other than acetate. These observations, coupled with the recent discovery of Nicolaides and Woodall (1962) that *Oncorhynchus tschawytscha* fry require trilinolein to develop proper skin pigmentation when raised initially on a fat-free diet suggest that fish require essential fatty acids.

## B. Hydrolysis of Lipids in Fish Muscles

A large proportion of the energy requirements of fish for migratory and maturation phenomena are, in the case of fatty fish at least, undoubtedly met by utilization of the depot lipids. In general this fraction occurs largely in the muscle. Recent investigations have revealed the presence in fish muscles of certain of the enzymes involved in utilization of the muscle lipids for energy purposes.

Work on hydrolysis of lipids in fish muscle has been carried out in connection with the need for technological information concerning formation and significance of free fatty acids in stored frozen muscle. However, the enzyme systems discovered in such investigations are probably functional *in vivo*.

Wood (1959a) briefly reviewed earlier literature dealing with the known slow hydrolysis of fats in fish muscles. He succeeded in preparing a lipase enzyme from frozen lingcod (*Ophiodon elongatus*) muscle. A 1 in 3 aqueous extract of the blended muscle was made to 60% saturation with magnesium sulfate and the precipitate was suspended in water and made to one-quarter of the original extract volume. Purification was 5- to 10-fold, and reprecipitation with magnesium sulfate gave no increase in specific activity. Only 18% of the original lipase activity of the muscle was recovered.

The preparation was unstable and, when it was diluted, lost much of its activity on standing overnight at 0°C, even when dialyzed against 0.01 *M* magnesium sulfate or cysteine. However, it could be kept 4 weeks at −20°C without loss of activity. The pH optimum was 8.2 and the enzyme hydrolyzed triacetin at an approximately linear rate at 5° to 45°C over a 1-hour period. Maximum hydrolysis was obtained at 45°C, though there were indications that the enzyme was being destroyed rapidly at this temperature. The tri- and monoacetic, propionic, and butyric acid esters of glycerol were all hydrolyzed effectively. Water-insoluble substrates such as trioctanoin, halibut liver oil, and lingcod liver oil were hydrolyzed feebly or not at all. This was assumed to be due to their insolubility since "Tween 80" (a monolaurate ester of a polyalkylene derivative of sorbitol) was hydrolyzed to yield lauric acid. Since hydrolysis of ethyl acetate and methyl acetate was extremely slow, it was concluded that the enzyme was not an esterase. It was also shown that the lipase activity of the muscle decreased very slowly on prolonged storage at −20°C (Wood, 1959b; Wood and Haqq, 1962). Like other lipase enzymes it was resistant to most of the usual enzyme inhibitors including azide, cyanide, ferricyanide, and *p*-chloromercuribenzoate.

Lovern (1961) has reviewed work dealing with hydrolysis of phospholipids (lipids of constitution) in fish. Since these usually occur in considerably lower concentrations in muscles of more fatty fish species, it would seem that they are probably much less available as energy sources than are the triglycerides. It is now well known that it is the phospholipids rather than the triglycerides that are hydrolyzed slowly in frozen fish (Lovern *et al.*, 1959). Bligh (1961) discovered that both phosphatidylcholine and phosphatidylethanolamine are hydrolyzed to yield free fatty acids by frozen cod muscle (*Gadus callarias*).

Yurkowski and Brockerhof (1965) homogenized Atlantic cod muscle with 4 parts of water, centrifuged the homogenate 1 hour at 1300 $g$, freeze-dried the supernate, and stored it at $-9°C$. This extract hydrolyzed lysolecithin. Reaction mixtures containing, in a final volume of 20 ml, 60 mg (0.11 m mole) of lysolecithin, 10 ml 0.125 $M$ tris buffer, pH 7.6, and 148 mg of enzyme preparation were incubated 2 hours at 25°C with agitation. Enzyme activity was measured by free fatty acids formed in the reaction:

Lysolecithin + H₂O → L-α-glycerylphosphorylcholine (GPC) + free fatty acid

Much of the lysolecithinase activity (56–60%) occurred in the muscle supernates, and there was a very marked variation in different fish, the specific activity as mμmoles of lysolecithin hydrolyzed per milligram of muscle (dry weight basis) per hour ranging from 0.34 to 6.73. The enzyme retained its activity in fish that had been frozen for 110 days. The Michaelis constant ($K_m$) was $2.7 \times 10^{-5}$ under the experimental conditions. The optimum pH was 7.6 and the optimum temperature 40°–42°C. Iodoacetate, KCN, NaF, and EDTA had little or no inhibitory effect. Oleic acid caused marked inhibition (71 to 82%).

The authors found, in preliminary work, that the lecithinase activity of cod muscle is quite labile, and disappeared when extracts were stored several weeks at $-9°C$.

Bilinski and Jonas (1966), realizing that the phospholipase activity in fish muscle is normally comparatively feeble, prepared ¹⁴C-labeled phospholipids as substrates for their investigations. Both labeled lecithin (phospholipid-choline-methyl-¹⁴C or PL-¹⁴C) and lysolecithin (lysophospholipid-choline-methyl-¹⁴C or Ly PL-¹⁴C) were employed. Using rainbow trout muscle slices or homogenates (500 mg), the hydrolysis of 5 mg of PL-¹⁴C or of 1.25 mg of Ly PL-¹⁴C in a final 5 ml volume was investigated at pH 6.5 over a 2-hour period at 35°C. Evidence was found for the presence of both lecithinase and lysolecithinase in trout muscles, the activity of the latter enzyme being considerably higher. Since GPC was a main product of hydrolysis, it was considered that hydrolysis of lecithin in trout muscles is due to activity of the two enzymes. Lysolecithin did not accumulate. The pH optimum for both enzymes was about 7.0 and the optimum temperature range 35°C–45°C. The activity was considerably higher in brown lateral line-muscle than in ordinary muscle. Free choline and phosphorylcholine were not formed, indicating that phospholipases C and D are absent from trout muscle. In view of the activity of lysolecithinase, there is at present no indication that phospholipase A is present in the muscle, and it is possible that an enzyme which liberates two fatty acids is present.

Cohen *et al.* (1967) have recently studied lysolecithinase from muscle of *Saurida undosquamis*. The comparatively fresh muscle was blended with 10 volumes of $H_2O$ and the suspension was then freeze-dried. For enzyme studies 100-mg portions of freeze-dried powder were added to 10 ml of diethyl ether, and the suspension was stirred 20 minutes at 0°C. The ether was decanted after centrifuging at 17,000 $g$ and the residue dried under nitrogen. The powder (100 mg), suspended in 15 ml of $H_2O$, was exposed to sonic oscillations for 1 minute. The resulting suspension was used in all studies. The enzyme preparation, pyridine-HCl buffer and lecithin were incubated together with shaking at 37°C, lysolecithinase being determined by the hydroxamate method.

Lysolecithin, and not lecithin, was hydrolyzed and the pH optimum was 5.0. Not all fish examined contained the enzyme, which appears to differ from that in cod muscle in the fact that lipid removal is required for activity. The pH optimum was quite different from that reported by the preceding investigators for cod and rainbow trout.

Jonas and Bilinski (1967) have recently succeeded in demonstrating lecithinase A activity in red (lateral) muscle of rainbow trout using a sensitive radioactive assay procedure. The results showed that the microsomal fraction of the muscle possessed about twice the activity of the mitochondria, and that the optimum pH was 7.5. The authors suggest that it is probable that lecithin breakdown occurs in two steps, first the formation of lysolecithin from lecithin by the above enzyme, followed by further hydrolyses of lysolecithin to GPC. The possibility that lecithin may be converted to GPC by a single diacylhydrolase enzyme (phospholipase B) has not yet been discounted.

The preceding results permit the conclusion that lecithin is hydrolyzed in fish muscles under postmortem conditions (Fig. 3).

The enzymic hydrolysis of other phospholipids of fish muscles, particularly phosphatidylethanolamine (cephalin), does not appear to have been investigated.

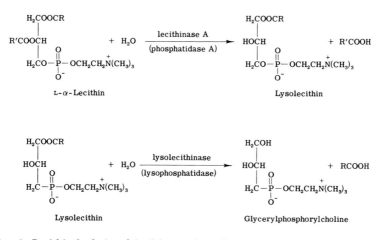

Fig. 3. Lecithin hydrolyzed in fish muscle under postmortem conditions, where R and $R^1$ are fatty acids.

## C. Oxidation of Fatty Acids

While specific enzymes responsible for the various steps in fat oxidation and synthesis have not been isolated in the case of fish, recent research has indicated that fatty acid oxidation proceeds along lines similar to those now accepted for the mammal.

Brown and Tappel (1959) prepared mitochondria from carp liver homogenates using conventional differential centrifugal techniques, and the ability of these to oxidize various saturated and unsaturated fatty acids was determined by accepted methods (Lehninger, 1957). When a tricarboxylic cycle intermediate such as succinate, oxalacetate, fumarate, malate, or $\alpha$-ketoglutarate was included in the medium as a "sparker," octanoic acid was oxidized actively by the mitochondria, but less actively in the absence of such intermediates. As with similar mammalian systems cytochrome $c$, magnesium, and adenosine triphosphate were required. No effect on the rate of fatty acid oxidation was observed by DPN, malonate, EDTA, cocarboxylase, coenzyme A, FAD, $Fe^{2+}$, and $Mn^{2+}$ in the concentrations used. Cysteine, $Cu^{2+}$, $Zn^{2+}$, and reduced glutathione were only slightly stimulatory and lipoic acid caused marked inhibition.

Both saturated and unsaturated fatty acids including butyrate, octanoate, palmitate, oleate, linoleate, linolenate, arachidonate, eicosapentaenoate, sorbate, crotonate, docosahexaenoate, and mixed fish oil fatty acids were oxidized but at different rates. Acetate and propionate were not oxidized. The long-chain unsaturated fatty acids were oxidized as rapidly by fish liver as by rat liver preparations, but a saturated fatty acid, oleic acid, was oxidized much more rapidly by the latter.

Experiments showed that less than the theoretical amount of acetoacetate was formed from octanoate and linoleate, since, in the presence of succinate as a "sparker" some of the acetoacetate was presumably metabolized via the TCA cycle. Dinitrophenylhydrazone, which has been used successfully as a "sparker" in mammalian systems and permits accumulation of theoretical amounts of acetoacetate, was not found satisfactory in the fish system. The results indicated that fatty acid oxidation in fish liver proceeds along lines similar to those in mammalian liver, but that, in general, the rates of oxidation are slower.

Bilinski (1963) investigated oxidation of saturated fatty acids by slices of both white and red (dark) muscle of rainbow trout. Warburg techniques and $^{14}$C-labeled fatty acids were used. When used in 0.1 or 1.0 m$M$ concentration, octanoate was oxidized fifty times as rapidly by the red as by the white muscle. Myristate (0.1 m$M$) was also oxidized much more rapidly by red muscle, but with hexanoate the differences in rates of oxidation by the two types of muscle were not so marked. The results are consistent with the general theory that the red or dark layers of muscle in fishes act as an organ rather than as ordinary muscle. It is now well known that red muscle is normally richer in glycogen, vitamins of the B complex, cytochromes, glycogen, and lipids and is more contractile and differs structurally (Buttkus, 1963) from white muscle.

Jonas and Bilinski (1964) studied fatty acid oxidation using slices of different tissues of both adult and juvenile sockeye salmon (*Oncorhynchus nerka*). No important differences were observed between tissues from adult and juvenile fish. Acetate and myristate were more actively oxidized than octanoate. The overall results indicate that, with a few exceptions, the ability of the various tissues to oxidize the three substrates decreased in the following order: kidney, liver, heart, red lateral line muscle, and brain, and last, dorsal muscle.

Following their work with tissue slices Bilinski and Jonas (1964) prepared subcellular particles, having the sedimentation characteristics of mitochondria, from red lateral muscle of rainbow trout and sockeye salmon and employed these particulate preparations to study oxidation of fatty acids. With myristate the rate of oxidation was linear for up to 90 minutes at 25°C, the pH range for active oxidation being 6.5 to 11.0, with an optimum of about 8.0. The various requirements for oxidation of octanoate by rainbow trout mitochondria, and of myristate by sockeye salmon mitochondria, were determined. Omission of $Mg^{2+}$ or ATP depressed oxidation markedly, and the latter could be largely replaced by ADP or AMP.

Omission of $\alpha$-ketoglutarate depressed oxidation to about the same extent as did omission of ATP. However, in absence of $\alpha$-ketoglutarate other TCA intermediates (succinate, oxalacetate, and fumarate) restored activity very considerably, the effects varying in different instances. Addition of DPN or DPNH had little effect, except in one case. Cytochrome $c$ and cysteine were without effect, and malonate inhibited oxidation strongly.

Coenzyme A accelerated oxidation of myristate, octanoate, and hexanoate, the optimum concentration being 0.1 m$M$. Comparative experiments showed that, on a protein nitrogen basis and with coenzyme A added, the particulate (mitochondrial) fraction oxidized myristate more actively than did whole muscle homogenates, and very much more actively than the supernate from the particulate fraction.

These results indicated that the fatty acid oxidizing system from fish lateral muscle had requirements similar to those of typical mammalian systems, except that the stimulating effect of added coenzyme A is unusual with the latter. It is of interest that, while cytochrome $c$ stimulated fatty acid oxidation by carp liver mitochondria (Brown and Tappel, 1959), it was without effect with the above muscle preparations.

## D. BIOSYNTHESIS OF LIPIDS

Malins (1966a) has recently reported that of the 31–56% of total lipid in the distal lobes of dogfish (*Squalus acanthias*) livers, 15–48% are diacylglyceryl ethers; 49–82% triglycerides; 1–2.2% phospholipids; 0.01–0.03% aldehydes of phosphatidyl plasmalogens; 0.02–0.06% plasmalogenic diglycerides; 0.01–0.02% nonesterified plasmalogens; 0.2–0.4% monoacylglyceryl ethers, and 0.36–0.38% diglycerides.

When palmitic acid-1-$^{14}$C was injected into dogfish, maximum radioactivity appeared in the liver lipid fraction 6–10 hours after injection. The triglycerides contained 79% of the recovered radioactivity, the phosphatides 15%, and the diacylglyceryl ethers 6%. From these and other results it was concluded that both alkyl and alkenyl ethers are formed from palmitic acid in these fish. It was felt that the comparatively high specific activity of the alkenyl ethers might mean that they are precursors of the alkyl ethers (Malins, 1966b).

Dogfish were injected intrahepatically with chimyl alcohol-1-$^{14}$C and the liver lipids were extracted after 4 and 10.5 hours (Malins, 1967). The following specific activities were found after 4 and 10.5 hours, respectively: nonesterified glyceryl ethers (NEGE), $9.6 \times 10^4$ and $1.8 \times 10^6$; monoacylglyceryl ethers (MAGE), $5.3 \times 10^3$ and $2.4 \times 10^4$; diacylglyceryl ethers (DAGE), not determined and 42; nonesterified vinyl ethers (NEVE),

5.1 $\times$ 10⁴ and 9.4 $\times$ 10⁵; monoacetylvinyl ethers (MAVE), 1.2 $\times$ 10⁴ and 1.1 $\times$ 10⁵; diacylvinyl ethers (DAVE), not determined and 3 $\times$ 10³; glyceryl ethers of phospholipids, not determined and 2.0 $\times$ 10⁴; and aldehydes of phospholipids, 8 $\times$ 10² and 2.2 $\times$ 10⁴. The specific activities of free fatty acids, obvious alternative precursors of glyceryl ethers in biosynthesis of vinyl ethers (plasmalogens), were 3.7 $\times$ 10³ and 2.76 $\times$ 10⁵, and these values were considerably greater than that of any esterified fatty acids examined. At 6 and 18.5 hours after injection of palmitic acid-¹⁴C the specific activities of the NEGE always exceeded those of the next active vinyl ethers, notably NEVE and MAVE. It was suggested that vinyl ethers may be derived directly from glyceryl ethers by enzymic degradation. It is also possible that vinyl ethers are formed from a discrete pool of fatty acids derived from chimyl alcohol.

### E. Occurrence of Ketone Bodies in Fish Blood

Starvation of salmon during spawning migration might be thought to favor ketogenesis. Studies with rainbow trout indicated that there was no pronounced change in ketone bodies (acetoacetate and $\beta$-hydroxybutyrate) during starvation. However, there were high concentrates of these in blood of naturally spawning sockeye salmon. Perhaps ketone bodies are formed as result of hormone changes or diesase rather than by starvation (Jonas and Bilinski, 1965).

## VII. Enzymes of Nucleic Acid Metabolism

Certain aspects of this subject have been reviewed largely from the standpoint of the importance of these enzymes in postmortem alterations that occur in fish (Tarr, 1966a, b).

### A. Deoxyribonuclease

Mannan and Tarr (1961) found that, of seven fish organs studied, exclusive of the gonads, kidney possessed the strongest deoxyribonuclease activity (at neutral pH). This enzyme proved very labile, being eliminated by mild methods of fractionation, as with ammonium sulfate, isoelectric precipitation at pH 4.5 or 5.0, and brief dialysis. A simple method of "purification" was used (0°–3°C) which did not increase the specific activity. Fresh salmon kidney was extracted with water, the mixture centrifuged, the supernate treated with 2% protamine sulfate to remove nucleic acids, and the clear supernate obtained after centrifuging used directly.

This preparation hydrolyzed crude salmon DNA to yield the deoxy-nucleosides of thymine, uracil, adenine, and guanine. These compounds were isolated in preparative amounts by ion-exchange chromatography of alcohol extracts of the enzyme reaction mixture.

McDonald (1962) found that salmon testes, presumably comparatively mature, contained three to five times as much deoxyribonuclease activity as calf spleen, and six to fifteen times as much as calf thymus. The enzyme was prepared as follows, all manipulations being carried out at 0°–3°C.

Minced salmon testes (50 pounds) were extracted with occasional stirring for 6–8 hours with 50 liters of 0.05 $N$ $H_2SO_4$. The mixture was filtered overnight by gravity to yield about 54 liters of filtrate (pH 5.4). The filtrate was made to 0.8 saturation with ammonium sulfate and the precipitate retained. The precipitate was suspended three times in pro-gressively smaller volumes of water with intermediate filtration. The com-bined aqueous extracts were adjusted to 0.65 saturation with ammonium sulfate and, after 18 hours, the precipitate was collected by filtration. At this stage the above procedure was repeated until the combined protein precipitate from 250 pounds of testes had been collected.

The following steps were carried out at room temperature. The combined protein precipitates were suspended in four times their weight of water, the suspension filtered, and the residue reextracted with a smaller volume of water. The combined aqueous extracts were brought to 0.7 saturation with ammonium sulfate and the precipitate collected after 18–24 hours. The filter cake was dissolved in 5 volumes of water and the solution ad-justed to 0.45 saturation with ammonium sulfate and the precipitate collected after 1 to 3 hours. The filtrate was adjusted to 0.7 saturation with ammonium sulfate and the precipitate was retained. This precipitate was dissolved in water and the protein fraction that precipitated between 0.45 and 0.7 saturation with ammonium sulfate was collected. At this stage the filter cakes were saved until material from 1000 pounds of testes was collected.

The above filter cake was dissolved in an equal weight of water, the solution adjusted to pH 3.8 with 1 $N$ sulfuric acid, and any precipitate which formed was removed by centrifugation. Saturated ammonium sulfate was added to the solution until incipient turbidity occurred and the mixture was left 1 week at 20°C. An inert crystalline precipitate of fine needles formed and these were removed by filtration and the filtrate was saved. The filter cake was suspended in twice its weight of water, which dissolved the crystalline, but not the amorphous material. The mix-ture was filtered and the precipitate was discarded. The filtrate was ad-justed to a stage of incipient turbidity with saturated ammonium sulfate solution and the crystalline material which formed in standing at 20°C was separated by filtration. The combined filtrates were made to 0.7 saturation with ammonium sulfate and the filtrate was discarded.

The filter cake from the above procedure was dissolved in twenty-five times its weight of water, the solution was then adjusted to pH 4.0, and heated rapidly to 65°C. After standing 15 minutes at this temperature it was cooled rapidly to 25°C and held 1 hour at room temperature. The denatured protein was removed by filtration, the precipitate being washed with water. The combined filtrates were adjusted to 0.7 saturation with ammonium sulfate and the precipitate was collected. The precipitate was dissolved in five times its weight of water and the solution was adjusted to 0.45 saturation with ammonium sulfate. The suspension was filtered and the filtrate made to 0.6 saturation with ammonium sulfate.

The filter cake was dissolved in four times its weight of water and dialyzed against running distilled water 24 hours at 1°–3°C. The solution was clarified, when necessary, by centrifugation and the fraction precipitating between 0–18% ethanol at 0°–2°C was collected, dissolved in a small volume of water, and stored at −20°C. The properties of this enzyme, which indicated that it was a "deoxyribonuclease type II" were as follows.

The preparation was comparatively homogeneous by paper electrophoresis, but contained some minor contaminating protein components. The enzyme was free from the protease, ribonuclease, phosphatase, and phosphodiesterase enzyme activities that were found in the crude extracts. The enzyme was most stable between pH 4 and 5, and was active at pH values between about 4.0 and 5.6, with an optimum of pH 4.8. Solutions containing > 1 mg protein per milliliter in 0.01 $M$ ammonium sulfate solution retained their full activity for 3 months at 3°C. The enzyme was readily inactivated at temperatures above 70°C. Deoxyribonucleic acid from thymus, salmon testis, and phage T2H were degraded at similar rates, but heat denaturation of these reduced the rate of degradation very markedly. Apurinic acid was not hydrolyzed. The activity was markedly accelerated by $Mg^{2+}$ or $Ca^{2+}$ ions (optimum concentration about $2 \times 10^{-3}$ $M$ for $MgCl_2$) and less by $Na^+$ and $K^+$ ($4.5 \times 10^{-2}$ $M$).

B. Ribonuclease, Phosphodiesterase, and Phosphomonoesterase
Activities

Tarr (1953, 1954) observed that free ribose was liberated from ribonucleic acid by ground lingcod muscle in 3–5 days at 0°C. The ribonucleic acid used was a rather crude commercial preparation. Later Tomlinson and

Creelman (1960) were unable to detect any decrease in the natural ribonucleic acid of muscle (Bluhm and Tarr, 1957) of whole eviscerated lingcod held for up to 3 weeks in ice. The same held true for pieces of muscle which were excised aseptically and were held 3 weeks at 0°C and for ground muscle held 5 days at 0°C. One explanation offered for these results is the possible inability of the ribonuclease enzymes present in the muscle (see below) to hydrolyze ribonucleic acid as present in fish muscles. Thus fish muscle ribonucleic acid may be loosely combined with protein, as in the case of nucleotropomyosin (Hamoir, 1951), and thus not be readily attacked.

Tomlinson (1958) investigated the ribonuclease, phosphodiesterase, and phosphomonoesterase activities of lingcod muscle. The ribonuclease enzyme preparation was obtained by adjusting an aqueous muscle extract to 0.8 saturation with ammonium sulfate, followed by dialysis, freeze-drying, and isoelectric precipitation at pH 4.5. This extract was freed from phosphomonoesterase activity by adjusting it to pH 9.0, and warming for 10 minutes at 58°C.

Paper electrophoresis of such extracts revealed two zones with phosphodiesterase activity and a single zone with ribonuclease activity. Attempts to separate the enzymes by chromatography using a cation-exchange resin (XE64) or Celite were unsuccessful. The pH activity relationships of the ribonuclease and phosphodiesterase were the same: there was a sharp optimum at pH 6.2 and rapid inactivation below pH 4.0 and above pH 9.0. Both ribonuclease and phosphodiesterase activities were inhibited by $Zn^{2+}$, $Cu^{2+}$, $F^-$, and iodoacetate. The ribonuclease activity was inhibited by $2.5 \times 10^{-2} M$ EDTA, while the diesterase activities were not affected.

The ribonuclease extracts degraded yeast ribonucleic acid more rapidly than they did fairly highly polymerized lingcod muscle ribonucleic acid. By appropriate electrophoretic and paper chromatographic techniques products of ribonucleic acid hydrolysis were identified as the 3′-phosphate esters of adenosine, guanosine, cytidine, and uridine. The presence of a ribonuclease was verified in muscle extracts of six other widely different fish species. Thus in many respects the enzyme appeared to be similar to mammalian spleen ribonuclease.

In later work Tomlinson (1959) carried out fractionation of the ribonuclease activity of lingcod muscle, and because of the rather broad specificity of the enzyme termed it a nuclease. He found that, because of its much greater capacity, the "free base" form of DEAE-cellulose was preferable to DEAE buffered with very low ionic strength *tris* solution for separating the various enzyme activities. Thus chromatography of lingcod muscle extracts on very small DEAE columns yielded three phosphodiesterase fractions and a single nuclease fraction on stepwise elution with increasing concentrations of *tris* buffers.

The nuclease hydrolyzed ribonucleic acid to yield the four nucleoside 3'-phosphate esters, and also hydrolyzed adenosine-3'-benzyl phosphate to yield adenosine-3'-phosphate. Thymidine-3'- and -5'-nitrophenyl phosphates were hydrolyzed with release of $p$-nitrophenol. No hydrolysis of deoxyribonucleic acid, adenosine-2'- or -5'-benzyl phosphates or of 2',3'-cyclic adenylic acid or 2',3'-cyclic uridylic acid was detected. Very slow hydrolysis of thymidine-5'-nitrophenyl phosphate was the single exception found to the otherwise apparent specificity of the enzyme which did not hydrolyze the 3'-linkage of either ribose or deoxyribose phosphate esters. No hydrolysis of $p$-nitrophenyl phosphate or of bis($p$-nitrophenyl) phosphate was detected.

Several investigators have noted the occurrence of acid or alkaline phosphomonoesterase activities in fish muscles (Ono and Nagayama, 1959; Simskaya and Karpliuk, 1957; Alfonsen and Bertran, 1954). Tomlinsom and Warren (1960) made a thorough study of the phosphomonoesterase activity of lingcod muscle. Crude, well-dialyzed ammonium sulfate fractions were applied to DEAE columns in the free base form. Five chromatographically distinct phosphomonoesterase activities, distinguished by their ability to hydrolyze $p$-nitrophenyl phosphate, were separated by eluting the column stepwise with tris buffers of from 0.0025 to 0.2 $M$ concentration. These enzymes were distinguished by their responses to EDTA, formate, fluoride, tartrate, heparin, and cysteine. Two of the enzymes required $Zn^{2+}$ and one $Mn^{2+}$ before they became active. The pH range of activity of the different enzymes was 3.0–8.2, with pH optima of 5.0–6.0. The substrate specificity of various enzymes was not determined.

## C. Adenosinetriphosphatases

The ability of fish muscles to degrade adenosine triphosphate has long been known. Thus early studies showed that adenosinetriphosphate (labile phosphate) rapidly disappears in fish muscles that are held postmortem (Tarr, 1950; Fujimaki and Kojo, 1955; Partmann, 1964). Tomlinson and Geiger (1962) reviewed some of the literature concerning postmortem changes in ATP concentration in fish muscles. ATP hydrolysis, as judged by a decrease in acid labile phosphorus, proceeded more rapidly in fish muscle brei than in whole muscle. It was also more rapid in thawing fish muscle than in thawing beef muscle (Partmann, 1961). Connell (1960) observed that the ATPase activity of cod muscle did not decrease during a 3-year storage at −29°C, but decreased at −22° and −14°C, and that the decrease was more rapid at the latter temperature. Partmann and Nemitz (1959) showed that heat inactivation of ATPase in carp muscle was independent of the water content above about 17% water. In freeze-dried muscle the stability of the enzyme increased as the water content decreased. A 17% water content was considered as constituting a boundary line between free and bound water.

These observations were carried out using whole fish muscles and no attempt was made to ascertain whether one or more enzymes was responsible. Engelhardt and Ljubimova (1939) were the first to demonstrate that "myosin" from mammalian muscles possessed ATPase activity; that is it could catalyze the reaction:

$$ATP + H_2O \rightarrow ADP + \text{orthophosphate } (P_i)$$

It is now known that the ATPase activities of actomyosin and myosin differ since, for example, at an ionic strength of 0.1 and pH 7.0 $1 \times 10^{-3}$ $M$ $MgCl_2$ activates actomyosin ATPase and inhibits myosin ATPase. The ATPase that is associated with the myosin molecule in mammals is stimulated by $Ca^{2+}$ and EDTA. In addition, mammalian muscle possesses a $Mg^{2+}$-activated ATPase (Kielley and Meyerhof, 1948). This enzyme is inhibited by $Ca^{2+}$ and is in the particulate fraction of muscle extracts which is rich in lipids. In mammalian muscles the ADP arising from ATPase activity yields AMP by the reversible reaction catalyzed by the soluble enzyme myokinase (adenylate kinase) (Kotel'nikova, 1949): AMP + ATP $\rightleftarrows$ 2 ADP. ADP may be involved in other enzymic reactions involving phosphorylation or dephosphorylation.

Several investigators have carried out investigations on ATPase activities in fish muscles at the "enzyme level." Reuter (1960) succeeded in isolating an ATPase of the Kielley-Meyerhof type from carp muscles and compared it with a similar enzyme isolated from rabbit muscles. In the case of both carp and rabbit this enzyme was associated with the sarcosomes. Carp muscle from freshly killed fish was frozen, finely sliced, homogenized with 4 volumes of 0.2 $M$ sucrose containing 0.03 $M$ Veronal buffer, pH 7.4, and centrifuged 15 minutes at 1500 $g$. This procedure removed cell debris, myofibrils, and mitochondria. After filtering the supernate through a sintered glass filter, the solution was centrifuged 2 hours at 21,800 $g$. The supernate contained a "soluble ATPase" and the sediment a "particulate ATPase." The latter was washed with and suspended in a small volume of the above medium.

The activity, as determined by liberation of orthophosphate from ATP at 20°C, was two to three times greater with carp particulate ATPase than with the similar rabbit enzyme. The activity of both carp and rabbit sarcoplasmic ATPases was markedly accelerated by $Mg^{2+}$ (optimum about $1.1 \times 10^{-3}\ M$) and only slightly by $Ca^{2+}$. DNP (dinitrophenylhydrazine), $5 \times 10^{-5}$ to $5 \times 10^{-3}\ M$ had no appreciable effect. The carp enzyme was rapidly inactivated at temperatures above about 35°C, while the rabbit enzyme was not inactivated until the temperature was raised to 42°C. If, instead of using a single centrifugation for 2 hours at 21,800 $g$, a series of different and increasing centrifugal gradients was employed, the "sarcoplasmic ATPase" was separated into two general ATPase fractions. These appeared to be associated with the mitochondria and sarcosomes, respectively.

The soluble ATPase that remained in solution after a 1-hour centrifugation at 100,000 $g$, was stable 2–3 days in the cold. However, it lost activity on dialysis against the extraction medium, and the activity was partially restored by addition of the dialysis medium. The soluble ATPase was obtained by ammonium sulfate fractionation (0–0.4 saturated). Reuter suggested that his results indicated that there may be three different sarcoplasmic ATPases, one associated with the mitochondria, another with the microsomes, and another partly soluble and associated with protein not sedimenting at 100,000 $g$.

Dingle and Hines (1960) were unable to identify a Kielley-Meyerhof type ATPase in the muscles of Atlantic cod. They did not, however, discount the possibility that such an enzyme is present. Possibly it may be present only in the red muscle, and, in any case, may well require differential centrifugation, such as Reuter employed, for separation.

The situation regarding myosin ATPases is also not entirely clear. Saito and Hidaka (1955a, b) prepared myosins A and B by 20-minute and 24-hour extractions, respectively, and purified these by reprecipitation. The ATPase activity of both preparations was accelerated about four times by $Ca^{2+}$ and inhibited about 50% by $Mg^{2+}$. These preparations were rapidly inactivated at 37°–45°C, but lost only a little activity after 48 hours at 1°–3°C. It is, however, difficult to assess the nature of such extracts.

Dingle and Hines (1960) prepared the fibrillar proteins from prerigor and postrigor cod muscle by two different procedures. Myosin was prepared from actomyosin by centrifugation, in the presence of ATP, at 42,000 $g$ for 1 hour at 0°C in a Spinco Model E ultracentrifuge. When studied in buffered solution at an ionic strength of about 0.1 and pH 7.3 the actomyosin ATPase activity was found to be strongly activated by $Mg^{2+}$. On the other hand, the myosin ATPase activity was suppressed by $Mg^{2+}$. These results parallel those reported for the fibrillar ATPases of mammalian muscles. Calcium ions occasioned some activation of the actomyosin ATPase activity of the cod actomyosin, but had a minor effect on that of myosin ATPase. The total ATPase activity of cod muscle was stable for months at $-23°C$, while the isolated enzyme–proteins were quite labile. Experiments of this sort are thus complicated by the great instability of fish muscle actomyosin and myosin preparations.

Kövér *et al.* (1963) fractionated skeletal muscle of the fish *Ameiurus nebulosus* into a fraction soluble in salt solutions of high ionic strength (myosin) and a second sarcoplasmic fraction obtained with low ionic strength (0.04 $\mu$) extraction. The myosin possessed marked ATPase activity equivalent to 0.4 mg orthophosphate liberated per milligram of protein per hour. Short tryptic digestion of rabbit myosin yields H and L meromyosins, but only a single component with a sedimentation coefficient similar to that of L meromyosin was found with the fish muscle preparation. This had a sedimentation coefficient similar to that of mammalian meromyosin. This fraction had both ATPase and acetylcholinesterase activities similar in activity to that in the original preparation and that of the trypsin digest. Thus fish myosin appears to differ from rabbit myosin. The myosin preparation had a cholinesterase activity corresponding to 3.5 mg of acetylcholine hydrolyzed per milligram of protein per hour. Evidently there is room for further investigation concerning the various ATPases in fish tissues.

### D. Myokinase (Adenylate Kinase)

This enzyme carries out the specific reaction: $2 \text{ ADP} \rightleftarrows \text{AMP} + \text{ATP}$. It is classically regarded as a "muscle enzyme," but has also been found in rat liver mitochondria. This enzyme almost certainly accounts for degradation of the ADP formed in fish muscles by ATPase activity to AMP. However, no detailed study of the enzyme appears to have been made. Jones and Murray (1961b) detected the enzyme in cod muscle homogenates or extracts using a recognized assay procedure. The occurrence of a myokinase-like activity in salmon testes is referred to in Section VII, H, 3 below.

### E. Deaminases

The deamination of both guanine and adenine or related compounds has been studied in fish muscles.

Nara and Saito (1959) prepared an adenylic acid deaminase from carp muscle by blending it with 4–5 volumes of 0.5 $M$ KCl or of Straub's solution (0.3 $M$ KCl, 0.09 $M$ KH$_2$PO$_4$, 0.06 $M$ K$_2$HPO$_4$; pH 6.6). The substrate (AMP) was used in $2.88 \times 10^{-3}$ $M$ concentration in 0.1 $M$ succinate buffer, pH 6.6. The activity was determined by following the ammonia liberated during deamination, and under the experimental conditions the reaction was linear with respect to enzyme concentration and time. A specific activity of 100 $\mu$g of NH$_3$ liberated per milligram of protein nitrogen per hour at 30°C was recorded.

Tarr and Comer (1964) investigated the deamination of adenine and related compounds and the formation of deoxyadenosine and deoxyinosine by a muscle enzyme preparation obtained from lingcod. An 0.8 saturated ammonium sulfate fraction of an aqueous extract of the muscle was dialyzed against water. The protein fraction thus obtained (crude enzyme) was absorbed on a small column of DEAE that had been equilibrated with 0.005 $M$ tris buffer, pH 7.5. The column was washed successively with 0.005, 0.1, and 0.2 $M$ tris buffers, the purified enzyme fraction being eluted at 0.3 $M$ concentration. The preparations contained 0.03 to 0.05 mg of protein nitrogen per milliliter and possessed both adenosine deaminase and purine nucleoside phosphorylase (Tarr, 1958b) activities. This fraction was quite unstable and was used within a few hours of preparation. The specific activity was only increased about twofold by the DEAE treatment. Dialysis reduced the activity rapidly and 2-mercaptoethanol did not protect the enzyme. Attempts to separate the deaminase and nucleoside phosphorylase activities in the preparation by treatment with alumina C$_\gamma$ or calcium phosphate gel were unsuccessful.

The crude enzyme possessed adenylic acid, adenosine, and deoxyadenosine deaminase activities. The adenylic acid deaminase was eliminated by flash-heating to 58°C while the adenosine and deoxyadenosine deaminase activities were unaffected by this treatment. Adenine was very slowly deaminated by both crude and purified preparations, the rate of deamination of deoxyadenosine being about 2300 times as rapid. Adenine proved a good substrate for the nucleoside phosphorylase activity, since deoxyadenosine was formed quite rapidly from adenine in the presence of deoxyribose-1-phosphate. The deoxyadenosine thus formed did not accumulate since it was deaminated rapidly to deoxyinosine. Thus, deamination of adenine was shown to play an insignificant role in formation of deoxyinosine or inosine. The nucleoside phosphorylase activity with adenine as substrate was about equal to that of the deaminase activity with deoxyadenosine or adenosine as substrates. These relationships are shown in the following diagram.

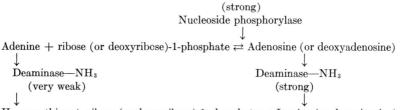

Lindahl and Svärd (1957) referred to previous investigations concerning the increase in free guanine that occurs in the skin of salmon parr during the transition to smolts, and to the fact that light stimulates this phenomenon. In their own experiments they employed clarified aqueous, or $1 \times 10^{-2}$ $M$ EDTA, extracts of ground skin of the roach (*Leuciscus rutilus* Lin.). This preparation deaminated guanine with formation of xanthine, and its activity was enhanced by use of EDTA. Especially at alkaline pH values $Cu^{2+}$ and $Zn^{2+}$ were strongly inhibitory. Thus, at pH 9.0 these cations in $6 \times 10^{-5}$ $M$ concentration completely abolished deaminase activity. However, iodoacetate and fluoride ($1 \times 10^{-2}$ $M$) were not inhibitory. The pH optimum was about 8.0, there being some variation in activity depending on the buffer used.

During an investigation of the nucleoside phosphorylase of lingcod muscle (Tarr, 1958b) it was observed that, when guanosine or deoxyguanosine was employed to synthesize ribose-1-phosphate or deoxyribose-1-phosphate, the solution became alkaline, presumably due to formation of ammonia arising from guanine deamination.

Roy (1966) subsequently prepared a guanine deaminase from muscle of this fish by heating an aqueous extract 1 minute at 58°C, cooling, removing denatured protein, and precipitating the crude enzyme with ammonium sulfate (0.4–0.6) saturated). This preparation, which was purified about sixfold, was employed for most experiments after dialysis for 4 hours. Adsorption on small DEAE columns, followed by stepwise elution, gave considerably greater purification (greater than 1950-fold, and specific activities of >280 in the most active fractions). The crude muscle extracts gave two pH optima for for guanine deaminase activity (5.6 and 8.5), while the partially purified (heated) preparation had a single pH optimum (6.0). The $K_m$ was $3.3 \times 10^{-5}$ $M$. Iodoacetate ($10^{-3}$ $M$) and $CuSO_4$ ($10^{-5}$ $M$) caused no inhibition, NaCN ($10^{-1}$ $M$) 45%, KF ($10^{-2}$ $M$) 75%, and $p$-hydroxymercuribenzoate ($10^{-4}$ $M$) complete inhibition. The crude preparation was stable for at least 3 weeks at 0°C, while the DEAE-cellulose fractions lost about 40% of their activity in 1 month at 0°C.

In the above work it was found that only guanine and 8-azaguanine were deaminated; adenine, guanosine, guanylic acid, 2-aminopurine, 2,6-diaminopurine, and 2-hydroxy-6-aminopurine were not substrates. Further work (Roy and Roy, 1967) showed that the enzyme removed chlorine from 2-chloro-6-hydroxypurine, hydrazine from 2-hydrazino-6-hydroxypurine, and methylamine from 2-methylamino-6-hydroxypurine, with formation of xanthine. The $K_m$ and $V_{\max}$ values with the different substrates varied considerably. The results obtained supported the view that the lactam tautomeric form of the substrate is necessary to support activity.

F. NUCLEOSIDE HYDROLASE

A nucleoside hydrolase enzyme was prepared from lingcod and rock cod
(*Sebastodes*) muscle by the following procedure carried out at about 0°C
(Tarr, 1955a). The muscle was blended with 3 volumes of water and NaCl
to adjust the suspension to 0.6 $M$ with respect to this salt. Sufficient 1 $N$
HCl was added to adjust the pH to 4.6 and the suspension was then centrifuged. The supernate was adjusted to pH 7.0 and was fractionated at this
pH with ammonium sulfate, the fraction precipitating between 0.4 and
0.6 saturation being retained. This fraction was dissolved in water and
dialyzed for 2 days against repeated changes of demineralized water to
yield a crude nucleoside hydrolase preparation.

The crude preparation was further purified by absorption on XE 64
cation-exchange resin at pH 7.3, washing the resin repeatedly with water,
and eluting the enzyme with 2.5 $M$ NaCl. The preparation was dialyzed
18 hours against water. The protein nitrogen content was about 16 $\mu$g
per milliliter. The specific activity increased as much as 1500 times by
purification, and the enzyme could be freeze-dried and stored at 37°C for
18 days with practically no loss of activity. Prolonged storage was not
studied.

The preparation possessed two distinct substrate-activity spectra when
different pH values were used in studies of nucleoside hydrolysis. At pH
8.6 only inosine was hydrolyzed actively by the purified enzyme. Adenosine,
but no other ribonucleosides inhibited this hydrolysis. At pH 5.5, adeno-
since, inosine, and guanosine were hydrolyzed rapidly, and xanthosine and
cytidine less rapidly; uridine was not hydrolyzed. Since there was no
additive effect when two nucleosides were present together, it was suggested that a single nucleoside hydrolase was responsible for the hydrolysis
at pH 8.6 and 5.5.

Hydrolysis of the nucleosides proceeded in absence of orthophosphate,
and D-ribose was isolated from guanosine hydrolysis, which indicated that
the enzyme was a nucleoside hydrolase and not a nucleoside phosphorylase.
Neither ribose-5-phosphate nor ribose-1-phosphate was hydrolyzed by
the enzyme. The fact that lingcod muscle hydrolyzes uridine with formation of ribose (Tarr, 1954) indicates that a uridine hydrolase may be
present.

G. NUCLEOSIDE PHOSPHORYLASES

A purine nucleoside phosphorylase was prepared from lingcod muscle
by Tarr (1955b, 1956, 1958b). The muscle was blended with 3 volumes of

water and sufficient 1 $N$ HCl to adjust the pH to 6.0. The suspension was centrifuged and the supernate fractionated with ammonium sulfate at pH 7.0, the fraction precipitating between 0 and 0.6 saturation being collected and dialyzed against demineralized water to remove ammonium sulfate. The crude preparation was further purified by passage through a cation-exchange resin (Amberlite XE-64) that had been equilibrated with 0.2 $M$ sodium phosphate buffer, pH 5.5. The nucleoside phosphorylase activity was not absorbed on the resin, and passed through as a single peak. The purification was only about threefold and about 75% of the total activity was lost. Attempts to purify the enzyme by use of DEAE (Tarr and Comer, 1964) as described above were even less successful from the point of view of obtaining an increase in specific activity. Other attempts to purify the enzyme further failed.

The specific activity ($\mu$moles of orthophosphate liberated from ribose-1-phosphate per milligram of protein nitrogen per hour in presence of hypoxanthine) varied from 20.3 to 32.3 for different preparations. The purified preparations were not homogeneous either in the ultracentrifuge or by electrophoresis. They possessed phosphoribomutase and phosphodeoxyribomutase activities which could not be eliminated by surface denaturation (Abrams and Klenow, 1953).

Both crude and purified nucleoside phosphorylase enzyme preparations were used to prepare deoxyribose-1-phosphate and ribose-1-phosphate by several different procedures. The enzyme was shown to be specific for $\alpha$-ribose-1-phosphate and was completely inactive toward $\beta$-ribose-1-phosphate and arabinose-1-phosphate. This property was used to verify the structure of chemically synthesized $\alpha$-D-ribofuranose-1-phosphate (Tener *et al.*, 1957) and of a mixture of $\alpha$- and $\beta$-deoxyribose-1-phosphates (MacDonald and Fletcher, 1960).

The enzyme was specific for purines, and possessed greatest activity for hypoxanthine, xanthine, 6-mercaptopurine, guanine, and 8-azaguanine. It also possessed slight activity with adenine (see also Tarr and Comer, 1964), 6-methylpurine and 2,6-diaminopurine. Recent experiments (H. Tarr, unpublished) have shown that 2,6-diaminopurine deoxyriboside is actually formed by reacting purified enzyme with deoxyribose-phosphate and 2,6-diaminopurine, but that the yield is very small indeed. Fifteen other substrates (purines and pyrimidines) were investigated and found to be inactive. The enzyme exhibited a fairly wide pH activity range (5.0–9.0) with optimum activity between about pH 6 and 7 for the crude, and 6.8 and 7.2 for the purified enzyme. In the system: hypoxanthine + ribose 1-phosphate $\rightleftarrows$ inosine + orthophosphate, the equilibrium was about 85% in favor of inosine.

When guanosine (or deoxyguanosine) and orthophosphate are reacted together the comparatively insoluble guanine forms and is largely deaminated to similarly insoluble xanthine. This fact tends to favor ribose-1-phosphate or deoxyribose-1-phosphate formation and was used in preparation of these compounds as mentioned above. Tests in which the enzyme was saturated with respect to either ribose-1-phosphate or deoxyribose-1-phosphate, and the opposite compound was then added, showed that such addition did not increase the formation of inosine from added hypoxanthine. It was, therefore, assumed that a single enzyme is responsible for the nucleoside phosphorylase activity. Low concentrations of $Mg^{2+}$, $Ca^{2+}$, and cysteine had no effect on the enzyme activity. The purified enzyme withstood heating for 3, but not for 5, hours at 50°C. It was inactive in absence of orthophosphate.

Recently a much greater purification of this enzyme was obtained, and it was shown that three "isoenzyme" forms are present in lingcod muscle, together with a very much weaker pyrimidine nucleoside phosphorylase (Tarr and Roy, 1967). A 0–0.6 saturated ammonium sulfate fraction of the muscle obtained as in earlier work (Tarr, 1958b) was dialyzed 16–20 hours against 0.01 $M$ phosphate buffer, pH 7.2. This crude preparation was quite stable, and could be frozen and stored months at $-30$°C without appreciable loss of activity. However, during further purification steps it was found that the enzyme lost activity very rapidly unless it was protected with 2-mercaptoethanol (0.025 $M$).

Thawed crude enzyme was centrifuged to remove denatured protein and was chromatographed on DEAE-cellulose columns, eluting them with a concave increasing gradient of 0.5 $M$ phosphate buffer, pH 7.2, into 0.01 $M$ phosphate buffer. Three different "peaks" of purine nucleoside phosphorylase activity were separated (isoenzymes) together with a much weaker pyridine nucleoside phosphorylase. The purine nucleoside isoenzymes were further purified by adsorption on alumina-$C_\gamma$ and elution. The most active fraction was purified about 120-fold and its specific activity (micromoles of inosine phosphorylated per milligram of protein per hour at 30°C) was 22. It utilized hypoxanthine, 6-mercaptopurine, guanine, 8-azaguanine, xanthine, adenine, 2,6-diaminopurine, and 6-methylpurine in presence of ribose-1-phosphate or deoxyribose-1-phosphate. Several other substituted purines tested were not utilized nor did they inhibit the phosphorylase activity of the enzymes. The $K_m$ with inosine as substrate in presence of excess orthophosphate was $3.2 \times 10^{-5}$ $M$. The pyrimidine nucleoside phosphorylase was very weak, the activity being only about one-thousandth that of the most active purine nucleoside phosphorylase preparation. It utilized uridine and thymidine, deoxyuridine feebly, but neither cytidine nor deoxycytidine. The purine and pyrimidine enzymes were inactivated by freezing and thawing and lost activity rapidly in absence of 2-mercaptoethanol.

Svärd (1957) prepared a crude guanosine phosphorylase by aqueous extraction of the skin of the roach (*Leuciscus rutilus* Lin.). The activity of the enzyme was determined spectrophotometrically in ultraviolet light with guanosine and orthophosphate as substrate. The results showed that the enzyme formed guanine and an unidentified labile phosphorus compound (presumably ribose-1-phosphate). The reaction did not occur in absence of orthophosphate. Neither the base (purine or pyrimidine) nor the sugar phosphate (ribose- or deoxyribose-1-phosphate) specificities of the enzyme were studied.

Mannan and Tarr (1961) observed that salmon liver, kidney, and spleen extracts, but not those of heart, stomach, or pyloric caeca, possessed pyrimidine nucleoside phosphorylase activity, liver being the most active. A crude nucleoside phosphorylase was obtained from salmon liver, but attempts to purify the enzyme were largely ineffective since it proved very sensitive to simple fractionation procedures, such as, isoelectric precipitation, ammonium sulfate fractionation, and dialysis against a number of solutions. Studies were therefore carried out with a preparation made by blending either sockeye or spring salmon livers with 2 parts of water and KF in 0.2 $M$ concentration. The clear liquid obtained on centrifuging 15 minutes at 40,000 $g$ was filtered through glass wool to remove floating particles, and 6 parts of 2% protamine sulfate solution were added. The suspension was centrifuged and the clear supernate was employed for nucleoside phosphorylase studies.

The following substrates were activated in presence of orthophosphate in the following order: deoxyuridine > thymidine > deoxyguanosine > deoxycytidine > deoxyinosine > deoxyadenosine > uridine > cytidine > adenosine > inosine > guanosine > xanthosine. The enzyme preparation thus exhibited wide specificity for purines and pyrimidines and for both deoxyribose-1-phosphate and ribose-1-phosphate. The preparation also possessed phosphodeoxyribomutase and phosphoribomutase activities.

Salmon liver pyrimidine nucleoside phosphorylase, which also contains deoxyribosyl transferase activity which was not separated during purification, has recently been purified and certain of its properties studied (Tarr *et al.* 1968). All procedures were carried out at 0°–3°C. Livers, removed from freshly killed rainbow trout, were blended briefly with 4 volumes of 0.01 $M$ phosphate buffer, pH 7.3, containing 0.025 $M$ 2-mercaptoethanol. Mercaptoethanol was used in all subsequent procedures, since the enzyme lost activity rapidly in its absence. The suspension was centrifuged 1 hour at 100,000 $g$, and the supernate made to 0.5 saturation with $(NH_4)_2SO_4$. The precipitated protein was dissolved in 0.01 $M$ phosphate buffer (about 10 ml for each 200–300 mg of protein) and the solution, after centrifuging to remove insoluble material, was chromatographed on a Sephadex G200 column. Phosphate buffer (0.01 $M$) was used as eluant since use of tris-HCl buffer resulted in very unstable preparations. The enzyme activity was eluted as a single peak, and the eluate was rechromatographed on DEAE-cellulose using a concave increasing gradient of 0.3 $M$ phosphate buffer into 0.01 $M$ phosphate for elution. The phosphorylase was eluted as a sharp peak. The eluate was concentrated to a small volume using a semipermeable membrane and nitrogen under 50 pound pressure, and the concentrate was adsorbed on a hydroxylapatite (0.001 $M$ phosphate, pH 6.8) column and eluted with phosphate buffer. The enzyme was removed by 0.03–0.05 $M$ phosphate buffer. The specific activity was 70–145 (micromoles uracil formed from deoxyuridine by 1 mg protein in 1 hour at 30°C) in different experiments and the purification 68- to 140-fold. It was observed that some livers gave preparations that possessed low specific activities throughout the purification procedure.

The enzyme utilized deoxyuridine, thymidine, 5-iododeoxyuridine, 5-bromodeoxyuridine, and 5-fluorodeoxyuridine, but not uridine, deoxycytidine, deoxyinosine, deoxyadenosine, or deoxyguanosine. The corresponding deoxynucleosides were synthesized from radioactive thymine, uracil, 5-iodouracil, 5-bromouracil, 5-fluorouracil, and xanthine (see below), in presence of deoxyribose-1-phosphate, but not from adenine, hypoxanthine, or cytosine. The deoxynucleoside which was formed from xanthine was identified as 3-deoxyribosylxanthine. The $K_m$ with deoxyuridine as substrate was $1.7 \times 10^{-3}$ $M$, and with thymidine $2 \times 10^{-2}$ $M$. Under conditions where equilibrium was very strongly in favor of deoxynucleoside phosphorylysis (e.g., high orthophosphate concentrations) marked deoxyribosyl transfer occurred between a number of deoxynucleosides and free pyrimidine bases. This transfer, as determined by use of radioactive pyrimidines, occurred between a number of 5-substituted pyrimidines and 5-substituted deoxynucleosides including: thymine and thymidine, uracil and thymidine, 5-halogen substituted uracils and thymidine and deoxyuridine, and xanthine and thymidine or deoxyuridine. Adenine, hypoxanthine, and cytosine were not utilized. The ratio of transferase: deoxynucleoside phosphorylase activity remained approximately constant during purification. The pH activity of the phosphorylase exhibited quite a sharp optimum with deoxyuridine and thymidine as substrates (pH 6.2–6.3), while transferase activity was not greatly different between pH 6.0 and 7.5. Thymine and uracil inhibited the phosphorylase (deoxyuridine substrate), inhibition, which was not competitive, being much more marked with thymine. Gel electrophoresis indicated that the preparation contained at least four protein bands, only one of which contained both deoxyuridine and thymidine phosphorylase activity.

Nucleoside phosphorylase enzymes have also been found in the male gonads (milts) of salmon (see Section VII, H below). The whole subject has been briefly reviewed (Tarr, 1967).

## H. Enzymes Involved in Deoxyribonucleic Acid (DNA) Formation

### 1. *Incorporation of Purines, Pyrimidines, and of Thymidine into Injected Immature Salmon Testis*

The enzymic mechanisms involved in biosynthesis of biologically important purines and pyrimidines, the corresponding nucleotides, and of DNA from the four deoxynucleoside triphosphates have been studied extensively during recent years (Kornberg, 1962; Smellie, 1962; Buchanan, 1960; Crosbie, 1960). However, no effort has been made to study biosynthesis of DNA in fish until very recently. Since the male gonads (testes) are the site of formation of large amounts of DNA, initial work has been concerned with these organs.

The incorporation of radioactive purines, pyrimidines, and related compounds into the DNA of salmon testes was first investigated (Tarr, 1964a). When adenine-8-$^{14}$C was injected into milts of an immature sockeye salmon which was then held 2 days before it was killed, the DNA became radioactive. When the DNA was hydrolyzed and the four constituent bases separated by paper chromatography, only adenine was radioactive. Thymine-2-$^{14}$C was not incorporated under these conditions. However, it was found in other experiments that this compound is rapidly degraded in live fish. Guanine-8-$^{14}$C was not incorporated, but the fish used was sexually mature.

In other experiments excised milts were injected with a number of different radioactive compounds and held for 2 or 4 days at 0°C or several hours at 30°C. Adenine-8-$^{14}$C, cytosine-2-$^{14}$C, guanine-8-$^{14}$C, and thymidine-methyl-$^{3}$H were all incorporated into the DNA. When the DNA was hydrolyzed and the individual purine and pyrimidine bases were separated by chromatography, it was found that radioactivity of constant specific activity occurred only in the base which had originally been injected. In several experiments injection of adenosine monophosphate, adenosine triphosphate, ribose-5-phosphate, ribose-1-phosphate, orotic acid, cytidine, and deoxyuridine did not occasion radioactivity in the DNA. These results indicated that enzymic mechanisms for incorporation of purine and pyrimidine bases into the DNA occur in salmon milts. In this work the gonads were probably too mature, in most cases, and subsequent work showed that by use of very immature gonads much better incorporation of radioactivity results.

Tarr and Roy (1966b) used slices of very immature testes of salmon and found that they incorporated radioactive purines, pyrimidines, and related compounds into DNA.

Good incorporation of tritiated thymine deoxyriboside occurred when this substrate was held 16–48 hours at 5°C with testes slices, and in most experiments a standard incubation of 24 hours at 5°C was used. Incorporation of radioactivity was largely prevented by exposing the tissue to vacuum or by KF treatment. In experiments using a large number of radioactive substrates the following results were obtained. Purine and pyrimidine bases, nucleosides, and nucleotides (and the corresponding deoxy compounds), were incorporated into DNA. It was found that the purine and pyrimidine bases of the extracted DNA were labeled in a manner which suggested that they were incorporated by recognized biosynthetic pathways utilizing preformed purines and pyrimidines or their derivatives. Under the experimental conditions carbonate-$^{14}$C, glycine-$^{14}$C, and formate-$^{14}$C were not incorporated into the purines of DNA, formate only causing labeling of thymine (presumably of the methyl group). It would appear unlikely that *de novo* biosynthesis of purine and pyrimidine rings occurs in fish testes. Labeling of the 2-deoxyribose of DNA occurred when the testes slices were incubated with radioactive C-1, C-6, or GL-glucose, myoadenylic acid, deoxyuridylic acid, ribose-5-phosphate or 5-phospho-$\alpha$-D-ribofuranosyl-1-phyrophosphate.

## 2. *Nucleotide Formation by Salmon Testis Pyrophosphorylases*

The role of 5-phosphoryl-$\alpha$-D-ribofuranose-1-pyrophosphate (PRPP) in the formation of inosinic acid by the *de novo* pathway and in the formation of ribomononucleotides from purine or pyrimidine bases is well established (Buchanan, 1960). Enzymic mechanisms that are able to utilize PRPP to form nucleotides have been demonstrated in immature salmon milts (Tarr, 1964b).

Soluble extracts were prepared from immature sockeye salmon milts by blending them in 0.66 $M$ lithium chloride solution to effect plasmolysis, followed by dilution to 0.1 $M$ concentration, and centrifuging to remove precipitated nucleoprotamine. Two micromoles of tritiated PRPP (460 $\times$ 10$^3$ cpm) were incubated 4 hours at 35°C with 2 $\mu$moles of $^{14}$C-labeled purine, pyrimidine, or orotic acid (0.44 to 2.6 $\times$ 10$^6$ cpm in different experiments), 20 $\mu$moles of MgCl$_2$, 200 $\mu$moles of tris buffer, pH 8.0, and 4.3

ml of the milt extract. The hypoxanthine used was not radioactive. The protein was removed by addition of trichloracetic acid and centrifugation. Carrier mononucleotide (20 μmoles) corresponding to the expected compound was added and the mononucleotides were then isolated as follows.

The nucleotides were precipitated as barium salts in the presence of ethanol. The crude barium salts were decomposed with Dowex 50-H$^+$ resin and the nucleotides were separated by chromatography on DEAE (carbonate form) using a gradient of ammonium bicarbonate as eluant. The pooled fractions containing the mononucleotides were evaporated several times *in vacuo* to remove ammonium bicarbonate and the residue dissolved in water. Portions of each solution were subjected to repeated paper chromatography in different solvent systems to ensure that the mononucleotides attained constant radioactivity. The results showed that $^{14}$C-labeled uridylic acid, cytidylic acid, thymidylic acid, adenylic acid, and guanylic acid were formed from the corresponding purine or pyrimidine bases. Orotic acid-2-$^{14}$C yielded $^{14}$C-labeled uridylic acid. Inosinic acid was not labeled since nonradioactive hypoxanthine had been used. However, this compound was radioactive in windowless gas flow counting due to presence of tritiated deoxyribose (see below).

The three radioactive purine mononucleotides were hydrolyzed 3 hours at 100°C in 1 $N$ HCl, and the ribose and free purine bases were isolated by paper chromatography. In all instances, the ribose was radioactive by windowless gas flow counting, but not by micromil window gas flow counting, showing that the ribose moiety was tritiated and therefore arose from the tritiated PRPP used. With the exception of hypoxanthine, which was not labeled initially, all the purine bases recovered were radioactive. The radioactivity was approximately constant on repeated paper chromatography. The results show that the system:

$$\text{PRPP} + \text{purine (pyrimidine)} \rightleftharpoons \text{ribomononucleotide} + \text{pyrophosphate}$$

is present in salmon milts, and that the pyrophosphorylase(s) involved has quite wide specificity.

### 3. *Nucleoside, Deoxynucleoside, and Mononucleotide Formation by Salmon Testes Enzymes*

In subsequent work (Tarr, 1964c) the formation of purine and pyrimidine nucleosides, deoxynucleosides, and of the corresponding mononucleotides by enzymes in a cell-free lithium chloride extract of immature rainbow trout testes was investigated. In these experiments the extract was adjusted to be 0.2 $M$ with respect of lithium chloride.

In one series of experiments 5 μmoles of tritiated ribose 1-phosphate

(14.5 $\times$ 10³ cpm) was incubated with ¹⁴C-labeled purine or pyrimidine
base (0.9 to 1.8 $\times$ 10⁶ cpm) plus 5 $\mu$moles of the corresponding nonradioactive base in 2 ml of milt extract at pH 7.2 for 2 hours at 35°C. The solutions were deproteinized by heating and 10 $\mu$moles of the corresponding
ribonucleoside was added as carrier. The products were chromatographed
repeatedly using different paper chromatographic solvent systems. The
results showed that ribosides of adenine, hypoxanthine, guanine, cytosine,
and uracil were all formed by the extract. Hydrolysis of the guanosine
and inosine and chromatographic separation yielded free ribose. The
ribose was radioactive (tritiated) as indicated by windowless counting,
and was free from ¹⁴C. The specific activities of the guanine and hypoxanthine were comparable to that of the parent nucleosides.

In a second experiment 10 $\mu$Ci of tritiated, or 0.5 $\mu$Ci of ¹⁴C-labeled
nucleosides or deoxynucleoside (1.6 to 910 m$\mu$moles in different experiments) were incubated under conditions rather similar to those of the
foregoing experiment with 1.4 ml of milt enzyme and 0.2 $\mu$moles of ATP.
After 3 hours at 35°C the solutions were deproteinized, 10 $\mu$moles of the
corresponding mononucleotide or deoxymononucleotide was added, and
the compounds were separated and their radioactive purity was determined
by repeated paper chromatography. The results showed that adenosine,
uridine, guanosine, cytidine, thymidine, and deoxyuridine all yielded the
corresponding nucleotide.

In other experiments ¹⁴C-labeled purines or pyrimidines, together with
5 $\mu$moles of the corresponding nonradioactive compounds, were incubated
as in the proceeding experiments with 4 ml of enzyme, 5 $\mu$moles of ribose-
1-phosphate or of tritiated deoxyribose-1-phosphate and 1 $\mu$mole of
adenosine triphosphate. The corresponding nucleosides, deoxynucleosides,
or mononucleotides were added after deproteinizing the solutions prior
to separating the compounds by repeated paper chromatography in different solvent systems. The results showed that inosine and inosinic acid
were formed from adenine (deamination of the adenine or derivative occurs), guanosine and guanylic acid from guanine, uridine and uridylic
acid from both uridine and orotic acid, thymine riboside and thymine
ribotide from thymine, and a small amount of cytidine and cytidylic acid
from cytosine in presence of ribose-1-phosphate and ATP. The corresponding deoxynucleosides and deoxynucleotides were formed from the bases
and deoxyribose-1-phosphate. Tritiated deoxyribose was isolated from
deoxyguanosine and deoxyadenosine, thus proving that the deoxyribose
in these compounds had come from the tritiated deoxyribose-1-phosphate
used.

Small-scale preparative experiments showed that thymidine (thymine deoxyriboside) resulted from the action of the milt enzyme nucleoside phosphorylase when thymine and deoxyribose-1-phosphate were present, and that thymine riboside was the product when ribose-1-phosphate was used.

These results when considered together show that immature salmon milts contain enzymes capable of forming a wide variety of purine and pyrimidine nucleosides, deoxynucleotides, and the corresponding mononucleotides. It is not known whether these systems, or the pyrophosphorylase system described previously, are singly or together responsible for nucleotide formation in milts.

### 4. Formation of Nucleoside Di- and Triphosphates from Nucleoside Monophosphates by Salmon Testes Enzymes

The nucleoside monophosphokinases and nucleoside diphosphokinases are a large and diversified group of enzymes whose function it is to transfer phosphoryl groups. The reactions involved are, respectively

$$\textit{Nucleoside} \text{ triphosphate } + \text{ nucleoside monophosphate} \tag{1}$$
$$\rightleftarrows \textit{nucleoside} \text{ diphosphate } + \text{ nucleoside diphosphate}$$

$$\text{Nucleoside triphosphate } + \textit{nucleoside} \text{ diphosphate} \tag{2}$$
$$\rightleftarrows \textit{nucleoside} \text{ triphosphate } + \text{ nucleoside diphosphate}$$

Certain of the enzymes are quite specific, thus myokinase transforms two molecules of adenosine diphosphate to one molecule each of adenosine mono- and triphosphates. Others are not at all specific and may carry out phosphoryl group transfers among a diverse group of nucleoside and deoxynucleoside phosphates.

Tarr and Roy (1966a) prepared an 0.2 $M$ lithium chloride extract of recently frozen immature sockeye salmon or trout milts as in previously reported work. This preparation possessed diverse phosphokinase activities. These extracts were carefully adjusted at 0°–3°C with 1 $M$ acetic acid to pH 4.6–4.8, centrifuged briefly to remove precipitated protein, and the clear supernates were adjusted to about pH 7.0 with 1 $N$ KOH. These preparations were very unstable (see below), and were used within a short time of preparation. They were practically free from adenine nucleotides. Further attempts at purification by treatment with alumina $C_\gamma$ or ammonium sulfate fractionation failed. The single purification step only caused about a twofold increase in specific activity but largely eliminated undesirable nucleoside triphosphatase activities. The specific activity of one purified preparation was 8.5 $\mu$moles of cytidine triphosphate formed from cytidine monophosphate by 1 mg of enzyme protein in 1 hour at 25°C. The enzyme lost 65% of its activity in 1 hour at 30°C and 85% in 2 days at 0°C.

The preparation was capable, under appropriate conditions, of forming nucleoside (or deoxynucleoside) di- and triphosphates from nucleoside (or deoxynucleoside) monophosphates. The reaction did not proceed in absence of ATP or other nucleoside triphosphate such as GTP, UTP, CTP, TTP, and ITP. The enzyme was most active at pH 7.4–8.0. The activity of the preparation was greatly enhanced by divalent cations, particularly by $Mg^{2+}$ and $Ca^{2+}$, and less by $Mn^{2+}$, $Co^{2+}$ and $Ni^{2+}$; $Hg^{2+}$, $Cu^{2+}$, $Ag^{2+}$, $Zn^{2+}$, iodoacetate, fluoride, EDTA, and $p$-hydroxymercuribenzoate were strongly inhibitory, and KCN was stimulatory. Glutathione and 2-mercaptoethanol were occasionally very slightly inhibitory but normally were without effect. The optimum pH range was 7.5–8.0. The most effectively utilized substrates were CMP, AMP, UMP, and dAMP. GMP and dCMP were not utilized as effectively, and IMP and TMP were poor substrates. When CDP, UDP, or ADP were employed as substrates in absence of ATP or other nucleoside triphosphate an equilibrium mixture of the corresponding mono-, di-, and triphosphate resulted, in which roughly one-half of the activity remained in the diphosphates. It was concluded that milts possess a very diverse monophosphokinase activity, but that the presence of a nucleoside diphosphokinase could not be excluded.

## 5. Nucleotides and Related Enzymes in Fish Livers

Tsuyuki et al. (1958) characterized the sugars, nucleotides, and related compounds of spring salmon (Oncorhynchus tshawytscha) liver. They identified the galactose, glucuronic acid, and N-acetylglucosamine derivatives of uridine diphosphate and suggested that the first two compounds might be implicated in enzymic conversion of inositol to glucuronic acid and in other coenzymic activities. Uridine diphosphate glucose did not appear in their ion-exchange chromatographic column eluates, and since fish livers have a rather high inositol content, it was thought that inositol might be a precursor of glucuronic acid in fish. Forrest and Hansen (1959) studied the acid-soluble nucleotides of livers of four different species of fish. They isolated and identified uridine diphosphate glucose, uridine diphosphate galactose, and uridine diphosphate acetylglucosamine, the glucose derivative being the major component. Using a procedure originally employed for calf liver they prepared uridine diphosphate glucose dehydrogenase and uridine diphosphate galactose-4'-epimerase from an acetone powder of salmon liver. Though these enzymes were not purified extensively they were separated and their ability to carry out the following reactions was verified.

Uridine diphosphate galactose $\rightleftarrows$ uridine diphosphate glucose
$$\uparrow$$
epimerase enzyme

Uridine diphosphate glucose $+ 2$ DPN$^+ \rightarrow$ uridine diphosphate glucuronic acid $+$
$$\uparrow \qquad\qquad\qquad 2\,\text{DPN} + 2\,\text{H}^+$$
dehydrogenase<br>enzyme

The finding that the ratio of uridine diphosphate glucose:uridine diphosphate galactose was 75:25 indicated that the epimerase enzyme is active in fish livers.

### 6. *Nicotinamide Hydrolase (NADase) (Transglycosidase)*

These enzymes cleave nicotinamide adenine dinucleotide (NAD) and nicotinamide adenine dinucleotide phosphate (NADP) at the N-ribosyl linkage:

OH: H
:

Adenine-ribose-P-O-P-ribose: nicotinamide

Adenosinediphosphate ribose + nicotinamide.

In the presence of isonicotinyl hydrazide (INH) a transfer reaction is catalyzed in which the INH replaces nicotinamide:

Adenine-ribose-P-O-P-ribose-nicotinamide + isonicotinylhydrazide
$\rightleftarrows$ Adenine-ribose-P-O-P-ribose-isonicotinylhydrazide + nicotinamide

It has been demonstrated that carp liver mitochondria possess a very active NADase (Raczynska-Bojanowska and Gasiorowska, 1963). The liver was fractionated so that mitochondria and microsome fractions were obtained, and these were disrupted in an homogenizer. Most of the NADase activity was in the mitochondria. About 9% was in the microsomes and supernate and 0.5% in the nuclei. The activity of NADase in carp liver mitochondria was about 100 times as high as that in rat liver mitochondria. By use of different analytical methods it was demonstrated that the activity in carp mitochondria was hydrolytic (glycohydrolase), while with rat mitochondria pyrophosphorylytic activity was also present. The activity of carp NADase preparations was about six times as high toward NAD as toward NADP. Thus, the Michaelis constants for these substrates were $2.2 \times 10^{-4}$ and $1.1 \times 10^{-3}$, respectively. As with NADase preparations from other sources nicotinamide was strongly inhibitory; 50% inhibition being occasioned by $5.5 \times 10^{-3}$ $M$ concentrations. The enzyme was not inhibited by $1 \times 10^{-2}$ $M$ INH, indicating that the carp enzyme might possess transglycosidase activity as indicated above. However, tests showed that the carp enzyme does not possess such activity.

Jones and Murray (1966) studied a soluble NADase prepared from muscle of Atlantic cod. It was somewhat purified using Sephadex G75 columns, and two poorly separated "peaks" of activity were obtained. The enzyme proved unstable to dialysis and was largely destroyed by freeze-drying. They noted that this enzyme appeared to differ from mammalian NADase in its ready solubility and in that it was not inhibited by nicotinamide. They reported that NAD *plus* NADH fell during exercise of the fish, and that after death there appeared to be a transient increase in the concentration followed by a decrease.

## VIII. Enzymes Concerned with Protein, Peptide, and Amino Acid Metabolism

### A. Enzymic Synthesis of Proteins

It has long been known that protamines occur late in maturation of Rhine salmon (*Salmo salar*) and more recently it has been reported that histones are replaced by protamines at the spermatid stage in developing salmon testes. Ingles *et al.* (1966) found, in testes of rapidly maturing rainbow trout at 27 days, one marked histone band by gel electrophoresis. After 52 days there were two histone bands and a faster moving protamine band. Biosynthesis of protamine was studied using light homogenates of cells from rapidly developing salmon testes in Hank's medium at 20°C in presence of arginine-$^3$H. The radioactivity of isolated protamine was used to detect arginine incorporation. Arginine incorporation increased over a 4-hour period; it was inhibited by puromycin but not by actinomysin D ($5 \times 10^{-5}$ $M$). Fifty percent inhibition was caused by only $1.4 \times 10^{-7}$ $M$ cycloheximide and by $1.9 \times 10^{-5}$ $M$ puromycin. Chloramphenicol was inhibitory in much higher concentrations. All these compounds are inhibitors of protein synthesis and their effect in the above system suggests involvement of mRNA, sRNA, and the ribosome system in protamine biosyntheses. The failure of actinomycin D to inhibit was linked with the possibility that the mRNA for protamine has a relatively long half-life; the site of action of this inhibitor is on the transcription of the DNA sequence into RNA.

### B. Proteolytic Enzymes

Considerable attention has been given to enzymes concerned in protein degradation in fish tissues postmortem, largely because of the technological importance of the subject. A useful review of this field has been published recently (Jones, 1962). In general there appears to be very slow proteolysis at the normal pH of fish muscle, and much more rapid proteolysis when the pH is adjusted to about 4.0. Though it is probable that the enzymes concerned are indigenous to the muscle, it is possible that in some cases diffusion of visceral enzymes into the muscle may be a factor. A few of the more recent contributions in this general field will be mentioned.

Siebert and Bottke (1963) rinsed the peritoneal cavities of freshly killed carp or trout with physiological saline and demonstrated that extracts thus obtained contained amylase, ribonuclease, catheptic protease (pH 4.5), neutral protease (tryptic enzymes; pH 7.5), acid protease (pepsin; pH 1.8), and certain glycolytic enzymes. They suggested that the enzymes diffuse into the visceral cavity from the various organs in the living fish.

Siebert (1958) found that the cathepsin activity (measured at pH 4.0) of sea fish kidney was exceptionally high and exceeded that of liver. Muscle had comparatively weak activity. The catheptic activities of the same organs obtained from several different mammals was much lower. Fish muscles were also shown to possess a glycylglycine dipeptidase. Neutral protease activity and decarboxylase activity for glutamic and aspartic acids were not found.

Intracellular autolytic proteases of animal tissues have been collectively called cathepsins, and kidney and spleen are normally rich sources of such enzymes. They have been generally classified according to their specificities: thus, cathepsin A is homospecific (has the same general specificity requirements) with pepsin, cathepsin B with trypsin, and cathepsin C with chymotrypsin. Cathepsin B and C have been studied in greatest detail and the latter is capable of carrying out transpeptidation reactions (replacement of the amine component of a CO—NH bond by another amine as in an amino acid).

Siebert *et al.* (1963) purified and studied the specificity of a new type of cathepsin from cod spleen. A clarified aqueous extract of cod spleen tissue was fractionated with ammonium sulfate (0.5–0.8 saturated) at pH 7.0. This fraction was dialyzed against 1% NaCl for 2.5 hours and was then fractionated with acetone at $-5°C$, the protein precipitating between 30 and 65% concentration being collected. This fraction was dissolved in 1% NaCl, refractionated at $-5°C$ between 45 and 58% acetone, the precipitate dissolved in 0.05 $M$ tris, pH 7.5, and clarified by centrifuging. This fraction was purified by DEAE chromatography, refractionated with acetone (45–58%), and then chromatographed a second time on DEAE. The enzyme was very unstable at pH values below 6.5, and was labile at high temperatures. It lost 50% of its activity in 1 week at 2°C in water solution. It was resistant to freeze-drying. The pH optimum was 5.0, and there was little activity below pH 4 and above pH 6.8. The enzyme was entirely inhibited by by $1 \times 10^{-3}$ $M$ $Hg^{2+}$ and $Cu^{2+}$, but not by $Co^{2+}$, $Zn^{2+}$, $Fe^{2+}$, $Mn^{2+}$, or $Mg^{2+}$. It was partially inhibited by $1 \times 10^{-3}$ $M$ $p$-chlormercuribenzoate. The enzyme was homogeneous in the ultracentrifuge. It had a sedimentation constant of $3.31 \times 10^{-13}$, a diffusion constant of $5.6 \times 10^{-7}$ and a molecular weight of $58,300 \pm 3\%$. The specificity of the enzyme was studied in detail. It was found to differ from cathepsin D, trypsin, pepsin, and chymotrypsin in its mode of action on the B chain of insulin. It behaved like an endopeptidase.

A proteolytic enzyme with the general properties of a cathepsin was prepared from albacore tuna (*Germo alalunga*) muscle by Groninger (1964). Tuna muscle was blended with two parts of water, and the crude suspension adjusted to pH 3.5 with 0.5 $N$ HCl and promptly returned to the original pH with 0.5 $N$ NaOH. Insoluble protein was removed by centrifugation at 800 $g$; the supernate was adjusted to pH 3.5 and the protein fraction that separated between 0.3 and 0.6 saturation with ammonium sulfate was dialyzed against several changes of 0.025 $M$ NaCl. This fraction was further purified by chromatography on DEAE-cellulose columns equilibrated with 0.025 $M$ NaCl, the protein fraction that was eluted in 0.05 $M$ NaCl in 0.01 $M$ phosphate buffer, pH 8.3, possessing most of the proteolytic enzyme activity. This fraction contained at least three protein components as judged by starch gel electrophoresis. Purification was about 260-fold and recovery only 2.3%. Dark muscle had an activity about three times that of white muscle. The optimum pH was about 2.5 with little activity at pH values below 1.5 and above 4.0. The purified enzyme was fairly heat sensitive, losing one third of its activity in 10 minutes at 55°C. Adrenalin, $Fe^{2+}$, $Co^{2+}$, EDTA, diisopropyl fluorophosphate, and soybean trypsin inhibitor were without effect in the concentrations used. $p$-Chloromercuribenzoate, iodoacetamide, and $N$-ethyl maleimide were inhibitory.

The enzyme was somewhat similar to the cod spleen cathepsin described by Siebert *et al.* (1963). However, it did differ in certain respects from this enzyme and from mammalian cathepsins C, D, and E. While the partially purified enzyme hydrolyzed tuna muscle extract, the purified fraction had lost this ability. So far this discrepancy has not been explained. Hemoglobin was used as substrate in the investigations since synthetic peptides were not hydrolyzed and casein was hydrolyzed by the purified but not by the partially purified enzyme.

More recently Siebert *et al.* (1965a) obtained a highly purified cod muscle cathepsin. The purification procedure involved holding a 1% KCl extract of frozen cod muscle at pH 4.6 for 10 minutes at 35°C; ammonium sulfate fractionation of the supernate (0.3–0.65 saturated fraction retained);

dissolving the fraction in water, holding it 10 minutes at 35°C (pH 4.1); cold acetone fractionation of the supernate (protein precipitating between 45 and 70% acetone retained); gel filtration (Sephadex G200) of an 0.1 $M$ phosphate buffer solution of the acetone precipitate (pH 6.0); adsorption on hydroxylapatite and elution, and column chromatography on carboxymethyl cellulose. The purification was 3000-fold with a 3% yield of enzyme, and the specific activity (micro moles tyrosine split from hemoglobin per hour per milligram enzyme protein) was 95.

The molecular weight of the cathepsin was 50,000, the pH optimum 4.6, and it contained two catalytically inactive SH groups per mole. Evidence was obtained indicating that histidine, but not serine, is involved in enzyme catalysis. The enzyme hydrolyzed several different proteins with an endopeptidase-like activity to yield peptides (average 4.5 amino acid residues) and free amino acids. The authors concluded that the strong catheptic activity of the muscle may in some way be connected with the breakdown of muscle proteins and use of the products for synthesis of reproductive organs (gonads). In support of this hypothesis they refer to the earlier results of their own laboratory in which it was shown that the catheptic activity of fish muscle was five to ten times that of mammalian muscle, and that this relationship also held for dipeptidases and transaminases. So far the apparent discrepancy between the pH optimum of this enzyme and its comparatively low activity at physiological pH values has not been explained.

## C. Anserinase

An enzyme capable of hydrolyzing the dipeptide anserine into its constituent amino acids was described by Jones (1955). An aqueous suspension of minced cod muscle was held 4 hours at 0°C, filtered, and the filtrate clarified by centrifugation. The extract was concentrated to somewhat less than 10% of its initial volume, dialyzed in presence of chloroform and toluene, the protein precipitate that formed was removed by centrifugation, and the supernate freeze-dried. This preparation hydrolyzed anserine to its constituent amino acids, $\beta$-alanine and 1-methyl histidine. The optimum pH for hydrolysis was 7.3. Zinc stimulated hydrolysis markedly, the optimum concentration being $1 \times 10^{-3.7}$ $M$. Above $1 \times 10^{-3}$ $M$, zinc became inhibitory. The hydrolysis was inhibited strongly by $Fe^{3+}$, $Ag^{2+}$, and $Pb^{2+}$, and weakly by $Mn^{2+}$ and $Co^{2+}$. The Michaelis constant was $3.8 \times 10^{-4}$ $M$. Anserinase was absent from rat muscle, and from that of certain other fish (Jones, 1956).

It was subsequently found that aqueous extracts of cod muscle contained a second zinc-activated dipeptidase with a pH optimum in the acid range (pH 3–4). This dipeptidase hydrolyzed anserine comparatively slowly, and also hydrolyzed glycylleucine, leucyltyrosine, alanylglycine, leucylglycine, and carnosine. If the cod muscle protein extracts were exposed to isoelectric precipitation or differential heating the pH 3–4 dipeptidase activity was removed as denatured protein, and the pH 7–8 dipeptidase activity remained in solution. These preparations hydrolyzed both anserine and other dipeptides actively indicating a broad specificity of the enzyme (Jones, 1956).

## D. Amino Acid Transaminases, Decarboxylases, Deaminases, and Dehydrogenases

Simidu *et al.* (1953) studied the enzymic decarboxylation of L-histidine. Muscle of mackerel or yellow-tail was ground with phosphate buffer, pH 7.4, and sea sand and centrifuged to yield a crude preparation. This was somewhat purified by use of alumina $C_\gamma$ gel.

Enzyme prepared from fresh muscle had an optimum pH of 7.5 and a temperature optimum of 45°C. The enzyme was also found in stomach, intestine, spleen, pyloric caeca, kidney, and liver. The authors concluded that histamine arising from this decarboxylation could be formed enzymically by histidine decarboxylase.

Siebert *et al.* (1965b) homogenized cod muscle in 0.1 $M$ phosphate buffer, pH 7.5 (50 gm per 100 ml), and centrifuged the homogenate 15 minutes at 1500 $g$. The supernate was homogenized with a second 50 gm of muscle and the mixture centrifuged as before. Where "soluble enzymes" were studied the homogenate was centrifuged 20 minutes at 20,000 $g$.

The homogenates carried out a very large number of different transaminase reactions between keto acids ($\alpha$-ketoglutarate, pyruvate, $p$-hydroxyphenylpyruvate, phenylpyruvate, $\alpha$-ketoisovalerate, $\alpha$-ketoisocaproate, oxalacetate) and various amino acids to yield an amino acid corresponding to the keto acid used. Thus $\alpha$-ketoglutarate reacted with eleven different amino acids to yield L-glutamic acid and, presumably the corresponding keto acid. In this system seven other amino acids were inactive.

They also studied the amino acid decarboxylase properties of the homogenate. They found that the extract was practically devoid of such enzymes. An exception was found in the case of L-aspartate which was slowly decarboxylated to yield $\alpha$-alanine. It was found that, of several compounds tested, only $\alpha$-ketoglutarate stimulated this decarboxylation of aspartate. This effect was demonstrated to be due to a sequence of reactions in which aspartate yielded oxalacetate in a transamination reaction with $\alpha$-ketoglutarate and this in turn was decarboxylated to pyruvic acid. Pyruvic acid in a second transaminase reaction yielded $\alpha$-alanine. The marked evolution of $CO_2$ with attendant formation of $\alpha$-alanine was thus explained.

A glutamic dehydrogenase, active in presence of either DPNH or TPNH, was present in the muscle extract. Both glutaminase I (phosphate activated) and glutaminase II (pyruvate requirement) were demonstrated. Neither D-amino acid oxidase nor monoamine oxidase were detected.

Arginase, the enzyme that hydrolyzes arginine to urea and ornithine, is largely concentrated in the deep-seated red muscle of tuna species, there being only a small amount in the superficial red muscle and none in the white muscle (Matsuura *et al.*, 1953). The enzyme was not found in the skeletal muscle of skates and one species of ray, but was present in both ordinary white skeletal and red lateral muscle of the lesser spotted dogfish (Connell, 1955). It would appear that in the rays and skates extrahepatic regulation of urea does not occur in the muscle.

Crystalline dogfish liver glutamate dehydrogenase was prepared from an acetone powder of the tissue in order to eliminate lipid before subsequent fractionation (Corman *et al.*, 1967). This procedure also gave a 15% higher yield of enzyme of twice the specific activity of that prepared from liver homogenates. Further purification was obtained by fractionation of acetone powder extracts with sodium sulfate and ammonium sulfate followed by DEAE-cellulose chromatography. The active eluate was treated with excess ammonium sulfate and the precipitate was dissolved in 0.1 $M$ phosphate buffer, pH 8.0 (protein concentration 18–20 mg per milliliter). Ammonium sulfate was added until slight turbidity occurred (about 0.25 saturation at 0°C), and crystallization occurred in 5–7 days at this temperature.

The dogfish enzyme was compared with mammalian and avian enzymes. The rates of cathodic migration in starch gel electrophoresis were dogfish > beef > chicken, and there were marked differences in abilities of the three dehydrogenases to utilize DPN, TPN, and certain substituted pyridine nucleotides. The dogfish enzyme in certain respects (stability during dialysis and in buffer at room temperature) appeared to be more stable than the other enzymes. The $K_m$ values differed, but the $V_{max}$ was of the same order under identical conditions (70 $\mu$moles of DPNH utilized per milligram of protein per minute).

## IX. Miscellaneous Enzymes

### A. ACETYLCHOLINESTERASE

Several investigators recognized that fish muscles possess cholinesterase activity, and that this appeared to be associated with ATPase activity

(Bezňak, 1944; Varga *et al.*, 1954: Siou, 1955) (see also Section VII, C above). Kövér *et al.* (1964) made a fairly detailed study of the acetyl- cholinesterase of the muscle of *Ameiurus nebulosus.*

White muscle was extracted in the cold with 0.2 $M$ $MgCl_2$ in 0.01 $M$ tris-maleate buffer, pH 7.0, and the clear supernate was then fractionated as follows. The solution was diluted with 11 volumes of cold water (ionic strength 0.04, pH 6.8). The precipitated protein was dissolved in a solution, the ionic strength of which was 0.6, using a solution of $MgCl_2$ in tris-maleate buffer, pH 7.0. The ionic strength of the rather viscous solution was adjusted to 0.23 with water (pH 6.8) and the protein precipitate was removed by centrifugation. The acetylcholinesterase activity remained in the clear supernate. Further purification was attained by precipitating the active enzyme protein by adjusting the ionic strength of the solution to 0.05, dissolving the precipitate in KCl ($0.6\mu$) (1% protein concentration), and removing denatured protein by centrifugation. The clear supernate obtained after adjusting the clear solution to pH 4.3 with acetic acid possessed strong acetylcholinesterase activity which was about thirty times that of the original muscle. The yield was about 10%. The specific activity was 75 mg acetylcholine hydrolyzed per hour per milligram of protein nitrogen at 37.5°C.

The purified preparation was homogeneous in the ultracentrifuge and had a sedimentation coefficient of 2.83 S. It was also homogeneous by moving boundary electrophoresis. The diffusion constant was $6 \times 10^{-7}$ cm$^2$ sec$^{-1}$, and the molecular weight 43,000.

## B. Enzymes Involving Folic Acid Metabolism

Whiteley (1960) investigated the distribution of enzymes involving tetrahydrofolic acid in animal tissues including those of several species of Pacific Ocean fish. Tetrahydrofolic acid ($FH_4$), a reduced form of folic acid, is an important coenzyme of cell metabolism for it serves as a carrier of carbon atom groups of the oxidation level of formate or formaldehyde which may be located at the N-5 or N-10 positions, or bridged between them. Certain of these derivatives are concerned with the biosynthesis of purines, pyrimidines, and amino acids. Enzymes mediating five important key reactions were studied, namely: (1) formate-activating enzyme (tetra- hydrofolate formylase); (2) deacylase; (3) cyclohydrase; (4) hydroxy- methyltetrahydrofolate dehydrogenase; (5) serine hydroxymethylase, and (6) reactions 4 and 5 measure as a "coupled reaction."

Enzyme (1) was present in quite variable amounts in all tissues of dog- fish (*Squalus suckleii*), rock sole (*Lepidopsetta bilineata*), sockeye salmon (*Onorhynchus nerka*), and a rockfish (*Sebastodes caurinus*). With a few exceptions the other enzyme systems all occurred in rockfish and sockeye salmon tissues. The specific activities of the various enzymes in the fish tissues were variable, and, in general, not vastly different from those of rabbit and chicken. Thus fish tissues, in common with those of mammals, contain the well-known enzymes involving folic acid derivatives.

## C. Alcohol Dehydrogenase

Alcohol dehydrogenase, found in yeast and in mammalian liver, was isolated from fish liver (Boeri *et al.*, 1954). The general reaction is:

$$\text{Alcohol} + \text{DPN}^+ \rightleftarrows \text{corresponding aldehyde} + \text{DPNH} + \text{H}^+$$

The enzyme was purified about five-fold from livers of eight widely different species of fish. The turnover numbers were much lower than that of yeast or horse liver alcohol dehydrogenase. In order of decreasing activity DPN$^+$, deamino-DPN$^+$, and TPN$^+$ acted as coenzymes. When tested in 0.1 $M$ pyrophosphate buffer, pH 9.0, at 20°C, the $K_m$ values (Michaelis constants) with different alcohols as substrates were: methanol, $1.4 \times 10^{-4}$ $M$; ethanol, $4.6 \times 10^{-4} M$; propanol, $2 \times 10^{-4} M$; butanol, $1.1 \times 10^{-4} M$; and isoamyl alcohol, $9 \times 10^{-5} M$. Thus the higher alcohols were better substrates than ethanol at low concentrations. The optimum pH was 9.0 and the enzyme was inhibited by the following SH reagents in the order given: $p$-hydroxymercuribenzoate > iodobenzoate > iodoacetate. GSH did not overcome inhibition by $p$-hydroxymercuribenzoate, but hydroxylamine inhibition was prevented by increasing ethanol concentrations.

## D. Enzymic Formation of and Decomposition of Oxalic Acid

The enzymic formation of oxalic acid and its decomposition in fish skeletal muscle were studied by Yamada and Suzuki (1952) and Yamada *et al.* (1959). An enzyme was prepared by extracting fish muscles with water, adsorbing the activity on calcium phosphate gel, and eluting it with pH 7.4 phosphate buffer. Oxalate was decarboxylated most actively at pH 4.0, especially by enzyme preparations made from fish muscles during the summer months. Muscle preparations from carp and seven species of marine fish were all active. Malonate was decarboxylated slightly by enzyme from two species, the maximum activity being at pH 5.0. The oxalate decarboxylase was destroyed at 60°C; the malonate enzyme at 80°C. The muscle extract formed oxalate from succinate and acetate, but not from tartrate, formate, oxalacetate or glyoxalate. Schmitt *et al.* (1966) obtained a clear extract from frozen Atlantic cod muscle by heating a 1% NaCl suspension at pH 5.1 for 10 minutes at 50°C and removing denatured protein by centrifugation. The solution was desalted by passage through Sephadex G25 gel and freeze-dried. The dry protein residue was taken up in 1% NaCl (20 mg of protein per milliliter), the fraction that precipitated between 0.3 and 0.5 saturation was dissolved in 0.05 $M$ phosphate buffer, pH 6.5, and insoluble protein was removed. Further purification by means of gel filtration on a Sephadex G100 column and column chromatography using carboxymethyl cellulose yielded an enzyme that was purified 95-fold with 34% yield.

The purification procedure removed malate dehydrogenase and the malic enzyme, but a trace of lactic dehydrogenase remained. The enzyme yielded equimolar quantities of $CO_2$ and pyruvate from oxalacetate. The molecular weight (gel filtration) was 130,000–150,000, the pH optimum 6.5–7.0, and the $K_m$ for oxalacetate $1 \times 10^{-3}$ $M$. The enzyme was strongly activated by manganese ($K_m = 3.6 \times 10^{-5}$ $M$) and magnesium ($K_m = 5 \times 10^{-4}$ $M$) ions. The SH agents $p$-chloromercuribenzoate and $Hg^{2+}$ caused 50% inhibition at $1 \times 10^{-4}$ and $5 \times 10^{-5}$ $M$ concentrations. The activation energy was 13.9 kcal/mole and the enzyme was strongly inhibited by oxalate.

## E. Inositol Metabolism

Tsuyuki and Idler (1961a, b) injected coho salmon with myo-inositol-2-[14]C. The specific activity of the inositol monophosphate, which they isolated from livers of injected fish, was very much higher than that of free glucuronic acid or of glucuronic acid from uridine diphosphate glucuronic acid. They discussed the possible significance of formation of this compound, and suggested that it might arise by direct phosphorylation of inositol as by a phosphokinase enzyme. It was suggested that glucuronic acid is among the first metabolites of inositol.

## F. Enzymes of Steroid Metabolism

Simpson *et al.* (1963) showed that 11-deoxycorticosterone (DOC) is present in high concentrations in the semen of spiny dogfish (*Squalus acanthias*), is largely (<85%) present in the nonfilterable portion of the seminal plasma, and may be bound to protein. Progesterone-4-[14]C, the key compound which undergoes transformation to corticosteroids, androgens, and estrogens, was incubated 24 hours at 20°C with dogfish semen (Simpson *et al.*, 1964a). About 60% of the recovered steroids had been converted to DOC. A minor constituent found was 3$\beta$-hydroxy-5$\alpha$-pregnan-20-one or its 3$\alpha$,5$\beta$-epimer. Unchanged progesterone was found, but no testosterone, 17$\alpha$-hydroxyprogesterone, androstenedione or corticosteroids. General evidence was obtained to support the fact that cholesterol is transformed by dogfish semen by a series of enzyme reactions, probably similar to those active in mammalian systems, to DOC via several intermediates including pregnenolone and progesterone. These results indicate that dogfish semen contains a 21-hydroxylase.

Simpson *et al.* (1964b) studied biosynthesis of steroids in sliced testis of dogfish, incubating preparations 20 hours at 20°C and checking them for bacteriological contamination. With progesterone-4-$^{14}$C as substrate DOC was obtained in large yield, and was accompanied by considerably smaller amounts of testosterone, Reichstein's substance S, 20$\beta$-hydroxypregnan-4-en-3-one, 20$\beta$, 21-dihydroxypregn-4-en-3-one, and 17$\alpha$, 20$\beta$, 21-trihydroxypregn-3-one. In other incubation experiments 3$\beta$-hydroxy-5$\beta$-pregn-20-one and 17$\alpha$,20$\beta$-dihydroxypregn-4-en-3-one were obtained. These results were taken to indicate clearly that the testis of dogfish contain a steroid 17$\alpha$-hydroxylase, a 21-hydroxylase, and a 20$\beta$-hydroxysteroid dehydrogenase.

## G. Biosynthesis of Trimethylamine Oxide (TMAO) and Its Enzymic Degradation

A useful review concerning the occurrence and significance of TMAO in marine animals was prepared fairly recently (Groninger, 1959).

It has long been known that fish and certain mammals are capable of converting TMA to TMAO. Baker and Chaykin (1962) prepared a microsome fraction from hog liver that oxidized TMA to TMAO in the presence of glucose-6-phosphate, its dehydrogenase and TPNH according to the following reaction:

$$(CH_3)_3N + O_2 + TPNH + H^+ \rightarrow (CH_3)_3NO + TPN + H_2$$

Later Baker *et al.* (1963) studied trimethylamine oxide biosynthesis by tissue homogenates with $^{14}$C-labeled TMA as substrate. The results indicated that this synthesis is restricted to vertebrates. Tissues of a large number of fishes (Elasmobranchii and Teleostei) were found to synthesize TMAO. However, the results were quite variable and in many instances no synthesis was obtained. The possibility that the assay conditions used were not optimum for some of the tissues studied was considered by the investigators.

Bilinski (1964) injected fish intraperitoneally with $^{14}$C-labeled trimethylamine, methylamine, betaine, $\gamma$-butyrobetaine, choline, DL-carnitine, L-methionine, glycine, sodium formate, sodium acetate, and bicarbonate. In a few experiments intravenous or intramuscular injections were made. The results showed that trimethylamine was the only really active precursor of TMAO. Very slight labeling of isolated TMAO occurred with betaine, γ-butyrobetaine, L-methionine, and traces with methylamine, carnitine, and sodium acetate. These results indicated that TMA is the probable precursor of TMAO in fish, but the enzyme system involved was not identified. Results were also obtained indicating that betaine is formed in fish by oxidation of choline. Ericson (1960) showed that fish possess a betaine-homocysteine-methyl transferase. Choline was a moderately effective TMAO precursor but this was possibly converted to TMA which was subsequently oxidized.

Amano and Yamada (1964) presented evidence that trimethylamine (TMA), dimethylamine (DMA), and formaldehyde were formed from added TMAO by blended pyloric caeca of cod in which bacterial action was presumably prevented by presence of toluene and chloroform, and suggested that enzymic mechanisms might be involved. No such activity was found in the muscle. Later the same authors, Yamada and Amano (1965a) found that a filtered aqueous extract of Alaska pollock pyloric caeca formed both formaldehyde and DMA from TMAO, the optimum pH for the reactions being about 6.1. Some activity was observed at pH 9.2 and at pH 5.4 and below pH 3.9 in case of DMA. Under the experimental conditions the enzyme system was most active at 26°C and was heat labile. Betaine and choline could not replace TMAO as substrate. Formaldehyde was not formed from DMA or TMA by the enzyme extract. Dialysis for 3 days eliminated the enzymic activity and the reaction was heat sensitive (Yamada and Amano, 1965b).

## X. Concluding Remarks

It has become evident through research that has been reviewed that fish muscle and organs do not differ radically from those of warm-blooded vertebrates in that they utilize certain of the well-known metabolic pathways for deriving energy from their metabolites. Only in a very limited number of cases have detailed comparisons between similar enzymes from fish and from warm-blooded vertebrates been made. The results, in some instances, have pointed to differences which appear to be consistent with evolutionary development. Fish enzymes have often been reported as being considerably more unstable to purification treatments such as dialysis, freeze-drying, and ammonium sulfate fractionation than their mammalian counterparts. However, there have been exceptions, some fish enzymes being reported as more stable than similar mammalian enzymes. Thus the overall picture is rather confused, and clarification must necessarily await the results of extensive and detailed studies of the as yet uninvestigated metabolic sequences and mediating enzymes in fish. There are indications that some enzymes may occur in certain fish tissues and not in similar tissues of warm-blooded vertebrates. A more intense study of such enzymes might eventually result in the uncovering of metabolic sequences or pathways that are unique to fish. It is to be hoped that this review may encourage increased and more imaginative research on fish enzymes, including studies on their metabolic significance and their role in postmortem changes.

# References

Abrams, A., and Klenow, H. (1953). *Arch. Biochem. Biophys.* **34**, 258.

Alfonsen, C. G., and Bertrán, E. C. (1954). *An. Inst. Invest. Vet. (Madrid)* **6**, 129.

Allison, W. S., and Kaplan, N. O. (1964). *J. Biol. Chem.* **239**, 2140.

Amano, K., and Yamada, K. (1964). *Bull. Jap. Soc. Sci. Fish.* **30**, 639.

Andreev, A. K. (1958). *Biokhimiya* **23**, 899.

Andreev, A. K. (1962). *C. R. Acad. Bulg. Sci.* **15**, 186.

Baker, J. R., and Chaykin, S. (1962). *J. Biol. Chem.* **237**, 1309.

Baker, J. R., Struempler, A., and Chaykin, S. (1963). *Biochim. Biophys. Acta* **71**, 58.

Barrington, E. J. W. (1957). *In* "The Physiology of Fishes" (M. E. Brown, ed.), Vol. 1, Academic Press, New York. pp. 109–161.

Bezňak, M. (1944). *Magy. Orv. Arch.* **45**, 1.

Bilinski, E. (1963). *Can. J. Biochem. Physiol.* **41**, 107.

Bilinski, E. (1964). *J. Fish. Res. Bd. Can.* **21**, 765.

Bilinski, E., and Jonas, R. E. E. (1964). *Can. J. Biochem.* **42**, 345.

Bilinski, E., and Jonas, R. E. E. (1966). *J. Fish. Res. Bd. Can.* **23**, 207.

Black, E. C. (1958). *In* "The Investigation of Fish-power Problems" (P. A. Larkin, ed.)., pp. 51–67. H. R. MacMillan Lectures in Fisheries, Univ. of British Columbia, Vancouver.

Black, E. C., Robertson, A. C., and Parker, R. R. (1961). *In* "Comparative Physiology of Carbohydrate Metabolism in Heterothermic Animals" (A. W. Martin, ed.), pp. 89–124. University of Washington Press, Seattle, Washington.

Bligh, E. G. (1961). *J. Fish. Res. Bd. Can.* **18**, 143.

Bluhm, H. M., and Tarr, H. L. A. (1957). *Can. J. Biochem. Physiol.* **35**, 767.

Boeri, E., Bonninchen, R. K., and Tosi, L. (1954). *Pubbl. Staz. Zool. Napoli* **25**, 427.

Boyer, P. D. (1953). *J. Cell. Comp. Physiol.* **42**, 71.

Brenner, R. E., Mercuri, O., DeTomas, M. E., and Peluffo, R. O. (1961). *In* "The Enzymes of Lipid Metabolism" (P. Desnuelle, ed.), pp. 101–108. Pergamon Press, Oxford.

Brodie, A. F., and Lipmann, F. (1955). *J. Biol. Chem.* **212**, 677.

Brown, W. D. (1960). *J. Cell. Comp. Physiol.* **55**, 81.

Brown, W. D., and Tappel, A. L. (1959). *Arch. Biochem. Biophys.* **85**, 149.

Buchanan, J. M. (1960). *In* "The Nucleic Acids" (E. Chargaff and J. N. Davidson, eds.), Vol. III, pp. 303–322. Academic Press, New York.

Burt, J. R. (1966). *J. Fish. Res. Bd. Can.* **23**, 527.

Burt, J. R., and Stroud, G. D. (1966). *Bull. Jap. Soc. Sci. Fish.* **32**, 204.

Buttkus, H. (1963). *J. Fish. Res. Bd. Can.* **20**, 45.

Cohen, M., Hamash, M., Atia, R., and Shapiro, B. (1967.) *J. Food Sci.* **32,** 179.

Connell, J. J. (1955). *Nature (London)* **175,** 562.

Connell, J. J. (1960). *J. Sci. Food Agr.* **17,** 245.

Cordier, D., and Cordier, M. (1957). *C. R. Soc. Biol. (Paris)* **151,** 1909.

Cori, G. T., Illingworth, B., and Keller, P. J. (1955). *In* "Methods in Enzymology" (S. P. Colwick and N. O. Kaplan, eds.), Vol. I, pp. 200–205. Academic Press, New York.

Corman, L., Prescott, L. M., and Kaplan, N. O. (1967). *J. Biol. Chem.* **242,** 1383.

Cory, R. P. and Wold, F. (1965). *Fed. Proc.* **25** (Pt. 1), 594.

Cory, R. P., and Wold, F. (1966). *Biochemistry* **5,** 3131.

Crosbie, G. W. (1960). *In* "The Nucleic Acids" (E. Chargaff and J. N. Davidson, eds.), Vol. III, pp. 323–348. Academic Press, New York.

Dingle, J. R., and Hines, J. A. (1960). *J. Fish. Res. Bd. Can.* **38,** 1437.

Drummond, G. I., and Black, E. C. (1960). *Annu. Rev. Physiol.* **22,** 169.

Ekberg, D. R. (1958). *Biol. Bull.* **114,** 308.

Engelhardt, V. A., and Ljubimova, N. M. (1939). *Nature (London)* **144,** 668.

Ericson, L. E. (1960). *Acta. Chem. Scand.* **14,** 2102.

Farkas, T., Herodek, S., Csaki, L., and Toth, G. (1961). *Acta Biol. Acad. Sci. Hung.* **12,** 83.

Fondy, T. P., Everse, J., Driscoll, G. A., Castillo, F., Stolzenbach, F. E., and Kaplan, N. O. (1965). *J. Biol. Chem.* **240,** 4219.

Forrest, R. J., and Hansen, R. G. (1959). *Can. J. Biochem. Physiol.* **37,** 751.

Fujimaki, M., and Kojo, K. (1955). *Bull. Jap. Soc. Sci. Fish.* **19,** 499.

Fujita, A. (1954). *Advan. Enzymol.* **15,** 389.

Geiger, E. (1948). *Forschr. Chem. Org. Naturst.* **5,** 267.

Ghankar, D. S., Bal, D. V., and Kamala, S. (1956). *Proc. Indian Acad. Sci.* **43B,** 134.

Groninger, H. S. (1959). *U.S. Fish Wildl. Serv. Spec. Sci. Rep. Fish. No.* **333,** 22 pp.

Groninger, H. S. (1964). *Arch. Biochem. Biophys.* **108,** 175.

Gubmann, M., Brown, W. D., and Tappel, A. L. (1958). *U.S. Fish. Wildl. Serv. Spec. Sci. Rep. Fish.* **288,** 51 pp.

Gubmann, M., and Tappel, A. L. (1962a). *Arch. Biochem. Biophys.* **98,** 262.

Gubmann, M., and Tappel, A. L. (1962b). *Arch. Biochem. Biophys.* **98,** 502.

Hamoir, G. (1951). *Biochem. J.* **50,** 140.

Hamoir, G. (1955). *Advan. Protein Chem.* **10,** 227.

Harris, R. S. (1951). *In* "The Enzymes" (J. B. Sumner and K. Myrback, eds.), Vol. I, Pt. 2, pp. 1186–1206. Academic Press, New York.

Hashimoto, T., and Handler, P. (1966). *J. Biol. Chem.* **241,** 3940.

Hashimoto, T., Joshi, J. G., del Rio, C., and Harder, P. (1967). *J. Biol. Chem.* **242,** 1671.

Hishida, T., and Nakano, E. (1954). *Embryologia* **2,** 67.

Hochachka, P. W. (1962). *Gen. Comp. Endocrinol.* **2,** 499.

Hochachka, P. W., and Hayes, F. R. (1962). *Can. J. Zool.* **40,** 261.

Horecker, B. L., and Smyrniotis, P. Z. (1953). *Biochim. Biophys. Acta* **12,** 98.

Horecker, B. L., Smyrniotis, P. Z., and Seegmuller, J. (1951). *J. Biol. Chem.* **193,** 383.

Hoskin, F. C. G. (1959). *Arch. Biochem. Biophys.* **85,** 141.

Ikeda, S. and Shimeno, S. (1967a). *Bull. Jap. Soc. Sci. Fish.* **33,** 104.

Ikeda, S., and Shimeno, S. (1967b). *Bull. Jap. Soc. Sci. Fish.* **33,** 112.

Ingles, C. J., Trevithick, J. R., Smith, M., and Dixon, G. H. (1966). *Biochem. Biophys. Res. Commun.* **22,** 627.

Jonas, R. E. E., and Bilinski, E. (1964). *J. Fish. Res. Bd. Can.* **21,** 653.

Jonas, R. E. E., and Bilinski, E. (1965). *J. Fish. Res. Bd. Can.* **22,** 891.
Jonas, R. E. E., and Bilinski, E. (1967). *J. Fish. Res. Bd. Can.* **24,** 2555.
Jones, N. R. (1955). *Biochem. J.* **60,** 81.
Jones, N. R. (1956). *Biochem. J.* **64,** 20.
Jones, N. R. (1958). *J. Sci. Food Agr.* **9,** 672.
Jones, N. R. (1962). *In* "Recent Advances in Food Science" (J. Hawthorn and M. Leitch, eds.), pp. 151–166. Butterworths, Washington, D.C. and London.
Jones, N. R., and Murray, J. (1961a) *Biochem. J.* **77,** 567.
Jones, N. R., and Murray, J. (1961b). *Z. Vergl. Physiol.* **44,** 174.
Jones, N. R., and Murray, J. (1966). *Bull. Jap. Soc. Sci. Fish.* **32,** 197.
Kanungo, M. S., and Prosser, C. L. (1959). *J. Cell. Comp. Physiol.* **54,** 265.
Katz, J., and Wood, H. G. (1960). *J. Biol. Chem.* **235,** 2165.
Kielley, W. W., and Meyerhof, O. (1948). *J. Biol. Chem.* **176,** 591.
Klenk, E., and Kremer, G. (1960). *Hoppe-Seyler's Z. Physiol. Chem.* **320,** 111.
Kövér, A., Szabolcs, M., and Benko, K. (1963). *Acta. Physiol. Acad. Sci. Hung.* **23,** 229.
Kövér, A., Szabolcs, M., and Csabai, A. (1964). *Arch. Biochem. Biophys.* **106,** 333.
Kotel'nikova, A. V. (1949). *Biokhimiya* **14,** 145.
Kornberg, A. (1962). Enzymatic Synthesis of DNA. "CIBA Lectures in Microbiological Chemistry." Wiley, New York.
Kwon, T. W., and Olcott, H. S. (1965). *Comp. Biochem. Physiol.* **15,** 7.
Lazarow, A., and Cooperstein, S. J. (1951). *Biol. Bull.* **100,** 191.
Lee, C. F., Nilson, H. W., and Clegg, W. (1955). *Commer. Fish. Rev.* **17,** 21.
Lehninger, A. L. (1957). *In* "Methods in Enzymology" (S. P. Colwick and N. O. Kaplan, eds.), Vol. I, p. 1545. Academic Press, New York.
Lindahl, P. E., and Svärd, P. O. (1957). *Acta. Chem. Scand.* **11,** 846.
Lovern, J. A. (1951). *Biochem. Soc. Symp. No.* **6,** 49–82.
Lovern, J. A. (1961). *In* "Fish in Nutrition" (E. Heen and R. Kreuzer, eds.), pp. 85–111. Fishing News (Books) Inc., London.
Lovern, J. A., Olley, J., and Watson, H. A. (1959). *J. Sci. Food Agr.* **10,** 327.
Ludovicy-Bungert, L. (1961). *Arch. Intern. Physiol. Biochim.* **69,** 265.
MacDonald, D. L., and Fletcher, H. G. (1960). *J. Amer. Chem. Soc.* **82,** 1832.
McDonald, M. R. (1962). *J. Gen. Bhysiol.* **45** (Pt. 2, supple), 77.
McGeachin, R. L., and Debnam, J. W. (1960). *Proc. Soc. Exp. Biol. Med.* **103,** 814.
MacLeod, R. A., Jonas, R. E. E., and Roberts, E. (1963). *Can. J. Biochem. Physiol.* **41,** 1971.
Malins, D. C. (1966a). *Biochem. J.* **100,** 31 pp.
Malins, D. C. (1966b). *Biochem. J.* **100,** 31–32.
Malins, D. C. (1967). *Biochem. J.* **103,** 29 p.
Mannan, A., and Tarr, H. L. A. (1961). *J. Fish. Res. Bd. Can.* **18,** 349.
Martin, G. -B., and Tarr, H. L. A. (1961). *Can. J. Biochem. Physiol.* **39,** 297.
Matsuura, F., and Hashimoto, K. (1954). *Bull. Jap. Soc. Sci. Fish.* **20,** 308.
Matsuura, F., and Hashimoto, K. (1955). *Bull. Jap. Soc. Sci. Fish.* **20,** 951.
Matsuura, F., Baba, H. J., and Mori, T. (1953). *Bull. Jap. Soc. Sci. Fish.* **19,** 893.
Mead, J. F., Kajama, M., and Reiser, R. (1960). *J. Amer. Oil Chem. Soc.* **37,** 438.
Murray, J., and Jones, N. R. (1958). *Biochem. J.* **68,** 9.
Nagayama, F. (1961a). *Bull. Jap. Soc. Sci. Fish.* **27,** 1026.
Nagayama, F. (1961b). *Bull. Jap. Soc. Sci. Fish.* **27,** 1029.
Nagayama, F. (1961c). *Bull. Jap. Soc. Sci. Fish.* **27,** 1018.
Nagayama, F. (1961d). *Bull. Jap. Soc. Sci. Fish.* **27,** 1961.

Nagayama, F., Osawa, H., and Takahashi, B. (1957). *J. Tokyo Univ. Fish.* **43**, 37.

Nara, S., and Saito, T. (1959). *Bull. Fac. Fish. Hokkaido Univ.* **10**, 68.

Nicolaides, N., and Woodall, A. N. (1962). *J. Nutri.* **78**, 431.

Ono, T., and Nagayama, F. (1959). *J. Tokyo Univ. Fish.* **45**, 153.

Ono, T., Nagayama, F., and Takahashi, B. (1957). *J. Tokyo Univ. Fish.* **43**, 37.

Paleus, S. (1954). *Acta Chem. Scand.* **8**, 971.

Partmann, W. (1954). *Z. Lebensm. Unters. Forsch.* **99**, 341.

Partmann, W. (1961). *Z. Ernahrungswiss.* **2**, 70.

Partmann, W. (1964). "Technology of Fish Utilization" (R. Kreuzer, ed.) pp. 4–13, Fishing News (Books) Inc., London.

Partmann, W., and Nemitz, G. (1959). *Z. Lebensm. Unters. Forsch.* **110**, 109.

Pesce, A., Fondy, T. P., Stolzenbach, F., Castillo, F., and Kaplan, N. O. (1967). *J. Biol. Chem.* **242**, 2151.

Raczynska-Bojanowska, K., and Gasiorowska, I. (1963). *Acta Biochim. Polon.* **10**, 117.

Renold, A. E., DiPietro, D. L., and Williams, A. K. (1964). *Proc. 3rd Inter. Symp. Stockholm*, **1963**, pp. 269–279. Pergamon Press, Oxford.

Reuter, A. (1960). *Arch. Intern. Physiol. Biochim.* **68**, 339.

Roberts, E., and Tsuyuki, H. (1963). *Biochim. Biophys. Acta* **73**, 673.

Roy, J. E. (1966). *Can. J. Biochem.* **45**, 1263.

Roy, J. E., and Roy, K. L. (1967). *Can. J. Biochem.*, **45**, 1263.

Saito, K., and Hidaka, T. (1955a). *Bull. Jap. Soc. Sci. Fish.* **21**, 925.

Saito, K., and Hidaka, T. (1955b). *Bull. Jap. Soc. Sci. Fish.* **21**, 929.

Schmitt, A., Bottke, I., and Siebert, G. (1966). *Hoppe-Seylers' Z. Physiol. Chem.* **347**, 18.

Sexton, A. W., and Russel, R. L. (1955). *Science* **121**, 342.

Shibata, T. (1958). *Bull. Fac. Fish. Hokkaido Univ.* **9**, 218.

Shibata, T., and Yoshimura, K. (1962). *Bull. Jap. Soc. Sci. Fish.* **28**, 514.

Shorland, F. B. (1962). *In* "Comparative Biochemistry" (M. Florkin and H. S. Mason, eds.), Vol. III, pp. 1–102. Academic Press, New York.

Siebert, G. (1958). *Experientia* **14**, 65.

Siebert, G., and Bottke, I. (1963). *Arch. Fischereiwiss.* **14**, 57.

Siebert, G., Schmitt, A., and Träxler, G. (1963). *Hoppe Seylers Z. Physiol. Chem.* **332**, 160.

Siebert, G., Schmitt, A., and von Malortie, R. (1965a). *Hoppe Seylers Z. Physiol. Chem.* **342**, 20.

Siebert, G., Schmitt, A., and Bottke, I. (1965b). *Arch. Fischereiwiss.* **15**, 233.

Simidu, W., Ikeda, S., and Kurokawa, Y. (1953). *Bull. Res. Inst. Food Sci. Koyoto Univ.* **12**, 49–56.

Simpson, T. H., Wright, R. S., and Gottfreid, H. (1963). *J. Endocrinol.* **26**, 489.

Simpson, T. H., Wright, R. S., and Renfrew, J. (1964a). *J. Endocrinol.* **31**, 11.

Simpson, T. H., Wright, R. S., and Hunt, S. V. (1964b). *J. Endocrinol.* **31**, 29.

Simskaya, A. M., and Karpliuk, I. A. (1957). *Vopr. Pitaniya* **16**, 63.

Siou, G. (1955). *C. R. Soc. Biol.* **149**, 1422.

Smellie, R. M. S. (1962). *In* "DNA, Structure, Synthesis and Function," p. 98. Pergamon, Oxford.

Svärd, P. O. (1957). *Acta Chem. Scand.* **11**, 854.

Tarr, H. L. A. (1950). *J. Fish. Res. Bd. Can.* **7**, 608.

Tarr, H. L. A. (1953). *Nature (London)* **171**, 344.

Tarr, H. L. A. (1954). *Food Technol.* **8**, 15.

Tarr, H. L. A. (1955a). *Biochem. J.* **59**, 386.

Tarr, H. L. A. (1955b). *Fed. Proc.* **14**, 291.
Tarr, H. L. A. (1956). *Fed. Proc.* **15**, 369.
Tarr, H. L. A. (1958a). *Annu. Rev. Biochem.* **27**, 223.
Tarr, H. L. A. (1958b). *Can. J. Biochem. Physiol.* **36**, 517.
Tarr, H. L. A. (1959). *Can. J. Biochem.* **37**, 961.
Tarr, H. L. A. (1960). *Can. J. Biochem.* **38**, 683.
Tarr, H. L. A. (1963). *Can. J. Biochem.* **41**, 313.
Tarr, H. L. A. (1964a). *Can. J. Biochem.* **42**, 51.
Tarr, H. L. A. (1964b). *Can. J. Biochem.* **42**, 575.
Tarr, H. L. A. (1964c). *Can. J. Biochem.* **42**, 1535.
Tarr, H. L. A. (1964d). "Technology of Fish Utilization," (R. Kreuzer ed.), pp. 26–31. Fishing News (Books) Inc., London.
Tarr, H. L. A. (1966a). *J. Food Sci.* **31**, 840.
Tarr, H. L. A. (1966b). *Bull. Jap. Soc. Sci. Fish.* **32**, 213.
Tarr, H. L. A. (1967). *In* "Methods in Enzymology" (L. Grossman and K. Moldave, eds.), Vol. 12A, p. 113. Academic Press, New York.
Tarr, H. L. A., and Comer, A. G. (1964). *Can. J. Biochem.* **42**, 1527.
Tarr, H. L. A., and Leroux, M. (1962). *Can. J. Biochem.* **40**, 571.
Tarr, H. L. A., and Roy, J. (1966a). *Can. J. Biochem.* **44**, 197.
Tarr, H. L. A. and Roy, J. (1966b). *Can. J. Biochem.* **44**, 1435.
Tarr, H. L. A. and Roy, J. E. (1967). *Can. J. Biochem.* **45**, 409.
Tarr, H. L. A., Roy, J. E., and Yamamoto, M. (1968). *Can. J. Biochem.* **46**, 407.
Taylor, J. F. (1955). In, "Methods in Enzymology" (Colwick, S. P. and Kaplan, N. O., eds.), Vol. I, p. 31, Academic Press, New York.
Tener, G. M., Wright, R. S., and Khorana, H. G. (1957). *J. Amer. Chem. Soc.* **79**, 441.
Tomlinson, N. (1958). *Can. J. Biochem. Physiol.* **36**, 633.
Tomlinson, N. (1959). *Can. J. Biochem.* **37**, 945.
Tomlinson, N., and Creelman, V. (1960). *J. Fish. Res. Bd. Can.* **17**, 603.
Tomlinson, N., and Geiger, S. (1962). *J. Fish. Res. Bd. Can.* **19**, 997.
Tomlinson, N., and Warren, R. A. J. (1960). *Can. J. Biochem. Physiol.* **38**, 605.
Tomlinson, N., Creelman, V., and Reid, K. G. (1960). *J. Fish. Res. Bd. Can.* **17**, 371.
Tsuyuki, H., and Idler, D. R. (1961a). *Can. J. Biochem. Physiol.* **38**, 1117.
Tsuyuki, H., and Idler, D. R. (1961b). *Can. J. Biochem. Physiol.* **39**, 1037.
Tsuyuki, H., and Wold, F. (1964). *Science* **146**, 535.
Tsuyuki, H., Chang, V. M., and Idler, D. R. (1958). *Can. J. Biochem. Physiol* **36**, 465.
Unemura, K. (1951a). *Igaku To Seibatsugaku* **18**, 108. (*Chem. Abstr.* **45**, 5327i).
Unemura, K. (1951b). *Igaku To Seibutsugaku* **18**, 204. (*Chem. Abstr.* **45**, 6232c).
Unemura, K. (1951c). *Nagoya J. Med. Sci.* **14**, 81. (*Chem. Abstr.* **46**, 5733h).
Varga, E., Szigeti, J., and Kess, E. (1954). *Acta Physiol. Acad. Sci. Hung.* **5**, 383.
Whiteley, H. R. (1960). *Comp. Biochem. Physiol.* **23**, 71.
Williams, R. T. (ed.) (1951). *Biochem. Soc. Symp.* **6**, 105.
Wilson, A. C., Kaplan, N. O., Levine, L., Pesce, A., Reichlin, M., and Allison, W. S. (1964). *Fed. Proc.* **23**, 1258.
Wood, H. G., and Katz, J. (1958). *J. Biol. Chem.* **233**, 1279.
Wood, J. D. (1959a). *Can. J. Biochem. Physiol.* **37**, 937.
Wood, J. D. (1959b). *J. Fish. Res. Bd. Can.* **16**, 755.
Wood, J. D., and Haqq, S. A. (1962). *J. Fish. Res. Bd. Can.* **19**, 169.
Yamada, K. and Amano, K. (1965a). *Bull. Jap. Soc. Sci. Fish.* **31**, 60.
Yamada, K., and Amano, K. (1965b). *Bull. Jap. Soc. Sci. Fish.* **31**, 1030.

Yamada, K., and Suzuki, T. (1950). *Bull. Jap. Soc. Sci. Fish.* **15,** 765.
Yamada, K., and Suzuki, T. (1952). *J. Agr. Chem. Soc. Jap.* **25,** 372.
Yamada, K., Suzu‚i, T., and Tanaka, M. (1959). *Bull. Agr. Chem. Soc. Jap.* **23,** 71.
Yamamoto, M. (1968). *Can. J. Biochem.* **46,** 423.
Yurkowski, M., and Brockerhof, H. (1965). *J. Fish. Res. Bd. Can.* **22,** 643.

# 7

# FEED FORMULATION AND EVALUATION

*W. H. Hastings and L. M. Dickie*

## I. Introduction

Demands for domestic fish for food and recreation have increased to such a volume that fish farming is emerging as a significant animal husbandry industry. In the United States during 1969 intensive fish culture produced over 36 million pounds of cold-water fish, 40 million pounds of warm-water food fish, 12 million pounds of bait fish, and 1.6 million pounds of exotic fish (Hastings, 1969a). Feed for this industry may be roughly estimated at twice the weight of fish produced, costing 10¢/pound for salmonid fish species raised in raceways and 5¢/pound for warm-water pond fish (U. S. Bureau of Sport Fisheries and Wildlife, 1968).

A farmer with capital, land, labor, and equipment can readily determine the monetary potential of the poultry, dairy, swine, and beef cattle industries by using the periodic U.S.D.A. "farm commodity-feed price" tables. These are ratios expressing the pounds of feed it is possible to purchase per unit of livestock or poultry products sold at the farm level. A quick calculation multiplying expected feed conversion by feed cost will reveal the equivalent value of feed available for management costs and profit. No such economic evaluation can be found for the production of fish. Parameters describing growth, survival, feed conversion, and other factors related to fish culture vary substantially with environmental conditions from species to species and even within strains of the same species. Limited knowledge of nutrient requirements of fish and the variability in response of fish in various impoundments make a fish "commodity-feed" ratio difficult and complicated to determine.

Fish trained to accept manufactured feeds have proved very efficient in converting forage, cereal grains, and concentrate by-product feedstuffs into edible meat. The relative growth and feed utilization of farm animals have been compared by Meyer and Nelson (1963). Weight gains reported during a period of rapid growth, with feed conversion values expressed as

TABLE I

Efficiency of Feed Utilization of Various Animal Species per 1000 Grams of Feed Intake

| Species | Live weight gain (gm) | Energy gain (kcal) | Protein gain (gm) |
|---|---|---|---|
| Rats | 322 | 663 | 62 |
| Chicks | 356 | 782 | 101 |
| Pigs | 292 | 1492 | 30 |
| Sheep | 185 | 832 | 22 |
| Steers | 163 | 748 | 26 |
| Channel catfish[b] | 715 | 935 | 118 |
| Brown trout[c] | 576 | 608 | 75 |

[a] From Meyer and Nelson, 1963.

[b] Data published in the 1963 Annual Report on Sport Fisheries Research, Dep. Interior Fish and Wildlife Service.

[c] Cortland Hatchery No. 21, 1962, pp. 31-ff.

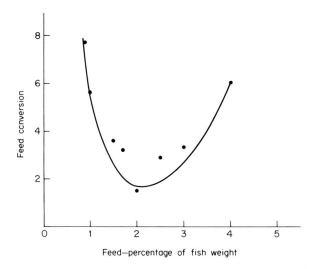

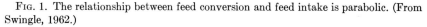

Fɪɢ. 1. The relationship between feed conversion and feed intake is parabolic. (From Swingle, 1962.)

energy gain and protein gain per unit of feed intake, are shown in Table I. Fish values are added by calculations from publications cited.

Animals which deposit large quantities of fat (e.g., pigs at 40% fat) show a more efficient energy conversion than lean animals. Fish are highest on the comparative list in terms of gross body weight gain and high in terms of protein gain per unit of feed intake. As fish feeds become better formulated to comply with research findings of balanced nutrient requirements and are texturized to improve acceptability and availability, they are likely to show improved utilization.

Fish are raised commercially under conditions of intensive stocking in an environment of limited productivity. Response to added feeds (Fig. 1) determines whether fish production is a feasible farm enterprise in competition for land and water with crops and livestock. This chapter attempts to set forth numerical coefficients of feed evaluation as guidelines for feed formulation, feed processing, and feeding management which will result in economical fish production.

## II. Nutrient Sources

### A. Water

Water has long been considered as both a nutrient and a nutrient carrier for fish (Schaeperclaus, 1933; Black *et al.*, 1961). For example, Wolf (1951) added no inorganic supplement to one of three test rations composed of purified organic ingredients and obtained no significant decrease in trout growth. Water contributes ionized salts which are apparently exchanged via gills and skin with those in the fish body through simple diffusion, active enzymatic or metabolic carriers, or by special cellular selection (Podoliak, 1962). The composition of fish body fluids depends somewhat on the aquatic environment, with transfer of $Ca^{2+}$, $Na^+$, $Co^{2+}$, $I^-$, $Cl^-$, and other dissolved minerals being regulated by threshhold concentrations and/or by species selectivity (Krogh, 1939; Mullins, 1950).

Criteria for the composition of freshwater that will support a good mixed fish fauna have been proposed by Ellis (1944) and Standler (1952). However, individual species requirements and the significance of some minerals are too little known for recommending a water chemistry formulation best adapted to fish production. The very low mineral content of high-altitude lakes, supplied largely from snow fields (Reimers, 1958), will support growth in the presence of natural food organisms. Once the established biomass was harvested, body condition of a small trout population declined.

A significant positive regression can be shown between total dissolved chemicals in water and the summed indexes of plankton, benthos, and fish standing crops (Frey, 1963; McIntire and Bond, 1962). However, the concentration of water-soluble material is not related directly to fish production (Hayes, 1963), but rather to fish food, indicating that fish are secondary and tertiary consumers of water nutrients. Only if food is deficient in chemicals and these are present in water in usable concentrations, are these removed and utilized directly in fish tissues.

Given suitable climatological conditions, fish food in unmanaged waters is restricted by the amount of available nutrients. The limited replacement of natural food in Sierra lakes (Reimers, 1958), estimated by the authors and by the method of Ivlev (1945) to contain 24 kcal/m², prevented reproduction of stocked fish. On the other hand, the rich waters of the Thames River provide an annual fish production of 426 kg/ha, requiring 704.5 kcal/m² (Mann, 1965).

## B. Planktonic and Benthoic Materials

Energy from dissolved organic matter added to a small stream was traced (Warren *et al.*, 1964) to the abundant growth of the bacterium *Sphaerotilus natans*, which in turn provided food for tendipedid larvae, the most important food organism for trout in the habitat studied. Other food chains have been traced for coastal waters (Hellier, 1962) and for coastal reefs in marine waters (Bardach, 1959). The conclusion was that, in general, the shorter the food chain involved, the more efficient is the transfer of photosynthetic products through the higher trophic levels in fish production.

The increased growth of minnows, exotic fish, and food fish in ponds provided with applications of inorganic phosphorus and nitrogen (Bennett, 1966, personal communication; Swingle, 1947) attests to the value of plankton as a direct and indirect fish food. Fry and small fish selectively capture micro- and macroscopic plant and animal life within the grasping ability of the mouth openings (Thorson, 1946). Many larger fish feed by brachial filtration. The utilization of this food as a primary source of nutrients and energy will vary with the quantity ingested, the balance provided by other food sources (Yashouv, 1956), and the digestibility of plant material by autolysis and gastrointestinal enzymes in fish. Vaas and Vass Van Oven (1959) have shown that significant amounts of *Chlorella* and *Scenedesmus* ingested by herbivorous fish (carp) remain viable after passage through the digestive tract.

Chemically, algae test high in nutritional value as animal food (see composition of *Chlorella*, Table VIII, Appendix). Lubitz (1963) found a protein efficiency ratio (PER) in rats of 2.19 for a powdered culture of *Chlorella pyrenoidosa*, compared with 2.90 for casein, and 4.01 for whole egg protein. Coefficients of digestibility for algae nutrient components were: crude protein, 96%, crude fat, 93%, total carbohydrate, 72%, and crude fiber, 15%. Nose (1960) reported weight gains of goldfish fed dried cultures of algae mixed with moist potato starch as equal to half that for fish fed casein plus potato starch, cellulose, and a salt mixture. Using the indirect method of measuring nitrogen retention ($Cr_2O_3$ added to the feed as an inert reference material), Nose found increased digestibility with a higher percentage of algae in the feed. At the ratio of algae to starch of 8:1, *Chlorella ellupsoideas* attained a digestibility of 57.4%.

## C. Animal Foods

Natural fish foods belonging to the animal kingdom include invertebrates, copepods, cladocera, insect larvae, aquatic insects, forage fish, and terrestrial animals. There is nothing common to these foods except that these contain chemical constituents which support animal life, have the ability to autolyze on death, and are presumably digestible. Mann (1961) tabulates the composition of several fish food animals, adding data on food conversion and the ratio of protein to total food. On a dry basis, these are calculated to contain 3260–4500 kcal/pound.

An analysis of forage organisms was carried out at the Fish Farming Experimental Station, Stuttgart, Arkansas. Approximately 1 acre-foot of water was screened through a U. S. No. 40 mesh sieve during June 24, 1963,

TABLE II

NATURAL ANIMAL FOOD OBTAINED BY SAMPLING FIVE PONDS JUNE 24, 1963

| Genus | Percentage by weight | Average weight (mg) | Daily number required for 100-gm fish[a] |
|-------|---------------------|--------------------|-----------------------------------------|
| Anax | 91.2 | 990 | 7 |
| Eulalia | 0.3 | 88 | 75 |
| Ephomera | 1.8 | 46 | 147 |
| Enallagma | 0.1 | 70 | 96 |
| Macrothemis | 0.4 | 100 | 68 |
| Ranatra | 0.2 | 200 | 34 |
| Culicoides | 0.3 | 100 | 68 |
| Chironomus | 5.5 | 10 | 680 |

[a] Based on expected conversion of natural food to fish weight gain during normal growth (Brown, 1957).

from five $\frac{1}{4}$-acre ponds. Bottom organisms were picked from dredge samples and drained areas of the shoreline. One kilogram each of daphnia and mixed insect larvae were harvested. Table II lists the insect larvae by generic name, the proportion each contributed to the total weight, and the average individual weights.

The chemical composition of mixed insect larvae and of daphnia is shown in Table III. Daphnia showed a selective concentration of vitamins A and $B_{12}$ (cobalamin), possibly because they were gorged with algae. During the fish growing season when water temperatures are suitable for insect hatches and bottom organism production, the carrying capacity of water impoundments, subject to natural biological control, amounts to about 400 pounds of assorted fish species (Swingle and Smith, 1950; Jenkins, 1958; Frey, 1963). This may be increased by pond fertilization and still more by the use of feeds. Hastings (1964) and Tiemeier et al. (1965) report yields of 2000 pounds/acre of channel catfish in still water by a program of heavy stocking and daily feeding. The ascending curve of total production showed no inflection, and it may be assumed that the carrying capacity of test ponds had not been reached. J. M. Martin (1967, personal communication) raised 4000 pounds of exotic fish per acre with a combination of pond fertilization and added feeds. H. Clemens (1966, personal communication) produced 13,000 pounds of tilapia per acre using cottonseed meal as a fertilizer feed material. Similar productions have been reported for carp (Kawamoto, 1957).

TABLE III

CHEMICAL COMPOSITION OF NATURAL FOODS AVAILABLE TO POND FISH[a]

| Nutrient | Mixed insect larvae (%) | Daphnia (%) |
|---|---|---|
| Moisture | 81.8 | 93.0 |
| Protein | 12.34 | 3.5 |
| Fat | 2.66 | 0.71 |
| Fiber | 2.20 | 0.45 |
| N.F.E. | 0.04 | 0.57 |
| Ash | 0.96 | 1.80 |
| Riboflavin ($\gamma$/gm) | 10.4 | 1.50 |
| Niacin | 34.9 | 18.0 |
| Choline | 954 | 501 |
| Pantothenic acid | 23.3 | 2.68 |
| Vitamin $B_{12}$ (m$\gamma$/gm) | 8.3 | 214 |
| Vitamin A activity | Less than 100 IU/100 gm | 720 IU/gm |
| $\beta$-Carotene (mg/gm) | Trace | 0.44 |

[a] From Hastings, 1964.

TABLE IV

MAXIMUM PERMISSIBLE DENSITY OF BROWN TROUT IN REARING TROUGHS[a]

| Water temp. (°F) | Pounds per cubic foot in troughs containing number of fish per pound | | | | | |
|---|---|---|---|---|---|---|
| | −2542 (−1)[b] | 2542− 304 (1–2) | 304− 88.3 (2–3) | 88.3− 37.8 (3–4) | 37.8− 19.7 (4–5) | 19.7− 11.6 (5–6) |
| 38 | 2.4 | 3.0 | 3.7 | 5.0 | 6.5 | 8.1 |
| 40 | 2.3 | 2.8 | 3.4 | 4.6 | 6.2 | 7.7 |
| 42 | 2.2 | 2.5 | 3.2 | 4.3 | 5.7 | 7.2 |
| 44 | 2.0 | 2.4 | 3.0 | 3.9 | 5.2 | 6.5 |
| 46 | 1.9 | 2.2 | 2.8 | 3.7 | 4.8 | 6.2 |
| 48 | 1.7 | 2.1 | 2.5 | 3.4 | 4.5 | 5.6 |
| 50 | 1.6 | 1.9 | 2.4 | 3.2 | 4.2 | 5.2 |
| 52 | 1.5 | 1.8 | 2.2 | 3.0 | 3.9 | 4.8 |
| 54 | 1.4 | 1.6 | 2.0 | 2.7 | 3.6 | 4.5 |
| 56 | 1.3 | 1.5 | 1.9 | 2.5 | 3.3 | 4.2 |

[a] From Haskell, 1955.
[b] Numbers in parenthesis give size in inches.

In running water fish production may exceed a million pounds per acre per annum (trout, Haskell, 1955; carp, Kawamoto, 1957). Haskell describes the carrying capacity of waters suitable for trout in terms of "pounds per cubic foot," the weight stocked in troughs being six times that in open ponds. Table IV shows values for the maximum density of trout raised in troughs to range from 1.3 to 8.1 pounds per cubic foot, depending upon water temperature and fish size. Animal production up to 15.7 pounds per cubic foot was reported (Haskell, 1955).

Since feed is necessary for the economical management of fish in most water impoundments (Lin and Chen, 1966), the formulation, utilization, and acceptability of manufactured foods (hereafter called "feeds") are subjects of research in areas of intensive fish culture.

## III. Formulation and Processing Fish Feeds

### A. HISTORICAL BACKGROUND

It is difficult to imagine a time when no information existed about fish feeds: Schaeperclaus (1933), Huet (1960), Lin (1959), and Wood (1953), reviewing the art of preparing feeds, show that early formulas were based on attempts to duplicate the composition of natural foods. This was laboriously accomplished by growing insects, harvesting small fish or other aquatic animals, or by processing culled domestic animals. For many years fresh and frozen animal products were the backbone of hatchery production rations. However, competition for this material with pet and mink feed industries, costs of preservation, storage, preparation, and loss on feeding, stimulated a continual search for substitutions which has resulted today in the common use of dry or semimoist feeds.

The objective of feed formulation is to supply the nutrient density for optimal animal production. Lacking a knowledge of detailed nutritional requirements of fish, formulation of fish feeds is in the "recipe" stage, certain ingredients and levels of vitamins being used because a successful feed contained them. Numerical coefficients are gradually being compiled to enable a computer to select ingredients on the basis of chemical and physical properties which will optimize fish production at low feed cost.

### B. WET FEEDS

For years it was hatchery practice to grow trout to stocking size on fresh or frozen beef liver. In 1927, McCay and Dilley attempted to grow trout fingerlings on various levels of purified protein, fat, carbohydrate, and salts supplemented with known vitamins. Only rations containing liver supported growth. McCay and Dilley (1927) postulated that "factor H," present in liver and distinct from then known vitamins, was essential for trout weight increase.

During the next 20 years, research efforts were focused along the line of economy, the objective being to develop a more economical ration than the 100% liver customarily used. In 1928, Titcomb *et al.* raised trout on mixtures of fish meal, vegetable oil meals, and frozen liver. Agersborg (1934) grew trout and salmon fingerlings on a formula consisting of 48% assorted ground fish, 28% sheep liver, and 24% salmon eggs. The Wisconsin Nevin State Hatchery (McLaren *et al.*, 1946) attained results equal to the use of fresh liver with a ration containing 47.5% fresh liver, 47.5% canned carp, and 5% dried brewer's yeast. This mixture was fed at the rate of 6% fish body weight by dropping chunks into water.

## C. MEAT–MEAL FORMULAS

In 1940 results of a number of years of research were published by Tunison describing the use of the Cortland dry feed mixture No. 6 as an additive to meat by-products. It served as a means of decreasing feed costs and improving the physical properties of wet meat rations. One method of feed preparation was grinding partially thawed hog spleen or combinations of hog spleen and beef liver, blending this with an equal weight of dry mixture and adding 30% water. This mixture was texturized by forcing it through holes in a potato ricer, forming wormlike particles. An alternate method of feed preparation was to use fresh organs or thawed frozen ones, adding the dry mixture and without blending additional water, passing the material through blades of a centrifugal air blower. Successive runs through the blades were necessary to texturize feed for small fish. Final consistency was described as similar to "moist sawdust" easily adapted to scattering by hand. A firmer texture and improved conversion were attained by storage of this moist feed for 24 hours in a refrigerated room at 3°C.

The dry constituents of the Cortland No. 6 fish feed recommended in 1940 are shown in Table V. A ration comprising this dry formula and equal parts hog spleen and beef liver analyzes about 27.8% protein and 42% water. On a dry basis, the protein content is about 48%. Under conditions existing at the Cortland Fish Hatchery, feed cost of producing trout was reduced from $0.22 per pound using beef liver to $0.12 per pound of fish using the Cortland No. 6 meat–meal mixture. By calculation, feed conversion was about 3.0.

The Cortland meat–meal (and other formulas) ration is nutritionally adequate and has proved quite acceptable to most fish. Several fish farmers

TABLE V

CORTLAND No. 6 DRY FEED
MIXTURE[a]

| Ingredients | Percentage |
|---|---|
| Dried skim milk | 24 |
| Whitefish meal | 24 |
| Cottonseed meal[b] | 24 |
| Wheat flour middlings | 24 |
| Salt | 4 |

[a] Tunison, 1940.
[b] Soybean meal is equivalent to cottonseed meal as a component.

who are near inexpensive supplies of fresh animal by-products (trash fish, chicken hatchery culls, offal) use modifications of the Cortland No. 6 dry mix along with wet, fresh animal products. It is generally digestible, succulent and, where a major component is available at low cost, results attained by handling this material are justified.

## D. PELLETED SEMIMOIST FEEDS

An example of a meat–meal feed successfully transferred from the hatchery to large-scale commercial production is the Oregon moist pellet. It was developed during 6 years of cooperative study by personnel of the Oregon State Game and Fish Commission and the Oregon Agricultural Experiment Station Seafoods Laboratory at Astoria (Hublou *et al.*, 1959). Feeding experiments with silver salmon (*Oncorhynchus kisutch*) conducted during the first year of testing production feeds, showed best acceptability, growth, and survival with a formula containing 40 parts meal mixture, 40 parts ground frozen turbot, and 20 parts ground frozen tuna liver. Later a mixture of 40% meat and/or wet fish material and 60 parts dry meal was adopted.

The presence of 37 to 40% water in the meat–meal feed assures a soft texture, yet one suitable for forming into a pellet by specialized equipment. The particle size has evolved from "chunks" formed by hand in the laboratory to pellets formed by high-capacity extruders. Modifications of the original formula are constantly being tested in feeding trials at state and federal hatcheries. A typical formula and processing specifications are shown in Table I, Appendix. If mixed into a tight dough, properly handled after extrusion, quick frozen, and stored at $-18°C$, pellets will remain separated without lumping. Satisfactory feed conversion, excellent survival of stocked fish, and a competitive price from several commercial companies have made the Oregon moist pellet a standard production feed for many hatcheries.

## E. Dry Feeds

### 1. *Cold-Water Fish Feeds*

For years it was believed by fish culturists that trout could not be raised without the inclusion of raw meat in the diet. A "factor H" (see Section II,B) was considered present in all raw meat, but limited in cooked and dried meat products. Other unidentified nutrients present in liver were labeled fractions "L" and "M" by Field *et al.* (1944). Lack of fresh or frozen meat caused cessation of growth, anemia, poor appetite, and susceptibility to disease. Early workers (Simmons and Norris, 1941; Tunison, 1940) postulated that the unknown factors were certain vitamin mixtures or vitamin precursors. Currently it is believed that the beneficial effects earlier attributed to unidentified nutrients in meat are results of a correct balance of several known vitamins plus a ration acceptability factor.

A logical step in the development of a complete dry feed was its use over extended periods with only occasional supplementation with fresh meat. This procedure was employed by Grassl (1956) to grow yearling rainbow trout to legal stocking size over a period of 28 weeks. The use of fresh liver and dried yeast mixture once a week and a dry pelleted concentrate for daily feeding resulted in growth and survival equal to that of a control group fed only a liver ration. Pioneer work in texturizing pelleted feeds for improved acceptability was done by Grassl (1956). Fish 4 inches long were offered a $\frac{3}{32}$-inch diameter pellet, and as fish grew larger they were offered $\frac{1}{8}$-inch pellet. Only 2 weeks were required for fish to become trained to accept the smaller pellet and to gain weight, whereas 4 weeks were needed to accustom fish to accept the larger pellets.

The first successful dry concentrate feed of known formulation used in raising trout through two generations was reported by Phillips *et al.* (1964). "At the end of 24 months the fish could be handled without loss and were, in general, satisfactory in appearance. They did not appear inferior to the other stock at the hatchery that were fed meat–meal mixtures or commercial fish food pellets." Formulas for pellets No. 1 and No. 6 in a series of dry concentrates tested as complete trout feeds are shown in Table VI. These have several features in common with the feeds of Grassl (1956) and commercial fish feeds offered as "complete feeds for trout raised in

TABLE VI

Composition of Dry Concentrates Tested as Complete Pelleted Trout Feeds[a]

| | Pounds per ton | |
|---|---|---|
| Ingredient | No. 1 | No. 6 |
| Bonemeal | 100 | 100 |
| Fish meal | 760 | 700 |
| Dried skim milk | 110 | 140 |
| Cottonseed meal | 300 | |
| Soybean meal | | 240 |
| Wheat middlings | 440 | 290 |
| Brewer's yeast | 200 | 200 |
| Corn fermentation solubles | | 240 |
| Vitamin mixture | 30 | 30 |
| A & D feedling oil | 60 | 60 |
| Total | 2000 | 2000 |

[a] From Phillips et al., 1963, 1964.

raceways," they contain from 35 to 40% fish meal, over 40% crude protein, about 3250 gross kcal per kilogram with 60% of this energy coming from protein. There was no significant difference in growth between formulas 1 and 6 during 18 months, but pellet No. 6 resulted in better feed conversion and less total feed calories per pound of fish gain.

The vitamins added to test feed No. 1 are identical to those found in fresh beef liver at approximately twice the level (Wolf, 1951) and described as "probably in most cases greatly in excess of the actual needs of trout and some are no doubt not necessary at all." The vitamins used in dry concentrate No. 6 contained twice the amounts of vitamins $B_{12}$, nicotinic acid, and ascorbic acid as used in feed No. 1, plus an antioxidant. The choline chloride was not premixed with other vitamins but added as a separate premix at the time of feed manufacture. Table VII shows the composition of vitamin mixtures used in Cortland dry pelleted feed Nos. 1 and 6.

Improved results with pellet No. 6 are ascribed to vitamin stability, particularly effective during the first few months in preventing "blue-slime" and possibly sunburn disease which had appeared previously (Phillips et al., 1963). Current specifications for trout feeds purchased by federal hatcheries in Region 2 include this special technique for preparing the vitamin mixtures (see Table III, Appendix).

TABLE VII

Vitamins Added per 1000 Pounds Pelleted Dry Concentrate Pellet No. 1[a,b]

| Ingredient | Amount[c] (gm) |
|---|---|
| Thiamin hydrochloride | 10.00 |
| Riboflavin | 33.00 |
| Pyridoxine hydrochloride | 10.00 |
| Choline hydrochloride | 1,500.00 |
| p-Aminobenzoic acid | 70.00 |
| Pantothenic acid | 55.00 |
| Nicotinic acid | 150.00 |
| Inositol | 250.00 |
| Biotin | 2.00 |
| α-Tocopherol | 75.00 |
| Ascorbic acid | 170.00 |
| 2-Methylnaphthoquinone | 10.00 |
| Folic acid | 2.80 |
| Cobalamin | 0.02 |
| Dried skim milk as carrier[c] | 10 |

[a] From Phillips *et al.*, 1963.

[b] Subsequent vitamin mixtures contained an antioxidant.

[c] All ingredients in gram values except for dried skim milk which is given in pounds.

TABLE VIII

Summary of Results from Feeding Pelleted Dry Feeds Nos. 1 and 6 to Brown Trout over an 18-Month Period

| Biological data | Pellet no. 1 | Pellet no. 6 |
|---|---|---|
| Initial weight ($W_o$) | 11 | 9 |
| Final weight ($W_n$) | 339 | 320 |
| Feed conversion | 1.76 | 1.56 |
| Calories/lb gain[a] | 2206 | 1841 |
| Grams protein/lb gain | 343 | 308 |

[a] Evaluation of energy as determined by Phillips *et al.* (1958): 3.9 cal/gm for protein, 8.0 cal/gm of fat, and 1.6 cal/gm of carbohydrate.

Fingerling trout fed pellet Nos. 1 and 6 were stocked at an average weight of 10 gm in raceways supplied with water at a temperature corresponding with the season. The growth constant calculated for two 180-day growing seasons was 1.0%. These fish continued on the same feed (although not on test) for another 3 months and spawned in November as 4-year brood stock. Survival of eyed eggs was 88.0%, with a resulting hatchability of 85.9%, comparable to fish fed routine hatchery "meat–meal" diet mixtures. Biological data associated with pellet Nos. 1 and 6 are shown in Table VIII.

The dry form of feed has almost completely replaced the wet and meat–meal formulas popular during the 1950's. Current research on formulation is focused on reducing cost via utilizing vitamins present in natural ingredients, thereby requiring lower levels in the added premix (See Appendix Table III ).

## 2. Warm-Water Fish Feeds

For years pond fish culturists have taken advantage of the natural biomass present in still waters and produced in abundance during warm weather. Early feeds for catfish, sunfish, buffalo, carp, and other species which accept artificial rations were supplemental to natural food harvested in the water. A typical pond fish feed recommended for intensive culture of catfish and minnows is the Auburn No. 2 (Swingle, 1958; Prather, 1958) containing the following ingredients: 35% soybean meal, 35% peanut meal, 15% fish meal, and 15% distillers solubles.

The Auburn No. 2 ration was fed as a meal to small fish and as a pellet to larger fish. Prather found that for fathead minnows weighing 1.75 pounds per thousand (approximately 1 inch long) the Auburn No. 2 pellet $\frac{3}{16}$-inch diameter produced significantly better growth with better conversion than the same formula produced either as a meal or a crumble or a complete trout pellet $\frac{1}{16}$-inch diameter. Total annual yield for channel catfish fed the Auburn No. 2 feed has been reported at over 3500 pounds per acre (Swingle, 1962). This was under conditions of heavy population density and heavy pond fertilization. The fish remained small and adapted to harvesting food organisms (copepods, chironomids) abundant in cyclic blooms throughout the season.

Although warm-water fish grow well on incomplete supplemental feeds, they grow better when fed a complete ration. Fish stocked at high population densities in a restricted area soon reach the carrying capacity (production limit). The nutrient most needed for weight gain is protein. Natural foods contain adequate amounts of vitamins and minerals to balance their caloric content, but when these become diluted by over-harvesting or are reduced by poor water fertility, it is economical to fortify added feeds for warm-water fish, as is done for trout in raceways. During the growing season fish become increasingly acclimated to routine feeding and, as a result, are sluggish in competing or searching for natural foods. Therefore, for warm-water fish culture where yields of 2000 pounds per acre and more are expected during a growing season, a complete feed is recommended. A tentative federal specification for pond fish feed is shown in Table IV in the Appendix.

Nutrient requirements for the production of domestic farm animals have been met by formula feeds. Elaborate restrictions have been worked out for amino acid levels, protein to calorie relationships, utilization coefficients, and animal response to ingredients which may be used in compounding least-cost formulas from materials commonly inventoried by feed mills. The complexity of applying these values to fish feeds is shown in the following sections.

## IV. Evaluation of Nutrients

### A. Chemical Evaluation

Although profitable animal production is implied in the sales program of a formula feed manufacturer, the only numerical guide to feed quality is found in the registration and labeling requirements of various state feed control agencies. Currently the label must guarantee nutrient classes in terms of "minimum percentage of crude protein (nitrogen $\times$ 6.25), minimum percentage of crude fat (ether extract), and maximum percentage of crude fiber." Values for ash, moisture and nitrogen-free extract (NFE) may be added. Feed control officials discourage the declaration of NFE because it is not measured by direct chemical analysis but by the difference between 100 and the sum of crude protein, crude fat, crude fiber, ash, and moisture. It represents the carbohydrate in a feed or an ingredient not classified as "crude fiber" and implies digestibility, whereas it may include nonnutrient components.

A computer searching for a "least-cost" formula at changing market prices of ingredients, using tag guarantees as restrictions, might easily go astray and develop a feed which would be unproductive. Feeds compounded solely on the basis of crude protein, fat, and fiber guarantees are no more than recipes which require further evaluation by chemical, biochemical, and subsequent biological testing.

Various tables of feed ingredient composition are used as guidelines in evaluating materials used in compounding formula feeds and in estimating performance. Publication No. 449 of the National Academy of Science (1956) lists the composition of concentrate by-product feedingstuffs in terms of fifty-eight chemicals and compounds, forty-five being specific nutrients and thirteen nutrient classes or organic constituents which relate to livestock and poultry production. These and similar tables of ingredient composition are used by many nutritionists in calculating formulas to comply with animal requirements not shown by tag guarantees.

The nutrient class which reflects most accurately the value of a feed is crude protein. A qualitative evaluation of proteins may be found from their amino acid constituents; those not biosynthesized are required in the feed at minimal levels. The first serious attempt to rate protein concentrates chemically in terms of their amino acid composition was proposed by Mitchell and Block (1946). An evaluation called the "chemical score" was found by comparing the essential amino acids in a single protein or in a mixed feed with those of whole egg protein, the "score" being defined as "100 minus the greatest percentage of deficit."

An extension of the chemical score is the "essential amino acid index" (EAA) developed by Oser (1951) and Mitchell (1954) which grades a protein on the basis of the relative quantities of all the essential amino acids, again using whole egg protein as a standard. The EAA shows greater correlation with the biological value of formula feeds than does the chemical score (Block and Weiss, 1956).

The chemical score as EAA of several feeds and feed ingredients as determined by Shanks (1964, personal communication) are shown in Table V in the Appendix. Although the correlation of chemical score, or EAA Index, with biological tests for fish has not been established, as it has for rats and chicks, the values in Table V may be useful in "arm chair" feed formulation.

Individual or total amino acids determined chemically on acid hydrolyzates of a product may be useful in detecting adulteration of raw material, but fail to measure the animal's ability to handle a product. The ability of digestive enzymes to release amino acids from protein is more accurately assayed by microbiological methods using enzymatic hydrolyzates (March *et al.*, 1949) or by assays with a proteolytic organism (Ford, 1962). These, however, have been classified under the heading "microbiological evaluations" and have not been sufficiently associated with biological tests with fish for general acceptance.

A chemical test which proves sensitive to processing and storage damage has been developed by Carpenter (1960). This is called the "available lysine test" and is based on the detection of the $\epsilon$-amino group of lysine by reaction with fluorodinitrobenzene (FDNB) to give a dinitrophenyl

(DNP) compound, measured colorimetrically as an ether-soluble dye. Fish meal and meat by-product meals have shown good correlation of this test with biological values measured as "net protein utilization" (Carpenter, 1963).

## B. BIOCHEMICAL EVALUATION

Attempts to improve on the obvious deficiencies of chemical tests for protein evaluation have been made for years. An *in vitro* method of evaluating animal protein concentrates using pepsin hydrolysis has been accepted by the Association of Official Agricultural Chemists (A.O.A.C.). This method, published in the A.O.A.C. Methods of Analysis (1960) was described by Almquist *et al.* (1935) and modified by Gehrt *et al.* (1957). Correlation of pepsin digestion values, available lysine, and biological tests on chicks was done for fish meals subjected to controlled conditions of heat damage (Meade and Altherr, 1966). Meade concludes, "Although we are inclined to accept the biological data as the more reliable, it is obvious that any of the methods will enable one to distinguish between good and bad meals."

## C. BIOLOGICAL EVALUATION OF FISH FOODS

In nature fish normally consume an array of food organisms which changes seasonally and with size or age (Keast, 1965, 1966; Keast and Webb, 1966). Such arrays appear to guarantee an adequate representation of the complex series of amino acids, vitamins, and other nutrients essential for normal growth, as well as a relatively standard supply of caloric energy per gram of intake (Golley, 1961; Slobodkin and Richman, 1961). Limitations on growth or of population production in nature seem, therefore, to result largely from restrictions in the total food supply. Slobodkin (1961) and Silliman (1968) have suggested, on the basis of experimental populations, that production, including growth and reproduction, of a culture of aquatic animals may be a rather simple function of total food supply, in some cases almost directly proportional to it.

Growth and production in fish culture is in a very different situation than natural production. Here the experimenter or fish farm manager can usually supply his fish with all the food they can eat. The problem then becomes one of finding an acceptable ration, ensuring that it is converted to fish flesh as efficiently as possible, and feeding as much of it to a particular group of fish as is consistent with high growth production. It is generally recognized, however, that as food intakes are increased, the growth rate per food intake is reduced. Furthermore, large fish can consume considerably less per body weight than small fish. Increasing the production by increasing the amounts of food will therefore frequently be at some sacrifice to growth efficiency. Changes in environmental conditions will also affect food intakes and growth efficiencies. To these nutritional complexities must be added the problem of shifting prices of the food mixtures and of the products. The combination of factors makes the problem of determining the point of optimum yield for intensive fish culture an extremely complex one, of which too little is yet known to permit calculations of the type being developed for some farm animals (Combs and Nicholson, 1964). However, the results of recent fish culture research give reason for optimism that such procedures are not far in the future. Some of the findings indicate areas where additional experimental work is required before it is possible to evaluate the suitability of various food types and amounts for maximizing fish production.

### 1. *Measuring Indexes of Growth and Food Intake*

The value of fish foods for production can ultimately be measured only by comparing some index of growth of a particular stock with an index of the food consumed. Ideally the two indexes must be in directly comparable terms, of which the two most frequently considered are calories or proteins. Relative merits of these two are still debated (cf., Gerking, 1967; Mann, 1967), either or both of which may be appropriate to the understanding of particular problems. Ostapenya and Sergeev (1963) found that in a number of natural foods there is a simple and regular relationship between the protein, fat, and carbohydrate composition of many naturally occurring foods and their caloric content, enabling the investigator to interpret results of experiments using natural foods in many cases where equivalents are not determined. In other cases, especially involving artificial food mixes, considerable detail is required.

### 2. *Growth Indexes*

Caloric and protein equivalents of growth of fishes are seldom directly determined, often for the very good reason that these require sacrifice of the experimental subjects. The most frequently observed parameters of growth are thus gain in wet body weight, or the gain in length. With certain restrictions either one may provide satisfactory approximations to the ideal, and must be known in any case, since they are the measures directly relevant to evaluation of the culture or farming operation. However, Phillips *et al.* (1963) and others have shown that if rearing takes place over periods of months, there may be significant changes in the water content and percentage ash in the body. Checks of the relationship of such parameters to wet weight provide a basis for improved approximations of the energy and protein equivalents (Winberg, 1956).

Measures of wet body weight gain, or of length, may be satisfactory indexes of growth but the literature contains unfortunately frequent calculations of percentage weight gains which when inappropriately used, or which when reported without correspondingly accurate data on actual weights or weight gains during the observation periods render interpretations of the results impossible. For example, the ratio of weight gain to initial weight in a short period of time, termed the "specific growth rate," is frequently convenient for describing growth patterns, since successive measurements over periods of months show it to be a monotonically decreasing function of time or age (Krüger, 1965). To compare growth rates at two different sizes would thus require the reference standard of the body weights. This simple fact is so frequently misunderstood as to justify further elaboration. Thus, for example, calculation of percentage growth implies that growth in weight ($\Delta W$) is proportional to body weight ($W$), that is that $\Delta W = CW^n$, where $C$ is a constant and $n$ is also a constant with a value of 1.0. It can be shown that this would result in exponential growth, a high rate which is rarely attained even under the best experimental conditions. A closer approach to reality would be achieved by determining values for $n$ which would normally be less than 1.0. Where it can be shown that $n$ is constant, the ratio $\Delta W / W^n = C$ would then provide comparison of growths. However, since $n$ changes almost continuously with growth, values of $C$ will vary depending on the size $W$. Thus any comparison of percentage growths requires exact knowledge of position on the growth curve. Percentage values without such corresponding weight measures cannot be interpreted.

A similarly unfortunate misuse of ratios and percentages occurs in the reporting of length and weight data, either in attempts to convert from length to equivalent weight measures, or in calculating the "condition factor." Brown (1946b) has illustrated the utility of the condition factor in studies of physiological growth rhythms, and, in a later paper (1957), briefly discusses its value as an index of fatness or body shape. In general, since length ($L$) is a linear or one-dimensional measure, and weight ($W$) is a volume or three-dimensional measure, the relationship between them is expected to be of the form $W = CL^n$, where $n = 3.0$ and $C$ is a constant, the value of which will be directly proportional to the "plumpness" of the animal. If, during growth, the shape of the animal normally changes slightly the value of $n$ will not be 3.0 but will still be constant over a wide range of sizes. Martin (1967, personal communication) and others have demonstrated that the value may well depend on feeding conditions at critical development periods, and for different habitats or species may take a stable value between 2.5 and 4.0. It is clear here, as an analogy to the discussion of percentage weights above, that in a reporting of the ratio $W/L^n = C$, the constant $C$ will be of considerable value where $n$ is correctly estimated. Where $n$ is incorrectly assumed to be 3.0 but is not, the estimate of $C$ differs from its true value depending on the absolute value of the length. Such errors are especially unfortunate where values of $W$ and $L$ are available over a sufficiently wide range to permit the validity of the estimate of $n$ to be checked by simple fittings of the logarithmic linear relationship: $\log W = \log C + n \log L$.

### 3. Measuring Food Intake

Measuring and reporting of food intakes of fish requires considerable skill, and poses particular problems in experimental work or in fish culture. In most pond culture or fish farming, feeds are administered at a rate proportional to the weight or size of the fish. If the initial percentage rate is low, a constant percentage may be maintained for long periods. However, experience has shown that constant percentage rates sooner or later exceed the appetite of the fish and lower percentage rates are required to prevent food wastage. Special care is required in order not to exceed such values in experimental work. Furthermore, it is known that appetites of individual fish vary in a rather regular rhythm which may sometimes be in phase for smaller groups (Brown, 1946b). Failure to take such changes into account may lead to food accumulations in particular periods which may be consumed later, giving rise to inexplicable changes in growth response. Tables of percentage rates of food administration such as published by Haskell (1955) are convenient guides in many situations. Interpretation of the results of experiments using them requires frequent observation and reporting of body weights of the fish involved.

The majority of modern foods are handled in "dry" conditions, but contain varying amounts of moisture and crude fiber or other indigestible bulk. Actual dry weights, caloric contents, protein sources, and vitamins, all of which may affect growth in complex fashion, require careful determination and reporting. Assessment of the digestibility of foods requires special experimental consideration and is discussed in more detail below.

### 4. Indexes of Food Utilization

Given reliably determined and appropriately reported measures of growth and food, indexes of food utilization for growth are generally derived as simple ratios. Two such ratios are commonly employed. The

first, familiar in hatchery and fish farm work, is generally in the form food
consumed per unit time/growth per unit time and is termed variously the
"food conversion factor," "absolute food quotient," "nutrient quotient,"
and other names. In what follows we shall use the readily understood term
"conversion factor." High values indicate that large amounts of food are
required to produce a unit of growth, and low values that a relatively small
amount is required. Ideally the measures of food and growth must be in
equivalent terms such as calories, protein, or at least dry weights. Since a
certain amount of food energy, generally one-half or more, is required to
support metabolic processes, the values of the conversion factor expressed in
these terms will rarely be less than 2.0 and values of 1.0 or less are a theoretical absurdity. In practice it has become almost convention to express
the foods in "dry" weights, and fish gains in wet body weight, in which case
a wide variety of values may appear. While such values may be useful
comparative "rules of thumb" in particular experiments, these may also
indicate lack of care in measurements and are of doubtful value in reporting
results unless exact equivalents are also determined and reported (Fig. 1).
Regrettably this has not been standard practice in the literature.

The second ratio used is simply the inverse of the first, i.e., growth per
unit time/food consumed per unit time. Again various terms are used to
describe it, such as "gross food utilization coefficient" or "energy coefficient
of growth." We shall term it simply the "gross growth efficiency." The
ratio calculated in this form is generally employed in reporting experimental
work since high values indicate a high proportion of food energy utilized
for growth and vice versa. As with the conversion coefficient, the units of
measure may be ordered to suit the purposes of an investigation, caloric or
protein equivalents being again the most useful. The results are, however,
commonly given in terms of dry or wet weights. Since up to one-half the
food energy intake is likely to be used for metabolic activities, values of the
gross growth efficiency greater than 0.50 are high and values of 1.0 or
greater are absurdities usually indicating faulty techniques. Values approaching 0.9 or greater are sometimes reported in the literature without
explanation and are sufficiently suspect to make any conclusions drawn
from them of questionable reliability (Winberg, 1956; Paloheimo and
Dickie, 1966a).

Depending on the use to be made of it, there are a number of forms of
either the conversion factor or growth efficiency expressions. It is believed,
for example, that a certain proportion of the energy of any ration ingested
is passed out in the feces or excreted in the urine without apparently
performing useful energetic work in the fish. It has therefore often been
suggested that a correction factor should be introduced to convert from

"ingested" to "digestible" rations. Other arguments are advanced for factors correcting "ingested" to "assimilated," or, in extreme cases, it has been suggested that corrections be introduced for the fraction of the food intake which is required under defined conditions to support the metabolic activity of the animal without growth (Pentelow, 1939; Brown, 1957; Swingle, 1958; Ivlev, 1966). The practical and theoretical difficulties inherent in definition and determination of this latter "corrected" efficiency—often referred to as "net growth efficiency"—are discussed by Brown (1957) and Paloheimo and Dickie (1966b).

Winberg (1956) reviewed the usage of growth efficiency correction factors by various earlier authors and concluded that a correction factor of the order of 0.8 was useful approximation for conversion from the energy equivalent of gross food ingested to an "assimilated" or "physiologically useful" ration (Brody, 1945). His correction term was accepted as a useful approximation by Ivlev (1960) and its use was supported by Paloheimo and Dickie (1966a) provided the true value was not much lower than this. A number of workers have determined appropriate values for a number of fish and feeding situations (Gerking, 1952; Davis and Warren, 1965) and have obtained rather stable values generally above 0.8. Results obtained by Davies (1964) suggest that caution must be exercised at low feeding levels, although he did not often encounter values lower than about 0.7. Growth efficiency may therefore, following Winberg (1956), be expressed as either

$$\frac{\Delta W}{R\Delta t} = K_1 \qquad \text{or} \qquad \frac{\Delta W}{pR\Delta t} = K_2 \tag{1}$$

where $\Delta W/\Delta t$ is growth per unit time, $R$ is the ingested ration during the time, and $p$ is the factor correcting from "ingested" to "physiologically useful" rations. While there are obvious theoretical reasons for preferring $K_2$ if there is sufficient experimental information to justify it, observational data are generally in the form of $K_1$ and in many cases it is a close enough approximation for interpretation of experimental results. Values of $K_2$ are, of course, higher than $K_1$, the equivalent forms being simply $pK_2 = K_1$.

Much experimental work is still devoted to the determination of an "assimilation" coefficient "$p$." There is need for reassurance in individual experiments that its value is of the order of 0.8 or greater and does not change remarkably with changes in feeding level, size or age of the fish, or with the type of food in particular experiments; checks are thus desirable. In general, however, the changes in $p$ which have been detected are small and of relatively little consequence to the study of food–growth relationships or for the development of optimum feeding systems. In our opinion other facets of the food–growth problem are of greater theoretical as well as practical importance.

### 5. *General Relationships between Food and Growth*

As was pointed out earlier, the problem of evaluating foods for growth requires knowledge of two basic biological processes. First, we need to know what it is that controls the total food intake, that is, the ration or appetite. Second, we need to know what determines the degree of utilization of this ration for growth. As was also suggested earlier, study of these two basic processes is not simple, partly because of the variety of factors which may be involved and the complexity of effects, and partly because these are interdependent rather than independent processes. The problem is actually a special case of study of the basic energy equation, which may be expressed in the form

Energy input = energy expenditure + energy accumulation

This truism has been recognized as a convenient starting point in food–growth studies for many years and has been applied in a more or less simple form to the study of production in populations or individuals (Lindeman, 1942; Ivlev, 1966; Patten, 1959; von Bertalanffy, 1964; Slobodkin, 1961; McLaren, 1963; Smith, 1963). The importance of equating the terms to clearly defined and measurable experimental variables seems to have been recognized most clearly by Winberg (1956) who proposed writing it in the form

$$pR = T + \Delta W/\Delta t \tag{2}$$

where $pR$ is again the physiologically useful ration, $T$ is the total metabolic expenditure, and $\Delta W$ the growth, all expressed in equivalent energy terms and all measured over the time interval, $\Delta t$. Winberg's extensive review gave adequate assurance that the variables so defined can be experimentally verified within experimental error limits that are sufficiently precise for deriving food–growth relationships. In this form, the problem of understanding food–growth relationships becomes one of studying the relationships of $pR$, $T$, and $\Delta W/\Delta t$ to each other and to an index of fish weight, $W$, under different environmental conditions. More specifically we wish to know what factors affect $R$, the food ration, and $(\Delta W)/(R\Delta t)$, the growth efficiency, and their interdependence through the basic energy equation. Recent reviews by Winberg (1956) and by Paloheimo and Dickie (1965, 1966a, b) are germane to this discussion.

### 6. *Food Intake*

Starting with the basic energy equation written as Eq. (2) Winberg (1956, 1961) demonstrated that an index of "routine" metabolism derived from the data of food–growth experiments as

$$T = pR - \Delta W/\Delta t \qquad (2a)$$

was essentially the same as has been well established in studies of oxygen consumption under rather similar experimental conditions. Specifically, he concluded that when this index of $T$ was plotted against body weight $W$, in the equation

$$T = \alpha W^\gamma \qquad (3)$$

or in logarithmic form

$$\log T = \log \alpha + \gamma \log W$$

which we will refer to in what follows as the $T$ line, the estimate of the slope of the log line, $\gamma$, was the same as has been found in oxygen consumption experiments under "standard" conditions (Beamish and Mookherjii, 1964), while the value for the intercept or level of metabolism, $\alpha$, was only slightly above the standard value for the same species. This agreement between results of respiration experiments which are generally run for periods of a few hours at most, and the results of laboratory feeding experiments which are generally maintained over periods of weeks or months gave needed assurance that both estimates were in fact reflecting features of the long-term energy budget. Winberg concluded from his food–growth studies that under normal nonstress living conditions in nature, a value of $\gamma$ of about 0.8 may be used to describe the relationship between metabolism and body weight in most fish species, and that the value of $\alpha$ is likely to be of the order of twice the "standard" value.

Paloheimo and Dickie (1966a) examined food–growth data published by a number of authors. In addition to verifying Winberg's conclusions respecting values of $\gamma$, they found that where fish were fed a maintenance ration, so that in the long-term they neither lost nor gained weight, the level of metabolism $\alpha$ was only slightly above the standard. By contrast, it appeared that when fish were fed *ad libitum*, the value of $\gamma$ appeared to remain unaffected but the value of $\alpha$ was raised by a factor of four or five times. In the few species where data were available, this level of $\alpha$ was, within experimental error, equivalent to the value characterizing "active" metabolism, defined by Fry (1957) and his associates as the level of metabolism exhibited by fish stimulated to their maximum sustained level of activity. Paloheimo and Dickie also concluded that if feeding opportunities for different sizes of fish were the same, but less than *ad libitum* feeding, intermediate values of $\alpha$ would be obtained. From such data they concluded that under constant ambient conditions, the level of food intake by fishes is reflected in the total metabolism through its effect on the level of metabolism $\alpha$. It was further noted, however, that the food–metabolism body-weight relationship was not one of simple proportionality. For example, feeding trout a constant proportion of body weight led to an apparently progressive rise in $\alpha$ with growth until the active level of metabolism was reached. The change in level reflected the ability of fishes to acclimate intake to feeding opportunities. At the point of active metabolism it appeared that the rate of food administration equalled the maximum ability of fish to consume it. Continued "feeding" in proportion to body weight led to accumulation of unused food in the tank. Determination of the level of food administration which would maintain fish at active or any other level of metabolism, requires knowledge of the relation of $pR$ and $T$ to the remaining term of the energy equation $\Delta W/\Delta t$.

## 7. Growth Efficiency

It has long been recognized among warm-blooded animals that increases in the ration lead to a decrease in the efficiency of production processes, an observation which has been well substantiated for brown trout by Brown (1946b, 1957). Kleiber (1947) appears to have been the first to suggest that this change in efficiency is independent of the body weight of the animal, although the frequent practice of comparing growth efficiency to rations expressed as a percentage of body weight, implies that many authors disagree with his hypothesis. Using the same data on which their metabolic study was based, Paloheimo and Dickie (1966b) reexamined the growth efficiency relationships. Their results led them to support Kleiber's generalization. That is, their analysis showed that when a food–growth experiment is carried out for a long period of time at one level of feeding, the ration and body weight are highly correlated, and there is a strong simple negative correlation between the logarithm of the gross growth efficiency and both rations and body weight. In such experiments the range of body weights is generally greater than the range of rations. A multiple correlation analysis then indicates that body weight is the better predictor of the efficiency change. However, where experiments are performed under different conditions, leading to different metabolic levels and food intakes, so that the correlation between ration and body weight is low, the multiple correlations indicate that the relationship between the logarithm of the growth efficiency and rations remained strong, but the relationship to body weight became insignificant. The relation between growth efficiency and amount of ration therefore appears to reflect some basic biological mechanism, the relation with body weight being incidental to the fact that body weight will often be correlated with the amount of ration.

From the data available, Paloheimo and Dickie (1966b) concluded that for a particular type of food the changes in the logarithm of the gross growth efficiency could be expressed as a simple linear function of the amount of rations. This relationship could be satisfactorily described by the equation

$$\log K_1 = \log \frac{\Delta W}{R\Delta t} = -a - bR$$

whence

$$\frac{\Delta W}{R\Delta t} = e^{-a-bR} \tag{4}$$

or

$$\frac{\Delta W}{\Delta t} = Re^{-a-bR}$$

That is, beginning at some low (not zero) level of rations, $R$, the growth efficiency, appears to approach a maximum defined by the term $e^{-a}$, and for each unit increase in ration decreases by a constant fraction defined by $e^{-b}$. There are practical limitations to the range of rations over which Eq. (4) applies for a given size of fish. Paloheimo and Dickie (1966b) concluded, however, that Eq. (4) which they termed the K line, describes the relationship between growth efficiency and food intake levels so long as the food intake maintained the fish within the normal biokinetic range. This range may be defined as metabolism lying within a lower limit exceeding the "maintenance level," and an upper limit which is the active metabolic level. That is the K line appeared to describe food–growth relations within what Fry (1957) termed the normal "scope for activity."

## 8. Food–Growth Equation

Some of the limitations of the T and K line equations for describing metabolic and growth efficiency relations have been pointed out in papers cited above and are further discussed by Beamish and Dickie (1967). In fact, while these are derived empirically from a number of experiments carefully conducted and reported in the literature, they are based on relatively few data, and, in some cases, the experiments were not specifically designed to offer information on the relationships. The K line, in particular, may have limited applications for interpreting events in nature where there are periodic or chronic shortages of food, leading to conditions of near starvation. In such situations a different functional form of the relationships may eventually prove to be more useful. Whatever the functional form finally adopted, however, the relationships so derived are a convenient vehicle for discussing food–growth relations and may, in any case, have direct utility in evaluating various feeds in fish culture work where limitations on the amount of food are not a problem.

Following Paloheimo and Dickie (1965) we may use these relationships to construct curves of growth of fishes in terms of rations. That is, from the energy equation we may write

$$pR = T + \Delta W/\Delta t \tag{2}$$

but from the K line we have

$$\frac{\Delta W}{\Delta t} = Re^{-a-bR} \tag{4}$$

whereas by substituting in (2)

$$T = \alpha W^{\gamma} = R(1 - e^{-a-bR}) \tag{5}$$

Once appropriate values of the parameters $\alpha$, $\gamma$, $a$, and $b$ are known for a particular food and fish, we can calculate from Eq. (5) the amount of food which will maintain a fish of size $W$ at a given level of metabolism $\alpha$. On this ration per unit time, Eq. (4) predicts the growth $\Delta W/\Delta t$, which then in turn may be used to arrive at a new body weight $W$ for a second calculation of ration $R$ in Eq. (5). In practice to determine the appropriate rations $R$ when the constants $a$ and $b$ are known, one would graph $R$ against $W$ using the relationship given in Eq. (5) at any desired level of $a$. This would eliminate the need to solve $R$ from Eq. (5) for given values of $W$, a procedure which can be done only numerically.

It should be noted here that in these equations we are using the gross ration, $R$, rather than the assimilated ration $pR$. However, since the original K line is in logarithmic form it is clear that since $pK_2 = K_1$, $\log K_1$ differs from $\log K_2$ only by the constant $\log p$, i.e., $\log K_2 + \log p = \log K_1$. That is, as long as $p$ does not change with $R$, the two K lines are parallel, differing only by the constant $\log p$ which may be absorbed in the value of $a$.

### 9. *Body Size, Food, and Growth on Different Rations*

If Eqs. (4) and (5) can be used to describe the growth of fishes over significant periods of their life, these may be used directly to predict the ration required to sustain a given growth rate, or to rear fishes to a given size in a particular length of time. Such information is basic to evaluation of various foods for production. The applicability of the equations and calculations depends upon two fundamental assumptions which can be verified experimentally. The first is that in a stable environment, a constant opportunity for feeding will give rise to a fixed level of metabolism, $\alpha$, in Eq. (5). The amount actually eaten will be different for different fish sizes, but from Eq. (5) will approach proportionality to $W^\gamma$, at higher rates of total intake. The second assumption is that with constant environmental conditions and a given type of food, the decrease in growth efficiency with increasing $R$ can be described over a significant range of body weights and rations by a single value of "$b$" in Eq. (4), which is not directly dependent on the body weight $W$. In the next section we discuss factors which seem likely to influence values of the parameters of the T and K lines, hence, the use of the equations in evaluating foods for fish culture. In the remainder of this section we briefly review calculated examples which illustrate the effects of changes in metabolism, growth efficiency, and food on growth curves.

Figure 1 shows a set of T lines, such as would describe the metabolic level of brook trout of different sizes held at a constant temperature and presented with different feeding opportunities. It is based on calculations reported by Paloheimo and Dickie (1965). The lower line with a value of

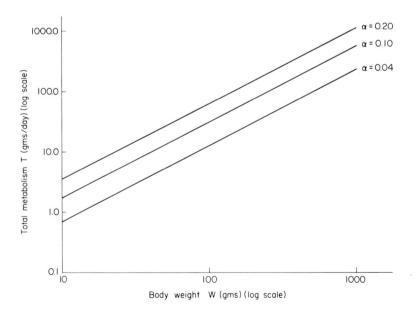

Fig. 2. The relationship of total metabolism per fish to body weight at various levels of feeding. (See also text.)

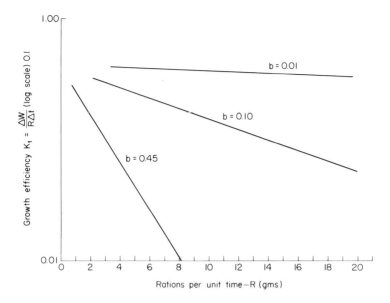

Fɪɢ. 3. Curves of growth efficiency in relationship to various types of ration.

$\alpha = 0.04$ corresponds with that characterizing a near maintenance ration. The upper line, with $\alpha = 0.20$ corresponds with an *ad libitum* or maximum feeding rate. An intermediate level of $\alpha = 0.10$ is also shown. In Fig. 2 are shown typical K lines for growth of brook trout fed on various diets. The steepest curve, $b = 0.45$, is close to that found for brook trout fed on a hatchery mash, as described by the Cortland Hatchery reports (Tunison *et al.*, 1939; Phillips *et al.*, 1940). The intermediate line, $b = 0.10$ is close to that exhibited by Surber's (1935) brook trout fed on live *Gammarus*. The remaining line, $b = 0.01$ is close to that shown by Baldwin's (1956) brook trout fed on live minnows.

Paloheimo and Dickie (1965) presented a series of growth curves scaled in terms of the parameters $\alpha$ and $b$ of the T lines and K lines. They also presented various scaling factors which may be used to construct curves of actual growth and rations, once appropriate values of $\alpha$ and $b$ are known. We have used these scaling factors together with parameter values given in Figs. 2 and 3 to construct curves of growth in weight ($W$) against time ($t$) in units of grams and days. The results are displayed in Figs. 4A, B, and C. The relationships have also been used to calculate the accumulated rations ($\Sigma R$) required to grow fish up to size $W$ in the time given. Values are shown on the growth curves. Several important features emerge. A comparison of the three panels for various values of $b$, shows that as the

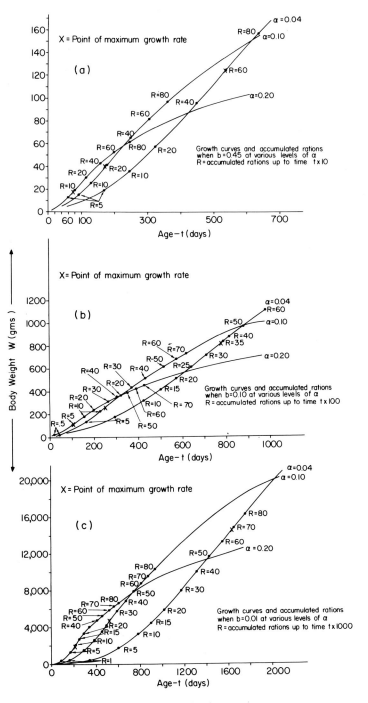

FIG. 4 (a–c).

K line slope decreases ($b$ becomes smaller), the growth rate increases markedly and the amount of accumulated ration required to reach a given size very rapidly becomes less. Panel A shows, furthermore, that the value of $\alpha$ affects the shape of the growth curve, hence the use of food for growth. In particular, a high metabolic level $\alpha = 0.20$, due to high rations intake, leads to a high initial growth rate. This soon falls off, however, leading to smaller sizes at higher food consumptions. This effect is reminiscent of observations in nature that the individuals or groups of a species which are faster growing when young tend to reach smaller average adult sizes. Growth curves resulting from all values of $b$ have similar patterns although with decreasing $b$ the points of intersection, hence the falling off of the faster growth rates at high levels of $\alpha$ will be at greater and greater body weights and ages. The graphs are based on data for brook trout. Panel C indicates that at the highest growth efficiency ($b = 0.01$) and lowest metabolic level ($\alpha = 0.04$) maximum growth rate occurs at a point beyond the usual size and age range of this species.

These relationships are set out in Fig. 5 in a form which is more directly appropriate to problems of fish culture. In this figure we show the logarithm of the ratio of body size ($W$) to the product of the accumulated rations ($\Sigma R$) and the age of the fish in days ($t$), plotted as a function of the accumulated ration up to that age. That is, we have plotted a kind of average growth efficiency curve for individual fish up to various ages. The results suggest a need for careful reconsideration of various feeding schedules and food types. For example, it is apparent from a comparison of panels A, B, and C in Fig. 4 that as $b$ decreases, the average efficiency of growth increases. Within each panel, however, the "crossing over" shown by the growth curves in Fig. 4 shows up in the efficiency curves as well, although at different points. Hence Fig. 4A shows that at $\alpha = 0.20$ size at age is higher than at $\alpha = 0.10$ up to an age of about 230 days, but that the accumulated rations are increasing rapidly. Figure 5A shows that the average growth efficiency at $\alpha = 0.20$ falls below that at $\alpha = 0.10$ by the time the accumulated ration reaches about 400 gm of food, which from Fig. 4A is at an age of about 160 days. Similar calculations can be made for other feeding levels by comparisons of the curves.

Interpretations of the practical consequences of these largely theoretical

---

Fig. 4. (a) Growth curves and accumulated rations when $b = 0.45$ at various levels of $\alpha$. $R$ = accumulated rations up to time $t$. (b) Growth curves and rations when $b = 0.10$ is at various levels of $\alpha$. $R$ = accumulated rations up to time $t$. (c) Growth curves and accumulated rations when $b = 0.01$ at various levels of $\alpha$. $R$ = accumulated rations up to time $t$. (X, point of maximum growth rate.)

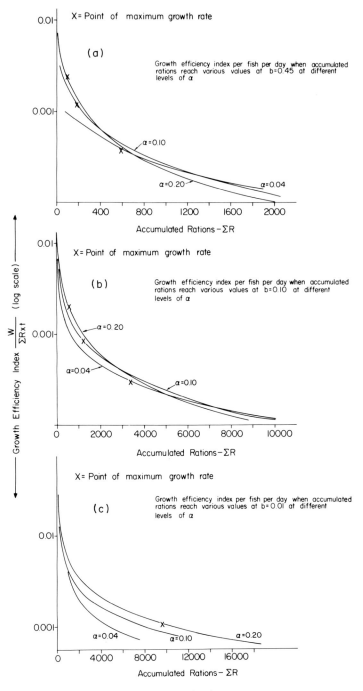

FIG. 5 (a–c).

calculations depend on further experimental observations designed to test them. There is little doubt that fish are capable of consuming the amounts of rations shown by some of the curves. Other parts of the curves may be outside the normal range of sizes and foods. In nature, for example, there are indications that fish normally change their diets to a different type of food, corresponding with a lower value of $b$, at about the time they reach maximum growth on that ration—the points marked X on the curves. Whether fish culture practice ordinarily achieves this is not known. We suggested above, however, that the hatchery practice of feeding a particular type of food in proportion to body weight leads to increasing levels of $\alpha$. The curves suggest that if the initial feeding rates so established result in initially low levels of $\alpha$, this system of increasing $\alpha$ with growth may result in considerable wastage of overall production efficiency. To what extent this potential effect is overcome by changes in food pellet size, which, as indicated below, may decrease $b$, is not known.

Any further discussion and speculation about the relationships revealed by these curves is out of place here. The data are at best suggestive of experiments which may lead to an increased understanding of factors which influence growth, and, hence, evaluation of foods for growth.

### 10. *Factors Influencing the Use of Food for Growth*

The foregoing discussion of the use of parameters of metabolic and growth efficiency relations for describing growth, indicates that the study of factors affecting growth, hence evaluation of foods, might best be accomplished by a study of effects of various foods on these parameters rather than on the amount of growth directly. The growth relations as described above, indicate moreover that it may be possible to categorize those factors in a comprehensible fashion. For example, the maximum sustained metabolic level was apparently characteristic of *ad libitum* feeding, even though the resulting growth pattern depended on levels of both $\alpha$ and $b$. In a sense it appears that for a given type of ration the level of $\alpha$ reflects the abundance of the food. The parameter $b$ may then be a reflection of the rewards in food intake for a given energy expenditure by the fish.

The meaning of the parameter $b$ is, however, not easily determined. For

---

Fig. 5. (a) Average growth efficiency per fish when accumulated rations reach various values at $b = 0.45$ at different levels of $\alpha$. X, marks the point of maximum growth rate. (b) Average growth efficiency per fish when accumulated rations reach various values at $b = 0.10$ at different levels of $\alpha$. (C) Average growth efficiency when accumulated rations reach various values at $b = 0.01$ at different levels of $\alpha$.

example, Ivlev (1960) speculated that rearing and feeding trout in fast-flowing raceways may be a waste of energy which could potentially be used for growth. The work of Brockensen (1966), reported by Warren and Davis (1967) suggested, however, that this is not so; cutthroat trout (*Salmo clarki*) reared in a stream had a higher growth efficiency than trout reared in aquariums. Brockensen noted that in aquariums the fish performed frequent "spontaneous" movements, and while direct metabolic measurements were not made, the explanation for lower efficiency in the aquariums almost certainly lies in the relatively high energy expenditures of spontaneous movements demonstrated by a number of workers (Sullivan, 1954; Brett, 1964; Smit, 1965). Thus the growth efficiency curve itself reflects elements of the behavior pattern and accompanying energy or metabolic expenditure. These are a reflection of suitability of food, not in the sense of a simple digestive efficiency but rather in the sense that they provide a measurement of behavioral efficiency. In fact, the data available lead to the conclusion that growth efficiency as measured by the parameters of the K line may primarily reflect those behavioral reactions to food which are often considered under the concept of "grazing" efficiency. It may frequently be of great importance to distinguish between physiological and grazing efficiency effects in food evaluation studies.

Considerations of this sort indicate that to understand how particular factors affect growth requires careful attention to the experimental techniques, not only as they affect characterization and measurement of food type, food intake, growth, and respiration, but also with respect to the behavior patterns evoked by the feeding. For example, Brett (1965) found that maximum forced activity in a respiration chamber resulted in greater proportionate increases in $O_2$ consumption by large than by small salmon, hence the estimate of $\gamma$ at active metabolism was higher than at the standard metabolism. Job (1955), Beamish (1964a), and others have suggested possibly similar effects of temperature. No such effect on $\gamma$ was detected by Paloheimo and Dickie (1966a) in relation to feeding. In the face of such apparent contradictions, it is important to determine what types of behavioral and physiological mechanisms the different experiments have been designed to study.

Unfortunately, even in cases where accurate food and growth data are available and appropriate experimental designs have been used, the methods of analysis and reporting adopted have often tended to obscure the effects which were being tested. For example, Paloheimo and Dickie (1966b) concluded that growth efficiency is not directly determined by body size, but rather by the ration intake. Yet in many reports of experimental results it is customary to compare growth efficiency with rations expressed as a function of body weight, usually a percentage of the weights, since this is the manner in which the feeds were administered. Equation (5) suggests that at one level of availability, hence one level of metabolism $\alpha$, the relation between the ration consumed and body weight will be approximately $R = W^\gamma$. In such a case plotting growth efficiency against $R/W^\gamma$ would be equivalent to plotting it against a single value of $R$, thereby simply providing a measure of residual variability or "error" in the experiment. Plotting against $R/W^{1.0}$ will give a line sloping upward to the right, but with the slope primarily determined by the degree to which $W^{1.0}$ differs from $W^\gamma$, or the corrected full expression in Eq. (5). As has already been noted, such reporting makes interpretation impossible when actual body weights are not available, as is frequently the case during the course of the experiments. Even where several levels of rations have been administered, so that $R$ and $W$ are no longer directly related, reliance on the percentage of body weight plot would seem a dangerous procedure which may obscure important effects. For this reason it would seem preferable to adopt some such system as the K line suggested here, unless further work demonstrates that body size itself is likely to influence the relationships.

## 11. *General Effects of Food Type on Growth*

A number of food–growth experiments which have been reported in the literature were reviewed by Paloheimo and Dickie (1966a, b). The results suggested some features of various foods and feeding systems which may influence the parameters of the T and K lines.

In the first place, the conclusion that growth efficiency is independent of body weight implies that growth efficiency is not determined by a given degree of stomach filling, and therefore is not a simple result of a change in digestive efficiency due to changes in either the bulk or the caloric content of various diets. This was demonstrated by Hatanaka *et al.* (1956a, b) on the feeding of individual plaice. Each plaice was fed to satiation each day on chunks of different types of food. The food contained different amounts of calories per gram, but the results could nevertheless be described by a single K line when the data were plotted in terms of calories, although not when wet weights or bulk of food was used (Paloheimo and Dickie, 1966b). Hatanaka's results further show that there may be substantial differences in growth efficiency for different species fed on the same diet. The relative unimportance of the degree of stomach filling is also indicated by observations of Rozin and Mayer (1961) that goldfish adjusted their rate of feeding to a nearly constant caloric intake per day despite a twofold increase in the bulk ingested.

The failure to discover major effects of the degree of stomach filling on growth efficiency, led to our earlier statements that the slope of the K line did not seem to be determined to a major extent by simple digestive efficiency. Digestive efficiency may, however, be an important factor in determining the value of $p$ or the intercept of the K line, measured by $a$. Variations in $a$, while having a direct influence on calculated growth efficiency, do not appear to be greatly different among diets and even rather large changes would appear to have a minor influence on growth, relative to the effects of changes in $b$ or in the metabolic level $\alpha$ (Paloheimo and Dickie, 1965).

Paloheimo and Dickie (1966b) concluded that differences of the sort exhibited by the slopes of the K lines most likely reflected differences in the efficiency of grazing on different foods. Ivlev (1961) had earlier demonstrated that a change in the variance of the distribution of food in a tank was equally as important in determining feeding success as was a change in abundance. A greater variance, i.e., greater degree of clustering of food particles, led to improve food intake per unit time. This finding may provide an explanation for differences in growth and feeding of trout fed on hatchery mash, on live *Gammarus*, and on live minnows (Fig. 2). The data showed that in each case the fish were at or near the active metabolic level. That is, they must have been taking their maximum possible ration on the various diets. In this situation there was a wide range of actual intakes. Ratios on the hatchery mash were generally low and although there was a high initial growth efficiency, the slope of the K line was large. Intakes on the *Gammarus* were higher and overlapped the lower range of intakes on minnows, but with a K line of apparently intermediate slope. Feeding on minnows was at the highest rate with a slope close to 0. Since there seemed no reason to assign major differences in caloric content per gram or in digestibility to these various foods, Paloheimo and Dickie speculated that the difference reflected a special case of the Ivlev experiments in which the variance increase is represented by the increase in particle size. That is, increasing the particle size increased the food intake and reduced the slope of the K line because it improved grazing efficiency at various levels of food intake.

Particle size has been recognized as of practical importance in fish culture for many years. Empirical rules have been worked out for determining an appropriate schedule of pellet sizes of prepared food with fish growth. However, the authors know of no experiments which have been deliberately designed to measure and provide an explanation of the role which food particle size plays in either fish culture or nature. If it is of possible major importance in controlling growth efficiency, information on its effects would appear essential for interpretation of other experiments dealing with the chemical nutrient quality of the food with which the particle size effects are likely to interact. That is, effects of grazing and physiological efficiency should be separated. In the trout experiments reviewed above particle size was furthermore completely confounded with fish density which may itself have an influence on efficiency. The interpretations of the growth parameters given here are thus still open to question until the influence of the various factors can be measured separately. At this juncture in the state of the art of fish feeding we can only conclude that characteristics of physical distribution and availability for grazing may have an influence on food value for growth, which are as important as substantial changes in the chemical nutrient or bulk characteristics.

## 12. *Effects of Temperature on Food–Growth Relations*

It has been known for over 50 years that temperature has rather predictable effects on the level of low routine or resting metabolism. Winberg (1956) and Hemmingsen (1960) found that the so-called Krogh correction applied over a wide range of temperatures and species. One of the most important extensions from the point of view of the food-growth work, however, was the conclusion of Fry (1957) and his co-workers that temperature may have a different effect on the standard and the active metabolism. Fry termed the difference between active and standard metabolic levels the "scope" for activity, and found that it appeared to reach a maximum at temperatures intermediate between the extremes that a particular species encountered. This pattern of variation with temperature is strikingly similar to the pattern of response of fish appetites to temperature (Hathaway, 1927; Kinne, 1960, 1962). Whether or not there is a direct or causal relationship between them, the similarity is strong enough to suggest that it is not a result of simple chance, and points to the measure of scope as a potentially powerful tool for determining optimum feeding and growth conditions.

Brown (1957) expressed the view that temperature was not of direct importance to growth efficiency, except through its general influence on metabolic rates and corresponding appetite. Her contention was supported by the analyses of Paloheimo and Dickie (1966b) who found several cases in which food–growth relations at different temperatures could be described by a single K line. An exception was, however, reported in the work of Menzel (1960) indicating the effects may not be simple in all cases. Further evidence of complications appeared from the work of Kinne where Paloheimo and Dickie found that the growth efficiency data for 15° and 35°C fell outside the growth efficiency relation apparent at the intermediate temperatures. Evidence from the metabolic calculations suggested that at these temperature extremes, even though the fish were still operating within the general limits of standard and active metabolism, the normal metabolism–size relationships no longer held, suggesting that the fish were subject to some extra stress, especially at the higher temperatures. Further complications may also appear if the suggestions in the work of Job (1955) and Beamish (1964a) that the response of metabolism to temperature may differ with body weight, are found to be statistically significant. There are already clear indications that large fish lose their appetite at high temperatures more readily than do the smaller fish, an effect which may partly be due to the rate of acclimation to high temperatures but which undoubtedly involves size differences in temperature tolerance as well. Interactions of these metabolic effects of temperature with the growth efficiency are not known, but cannot be expected to be as simple as appears to be the case in the intermediate temperature range, where the influence on appetite seems to predominate.

## 13. *Effects of Food Quality on Growth*

Much of the experimental work on evaluating foods for growth has been concerned with variations in the chemical quality along much the same lines as have been pursued in research on husbandry of warm-blooded animals. Such work has verified the necessity for the presence of a large number of specific amino acids, vitamins, and minerals for normal growth. Detailed consideration is given in other chapters of this volume and does not require repetition here. However, the relationships among these constituents, and the bearing on general body growth, is complex and still not well understood. In some instances, there are significant interactions with food characteristics and environmental factors described above. We therefore review some of them briefly.

It is generally conceded that fish, as most other animals, exhibit a wide degree of homeostatic control of body condition under a variety of feeding conditions (Brown, 1946b). Gerking (1955), for example, studied the relations among composition of the food, fish flesh, and growth efficiency. He found that protein retention was increased steadily with increase in the protein content of the food. It is of no little importance, however, that when his data are calculated in terms of gross growth efficiency and rations in energy units the characteristic K line appeared (Paloheimo and Dickie, 1966b). The difference between the protein and gross energy calculations may be a result of the fact that the food used by Gerking had a lower protein per gram content than the fish flesh. The increased protein retention may therefore have reflected a greater demand for replacement during greater activity, but under nonequilibrium conditions, resulting in an actual diminution in the fish protein content. Such effects illustrate the remarkable homeostatic capacity of fishes to digest and utilize food of widely different compositions, so long as the requisite total energy is supplied to various metabolic sites and the body composition is not altered beyond certain limits. However, critical combinations of dietary constituents may be frequently encountered in prolonged feeding on artificial diets. For example, Brown (1951) found that on certain diets fish appeared to grow normally for considerable periods of time after which they rapidly developed pathological symptoms and died. The effect was reminiscent of an accumulation of toxic substances. Phillips *et al.* (1948) reported that above a "safe" level of digestible carbohydrate of about 9% wet weight (about 33% dry weight basis), fish livers became smaller, glossy, and pale in color. Liver damage may apparently be reduced by addition of vitamin supplement to a high carbohydrate diet (McLaren *et al.*, 1946), although DeLong, *et al.* (1958) found no signs of such damage in diets containing as high as 61% carbohydrate. They suggest that their results may have been due to adequate vitamins and a relatively high temperature, the combination being necessary to permit metabolism of the diet.

Excessively high protein levels have also been found deleterious especially to small fish. DeLong *et al.* found in temperatures of 47°F (8.3°C) growth rates of 2-gm chinook salmon were maximal for that temperature on 40% protein. Growth was less at both lower and higher protein levels. No such growth depression was noted at a higher temperature (58°F = 14.4°C) or among larger salmon (average weight about 6 gm). At all sizes and temperatures mortalities during the experiments were at a minimum at about the 40% protein level, although at the colder temperatures they were probably not significantly higher for larger fish up to the highest protein content tested (65%).

The data of DeLong *et al.* show further possible important interactions of size and temperature with diet. Thus at 25% protein an increase in temperature by 11°F (6.1°C) increased percentage growth of the smaller fish by about $2\frac{1}{2}$ times but increased the growth of the larger fish by nearly four times. At the highest protein content the same temperature change increased the percentage weight gain of the small trout by more than seven times, whereas the large fish growth was only about $2\frac{1}{2}$ times higher. Such differences in the growth response of large and small fish to different temperatures are reminiscent of the metabolic responses studied by Job (1955) and Fry (1957). The results of DeLong *et al.* are consistent with the general finding of greater ability of small fish to respond to high temperatures, but interaction with protein is involved.

TABLE IX

Data Showing the Interrelationship between Feed Conversion and Water Temperature for Several Levels of Protein in Test Diets for Channel Catfish[a]

| | Feed Conversion | |
| Percent protein | 76°F (24.4°C) | 69°F (20.6°C) |
|---|---|---|
| Casein | | |
| 11.7 | 2.2 | 2.8 |
| 17.1 | 1.6 | 1.7 |
| 22.5 | 1.1 | 1.3 |
| 28.3 | 0.9 | 1.1 |
| 33.6 | 0.9 | 1.1 |
| 39.0 | 0.9 | 1.0 |
| 50.4 | 0.8 | 1.3 |
| Wheat gluten | | |
| 11.3 | 1.8 | 2.6 |
| 16.1 | 1.7 | 2.9 |
| 21.1 | 1.4 | 2.9 |
| 26.1 | 1.2 | 2.6 |
| 30.2 | 1.1 | 4.3 |
| 34.6 | 1.0 | 4.3 |
| 43.5 | 2.1 | — |
| Soybean protein | | |
| 11.6 | 2.4 | 3.6 |
| 22.1 | 1.8 | 3.4 |
| 27.7 | 1.3 | 2.9 |
| 32.6 | 1.2 | 2.2 |
| 37.7 | 1.1 | 1.5 |
| 47.9 | 1.2 | 2.3 |
| | 1.6 | 2.7 |

[a] From Dupree and Sneed, 1966.

These interactions of feed composition and temperature are further illustrated by recent work of Dupree and Sneed (1966) on fingerling channel catfish. They tested various levels of three different protein sources at two temperatures. Their results, summarized in Table IX, are given in terms of food conversion coefficients, calculated as dry weight of diet per unit wet weight gain of the fish (thus, the apparently absurd values of less than 1.0 for food conversion). The table shows that increased casein and soybean sources of protein appeared to result in maximum growth per food intake at about the 40% protein level in both the higher and lower temperatures, with the higher temperatures showing generally improved efficiency of conversion (i.e., lower food coefficients). The same general pattern emerged for wheat gluten protein at the higher temperature; however, in low temperatures the effect was reversed, the lowest protein content giving best growth.

The majority of the above results suggest that a level of crude protein of about 10% of the diet is satisfactory for feeding under a variety of conditions and for a number of species. However, because of the expense of the protein constituents it is sometimes economically desirable to administer rations of lower protein content, even where this may decrease growth rates and increase the total food requirement (Dunkelgod *et al.*, 1961). Of particular interest in this respect is the so-called "protein sparing" action of increased proportions of available carbohydrate at lower levels of protein. The effect is illustrated by the results of Nail (1962) who tested the protein and total food conversion values for four different protein levels at two levels of carbohydrate. His results summarized in Table X show that as the level of protein was increased, both the protein conversion efficiency and total food conversion factors were decreased (lower food amounts were required per unit growth). At the highest protein levels tested, changes in the carbohydrate content did not affect either the protein or total food conversion rates. However, at the lower protein levels, increases in the carbohydrate content led to improvement in both the

TABLE X

VARIATIONS IN PROTEIN AND FEED CONVERSIONS FOR CHANNEL CATFISH FED DIFFERENT LEVELS OF CASEIN AT TWO LEVELS OF CARBOHYDRATE[a]

| Percentage Protein | Percentage carbohydrate | Protein conversion[b] | Feed conversion |
|---|---|---|---|
| 6.3 | 9.3 | 3.75 | 6.65 |
| 15.8 | 9.3 | 4.1 | 2.3 |
| 25.3 | 9.3 | 2.4 | 1.4 |
| 34.8 | 9.3 | 3.1 | 1.25 |
| 6.3 | 18.6 | 2.45 | 4.0 |
| 15.8 | 18.6 | 1.9 | 1.8 |
| 25.3 | 18.6 | 2.1 | 1.23 |
| 34.8 | 18.6 | 3.0 | 1.23 |

[a] Nail, 1962.
[b] Protein conversion was calculated by dividing the amount of protein deposited into the amount of protein fed.

protein conversion and total food conversion values. Shanks (1966) found
the same effect with trout.

Experimental results of this sort demonstrate clearly that nutritional
quality of foods, once a certain minimum content is supplied, may show a
remarkable complexity of interaction with other factors, and may affect
growth efficiencies in a complex manner. To date there have been few
attempts to measure the effects of such variables except through their
direct influence on growth and even in such cases the results are too often
discussed inappropriately as percentages of body weights. The remarkable
capacity for homeostasis of the general fish body condition suggests that
despite the apparent complexity some degree of generalization will be
possible. The discussion of foregoing sections further implies that there
may be profit in considering the effects of nutrient constituents and sources
in terms of both metabolic and growth efficiency effects. Where size
variations are involved, calculations of the effects in terms of the parameters
of the T and K lines may prove advantageous.

14. *Effects of Crowding*

As noted earlier the change in growth efficiency with change in size of
food particle, deduced by Paloheimo and Dickie (1966b) from a comparison
of three different sets of trout data, also involved a change in the density
of fish involved in the experiment. Density was, in fact, totally confounded
with particle size, the hatchery mash feedings having been carried out
with thousands of small trout in a rearing trough, the *Gammarus* feedings
of Surber involved groups of five fish each, while the minnow feeding
experiments were performed with single trout in an aquarium. Thus while
there seems to be evidence that food particle size is important, its effects
in this case cannot be separated from effects of crowding.

Effects of crowding are difficult to specify from the data available. It
is known, for example, that crowding affects metabolic level, and will have
an influence on appetite or food consumption rate. Brown (1946a, b) found
that there was an intermediate optimum density of fish for optimum food
intake and growth. At both lower and higher densities, food intake was
lower, as was growth. There is no way of knowing in these cases whether
the growth effect involved a change in the growth efficiency curves in
addition to the metabolic level effect.

Kinne (1960, 1962) and Menzel (1960) used different group sizes in
various experiments carried out by them, yet growth efficiency, calculated
from their data, shows no signs of a relationship with group size. This
suggests that within certain narrow limits crowding may not directly
affect the growth efficiency curves, the total effect of crowding, therefore,

being ascribed to its effect on appetite, and the basic effects of food intake on growth efficiency, described by the K line. However, a wide range of initial stocking densities was examined by Hastings (1969b). He stocked channel catfish of various ages at various rates in ponds. Food was administered to the ponds at a constant percentage of the body weight of the fish, as is general hatchery practice, with the initially smaller fish receiving a higher proportion per body weight than the initially larger fish. Experiments were run for about 200 days.

Since the ponds were not closed to a certain amount of natural food production, it is not certain to what extent the effects of stocking density and feeding interacted with the natural food production. The results indicated, nevertheless, that over the whole range of initial stocking densities, production was increased by only 0.32% for each 1% increase in stock density, indicating a marked decline in growth efficiency with density. Since all feeding was at more or less the same level per fish, the effect may have been one of changing the intercept "*a*" of the K line. The effect on *b* cannot be judged from the results. Davis and Warren (1965) showed that with "natural" food production in a stream, there is an intermediate optimum density for production, above which predation rates exceeded natural food production rates, leading to an overall decrease in total sculpin growth. In this situation the data suggest a single K line at different densities, but a comparison of their winter and summer data indicates a change in the K line with season.

## 15. *Other Factors in Growth*

There are undoubtedly many other factors which influence metabolic level and growth efficiency curves. Social hierarchies may have at least a modifying influence on density effects. Hormone production in different situations, especially seasonal changes associated with maturation of gonads, have been shown by Wohlschlag and Juliano (1959) and Beamish (1964b) to have a pronounced effect on the standard and total metabolism, and are certain to alter feeding behavior as well. Effects of light are also associated with growth efficiency (Brown, 1946b). Phillips *et al.* (1957) found that an increase in light intensity increased food intake by 30% without a change in growth rate. Unfortunately, despite the very large body of information bearing on such factors, experimental designs and reports do not offer information which permits us to judge whether such factors affect the efficiency solely through indirect effects on food intake or whether they alter the parameters of the K line as well. At least some of them have undoubtedly complex effects on the production processes.

### 16. *Other Factors in Production*

In the preceding discussion we have dealt with production of fish from their food as though production were a simple function of the growth of individuals. However, production, which we may define with Ivlev (1966) as the total elaboration of new biomass by a group of organisms per unit time, irrespective of the fate of that "production," is obviously dependent on both growth and reproduction of new organisms. In fish culture, the reproduction part of the production is generally a factor which can be controlled by the stocking density, and hence can be largely disregarded in our discussion except insofar as the density of fish themselves affects the food intake and use for growth of the individual. Unfortunately, very little precise information on density effects is available, so that our discussions can hardly come to a more significant conclusion than that further experimental study is required.

Production defined as above is also to be distinguished from the yield or what might be termed "commercial production." This latter quantity obviously depends on survival of the growing fish up to the time of harvest. Information available at present indicates that the probability of survival may not be entirely independent of growth, so that special experimental consideration of these relationships is also necessary. While effects of food quality on survival have been noted briefly in many experiments, our lack of knowledge again restricts our discussion of factors which will affect the value of food primarily to a study of the growth parameters. In fish culture work this may not be a serious limitation in evaluation of foods, provided favorable environmental conditions are maintained. However, the balance of production processes by mortalities in nature is an essential part of population control, determining the biomass of a particular group in a community. Further study of the interaction of mortalities and food with growth parameters in experimental fish culture work may therefore provide essential information on the balance of natural animal populations.

### References*

Agersborg, H. P. K. (1934). *Trans. Amer. Fish. Soc.* **64**, 155–162.
Almquist, H. J., Stokstad, E. L. R., and Halbrook, E. R. (1935). *J. Nutr.* **10**, 193–211.
Baldwin, N. S. (1956). *Trans. Amer. Fish. Soc.* **86**, 323–328.
Bardach, J. E. (1959). *Limnol. Oceanogr.* **4** 77–85.
Beamish, F. W. H. (1964a). *Can. J. Zool.* **42**, 177–188.
Beamish, F. W. H. (1964b). *Can. J. Zool.* **42**, 189–194.
Beamish, F. W. H., and Dickie, L. M. (1967). *In* "The Biological Basis of Freshwater Fish Production" (S. D. Gerking, ed. pp. 215–242). Blackwell, Oxford.

* References designated as *Fish. Res. Bull.* are published by the New York State Conservation Department, Albany, New York.

Beamish, F. W. H., and Mookherjii, P. S. (1964). *Limnol. Oceanogr.* **42**, 161–175.
Black, E. C., Robertson, S. C., and Parker, R. R. (1961). *In* "Comparative Physiology of Carbohydrate Metabolism in Heterathermic Animals" (A. W. Martin, ed.,) pp. 89–124. University of Washington Press, Seattle.
Block, J. R., and Weiss, K. W. (1956). "Amino Acid Handbook," p. 138. Thomas, Springfield, Illinois.
Brett, J. R. (1964). *J. Fish. Res. Bd. Can.* **21**, 1183–1226.
Brett, J. R. (1965). *J. Fish. Res. Bd. Can.* **22**, 1491–1501.
Brockensen, R. W. (1966). "Influence of Competition on Food Consumption and Production of Animals in Laboratory Stream Communities." M.S. Thesis, Oregon State University, Corvallis.
Brody, S. (1945). "Bioenergetics and Growth." Reinhold, New York.
Brown, M. E. (1946a). *J. Exp. Biol.* **22**, 118–129.
Brown, M. E. (1946b). *J. Exp. Biol.* **22**, 130–144.
Brown, M. E. (1951). *J. Exp. Biol.* **28**, 473–491.
Brown, M. E. (1957). *In* "The Physiology of Fishes" (M. E. Brown, ed.), Vol. 1. Academic Press, New York.
Carpenter, K. J. (1960). *J. Biochem.* **77**, 604–610.
Carpenter, K. J. (1963). *Nat. Acad. Sci. Food Nutr. Bd. Pub.* **1100,** 74.
Chugunova, N. I. (1959). "Age and Growth Studies in Fish," p. 132. Translations published by Nat. Sci. Found., Washington, 1963, by the Israel Program for Scientific Translations.
Combs, G. F., and Nicholson, J. L. (1964). *Maryland Agr. Exp. Sta. Misc. Pub. No.* **52.**
Davies, P. M. C. (1964). *Comp. Biochem. Physiol.* **12**, 67–79.
Davis, G. E., and Warren, C. E. (1965). *J. Wildl. Manage.* **29**, 846–871.
DeLong, D. C., Halver, J. E., and Mertz, E. T. (1958). *J. Nutr.* **65**, 589–599.
Dunkelgod, K. E., Gleaves, E. W., Tonkinson, L. V., Thayer, R. H., Sirny, R. J., and Morrison, R. D. (1961). *Okla. State Exp. Sta. Processed Series* P-391.
Dupree, H. K., and Sneed, K. E. (1966). *"U.S. Dep. Interior Fish Wildl. Serv. Tech. Paper* **9,** 21.
Ellis, M. M. (1944) *U.S. Dep. Interior Spec. Sci. Rep.* **2.**
Field, J. B., Herman, E. F., and Elvehjem, C. A. (1944). *Proc. Soc. Exp. Biol. Med.* **55,** 222–225.
Ford, J. E. (1962). *Brit. J. Nutr.* **16**, 409–425.
Frey, D. (1963). "Limnology in North America," p. 734. Univ. of Wisc. Press, Madison, Wisconsin.
Fry, F. E. J. (1957). *In* "The Physiology of Fishes" (M. E. Brown, ed.) Vol. 1, p. 51. Academic Press, New York.
Gehrt, A. J., Caldwell, M. J., and Elmslie, W. P. (1957). *J. Ass. Off. Agr. Chem.* **40,** 606–617.
Gerking, S. D. (1952). *Physiol. Zool.* **25**, 358–372.
Gerking, S. D. (1955). *Physiol. Zool.* **28**, 267–282.
Gerking, S. D. (ed.) (1967). "The Biological Basis of Freshwater Fish Production," pp. xl–xlv. Blackwell, Oxford.
Golley, F. B. (1961). *Ecology* **42**, 581–584.
Grassl, E. F. (1956). *Trans. Amer. Fish. Soc.* **86**, 307–322.
Grimalskii, V. L. (1962). *Zh. Biol.* **16**, 169. (Translation, *Biol. Abstr.* **42** , No. 12874.)
Haskell, D. C. (1955). *Progr. Fish Cult.* **17**, 117.
Haskell, D. C. (1959). *N. Y. Fish Game J.* **6**, 204.
Hastings, W. H. (1964). *U.S. Dep. Interior Circ.* **210**, 48–57.

Hastings, W. H. (1967). *Proc. Comm. Fish Farming Conf., College Station, Texas*, pp. 27–34.

Hastings, W. H. (1969a). *Div. Fish. Res., Res. Pub.* **77**, pp. 223–230.

Hastings, W. H. (1969b). *Proc. Am. Feed Manufacturers Assoc. Nutr. Council*, Dec. 2.

Hatanaka, M., Kosaka, M., and Sato, Y. (1956a). *Tohoku J. Agr. Res.* **7**, 151–162.

Hatanaka, M., Kosaka, M., and Sato, Y. (1956b). *Tohoku J. Agr. Res.* **7**, 163–174.

Hathaway, E. S. (1927). *Ecology* **8**, 428–434.

Hayes, F. R. (1963). *Proc. 6th Conf. Great Lakes Res. Univ. Mich., Ann Arbor Pub.* **10**, 112–117.

Hellier, T. R., Jr. (1962). *Inst. Marine Sci.* **8**, 1–22.

Hemmingsen, A. M. (1960). *Rep. Steno. Mem. Hosp. Nord. Insulin. Lab. (Copenhagen)* **9** (2), 3–110.

Hublou, W. F., Wallis, J., McKee, T. B., Law, D. K., Sinnhuber, R. O. and Yu, T. C. (1959). *Res. Briefs*, Oreg. Fish Comm. **7**(0), 28–56.

Huet, M. (1960). "Traite de Pisciculture," Article III, p. 369.

Ivlev, V. (1945). *Adven. Mod. Biol.* **19**, 98–120. (Transl. by W. E. Ricker.)

Ivlev, V. S. (1960). *Z. Fischerei Hilfwiss.* **9**, [N. F.], 281–289. (*J. Fish. Res. Bd. Can. Transl. Ser.* 374.)

Ivlev, V. S. (1961). "Experimental Ecology of the Feeding of Fishes." Yale Univ. Press, New Haven, Connecticut.

Ivlev, V. S. (1966). *J. Fish. Res. Bd. Can.* **23**, 1727–1744.

Jenkins, R. M. (1958). *Proc. Okla. Acad. Sci.* **38**, 157–172.

Job, S. V. (1955). *Univ. Toronto Biol. Ser. No. 61 Pub. Ontario Fish. Res. Lab. No.* 73.

Kawamoto, N. Y. (1957). *Progr. Fish Cult.* **19**, 26–30.

Keast, A. (1965). "*Great Lakes Res. Div. Univ. Mich. Pub. No.* **13**, 106–132.

Keast, A. (1966). *Great Lakes Res. Div. Univ. Mich. Pub. No.* **15**, 51–79.

Keast, A., and Webb, D. (1966). *J. Fish. Res. Bd. Can.* **23**, 1845–1874.

Kinne, O. (1960). *Physiol. Zool.* **33**, 288–317.

Kinne, O. (1962). *Comp. Biochem. Physiol.* **5**, 265–282.

Kleiber, M. (1947). *Physiol. Rev.* **27**, 511–541.

Knautche, C. (1898). *Z. Fischerei* **6**, 317.

Krogh, A. (1939). "Osmotic Regulations in Aquatic Animals," p. 132. Cambridge Univ. Press, London.

Krüger, F. (1965). *Helgolaender Wiss. Meeresunters.* **12**, 78–136. (*J. Fish. Res. Bd. Can. Transl. Ser. No.* 824.)

Lin, S. Y. (1959). "Pond Culture of Warm-Water Fishes," UNESCO Conf., Warm Springs, Georgia.

Lin, S. Y., and Chen, T. P. (1966). *FAO World Symp. Warmwater Pond Fish Culture*, Rome **2**/E-11, 1–16.

Lindeman, R. L. (1942). *Ecology* **23**, 399–418.

Lubitz, J. A. (1963). *J. Food Sci.* **28**, 229–232.

McCay, C. M., and Dilley, W. E. (1927). *Trans. Amer. Fish. Soc.* **57**, 250–260.

McIntire, D. C., and Bond, C. E. (1962). *Trans. Amer. Fish. Soc.* **91**, 303–312.

McLaren, B. A., Herman, E. F., and Elvehjem, C. A. (1946). *Arch. Biochem. Biophys.* **10**, 433–441.

McLaren, I. A. (1963). *J. Fish. Res. Bd. Can.* **20**, 685–727.

Mann, H. (1961). *In* "Fish as Food" (Borgstrom, ed.), Vol. 1, pp. 77–102. Academic Press, New York.

Mann, K. H. (1965). *J. Animal Ecol.* **34**, 253–275.

Mann, K. H. (1967). *In* "The Biological Basis of Freshwater Fish Production," (S. D. Gerking, ed.), pp. 243–257. Blackwell, Oxford.

March, B. E., Stupich, O., and Biely, J. (1949). *Poultry Sci.* **28,** 718–724.

Meade, T. L., and Altherr, F. (1966). *Proc. 21st Annu. Texas Nutr. Conf.,* Austin, pp. 136–140.

Menzel, D. W. (1960). *J. Cons. Cons. Perma. Int. Explor. Mer.* **25,** 216–222.

Meyer, J. H., and Nelson, A. O. (1963). *J. Nutr.* **80,** 343–349.

Mitchell, H. H. (1954). "Methods for Evaluation of Nutritional Adequacy and Status," Chicago Quartermaster Food and Container Institute, Chicago.

Mitchell, H. H., and Block, R. J. (1946). *J. Biol. Chem.* **163,** 599–620.

Morgulis, S. M. (1918). *J. Biol. Chem.* **36,** 391–413.

Mullins, L. J. (1950). *Acta. Phys. Scand.* **21,** 303.

Nail, M. L. (1962). *Proc. 16th Annu. Conf. S. E. Ass. Game Fish Comm.* Columbia, South Carolina, pp. 307–316.

Nose, T. (1960). *Bull. Freshwater Fish Res. Lab. (Tokyo)* **10,** 1–10.

Oser, B. L. (1951). *J. Amer. Diet. Ass.* **27,** 396–402.

Ostapenya, A. P., and Sergeev, A. I. (1963). *Vopr. Ikhtiol.* **3,** 177–183. (*J. Fish. Res. Bd. Can. Transl. Ser. No.* 874.)

Paloheimo, J. E., and Dickie, L. M. (1965). *J. Fish. Res. Bd. Can.* **22,** 521–542.

Paloheimo, J. E., and Dickie, L. M. (1966a). *J. Fish. Res. Bd. Can.* **23,** 869–908.

Paloheimo, J. E., and Dickie, L. M. (1966b). *J. Fish. Res. Bd. Can.* **23,** 1209–1248.

Patten, B. C. (1959). *Ecology* **40,** 221–231.

Pentalow, F. T. K. (1939). *J. Exp. Biol.* **16,** 446–473.

Phillips, A. M., Jr., Tunison, A. V., Fenn, A. H., Mitchell, C. R., and McCay, C. M. (1940). *Cortland Hatchery Rep. No.* **9,** 32.

Phillips, A. M., Jr., Tunison, A. V., and Brockway, D. R. (1948). *Fish. Res. Bull.* **11,** 44.

Phillips, A. M., Jr., Brockway, D. R., and Vaughn, R. R. (1957). *Fish. Res. Bull.* **21,** 14–16.

Phillips, A. M., Jr., Podoliak, H. A., Brockway, D. R., and Vaughn, R. R. (1958). *Fish. Res. Bull.* **21,** 93.

Phillips, A. M., Jr., Podoliak, H. A., Dumas, R. F., and Thoesen, R. W. (1959). *Fish. Res. Bull.* **24.**

Phillips, A. M., Jr., Podoliak, H. A., Poston, H. A., Livingston, D. L., Booke, H. E., Pyle, E. E., and Hammer, G. L. (1963). *Fish. Res. Bull.* **26,** 31.

Phillips, A. M., Jr., Podoliak, H. A., Poston, H. A., Livingston, D. L., Booke, H. E., Pyle, E. E., and Hammer, G. L. (1964). *Fish. Res. Bull.* **27.**

Podoliak, H. (1962). "Refresher Course for the In-Service Training School," pp. 1–7. Bureau of Sport Fisheries and Wildlife, Cortland, New York.

Prather, E. E. (1958). *Proc. 12th Annu. Conf. S. E. Ass. Game Fish Comm.*

Reimers, N. (1958). *Calif. Fish Game* **44,** 319–333.

Rozin, P., and Mayer, J. (1961). *Amer. J. Physiol.* **201,** 968–974.

Schäperclaus, W. (1933). *U.S. Dep. Interior Fish Wildl. Serv. Fish. Leafl. No.* 31, p. 261.

Silliman, R. P. (1968). *U.S. Fish. Wildl. Fish. Bull. No.* **66,** 425.

Simmons, R. W., and Norris, E. R. (1941). *J. Biol. Chem.* **140,** 679–680.

Slobodkin, L. B. (1961). *Amer. Natur.* **95,** 147–153.

Slobodkin, L. B., and Richman, S. (1961). *Nature (London)* **191,** 299.

Smit, H. (1965). *Can. J. Zool.* **43,** 623–633.

Smith, F. E. (1963). *Ecology* **44,** 651–663.

Standler, G. J. (1952). *S. Afr. Ind. Chem.* **6**, 118.

Sullivan, C. M. (1954). *J. Fish. Res. Bd. Can.* **11**, 153–176.

Surber, E. W. (1935). *Trans. Amer. Fish. Soc.* **65**, 300–304.

Swingle, H. S. (1947). *Agr. Exp. Sta. Ala. Polytech. Inst.* **264**, 1–34.

Swingle, H. S. (1958). *Proc. 12th Annu. Conf. S. E. Ass. Game Fish Comm.* pp. 63–72.

Swingle, H. S. (1962). *Fish. Res. Annu. Rep.* 163–211 (not published), Auburn Univ., Auburn, Alabama.

Swingle, J. D., and Smith, E. V. (1950). *Agr. Exp. Sta. Ala. Polytech. Inst. Bull.* **254**, 30.

Thorson, G. (1946). *Plankton* **4**, 1–523.

Tiemeier, O. W., Deyoe, C. W., and Wearden, S. (1965). *Trans. Kansas Acad. Sci.* **68**, 180–186.

Titcomb, J. W., Cobb, E. W., Crowell, M. F., and McCay, C. M. (1928). *Trans. Amer. Fish. Soc.* **58**, 205–231.

Tunison, A. V. (1940). *N. Y. State Cons. Dep. Bur. Fish.* p. 17.

Tunison, A. V., Brockway, D. R., Maxwell, J. M., Dorr, A. L., and McCay, C. M. (1942). *N.Y. Cons. Dept. Fish. Res. Bull.* **4**. 45.

Tunsion, A. V., Phillips, A. M. Jr., McCay, C. M., Mitchell, C. R., and Rodgers, E. O. (1939). *Cortland Hatchery Rep. No. 8.*

U.S. Bureau of Sport Fisheries and Wildlife (1968). *Ann. Rep. Div. Hatcheries*, p. 22.

Vaas, K. F., and Vass Van Oven, A. (1959). *Hydrobiol. Acta Hydrobiol. Limnol. Protistol.* **12**, 308–392.

von Bertalanffy, L. (1964). *Helgolaender Wiss. Meeresunters.* **9**, 5–37.

Warren, C. E. and Davis, G. E. (1967). *In* "The Biological Basis of Freshwater Fish Production" (S. D. Gerking, ed.), pp. 175–214. Blackwell, Oxford.

Warren, C. E., Wales, J. H., Davis, G. E., and Doudoroff, P. (1964). *J. Wildl. Manage.* **28**, 617–660.

Winberg, G. G. (1956). *J. Fish. Res. Bd. Can. Transl. Ser.* **194**, 202.

Winberg, G. G. (1961). *J. Fish. Res. Bd. Can. Transl. Ser.* **362**, 11.

Wohlschlag, D. E., and Juliano, R. O. (1959). *Limnol. Oceanogr.* **4**, 195–209.

Wolf, L. E. (1951). *Progr. Fish Cult.* **13**, 17–24.

Wood, E. M. (1952). "Methods for Protein Studies with Trout with Application to Four Selected Species." Thesis, Cornell University, Ithaca, New York.

Wood, E. M. (1953). *Progr. Fish. Cult.* **15**, 147–162.

Yashouv, A. (1956). *Bamidgen* **8**, 79–87. Methods of Analysis (1960). 9th ed., pp. 286–287. Ass. Off. Agr. Chem. Washington, D.C.

# 8

## SALMONID HUSBANDRY TECHNIQUES

*Roger E. Burrows*

## I. Introduction

The exploration and evaluation of the principles of salmonid nutrition by means of feeding trials creates problems not ordinarily encountered in animal husbandry. Unless the investigator is aware of these problems many erroneous conclusions can be drawn from what appears to be clear-cut experimental evidence. As a result, the early literature on salmonid nutrition, as reviewed by Karrick (1948), is rife with paradox and contradiction. The purpose of this chapter is to define the problems to be encountered in feeding trials so that these variables may be recognized and thereby either controlled or measured.

The problems encountered are principally those of the rearing environment and the ability or inability of the environment to meet the requirements of the fish. Such anomalies may distort the normal response. Without normal response the conclusions drawn from feeding trials or any other investigation measuring the normal reactions of fish may be invalidated by the effect of stress.

The principal practical objective of research into salmonid nutrition is to improve the diets fed in artificial propagation. The normal environment of the animal then becomes the crowded conditions encountered in intensive fish culture and not that of the stream or lake. At the same time, except on commercial trout farms, the final objective is to produce a fish which will survive in both environments and ultimately either reproduce itself or enter the fisherman's creel.

Salmonid dietetics, then, become dependent, in part, on the ability of the investigator to reproduce the conditions created by good fish cultural practice. In addition, of course, there are numerous differences to be encountered in the experimental techniques of salmonid feeding trials which differ markedly from those employed in other forms of animal husbandry. This chapter will attempt to define, first, the characteristics of good fish cultural practice and, second, the experimental design and procedures best suited for feeding trials.

## II.  Fish Cultural Practices

Fish are aquatic animals and, as such, must live and be fed within a water environment. This environment imposes certain restrictions both of itself and through facilities employed in feeding trials. Unfortunately, salmonids are one of the most sensitive groups of fishes and therefore have some of the most demanding environmental requirements for normal growth. They are not, however, the most difficult to feed in that they adapt readily to very artificial diets. Salmonids, also, are quite adaptable to various types of rearing facilities. Fingerling survival, however, is not necessarily a measure of optimum conditioning. Facilities which do not provide adequate exercise produce fish of low stamina and poor adaptability to stream conditions. Good fish cultural practice in diet trials, then, produces an environment, facilities, and techniques which are conducive to growth and survival of the animal, at least comparable to that achieved in artificial propagation.

### A.  Environmental Requirements

The optimum environment of salmonids is cool, well-aerated, uncrowded water, containing a minimum of pollutants. While this statement is an obvious oversimplification of the facts, it is still generally true that water temperature, oxygen content, density, and degree of pollution regulate the carrying capacities of water supplies. For practical purposes, these are the factors which determine feasibility and limitations of experiment.

### 1. *Water Temperature*

Fish are poikilothermic and, as such, the metabolic rate is directly correlated with water temperature. Optimum temperatures, then, become those most favorable to the metabolism of the animal. Brett (1956, 1959) has reviewed the literature on thermal requirements of fishes and particularly salmonids. The Salmonidae have the lowest thermal tolerance of the freshwater fishes and, in general, trout (*Salmo, Salvelinus*) are more resistant to high temperatures than are salmon (*Oncorhynchus*).

The optimum temperature range of salmonids is between 10° and 15°C (50°–59°F) (Brett, 1952). It is in this range where maximum food conversion and growth rate occurs. At temperatures above 60°F, the metabolic rate increases to the point where a greater portion of the food intake is required for maintenance and less is available for growth. At temperatures below 50°F the metabolic rate progressively declines and, as a consequence, the growth rate is reduced. Unfortunately most fish cultural stations are not capable of maintaining optimum temperature ranges throughout the rearing cycle and, for this reason, feeding trials should not be confined to optimum temperatures. As the temperature changes the food intake of the animal changes due to alteration in the metabolic activity. In fingerling chinook salmon (*O. tshawytscha*) an increase of 1°F results in a 7% increase in growth rate per month within the temperature range of 40° to 60°.

The reaction of different species of salmonids to temperatures, other than optimum, differ. Brett (1959) states that coho salmon (*O. kisutch*) fingerlings are much more active in the upper temperature tolerance range than are sockeye salmon (*O. nerka*). Burrows (1963) reports that sockeye salmon fingerlings grow at a faster rate between the temperatures of 40° and 60°F than do chinook fingerlings. The varying responses of other salmonids as determined by other investigators have been summarized by Brett (1952).

Differences in the thermal response of salmonid species make it mandatory that feeding trials be conducted in the tolerance as well as the optimum range. Phillips *et al.* (1947, 1948, 1950) have reported that the requirement of trout for B-complex vitamins is a function of body weight. The vitamin intake of salmonids, however, is controlled by the food intake and the vitamin content of the diet. When food intake is high, the vitamin content per unit of diet weight can be lower than when the intake is reduced which is probably due to increased efficiency of diet utilization during periods of rapid growth at higher temperatures. Diets which prove satisfactory when tested at the optimum temperature range should be further tested in the lower tolerance range before these are considered satisfactory for production use.

Unfavorable temperatures at either end of the tolerance range produce another problem in that a loading stress (Brett, 1958) is created and, as a result, prolonged exposure results in lowered resistance and greater susceptibility to disease. Most diseases are more virulent in the tolerance rather than the optimum temperature range of the fish.

The diet requirements of the animal vary with temperature and, therefore, diet composition must vary if optimum utilization is to be achieved. Temperatures both above and below the optimum range call for changes in the protein calorie–energy relationship with lipids and carbohydrates increased to meet the increased energy requirement.

The response of salmonids to water temperature are many and varied and because temperature has a direct effect on metabolism, it cannot be ignored in the design, conduction, and interpretation of results of feeding trials.

## 2. *Oxygen Requirements*

The oxygen consumption of fingerling salmonids is affected by water temperature, fish size, pollutants, food metabolized, and both physical or other physiological activity. An increase in water temperature is accompanied by an increase in metabolic activity of the fish and, as a result, an increase in the oxygen demand of the animal. At the same time that oxygen demand is increasing the oxygen carrying capacity of the water is decreasing. If the number of fish is small, the oxygen content of the water never becomes a limiting factor but, in intensive fish culture and in some feeding trials, an increase in water temperature can result in growth inhibition due to oxygen deficiency.

The inhibitory effect of oxygen deficiency on oxygen consumption is defined as respiratory dependence. At what oxygen level respiratory dependence becomes active has been explored by numerous investigators and reviewed by Fry (1957) and Jones (1964). Jones defines this point as the critical level.

The critical oxygen level is of significance in fish culture and in nutritional investigations because below this point the fish is in a subnormal environment. Reductions in oxygen consumption indicate a reduction in both physical and metabolic activity which is reflected in a decrease in growth rate and a change in the dietary requirements of the animal. In actuality, the critical oxygen level must be above that at which growth inhibition can be measured.

The measurement of reduction in both cruising speed and oxygen consumption in an attempt to determine the critical level of respiratory dependence has been reported by Fry (1957). Job (1955) and Fry (1957) have established the critical level for brook trout (*S. fontinalis*) at between 6 and 7 ppm of oxygen (6–7 mg $O_2$/liter). Hermann *et al.* (1962) presents data for coho salmon which indicates a significant reduction in growth rate when the oxygen level drops below 5 ppm. Shaw (1946) states that 5 ppm is the minimum level of oxygen at which trout should be held. Our experience with chinook salmon fingerlings has been that in waters containing 5 ppm of oxygen, the food intake is measurably reduced and, below this level, the fish move into a conservation phase in which both activity and oxygen consumption are reduced. All the available evidence indicates the critical oxygen level for salmonids within the optimum temperature range to be at approximately 6 ppm.

Fish size also affects the oxygen requirements of salmonids. Fortunately as the fish increase in size the requirement is reduced but not at a rate sufficient to compensate for the increase due to the gain in weight. In hatchery practice and in feeding trials the growth rate of the animal must be taken into consideration so that the fish do not outgrow the capacity of the environment and encounter the effects of respiratory dependence.

A complicating factor in the determination of oxygen requirements is the effect of activity on these requirements. Fry (1957) has defined three metabolic levels as standard, routine, and active metabolism. Shaw (1946) has determined the oxygen requirements of trout at minimum, normal, and maximum levels, although the activity levels used in these determinations are not defined.

In fish culture, the standard metabolic rate is of little or no significance because it is practically impossible to attain. Metabolism also varies in the crowded conditions of artificial propagation. Active metabolism is the normal condition of reared salmonids. Obviously there are differences in the activity level. The normal activity level is defined as that at which oxygen consumption is fairly stable and the fish, as a group, are in a relatively quiescent state. At this activity level there is no massive response by the population to external stimuli. Such a condition, however, does not preclude individual activity. The maximum activity level is that at which oxygen consumption is at its peak. This level occurs principally during feeding or handling which involves a general response by the entire population.

The difference between the oxygen requirements of the two levels of activity is of significance in that the maximum carrying capacity of the water is determined from the oxygen content of the water, the critical oxygen level, and oxygen requirement of the fish at the normal activity level. At maximum loading, any increase in the oxygen requirement above that of the normal activity level creates a condition of respiratory dependence and an increasingly unfavorable environment. Shaw (1946) and Davis (1947) report increases in the oxygen consumption of trout of more than 100% after feeding. With the oxygen level of the water at 6 ppm, at maximum loading and normal activity, a decrease in the oxygen level to 3 ppm due to feeding could be expected during the period of maximum oxygen consumption. The exposure to this level would be of short duration and probably not inhibiting other than to physical activity. At less than maximum loadings the oxygen consumption of 15-gm fall chinook fingerlings returns to normal within 3 hours after feeding. Fish of this size are not fed more than twice a day and the oxygen content of the water will be above the critical level before the next feeding and subsequent depletion. Prolonged exposure, more than 12 hours per day, to oxygen levels below 5 ppm should be avoided. In fact, maximum loadings are undesirable and not conducive to optimum growth. In feeding trials the carrying capacity of the water may be approached but not exceeded.

## 3. *Carrying Capacity of Water*

The limitation which determines the carrying capacity of water is principally composed of an interrelationship between the available oxygen and the population density. Sufficient oxygen must be supplied from the water to support the physical and physiological activity of the animal. In feeding trials, this oxygen level should be sufficient to maintain normal growth. In order to attain this objective the carrying capacity of the water must not be exceeded. To determine the carrying capacity it is necessary to know the oxygen content of the water, the rate at which it is supplied, the water temperature, and the oxygen requirements of the fish. With these data the carrying capacity of water in terms of oxygen maintenance may be calculated.

Elliott (1969) has determined the oxygen consumption of fall chinook fingerlings at three fish sizes, several water temperatures, and at normal activity levels. From these data the carrying capacities of oxygen-saturated water at five water temperatures, and several fish sizes have been calculated and delineated in Fig. 1. The determinations for available oxygen are based on the difference between the saturated and critical levels. The saturated level is determined from sea level measurements and the critical

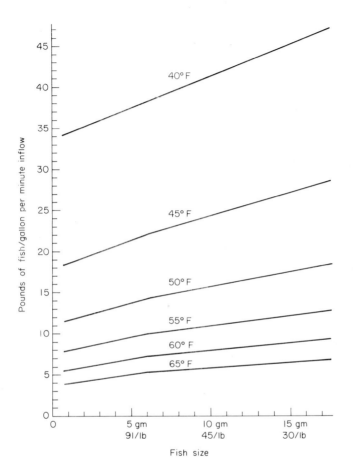

Fig. 1. Carrying capacity of oxygen-saturated water at normal activity level of fingerling chinook salmon as affected by water temperature and fish size.

oxygen level is established at 6 ppm. Shaw (1946) used a similar approach to calculate carrying capacity of water for several species of salmonids. He apparently encountered difficulty with the activity of the fish when determining oxygen consumption rate because he concluded that differences within species obscured differences between species and that no significant difference existed due to fish size. He selected a critical oxygen level of 5 ppm for his calculations. His measurement of temperature effect on carrying capacity is in surprisingly close agreement with that shown in Fig. 1 for 1-gm chinook fingerlings. Because Shaw's measurements were conducted on several species of trout and at least one species of salmon and these measurements are in essential agreement with those of Fig. 1, for all practical purposes, the carrying capacities of water as shown in Fig. 1 should be generally applicable to most salmonids.

In addition to the limitations imposed by the available oxygen, the density of the population can increase to the point of growth inhibition. Physical overcrowding usually becomes active at water temperatures below 55°F when oxygen requirement is low and oxygen content of the water is high. Crowding is actually the effect of numbers of fish and should be expressed in terms of density of the population. The pounds of fish per cubic foot of water is the most generally applied measure of density and the one used in this discussion.

Overcrowding can result in a reduction in growth rate due to stress and in poor food utilization caused by wastage. Both effects are highly undesirable in nutritional experiments.

As fish increase in size, the density of the population per cubic foot of water increases and the number of fish which can be carried per cubic foot decreases but, paradoxically, pounds of fish which can be carried per cubic foot increases. Figure 2 demonstrates the increase in density which is possible as fish increase in size. From this graph it is obvious that fish

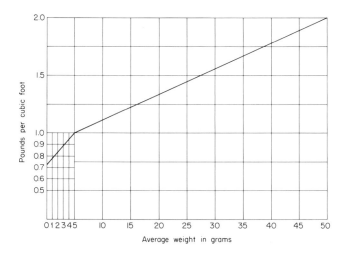

FIG. 2. Effect of fish size on maximum loading density of salmonids, expressed as pounds of fish per cubic foot of water.

less than 5 gm in average weight are much more sensitive to overcrowding than are larger fish. Comparing Figs. 1 and 2, it is apparent that there is an interaction between the oxygen requirements and the density of stocking on the carrying capacity of water. With small fish, less than 5 gm, and warm water, 55°F and above, available oxygen is usually the limiting factor in carrying capacity. With larger fingerlings and colder water the density of stocking is usually limiting.

It must be emphasized that both graphs do not depict desirable stocking rates but rather the maximum pounds of fish per gallon per minute of inflow or per cubic foot of water which must not be exceeded if normal growth rates are to be maintained. To determine desirable stocking rates it is necessary to establish the length of the experimental period and the expected rate of growth. From these data it is possible to estimate the size and weight of fish at the conclusion of the experiment and thereby determine the initial stocking rate which is necessary in order that the carrying capacity is not exceeded at the conclusion of the experiment.

Not all species of salmonids are affected equally by crowding. Burrows and Chenoweth (1955) report experiments conducted with sockeye salmon averaging 4 gm each which indicated that densities in excess of 5 pounds per cubic foot could be carried in deep troughs with no reduction in growth rate. Davis (1947) reported similar results in experiments with rainbow trout. Under such circumstances the mechanics of maintenance become limiting and disease epidemics could become disastrous. Only the more gregarious species can be subjected to such densities. In fact, some of the more solitary species are affected by a *space factor* in addition to overcrowding. The response seems to be an inherited inhibition to confinement and is not associated with density per se. Johnson and Gastineau (1952) report a reduction in growth rate in chinook fingerlings reared in deep troughs when compared to either 6-foot circular tanks or 15 × 140 foot raceways after the fish reach 8 gm in average weight. Palmer *et al.* (1952) demonstrate that there is no inhibitory effect on the growth of chinook fingerlings when reared in 3-, 4-, or 5-foot circular tanks. In these experiments no group was loaded at a rate of more than 0.5 pound per cubic foot, yet only where freedom of lateral movement existed was the growth rate normal. It is assumed that other species of salmonids are affected by this *space factor* but no references to this phenomenon have been discovered in the literature.

In diet trials, factors which influence carrying capacity must not be allowed to become inhibitory. A general retardation in growth rate within an experiment can obscure true differences in diet response due to the variability imposed by biological variation and experimental error.

4. *Effect of Pollutants*

Industrial wastes and domestic sewage generally do not affect salmonid dietetics. Laboratories should have water supplies which are free of contamination from these sources. The pollutants with which the researcher is concerned are those associated with water quality and metabolic waste and consist principally of heavy metals and inorganic gases.

Water supplies which have a pH of 7 or below or contain 10 ppm or less of calcium bicarbonate have a tendency to pick up copper, zinc, and lead from the supply pipes in quantities sufficient to be either latently toxic or immediately lethal to the fish. A lethal response is obvious but toxicity which is sublethal can invalidate diet trials by introducing extraneous stress with a resultant reduction in the growth rate plus abnormal physiological changes.

The problem of toxicity from heavy metals can be circumvented if care is taken to avoid galvanized or copper or lead pipe and fittings. Iron or plastic pipe may be used and plastic or stainless steel valves. According to Smith (1966) polyethylene and polyvinylchloride piping should be used with caution in that manufacturing processes differ in the amount of contaminants introduced. Plastic piping suitable for domestic water supplies should be satisfactory for fish rearing but probably should be tested with small fish before exposing a valuable group to this environment.

Water supplies with a pH above 7.5 and calcium bicarbonate above 50 ppm are less subject to contamination with toxic forms of heavy metals. Lloyd (1960, 1961) and Sprague (1964a) report on reduction in toxicity of copper and zinc compounds in hard waters and the additive and synergistic effects of copper and zinc compounds when both are present in the water supply. In water supplies of this type, galvanized piping and brass valves may be used with impunity providing that retention time within the pipeline is not prolonged due to oversize pipe and low flows. Sprague (1964b) reports an increased alkalinity in a soft water supply due to prolonged retention of 18 hours in concrete pipe. At the Salmon-Cultural Laboratory, we encountered zinc toxicity from a galvanized domestic supply line during the winter months when the interchange rate was low, even though the pH of the water was 8.0 and the carbonate alkalinity 50 ppm.

Sprague and Ramsay (1965) report incipient lethal levels of copper sulfate at 32 ppb and zinc sulfate at 420 ppb for Atlantic salmon (*S. salar*) fingerlings in soft water. Normal surface waters do not contain either metal in these quantities. Springs and well water supplies can contain toxic levels of heavy metals and should be checked thoroughly before acceptance as a laboratory water supply.

The principal inorganic gas in normal water supplies which is not associated with the catabolic products of metabolism is chlorine. Chlorine is introduced into domestic water supplies as a disinfectant and can prove extremely toxic to fish. Merkins (1958) estimates the safe tolerance level for trout to be approximately 4 ppb. The most practical method for the removal of chlorine from a water supply is by means of an activated charcoal filter as described by Sharp (1951). Such filters may be regenerated by back flushing and thereby provide continuous dechlorination. The neutralization of chlorine with sodium thiosulfate as described by Rodgers (1949) and Pyle (1960) is not as reliable a procedure.

The relatively large numbers of fish confined in small areas with limited water interchange as practiced in feeding trials can cause pollution problems from catabolic products, principally ammonia. While carbon dioxide is a catabolic product and can cause problems in polluted water as reviewed by Jones (1964), under normal conditions of rearing it is not a significant factor. Burrows (1964) has reported a cyclic phenomenon of urea and ammonia excretion and the dominance of ammonia as the carrying capacity of the water is approached. In diet trials the primary concern is that the ammonia exposure is not sufficient to result in a reduction in growth rate. Unionized ammonia ($NH_3$) is of no consequence if the pH is 7 or below but as pH increases the deleterious effect of the ammonia content of the water increases. At a pH of 7.8 and a water temperature of 65°F, ammonia can become a limiting factor when the fish loading rate is 8 pounds per gallon per minute of inflow.

At ammonia levels normally encountered in artificial propagation, ammonia acts as an irritant rather than producing lethal effects. Prolonged, constant exposure to unionized ammonia causes proliferation of the gill epithelium in salmon fingerlings resulting in reduced stamina, growth, and disease resistance. Because the length and strength of ammonia exposure is of importance, the hydraulic characteristics of the rearing container also assume importance. Burrows and Chenoweth (1955) have correlated disease resistance with the hydraulic characteristics of three types of rearing ponds. The containers used for nutritional studies, although usually smaller, can similarly influence the results of nutrition studies.

### 5. Types of Rearing Facilities

In addition to quality of the inflowing water, the rearing environment is influenced by the type of rearing facility employed. Most laboratories are reluctant to devote sufficient space or water to the rearing facilities and, as a result, create abnormal environments for the experimental animals. Small rectangular troughs or tanks are used in an effort to conserve space and inflows are reduced to a minimum in an effort to conserve water. As a result much of the work produced by such laboratories can be both nutritionally and physiologically invalid.

Small troughs or tanks, usually 4–6 feet in length and 12–16 inches in width with water depths ranging from 3–18 inches, can be used for experimental rearing providing water inflows are adequate to meet ultimate requirements of the fish at the conclusion of the experiment and the species under test is adapted to trough rearing. Some salmonid species are normally stream dwellers while some inhabit lakes habitually. Some species are gregarious and some are solitary. Some species adapt readily to troughs, some do not.

Those species which require fast water currents or more space than is provided in troughs should be reared in circular tanks. Chinook salmon appear to be one of the most sensitive salmonids to rear, in that increased water current increases growth rate and trough confinement retards growth. Johnson and Gastineau (1952) demonstrate no retardation of growth rate of chinook fingerlings reared in circular tanks as compared to raceway ponds but show a retardation in fish reared in troughs. Palmer *et al.* (1952) show no reduction in growth rate of chinook fingerlings reared in 3-, 4-, 5-, or 6-foot circular tanks when compared to Foster-Lucas ponds. The circular tank seems to meet the environmental requirements of this species and, very probably, those of the other more difficult to rear salmonids.

The size of the rearing container assumes importance in that stunting, due to overcrowding, can become active if the initial number of fish in the experiment is too large and the fish outgrow the carrying capacity of the facility before the conclusion of the experiment.

The amount of inflowing water also limits carrying capacity of the equipment in relation to oxygen supply. In addition, the hydraulic pattern within the container determines the degree of short circuiting and expulsion rate of the catabolic products. Increasing the depth of a tank does not necessarily increase the carrying capacity. If the inflow is not increased, the water tends to short circuit and the flow to laminate. Under such conditions ammonia can accumulate in areas of low flow, cause deleterious conditions, and inhibit growth rate.

The most efficient container for laboratory use is the circular tank in that the current velocity in the tank can be controlled to suit the type of fish being reared. The size of the tank would be dependent on the size of the sample and the duration of the experiment. Such tanks take up more space than either troughs or deep tanks. As some species grow quite well in troughs the space-saving factor must be considered. Only rarely, however, can deep tanks be justified because of their increased water demand, inefficiency, and danger of overloading.

### 6. *Reconditioning of Water for Reuse*

Most laboratories are handicapped in conducting feeding trials by the quantity and quality of water available and the lack of environmental control. One solution to these problems is reconditioning of water for reuse. Experimentation at the Salmon-Cultural Laboratory has demonstrated that reconditioning of water is entirely practicable even for large-scale production operations.

In reuse of water the principal problem is the accumulation of ammonia. Fortunately, nitrifying bacteria are present in the soil and water which convert ammonia to nitrites and then to harmless nitrates. When provided with a favorable environment these bacteria develop to the point where they will handle surprisingly large quantities of ammonia. This application of nitrification to alteration of water quality is not new. Hawkes (1963) has reviewed the development and application of bacterial beds for nitrification in sewage treatment plants. Atz (1964) describes closed-circuit systems for seawater aquariums and the role of nitrifying bacteria in the reconditioning of water. In freshwater semi-closed systems, a combination filter and bacterial bed is used to remove both the solid and liquid waste products. Crushed oyster shell as the filter material creates a fast filter, supplies calcium and trace minerals, and maintains a desirable pH of between 7.6 and 8.0. Beneath the crushed shell a bacterial bed consisting of sharp rock, sized $\frac{1}{2}$ to 3 inches, creates an undisturbed, porous area for the development of the nitrifying bacteria. These filters, when operated at a capacity of 1 gallon per minute per square foot of filter surface area, will support salmonids at the density levels shown in Fig. 2 providing that adequate oxygen levels are maintained.

Oxygenation of depleted water in a reuse system is accomplished by aspiration and discharge under pressure into a depth of water. This approach eliminates supersaturation and prevents accumulation of carbon dioxide. A schematic diagram of a tested reconditioning system is presented in Fig. 3. This type of system is adaptable to both laboratory and production operations.

In a semi-closed system, supplemental water is added to remove the accumulation of nitrates, to replace leakage and evaporation, and to control temperature providing temperature control equipment is not available and

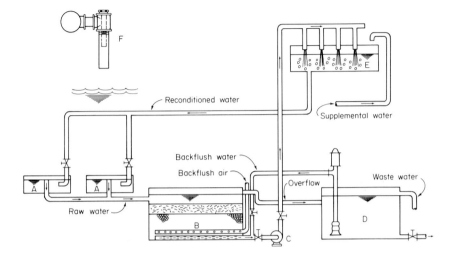

Fɪɢ. 3. Schematic diagram of water reconditioning system. (A) Experimental tanks: Water flow through tanks and number of tanks determines size of reconditioning system. Two to ten percentage supplemental water required dependent on water temperature. Four degree rise in ambient temperature causes 1° rise in recirculating water temperature above that of supplemental water. (B) Filter and reconditioning tanks: One square foot of filter area required per gallon per minute of water flow through filters. Crushed oyster shell, $\frac{1}{4}$- to $\frac{3}{4}$-inch size forms filter bed. Depth of bed varies from 3 to 12 inches dependent on size reconditioning system. Crushed rock $\frac{1}{2}$ to 3 inches forms bacterial bed below shell. Depth of rock varies from $1\frac{1}{2}$ to 4 feet dependent on nitrification load of system. Raw water enters top of filter and reconditioned water exits through perforated pipe at bottom of filter. Backflush water and air introduced through two pipes at bottom of tank in reverse circulation for cleaning. (C) Circulating pump: Supplies 10 psi pressure at aerators. (D) Wash water sump and pump: Collects waste water for use in backflushing filters. Not required if adequate source of backflush water available. (E) Aeration tank: Aspirators drive into 5 feet of water. (F) Aspirator: $1\frac{1}{2}$ inch outlet, $\frac{3}{4}$-inch air pipe, at 10 psi delivers 125 gpm, requires 4 square feet of area per aspirator, 90–95% efficient.

the temperature of the supplemental water is satisfactory. With temperature control equipment the minimum amount of supplemental water required is 2% of the amount of recirculated water. Without temperature-control equipment, the amount of supplemental water required would be dependent on its temperature, the desired temperature range of the recirculated water, and the range of the ambient temperature. With 10% of supplemental water, a 4°F change in ambient temperature causes a 1°F change in water temperature.

Controlled temperature equipment combined with a reconditioning system provide very versatile research facilities for nutritional studies. Several independent systems would provide any series of temperature gradients desired.

In addition to temperature control the reuse of water allows introduction of adequate quantities of water per tank and makes sterilization of the supplemental water supply practicable. The disinfection of water in basic nutrition work is highly desirable in that danger of experimental loss due to extraneous diseases is eliminated. With the relatively small amounts of water involved, both mechanical filtration and chemical disinfection are practical.

Reconditioning systems have a definite place in the design of facilities for nutritional investigations. The potentialities are only beginning to be exploited.

## B. Dietary Methods

Salmonid diets must be adapted to the aquatic environment otherwise the diet evaluation may be distorted by losses of water-soluble components. The water-soluble vitamins and proteins are particularly vulnerable to such loss. Diet preparation and presentation can become as important as the diet constituents in that results may become distorted due to loss of the water-soluble components.

### 1. *Diet Preparation*

There has been a radical change in diet composition in the last 15 years due to the development of more adequately bound diets. The problems encountered with preparation of meat, and meat–meal diets have been ably discussed by Phillips (1956). Fortunately these problems have been circumvented by the development of the gelatin-bound purified diets of Wolf (1951) and Halver (1957, 1967) and the several types of pelleted foods recently developed.

The purified diet was made possible by the use of gelatin as the binding agent and has proved a most useful tool in basic research. Neither the gelatin binder nor the purified ingredients are practical for production diets; the gelatin provides too much volume and the ingredients are too costly. With the development of pressurized pelleting of dry meals for poultry feeding, diet preparation for trout feeding changed radically. Several commercial companies found that this type of pellet could be adapted to trout feeding. As a result numerous, closed-formula, pelleted, trout foods are available commercially and a few open-formula pellets have been developed. This type of pellet consists of dry ingredients which are formed into pellets by pressure. Investigators conducting studies on potential pellet formulations use commercially available pellet presses.

The Oregon Fish Commission Laboratory has developed a moist pellet (Hublou, 1963) which the salmons will eat. This pellet consists of 40% of raw or pasteurized fish products combined with fish and vegetable meals together with a vitamin supplement and a kelp meal binder. The pellet is formed by extrusion through a spaghetti press and is quick frozen and stored under refrigeration.

The Salmon-Cultural Laboratory has developed a third type of pellet derived from a reconstituted dry meal diet developed at this laboratory and fed through a ricer (Fowler *et al.*, 1966). This diet consists of a mixture of dry animal and vegetable products, a vegetable oil and a vitamin supplement. It is partially reconstituted with water and bound by the addition of carboxymethyl cellulose (CMC). After extrusion through a spaghetti press, the pellets are quick frozen and kept in frozen storage. The soft pellet produced by this formulation is consumed readily by salmon fingerlings. It is particularly adapted for feeding trials in that the protein intake of the fish may be controlled by the amount of water added to the diet and the caloric intake adjusted by the amount of oil added.

More recent investigations indicate that diets of this type may be pressure-pelleted and used in salmon propagation (Fowler and Burrows, 1971). With the deletion of the added water, some inert ingredient is added in order to maintain desired or comparable nutrient levels in diet studies.

All three types of pellets are much superior to any of the meat or meat–meal diets in the conservation of the water-soluble components even when the meat diets are bound to maximum consistency by addition of salt or other binders. Willoughby (1953) reports an increase of 50% in growth in fish fed a dry pellet compared to a ricer-fed, identical diet over a 5-month period. A similar experiment with the soft pellet has demonstrated a 30% increase in gain over a 2-week period. All of the pelleted diets have proved equal to or better than the best of the meat–meal, bound, and ricer-fed combination in producing growth. Some of the hard pelleted products, however, have not proved to be nutritionally adequate when fed exclusively over prolonged periods.

While pellets are made in several sizes and fed in correlation with size of fish, difficulty is still experienced in starting salmonids to feed on even the smallest pellets available. Several agglomerate feeds have been developed which are mixtures of meals, oil, and vitamin supplements. These agglomerates have proved to be equal or superior to liver as a starting diet. Small salmon fingerlings cannot consume hard pellets of the same size as soft pellets and must be fed granules one to two sizes smaller.

Water temperature, also, affects the consumption of hard food particles. Cold water tends to inhibit both the appetite and activity of the fish. Most starter feeds, however, are softened and made more palatable by the addition of vegetable or fish oils to the dry meals and are consumed quite readily at temperatures below 8°C. After conversion to hard pellet granules, small salmon fingerlings, less than 1.0 gm average weight, may refuse to feed if the water temperature drops below 4°C and remains there for periods of a week or more. Extremely emaciated fish, "pinheads," may develop in as much as 50% of a lot during prolonged periods of cold water. Such fish rarely recover and eventually enter the mortality. Diet studies are best conducted in controlled environments at water temperatures above 10°C.

It is highly probable that little if any nutritional research in the future will be conducted with meat or meat–meal, ricer-fed, combination diets. The gelatin-bound, purified ration and the pelletized combination diets eliminate so many of the potential variables that these are by far the best vehicles for diet studies.

### 2. Feeding Levels

The amount of food which fish should be fed in order to achieve optimum utilization is related to species, fish size, diet quality, and water temperature. For optimum utilization fish should be fed slightly less than maximum consumption. This level for meat and meat–meal diets has been determined for several species of trout and salmon on a trial and error basis. The variation in consumption of several species is depicted in Fig. 4. Actually these levels are very accurate for these species and represent close analyses of numerous production operations. For feeding levels for other species of

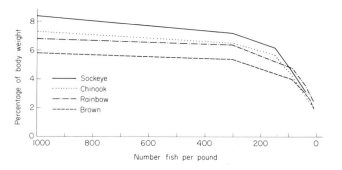

Fig. 4. Consumption of meat and meat–meal diets by several species of salmonids at 50°F water temperature. Sockeye salmon after Burrows *et al.* (1951), chinook salmon after Burrows *et al.* (1952), and rainbow and brown trout after Tunison (1945).

trout reference should be made to Phillips *et al.* (1963). Coho salmon are
fed at the same rate as chinook salmon. No feeding levels have been developed for other species of salmon primarily because these have not been
reared extensively in hatcheries. Both pink salmon (*O. gorbuscha*) and the
chum salmon (*O. keta*) are very voracious feeders as fingerlings. There is
every reason to believe that these species should be fed at even a higher
rate than the sockeye salmon.

Figure 4 also shows the effect of fish size on food consumption. As fish
increase in size the rate of growth declines and protein requirement also
declines. The diet composition and the protein-energy calorie ratio in the
diet therefore should change with the changing requirements of the fish.

The quantity and quality of the protein fed affects food consumption by
the fish. Most feeding charts were developed for meat or meat–meal diets.
Since the introduction of dry meal diets, it is possible to increase the level
of high quality protein well above the 18–20% encountered in meat diets.
The feeding level on high-protein diets should be reduced if the feeding
charts are to be applicable. If the protein quality of the diet is equal to
that of a meat diet and the protein content is significantly higher, the
amount fed should vary inversely with protein content. The protein quality
of most dry meal diets is rarely equal to that of meats and the feeding level
must be increased over the indicated reduction to conform with what the
fish will consume. Figure 5 demonstrates the effect of protein content on
the food intake of chinook salmon fingerlings. It will be noted that the

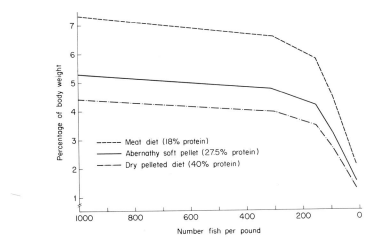

FIG. 5. Effect of protein content of diet on food consumption of chinook salmon
fingerlings at 50°F water temperature.

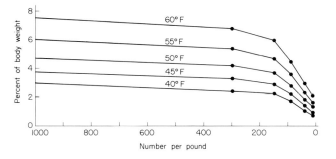

Fɪɢ. 6. Effect of water temperature on food consumption of chinook salmon fingerlings fed the Abernathy soft pellet (27.5% protein).

protein quality of the Abernathy diet is very comparable to that of meat but that of the hard pellet is much inferior in that a protein content of 40% would indicate a feeding level 45% of the meat level. Actually, the hard pellets are fed at 60% of the meat level.

The effect of water temperature on salmonids has been previously discussed. Because temperature does affect metabolism it also affects food intake. The effect of temperature on the food intake of chinook fingerlings is shown in Fig. 6. Above 60°F the fish are not in an optimal environment and the food intake should not be increased above the 60°F level. Below 40°F, chinook fingerlings become sluggish and feed slowly responding best during the diurnal period of rising temperature. Other species of trout and salmon respond differently at the limits of the temperature range, but all are affected by temperature and respond best in the optimum range of 50°–60°F (10°–15°C).

### 3. Feeding Frequency

In any diet trial it is highly desirable that all test animals have an equal opportunity to feed and are assured of an equal portion. When feeding salmonids the frequency of feeding regulates the availability of the diet to the fish. Bulky diets such as meats or partially reconstituted pellet feeds should be fed frequently particularly to small fish. Palmer *et al.* (1951) have demonstrated the use of frequent feeding of meat diets as a means of ensuring equal distribution of feed as well as preventing wastage of feed from infrequent feeding. Best utilization was found by feeding eight times per day up to the time the fish reached 100 per pound (4.5 gm average weight). These tests were conducted in low-velocity troughs. In tanks and ponds with water velocities from 0.5 to 1.0 foot per seconds, the feeding frequency may be more rapidly reduced due to the more efficient distribution of the feed by the current and better distribution of the fish in the pond. Salmonids more than 500 per pound should be fed at least eight times per day; between 500 and 150 per pound, five times per day; between 150 and 90 per pound, three times per day; and less than 90 per pound, two times per day providing that water temperatures are above 45°F. Colder temperature require more frequent feeding. The fish should consume their allotment within 10–15 minutes after being fed. If consumption is too rapid the number of feeds should be reduced and the allotment per feed increased. The reverse procedure should be used if consumption is too slow.

Concentrated feeds present a different problem particularly if the protein is of poor quality and it is desired to feed on an isoprotein basis. Under these circumstances the more aggressive, voracious fish are capable of consuming all of the feed if frequent feeding intervals are used. As a result some of the fish do not receive their portion and may either actually starve to death or, at best, be stunted. To avoid this development the allotment of feed must be increased and the frequency reduced. Many times, under these circumstances, it is necessary to reduce to one feeding per day.

## III.  Experimental Procedures

Fish present handling and manipulation problems not ordinarily encountered in other types of feeding trials which, of necessity, affect both the experimental techniques and the design of experiment. As compensation, feeding trials using fish as the test animal have several advantages in that the animals are small leading to use of relatively large groups and allowing for complete analyses of the animal produced.

### A. Experimental Techniques

Weight is the initial and most readily available measure used in feeding trials. The determination of accurate weights presents problems in that the fish cannot be removed from the water indefinitely and therefore a certain residual amount of water remains on the fish in the weighing process. The problem is to standardize this residual without jeopardizing the well being of the fish. In production operations, Griffiths *et al.* (1941) recommended a 5- to 10-second draining period. Our experiments indicate rather erratic results with this short and unstandardized period. Burrows *et al.* (1951) recommended a 15-second draining interval for fish held in drain nets. The 15-second draining interval removes most of the water from both the fish and the net and the residual is a relatively uniform amount. Weights taken in this manner can usually be reproduced within 5 gm at total group weight 1–10 kg.

In diet trials each experimental lot is weighed at biweekly intervals (Fig. 7). The procedure is as follows:

1. Fish are drained from rearing tank and retained in tub.

2. Fish are poured from tub into drain net, the drain net is removed from the water, and allowed to drain for a full 15-second interval.

3. Fish are poured from net into tared tub containing 2–3 inches of water.

4. Fish are weighed to nearest gram on triple-beam, 30 kg-capacity balance.

5. Fish are returned to rearing tanks in weight tubs.

In routine operations the elapsed time from removal to return of the fish to the rearing tank is approximately 2 minutes.

A second problem is the procurement of unbiased samples for the initial populations composing the experimental lots. Fish derived from the same female or the same day's egg take while still of the same race and species and as near homogeneous as possible do not have the same growth rates and are therefore of different sizes. Grading of the population to minimize variation imposes selectivity and can invalidate the results of some experiments. Selectivity may be unintentionally imposed by the method of sampling. As described by Hewitt and Burrows (1948), samples within a population may differ markedly dependent on when and how the samples are taken. The vertical sampler developed by these authors and later modified to contain four removable closed pockets (Burrows *et al.*, 1951) selects unbiased samples for experimental work (Fig. 8). The experimental sampler consists of four, pie-shaped, rod-framed nets supported by a circular frame which fits inside a tub. The collapsed nets and frame are placed in the tub and water and fish added. The sampler is drawn rapidly upward through the milling fish to secure unbiased samples of the population. By quartering and requartering the initial population until the desired sample size is attained, bias in sample selection is eliminated.

The techniques of experiment for the Cortland Laboratory have been described by Tunison *et al.* (1940), Phillips *et al.* (1953), and for the Salmon-Cultural Laboratory by Burrows *et al.* (1951, 1952). In general the techniques of experiment are similar but designs of experiment are different.

Fig. 7. Equipment and procedure for weighing fish. (a) Diet tanks showing center screen assembly in place and jump guard removed. (b) Removal of screen assembly allowing fish to flow through center outlet to be trapped in drain tub beneath. (c) Drain tub and cart containing fish to be weighed. (d) Portable receiving trough, framed drain net, and triple-beam balance. Tub on balance contains about 2 inches of water which is included in the tare. (e) Fish removed from water and allowed to drain for 15-second interval prior to weighing. (f) Drained fish being poured into weigh tub. Total weigh will be recorded and fish returned to tank. Four men can weigh forty-two tanks of fish in $1\frac{1}{2}$ hours using this procedure.

Fig. 8. Method for selection of samples for diet experiments. (a) A quarter sampler with removable pockets. (b) Sampler in place in tub prior to introduction of fish. Water depth is about 2 inches. (c) Fish and water have been poured into sampler and sampler is being drawn upward through fish. (d) One of the sampler pockets has been removed, the fish drained for 15 seconds in the pocket, and the fish are being poured from the net into the tub until a predetermined weight is reached. Man on right is tapping tub to forewarn of approaching weight. Weighed fish will be distributed into tanks by system of random numbers.

## B. Design of Experiment

The design of experiment for salmonid feeding trials is not essentially different from those of other animal husbandry experiments. The statistical applications are the same. Because of the numbers of fish used per sample population the individual trials may be conducted in duplicate. Only when six or less diets are to be tested is it necessary to conduct the trials in triplicate.

The biological variation encountered within an experiment varies between species and between years of experiment. The experimental error is relatively fixed providing that the same techniques are used. The combination of experimental error and biological variation usually ranges between 5 and 10% of the weight of fish dependent on the species, rate of growth, and duration of experiment.

Weight is the criterion of measurement used during experiments to determine amount to feed. Fish are usually stocked at a fixed weight and weighed at biweekly intervals to determine the rate of gain.

Two approaches have been used for conducting feeding trials with salmonids. In the experiments at the Salmon-Cultural Laboratory the tanks are stocked at the rate of 1000 gm per 6-foot circular tank or 16-foot deep trough for 12-week experiments and 500 gm per tank or trough for 24-week experiments. These stocking levels are based on the fact that chinook and sockeye salmon fingerlings fed good diets in the 50° and 60°F temperature range will double in weight every 6 weeks, on the average. At these stocking levels there is not danger of an inhibition in growth rate due to overcrowding.

The Cortland Laboratory uses another approach. Here small troughs are stocked with equal weights of trout at levels approaching the carrying capacity of the equipment. According to Tunison *et al.* (1940), at each biweekly weigh period the number of fish in each group is reduced so that the new period starts with the same weight of fish per cubic foot of water. Phillips *et al.* (1953) defend this procedure on the basis that the small troughs make it impossible to stock with a significant initial population if it is necessary to carry the entire sample through to the termination of the experiment. He justifies the procedure on the basis that it works. The reason that it works is that this laboratory is very successful in procuring an unbiased sample every time each population is reduced. Many of the major contributions to salmonid nutrition have been derived from feeding trials conducted at the Cortland Laboratory attesting to the success of this approach. If space and facilities were available, however, probably none of these investigators would favor this experimental design over that of the retention of entire samples throughout the experimental period.

The evaluation of experimental results in salmonid feeding trials has become much more sophisticated in recent years. While gain in weight is the principal criterion used during the experiment, it assumes but secondary importance in the evaluation of final results. Numbers and size of fish available at the conclusion of feeding trials make chemical analyses of sample groups from each population practicable. Growth is no longer measured by gain in weight but by protein deposition in the fish. By chemical analyses of both the food fed and the fish produced it is possible to determine protein utilization, optimum caloric levels, protein-energy calorie ratios, and many other measurements much more accurately than can be achieved in other forms of animal husbandry where fewer and larger animals are used in the experiments.

With the development of more refined methods of measurement the design of experiments may change. Ultimately the quality of the fish produced in feeding trials will be correlated with adult survival. In this manner quality standards may be defined and quality control applied–quality control not only in terms of diet and environment but also logically applied to the end product, the fish produced.

## IV. Summary

Salmonid husbandry requires employment of sound fish cultural practices and good experimental techniques if the results are to be applicable to artificial propagation. These requirements may be summarized as follows:

1. The objectives of sound fish cultural practice are to produce an environment, facilities, and techniques which are conducive to normal growth and survival of the test animals.

2. Water temperature affects the growth and activity of the fish. Optimum temperatures are between 10° and 15°C for salmonids. Feeding trials should be conducted at both the optimum and tolerance temperature ranges in order to determine the effect of changes in metabolic activity on the dietary requirement.

3. Oxygen consumption of fingerling salmonids is affected by water temperature, fish size, pollutants, food metabolized, and both physical and physiological activity. The critical level of respiratory dependence is at an oxygen level of 6 ppm. Oxygen levels should not be allowed to drop below 6 ppm when fish are in a state of normal activity.

4. The factors limiting the carrying capacity of water are an interrelationship between the available oxygen and the population density.

5. The principal pollutants of concern are those associated with water quality and metabolic wastes. Salmonids held in soft water are subject to copper, zinc, and lead toxicities. Soft water supplies should not be allowed to contact these heavy metals. The principal deleterious product of salmonid excretion is unionized ammonia. In diet trials the primary

concern is that the unionized ammonia does not accumulate to the point that the growth rate is inhibited. At 65°F, in hard waters, unionized ammonia can become a limiting factor when the loading rate exceeds 8 pounds per gallon per minute of inflow.

6. Small troughs or circular tanks have proved to be the most acceptable fish containers for diet trials. Of the two, the circular tanks are the most versatile.

7. Water may be reconditioned by action of nitrifying bacteria and aerated for reuse. In such systems the amount of supplemental water required varies from 2–10% of the amount recirculated. Reconditioning and recirculating makes temperature control practicable for feeding trials.

8. Gelatin-bound purified rations and three or more types of pelleted diets are available for feeding trials. The purified ration is most suitable for basic research and the pelleted products for applied research.

9. The amount of food which salmonids should be fed for optimum utilization is related to the species, fish size, diet quality, and water temperature. As the fish increase in size the rate of food consumption decreases. In proteins of equal quality an increase in the protein content of the diet results in a reduction in the total diet intake. Within limits, as the temperature increases the food intake increases.

10. The frequency of feeding regulates distribution of the diet to the fish. Small fish, more than 500 per pound, should be fed at least eight times per day. Large fish, less than 90 per pound (5 gm each) should be fed twice daily.

11. The weight of the fish is the most reliable measure for use during feeding trials. A 15-second draining interval has proved the most practical procedure for consistent removal of water.

12. Unbiased samples are best secured by use of a vertical pie sampler.

13. Statistical procedures developed for agricultural experiments are directly applicable to salmonid feeding trials. Duplicate samples and retention of initial samples throughout the experiment are the recommended procedures.

## References*

Atz, J. W. (1964). *U.S. Bur. Sport Fish. Wildl. Res. Rep.* No. **63**, 1–16.

Brett, J. R. (1952). *J. Fish. Res. Bd. Can.* **9**, 265–323.

Brett, J. R. (1956). *Quart. Rev. Biol.* **31**, 75–87.

Brett, J. R. (1958). *In* "The Investigations of Fish-Power Problems" (P. A. Larkin, ed.), pp. 69–83. H. R. McMillan Lectures in Fisheries, Univ. of British Columbia, Vancouver.

* References designated as *Fish. Res. Bull.* are published by the New York State Conservation Department, Albany, New York.

Brett, J. R. (1959). *Trans. 2nd Seminar Biol. Problems Water Pollution, U.S. Public Health Ser., Robt. A. Taft San. Eng. Center,* Cincinnati Ohio.

Burrows, R. E. (1963). *Proc. 12th Pacific Northwest Symp. Water Pollution Res. Water Temperature—Influences, Effects, and Control, U.S. Dept. Health Education and Welfare, Public Health Ser., Pac. N.W. Water Lab.,* pp. 29–35.

Burrows, R. E. (1964). *U.S. Bur. Sport Fish. Wildl. Res. Rep. No.* **66,** 12 pp.

Burrows, R. E., and Chenoweth, H. H. (1955). *U.S. Fish Wildl. Serv. Res. Rep. No.* **39,** 29 pp.

Burrows, R. E., Robinson, L. A., and Palmer, D. D. (1951). *U.S. Fish Wildl. Ser. Spec. Sci. Rep. Fish. No.* **59,** 39 pp.

Burrows, R. E., Palmer, D. D., Newman, H. W., and Azevedo, R. L. (1952). *U.S. Fish Wildl. Ser. Spec. Sci. Rep. Fish. No.* **86,** 23 pp.

Davis, H. S. (1947). *U.S. Dep. Interior Fish Wildl. Ser. Res. Rep. No.* **12,** 98 pp.

Elliott, J. W. (1969). *Progr. Fish Cult,* **31,** 67–73.

Fowler, L. G., and Banks, J. L. (1966). *U.S. Dep. Interior Fish Wildl. Serv. Tech. Pap.* **13,** 1–18.

Fowler, L. G., and Burrows, R. E. (1971). *Prog. Fish Cult.* **33,** 67–75.

Fry, F. E. J. (1957). *In* "The Physiology of Fishes" (M. E. Brown, ed.), Vol. I, pp. 1–63. Academic Press, New York.

Griffiths, F. P., Jarvis, W., Smith, A. B., and Lockwood, C. A. (1941). *Trans. Amer. Fish. Soc.* **70,** 275–281.

Halver, J. E. (1957). *J. Nutr.* **62,** 225–243.

Halver, J. E. (1967). *U.S. Bur. Sport Fish. Wildl. Res. Rep. No.* **70,** 78–102.

Hawkes, H. A. (1963). "The Ecology of Waste Water Treatment," 203 pp. Macmillian, New York.

Hermann, R. B., Warren, C. E., and Doudoroff, P. (1962). *Trans. Amer. Fish. Soc.* **91,** 155–167.

Hewitt, G. S., and Burrows, R. E. (1948). *Progr. Fish Cult.* **10,** 23–27.

Hublou, W. F. (1963). *Progr. Fish Cult.* **25,** 175–180.

Job, S. V. (1955). *Univ. Toronto Stud. Biol. Ser. No. 61. Publ. Ontario Fish. Res. Lab.* **73,** 39 pp.

Jones, J. R. E. (1964). "Fish and River Pollution." Butterworth, Washington, D.C.

Johnson, H. E., and Gastineau, A. C. (1952). *Progr. Fish Cult.* **14,** 76–78.

Karrick, N. (1948). *U.S. Dep. Interior Fish Wildl. Serv. Fish. Leafl.* **325,** 1–23.

Lloyd, R. (1960). *Ann. Appl. Biol.* **48,** 84–94. (*Biol. Abstr.* **35,** No. 46741.)

Lloyd, R. (1961). *Ann. Appl. Biol.* **49,** 535–538. (*Biol. Abstr.* **57,** No. 17007,) 1962.

Merkins, J. C. (1958). *Water Waste Treat.* **7,** 150–151.

Palmer, D. D., Robinson, L. A., and Burrows, R. E. (1951). *Progr. Fish Cult.* **13,** 205–212.

Palmer, D. D., Newman, H. W., Azevedo, R. L., and Burrows, R. E. (1952). *Progr. Fish Cult.* **14,** 122–124.

Phillips, A. M., Jr. (1956). *Progr. Fish Cult.* **18,** 113–119.

Phillips, A. M., Jr., Brockway, D. R., Rodgers, E. O., Sullivan, M. W., Cook, B., and Chipman, J. R. (1947). *N. Y. State Conserv. Dep. Fish. Res. Bull. 9 Cortland Hatchery Rep.* **15,** 21 pp.

Phillips, A. M., Jr., Brockway, D. R., Rodgers, E. O., Robertson, R. L., Goodell, H., Thompson, J. A., and Willoughby, H. (1948). *Fish. Res. Bull.* **10,** 35 pp.

Phillips, A. M., Jr., Brockway, D. R., Bryant, M., Rodgers, E. O., and Maxwell, J. M. (1950). *Fish. Res. Bull.* **13,** 31 pp.

Phillips, A. M., Jr., Lovelace, F. E., Brockway, D. R., and Balzer, G. C., Jr. (1953). *Fish. Res. Bull. No.* 16, 46 pp.

Phillips, A. M., Jr., Tunison, A. V., and Balzer, G. C. (1963). *U.S. Bur. Sport Fish. Wildl. Circ.* 159, 38 pp.

Pyle, E. A. (1960). *Progr. Fish Cult.* 22, 30–33.

Rodgers, E. O. (1949). *Prog. Fish Cult.* 11, 82–84.

Sharp, R. W. (1951). *Prog. Fish Cult.* 13, 146.

Shaw, P. A. (1946). *Calif. Fish Game* 32, 3–12.

Smith, V. C. (1966). *Lab. Manage.* Feb., p. 26.

Sprague, J. B. (1964a). *J. Fish. Res. Bd. Can.* 21, 17–26.

Sprague, J. B. (1964b). *Prog. Fish Cultur.* 26, 111–114.

Sprague, J. B., and Ramsey, B. A. (1965). *J. Fish. Res. Bd. Can.* 22, 425–432.

Tunison, A. V. (1945). *U.S. Fish Wildl. Serv.* 23 pp. (mimeo.).

Tunison, A. V., Phillips, A. M., McCay, C. M., Mitchell, C. R., and Rodgers, E. O. (1940). *N. Y. State Conserv. Dep. Cortland Hatchery Rept. No. 8 the Year 1939*, 33 pp.

Willoughby, H. (1953). *Progr. Fish Cult.* 15, 127–128.

Wolf, L. E. (1951). *Progr. Fish Cult.* 13, 17–24.

# 9

## NUTRITIONAL FISH DISEASES

*S. F. Snieszko*

## I. Introduction

Nutritional fish diseases are defined as those which can be attributed to deficiency, excess, or improper balance of components present in the food available. Such diseases usually have a gradual onset because symptoms do not appear until one or more of the components of a diet drop below the critical level of the body reserves. Also, if food contains all necessary components in proper balance a nutritional disease is possible. For example, in the case of insufficient food supply an animal is starved, or if too much food is available the excess may be converted to fat and deposited in various tissues or organs. In fishes, which are ectothermic animals, the rate of metabolism depends on the temperature of the environment. Since fishes do not have to maintain body temperature above that of the environment, insufficient feeding results primarily in reduced growth rate which may be followed by starvation. Fish usually grow through their entire life-span. The rate of growth depends largely on the rate of metabolism which in turn depends on temperature within certain amplitude limits characteristic for various groups or species.

When one thinks about nutritional diseases of fishes, it must be remembered that there are more species of fishes than of all other vertebrates combined. Different taxonomical or ecological groups of fishes may have extremely different food requirements or feeding habits. Very little is known about fish diseases caused solely by malnutrition. The bits of information available on nutritional fish diseases are, in general, limited to those species raised for food, sport, or hobby.

Very few species of fish cultivated by man depend entirely on natural food found in their environment. The majority receive part, or all, of their food in a prepared form. Such prepared feeds differ greatly from the natural food. Most of the research on fish nutrition during recent years was limited to salmonids in the United States and to cyprinids in Europe.

Nutritional fish diseases have received very little attention. In the recently published textbook on fish diseases by Reichenbach-Klinke (1966) only 4 of 389 pages are devoted to nutritional diseases. Nutritional diseases are not listed in the last edition of Schäperclaus' (1954) textbook. Metabolic and deficiency diseases are briefly discussed in Amlacher's fish disease compendium (1961) under the heading "Metabolic Disorders."

Very little is known about nutritional diseases of pond fishes in America because production of such fish based on intensive artificial feeding is a recent development.

The only English review on nutritional diseases of salmonids is that by Halver (1954).

## II.  Thyroid Tumor

### A. HISTORICAL BACKGROUND

At the turn of the century thyroid tumors in hatchery-raised salmonids occurred in epizootic proportions and were originally described as adenocarcinomas or carcinomas. Later most, but not all, of these tumors were recognized as thyroid hyperplasia or goiter caused by iodine deficiency. The early historical review is contained in a monograph by Gaylord *et al.* (1914) as well as the most complete review of pathology and histopathology of this disease up to 1912. Numerous epizootics of this disease were reported from Europe, New Zealand, and United States. In all cases it was described as a typical cancer of unknown etiology, but Gaylord *et al.* (1914) suspected an infection as the cause of the disease.

Studies by Marine and Lenhart (1910, 1911) and Marine (1914) indicated that the presence of iodine in water or in the diet drastically reduced the incidence of the disease, halted the progress of the development of the goiters, and even resulted in regression. Nigrelli (1954) indicated that the majority of thyroid tumors in salmonids represent simple hyperplasia, but occasionally the adenomas and adenocarcinomas of undetermined etiology occur. The genetic predisposition to thyroidal tumors in the swordtail (*Xiphophorus*) was reviewed by Gordon (1954). Nevertheless, iodine deficiency is recognized as the most frequent cause of simple hyperplastic thyroid tumor in salmonid fishes.

MacIntyre (1960) includes synopsis of thyroid tumors in captive and free-living teleosts. It is evident from this review that thyroid tumors may affect many families of fishes.

### B. CAUSES

Epizootic outbreaks of thyroid tumors have been reported only from fish hatcheries and apparently resulted from iodine deficiency. The relationship between goiter and iodine deficiency is a well established fact. This is further supported by an observation that thyroid tumors are rare

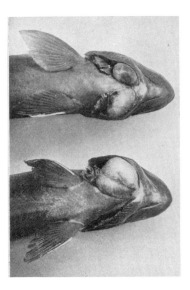

Fig. 1. Advanced thyroid tumors in rainbow trout, ¾ their natural size (Marsh, 1911).

in nature (MacIntyre, 1960). Thyroid tumors are rare in hatcheries at present because fish feed contains iodine added in the form of solution, iodides, or iodized table salt. Thyroid tumors in fishes usually regress under the influence of iodine and should, therefore, be classified as goiters. In some cases, goiters become malignant with metastases to other organs. It is generally agreed that goiter usually precedes thyroid carcinoma. "Tumors of the thyroid gland have been investigated more thoroughly than most other types of teleostean tumors, principally because of the economical value of many of the fishes involved and the similarities to goitrous conditions in man. The genetic and environmental causes of atypical thyroid growth in fishes are still not fully understood, however" (MacIntyre, 1960).

## C. Signs and Symptoms of the Disease

The normal thyroid follicles in fish resemble those of mammals. The gland is not well delineated but diffused in the lower jaw between the first and third gill arches. Therefore the proliferation of the thyroid tissue results in invasion of the surrounding tissues. The first evidence of visible tumors is hyperemia on the floor of the mouth and protrusions at the branchial junction. This is followed by tumors in the floor of the mouth and in the gill region. The neoplastic tissue grows between muscle planes and fills areolar spaces. Since karyokinetic figures are common and metastases occur, this tumor has some characteristics of a malignancy (Gaylord *et al.*, 1914). The thyroid tumor of salmonids approximate the three forms of thyroid tumor in mammals, namely proliferating, carcinomatous, and malignant struma. Advanced thyroid tumor can be tentatively diagnosed on the basis of its appearance and location, but firm diagnosis is possible only by histopathological examination.

The most detailed description of thyroid tumor is that of Gaylord *et al.* (1914) which contains many excellent black and white and color illustrations. The first sign is an appearance of red area in the middle of the floor of the mouth. With time the tumor may fill the mouth and protrude between the gill arches becoming clearly visible because gill covers are lifted by the tumor (Fig. 1). Exophthalmus may occur at all stages of the tumor development. Histologically the fish goiter shows hyperplasia of thyroid tissue with greatly increased storage of colloid in the follicles (Fig. 2).

According to Schlumberger (1955) separation of goiter from malignancy

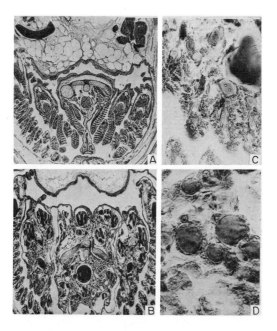

Fig. 2. Tumor of thyroid gland in teleost fishes, *Girardinus falcatus*. (A) Normal thyroid tissue. Four small follicles (60×). (B) Hyperplastic thyroid around ventral aorta. Numerous follicles (60×). (C) Hyperplastic thyroid tissue in the gills (300×). (D) Detailed view of hyperplastic thyroid (970×) (MacIntyre, 1960).

in the thyroid is particularly difficult in fish where the thyroid tissue is scattered over a wide area and proliferation in separate follicles may be interpreted as metastasis. Nevertheless, true metastases on the wall of the rectum and a nodule on the mandible were recorded by Gaylord *et al.* (1914). Confirmed malignant thyroid tumors seem to be rare in fishes.

## D. Species Affected

Thyroid tumors occurred most often among salmonids. The most acute outbreaks were reported among hatchery fish. Thyroid tumors are rare in wild fish and have been reported only in nine families. Their incidence is much higher in captive fishes, particularly if maintained in an environment deficient in iodine (all reports up to 1960 were listed by MacIntyre, 1960).

## E. Remedial Measures

In nonmalignant outbreaks of thyroid tumor in fishes, addition of iodine or iodide to fish food, or water, will either prevent the occurrence or cause tumor regression. Treatment with potassium iodide was recommended by Marsh (1911) who reported that mercury was also beneficial. The latter observation was not confirmed. The use of iodized salt in feed is as effective in prevention of goiter in fish as in other vertebrates.

Davis (1953) recommended addition of a tablespoon of Lugol's iodine solution to each 25 kg of feed. Woodall *et al.* (1964) determined the iodine requirements of chinook salmon to be 0.6 $\mu$g of iodine per gram of dry feed. They also observed that chinook salmon receiving food containing 10.1 $\mu$g of iodine per gram of diet were the only ones to be free of corynebacterial kidney disease. This is another observation on the relationship between the presence of minerals in the environment and the occurrence of kidney disease as reported by Warren (1963).

## III. Nutritional Gill Disease

## A. Historical Background

Nutritional gill disease was first observed by Fish (1935) but its etiology was not recognized. Tunison *et al.* (1944) were the first to associate gill clubbing with pantothenic acid deficiency. L. Wolf (1945) believed that deficiency of this vitamin was the only cause of gill disease and minimized the bacterial etiology reported by Davis (1926). Deficiency of pantothenic

TABLE I

Effect of vitamin Supplement and Occurrence of Gill Disease (Nutritional) in Fingerling Rainbow Trout in a Test Lasting 112 Days[a]

| Supplement to the basal diet[b,c] | Mortalities (%) | With gill disease (%) |
|---|---|---|
| None | 36 | 33 |
| Yeast | 19 | 0 |
| Four vitamins without thiamine | 19 | 0 |
| Four vitamins without riboflavin | 45 | 0 |
| Four vitamins without niacin | 26 | 0 |
| Four vitamins without pantothenate | 29 | 40 |
| Four vitamins without pyridoxine | 48 | 0 |
| All 5 vitamins added | 36 | 0 |
| Without riboflavin and niacin | 19 | 0 |
| Without riboflavin and pantothenate | 75 | 50 |
| Without niacin and pantothenate | 28 | 22 |
| Without pyridoxine and pantothenate | 56 | 50 |
| Without thiamine, riboflavin, and pyridoxine | 92 | 0 |

[a] Abbreviated after Wolf, 1945.

[b] Basal diet, Tapioca, pork spleen, meat meal and water.

[c] Vitamins tested, thiamine, riboflavin, niacin, calcium pantothenate, and pyridoxine.

acid was confirmed as the cause of nutritional gill disease in salmonid fishes in subsequent investigations (Rucker *et al.*, 1952; Halver, 1954).

## B. Causes

Deficiency of pantothenic acid in the diet is the cause of nutritional gill disease in salmonid fishes. Convincing experimental evidence was furnished by L. Wolf (1945) (Table I; Figs. 3 and 4).

## C. Signs and Symptoms of the Disease

There are no striking differences in signs and symptoms of gill diseases of different etiology. Fish experience respiratory difficulties in all gill diseases: loss of appetite, congregating near the inflow of water, turning toward the current, remaining almost motionless unless disturbed, and tending to remain at equal distances from each other thereby best utilizing the space available for each fish. If tanks are in tandem, the earliest and most severe signs are in the lowest tanks. In water containing metabolic wastes and an oxygen deficiency, fish become weak and are carried toward the lower end by the current. Gills may be hyperemic in the initial stages of the disease. With the advance of proliferation of the gill epithelium and clubbing and fusing of the gill filaments, gills appear pale and respiration is accelerated.

The differences between gill disease caused by infective agents and malnutrition can be detected by microscopic examination of gill lamellae. In the early stages of nutritional gill disease, the epithelial hyperplasia resulting in clubbing begins at the distal end of the gill filament (Wood and Yasutake, 1957). Examination of gills is the best diagnostic method for presence of myxobacteria in bacterial gill disease. Another indication of nutritional gill disease is the lack of response to disinfectants used for the control of bacterial gill disease.

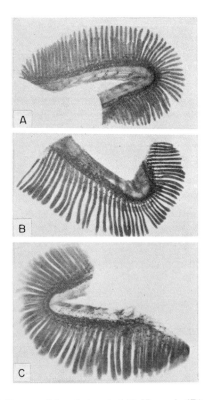

Fig. 3. Dietary gill disease of brook trout. (A) Normal; (B) moderate gill disease; (C) severe gill disease (Wolf, 1945).

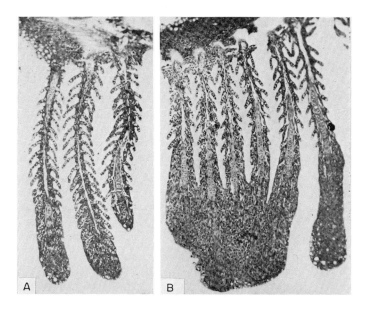

Fig. 4. (A) Section through part of gill showing lamellae grown together at tips of filaments. (B) Section through severely diseased gill with filaments grown together at tips (Wolf, 1945).

Microscopic differentiation among nutritional, bacterial, and improperly named "hemorrhagic" gill disease was described and illustrated by Wood and Yasutake (1957). The most detailed description of nutritional gill disease is that by Wolf (1945).

### D. Species Affected

All salmonid fishes are susceptible to nutritional gill disease. Sufficient information is lacking on the relative susceptibility of different species of salmonids. "Of all the vitamin deficiences, a deficiency in pantothenic acid is probably the most common among trout" (Phillips and Podoliak, 1957).

### E. Remedial Measures

A remedial measure is feeding a diet containing sufficient quantities of pantothenic acid. The daily requirement has been tentatively established between 0.97 and 1.25 mg per kilogram of body weight per day. Vitamin supplement, beef liver. brewer's yeast, dried skim milk, and distiller's solubles are good sources of pantothenic acid.

## IV.  Nutritional Anemia

Anemia is characterized mainly by depressed values for erythrocytes and hemoglobin. These values vary greatly in normal fishes depending on species, age, water temperature, and sex. Some marine fishes in arctic areas have such low oxygen requirements that plasma alone can supply the respiratory needs and these fish do not have erythrocytes (Ruud, 1965). Therefore nutritional anemia as such can be diagnosed only if the values for hemoglobin and erythrocytes are below the normal values and beyond the normal amplitudes of variation as established for any species of fish under any specific environmental conditions. Many infectious, parasitic, and neoplastic diseases are known to cause anemia in fishes. One can classify as nutritional anemia only those cases attributed to malnutrition and these can be corrected by alleviating the nutritional deficiencies.

A considerable portion of the research on causes of nutritional anemia in salmonid fishes was conducted by Tunison, Phillips, and associates at the Eastern Fish Nutrition Laboratory, Cortland, New York. The results were described in numerous reports from the laboratory (Index by Hublou, 1960), and recently the Western Fish Nutrition Laboratory reported on folic acid deficiency anemia in salmon (Smith, 1968).

Nutritional anemia may have two basic causes. One may be the lack of elements permitting fish to produce blood and, second, nutritional diseases which affect hematopoietic organs. Some of the essential vitamins, minerals, and possibly also amino acids, belong to the first group. Fatty degeneration of the liver, visceral granuloma, hepatoma in terminal stages, and possibly others belong to the second group. Most communicable diseases in their acute form also may result in anemia.

Anemia is usually considered one of the symptoms of many nutritional diseases or disorders. Therefore anemia is described in this chapter as one of the symptoms of nutritional diseases under vitamin deficiencies, degenerative liver diseases, visceral granuloma, and starvation.

## V.  Vitamin Deficiency Diseases

### A. INTRODUCTION AND GENERAL HISTORICAL REVIEW

Recognition of vitamin deficiency diseases followed the introduction of artificial feeds to intensive fish culture. At the turn of the century intensive trout culture was introduced in Europe and the United States and artificial feed consisted mainly of livers, spleens, and other organs of slaughtered farm animals or raw marine fishes. Large-scale pond fish culture, mainly of carp, also developed in Europe, and regular use of artificial feeds was introduced about 50 years ago. This resulted in many catastrophic mortalities in fish farms and hatcheries and thereby stimulated fish nutritional research. In 1930, a trout nutrition laboratory was established at Cortland, New York, and was operated jointly by the U.S. Fish and Wildlife Service and the New York State Conservation Department. Research results have been published annually since 1932. An index to the Cortland hatchery reports is available from 1932 through 1958 (Hublou, 1960).

The history of early investigations on nutritional trout diseases attributed to vitamin deficiencies was thoroughly reviewed by L. Wolf (1942) and is briefly summarized below.

European investigators reported that originally the deleterious effects of feeding raw fish were attributed to parasites transferred with fishes used as food. The high fat content was also considered nutritionally harmful. Herring and smelt were therefore considered unsuitable as trout food. A considerable number of research reports were published on the effect of high fat diets for trout. These reports indicated that high fat diets did not have as harmful an effect on trout as raw herring or smelt.

About 1940, it was reported that there were resemblances between a disease of foxes caused by vitamin $B_1$ deficiency and the fish diet disease of trout. Alexander *et al.* (1941) found that carp, quillbacks, mullets, suckers, and Atlantic whiting contained a substance which destroyed thiamine. Spitzer *et al.* (1941) found such a substance in fish flesh. It is an enzyme called thiaminase.

Vitamin requirements were first studied by determination of vitamins in trout livers or by supplementing fish food with certain vitamins to find empirically which would alleviate disorders suspected as signs of vitamin deficiencies.

This was followed by introduction of diets of known composition as used by McLaren *et al.* (1947) or vitamin-free diet developed for fish nutritional research by L. Wolf (1951). This diet was further improved by Halver and Coates (1957), and Coates and Halver (1958). It is now possible to maintain salmonids on a synthetic diet for generations without any visible undesirable effects.

In the discussion on diseases associated with deficiency or excess of vitamins, emphasis will be given to reports published during the last 30 years when diets of known composition were used (McLaren *et al.*, 1947).

Nomenclature of vitamins and their order will be the same as used by Mitchell (1964).

## B. FAT-SOLUBLE VITAMINS

### 1. *Vitamin A*

The only pathological conditions attributed to vitamin A deficiency were reported in channel catfish. They were exophthalmos, ascites, edema, and hemorrhagic kidneys (Dupree, 1966). This vitamin was recommended as treatment for ichthyophthiriasis of Atlantic salmon fingerlings. It was added at a rate of 30,000 IU per kilogram of food (Malikova *et al.*, 1961).

### 2. *Vitamin D*

Absence of codliver oil in the diet of rainbow trout resulted in a necrotic appearance of the kidney. Addition of ergosterol and 7-dehydrocholesterol resulted in somewhat better hemoglobin level and absence of kidney necrosis (McLaren *et al.*, 1947).

The hemoglobin level in Atlantic salmon fingerlings fed a diet deficient in vitamin D was 21% lower than in control fish (Chudova, 1961).

### 3. *Vitamin E (The Tocopherols)*

Critical research on the requirements of tocopherols for fish was made possible when a tocopherol-free fat became available for the preparation of test diets. Woodall *et al.* (1964) observed pathological changes in chinook salmon (*O. tshawytscha*) fed a diet containing highly purified trilinolein. Salmon maintained on a diet very low in tocopherols developed exophthalmia and accumulation of ascites to such an extent that the abdomen was visibly distended. There was advanced anemia with red cell numbers and hemoglobin reduced to less than half of the values present in controls. Also erythrocytes were smaller with a relative increase in the number of polychromatocytes. Histopathological changes were insignificant. Gill lamellae were clubbed and occasionally fused similar to those in fish suffering from a pantothenic acid deficiency.

Symptoms of tocopherol deficiency in brown trout fingerlings consisted of anemia with onset of severe anemia in 8 weeks; heavy mortalities occurred when the hematocrit level dropped to about 20% of normal. Diseased trout recovered when placed on a diet supplemented with 370 ppm of *dl*-α-tocopheryl acetate (Poston, 1964b). According to Faktorovich (1960), accumulation of ceroid in fish liver and other tissues is caused by a vitamin E deficiency which prevents oxidation of unsaturated fats in ceroid. Depletion of vitamin E by its antioxidative properties present in

TABLE II

Summary of Hematological Data from Chinook Salmon Fed Diets with and Without Vitamin E[a]

|  | Diet | |
| --- | --- | --- |
|  | With vitamin E | Without vitamin E |
| Hemoglobin (gm/100 ml) | 12.2–12.8 | 6.2 |
| Hematocrit | 40.3–43.7 | 21.4 |
| Erythrocyte area ($\mu^2$) | 96.4–98.2 | 71.2 |
| Immature erythrocytes (%) | 2.6–3.6 | 17.6 |

[a] After Whitmore, 1965.

fish tissues may be caused by an excess unsaturated fat in the fish diet. Plehn (1924) indicated that feeding rainbow trout raw fish containing much fat should be avoided. Faktorovich (1960) indicated that the spoiled raw fish contain unsaturated fatty acids which destroy vitamin E. When such food is being fed, vitamin E deficiency develops which results in lipoid liver degeneration and deposition ceroid.

Anemia was often observed in chinook salmon raised on a diet of Oregon moist pellets (Whitmore, 1965). It was suspected that anemia was caused by feeding rancid pellets. $d$-$\alpha$-tocopheryl was added at a rate of 50 mg/100 gm of dry diet to prevent rancidity. On the basis of the hematological observations present in Table II, microcytic anemia was diagnosed in salmon fed a rancid diet. When anemic salmon were again fed a diet enriched with vitamin E, all blood indexes returned to normal within 20 days.

### 4. *Vitamin K*

It is generally accepted that vitamin K, essential for blood coagulation, is furnished by intestinal bacterial flora. Therefore any drug which suppresses bacterial reproduction in the intestinal tract may contribute to vitamin K deficiency. This was confirmed by Phillips *et al.* (1962) for brook trout maintained on a synthetic diet without vitamin K (2-methyl-3-phytyl-1,4-naphthoquinone). Such trout developed mild anemia, as determined by microhematocrit, and a slight increase in the blood coagulation time. Similar effects were produced by addition of sulfaguanidine to the diet which depresses intestinal bacterial flora (Poston, 1964a).

Vitamin K deficiency caused mild cutaneous hemorrhages in channel catfish (Dupree, 1966).

## C. B Vitamins

### 1. *Thiamine ($B_1$)*

Literature is more complete on thiamine requirements by fish and on deficiency symptoms than on any other vitamin. The early history of research on thiamine deficiency disease in fishes can be found in a report by L. Wolf (1942) and a recent review was written by Coble (1965). Thiamine was found to be essential to all species of fish in which it was tested. The most detailed description of $B_1$ deficiency signs and symptoms in brook, brown, and rainbow trout were given by L. Wolf (1942, 1952) and are summarized below.

Loss of balance progresses slowly from occasional instability to complete inability to maintain normal position. Eventually trout stay at the bottom, swim on their sides, or are vertically oriented. There is a slow onset of anorexia but even trout which cannot maintain their normal positions take some food. Trout become very excitable and undergo periods of frantic activity as turning, twisting, and leaping. Frightened fish become more violent. The air bladder may be over- or underinflated and gas may be present in the stomach. The position of the bladder may be changed and peritoneum ruptured. The cornea of the eye may become opaque but the lens remains clear. Older trout may become blind and dark in color. Death usually follows an almost complete paralysis of voluntary muscles.

All symptoms may be aggravated by transferring trout to colder water. Brain lesions in trout were the same as in higher vertebrates suffering from thiamine deficiency. They consisted of vascular degeneration, proliferation, and hemorrhages (Alexander *et al.*, 1941).

Rainbow trout fingerlings fed canned carp developed typical symptoms of $B_1$ deficiency (Woodbury, 1943). Some of these trout were treated with thiamine by parenteral injection of 2 mg of the vitamin per trout. A single injection resulted in recovery and an increase in oxygen intake which was 3.5 greater than in untreated trout—convincing evidence that symptoms were attributed to $B_1$ deficiency.

Symptoms of thiamine deficiency described by Wolf were also reported by others. McLaren *et al.*, (1947), Halver (1954), and Phillips and Brockway (1957) observed similar symptoms in all tested salmonid fishes. Livers were occasionally found to be pale or yellow, some trout were covered with a purplish sheen, were anemic, and had abdominal edema.

Blueback salmon fingerlings fed fresh herring developed similar external and internal symptoms and hemoglobin levels were 20% lower than in controls (Burrows *et al.*, 1952).

According to Harrington (1954), thiamine requirements differ among fishes. A species of catfish, *Nocturus* (*Schilbeodes*) *mollis* and a sunfish *Ennescanthus obesus* were maintained on a diet of carp eggs. Within a month catfish showed signs of thiamine deficiency and died while sunfish remained normal. Catfish showing signs of athiaminosis recovered when carp-egg diet was enriched with thiamine. Signs of athiaminosis were swifter and more widespread under longer and brighter illumination. Channel catfish (*Ictalurus punctatus*) (Dupree, 1966) fed a $B_1$-deficient diet developed lethargy and difficulty in maintaining equilibrium.

Anemic conditions in rainbow trout were reported by McLaren *et al.* (1947) and $B_1$ deficiency in Atlantic salmon fingerlings resulted in 30% lower hemoglobin levels than the controls (Chudova, 1961).

## 2. *Riboflavin* ($B_2$)

In rainbow trout fed a riboflavin-deficient diet, disease symptoms consisted of hemorrhagic eyes, nares, and operculum. About 40% died apparently because of this deficiency (McLaren *et al.*, 1947). Subsequent experiments by Phillips *et al.* (1952, 1957, 1958) indicated that riboflavin deficiency caused high mortalities in brook trout and Atlantic salmon. Eye clouding occurred in brook trout. In chinook salmon there was clouding of lens, eye hemorrhages, photophobia, dim vision, discoloration of the iris, darkening of the skin, and incoordination of movements (Halver, 1954). Opaqueness of the eye lens was also observed in channel catfish deprived of riboflavin (Dupree, 1966).

In conclusion, riboflavin deficiency results in high fish mortalities with eye opaqueness the most frequently observed external sign.

## 3. *Nicotinic Acid*

Nicotinic acid is essential for good growth of brook and brown trout (Phillips and Brockway, 1957) but disease symptoms were reported only in chinook salmon (Halver, 1954). They consisted of incoordinated movements, intestinal lesions, edema, swollen but not clubbed gills, and muscle spasms. In channel catfish (Dupree, 1966), deficiency signs included photophobia, tetany, lethargy, and reduced coordination. Anemia and swollen gills were also observed in rainbow trout (McLaren *et al.*, 1947).

*Nicotinic Acid and Sunburn.* It is well known that various chemicals and drugs, particularly those which fluoresce under ultraviolet light, may sensitize people or animals to sunburn. Niacin-deficient persons with pellagra are more sensitive to sunburn. When chinook salmon fed niacin-deficient or control diets were exposed to sunlight under hatchery conditions the niacin-deficient salmon developed sunburn. When niacin was returned to the diet they recovered (DeLong *et al.*, 1958).

The value of fish diet with niacin supplement to prevent sunburn was tested in lake trout (Allison, 1960) and landlocked Atlantic salmon (Corson and Brezosky, 1961). The results were inconclusive in both cases.

It should be mentioned that the use of phenothiazine, an antagonist of niacin, was apparently associated with sunburn in trout treated with phenothiazine used to control an infection with Hexamita (Rucker, 1958).

## 4. *Pyridoxine* ($B_6$)

Pyridoxine is essential for survival of the following fishes which have been tested: brook, brown, and lake trout (Phillips and Brockway, 1957), Atlantic salmon (Phillips *et al.*, 1958), chinook salmon (Halver, 1954), rainbow trout (McLaren *et al.*, 1947), and channel catfish (Dupree, 1966).

Nervous disorders were among disease symptoms most generally observed. Halver (1954) also observed anemia, abdominal edema with colorless ascites, and blue green discoloration of the dorsal area in chinook salmon. Disturbances in locomotion, and spasms were observed in channel catfish (Dupree, 1966).

Interesting observations were made on the relationship among the protein contents of diet, pyridoxine, and trout survival (Phillips *et al.*, 1959). Brook trout maintained on a diet containing from 23 to 28% protein and deficient in pyridoxine died while losses of the same trout at the same time were half as large when fed a diet containing only 11.5% protein.

When pyridoxine requirement tests were performed in brook trout year around at a uniform temperature of 8.3°C, survival was better during fall and winter than during spring. This may be associated with sexual activity or simply age and size of fish which varied from 3.6 to 170 gm (Phillips and Livingston, 1965).

## 5. *Pantothenic Acid*

Deficiency of this vitamin is associated with a number of pathological conditions in fishes. Nutritional gill disease has been studied in greatest detail and the observations are very well documented. It is previously described in this chapter.

There are other signs of pantothenic acid deficiency; Halver (1957) reported loss of appetite, necrosis and scarring, cellular atrophy, exudate on gills, and sluggishness in chinook salmon. In channel catfish there were necrotic jaws, barbels and fins, "mummy" textured skin, and lethargy (Dupree, 1966). It seems also that deficiency of this vitamin may be a cofactor with biotin in production of "blue slime" disease in brown trout.

### 6. *The Cobalamin Derivatives* ($B_{12}$)

Deficiency of this vitamin in chinook salmon (Halver, 1957) is reflected in erratic hemoglobin levels, erythrocyte counts, and cell fragmentation. There is no evidence that vitamin $B_{12}$ deficiency is a significant cofactor with folic acid deficiency as cause of anemia in brook trout (Phillips, 1963).

### 7. *Pteroylglutamic Acid (Folic Acid)*

It has been known for a long time that salmonid fishes grown in hatcheries often became very anemic and died unless beef liver was included in the diet. McCay and Dilley (1927) confirmed that trout anemia was a nutritional disease caused by the lack of an unknown antianemia factor "H" in fish diet. McLaren *et al.* (1947) considered folic acid with biotin as the antianemia factors for rainbow trout. L. Wolf (1951) also found that lack of folic acid or inositol caused anemia in rainbow trout.

Research on folic acid as a possible antianemia factor was complicated by batches of "vitamin-free" casein which may have contained traces of this vitamin and its use sometimes produced conflicting results.

In a series of experiments on brook trout fed a synthetic diet from which folic acid was withheld, in combination with vitamin $B_{12}$, riboflavin, and niacin evidence pointing to folic acid as the antianemia factor became much clearer (Phillips *et al.*, 1960) (Table III). In a subsequent investigation, the vitamin selection was narrowed to folic acid and $B_{12}$. Brook trout fed diet without folic acid developed anemia, while trout deprived of $B_{12}$ remained normal. In the early stages of the experiment, there was an indication that $B_{12}$ was enhancing the development of anemia (Phillips, 1963). Subsequent research indicated that the omission of either *p*-aminobenzoic acid or folic acid, or both, from the diet of brook trout fingerlings resulted in anemia. There was a slight additive effect when both vitamins were lacking (Phillips *et al.*, 1963).

Folic acid deficiency in chinook salmon also resulted in anemia, fragility of caudal fin, dark coloration, and lethargy (Halver, 1957). Decreased appetite and lethargy were observed in channel catfish (Dupree, 1966).

### 8. *Biotin*

Blue slime (or blue slime patch) disease is the most frequently observed pathological sign of biotin deficiency. This disease occurs in brown trout and to some lesser degree in brook and rainbow trout. It is characterized by the gradual appearance of a bluish film covering the body and it may slough off in patches. Davis (1953) reported that this disease appeared about the same time every year and later disappeared without causing

TABLE III

Effect of Dietary *p*-Aminobenzoic Acid (PABA) and Folic Acid on Microhematocrit Values in Fingerling Brook Trout[a]

| Weeks from the start | Microhematocrit values in diets | | | |
|---|---|---|---|---|
| | Complete | Less PABA | Less folic acid | Less PABA and folic acid |
| 6 | 42 | 41 | 35 | 40 |
| 12 | 40 | 37 | 35 | 33 |
| 20 | 40 | 35 | 35 | 31 |

[a] Summary of data from Phillips *et al.*, 1963.

any mortalities. On other occasions, it caused heavy mortalities in brown
trout in hatcheries.

I have observed this disease year after year in 1-year-old brook trout at
the Leetown National Fish Hatchery. It seems the disease may not be
nutritional but may be associated with the season of the year, or sexual
cycle, because it regularly appeared during the winter months. It occurred
when trout were fed the soft meat–meal or dry pelleted diets and its appearance and disappearance could not be correlated with any changes in
feeding. Brown trout at Leetown were fed the same diet but never developed
this seasonal "blue slime" disease. It is interesting that brown trout which
have greater biotin demands than brook trout did not show this blue slime.

Experimentally the blue slime disease was produced in brook (Phillips
*et al.*, 1952) and in brown trout (Phillips *et al.*, 1955). Removal of biotin
from the diet by addition of raw egg white also resulted in blue slime
disease (Phillips *et al.*, 1950).

In chinook salmon (Halver, 1957) and channel catfish (Dupree, 1966),
biotine deficiency caused darker skin coloration, muscle atrophy, and
fragmentation of erythrocytes. Biotin may also contribute to anemia in
rainbow trout (McLaren *et al.*, 1947).

## 9. *Choline*

Anemia and hemorrhagic kidney and intestine were reported as pathological changes resulting from choline deficiency in rainbow trout (Mc-
Laren *et al.*, 1947) and chinook salmon (Halver, 1957).

## 10. *Inositol*

Symptoms described as a result of inositol deficiency in rainbow trout (McLaren *et al.*, 1947) and chinook salmon (Halver, 1957) consisted of fin necrosis, anemia, and distended stomach.

## 11. *Vitamin B Deficiency in Carp*

Zobairi (1956) performed a very interesting experiment on the importance of B complex vitamins for carp. Carp fingerlings weighing 31 gm each at the beginning of the test were started on a deficient diet consisting of ten parts peanut meal and one part fish meal. In about 180 days carp started to develop deficiency symptoms among which the most striking was nervousness. In some of the carp, fins contained air bubbles, fish lost equilibrium, and rested at the bottom. Some had bloodshot eyes and exophthalmus. Occasionally eye cornea became opaque, and soft tissue in fins started to disintegrate.

Injection of $B_1$ alone had no beneficial effect. Other fish received one intraperitoneal injection of 1 mg per fish of each of the following B complex vitamins: pyridoxine, folic acid, calcium pantothenate, riboflavin, $B_{12}$, and 50 mg of choline. This resulted in diappearance of all deficiency symptoms within several days.

## D. Ascorbic Acid

In the early nutritional studies, this vitamin was not considered essential for salmonid fishes, with the exception of McLaren *et al.* (1947) who observed hemorrhagic kidney, liver, and intestine in rainbow trout fed a diet deficient in ascorbic acid. Kitamura *et al.* (1965) observed lordosis and scoliosis in rainbow trout fed a diet deficient in ascorbic acid. Halver *et al.* 1969) have shown that this vitamin is essential for rainbow trout and coho salmon (*Oncorhynchus kisutch*). The minimum amount of ascorbic acid was 10 mg for 100 g of dry diet. In the absence of this vitamin wound repair was also delayed.

## E. Hypervitaminosis

### 1. *Vitamin A and Codliver Oil*

Excess of this vitamin in fish diet may cause toxic effects. Blueback salmon developed hemorrhagic, swollen, necrotic, or misformed gill lamellae and pale livers (Burrows *et al.*, 1952), when whole liver was used as the sole diet.

Brook trout fed a pelleted diet containing up to 2.5 million units of vitamin A, palmitate, or acetate per kilogram of pellets had eroded and necrotic caudal fins. There was also a slight reduction of hematocrits from 44 to 37 or 38 (Poston, 1966b).

## VI. Lipoid Liver Degeneration and Viral Hemorrhagic Septicemia

### A. HISTORICAL REVIEW

Nutrition of salmonid fishes, freshwater trout, in particular, differs greatly depending on the habitat. Wild trout in streams, rivers, and lakes feed upon other fish or invertebrate animals. In hatcheries or fish farms food consisted (and still consists, in some measure) of warm-blooded domestic vertebrate organs, marine or freshwater fish preserved by freezing, or more or less spoiled by decomposition, and with, or without, addition of meals of animal and plant origin. During the last 10 years pelleted dry fish food has been used in increasing quantities. It was only natural to expect that nutritional disturbances would be common until nutritional research would come up with a well-balanced diet. Diseases attributed to malnutrition plagued, and in a lesser measure still hamper, intensive fish culture, trout culture, in particular.

Rainbow trout, because of its popularity in trout culture and its specific susceptibility to liver damage caused by malnutrition, were particularly often affected by diseases characterized by liver and kidney damage and anemia.

Rainbow trout are also very susceptible to a viral disease described under different names as: swelling of the kidney and liver degeneration (INL) (Schäperclaus, 1954), pernicious anemia (Besse, 1956), lipoid liver degeneration (Plehn, 1924), Egtved disease (Rasmussen, 1965), or viral hemorrhagic septicemia (Ghittino, 1965).

Since many of the symptoms of purely nutritional disease and viral disease are similar, and malnutrition according to some observers predispose trout to viral disease or vice versa, many reports were published on liver diseases in trout. An attempt will be made to bring some clarity to this still confused situation.

The most recent and complete reviews on liver diseases of trout of nutritional, viral, or mixed etiology, are by Amlacher (1961), Ghittino (1962, 1965), and Rasmussen (1965). Each of these reports contains extensive bibliographies. The most extensive review on anemia, in general, and fish, in particular, is that by Besse (1956).

## B. CAUSES

Typical viral hemorrhagic septicemia (VHS) is caused by the Egtved virus (K. Wolf, 1966). Thorough investigations by Rasmussen (1965) have shown this disease could not be caused by malnutrition or cured by nutritional manipulation. This makes it clear that VHS is etiologically different from the lipoid liver degeneration.

Causes of lipoid liver degeneration are complicated, poorly understood, and probably multiple. According to Besse (1956), the main cause is feeding rainbow trout spoiled marine fishes. Such material is alkaline, contains toxins, neutralizes stomach acid, and results in anemia of the same type as pernicious anemia in humans. Faktorovich (1961b) fed rainbow trout three experimental diets consisting of: (1) meat–bone meal with barley meal; (2) the same plus synthetic vitamins A, $B_1$, $B_2$, $B_{12}$, D, C, and niacin; and (3) the same as (1) enriched with 50% peptone–corn–agar containing culture of microorganisms rich in vitamins A, $B_1$, $B_2$, $B_{12}$, and D. Only trout fed the last diet had normal livers. Trout fed the other two had fatty livers. Three previous reports by Faktorovich (1956a, 1958, 1959b), available in English translation, describe the progress of fatty liver degeneration when poor diets consisting of decomposing fish, silk worm pupae and fish and bone meal were fed. When trout were returned to a satisfactory diet consisting of fresh fish, or other complete diets containing all required vitamins, livers slowly regenerated and ceroid was removed by leukocytes. Accumulation of fat and ceroid in the livers of hatchery-raised rainbow trout was reported recently in Austria by Weisser and Otte (1964).

In countries with highly developed silk industry, as Japan, spent silk worm pupae are used as animal food high in proteins and fat. One has to note here that fat present in the dried pupae is usually rancid. In a series of experiments between 1960 and 1963, Kawatsu reported on the value of this material as a component of a practical diet for rainbow trout (Kawatsu, 1960, 1961, 1963, 1964). When as much as 43% of the animal food component consisted of pupae, fatty livers, but no anemia, occurred. If such food was given sparingly, there were few mortalities but when it was given abundantly, losses were high.

When defatted pupae were used, mortalities were much lower, there was no anemia, droplets of fat in the liver were smaller, and kidney damage was absent or slight (Kawatsu, 1961).

In another series of tests, the value of various vitamins was tested for the control of liver and kidney damage caused by rancid pupae (Kawatsu, 1964). None of the vitamins as riboflavin, pyridoxine, pantothenic acid, folic acid, thiamine, nicotinic acid, choline, or $B_{12}$ prevented anemia caused by feeding rancid fat. A combination of riboflavin, pyridoxine, pantothenic acid, and folic acid maintained hematopoiesis at a somewhat higher level for longer periods of time. Tocopherols, which are known to prevent oxidation and rancidity of fats, prevented anemia caused by feeding rancid pupae.

One of the proposed reasons for the high susceptibility of salmonids, rainbow trout, in particular, is that under wild conditions livers of these trout do not contain reserve fat and therefore are not equipped to utilize fats which accumulate in the livers under hatchery conditions. This high content of unsaturated fatty acids creates favorable conditions for auto-oxidation and deposition of ceroid (Wood and Yasutake, 1956); Nigrelli and Jakowska, 1961; Mandelli and Grimaldi, 1958). Wunder (1967) observed that in adult female carp with poorly developed ovaries there was 32–45% fat by weight in the livers. In males of the same age with well-developed testicles there was no fat in the liver and very little in the abdomen. Fatty carp were not considered as diseased, but only as undesirable for marketing.

Finally a report on a typical case of lipoid liver and kidney degeneration which occurred at the Leetown National Hatchery should be mentioned. One year, contrary to previous practice, fat was not trimmed from beef spleens used as the meat component of meat–meal diet. Rainbow trout fingerlings, but not brook or brown trout, developed typical symptoms of the disease. Anemia was so advanced that gills were almost colorless and hematocrit values were between 10 and 20. Fish were so weak that any disturbance or handling resulted in instant mortalities.

Similar conditions occurred when pelleted floating diet was used. During the first year and a half this diet produced excellent growth. During the second year, rainbow trout developed discolored livers and kidneys with advanced anemia and mortalities. At that time these trout were divided in two lots. One was continued on floating pellets, while the other received these pellets mixed with 50% beef liver by weight. Fish fed all pellet diets died while a very slow recovery took place in trout fed pellets supplemented with beef liver.

## C. Signs and Symptoms of the Disease

Signs and symptoms of nutritional and viral liver diseases are similar. It is believed that viral hemorrhagic septicemia can be diagnosed with some degree of certainty only if the presence of Egtved virus is demonstrated in the diseased fishes. Even this does not give certain diagnosis because nutritional and viral disease may be present simultaneously, or fish with nutritional disease may be carriers of the Egtved virus. Therefore, virological examination, detailed epidemiological information, history of the disease outbreak, and detailed record of feeding may be needed for dependable diagnosis of the disease and its causes.

For comparison with nutritional liver disease, symptoms of Egtved disease are summarized by Rasmussen (1965).

Diseased fish have reduced appetitie, separate from the rest of the fish, and tend to float near the shore. They may be darker than healthy fish or be completely black. There is often exophthalmos and abdominal distention caused by edema. The gills are pale. On other occasions trout may display motor disorders in the form of sudden leaps and twists. Such fish are lean and gills may have normal red color.

Internally there is ascites in the abdomen and tissues may be edematous. The stomach is distended, often empty with fluid which is neutral or nearly so (pH 6–7); in healthy fish it is acidic (pH 1–4). The intestine may be filled with yellow mucus, while the liver is pale, yellow or yellow-gray. *The kidney, particularly the posterior end, may be swollen with a wavy appearance and also hemorrhagic. Small hemorrhages may be present in all organs, peritoneum, and musculature.* Fish are unusually anemic, gills may be almost colorless, and hematocrit readings are in the range of 10 to 20. One should be alerted to the fact that most of these symptoms can also be found in various vitamin deficiency diseases described elsewhere in this chapter.

Symptoms of viral hemorrhagic septicemia can be compared with those of liver lipoid degeneration as described by Davis (1953). It affects chiefly rainbow trout. In advanced stages fish are dark and swim listlessly at the surface of the water. Gills are pale and and fish may have light to advanced anemia and stomach and gut empty with pale yellow fluid. The body is distended with fluid in the abdomen and there is exophthalmos; the liver is yellow or gray. *There are no hemorrhages and the kidney is not swollen but the gut may be inflamed.* The liver glycogen is usually replaced by lipids which cause liver cell degeneration in advanced cases. Such liver lipoid degeneration was recently described by Wood and Yasutake (1956a), Faktorovich (1960), and Ghittino (1962) with detailed histopathological documentation (Fig. 5). Ceroid is the substance found in livers of fish with typical liver lipoid degeneration. It should be added that the chief difference in symptoms between the viral and nutritional liver degeneration in rainbow trout are the presence of petechiae and swollen kidney in trout with the viral disease.

Fig. 5. A rainbow trout with a typical case of lipoid degeneration of the liver caused by malnutrition (Ghittino, 1961).

## D. Species Affected

It is generally accepted that rainbow trout are particularly susceptible to liver lipoid degeneration and VHS. Recently Ghittino and Leon (1963) reported that brook trout in Italy are also affected by lipoid liver degeneration. They seem to be less susceptible than rainbow trout and degeneration progresses more slowly with advanced cases found in 4- to 5-year-old fish.

This disease also occurred in chinook salmon fingerling fed diets containing different fats. Fish fed diets containing hard beef spleen fat developed acute lipoid liver degeneration with advanced anemia within 26 weeks. The hematopoietic part of the kidney was also affected which explained the presence of acute anemia resulting in mortalities. When diseased fish were given a soft fat diet, little or no recovery was observed (Burrows, 1964). This observation, and the one made at Leetown on rainbow trout fed beef spleen with fat, indicated that inclusion of hard beef fat in the diet of salmonid fishes may result in liver and kidney degeneration resulting in death of affected fish.

Livers in channel catfish that had been fed artificial diets and held in production ponds were usually larger and more vacuolated than those of wild fish (Judd and Cross, 1966). Livers of wild catfish had an average

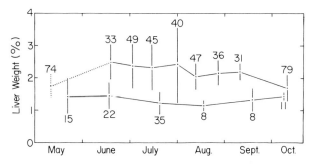

Fɪɢ. 6. Liver weight of channel catfish expressed as percentage of body weight. Upper line shows weight of liver of catfish kept in ponds. Lower line shows weight of liver in wild catfish. (Judd and Cross, 1966.)

weight of 1.3% of body weight; those raised in ponds varied from 1.3 to 2.2% (Fig. 6).

Damage to the livers visible as vacuolation was proportionate to the weight of the liver; the larger the liver the greater the damage. Livers of pond fish weighing approximately 1.3% of body weight were similar in histological appearance to the livers of wild catfish. The authors express the opinion that diet alone may not have been responsible for the fatty liver degeneration. They suspected that low oxygen levels, fluctuation in dissolved oxygen from 2 to 12 ppm, and high temperatures may have reduced the fat utilization by the catfish.

E. Remedial Measures

In conclusion, it may be said that salmonid fish, rainbow trout in particular, must receive a well-balanced diet free from excessive fat, hard animal fat, or rancid fat, in particular, if liver lipoid and kidney degeneration is to be avoided (Phillips and Podoliak, 1957).

## VII.  Visceral Granuloma

This disease was described as a mycosislike granuloma by Wood *et al.* (1955). It seems likely that neurilemmoma reported in brook trout by Young and Olafson (1944) was the first described case of this disease. Subsequently to results described by Wood *et al.* (1955), K. Wolf and Dunbar* carried

* Eastern Fish Disease Laboratory, Kearneysville, W. Va. Unpublished results.

out extensive work aiming at isolation of the hypothetical fungus causing this disease. They came to the conclusion that a fungus was not involved.

Investigations conducted during the past 3 years by Dunbar (1966) at the Eastern Fish Disease Laboratory indicated that this disease has a nutritional etiology as was suspected by Wood and Yasutake (1956b). In the initial experiments by Dunbar (1966), visceral granuloma occurred within 2–3 months in brook trout fed the wet meat–meal diet and some commercial pellets, but after 18 months granuloma was uniformly absent in brook trout fed the synthetic diet of L. Wolf (1951) modified by Halver and Coates (1957). Further investigations by Dunbar† have shown that the incidence of visceral granuloma varied from 5 to 91% depending on the composition of the dry meal portion of the meat–meal diet. The disease was absent in control trout fed the above named synthetic diet. At this time it is not known if some vegetable or animal meal components of the test diet, or the presence of toxic substances developing in the meals during storage may be contributing factors to the etiology of this disease. Brook trout raised in hatcheries are particularly susceptible to this disease, while rainbow and brown trout are resistant. The incidence is very high in 1-year-old or older brook trout. Diseased fish grow progressively weaker, become very anemic, and seldom survive the second year.

The gross pathological picture and histopathology was described in detail by Wood et al.* (1955). This disease usually begins as barely visible papillae projecting from the serosa of the stomach. It gradually spreads to other internal organs, except liver and lower gut. The affected kidney is swollen and contains numerous hard nodules of light gray color. In advanced cases there is ascites in the abdomen which may be distended due to proliferation of granulomatous tissues and accumulated fluid. Trout are usually anemic, serum proteins are reduced, and serum albumin is particularly low. The ultimate cause of death is probably advanced anemia. Hematocrit level in moribund trout was found to be within 10–15 limit.

In the original report by Wood et al. (1955), kidney disease and visceral granuloma were present. This was purely coincidental, because in most cases of visceral granuloma in brook trout since then examined, no complications caused by other diseases were observed. Visceral granuloma is a slowly progressing disease. From the time the first papillae appear on the serosa of the stomach to the development of massive granuloma may take a year or more. To our knowledge the disease is always fatal for 2- to 3-year-old brook trout. It affects about 75% of the 16- to 18-month-old

---

† Personal communication.

* Dunbar et al., 1971.

brook trout at the Leetown National Fish Hatchery. Survival chances of these trout for another year are negligible.

## VIII. Pathological Consequences of Starvation

Starvation is a common condition among wild freshwater fishes. When the food supply contains all necessary components, but is not adequate for any species of fish under specific environmental conditions, the growth of the fish slows down or stops. In fish culture it is customary to adjust the amount of food to control the growth rate of fishes. This is most frequently done with aquarium fishes which may easily outgrow aquariums if fed more than at the maintenance level. Starvation takes place if fish are fed below the maintenance level, that is when the body weight decreases.

Freshwater fishes, pond fishes in particular, are often exposed to starvation in areas where temperature differences are considerable between summer and winter. In some areas of North America, Europe, and Asia the water temperature restricts active feeding of some fish species to three or four months of the year. During the remaining months fish eat very little and their survival depends on reserves accumulated during summer. Fish do not hibernate as some warm-blooded vertebrates do. Their metabolism and feeding rate gradually increases or decreases, depending on the temperature within the survival temperature amplitude which is species characteristic.

The relationships between food and growth and starvation of salmonid fishes was reviewed by Phillips *et al.* (1953) and Brown (1957), and for cyprinid fishes by Steffens (1964). Starved brook and rainbow trout metabolized actively at 8° to 12°C, with about 40% weight loss in 14 weeks. Mortalities were high near the end of the test. There was some loss of vitamins from the tissues and reduction in fat and glucose. Detailed pathological examination was not carried out.

In rainbow trout fingerlings exposed to starvation at 15°–17°C for 12 weeks, there was an initial increase in hemoglobin and red cell counts. This was followed by hemoglobin drop from 9.5 to 6.0 gm per 100 ml and red cells from 1.7 million to 0.9 million per mm³. Erythrocytes became smaller indicating that starving brook trout had symptoms of microcytic anemia (Kawatsu, 1966).

The review paper by Steffens (1964) is concerned with conditions developing in carp during the winter. It is a well-established fact that carp, as well as other pond fishes which feed little or not at all in the winter, are

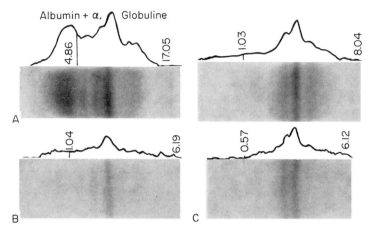

Fɪɢ. 7. Electrophorogram of carp serum. (A) Serum of normal healthy carp; (B) and (C) sera of carp in various stage of globulin depletion with almost total depletion of albumin. (Liebmann *et al.*, 1960.)

often affected by diseases and high losses in spring when the water temperature increases to the level where fish become active again. Survival during winter and disease resistance in spring depends largely on the nutritional and health condition during the preceding summer and fall and the conditions existing in the ponds during winter.

Offhaus *et al.* (1955) and Riedmüller (1965) reported on electrophoretic studies with carp serum. They found that in healthy 2-year-old carp there was about 30% albumin and 70% globulins with albumin to globulin ratio (A:G) about 0.40. In very sick carp the A:G was 0.12 to 0.0 (Fig. 7). On the basis of the A:G ratio compared with the state of health of carp and their subsequent survival, they suggested that carp be divided in four groups:

| State of health and survival | A:G ratio |
|---|---|
| Very good | 0.40 to 0.28 |
| Good | 0.28 to 0.21 |
| Poor | 0.21 to 0.12 |
| Very poor | 0.12 to 0.00 |

They found that carp in the first two categories only were satisfactory as brood stock.

I should like to add that carp having a low A:G ratio are usually very anemic. Red cell counts, hematocrit, or hemoglobin determination may

TABLE IV

Changes in Serum Protein of Carp during Overwintering[a]

| Date | Protein in serum (%) | Composition of musculature | | | Condition of fish maintenance |
|---|---|---|---|---|---|
| | | Water (%) | Protein (%) | Fat (%) | |
| October 20 | 3.8–4.0 | 79.8 | 16.6 | 2.9 | At the start |
| December 24 | 3.7–3.8 | 80.9 | 16.0 | 2.4 | Two months in a winter pond |
| March 1 | 2.7–2.8 | 82.9 | 15.1 | 1.1 | Four months in a winter pond |
| March 15 | 1.98–2.0 | 88.0 | 10.8 | 1.05 | Until December in a winter pond followed by three months starvation in an aquarium |
| November 20 | 3.72–3.84 | 84.0 | 13.1 | 1.5 | After three months starvation and six months feeding in an aquarium |

[a] Sorvatchev, 1957b, as quoted by Steffens, 1964.

TABLE V

Electrophoresis of Sera of Carp Maintained under Various Conditions[a]

| Condition of fish maintenance | Serum protein fractions | | | |
|---|---|---|---|---|
| | Albumin (%) | $\alpha$-Globulin (%) | $\beta$-Globulin (%) | $\gamma$-Globulin (%) |
| Before overwintering Serum protein 3.84% | 22.0 | 43.8 | 24.6 | 9.6 |
| Six-month starvation under normal conditions Serum protein 2.73% | 15.0 | 26.3 | 34.2 | 24.5 |
| Three-month starvation under natural conditions plus 3-month starvation in aquarium Serum protein 2.0% | 7.7 | 16.6 | 18.3 | 57.4 |
| Six-month starvation followed by 6-month feeding Serum protein 3.72% | 15.6 | 30.7 | 28.9 | 24.8 |

[a] Sorvatchev (1957a, b) as presented by Steffens (1964).

also be used to estimate the state of health. Refractometric serum protein determination is also very useful.

A brief summary from the excellent review by Steffens (1964) on the overwintering and winter starvation of carp from a physiological point of view follows. The protein content of the musculature was highest in September, 16.41%, and the lowest in March, 15.20%. Vitamin A contents of of the carp liver was low in winter and was further depressed under crowded conditions (Tables IV and V).

The hemoglobin and red cell numbers in overwintering carp were influenced by water conditions during the winter. Contents of dissolved oxygen had strong influence as given in a summary table from data of Ivlev and quoted by Steffens (1964) (Table VI).

Under favorable conditions (dissolved oxygen 3.7 ppm), there was a steady decline in red cell and hemoglobin levels until March, followed by recovery in April. Under average conditions (dissolved oxygen 2.5–2.6 ppm) fish were well enough to compensate for reduced oxygen by maintaining high red cell and hemoglobin levels. Under poor conditions fish were able to compensate for low oxygen level of 1.8 to 1.9 ppm through the middle of February. There was a sudden collapse in compensatory ability in March with a slow recovery in April. In pike perch the hemoglobin and erythrocytes declined gradually during the winter. In silurid fishes, there was a slight rise in mid-February followed by a drop (Ivlev, 1955).

TABLE VI

SUMMARY OF DATA ON HEMOGLOBIN LEVELS AND RED CELL COUNTS IN BLOOD OF WILD CARP OVERWINTERING IN WATER WITH THREE DIFFERENT LEVELS OF DISSOLVED OXYGEN[a]

|  | Dissolved oxygen | | | | | |
|  | 3.7 ppm | | 2.5–2.6 ppm | | 1.8–1.9 ppm | |
| Month | Hemo-globin | Red cells (millions) | Hemo-globin | Red cells (millions) | Hemo-globin | Red cells (millions) |
|---|---|---|---|---|---|---|
| November | 11.0 | 2.82 | 10.9 | 2.77 | 10.7 | 2.82 |
| January | 6.2 | 1.58 | 9.6 | 2.42 | 8.3 | 2.49 |
| February | 4.5 | 1.15 | 11.7 | 2.92 | 13.1 | 3.33 |
| March | 4.3 | 1.11 | 11.8 | 2.98 | 1.0 | 0.23 |
| April | 8.2 | 2.04 | 7.5 | 1.90 | 2.1 | 0.53 |

[a] Ivlev, 1955 as quoted by Steffens, 1964.

The best overwintering conditions were in water with a high oxygen level when the hemoglobin and red cell numbers could adjust themselves to the lower metabolic requirements of fish in cold water. In the other two bodies of water, fish had to maintain high hemoglobin and red cell counts to best utilize the low dissolved oxygen.

According to Steffens (1964), the appearance of internal organs was greatly changed in carp starved under experimental conditions or surviving unfavorable overwintering conditions in ponds. Such carp usually had an accumulation of yellow or pink exudate in the abdomen, the gut was thin and parchmentlike, transparent and flabby, and in some carp was inflamed and ulcerated with sloughing epithelium. The gall bladder was overfilled and liver was green. Such debilitated fish became easily infected with bacteria belonging to the genera *Aeromonas* and *Pseudomonas* with resulting hemorrhagic septicemia and high mortalities.

The best remedial measures against winter starvation of pond fishes is to provide optimum conditions during the period when water is warm and the growth is rapid, to have well aerated and clean winter ponds, and to avoid overcrowding.

## IX. Miscellaneous

### A. Nutritional Impairment of Pigmentation

Previously unfed chinook salmon fry were used in an experiment on fatty acid requirements. Precautions were taken to prevent oxidation, or any other deterioration of fatty acids, used in this experiment. Fish not fed trilinolein were lighter in color than those receiving it. Linoleic acid was used for growth but did not support normal pigmentation. This nutritional depigmentation was caused by affecting the melanin-producing cells. Repigmentation during the recovery experiment was most rapid in the subgroup fed a diet containing 3% trilinolein (Nicolaides and Woodall, 1962).

*Linseed oil cake and soybean groats* were used as a supplementary food for fingerling carp. Apparently these materials were not entirely satisfactory because their use resulted in reduced red cell counts and elevated numbers of monocytes and polymorphonuclear leukocytes (Kudryashova, 1963).

### B. Nutrition and Resistance to Ichthyophthiriasis

Atlantic salmon (*Salmon salar*) raised in northwest Russia became anemic with reduced red cell counts, increased number of polymorphonuclear leukocytes and monocytes, and reduced levels of B vitamins in the organs. Double doses of B vitamins resulted in lower mortalities and restoration of normal hematology. Also a double normal dose of vitamin A amounting to 30,000 IU per 1 kg of food was very effective in the control of ichthyophthiriasis (Malikova *et al.*, 1961).

## C. Indispensable Amino Acids

During investigations on the amino acids essential for salmonids, sockeye salmon fed a diet deficient in tryptophan developed scoliosis within 4 weeks. The same symptoms appeared in 25% of rainbow trout fed a diet without tryptophan. Scoliosis disappeared upon restoration of this amino acid indicating that the damage caused by deficiency was not permanent (Shanks *et al.*, 1962). No other specific pathology was noted in chinook salmon fed specific amino acid-deficient diets for 10–12 weeks although no growth occurred on these diets during the experimental period (Halver *et al.*, 1957).

## References

Alexander, L., Green, R. G., Evans, C. A., and Wolf, L. E. (1941). *Trans. Amer. Neurol. Ass.* pp. 119–122.

Allison, L. N. (1960). *Progr. Fish Cult.* **22,** 114–116.

Amlacher, E. (1961). "Taschenbuch der Fischkrankheiten." XI and 286. Gustav Fischer, Jena.

Besse, P. (1956). *Appliquée* **6,** 441–467.

Brown, M. E. (editor) (1957). In "Physiology of Fishes," Vol. 1, Chap. IX, pp. 361–400. Academic Press, New York.

Burrows, R. E. (1964). *Bur. Sport Fish. Wildl. Prog. Sport Fish. Res. Circ.* **210,** 59.

Burrows, R., Palmer, D. D., Newman, H., and Azevedo, R. L. (1952). *U.S. Dep. Interior Fish Wildl. Serv. Spec. Sci. Rep.* **86,** 24.

Chudova, Z. I. (1961). *Biol. Abstr.* **44,** No. 17795.

Coates, J. A., and Halver, J. E. (1958). *U.S. Dep. Interior Fish Wildl. Serv. Spec. Sci. Rep.* **281,** 9.

Coble, D. W. (1965). *Can. Fish Cult.* **36,** 27–34.

Corson, B. W., and Brezosky, P. E. (1961). *Progr. Fish. Cult.* **23,** 175–178.

Davis, H. S. (1926). *Trans. Amer. Fish. Soc.* **56,** 156–159.

Davis, H. S. (1953) "Culture and Diseases of Game Fishes," pp. 1–332. Univ. of California Press, California.

DeLong, D. C., Halver, J. E., and Yasutake, W. T. (1958). *Progr. Fish Cult.* **20,** 111–113.

Dunbar, C. E. (1966). *Progr. Sport Fish. Res. Bur. Sport Fish. Wildl. Res. Pub.* **17.**

Dunbar, C. E., and Herman, R. L. (1971). *J. Nutr.* **101,** 1445–1451.

Dupree, H. K. (1966). *Bur. Sport Fish. Wildl. Tech. Pap.* **7,** 1–12.

Faktorovich, K. A. (1956a). *Vopr. Ikhtiol.* **6,** 156–164.

Faktorovich, K. A. (1956b). *Tr. Soveshch. Fiziol. Ryb,* pp. 237–243. (Engl. transl. OTS 61-31048).

Faktorovich, K. A. (1958). *Tr. Soveshch. Ikhtiol. Komis. Akad. Nauk. SSSR* **8**, 237–243. (Referat. *Zh. Biol.* 1959, No. 39916; Transl. *Biol. Abstr.* **45**, No. 67926. 1964.)

Faktorovich, K. A. (1959a). *Tr. Soveshch. Ikhtiol. Komis. Akad. Nauk SSSR* **9**, 69–73. *Biol. Abract Abstr.* **36**, No. 47412. 1961).

Faktorovich, K. A. (1959b). *Proc. Conf. Fish Dis.* (English transl. OTS 61-31058, pp. 70-74, 1963.)

Faktorovich, K. A. (1960). *Z. Fischerei Hilfswiss.* **9**, 95–99.

Faktorovich, K. A. (1961a). *Bull. State Sci. Res. Inst. Lakes Rivers* **51**, 37 46.

Faktorovich, K. A. (1961b). *Izvest. Gos. Nauchn. Inst. Ozernogo Rechnogo Rybn. Khoz.* **51**, 47–51, 268. (Referat. *Zh. Biol.*, 1963, 714; *Biol. Abstr.* **44**, No. 13925, 1963.)

Fish, F. F. (1935). *Trans. Amer. Fish. Soc.* **65**, 85–87.

Gaylord, H. R., Marsh, M. C., Busch, F. C., and Simpson, B. (1914). *Bull. U.S. Bur. Fish.* **32**, 363–524.

Ghittino, P. (1962). *Vet. Ital.* **13**, 457–489.

Ghittino, P. (1965). *Ann. N. Y. Acad Sci.* **126** ,468–478.

Ghittino, P., and Leon, J. I. (1963). *Atti. Soc. Ital. Sci. Vet.* **17**, 569–574.

Gordon, M. (1954). *Trans. Amer. Fish. Soc.* **83**, 229–240.

Halver, J. E. (1954). *Trans. Amer. Fish. Soc.* **83**, 254–261.

Halver, J. E. (1957). *J. Nutr.* **62**, 225–243.

Halver, J. E., and Coates, J. A. (1957). *Progr. Fish. Cult.* **19**, 112–118.

Halver, J. E., D.C. DeLong, and Mertz, E. T., (1957). *J. Nutr.* **63**, 95–105.

Halver, J. E., L. M. Ashley, and R. R. Smith. (1969). *Trans. Am. Fish. Soc.*, **98**, 762–771.

Harrington, R. W., Jr. (1954). *J. Fish. Res. Bd. Can.* **11**, 529–534.

Hublou, W. F. (1960). Index Cortland Hatchery Reports, Nos. 1–27 for the years 1932–58. N. Y. State Conserv. Dep., Albany, pp. 1–15.

Ivlev, V. S. (1955). *Byull. Mosko. Obshchest. Ispyt. Prir. Otd. Biol.* **60**, 73–78, (*Biol. Abstr.* **31**, No. 20,000, 1957.)

Judd, C. E., and Cross, F. B. (1966). *Trans. Kansas Acad. Sci.* **69**, 48–57.

Kawatsu, H. (1960). *Bull. Freshwater Fish. Res. Lab.* **10**, 41–52.

Kawatsu, H. (1961). *Bull. Freshwater Fish. Res. Lab.* **11**, 29–38.

Kawatsu, H. (1963). *Bull. Freshwater Fish. Res. Lab.* **13**, 51–56.

Kawatsu, H. (1964). *Bull. Freshwater Fish. Res. Lab.* **14**, 1–9.

Kawatsu, H. (1966). *Bull. Freshwater Fish. Res. Lab.* **15**, 167–173.

Kudryashova, Y. V. (1963). *Dokl. Mosk. Sel'skokhoz Akad.***85**, 363–366 (Referat. *Zh. Biol.*, 3963, No. 14176; Transl. *Biol. Abstr.* **45**, No. 76468.)

Kitamura, S., Ohara, S., Suwa, T., and Nakaguwa, K. (1965). *Bull. Jap. Soc. Sci. Fish.* **31**, 818–826.

Liebmann, H., Offhaus, K. and Riedmüller, S. (1960). *Schweiz. Zeitschr. Hydrol.* **21**, 507–517.

McCay, C. M., and Dilley, W. E. (1927). *Trans. Amer. Fish. Soc.* **57**, 250–260.

MacIntyre, P. A. (1960). *Zoologica* **45**, 161–170.

McLaren, B. A., Keller, E., O' Donel, J., and Elvehjem, C. A. (1947). *Arch. Biochem. Biophys.* **15**, 169–177, 179–185.

Malikova, E. M., Apine, S. O., and Shaldaeva, R. E. (1961). *Tr. Nauchn. Issled Inst. Rybn. Khoz. Latviisk.* **3**, 445–452. (Referat. *Zh. Biol.* 1963, 7172; Transl. *Biol. Abstr.* **45**, No. 32062. 1964.

Mandelli, G. and Grimaldi, E. (1958). *Atti Soc. Ital. Sci. Vet.* **12**, 391–394.

Marine, D. (1914) *J. Exp. Med.* **19**, 70–88.

Marine, D., and Lenhart, C. H. (1910). *J. Exp. Med.* **12**, 311–337.

Marine, D. and Lenhart, C. H. (1911). *J. Exp. Med.* **13**, 455–475.

Marsh, M. C. (1911) *Trans. Amer. Fish. Soc.* **40**, 377–391.

Mitchell, H. H. (1964). "Comparative Nutrition of Man and Animals," Vol. 2, pp. 1–840. Academic Press, New York.

Nicolaides, N., and Woodall, A. N. (1962). *J. Nutr.* **78**, 431–437.

Nigrelli, R. F. (1954). *Trans. Amer. Fish. Soc.* **83**, 262–296.

Nigrelli, R. F., and Jakowska, S. (1961). *Zoologica* **46**, 49–55.

Offhaus, K., Brunner, G., and Riedmüller, S. (1955). *Arch. Fischerei.* **6**, 316–327.

Phillips, A. M. (1963). *Progr. Fish. Cult.* **25**, 132–134.

Phillips, A. M., and Brockway, D. R. (1957) *Progr. Fish. Cult.* **19**, 119–123.

Phillips, A. M., and Livingston, D. L. (1965). *Fish. Res. Bull.* **29**, 15–16.

Phillips, A. M., and Podoliak, H. A. (1957). *Progr. Fish. Cult.* **19**, 68–75.

Phillips, A. M., Brockway, D. R., and Rogers, E. O. (1950). *Progr. Fish. Cult.* **12**, 67–71.

Phillips, A. M., Lovelace, F. E., Brockway, D. R., and Balzer, G. C. (1952). *Fish. Res. Bull.* **16**, 1–46.

Phillips, A. M., Brockway, D. R., and Balzer, G. C. (1953). *Fish. Res. Bull.* **17**, 1–31.

Phillips, A. M., Lovelace, F. E., Podoliak, H. A., Brockway, D. R., and Balzer, G. C. (1955). *Fish. Res. Bull.* **19**, 1–56.

Phillips, A. M., Podoliak, H. A., Dumas, R. F., and Thoesen, R. W. (1958). *Fish. Res. Bull.* **22**, 1–87.

Phillips, A. M., Podoliak, H. A., Livingston, D. N., Dumas, R. F., and Thoesen, R. W. (1959). *Fish. Res. Bull.* **23**, 1–83.

Phillips, A. M., Podoliak, H. A., Livingston, D. L., Dumas, R. F., and Hammer, G. L. (1960). *Fish. Res. Bull.* **24**, 1–76.

Phillips, A. M., Podoliak, H. A., Poston, H. A., and Livingston, D. L. (1962). *Fish. Res. Bull.* **26**, 1–87.

Phillips, A. M., Podoliak, H. A., Poston, H. A., Livingston, D. L., Booke, H. E., Pyle, E. A., and Hammer, G. L. (1963). *Fish. Res. Bull.* **27**, 1–111.

Plehn, M. (1924). "Praktikum der Fischkrankheiten," pp. 1–179. Stuttgart, Germany.

Poston, H. A. (1964a). *Prog. Fish. Cult.* **26**, 59–64.

Poston, H. A. (1964b. *Fish. Res. Bull.* **28**, 6–10.

Poston, H. A. (1966a). *Progr. Sport Fish. Res.* **1965**. *Bur. Sport Fish. Wildl. Res. Publ.* **17**, 17–18.

Poston, H. A. (1966b). *Prog. Sport Fish. Res.* **1965**. *Bur Sport Fish, Wildl. Res.* 17–18.

Poston, H. A. (1967). *Fish. Res. Bull.* **30**, 46–51.

Rasmussen, C. J. (1965). *Ann. N. Y. Acad. Sci.* **126**, 427–460.

Reichenbach-Klinke, H. H. (1966). "Krankheiten und Schädigungen der Fische," pp. 1–389. Fischer Verlag, Stuttgart.

Riedmüller, S. (1965). *Allg. Fischwirtschaftsztg.* **18**, 28–35.

Rucker, R. R. (1958). *Trans. Amer. Fish. Soc.* **87**, 376–379.

Rucker, R. R., Johnson, H. E., and Kaydas, G. M. (1952). *Progr. Fish. Cult.* **14**, 10–14.

Ruud, J. T. (1965). *Sci. Amer.* **213**, 108–114.

Schäperclaus, W. (1954). "Fischkrankheiten," 3rd Ed., pp. 1–708. Academie Verlag, Berlin, Germany.

Schlumberger, H. G. (1955). *Ohio J. Sci.* **55**, 23–43.

Shanks, W. E., Gahimer, G. D., and Halver, J. E. (1962). *Progr. Fish Cult.* **24**, 68–73.

Smith, C. E. (1968). *J. Fish. Res. Bd. Can.* **25**, 151–156.

Sorvatchev, K. F. (1957a). *J. Zool.* **36**, 737–741 (Russian).

Sorvatchev, K. F. (1957b). *Biochemistry* **22**, 872–878 (Russian).

Spitzer, E. H., Coombes, A. I., Elvehjem, C. A., and Wisnicky, W. (1941). *Proc. Soc. Exp. Biol. Med.* **48,** 376–379.

Steffens, W. (1964). *Z. Fischerei. Hilfswiss.* **12,** 97–153.

Tunison, A. V., Phillips, A. M., Shaffer, H. B., Maxwell, J. M., Brockway, D. R., and McCay, C. M. (1944). *Fish. Res. Bull.* **6,** 1–21.

Warren, J. W. (1963). *Progr. Fish. Cult.* **25,** 121–131.

Weiser, M., and Otte E. (1964). Wiener *Tierärztl. Monatschr.* **51,** 98–106.

Whitmore, C. M. (1965). *Fish. Comm. Oregon, Contrib. No.* **29,** 1–31.

Wolf, K. (1966). *Advan. Virus Res.* **12,** 35–101.

Wolf, L. E. (1942). *Fish. Res. Bull.* **2,** 1–16.

Wolf, L. E. (1945). *Fish. Res. Bull.* **7,** 1–30.

Wolf, L. E. (1951). *Progr. Fish. Cult.* **13,** 17–24.

Wolf, L. E. (1952). *Progr. Fish. Cult.* **14,** 110–112.

Wood, E. M., and Yasutake, W. T. (1956a). *Amer. J. Pathol.* **32,** 591–603.

Wood, E. M. and Yasutake, W. T. (1956b). *Progr. Fish. Cult.* **18,** 108–112.

Wood, E. M., and Yasutake, W. T. (1957). *Progr. Fish. Cult.* **19,** 7–13.

Wood, E. M., Yasutake, W. T., and Lehman, W. L. (1955) *J. Infec. Dis.* **93,** 262–267.

Woodall, A. N., and LaRoche, G. (1964). *J. Nutr.* **82,** 475–482.

Woodall, A. N., Ashley, L. M., Halver, J. E., Olcott, H. S., and van der Veen, J. (1964). *J. Nutr.* **84,** 125–135.

Woodbury, L. A. (1943). *Trans. Amer. Fish. Soc.* **72,** 30–34.

Wunder, W. (1967). *Arch. Fischerei.* **17,** 114–121.

Young, G. A., and Olafson, P. (1944). *Amer. J. Pathol.* **20,** 413–419.

Zobairi, A. R. K. (1956). *Progr. Fish. Cult.* **18,** 88–91.

# 10

## NUTRITIONAL PATHOLOGY

*Laurence M. Ashley*

## I. Introduction

Nutrition and pathology are related disciplines which should be considered together. "Every disease has a nutritional aspect. . . . Nutrition thus has relations with all branches of medicine" (Gounelle, 1961). The pathology that occurs in fishes incident to oral ingestion of foods and, in some instances, to branchial (gill) absorption may be termed nutritional as opposed to pathology induced by noningested bacteria, viruses, parasites, or other nonnutritional disease entities.

While deficiency syndromes represent symptom complexes of various dietary disturbances, pathology is concerned with specific disease processes and resultant tissue changes in the individual whatever its systematic position. Many nonnutrient dietary components, although at times useful in the dietary, may contribute either directly or indirectly to nutritional disease and the number of such components is legion (see Chapter 5). In addition, certain nonnutrient, *nondietary* materials may be ingested inadvertently, or absorbed via gills or skin with resultant traumatism, toxic response, or other pathology. In a broad sense nutritional pathology comprises a considerable and varied segment of fish husbandry.

Fish environments are generally quite constant as compared with those of terrestrial vertebrates and when free from serious contamination are relatively well balanced. Food webs usually remain more or less constant within seasonal limits. Likewise, nutritional deficiencies may vary over a considerable range on a seasonal basis in relatively wild or undisturbed waters.

Currently, earth's exploding human population poses many problems of water contamination, often resulting in the direct or indirect damage and possible destruction of aquatic populations. Sometimes fish are killed outright in great numbers when oils, pesticides, or other products of man's economy happen to be spilled into rivers, large lakes, or along the seashore. Should fish survive such an insult, it is probable that certain food organisms would have been simultaneously destroyed, thus precipitating a nutritional crisis for fish and other aquatic organisms. Under such conditions, fish may go "off feed" and suffer from inanition. Problems resulting from fish exposure to many new industrial chemicals and other compounds are only now beginning to receive their just share of attention by government and private research agencies. Only recently has the public become cognizant of these real and potential dangers to fish and wildlife.

Historically, nutritional deficiency syndromes were often observed in hatchery fish in the form of growth retardation, anorexia, anemia, and other conditions long before the causes were discovered. In the early 1920's, efforts to improve growth of trout were made by means of adding vitamins to the diet. In America, this work was pioneered by Davis and James (1924). A factor "H" believed necessary in the prevention of trout anemia was proposed by McCay et al. (1927) but proof that factor "H" was largely folic acid with supplemental vitamin $B_{12}$ was not forthcoming until Wolf (1951), Halver (1957), and Phillips (1963) reported this fact.

Specific information on the contributions made to this subject in the various countries where fish culture is widely practiced is scattered and often unavailable. However, recent reports indicate some progress is being made in most parts of the world today.

## II. Imbalance of Specific Micronutrients

Various clinical signs, symptoms, and lesions may occur as a result of partial or complete deficiency of one or more essential micronutrients (vitamins). Omission of any essential vitamin from the diet will to a greater or lesser extent impair normal body processes, depending upon which vitamin is lacking. Except in controlled deficiency experiments, the total lack of a given vitamin in hatchery fish is probably rare. Marine fish generally seem to obtain rather complete and well-balanced rations in the natural environments. Certain stream and lake fish may suffer from dietary imbalance at least periodically from recurrent floods, drought, freeze-ups, or other climatic extremes. A common symptom resulting from deficiencies of micronutrients is growth retardation often associated with impaired appetite. The specific qualitative and quantitative vitamin requirements of most species of food and game fishes remain to be determined. Excesses of specific micronutrients, if such occur in fishes, are little understood at present.

### A. Avitaminoses

The avitaminoses include those deficiency syndromes, lesions, and anomalies resulting from inadequacy of one or more water-soluble vitamins, mainly those of the B-complex and vitamin C (ascorbic acid) or of one of the fat-soluble vitamins A, D, E, K, or P. Deficiency syndromes have been demonstrated and described for most of the essential water-soluble vitamins for chinook salmon (*Oncorhynchus tshawytscha*) (Halver, 1957) and for silver salmon (*O. kisutch*) (Coates and Halver, 1958). The various comparative anomalies reported for each vitamin deficiency syndrome are given in Table I. These are compared with those of other animals as found in column 2, Table I. These comparisons reveal the gross similarities between fish and higher vertebrates with respect to the vitamin deficiency syndromes. Other salmonids now known to be essentially similar to chinook and silver salmons in requirements for the essential water-soluble vitamins and in response to deficiencies of these vitamins include the following trouts: rainbow (*Salmo gairdneri*), brook (*Salvelinus fontinalis*), brown (*Salmo trutta fario*), and lake (*Salvelinus namaycush*). A beginning has been made on some other trout and salmon species, one

TABLE I

COMPARATIVE NUTRITIONAL DEFICIENCY PATHOLOGY OF FISH AND OTHER VERTEBRATES[a]

| Nutrient | Fish | Other vertebrates |
|---|---|---|
| Thiamine | Anemia,[1-7] anorexia,[1,2,5-7] ataxia (terminal),[2,5-7] convulsions (when moribund),[1,2] corneal opacities,[5-7] degeneration of vestibular nerve nucleus,[1,2,5-7] fatty liver,[5-7] hemorrhage of midbrain or medulla,[5-7] loss of equilibrium,[2,5-7] melanosis in older fish,[5-7] muscle atrophy,[1,2] paralysis of D and P fins,[2] rolling, whirling motion,[2,5-7], vascular degeneration,[5-7] weakness[5-7] | Anorexia,[25] ataxia (terminal),[16,20] chromatolysis and necrosis of neurons,[20] convulsions (when moribund),[16,20] degeneration of vestibular nerve nucleus,[17] hemorrhage of midbrain or medulla,[12,14-20] incoordination,[16] inflammation in heart muscle,[11-13,16,17] loss of patellar and achilles reflexes,[25] neuritis,[25] ptosis,[16] scarring among intact heart muscle fibers,[11-13,16,17] tremors,[16,25] weakness,[16,25] vomition[25] |
| Riboflavin | Anorexia,[1] cloudy lens,[6,10] darkened skin,[1] dim vision,[1] discolored iris,[1] hemorrhage in eyes, nares or operculum,[5,8] incoordination,[1] lens cataract,[2] mortalities,[4] photophobia,[1] xerophthalmia[2] | Alopecia,[15,17] angular stomatitis,[25] atrophy of sebaceous glands and hair follicles,[17] cloudy lens,[12] congenital skeletal anomalies,[17] corneal lesions,[12,17,18] creatinuria,[17] depigmentation,[13] fatty liver and/or kidney,[11,12] lens cataract,[11,17] oral dermatitis,[19] scaly atrophy of epidermis,[11,12,16,18] scrotal skin lesions,[25] seborrheic dermatitis,[25] spastic paralysis of hind quarters with excess dietary fat,[17] toxicity of excess dietary proteins,[17] xeroderma[17] |
| Pyridoxine | Anorexia,[2] ascites,[2] ataxia,[1] convulsions,[1,2] flexing of opercles,[1] hyperirritability,[1,2] indifference to light,[2] microcytic, hypochromic anemia,[1] rapid, jerky breathing,[1] rapid onset of rigor mortis,[2] spasms,[10] weight loss, nervous disorders, increased mortalities[8] | Anemia and anorexia,[25] anisocytosis,[11] arterial sclerosis,[16] ataxia,[10,11] alopecia late in disease,[17] cheilosis,[25] convulsions,[11,12,15,25] dental caries,[16] demyelination of peripheral nerves,[11] drowsiness,[25] edema of eyelids,[16] elevated serum iron,[11,12] enteritis,[12] epileptiform fits,[12,17] erythema on dorsum of paws,[17] erythema and edema of corium,[17] fissures in hands and feet,[16] gastritis,[12] glossitis,[25] hair follicles degenerate (late),[17] hemorrhagic kidney degeneration,[12] hemosiderin rise, spleen, marrow,[11] hyperkeratosis with scaling,[17] hyperplastic |

TABLE I (continued)

| Nutrient | Fish | Other vertebrates |
|----------|------|-------------------|
| | | bone marrow,[11] impaired antibody production,[17] impaired chondrogenesis, osteogenesis, and hematopoiesis,[17] impaired metabolism of protein,[17] leukocytes infiltrate corium,[17] liver fat increased,[11,16–18] microcytic, hypochromic anemia,[11,12,17,25] nausea,[25] oral dermatitis,[19] prostration,[12] resorption of embryos *in utero*,[17] sebaceous glands affected late,[17] seborrheic dermatitis of nasolabial folds, periocular-eyebrow and oral-angular tissues,[25] serum transaminase reduced,[16] swollen digits,[17] thymic atrophy,[17] vascular proliferation of cornea,[17] weight loss[16] |
| Folic acid | Anemia,[1,6] anorexia,[10] ascites,[2] dark coloration,[1,2] erythropenia,[2] exophthalmia,[2] fragility of caudal fin,[1] lethargy,[1,10] macrocytic anemia,[2] pale gills,[2] poor growth[1,2] | Various developmental anomalies[17], leukopenia and granulocytosis,[11,17] macrocytic anemia[16] |
| Pantothenic acid | Anorexia,[1,2] clubbed gills,[1,2] flared opercula,[2] gill exudate,[1,2] general "mumpy" appearance,[1,10] lethargy,[1,2,10] necrosis of jaw, barbels, and fins,[10] prostration,[1,2] poor weight gain[8] | Adrenal enlargement and hemorrhage,[21] alopecia of circumocular, snout and ear areas,[16,17] achromotrichia,[17] ataxia,[16] cardiovascular instability,[25] cellular atrophy of epidermis,[18] chromatolysis of dorsal root ganglion cells,[11] colonic lesions,[11] dermatitis,[23] diarrhea,[11,25] gingival necrosis,[17] hemorrhagic necrosis of adrenals,[17] hyperkeratosis,[18] neuromotor disorders,[25] oral encrustations,[17,19] physical and mental depression,[25] poor growth,[17] prostration,[11,12] repeated infections,[25] spastic hind quarters,[12] weak extremities,[15] reproductive failures and birth defects[17] |
| Inositol | Anemia,[1,5] bloated stomach,[1,5] poor growth,[2,8] anorexia,[8] skin lesions[8] | Alopecia of corpus[18] |
| Biotin | Anemia,[5] anorexia,[1,2] blue slime disease, [5–7] colonic lesions,[1] contracted caudal fins,[2] dark | Alopecia,[11,17,18] anorexia,[25] atrophy of lingual papillae,[25] erythema,[17] graying coat,[18] hyperkeratosis,[17] |

TABLE I (continued)

| Nutrient | Fish | Other vertebrates |
|----------|------|-------------------|
| | coloration,[1,10] erythrocyte fragmentation,[1] mortalities,[7] muscle atrophy,[1,10] poor growth,[2] spastic convulsions[1] | inflamed oral mucosa,[11] lethargy,[25] lusterless coat,[17] muscle atrophy,[17] muscle pain,[25] paralysis of hind limbs,[15] peculiar gait and attitude,[17] poor growth,[15] scaly dermatitis[16,25] skin lesions[17] |
| Choline | Anemia,[5] poor food conversion,[1,2] poor growth,[1,2] vascular stasis and hemorrhage in kidney and intestine[1,5] | Anemia,[17] cirrhosis of liver,[17] edema,[17] enlarged kidneys with necrosis of tubular epithelium,[17] fatty infiltration of liver,[12] fatty infiltration of kidney,[17] vascular stasis and hemorrhage in kidney,[17] hypertension,[17] liver shrunken,[17] liver dark reddish brown,[17] mortalities of young,[12] muscular dystrophy,[22] neoplasms in lungs, liver and other tissues,[17] subcapsular renal hemorrhages[17] |
| Nicotinic acid (niacin) | Anemia,[5] anorexia,[1,8] colonic lesions,[1] edema of stomach and colon,[1] incoordination,[10] jerky movements,[1] muscle spasms,[1,10] lethargy,[1,10] photophobia,[1,10] swollen gills,[5] tetany,[10] skin hemorrahge,[8] high mortality[8] | Brain and peripheral ganglion damage,[17,18] diarrhea[11,15,25] (if diet is low in tryptophan, the following functional and organic anomalies may also arise: amenorrhea, angular stomatitis, apathy, cheilosis, glossitis, lesions of nasolabial folds, and mental depression) |
| *p*-Amino-benzoic acid | No significant change in growth, appetite or survival | Alopecia,[17] poor growth [23] |
| Cobalamin (B$_{12}$) | Anorexia,[1] erratic hemoglobin and erythrocyte counts,[1] fragmentation[1] | Alopecia,[17] anemia,[11,17] capillary fragility,[17,21] developmental anomalies,[21] hyperplastic marrow,[11] megaloblastosis,[21] normocytic anemia,[11] poor growth,[11,17,21] reduced cytochrome oxidase in young of deficient mothers,[21] "scurvy" [17,21] (combined folic acid and cobalamin deficiency accentuates the anemia factors) |
| Vitamin A | Ascites,[10] edema,[10] exophthalmos,[10] hemorrhagic kidneys[10] | Damage to epithelia of salivary glands, pancreatic ducts, linings of mouth, pharynx, genitourinary tract, eyes and thymus,[11–13,15–18,20,21] intrauterine development im- |

TABLE I (continued)

| Nutrient | Fish | Other vertebrates |
|---|---|---|
| | | paired, fetus resorbed or aborted,[17,23] herniation of spinal nerve roots,[17] xerophthalmia[25] |
| Vitamin C (ascorbic acid) | Anorexia,[2,5] impaired collagen production,[2,5] impaired wound healing,[2,5] lordosis with dislocated vertebrae and focal hemorrhage,[2,5] poor growth,[2,5] scoliosis with hemorrhage in severe cases,[2,5] twisted deformed hyaline cartilage in gill filaments and sclera of eyes[2,5] | Anorexia,[21] costo-chondral junctions enlarge, may disengage,[21] impaired wound healing,[21] paralysis with swelling of hind legs,[21] periosteum loosely attached,[21] poor growth,[21] ruffled coat,[21] keratosis, hyperemia, and hemorrhage of hair follicles, erythema, swelling, hemorrhage and sagging of gums (scurvy)[25] |
| Vitamin D | Reduced conversion[5,7] | Defective bone development, impaired ossification (rickets),[17,25] necrosis of kidney[17] |
| Vitamin E (α-tocopherol) | Anemia,[7] ascites,[1] ceroid in liver, spleen, kidney,[1] clubbed gills,[1] epicarditis,[1] exophthalmia,[1] microcytic anemia,[1] mortalities,[7] pericardial edema,[1] poor growth,[1] red blood cell fragility[1] | Atrophy of motor end plates,[17] ceroid deposits in adipose tissue,[17,22] massive necrosis of liver on high fat diets,[17] nutritional cardiac and skeletal muscular dystrophy,[11,12,15-18,21] pigment loss from incisor teeth,[17] reproductive anomalies[11,17,18,21] |
| Vitamin K | Anemia,[6] coagulation time prolonged[6] | Early uterine hemorrhages and abortions,[22] hemorrhages of subcutaneous tissues, thymus, bladder, adrenal, eye, kidney, testis, brain[17] |

[a] Superscript numbers indicate kind of fish or animal as follows: 1, chinook, 2, coho, 3, sockeye, 4, Atlantic salmon, 5, rainbow trout, 6, brook trout, 7, brown trout, 8, carp, 10, channel catfish, 11, swine, 12, dog, 13, fox, 14, sheep, 15, calves, 16, monkey, 17, rat, 18, mice, 19, hamster, 20, cat, 21, guinea pig, 22, rabbit, 23, chick, 25, man.

of which is the Atlantic salmon (*Salmo salar*). The water-soluble vitamin requirements of carp (*Cyprinus carpio*) are being studied in Japan by Aoe and co-workers (Aoe *et al.*, 1967). However, much remains to be learned about the specific nutritional requirements of most species of food and game fishes.

## 1. *Thiamine Deficiency Syndrome*

A thiamine deficiency syndrome in young silver salmon appeared after 12 weeks on a thiamine-deficient diet. Feeding gradually ceased and many emaciated "pin head" fish with typical "pinched" or severely concave abdomens appeared. Moribund fish lost control of dorsal and of pectoral fins. Locomotion was characterized by slow, rolling movements and by a general loss of equilibrium, suggesting marked changes in certain areas of the central nervous system. Affected fish suffered a loss of normal dark hue at the onset of clinical symptoms. This depigmentation progressed to a somewhat transparent condition when fish were moribund, or at death (Coates and Halver, 1958). Deficient chinook salmon fingerlings have poor appetites, muscle atrophy, convulsions prior to death, and loss of equilibrium suggestive of neurological changes. Rainbow trout deficient in this vitamin have livers with twice the amount of fat found in control livers or in those of wild trout (McLaren *et al.*, 1947). Young carp fed a thiamine-deficient diet for 13 weeks failed to show any deficiency symptoms (Aoe *et al.*, 1967). The clinical syndrome for thiamine-deficient rainbow trout includes nervous disorders such as loss of equilibrium and whirling, melanosis, anorexia, weakness, and ultimately, paralysis (Woodbury, 1943). Again, central nervous system disorders are implied but the exact nature remains unknown.

Changes in the myocardium of several species of mammals have been reported and the most definite changes occurred in pigs where scarring appeared among intact heart muscle fibers, and in some instances acute or subacute inflammation occurred (Follis *et al.*, 1943) (Fig. 1). These changes have not yet been confirmed for thiamine-deficient fishes.

Although laboratory mammals and humans have been more thoroughly studied in thiamine deficiency states than have fish, the gross and microscopic pathology of this syndrome is still somewhat confused. Conflicting reports have appeared, some of which were not based on well-controlled experiments. A diet of raw fish will induce Chastek paralysis in foxes, a disease similar to Wernike's hemorrhagic encephalitis in man, and this led to the discovery of a thiamine-destroying enzyme in raw fish (Krampitz and Woolley, 1944). Foxes on a thiamine-adequate diet without raw fish recover readily.

Lesions in brain, spinal cord, cranial, and peripheral nerves in thiamine-deficient animals, including fishes, need further study. In all such work on the nervous system, careful microtechnical work is essential. Methods are exacting and must be meticulously carried out if comparable results by various workers are to be obtained.*

---

* See methods of various authors in works on histopathological technique.

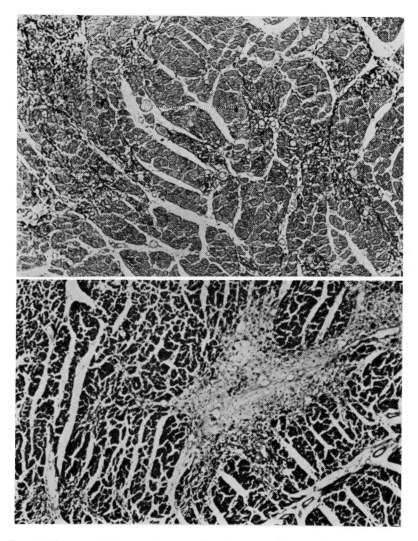

Fig. 1. Thiamin deficiency, pig heart. Top, fine scarring between intact ventricular myofibers in animal 320 days on low thiamine diet. Inflammatory lesions here are slight but in other areas acute lesions occurred (×75). Bottom, large scar in myocardium of animal on low thiamine diet for 254 days (×60). From Follis, (1958). Courtesy of Charles C. Thomas, Springfield, Illinois.

Hemorrhagic foci and chromatolysis of Nissl substance in nerve cells of the solitary, vestibular, Deiter's and Bechterew's nuclei were seen in thiamine-deficient rats (Prickett, 1934) while deficient mice had hemorrhages in the medulla (Dunn *et al.*, 1947). Whether or not fish get similar neurological lesions when fed thiamine-deficient diets remains to be determined.

The beri beri syndrome, once believed to be a result of thiamine deficiency, is now recognized as a result of multiple vitamin deficiencies. "When the literature of the last 10 years is considered in perspective, the conclusion is inescapable that thiamine has never deserved the title of 'Antineuritic vitamin,' and has not yet shown itself capable of filling completely the role that was formerly assigned to the hypothetical Antiberiberi vitamin" (Meiklejohn, 1940). Furthermore, "Inanition control animals must always be included in experiments which study thiamine deficiency" (Follis, 1958).

### 2. *Pyridoxine Deficiency*

The clinical syndrome for pyridoxine deficiency in chinook and in silver salmon is essentially similar, being characterized by anorexia, anemia, nervous disorders, including convulsions, and a gasping respiration (Halver, 1957; Coates and Halver, 1958). The histopathology has not yet been described, but Smith (1968) found a tendency for hypochromic anemia in pyridoxine-deficient rainbow trout. Weight losses and subsequent mortalities were common among deficient fish. Erythrocyte transaminase was reduced by about 50% over a period of about 60 days. Controls remained normal. By the end of nearly 3 months on test, thirty controls averaged 288 gm while twelve deficient fish averaged 204 gm in weight. Failure of deficient rainbow trout to judge distance in efforts to capture or grasp food (McLaren *et al.*, 1947), together with the aforementioned neurological disorders, strongly indicate some type of brain and/or nerve damage. Effects of pyridoxine deficiency on young carp were reported by Ogino (1965) who found deficient fish, after a 10-week period, had weight loss, increased mortalities, and nervous disorders when no pyridoxine was added to the diet. Deficient fish given deoxypyridoxine suffered from edema, hemorrhage, exophthalmos, and skin disorders. All carp in these experiments were reared in 25°C dechlorinated city water. In nearly a dozen species of mammals deficient in pyridoxine, various pathological changes occur. Among these are hyperkeratosis of the extremities, degeneration of myelin sheaths and axons in the dorsal columns of the spinal cord and in the dorsal roots, but not in the ventral roots, of spinal nerves, and atrophy of dorsal root ganglion cells (Figs. 2 and 3). These changes in the nervous system are accompanied by such nervous anomalies as epileptiform seizures, weakness, twitching, and muscle spasms (Chick *et al.*, 1940). Deficient swine undergo fatty infiltration of the liver and some livers become cirrhotic (Wintrobe *et al.*, 1943). Affected Rhesus monkeys have increased dental caries (Reinhart and Greenberg, 1956). Much re-

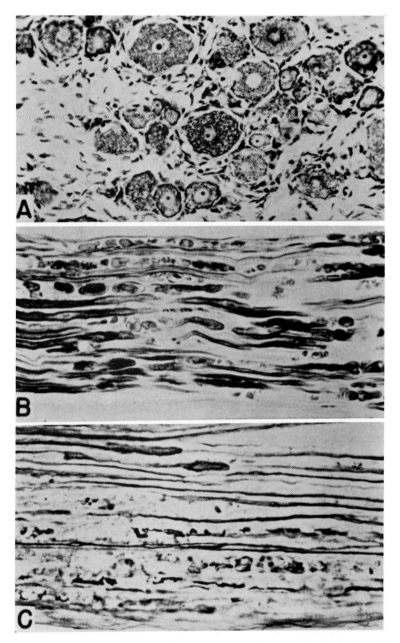

FIG. 2. Pyridoxine deficiency of sensory neurons and nerves of pig. A, Dorsal root ganglion cells showing atrophy but no chromatolysis. B, Myelin stain. C, Silver stain showing degeneration of myelin and of axis cylinders respectively. From Follis, (1958). Courtesy of Charles C. Thomas, Springfield, Illinois.

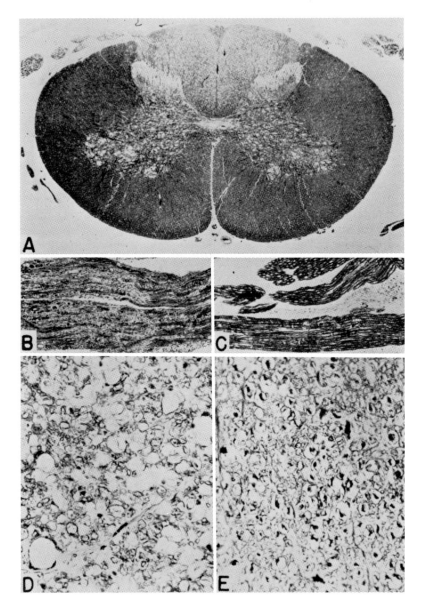

FIG. 3. Pyridoxine deficiency of pig spinal cord. A, Section from lumbar cord showing degeneration of dorsal (sensory) columns. B, Dorsal root is damaged. C, Ventral
root is normal. D and E, High power of dorsal and of lateral columns with damage
limited to the former. From Follis (1958). Courtesy of Charles C. Thomas, Springfield,
Illinois.

search is needed before the full extent and kinds of pathology resulting from pyridoxine deficiency in fishes is completely described.

### 3. *Folic Acid Deficiency*

Although Phillips (1963) reported finding folic acid to be an antianemic factor for brook trout, work on silver salmon (Coates and Halver, 1958) disclosed no gross anemia from a lack of folic acid, or was any clinical syndrome discovered. However, when this group was divided, the fish receiving folic acid in the complete diet experienced direct benefit from the added vitamin—these began to grow rapidly and showed a significant weight gain over the deficient lot. Thus, folic acid may be considered essential for normal growth of silver salmon. McLaren *et al.* (1947) held that folic acid and/or biotin is specific in the prevention of rainbow trout anemia, but after numerous experiments, Phillips *et al.* (1962) concluded that the effective antianemia vitamin, long designated as factor "H," was folic acid and that vitamin $B_{12}$ was supplemental to its antianemia properties. Recent work with these two vitamins is of interest. Rachmilewitz *et al.* (1965) reported a severe macrocytic anemia in a group of parturient Burmese women which was traced to folic acid alone by means of folic acid activity studies on both blood serum and on whole blood. These authors stress the importance of whole blood assays since they found 90% of all folic acid metabolites in the red blood cells and only 10% in the serum. The same authors also reported finding a nutritional macrocytic anemia due to vitamin $B_{12}$ deficiency in another group of patients. Recent work with folic acid-deficient silver salmon (Smith, 1968) showed that macrocytic anemia with poikilocytosis appeared in fish within 5 months after being fed the deficient diet (Fig. 4). The red blood cell count was significantly lower in deficient fish. The mean corpuscular volume was significantly higher (about 25%) in deficient fish, and the mean corpuscular hemaglobin was correspondingly greater in proportion to the increase in erythrocytic size. Fish fed the recovery diet regained a normal blood picture within 9 weeks. Red blood cells of deficient fish were frequently either attenuated or segmented as seen in Fig. 4.

### 4. *Biotin*

A biotin deficiency syndrome in silver salmon is characterized by loss of appetite, emaciated bodies, and by caudal fins contracted to form a triangular point. Deficient fish ingest less feed but nevertheless remain fairly active. The recovery group regained normal appetite and weight quickly, and within 2 weeks fish appeared normal. Mortalities, fairly consistent in other groups, were virtually absent from the biotin recovery

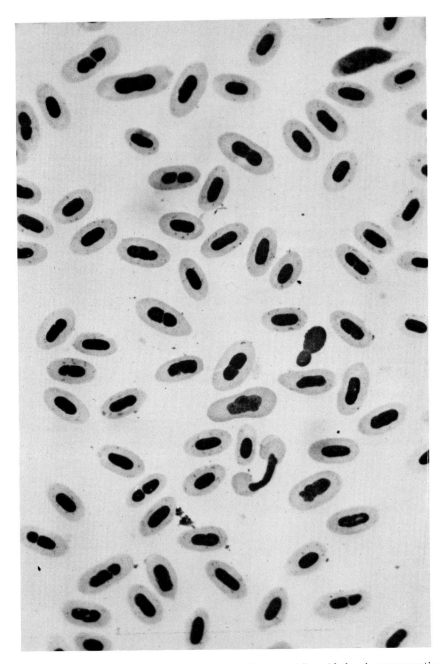

FIG. 4. Blood smear of young coho salmon deficient in folic acid showing macrocytic anemia with poikilocytosis which appeared after 5 months on test. Leishman stain (× 2300). (Smith, 1968).

group after restoration of the missing biotin to the diet (Coates and Halver, 1958). Biotin-deficient chinook salmon acquire increased coloration, colonic lesions, muscle atrophy, spastic convulsions, erythrocyte fragility, and anorexia (Halver, 1957). In the case of brown trout on biotin-deficient diets, blue slime patch disease appeared with characteristic sloughing lesions on the back and body of affected fish (Phillips *et al.*, 1951; Davis, 1953).

### 5.  *Pantothenic Acid*

Pantothenic acid deletion experiments on fish have been restricted to only a few species. Occasional atrophy and scarring of cardiac muscle fibers was reported by Halver (1957), who also noted cellular atrophy in various organs but apparently this followed no consistent pattern. Several clinical symptoms were also described in the pantothenic acid syndrome

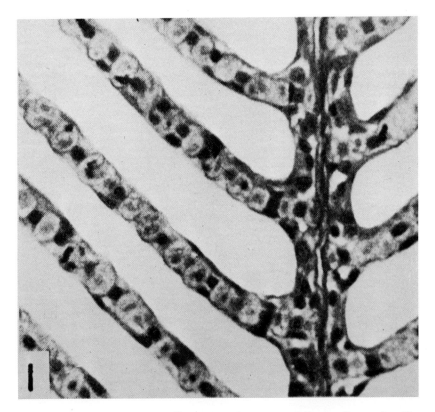

Fig. 5. "Normal" gill of hatchery salmonid showing portions of well spaced, uniform gill lamellae extending from the heavier gill filament. Hematoxylin and eosin (H and E) (×450).

for salmonids. The condition of clubbed gills and hyperplasia of gill epithelium comprise the essential lesions of nutritional gill disease which was described and compared with bacterial gill disease by Wood and Yasutake (1957). Nutritional gill disease can usually be distinguished from the bacterial type since the hyperplasia in the former originates on the gill filament proper between the bases of the gill lamellae (Figs. 5 and 6). Hyperplasia of the gill epithelium thus appears to be the cause of the characteristic fusions of the adjacent gill lamellae which tend to cluster about the apices of the filaments (Figs. 7 and 8). In the bacterial form of gill disease the epithelial hyperplasia normally begins near the tips of the lamellae and the fusions tend to be sporadic in distribution over the filaments. These two forms of gill disease may occur simultaneously, and a deficiency

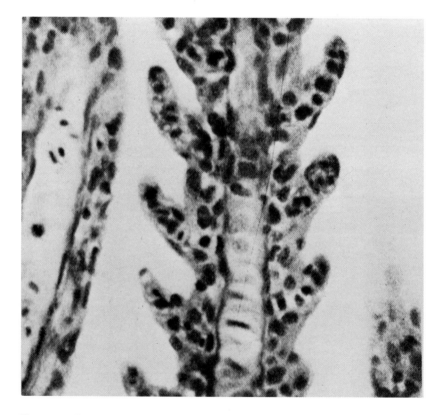

Fɪɢ. 6. Early stage of nutritional gill disease in pantothenic acid-deficient salmonid showing moderate hyperplasia of filamentar epithelium between bases of gill lamellae. Hematoxylin and eosin. (×450).

Fig. 7. Nutritional (deficiency) gill disease showing fusion of distal gill lamellae in gills of pantothenic acid-deficient salmonid fish. H and E (×180).

of pantothenic acid may predispose the fish to an attack of the bacterial disease which thus complicates the diagnosis of the nutritional form. (See also toxic gill disease under Section IV,B,4.) Pantothenate-deficient fish returned to a recovery diet regain appetites, gill damage is repaired, and they soon begin gaining weight. McLaren *et al.* (1947) reported growth retardation and clubbed gills in rainbow trout lacking pantothenic acid, and it is possible that the symptoms of this deficiency syndrome would be similar in many unstudied species of fish should they become deficient in this vitamin. Ogino (1967) reported very poor weight gain in 6-week feeding trials of young carp deficient in calcium pantothenate.

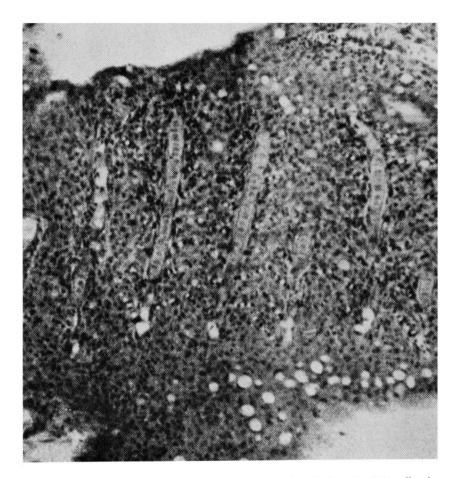

FIG. 8. Advanced nutritional gill disease with complete fusion of gill lamellae in portion of gill filament. Pantothenic acid-deficient salmonid. H and E (×200).

Rats and mice deficient in pantothenic acid have been shown to acquire hyperacidity (Zucker and Zucker, 1964) and duodenal ulcers (Seronde, 1964). Rats had greying and alopecia about the nose, ears, and eyes (Sullivan and Nicholls, 1942), acquired extensive, scaly, erythematous dermatitis prior to alopecia, the dermatitis being characterized by a moderate hyperkeratosis and acanthosis (scaling), and occasional epidermal vesicles and crusting, especially in relation to small eczematous foci. Hair follicles dilated along the entire length of the hair just before alopecia occurred. In terminal stages of the syndrome in rats sebaceous glands often atrophy (Vohra and Kratzer, 1956). Besides ulcers, rats have also had gingival and periodontal necrosis, and hyperkeratosis of the oral mucosa (Wainwright and Nelson, 1945). In swine colonic lymph nodes were sometimes infiltrated with leukocytes or were abscessed and later ulcerated. These lesions healed readily when the deficient animals were returned to a recovery diet (Wintrobe *et al.*, 1943; Sharma *et al.*, 1952;

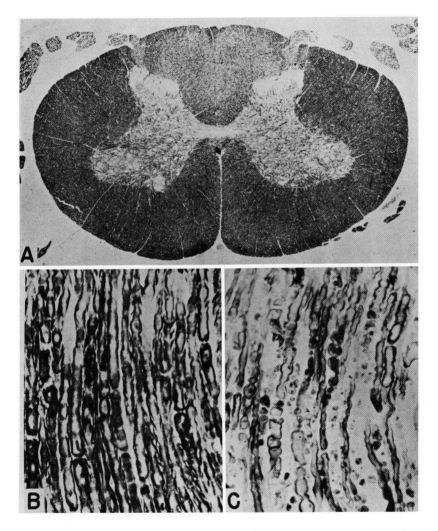

FIG. 9. Pantothenic acid deficiency of spinal cord of pig. A, Loss of myelin in dorsal columns of lumbar segment in animal fed a deficient diet for 99 days. B and C, Sections of ventral and dorsal roots, respectively, showing loss of myelin in latter but no myelin loss in former. From Follis (1958). Courtesy of Charles C. Thomas, Springfield, Illinois.

Stothers *et al.*, 1955). Deficient swine develop a jerky gait and this is followed by prostration. Histopathology in these animals shows chromatolysis of dorsal root ganglion cells, loss of Nissl granules, with damage to neurons of all sizes, and after 90 days on a deficient diet, degeneration of myelin in afferent sensory nerves of the cord (Follis and Wintrobe, 1945) (Fig. 9).

Another striking lesion in pantothenic acid-deficient rats is hemorrhagic necrosis of the adrenal cortex (Ralli and Dumm, 1953; Ashburn, 1940). This type of adrenal lesion was also reported for guinea pigs and for dogs (Schaefer *et al.*, 1942). Deficient rats (Nelson and Evans, 1946) and swine (Ullrey *et al.*, 1955) suffer from reproductive failure which includes faulty implantation, resorption of ova, and defective litters. Deficient mice have normal adrenals but have dermatosis and myelin degeneration of sciatic nerves, posterior nerve roots, pyramidal tracts, and both fasciculus gracilus and fasciculus cuneatus (Lippincott and Morris, 1941).

In general, deficient animals experience reduction in antibody formation, some have corneal vascularization (Bowles *et al.*, 1949), and some have endochondral bone dysplasia (Nelson *et al.*, 1950). It is obvious that further controlled deletion experiments with this vitamin need to be done on fishes before this deficiency syndrome can be adequately compared with that of mammals.

### 6. *Inositol*

Inositol-deficient silver salmon have reduced appetites and diminished growth, although a constant weight gain may occur. Fish returned to the vitamin complete diet showed a significant growth response and a corresponding decrease in mortalities (Coates and Halver, 1958). Rainbow trout lacking inositol developed fin degenerations closely resembling fin rot, which on microscopic examination shows tissue necrosis with sloughing (McLaren *et al.*, 1947). Inositol deficiency in young carp induced skin lesions which were less severe as fish grew older. These lesions were accompanied by anorexia and retarded growth (Aoe and Masuda, 1967). The carp responded well on a recovery diet. Further work appears to be necessary with regard to inositol deficiency in fishes.

### 7. *Niacin*

Besides anorexia, jerky or labored movements and muscular spasms when at rest, colonic lesions, and edema of stomach and colon occurred in deficient chinook salmon (Halver, 1957). Silver salmon did not develop this syndrome but the fish in the experiment had a heavy infestation of *Hexamitus salmonis* and more or less myxobacterial infection as well

(Coates and Halver, 1958). There is the possibility that intestinal parasites and bacteria may synthesize certain vitamins; thus the deficient diets of these fish may have been inadvertently supplemented in some cases. McLaren *et al.* (1947) reported severely swollen gills in niacin-deficient trout. DeLong *et al.* (1958) observed a tendency of niacin-deficient chinook salmon fingerlings to "sunburn" or to develop a "back peel" dermatitis on exposure to sunlight for periods between 2 and 3 weeks. Young carp fed niacin-deficient test diets for 8–10 weeks suffered from anorexia, skin hemorrhages, and high mortality (Aoe, 1967).

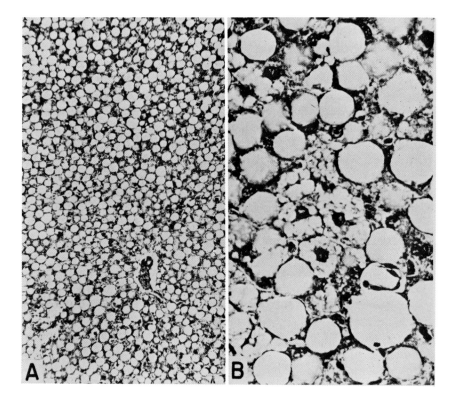

Fig. 10. Choline deficiency in rat liver. Diffuse fatty infiltration of entire liver a portion of which is shown in A (×90). Most liver cells are distended with large fat vacuoles but some include clusters of small vacuoles as shown in B (×405). H and E. From Follis, (1958). Courtesy of Charles C. Thomas, Springfield, Illinois.

## 8. *Choline*

A lack of dietary choline results mainly in poor growth and in poor food conversion in chinook and in silver salmon (Halver, 1957; Coates and Halver, 1958). Chinook salmon also had hemorrhagic kidneys and intestines but these lesions were not found in the silver salmon. Chronic choline deficiency in rats and in chickens induced many cases of fatty infiltration (Fig. 10) and of cirrhosis. Some tumors occurred in the livers together with pulmonary metastases in two rats. Both rats and chickens had increased hemosiderin pigmentation of livers and spleens, with chickens having the most pigmentation (Salmon and Copeland, 1954). Choline-deficient young rats developed, in 6 to 10 days, lassitude, distended abdomens, swollen kidneys, dyspnea, coma, and sometimes ocular hemorrhages and vertigo. Histological studies disclosed massive renal cortical hemorrhages and varying amounts of hemorrhage in lungs, lymph nodes, adrenals, and myocardium, besides heavy fat deposits in the liver and thymic atrophy (Engel and Salmon, 1941). Further choline deletion studies on rats with different diets than those fed in the preceding experiments resulted in one or more types of neoplasms in 14 out of 18 rats fed these diets for 5 to 11 months. Control rats failed to develop neoplasms (Engel *et al.*, 1947). Rainbow trout on a choline-deficient diet had hemorrhagic intestines and also suffered from kidney degeneration (McLaren *et al.*, 1947).

## 9. *Riboflavin Deficiency*

Riboflavin-deficient chinook salmon had characteristic eye lesions with accompanying "photophobia," dim vision, incoordination, and more or less blindness. Corneal vascularization, cloudy lenses, and at times, hemorrhage in the eyes occurred while poor appetite was associated with striated constrictions of abdominal wall and darkened body coloration. Rainbow, brook, and brown trout deficient in riboflavin developed opaque eyes (Phillips *et al.*, 1959). Other animals (West and Todd, 1961) have had, in addition, cataracts, scleral congestion, abnormal pigmentation of iris, cheilosis, angular stomatitis, and impaired erythrocyte formation. Hemorrhages of nares, eyes, and operculum were reported for riboflavin-deficient trout (McLaren *et al.*, 1947). Ogino (1967) reported hemorrhage in various body regions of young carp deficient in riboflavin after 6 weeks on test.

## 10. *Vitamin B$_{12}$ (Cobalamin) Deficiency*

Lack of vitamin B$_{12}$ was mentioned above under folic acid with which it seems to be more or less synergistic in action. The deficiency syndrome in salmonids includes poor appetite, reduced hemoglobin, and erratic erythrocyte counts and fragmentation of erythrocytes (Halver, 1957; Coates and Halver, 1958). Pernicious anemia, macrocytic anemia, sprue, and retarded growth in the young have been reported for some of the higher vertebrates.

## 11. *Vitamin B Complex Deficiency*

Carp reared in dechlorinated city water supplied via galvanized pipes and fed nine parts peanut meal plus one part fish meal in water ranging from 80° to 86°F acquire symptoms of general vitamin B complex deficiency. Fish suffer nervous excitability, loss of equilibrium, bloodshot eyes, and swim belly up or lay on their sides on the bottom. Ultimately fin membranes fray and disintegrate and mucus sloughs from the body, especially along the lateral line. A high mortality of 75% during the 34th week was reported by Zobairi (1956) and the survivors developed "pop-eye." These fish recovered in about 6 days after being given an intraperitoneal injection of a B-vitamin supplement consisting of either pyridoxine, pantothenic acid and folic acid, or of riboflavin, cyanocobalamin (B₁₂), and choline in distilled water.

## 12. *Ascorbic Acid Deficiency*

Vitamin C (L-ascorbic acid) deficiency has long been recognized as the principal cause of scurvy in man. Experimental "C" deficiency, after 10 to 20 weeks or more, results in a deficiency syndrome somewhat unlike

Fig. 11. Scoliosis (upper) and lordosis (lower) in coho salmon fingerlings deficient in ascorbic acid for 22 weeks. Middle fish is normal coho fed complete test diet. From Halver *et al.* (1969).

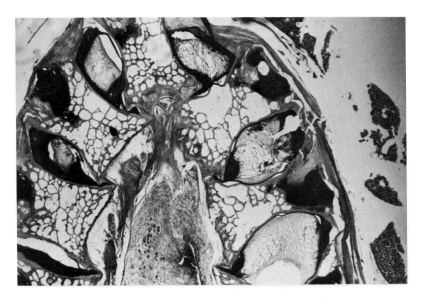

Fig. 12. Mid-sagittal section through spine of coho with severe lordosis showing displaced vertebrae with up to 80° misalignment and pinched spinal cord with hemorrhagic areas (black) in some places. H and E (×45). From Halver *et al.* (1969).

scurvy and yet the two are similar in basic pathology. This similarity is dependent upon a failure of the normal production of collagen—a tough, fibrous component of most connective tissue, of cartilage, and of bone. Perhaps the most obvious pathology in deficient rainbow trout (Kitamura *et al.*, 1965), brook trout (Poston, 1967), and coho salmon (Halver *et al.*, 1969) is the appearance in from 20 to 30 weeks of spinal anomalies. Halver *et al.* (1969) reported severe scoliosis and lordosis in coho salmon and rainbow trout after 20 weeks on L-ascorbic acid-deficient diets fed in 15°C water. Histopathology of these lesions shows extensive hemorrhage in and around the spinal cord which was severely distorted by the displaced vertebrae in the area of dorso-flexion (Figs. 11 and 12). Another skeletal anomaly observed in coho salmon fingerlings on the vitamin C-deficient diet for 20 weeks was discovered in the gills where the hyaline cartilage supports of the gill filaments were often twisted or bent into zig-zag or spiral configurations (Fig. 13). Less marked, but definite, cartilage anomalies also occurred in the ocular cartilages of many deficient fish (Halver *et al.*, 1969).

Wounding experiments on coho fingerlings may be compared with those done on guinea pigs (Wolbach, 1933) deficient in L-ascorbic acid in which skin incisions failed to develop collagen after 9 days while controls had an abundance of collagen in the healing incisions (Fig. 14). Coho salmon incisions 1 cm long were made into either the skeletal muscle, about 1 cm below the dorsal fin, or through the abdominal wall. The wounds were closed with gut sutures. Controls healed well in 3 weeks, sutures dropping out in the usual manner; deficient fish wounds failed to heal. These wounds were inflamed through most of the post-incision period. About one-half of these fish died. Those with the abdominal incisions suffered from water infusing the peritoneal cavity via the unhealed wounds (Halver *et al.*, 1969) (Figs. 15 and 16).

Fractured ribs in deficient guinea pigs will not begin to heal until about 24 hours after vitamin C has been restored to the diet (Wolbach, 1933). Wolbach further states that "matrix formation of epiphyseal cartilage cells ceases as a result of ascorbic acid deficiency just as promptly and conspicuously as does the matrix formation of bone and connective tissue cells and . . . cartilage cells do not mature until ascorbic acid is given." Ikeda and Sato (1965) showed from radioactive carbon studies that carp can synthesize only part of the ascorbic acid requirement. The ability of

Fig. 13. Gill filaments of coho salmon deficient in ascorbic acid for 20 weeks showing distorted (twisted and spiraled) cartilages (black) of varying thicknesses. Normal fish have straight or slightly curved cartilages of uniform thickness. Giemsa stain (×45). From Halver *et al.* (1969).

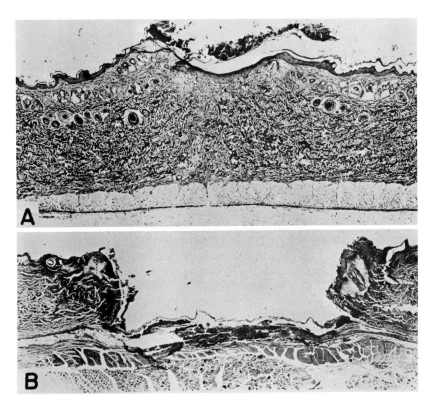

FIG. 14. Ascorbic acid deficiency. A, Skin of guinea pig. Skin from normal animal in which a central incision had been made 9 days previously. Hair follicles are absent and epithelium is increased in thickness and is overlain by debris. The wound is fully healed. B, Skin from guinea pig with acute scurvy in which a similar incision had been made 9 days earlier. The wide defect indicates complete lack of healing. H and E (×6). From Follis (1958). Courtesy of Charles C. Thomas, Springfield, Illinois.

coho salmon in this regard remains unknown but recent data indicate that at least part of the vitamin C requirement for coho fingerlings must be supplied in the diet (Halver *et al.*, 1969).

## 13. *Fat-Soluble Vitamins A and D*

Knowledge of minimum requirements of fishes for the several fat soluble vitamins, A, D, E, K, and P, remains very incomplete. Some work has been done but much of it lacks clear-cut results. For example, with rainbow trout, McLaren *et al.* (1947) fed a crude mixture of vitamin $A_1$ and $A_2$ extracted from freshwater fish livers (more or less equivalent to the

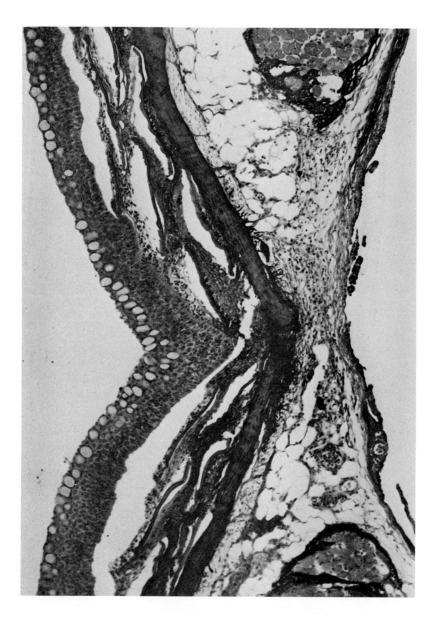

FIG. 15. Normal wound healing in belly wall of ascorbic acid adequate coho salmon fingerling 3 weeks after wounding. Dermal collagen layer incompletely healed but epidermal layer is essentially healed. H and E ($\times$ 315).

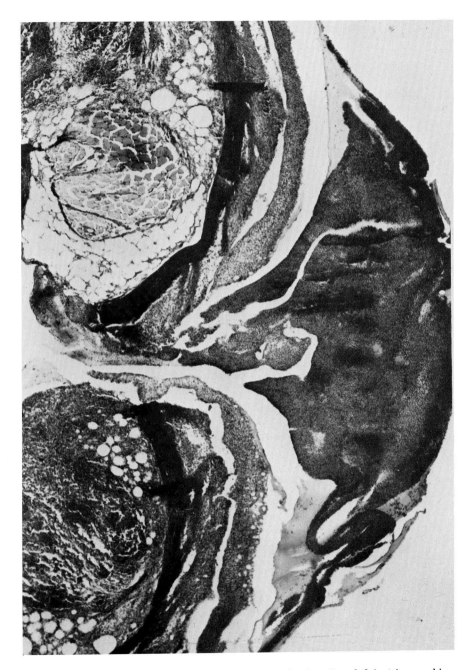

Fɪɢ. 16. Failure of wound to heal in belly wall of coho fingerling deficient in ascorbic acid 23 weeks. Fish wounded 3 weeks prior to sacrifice. Note the large hemorrhagic blood mass above the wound which remains open and unhealed. H and E (×150).

amount of vitamin A in 2% cod liver oil) and obtained only a moderate growth response. Feeding β-carotene elicited a toxic response. However, feeding vitamin A (palmitate) at doses of 3,000, 30,000, or 300,000 I U failed to elicit a toxic response in brook trout held in water at 47°F (Phillips *et al.*, 1964). In vitamin A-deficient rats, infections were more frequent and were histologically more extensive than in controls (Finkelstein, 1932; Dubos, 1955). This protective mechanism in rats has apparently not yet been demonstrated for vitamin A-sufficient fish. Mellanby (1947) cited extensive experimental evidence showing the effectiveness of vitamin A in controlling shape and histological molding of growing bone in young mammals.

Feeding 1% cod liver oil supplement gave a growth response equivalent to that from the basal ration but poorer growth was obtained from feeding 0.5% cod liver oil than when the diet was completely lacking in cod liver oil. Furthermore, vitamin $D_3$ (irradiated 7-dehydrocholesterol) seemed to be more effective than vitamin $D_2$ (irradiated ergosterol) as a source of vitamin D. However, fish on a cod liver oil-free diet grew very slowly, although continuously. Much more needs to be learned concerning the possible synthesis, sparing, and metabolic particulars of the fat-soluble vitamins in fish. Schäperclaus (1954) believes vitamin D plays an important role in phosphorus and calcium metabolism in fish. He feels that some of the abnormal gill covers of artificially reared fish are attributable to avitaminosis D.

### 14. *Tocopherols*

Vitamin E (α-tocopherol)-deficient chinook salmon develop a syndrome exhibiting poor growth, exophthalmia, ascites, erythrocyte fragility, anemia, clubbed gill, epicarditis, and ceroid deposition principally in the spleen (Figs. 17 and 18). Feeding 5% stripped herring oil supplement aggravates these symptoms, but these are also evident when only 1% herring oil supplement is included in the diet. Fish fed diets supplemented with α-tocopherol lack these symptoms (Woodall *et al.*, 1964). In rats deficient in vitamin E, mucosal changes in the intestine consisting of thickened duodenal walls mainly due to large "lipid"-filled cells in the lamina propria are observed. This change is preventable by feeding vitamin E, methylene blue, or saturated fats. Cell inclusions in the altered gut mucosa, tested histochemically, are positive for mucopolysaccharides, the significance of which is unclear (Emmel and Bisett, 1965). Using special perfusion-fixation methods, Parnell-King (1964) found pathological changes in neural tissues of mice fed vitamin E-deficient diets. The experiment ran 139 days using diets representing all possible combinations of vitamin E, neutral fat, and essential unsaturated fatty acids. Controls received com-

FIG. 17. Clubbing and hyperplasia of chinook salmon gills in α-tocopherol-deficient fingerlings. Note resemblance to nutritional gill disease of pantothenic acid deficiency, Fig. 6–8. H and E (×200).

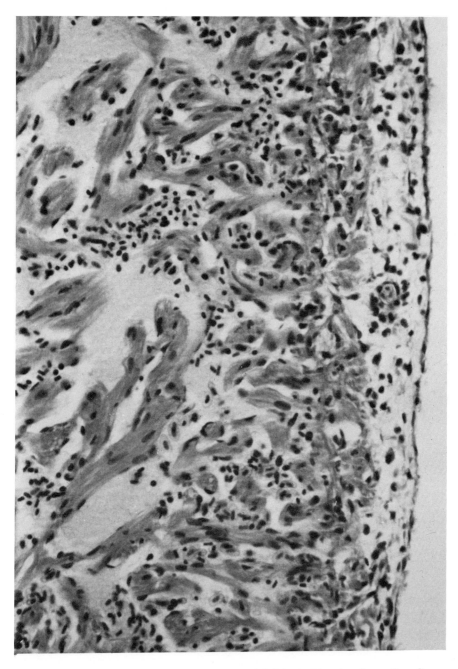

FIG. 18. Subepicardial edema in α-tocopherol-deficient chinook salmon fingerling. H and E (×350).

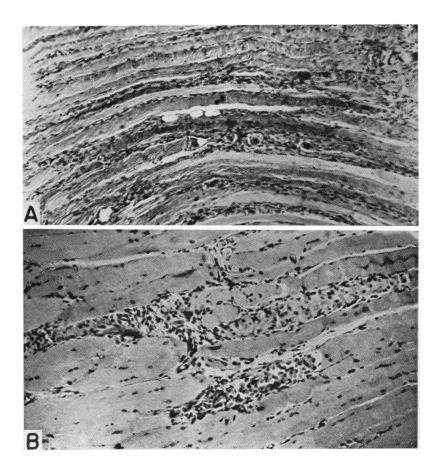

Fig. 19. Vitamin E deficiency in skeletal muscle. A, Destruction of rabbit myofibers with cellular infiltration and proliferation of sarcolemma nuclei. Fat vacuoles are evident. H and E (×130). B, Similar changes in hamster muscle fibers with cellular infiltration and myofiber destruction. Macrophages filled with acid-fast pigment (ceroid) are common but poorly shown in this photomicrograph (×150). (Courtesy of Dr. Karl E. Mason.) From Follis, (1958). Courtesy of Charles C. Thomas, Springfield, Illinois.

mercial rat chow and synthetic diets. Vitamin E-deficient mice have hyperchromatic nerve cells, fragmentation and disintegration of Nissl substance, and acid-fast free and nonfluorescent cytoplasmic vacuoles. Nuclear membranes and polar bodies are accentuated—the changes appearing in the anterior horn cells (spinal cord) and in the neurons of the nucleus proprius. Combinations of vitamin E deficiency with deficiencies of either unsaturated fatty acids or neutral fat appeared to augment

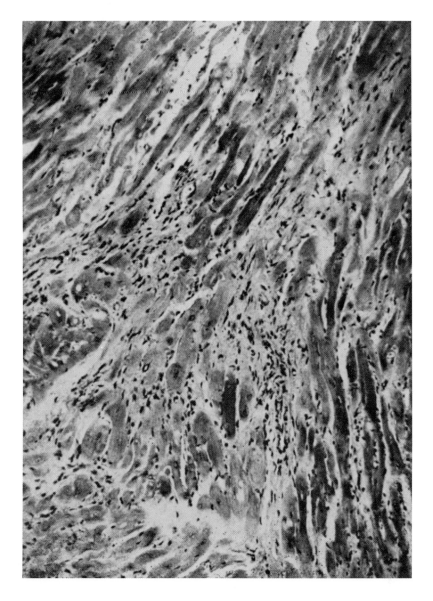

Fig. 20. Vitamin E deficiency in the heart of rat. Extensive scarring and myocardial fiber degeneration in a rat on a vitamin E-deficient diet for more than 1 year. Ceroid containing macrophages are common in areas of marked cellular infiltration. No evidence of recent fiber necrosis appears (×150). (Courtesy of Dr. Karl E. Mason.) From Follis (1958). Courtesy of Charles C. Thomas, Springfield, Illinois.

disintegration of Nissl substance and the disruption of the cell membrane. Schwartz (1965) reported that vitamin E and selenium are "essential cofactors at specific sites of intermediary metabolism." He cited three groups of diseases, the first of which are those strictly responsive to vitamin E and not affected by selenium supplements. Examples given are: (1) resorption sterility of rats, (2) muscular dystrophy of rabbits (Fig. 19), (3) encephalomalacia of chicks, and (4) necrosis and scarring of heart muscle fibers in rats (Fig. 20). Group two diseases are responsive to either vitamin E or selenium and include: (1) dietary necrotic liver degeneration of rats, (2) multiple necrotic degeneration of mice, (3) exudative diathesis of chicks, and (4) hepatosis dietetica of swine plus numerous other deficiency diseases in other species. Many of these diseases were formerly believed to be caused by lack of vitamin E only. The diathesis of Schwartz's third group was caused by lack of selenium alone and will not be discussed here.

### 15. *Vitamin K (Antihemorrhagic)*

Most of the work on the K vitamin fractions has been done on rats and chicks. Nutritional pathology observed on rats and chicks with vitamin K-deficient diets includes hypoprothrombinemia with hemorrhage throughout much of the body, especially the thymus, thorax, retroperitoneal region, gonads, and epididymal fat pads. This syndrome was alleviated by feeding small amounts of either $K_1$ or $K_3$ which resulted in a return of prothrombin times to normal (Doisy, 1961). While more needs to be done on the response of fish to vitamin K deficiency, Poston (1964) has shown that immature brook trout do respond to this deficiency by developing, within 16 weeks, a prolonged coagulation time and a lowered microhematocrit, both of which are significantly different from those of controls.

### B. Hypervitaminoses

### 1. *Hypervitaminosis A*

Excesses of vitamin A in rats have often been reported. Anomalies have included proteolysis (Rodahl *et al.*, 1965), overstimulation of bone growth in the young (Sherman and Lanford, 1957), toxic responses, and spontaneous bone fractures (Moore and Wang, 1943, 1945). Cohan (1954) reported litter failures in rats with excess vitamin A; and if litters came to term, many young were malformed with such anomalies as brain deformities, abnormal eyes, cleft palates, shortened jaws, spina bifida with meningocoele and with hydrocephalus. While 52% of these young had malformations, the 1201 controls had no congenital anomalies. Burrows *et al.* (1952) found hypervitaminosis A in salmon fed vitamin A-rich whale liver in the diet. A syndrome including eye inflammation and nervous disorders was identified. After repeated experiments feeding vitamin A (both the acetate and the palmitate) to brook trout at levels of 3000, 30,000 or 300,000 units per pound of diet failed to elicit significant effects such as reported for mammals, these authors increased the dose of vitamin A to 1,100,000 units per pound of feed. After 16 weeks on this regimen trout showed increasing growth retardation until the experiment ended after 24 weeks. Mortalities were not significantly increased over those of controls. Experimental fish had a severe fin anomaly typified by extensive erosion and necrosis of the caudal fin in about 69% of the fish examined. The controls all had uneroded, healthy fins (Poston *et al.*, 1966).

## 2. Hypervitaminosis D

Specific data on hypervitaminosis D are either unavailable or are very scanty regarding most species of animals, and this appears to be especially true of fishes. Clinical pathology of hypervitaminosis D may be negligible or absent in a given series of treated animals, but at the same time subclinical or histopathological changes may be considerable (Cowdry and Scott, 1936). In the absence of clinical findings these authors, working with monkeys (*Macacas rhesus*), observed such tissue changes as fragmentation and calcification of the arterial inner elastic membranes of one monkey, infiltration of parathyroid glands with eosinophils in two others, renal tubular leukocytic invasion in three, renal tubular degeneration in two, and calcification in one. In addition, some of the experimental animals revealed: (1) reduction in number of cytoplasmic basophilic bodies in the parathyroid glands, (2) nuclear inclusion bodies in cells of renal tubules, and (3) intimal thickenings in certain blood vessels. None of the controls had any of these changes. It is not possible to extrapolate these observations to fishes in any general sense since the authors noted carefully that two mature monkeys of the species *Cebus fatuellus* reacted very differently from rhesus monkeys to the same excessive doses, which in the rhesus monkeys ranged from a minimum of 5 ml for 4 days to 133 ml for 134 days of a concentrate of approximately 1 million USP units per gram in comparison to the usual dose of 10,000 units per gram. However, since fishes do respond in a manner similar to mammals, when challenged by various disease inducing entities, one may assume that some of the more responsive species of fishes, at least, would show histopathological changes of varying degrees to excessive doses of certain vitamins. In man and in experimental animals, excess vitamin D induces mineral mobilization from the skeleton and metastatic deposits of calcium in certain soft tissues, the kidneys, in particular. These effects are somewhat conditioned by factors such as dietary calcium, phosphorus, and vitamin A. Large excesses of vitamin D almost always retard growth (Holman and McCance, 1956).

## III. Imbalance of Macronutrients

### A. Deficiencies

#### 1. *Protein*

Nutritional and pathological effects resulting from protein deficiency are largely nonspecific in character—the anomalies are akin to those arising from several essential amino acid deficiencies.

Perhaps the most striking effect of protein deficiency is growth retardation. This is histologically exhibited by subnormal bone and cartilage development characterized by dystrophy of epiphyseal cartilages and by an osteoporotic anomaly of the bone matrix. Protein deficiency reduces chondroblastic and osteoblastic activity, apparently to a point where neither cartilage nor bone can form in the normal manner (Follis, 1956). Even in adult rats, protein deficiency induces a rarefaction of the bones (Estremera and Armstrong, 1948), teeth, and periodontal tissues (Hunter, 1950; Frandsen *et al.*, 1953).

Further changes may include atrophy of most lymphoid tissues, nonspecific changes in endocrine glands, malformation and malfunction of both formative and formed elements of the blood (Whipple and Robscheit-Robbins, 1940; Lucas and Orten, 1954), and depletion of plasma proteins (Madden *et al.*, 1945; Miller *et al.*, 1951). Nelson and Evans (1953) and Goettsch (1949) found protein-deficient rats suffered reproductive failures. Corneal vascularization of rats, originally observed after riboflavin deprivation (Bessey and Wolbach, 1939), is now known to occur in deficiencies of each of the ten essential rat amino acids (Sydenstricker *et al.*, 1947).

Lens pathology in the form of cataract may also develop under protein deprivation and also under deficiency of tryptophan, histidine, and phenylalanine (Hall *et al.*, 1948). Lack of either leucine or threonine may cause less severe lens anomalies. Furthermore, haziness of the lens was reported to result from a lack of isoleucine, lysine, methionine, and valine.

Fish are now known to require the same ten amino acids needed by growing rats (Halver *et al.*, 1957). However, the histopathology of fish rendered deficient by the deletion of single amino acids from a basal ration remains largely unexplored. Scoliosis has been reported in tryptophan-deficient sockeye salmon (*Oncorhynchus nerka*). This anomaly appeared after 21–28 days without tryptophan. Scoliotic fish recovered in 7–14 days after tryptophan was returned to the rations (Halver and Shanks, 1960). Aside from scoliosis, growth retardation is about the only anomaly reported for fish deficient in single amino acids.

Rats deficient in either valine, leucine, tryptophan, isoleucine, or phenylalanine developed tremors (Sebrell and McDaniel, 1952). However, neurological lesions were not described for these rats and it appears likely that such lesions as those reported for rats deficient in pantothenic acid or in pyridoxine do not seem to appear when only one or a few amino acids are lacking in the diet. More significant lesions in rats do appear when the animals are deprived of cystine and methionine. This syndrome includes anorexia, anemia, hypoproteinemia, and massive hepatic necrosis. Rats devoid of methionine only do not develop the hepatic necrosis but do get all of the other anomalies resulting from lack of cystine and methionine. When the diet lacks cystine but contains small amounts of methionine, growth and appetite are only moderate. The rats do not get anemia or hypoproteinemia but die with massive hepatic necrosis. When the diet contains large amounts of methionine, but no cystine, growth is excellent and no pathological lesions appear. The anemia, in rats receiving no methionine, is characterized by severe anisocytosis, poikilocytosis, polychromasia, hyperchromicity, and macrocytosis. It is associated with hyperplasia of type A normoblastic cells in the marrow and is accompanied by a marked reticulocytosis (Glynn *et al.*, 1945).

Glynn *et al.* (1945) deprived rats of the sulfur-containing amino acids cystine and methionine. He concluded (1) that cystine deficiency causes massive necrosis of the liver, and (2) that methionine deficiency results in anorexia, arrested growth or even wasting, and when severe, causes hypoproteinemia and a special kind of anemia. György and Goldblatt (1942) observed that rats on diets low in casein with high fat content, but without choline, regularly developed hepatic necrosis and cirrhosis with or without ascites after from 100 to 150 days. Adequate supplements of L-cystine plus choline or of DL-methionine proved highly effective in preventing liver damage. It would be interesting to know whether or not comparable experiments on fish would yield similar pathological results. Sidransky and Verney (1965) found all rats deficient in threonine had fatty livers, increased liver glycogen, and atrophy of pancreas, thymus, submaxillary, spleen, and stomach, regardless of whether other essential amino acids were fed at low, normal, or at high levels.

Electron micrographical studies of lysine-deficient rats have recently shown changes in the exocrine pancreas cells. Zymogen granules were lessened in number and, in many instances, their bounding membranes ruptured. Large aggregations of lipid droplets were seen at the bases of the cells. Mitochondria were swollen and malformed with displaced cristae and with altered myelin bodies. These lysine deficiency changes accompanied nonspecific regressive anomalies due to partial inanition (Scott, 1966). In bronze turkey poults a failure of feather pigmentation occurred when birds were fed a high percentage (10%) of cottonseed meal or of corn gluten meal in the ration. The addition of crystalline lysine to corn gluten meal prevented appearance of the white feather syndrome. Soy bean meal did not induce depigmentation of feathers, apparently owing to its adequate lysine content (Fritz *et al.*, 1946).

Hunter (1950) found lysine-deficient black rats to have "diluted" coats of finer textured fur than occurred in control black rats in twice confirmed experiments. Hunter concluded that lysine plays a role in melanin synthesis in rats as well as in turkey poults. Since most fish produce considerable melanin, it may be that lysine plays a similar melanogenic role in fish as in mammals. It remains largely for the future to determine what effects, if any, may occur in experimental fishes rendered deficient of single amino acids while receiving an otherwise adequate basal diet.

## 2. *Lipids*

Lipids lacking in the dietary of growing pigs result in retarded growth, dermatitis, loss of fur, skin ulcers, and increased mortality. Other anomalies in lipid-deficient mammals are priapism, dystrophic spleen, testes, and gall bladders, enlargement of livers, kidneys, adrenals, and hearts, and reddening of muscles (Reid and Martin, 1959). These authors also reported anemia in some deficient pigs but stated that the blood picture was unaltered except for a slight microcytosis. Fat-deficient young rats, on the other hand, acquire hyperkeratosis with epidermal cells increased from 2 to 12 cells in thickness. The stratum granulosum cells become hypertrophic and collagen fibers in the dermis become edematous (Williamson, 1941; Ramalingaswami and Sinclair, 1953). Hair follicles are increased in size and the hair fragility is increased (Kramer and Levine, 1953). In male rats testicular atrophy occurs. Histologically, the tubular epithelium of the testis degenerates and giant cells are increased in number. Return of deficient animals to an adequate diet results in prompt recovery (Deuel and Reisser, 1955). In another study, Hands *et al.* (1965) found that rats lacking dietary fat suffer loss of visual acuity. Controls could discriminate between black and white stripes at 0.002 ft, but deficient rats could not. Controls have fourteen times the amount of docosahexaenoic acid in retinal fats and deficient rats have no liver stores of vitamin A while controls have 190 IU/gm of this vitamin. In histochemical studies of fat-deficient rats these authors found that neutral lipid content of liver mitochondria was twice that of controls.

Few fat deficiency studies have been reported on fish, but Nicolaides and Woodall (1962) reported impaired pigmentation of chinook salmon fry fed a fat-free ration from first feeding to 16 weeks. Depigmentation was at its maximum at 24 weeks on test. A similar pigmentation anomaly was seen when triolein or linolenic acid was included in the diet, but most pigment loss was prevented by the inclusion of trilinolein. More severe skin lesions were reported by Higashi *et al.* (1966) in rainbow trout fed fat-free diets, but the nature of the lipids involved was not assayed.

### 3. *Minerals*

According to Phillips (1959), "Mineral studies upon fish will surely be productive, and such information should result in a more vigorous and healthy animal." Phillips further noted that, "The establishment of mineral requirements of higher animals has overcome many formerly incurable diseases." Among these are: (1) dietary anemia, overcome with iron, cobalt, copper, and others; (2) subnormal bone development, overcome with calcium, fluorine, phosphorus, and magnesium; (3) poor hair development, controlled with zinc; (4) improper blood coagulation, prevented by calcium; and (5) numerous problems of growth, controlled by various combinations of minerals. To date very little has been added to the literature on the mineral requirements of fishes, although a little work is known to be in progress. Phillips also stated that many required minerals can be absorbed through gills or other body surfaces by fishes but that soft waters which are poor in minerals necessitate either (1) fertilization of the water with the needed minerals or (2) suitable mineral supplementation of the fishes' diet. Obviously the second method is more practicable when fish, such as trout, must be reared in flowing water.

All minerals essential to adequate nutrition of higher animals can be considered essential for fish until proved otherwise. Specific mineral deficiency syndromes of fishes are still little known, but a few which have been more or less worked out are detailed below. Some of these are compared with mineral deficiency syndromes of higher vertebrates.

*a. Iodine Deficiency.* This deficiency was, according to Gaylord and Marsh (1914), reported for brook trout as early as 1891 by Scott who identified the throat lesions as a form of cancer. Marine and Lenhart (1910) held that this disease was a form of goiter, but Gaylord and Marsh

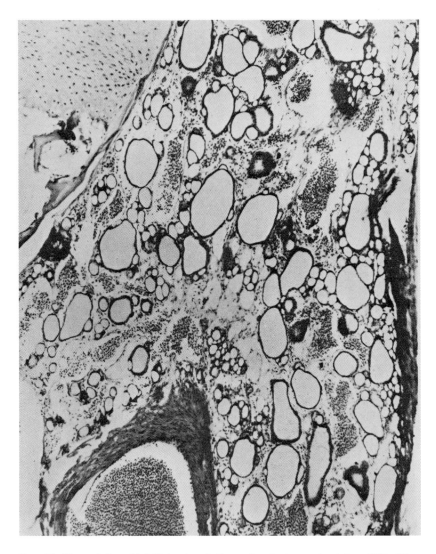

Fig. 21. Normal thyroid follicles in adult sea trout. Approximately ×200. (From Gaylord and Marsh, 1914.)

believed it to be a neoplastic disease, as had Scott. After much controversy as to its etiology and many experiments later, the diagnosis of goiter was confirmed. It was shown conclusively that the disease could be controlled by the administration of minute quantities of dietary iodine. Davis (1953) explained the confusion that had attended the fish goiter controversy by pointing out the diffuse nature of the teleost thyroid tissue which is scattered along the course of the ventral aorta and its main branches to the gills, especially the second and third branchial arches (Fig. 21). Hyperplasia of the thyroid or goiter thus presented a picture remarkably similar to that of an invasive neoplasm of the branchial arch region (Figs. 22 and 23). Goiter in fish is indeed rare today since iodine is recognized as an essential mineral nutrient and one teaspoonful of Lugol's solution/50 pounds of feed prevents goiter. Fish meal in the dietary usually contains enough iodine to prevent the disease. Subclinical evidence of iodine deficiency was recently provided by Woodall and LaRoche (1964) who failed

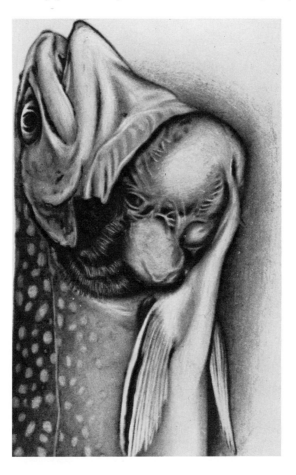

Fɪɢ. 22. Large thyroid goiter (termed a tumor by Gaylord and Marsh) in an iodine deficient brook trout 2 years of age. (From Gaylord and Marsh, 1914.)

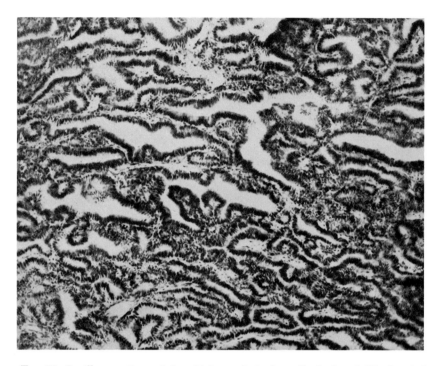

Fɪɢ. 23. Papillary pattern of thyroid hyperplasia from Gaylord and Marsh, 1914. Species of fish not given but most cases figured by these authors were from brook trout reared in hatcheries.

to find goiter in chinook salmon deficient in iodine but who found subclinical thyroid hyperplasia upon histological examination.

*b. Iron, Copper, and Cobalt Deficiencies.* Deficiencies of these minerals may induce anemia. Iron, as an essential mineral component of hemoglobin, except in molluscs and in certain arthropods, heads the list of antianemic minerals, but traces of copper and of cobalt, the latter as part of the cyanocobalamin (vitamin $B_{12}$) molecule, also appear to be essential. Some fish are so deficient in iron that when fed to mink (or to other fish) induce anemia. Cooking with 16 mg organic iron added per week (for mink) prevents anemia. Since cyanocobalamin is essential in erythrocyte maturation, the need for traces of cobalt is obvious. Helgebostad and Martinsons (1958) attributed anemia in mink kits to an iron deficiency acquired when mink were fed raw, gutted ocean fish, coalfish (*Gadus virens*), and whiting (*G. merlangus*). The anemia in these mink was characterized by low red blood cell count (average 7.8 million/mm³), low hemoglobin (average

10.6 gm%), an increased reticulocyte count of 2.3%, and an increased leukocyte count (average 14.66 thousand/mm³). When the same species of fish were boiled and then fed, no anemia appeared. An interesting case of nutritional anemia in trout is related by Sadkovskaya (1957) in which clinical symptoms were most severe and mortalities unusually high. Malnutrition was suspected, and after tests for bacteria and viruses proved negative, the disease was successfully prevented by feeding live crustaceans (*Gammarus*). Affected fish showed gradual paling of gills and fading of liver until gills were white and livers yellow-gray. Intestinal walls thinned and became translucent while eyes became protruded, cloudy, and sometimes hemorrhagic until blindness ensued and fish no longer reacted to men walking along the bank of the ponds. Lateral line involvement was evident by the fact that moving the hand back and forth in the water failed to elicit avoidance reactions in the blind fish.

Iron-deficient rats may show marked anomalies of red blood cells on microscopic inspection of blood films (Smith and Medlicott, 1944) (Fig. 24).

*c. Potassium Deficiency.* Animals, rats, rabbits, calves, and dogs, fed as little as 0.01% potassium in an otherwise adequate diet, get well-defined heart and kidney lesions. Follis *et al.* (1942a) found such lesions plus growth retardation in rats which became acutely deficient; some even died within 1 week. Gross cardiac lesions consisted of minute gray opacities in the ventricles. Stained sections of these lesions revealed hyaline degeneration and necrosis of myocardial fibers. There was proliferation of sarcolemmal nuclei and leukocytes often filled the interstices between muscle fibers (Smith *et al.*, 1950; Cohen *et al.*, 1952; Hove and Herndon, 1955). The largest lesions encompassed several low power fields (Fig. 25). The atrial myocardium was only mildly affected. Similar pathology of the kidneys was observed by Follis *et al.* (1942a), MacPherson and Pearse (1957), and Milne *et al.* (1957). After a week on potassium-deficient diets, rat kidneys were grossly pale and swollen. Later on the still enlarging kidneys developed finely pitted surfaces. Histologically there were fat accumulations in renal tubular epithelial cells showing first in the basal cytoplasm as small sudanophilic droplets. With additional droplet deposition these cells became necrotic after which cellular debris was discharged into the lumens (Fig. 26). Calcification of tubular epithelia and calcareous casts in the lumens sometimes appeared later. No glomerular lesions were noted by any of the above authors (Iacobellis *et al.*, 1954). Potassium-deficient calves had varying degrees of granular degeneration and vacuolation of cardiac Purkinje fibers together with altered electrocardiograms (Sykes and Moore, 1942).

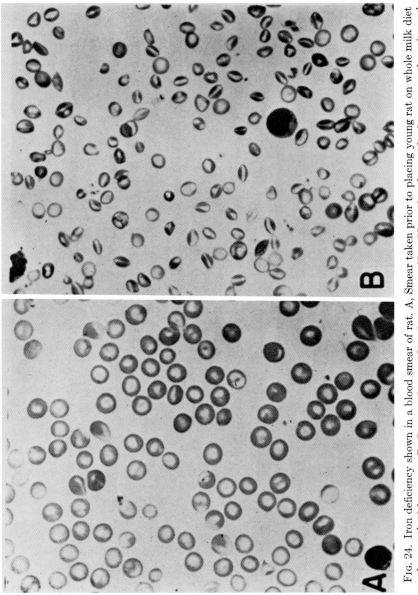

Fig. 24. Iron deficiency shown in a blood smear of rat. A, Smear taken prior to placing young rat on whole milk diet supplemented with copper. B, Smear taken 40 days later, at sacrifice. Note abundance of microcytes, achromia, and poikilocytosis. The blood values were: R.B.C., 4,290,000; Hb, 1.7 gm, MCV, 44 $\mu^3$; MCHC, 19%; MCH, 8.6 $\mu^2$. Wright stain ($\times$600). From Follis (1958). Courtesy of Charles C. Thomas, Springfield, Illinois.

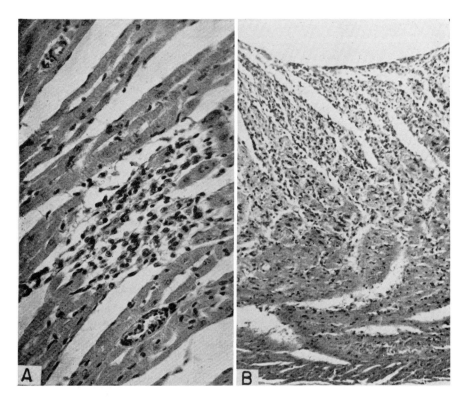

Fig. 25. Potassium deficiency in a rat heart. A, Small focus of necrotic fibers in wall of left ventricle from rat on deficient diet for 9 days (×270). B, Section through entire wall of right ventricle of rat on deficient diet for 12 days (×135). From Follis (1958). Courtesy of Charles C. Thomas, Springfield, Illinois.

*d. Sodium Deficiency.* Since sodium is normally obtained in rock salt, it may rarely be deficient. Rats fed low sodium diets acquired conjunctival hyperkeratosis of the palpebral areas and the Meibomian gland ducts were dilated. Later on the Harderian glands became swollen. The corneal substantia propria (fibrous tissue) had leukocytic infiltration and capillary vascularization while the corneal epithelium became keratinized (Follis *et al.*, 1942b).

*e. Calcium Deficiency.* Calcium is well known as a major mineral element required for bone development together with magnesium and certain other mineral cations. A deficiency of calcium alters various physiological processes and also results in morbid changes in developing bone. The epiphyseal cartilages become widened, and the chondrocytes become

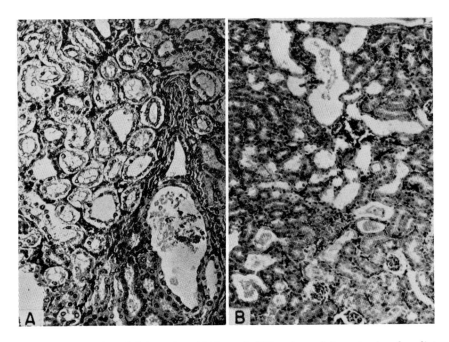

Fig. 26. Potassium deficiency in rat kidney. A, This rat was fed a potassium low diet for 15 days. Note vacuolated epithelial cells, some with fat. A dilated tubule contains desquamated cellular debris (×150). (Courtesy *Amer. J. Pathol.*) B, This rat was fed the same ration for 5 weeks. Note dilated tubule lined by flattened, regenerated epithelium (×123). From Follis, (1958). Courtesy of Charles C. Thomas, Springfield, Illinois.

hypertrophied and deranged. The bony spicules are diminished in number while osteoid increases in width, there being too little calcium to convert it into bone. The role of vitamin D was demonstrated in early calcium deficiency experiments, but later uncomplicated experiments first clearly showed the nature of the true deficiency syndrome (Martin, 1937). Martin showed that deficient dogs got osteoporosis, widespread hemorrhage, and inflammation of the gastrointestinal tract. Similar lesions appear in calcium-deficient rats and many animals die in paralysis after galvanic stimulus (Boelter and Greenberg, 1941). These authors also found that rats on a low-calcium diet soon fail to mate and newborn litters may die because their mothers lack sufficient milk. Calcium-deficient rabbits get lens opacities and the lenses thus affected have histologically demonstrable vacuoles, clefts, and dots near the lens' equator. Such opacities may spread toward the anterior and posterior suture lines and blindness may result (Swan and Salit, 1941). The literature is very meager regarding tissue changes in calcium-deficient fishes, but since fish bones are less highly calcified than are those of mammals, changes such as osteoporosis might not develop as readily or appear so obvious in deficient fish as in mammals. Fish often absorb calcium cations directly via the gills (Phillips *et al.*, 1956). Lens opacities, however, might appear in fishes as reported when deficient in riboflavin, vitamin A, tryptophan, histidine or phenylalanine, or after thioacetamide intoxication. Phosphorus deficiency results in changes akin to those of rickets in vitamin D deficiency in which impaired bone development results in a deformed skeleton, at least in mammals. A ricketic syndrome has not been described for fishes, although fish do need cod liver oil for normal growth.

The need for various trace minerals for adequate carp nutrition was shown by Gordeev (1964) who either fed or added to the pond water, salts of cobalt, copper, and manganese in amounts of 0.08, 0.04, and 0.02 mg/kg of live fish during the periods of active growth and feeding of the carp. Fish on trace mineral supplements exceeded controls in weight by from 5 to 30% at the end of the experiment. Control fish were not significantly subnormal but the experiment points up the desirability of certain trace minerals in fish nutrition in order to ensure optimum growth.

*f. Copper Deficiency.* This mineral was reported as a dietary essential for mammals, birds, and fishes by McHargue (1925) who found that fetuses and newborn mammals contained up to more than twice the amount of copper as did their parents. An interesting experiment comparing normal with copper-deficient diets fed 6 weeks to 1-day-old chicks (Simpson and Harms, 1964) resulted in hemorrhages in moribund copper-deficient chicks. Electron microscope studies demonstrated the presence of a progressive degeneration of aortic elastic fibers which began peripherally and progressed centrally. Affected elastic fibers swelled, softened, and underwent dissolution, finally resulting in the terminal hemorrhages. Copper occurs in blood cells and in many other tissues, and its lack impairs or prevents the use of iron by many animals. Black sheep become depigmented, lambs incoordinated, and female rats and cattle fail to reproduce. However, normal needs are amply met in a balanced adequate diet (Pfizer Spectrum, Spring, 1965). Aortic lesions in copper-deficient chicks were reported by O'Dell *et al.* (1966) who noted large accumulations of nonelastin, noncollagen protein together with excessive amounts of soluble collagen. Controls had about 47% elastin as compared with about 26% in deficient aortas. Copper-deficient pigs have hyperplasia of red bone marrow and dysplasia of developing bone characterized by acellularity and diminished osteoid and bone matrix (Figs. 27 and 28). Hunt and Carlton (1965) fed a synthetic copper-deficient diet to Dutch belted rab-

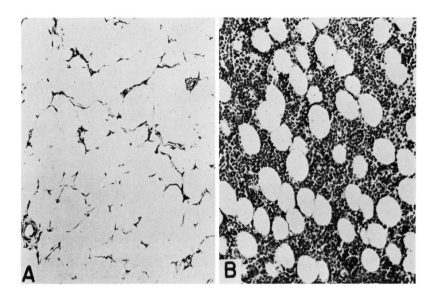

Fig. 27. Marrow from pig rib. A, Normal marrow composed mostly of fat but with scattered foci of cellular elements. B, Copper-deficient pig showing hyperplasia of hemapoietic elements—mainly erythroid tissue. H and E. (×120). From Follis, Richard (1958). Courtesy of Charles C. Thomas, Springfield, Illinois.

bits and found reduced growth, lowered hemoglobin and hematocrit levels, depigmented hair (achromotrichia), alopecia, and dermatosis in the deficient animals. Gross lesions included calcific nodules in the hearts of some rabbits. Microscopic, noninflammatory, necrotic myocardial fiber lesions with dystrophic calcification were noted. Loss of elastic fibers, calcification, and fragmentation of the internal elastic membrane in muscular and elastic arteries also occurred. In some muscular arteries, calcification of the tunica media occurred. Rabbits receiving 3 ppm copper had little evidence of deficiency.

Some fish, cold water forms in particular, seem able to adjust to copper, and perhaps other mineral deficiencies, for considerable periods without apparent ill effects other than growth retardation. However, more work is needed and it would appear most desirable to work with warm water fishes in aquariums made of inert material so that water chemistry as well as food ingredients might be kept deficient in the mineral under investigation.

It should be admitted, however, that most natural waters contain copper and other minerals in adequate amounts to meet the needs of fishes regardless of (or together with) those minerals present in the food. Therefore, mineral deficiency syndromes and their associated histopathology, as observed in the higher vertebrates, are, in general, much less a cause for concern for fishes.

*g. Zinc Deficiency.* This is another essential trace mineral, excessive in chronic lymphatic leukemia and in osteomyelosclerosis, but decreased in chronic myelogenous leukemia, acute myelogenous leukemia, plasmacytoma, and Hodgkin's disease (Szmigielski and Litwin, 1964). Little mention of zinc requirements in fishes can be found in the literature, but several cases of Egyptian dwarfism in young humans have been traced to zinc deficiency (Pfizer Spectrum, Spring, 1965). Fishes usually obtain sufficient zinc from the feed or directly from the water.

*h. Magnesium Deficiency.* This deficiency in mammals is well known. Rats, cattle, and humans lacking the Mg cation may develop tetany, convulsions, and lesions in the kidneys which may include necrosis and inflammation with occasional calcareous casts in the renal tubules. In man, Mg deficiency has been associated with idiopathic epilepsy, eclampsia, chronic nephritis, and other disorders (Wacker and Vallee, 1961).

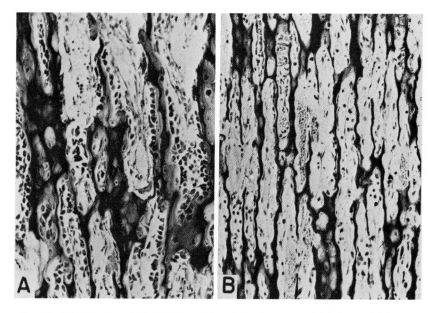

Fɪɢ. 28. Metaphysis of pig. A, Normally calcified bony matrix about which many osteoblasts appear to be generating osteoid. B, Similar area from copper-deficient pig showing acellularity, increased density, and lack of bone deposition. H and E. (×130). From Follis (1958). Courtesy of Charles C. Thomas, Springfield, Illinois.

MacIntyre and Davidson (1958) induced nephrocalcinosis and hyper-calcemia by feeding Mg deficiency diets to rats; the deficient animals also manifested secondary potassium depletion and sodium retention. After only 12 days on the deficient diet, edema and peripheral vasodilatation occurred and lasted 7–10 days. Within 3 weeks femoral Mg declined to about half that of control femurs. The potassium depletion of Mg-deficient rats was believed due to impaired function of mitochondria. Smith *et al.* (1962) observed very similar changes in Mg-deficient rats but noted in addition that in late stages of this syndrome rats have coarse, dull hair, and patchy, scaly dermatitis about the eyes and ears. While fish are be-lieved to require essentially the same minerals as mammals for good growth and development, it remains for future research to show to what extent pathological changes will occur in fishes deficient in one or more essential minerals.

*i. Sulfur Deficiency.* This is an essential mineral to animal life but owing to complexities in the biochemistry of sulfur metabolism, it is best that the pathology of its deficiency states be considered under the prin-cipal sulfur-bearing amino acids, methionine and cystine (Section III, A, 1).

*j. Vanadium Deficiency.* Although rather toxic, vanadium has useful functions in animals, and presumably also in fish. Foremost among these is inhibition of cholesterol and lipid synthesis (Curran, 1965). Curran lowered serum cholesterol as much as 20% by adding vanadium to the diets of young men with normal cholesterol levels. Workmen exposed to vanadium have rather low cholesterol levels. Death rates for coronary disease in men in the United States correlate well with the geographic distribution of vanadium. While atherosclerosis in fish is still little known, a few cases have been reported (Vastesaeger *et al.*, 1962). Vanadium de-ficiency is also known to impair mineralization of dental enamel. Future vitamin-mineral preparations for both man and beast (fishes included) may well include traces of vanadium.

*k. Fluorine Deficiency.* Fluorine is another trace mineral the absence of which favors dental caries. This may be due in part to its protective effect on the function of vanadium. It is believed that molybdenum may also enhance the protective effect of vanadium on dental health.

*l. Selenium Deficiency.* The deficiency of selenium in various farm animals and in trout was reported by Schwartz (1961). He indicated that deficiencies of factor 3 selenium resulted in a variety of pathological changes for various species such as poor growth, liver, heart and kidney necrosis, calcifications, muscular dystrophy, pancreatic atrophy, serum protein and exudative diathesis, and hemorrhagic lungs.

The antioxidant role of selenium serves to prevent muscular dystrophy in sheep. Lambs fed liquid diets containing stripped lard and torula yeast develop gross and microscopic lesions of nutritional muscular dystrophy in 16 to 36 days and high levels of serum glutamic-oxalacetic transaminase. When this diet is supplemented with selenium, growth is stimulated more than with α-tocopherol and clinical symptoms of dystrophy fail to appear (Hopkins *et al.*, 1964). Effects of dietary selenium on fishes are little known although some limited observations have been made. Coates *et al.* (1967) fed 0.1 ppm selenium to rainbow trout for 1 year without inducing hepatoma. No significant pathology was observed in these fish after 16 months on test.

*m. Manganese and Molybdenum Deficiencies.* The lack of these minerals tends to result in abnormal metabolism in mammals. Little if any published information relating to the needs of fishes for these minerals exists. Manganese is sometimes useful in vitamin deficiency for it has a sparing action on thiamine and it may relieve a kind of paralysis of vitamin E-deficient animals. It may also provide other forms of protection in animals. Molybdenum in adequate amounts protects young animals and children from dental caries. It appears to serve as an adjunct to iron in prevention of anemia. Although Mn and Mo are but slightly toxic, an excess of either may upset normal metabolism.

In summary, it may be said that few syndromes and histopathological effects are clearly established for specific mineral deficiencies of fishes.

## B. Excesses

### 1. *Protein*

An excess of protein in an otherwise adequate fish diet is unlikely in either natural or hatchery conditions. Should such an excess exist, the organism may exhibit moderate to slight growth retardation because of energy losses incident to the elimination of excess nitrogen. Fish are less handicapped by nitrogen excesses than are higher vertebrates because fish have the added mechanism of nitrogen elimination via the gills. Therefore, one may assume that nutritional pathology in fish getting an excess of good protein would be negligible or lacking. Even a surplus of poor quality protein would not ordinarily result in significant pathology unless one or more essential amino acids were largely absent from the diet, in which case the resulting pathology would be caused by a deficiency.

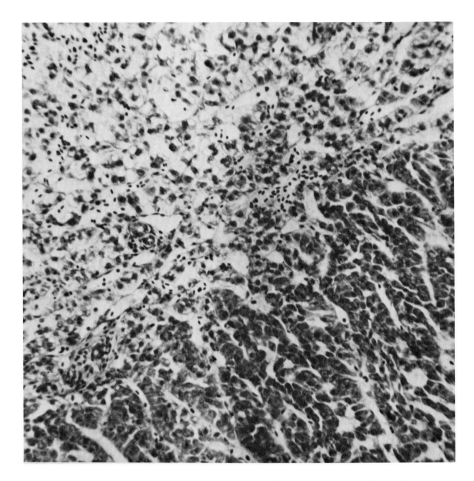

FIG. 29. Heavily vacuolated, formerly glycogen-filled rainbow trout liver adjacent to nonvacuolated neoplastic cells of liver cell carcinoma. Fish fed Dollar's diet XIII for 18 months. H and E (×200). Courtesy of Dr. Raymond Simon, Oregon State University, Corvallis, Oregon.

### 2. Carbohydrate

Hess (1935) reported that livers had a great infiltration of glycogen in overfed fish, especially when lard or lard and cornstarch were added to the diet (Figs. 29 and 30). Furthermore, pancreatic tissue had progressively more fat infiltration and pancreatic islets were proportionally diminished in fish with increased food intake, especially with fat and carbohydrate additives and in those getting less exercise because of reduced water flow. Histological study of pancreatic islets in sluggish overfed fish showed a rather uniform cellular degeneration with nuclear pyknosis somewhat akin to conditions which occur in mammals preceding the onset of, or during, incipient (sugar) diabetes. No mention was made of lipoid degeneration of the liver in these fish but the condition appears somewhat related to liver lipoid disease (ceroid) discussed below (Section III, B, 3). Liver glycogenosis, described above, is a common finding in hatchery fish since overfeeding is commonly practiced in an effort to increase production. Overfeeding may be only a relative term but when the quantity of food consumed by hatchery fish is compared with that ingested by wild

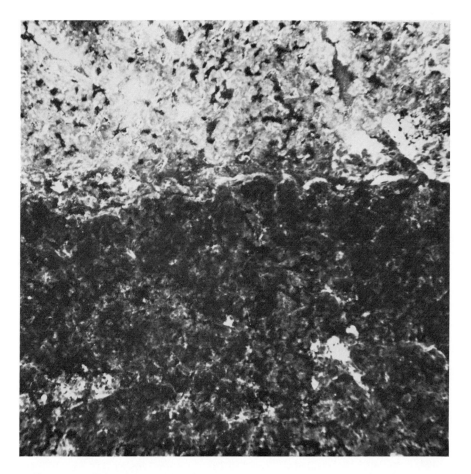

Fig. 30. Periodic acid Schiff (PAS)-stained section from same liver as Fig. 29 showing strong PAS reaction in glycogen-filled hepatocytes and lack of glycogen in tumor cells. (×200). Courtesy of Dr. Raymond Simon, Oregon State University, Corvallis, Oregon.

fish of the same species, one finds more food eaten by the former, but for exceptional occasions when wild fish have an opportunity to gorge.

Tannenbaum (1959) reported mammary tumors in mice did not occur when caloric intake was restricted from full fed controls to $\frac{2}{3}$-fed mice, and these mice continued to have no tumors even after 100 weeks when only 29 of 50 animals remained alive. These had fewer diseases of kidneys, heart, liver, and other organs than did full-fed mice. Experiments in which 12.5–25% butter fat was fed increased the tumor incidence in mice. Tannenbaum concludes that chronic caloric restriction inhibits the genesis of many kinds of tumors, decreases the incidence of neoplasia and also delays the time at which tumors appear.

With regard to fish, insufficient data are available to judge the possible extent to which Tannenbaum's observations may apply to the relationship between overeating and neoplasia in fishes.

### 3. *Fiber*

Phillips *et al.* (1962) wrote: "The reduction of the calorie content of a standard type trout diet by replacement of fractions of the diet with inert cellulose flour reduced the growth rate of brook trout." Buhler and Halver (1961) obtained similar results with chinook salmon when dietary bulk was increased with high concentrations of $\alpha$-cellulose. However, protein utilization was improved when small amounts of this fiber were included in the dietary. Graham (1964) found that the net available metabolizable energy for maintenance and for fattening of sheep decreases directly as the quantity of digestible fiber increases. This should not be taken to mean that digestible fiber is undesirable but rather, that such fiber in excess of a certain optimum quantity is undesirable. According to Hungate (1950), ruminant and equine species are able, with the help of intestinal bacteria, to degrade cellulose, thus converting it to digestible compounds. A similar phenomenon is accomplished in swine and in rats by virtue of their intestinal floras (Dukes, 1942; Maynard and Loosli, 1956). Fish may have a similar ability for degradation of some cellulose by virtue of intestinal flora.

### 4. *Excess Fats*

Unsaturated and/or oxidized fats have been found by fish culturists to have harmful effects when fed in quantity to rainbow trout. Brook trout are less affected and brown trout are rarely affected by such poor quality feeds. The disease resulting, especially in rainbow trout, is termed liver lipoid disease (LLD) or ceroidosis. It is characterized by the accumulation of pigmented insoluble fat (ceroid) in liver macrophages, Kupffer cells, or parenchyma cells. Spleen, kidney, and adrenal cortical tissues have also been observed with ceroid deposits (Wood and Yasutake, 1956b; Faktorovich, 1956, 1960; Ghittino and Ceretto, 1962). Faktorovich considers LLD to be a serious disease of rainbow trout and notes that carp in public ponds, when fed quantities of bread, often suffer from this disease. This suggests that nutritional imbalance may be a factor in addition to rancid fats resulting from prolonged and inadequate storage of fatty fish or cereal products prior to feeding. Wood and Yasutake reported ceroid in various organs of fish (mostly salmonids) suffering from nutritional deficiencies as well as fish with various infectious diseases of both viral and bacterial origin. Davis (1953) noted that the disease is often characterized by anemia.

Plehn (1924), who first reported LLD, Faktorovich (1956), and Ghittino and Ceretto (1962) all compared the pale yellow-brown livers of affected trout with the red-brown livers of healthy trout. The latter authors described and illustrated the gross and microscopic pathology of the

Fig. 31. Liver lipoid disease of rainbow trout (LLD). Lower fish shows yellowish-brown liver typical of LLD. Upper fish has reddish-brown liver typical of normal trout. Courtesy of Dr. Pietro Ghittino, Instituto Zooprofilattico Sperimentale, Torino, Italy.

Fɪɢ. 32. Rainbow trout with severe case of liver lipoid disease (LLD). Much of the liver is a pale tan color indicative of altered liver parenchyma cells rich in ceroid. Courtesy of Dr. Ghittino.

disease, particularly as it affects the liver (Figs. 31–33). Affected livers may have nearly all parenchymal cells damaged or destroyed by ceroid deposits. These may also reveal increased fibrosis, widened liver cords (muralia), and generally altered liver architecture. Gaschott (1929) reported finding angular masses of lipoid deposited on the heart in addition to that found in the liver. In more advanced cases frank hepatoma may appear (Ghittino and Ceretto, 1962).

There is a need for further research into the etiology of ceroidosis (LLD) in trout. Such experiments should involve sizable numbers of control and experimental fish and should seek to determine the types and combinations of feedstuffs and other factors which may induce liver lipoid disease. Sinnhuber (1969) has recently reviewed the role of excess fats and type of fats metabolized by fish.

## IV. Toxicants

Toxicants may be either swallowed or absorbed by fish with resultant pathology varying from mild toxic response to severe hemorrhage and

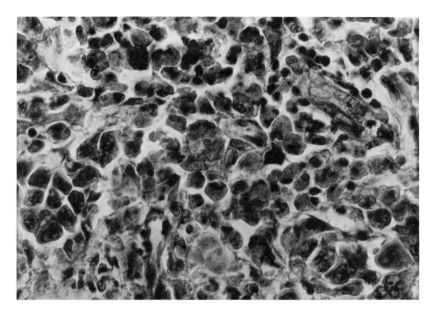

Fig. 33. Histopathology of liver lipoid disease (LLD). Note destruction of normal liver architecture. Many parenchymal cells are engorged with ceroid pigment which, being sudanophilic, stains an orange-brown color. Liver cords (muralia) tend to be more than two cells wide and sinusoids diminished in number. Increased fibrosis is also typical of livers with ceroidosis. Sudan III and hematoxylin (×975). Courtesy of Dr. Ghittino.

tissue destruction, terminating in death. Histological changes are often obvious in both chronic and acute toxicoses. Ellis (1937) bioassayed scores of potentially toxic agents using goldfish and daphnia as test organisms. More recently hundreds of organic pesticides, herbicides, and fungicides are being employed and extensive research is now underway to determine the relative toxicities and lethalities of each. Since crustaceans and other aquatic food organisms in addition to certain terrestrial organisms eaten by fish may concentrate toxins, it is highly probable that certain species of fish may indirectly ingest injurious amounts of such chemicals from time to time. Besides this source of poisoning, fish may absorb many kinds of toxins directly from their environment. Only a few examples of toxicants harmful to fish are included in this chapter.

## A. Inorganic Toxicants

### 1. *Arsenic*

Evidence is gradually accumulating to show that various arsenic compounds may be toxic to animal life and fishes are no exception. Some of these, while not highly toxic, are known to cause damaging results when fish or mammals are exposed for prolonged periods of time to either ingested or absorbed arsenicals. Besides the more toxic arsenates and arsenites, certain arsenic compounds have been known to cause some damage in prolonged use as vermifuges. Thuman (1940) found great variation in resistance to arsenicals in various species of fishes. She noted that resistance varied directly with the fishes' ability to store arsenic in their tissues. Halver and Ashley (unpublished data) found a $\frac{5}{14}$ incidence of hepatoma in rainbow trout fed an arsenic compound (Carbarsone) at 7.5 mg/100 gm of dry diet for 12 months. The classical trabecular, basophilic neoplasms were microscopic in size but probably would have grown larger had the fish lived longer. Length–weight records of young-of-the-year bluegills (*Lepomis macrochirus*) indicate growth to be inversely proportional to the concentration of sodium arsenite in hatchery pools. Adult bluegills lost weight in direct proportion to arsenite concentration. Pathological change after prolonged exposure included liver and kidney damage and suspected degenerative changes in the ovaries. No histopathology was reported (Gilderhus, 1966).

### 2. *Hexavalent Chromium*

Large-mouth black bass (*Micropterus salmoides*) were found to react to hexavalent chromium with marked sloughing of mucus from the anal area and coughing movements were increased. Extensive pathological changes were found in the intestine but the gills showed no histological change (Fromm and Schiffman, 1958).

### 3. *Lead*

Lead cations in excess may be toxic to certain fish species as well as to certain species of ducks. Coburn *et al.* (1951) reported lead poisoning in ducks that feed by straining mud from the substratum. The minimum lethal dose of lead for these water fowl was approximately 8 mg/kg body weight. Affected birds were anemic and emaciated. The livers were usually smaller than normal and histological examination revealed a diffuse necrosis that was, in part, responsible for the atrophy. Atrophy of gizzard muscles and flabby skeletal and heart muscles were present in most birds. Recent research on golden hamsters injected intravenously with various lead salts revealed significant numbers of a variety of congenital anomalies among the offspring (Ferm *et al.*, 1967). Whether or not fish may be poisoned by ingested lead, as shot or in other forms, needs further investigation.

## 4. *Copper*

Copper may be absorbed or adsorbed by the gills in harmful amounts as when hatchery waters ionize copper from bronze or brass fittings or when copper sulfate is used excessively as an algicide in ponds. Reports of histopathological studies on hatchery fish having died of copper poisoning are seldom encountered in the literature, but growth retardation and pigmentation changes have been noted in experimental rainbow trout and coho salmon ingesting 1 mg/gm dry diet ingredients (from 100 to 200 times the dietary requirements) of copper (W. Zaugg, 1967, personal communication). Much smaller quantities in the aquarium water were toxic to trout. Calventi and Nigrelli (1961) reported the effects of copper acetate and copper citrate on the killifish (*Fundulus heteroclitus*). They found 0.4 ppm of copper was nontoxic for 18 days. Fish survived 1 ppm for 3 days and for 5 days following single injections of 25 $\mu$g of copper as copper sulfate or copper acetate. More than 50 $\mu$g of copper were lethal within 24 hours.

Affected fish usually had some degree of congestion in gills, livers, and lower digestive tracts. Increased skin pigmentation was commonly accompanied by lateral tail flexion and loss of response to touch stimuli, suggesting a neurotoxic effect of copper.

Fish exposed to higher concentrations (1, 5, and 10 ppm) of copper or injected with from 50 to 100 $\mu$g revealed significant histological changes. Vacuolated liver cells with nuclei exhibiting karyorrhexis were common. Kidneys had extreme granulocytopoietic activity and erythrocyte fragility was evident. Eosinophilia occurred for about 3 days in fish immersed in water containing 2 ppm, and for 1 day or more after one injection per fish of either 50 or 75 $\mu$g of copper. Copper treated fish also acquired a bacterial infection by activation of gram-positive, nonmotile, diphtheroid rods, the significance of which remains unclear.

## 5. *Cadmium*

Cadmium was shown to be toxic to rainbow trout fingerlings by Roberts (1963). Fish apparently absorbed the Cd cations via the gills and died within 24 hours after being placed in a plastic tank into which water was filtered through a cadmium-plated screen. Since mortalities occurred within 1 day, fish died of acute toxic responses but neither gross nor microscopic tissue changes were noted by the author. Injected cadmium, as well as many other kinds of metallic salts, have been shown to be toxic, and/or carcinogenic in various species of animals as reported by Gunn *et al.* (1964). Cadmium chloride wastes may enter streams from pigment and dye works.

## 6. *Selenium*

Selenium salts are sometimes toxic to livestock (blind staggers disease), less so to chicks and poults, and of variable toxicity to fish. Nesheim and Scott (1961) reviewed the effects in cattle and in poultry, noting that slight amounts were beneficial in preventing exudative diathesis when only 0.05–0.1 mg/kg of diet was fed. However, 5 ppm of selenium in the diet caused stunting in poultry and 20 ppm was lethal, according to Gilbert (1957). Ellis *et al.* (1937) found small amounts of selenium leached from smelters were toxic to goldfish and 2 ppm of sodium selenite in river water was lethal to goldfish. The first mortality occurred on the 18th day and additional deaths rose at an ever increasing rate until all fish were dead by the 46th day. These authors further reported histological changes in selenium poisoned catfish (*Ictalurus punctatus*). Three milligrams per kilogram body weight of sodium selenite or 0.15 mg/fish was fatal in less than 48 hours, usually in less than 7 hours in 10°C water. Toxicity increased greatly when water at 27°C was used. At this temperature selenium at 0.35 mg/kg or 0.018 mg/fish, killed in 24 hours or less.

A general edematous condition occurs in cases of chronic selenium toxicity and becomes progressively worse. Fish have a worsening exophthalmia and protruding abdomens with more or less bloody ascites. The red blood cell count is moderately reduced but the hemoglobin (Sahli) is reduced from a normal of 9.8 gm to 6.9 gm/100 ml in selenized fish, suggesting that selenium toxicity interferes with hemoglobin formation. Many immature red cells are in the blood of toxic fishes and the white blood cell count is elevated about 4000/mm$^3$ from the normal. Lymphocytosis is also present with 82% lymphocytes in the differential count. Severe edema occurs in spleen, kidney, skeletal muscle, stomach, and ovary.

## 7. *Ammonia*

Ammonia concentration in the watery environment may be toxic to fish as pointed out by Burrows (1964). The most severe tissue damage appears to be hyperplasia of the gills. Wolf (1957) reported increased incidences of blue sac disease among trout and salmon eggs and sac-fry exposed to water containing added ammonia with or without added urea. Vamos (1963) reported that carp can withstand up to 0.5 mg of ammonia per liter of water. Above this amount, distress reactions appear and are followed by sinking of affected fish which appear lethargic or comatose. These carp can be revived in freshwater. Evidence of internal tissue damage in fish from ingested ammonia is not yet available but it is not unlikely that under certain conditions fish will swallow water with a high ammonia content and tissue damage may result.

### 8. *Bentonite*

Bentonite, a colloidal native hydrated clay (aluminum silicate), is reportedly toxic to *Tilapia macrocephala*, a cichlid fish. Fish fed a 1:1 mixture of ground trout pellets and bentonite for 3 months showed increasing emaciation, gross changes in gall bladder, spleen, and liver, and hypochromic anemia. The distended stomach was found filled with the bentonite-feed mix which appeared undigested a week after feeding. Imprints of liver and spleen stained with Wright's showed most liver parenchymal cells destroyed and liver macrophages were filled with bentonite. Other fish fed tubificid worms or the trout pellets were unaffected (Jakowska, 1956). Wilson (1954) reported the induction of hepatomas in mice fed a diet containing 50% bentonite. He reported liver histopathology in these mice as similar to that of mice fed a choline-deficient diet and concluded that the cation-exchange property of bentonite apparently removes choline from the food during digestion, preventing its absorption by the body, thus inducing a choline deficiency.

### 9. *Zinc*

Zinc is a required trace mineral and in high concentrations may be toxic, but copper is more toxic to salmon fry than is zinc as judged by subclinical histopathology (A. N. Woodall and M. J. Tripp, personal communication). Fortunately there exists a rather wide range of concentrations between nutritional and toxic levels of these mineral metabolites. Pond (1965) reported young pigs suffer severe anemia, hemopoietic dystrophy, and growth failure when given zinc in amounts greater than 0.1% in the diet. Above this level growth depression and hemorrhages in axillary spaces, lymph nodes, spleen, and brain ventricles occurred. (A. N. Woodall and M. J. Tripp, personal communication) determined the $LD_{50}$'s of chinook, silver and blueback (sockeye) salmon, and of rainbow trout fry based on metered amounts of zinc solutions into 10°C aquarium water. The $LD_{50}$ at 0.2 ppm of zinc was 40 hours for chinook, 96 hours for silver, 75 hours for blueback, and 72 hours for rainbow trout. Toxicity to dietary zinc has not been reported for any of these species. The histopathology of toxic dietary levels of zinc remains to be determined for these and most other fish species.

## B. ORGANIC TOXICANTS

### 1. *Tannic Acid*

Tannic acid fed daily to rainbow trout in doses of from 7.5–480 mg/100 gm of dry diet induced histologically confirmed hepatocellular carcinoma as basophilic micronodules after 12–20 months on test. Tumor incidences ranged from $\frac{0}{10}$ to $\frac{6}{10}$ for different dosages. Controls were consistently negative for all forms of neoplasia (Halver *et al.*, 1963; Halver, 1967).

## 2. *Gossypol*

Gossypol, a yellow pigment from the glands of cottonseed, when fed to various fish species has been known to result in anorexia and deposition of focal to massive sudanophilic substance grossly visible in the liver. These deposits are probably composed of "ceroid" which has been identified in the livers of at least six species of fish as reported by Wood and Yasutake (1956b). Sinnhuber *et al.* (1968) have reported a cocarcinogenic effect from gossypol added to a test diet containing aflatoxin $B_1$. To avoid the toxic effect of gossypol in diets including cottonseed meals, a so-called "glandless" strain of cotton has been developed. Otherwise, cottonseed meal processors must keep the gossypol content down to an established minimum by special methods of processing cottonseed.

## 3. *Aflatoxins*

Aflatoxins are toxic metabolites of *Aspergillus flavus* Link, a mutant variety of common blue-green mold that may occur as a contaminant in oilseed meals. Aflatoxins were unknown in cottonseed meals when Wolf and Jackson (1963) showed that these meals contained one or more unidentified rainbow trout hepatocarcinogens. Ashley *et al.* (1964, 1965) and Halver (1965), reported that aflatoxins were powerful hepatocarcinogens causing trout liver cell carcinomas and that these carcinogens occurred in certain lots of cottonseed meals. These discoveries led to the initiation of controls for the elimination of dangerous levels of aflatoxins from commercial trout feeds and marked the beginning of the end for a worldwide epizootic of rainbow trout hepatoma.

Trout hepatomas arise after 4–6 months of feeding aflatoxin-contaminated oilseed meals with as little as 0.1–0.5 ppb of aflatoxin $B_1$ in the total feed mix. Purified aflatoxins other than $B_1$ also induce rainbow trout hepatoma and, in order of diminishing potencies, are designated $G_1$, $B_2$, and $G_2$. The hepatocarcinogenicity of yet other fractions remains undetermined or is insignificant. Aflatoxin $B_1$ in amounts of 80 ppb or more induces rapid toxic changes and when 0.5 mg/kg body weight of this toxin is force fed for one to five times to rainbow trout, the fish may die within 3–10 days with necrotic pale yellow or creamy colored livers which are more or less mottled by hemorrhages (Figs. 34 and 35). The gills become severely edematous after force feeding as little as 0.1 mg/kg five times on successive days. Stained histological sections of this lesion show the gill epithelium (mucosa) markedly displaced leaving serum-filled spaces

FIG. 34. Rainbow trout liver showing necrotic area (white), other pallid areas near the margin (prenecrotic), and several dark, hemorrhagic streaks typical of acute aflatoxicosis. Trout force fed single dose of 1 mg/kg body weight crude aflatoxin and sacrificed on the eighth day following.

between epithelium and lamellar capillaries (Fig. 36). In the most severe cases visceral fat, digestive, and other internal organs may show hemorrhagic spots and necrosis of epithelial cells (Fig. 37). Severely affected livers are almost completely necrotic in these cases. However, coho salmon and channel catfish are less sensitive to high levels of aflatoxins and the livers show less hemorrhagic lesions, but cellular degeneration and moderately severe necrosis do occur (Halver *et al*, 1969). Aflatoxin $B_1$ is 900 times more potent than butter yellow (DAAB or dimethylaminoazobenzene) and is 75 times more potent than dimethylnitrosamine (DMNA) as a rat hepatocarcinogen (Butler, 1965). While the great epizootic of rainbow trout hepatoma of the 1960's led to the discovery of aflatoxins as the primary carcinogen, an earlier epizootic of rainbow trout hepatoma which occurred in the late 1930's was recently reported by Wales and Sinnhuber (1966). It was assumed to have been caused, at least in part, by aflatoxins in mold-contaminated oilseed meals fed to these trout.

Additional organic toxicants inducing hepatoma in rainbow trout include dimethylnitrosamine fed at from 7.5 to 1920 mg/100 gm of dry diet, acetylaminofluorene, aminoazotoluene, dimethylaminoazobenzene, diethylstilbestrol, urethane, tannic acid, carbon tetrachloride, thiourea,

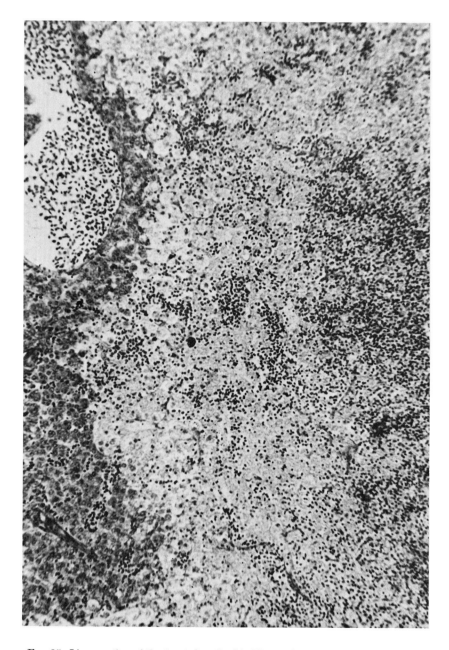

FIG. 35. Liver section of the trout described in Fig. 34, large area of necrosis in which numerous nucleated red blood cells are indicative of hemorrhagic necrosis and partial sparing of hepatocytes adjacent to portal vein; however, necrotic pattern was not typically zonal. H and E (×250).

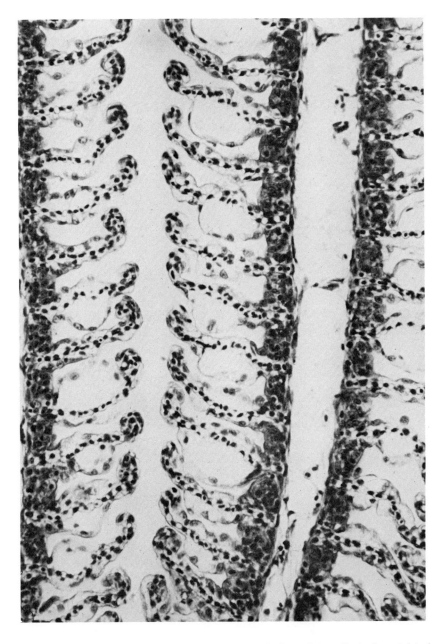

Fɪɢ. 36. Gill edema in rainbow trout force fed single dose of 5 mg/kg body weight of crude aflatoxin. The delicate lamellar epithelium is forced away from the lamellar capillary in many gill lamellae. Fish force fed 5 mg/kg body weight of crude aflatoxin in one dosage. H and E (×200).

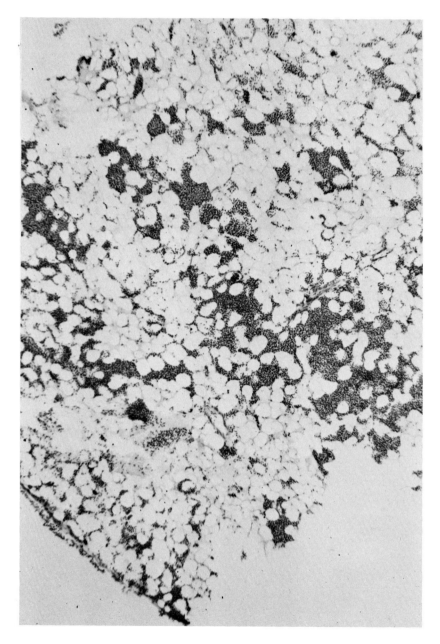

Fig. 37. Visceral adipose tissue showing hyperemia and hemorrhage typical of acute aflatoxicosis in rainbow trout force fed single dose of 5 mg/kg body weight crude aflatoxin. H and E (×150).

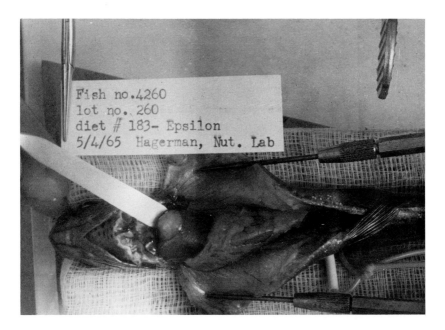

Fig. 38. Typical gross liver cell carcinoma (hepatoma) in rainbow trout fed a neutral lipid fraction of suspect commercial pellet feed believed to contain aflatoxins. Fish sacrificed after 20 months on test. (Tip of spatula indicates tumor).

dichlorodiphenyltrichloroethane (DDT), and probably others. Of those listed, dimethylnitrosamine is probably the most potent. It induced gross, sometimes massive, liver neoplasms in 12–20 months (Figs. 38 and 39). Aminotriazole, an effective hepatocarcinogen in certain mammals, apparently is noncarcinogenic in rainbow trout as is thioacetamide, but the latter induced a high incidence of cataract in trout (see under Section IV, B, 14).

Other mycotoxins and fungal metabolites may also cause fish diseases (Kraybill and Shimkin, 1964). Wood and Yasutake (1956a) described granulomatous lesions in the gastric wall in hatchery rainbow trout (Fig. 40). The lesions sometimes showed hyphalike structures but these were not seen consistently and a fungal etiology for the granuloma could not be supported. However, it is possible that a food-borne mycotoxin, as yet unidentified, is involved in the etiology of this lesion. Wild trout were free from granulomata but hatchery trout increasingly fed "dry feed products" frequently had the disease.

*Visceral Granuloma.* Recently, Dunbar and Herman (1971) reported

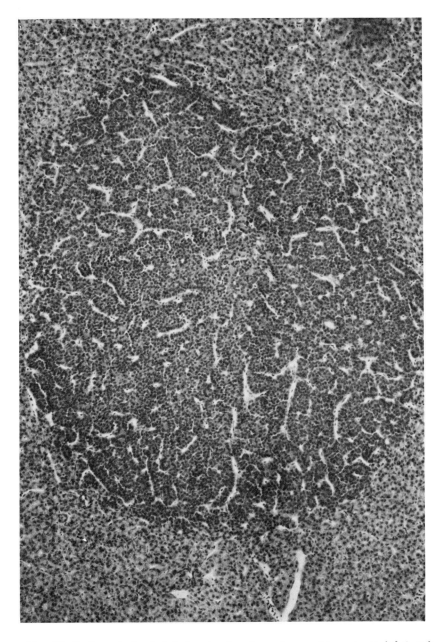

FIG. 39. Section of classical trabecular hepatoma from rainbow trout fed 8 ppb aflatoxin $B_1$ for 12 months. H and E ($\times$150).

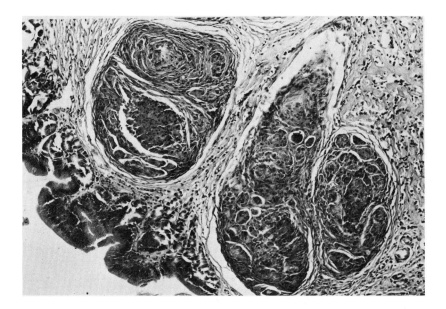

FIG. 40. Granulomas in stomach wall of brook trout. Histological evidence suggested a fungal etiology but this could not be positively established. H and E (×98).

having fed a synthetic diet with suspect diet components added or a meat–meal diet with individual components removed to determine their effects on the incidence of visceral granuloma. Visceral granuloma occurred in fish fed a cottonseed meal diet (21%), a meat–meal diet (84.5%), and a gossypol (cottonseed toxin) diet (2.6%). Omission of cottonseed meal resulted in the smallest incidence of visceral granuloma. Both the pathogenesis and histopathology of visceral granuloma were described in detail. Briefly, the disease is histologically characterized by the appearance of many Langhans-type giant cells and Schaumann-body type concretions presenting a picture similar to that of sarcoidosis in man. Grossly, papillary proliferations occur on the stomach surface and calcifications occur in the posterior kidney. Severe cases may present lesions throughout the visceral mass. The authors consider visceral granuloma in brook trout to be similar to nephrocalcinosis in rainbow trout.

Further research in this broad area should be rewarding and it is gratifying to note that considerable interest in the subject of mycotoxins in foodstuffs has been aroused by the discovery of the aflatoxins and certain newly described toxins derived from *Penicillium* sp.

### 4. Toxic Gill Disease

Dietary and/or contact exposures of fish to various toxins and carcinogens such as thiourea (Mathur, 1967), DDT, and aflatoxins (Ashley, unpublished data), may result in gill damage typified by epithelial hyperplasia and blood engorgement of gill lamellae resulting in gross, globular
or spheroid red dots on the gills. This condition, originally termed "hemorrhagic" gill disease, was shown not to be truly hemorrhagic (Wood and
Yasutake, 1957). The blood-filled gill lamellae when studied in histological
sections showed no evidence of rupture or hemorrhage; and since most
cases reported have been known to be related to a toxic condition either
in the feed or in the water, the term *toxic* gill disease would seem appropriate. The blood engorged gill lamellae in this disease are actually capillary angiomata or branchial telangiectases (Figs. 41 and 42). This form
of gill disease differs in its etiology as well as in its pathology from both
the nutritional and the bacterial types of gill disease. The nutritional type
is described under Section II, A, 7 in this chapter. Toxic gill disease has
been experimentally induced in rainbow trout fed aflatoxin $B_1$ at 480
mg/100 gm of dry diet for 4 to 8 weeks, and by force feeding a single dose
of 0.1 mg/kg body weight. The latter dosage resulted in toxic gill lamellae
within 3 to 10 days. DDT appeared to be more toxic to the gills than to
the liver, but aflatoxin $B_1$ appeared to be more toxic to the liver than to
the gills.

### 5. Cyclopropenoid Fatty Acids

Recent work with cyclopropenoid fatty acids fed with 4 ppb aflatoxin
$B_1$ to rainbow trout for 15 months has shown a tumor initiating and aug-
menting effect (Sinnhuber *et al.*, 1968). These fatty acids function as
cocarcinogens with aflatoxin in the induction of trout liver neoplasms
(hepatomas). Aflatoxin alone fed at 4 ppb induced hepatomas in 20% of
the trout while the addition of 220 ppm Sterculia foetida oil to the diet
induced tumors in 90% of the fish. Other cocarcinogens found effective
in this way when fed with 4 ppb aflatoxin $B_1$ were: 250 ppm gossypol,
60% hepatoma; 50 ppb 3-methyl coumarin, 55% hepatoma; and 0.5%
polymerized vegetable oil, 25% hepatoma. Each diet group was fed for 15
months and it was concluded that cyclopropenes with aflatoxin $B_1$ caused
tumors to appear much earlier, besides resulting in greater liver damage
than the other compounds tested (Lee *et al.*, 1966) (Fig. 43).

### 6. Toxic Algae

Algal toxins concerned with fish poisonings have been little studied to
date, but few species of these lower plants have been incriminated. Poison-

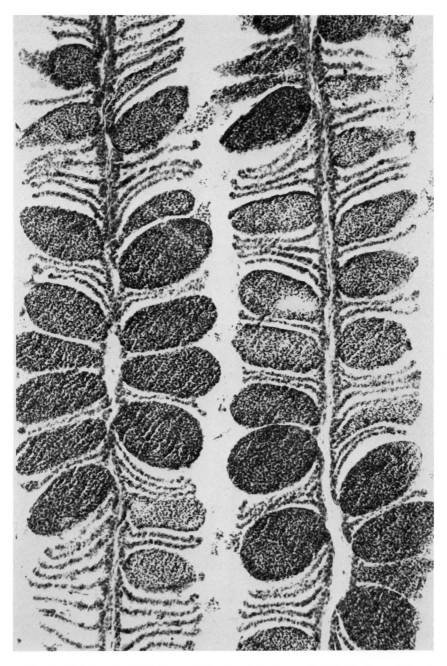

Fig. 41. Rainbow trout gill filaments showing toxic (hemorrhagic) gill disease induced by DDT fed at 7.5 mg/100 gm dry diet for 12 months. H and E (×100).

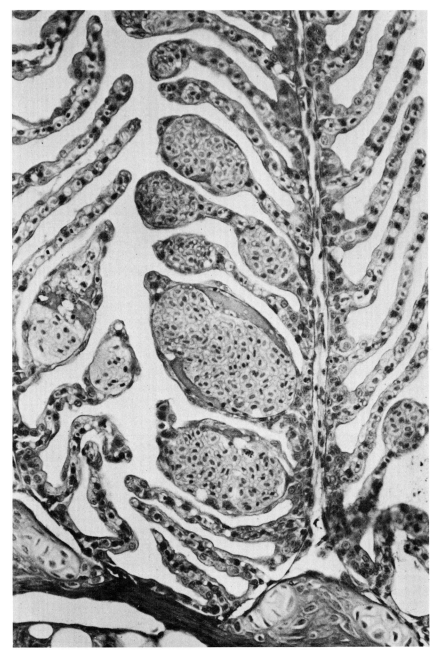

Fig. 42. Variant form of toxic gill disease in fingerling brook trout given granuloma disease via inoculation. Fish was moribund and also had hyperemic kidney and focal liver hyperemia. Etiology of gill condition may have been due to moribundity or associated with granulomatous condition of fish

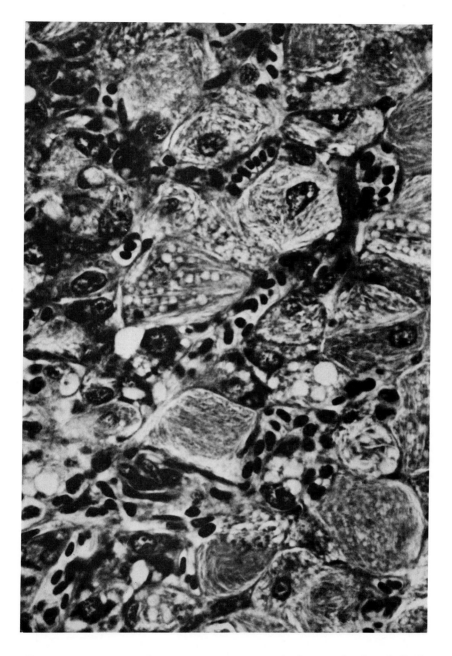

FIG. 43. Rainbow trout liver section showing peculiarly vacuolated and fibrillar cytoplasm in bizarre hepatocytes. Fish fed cyclopropenoid fatty acids derived from cottonseed meal. Courtesy of J. H. Wales, Oregon State University, Corvallis, Oregon.

ous freshwater algae include *Anabaena flos-aquae, Aphanizomenon flos-aquae,* and *Microcystis aeruginosa* (in certain circles referred to as "Annie, Fannie, and Mike") as the most toxic species (Kingsbury, 1964). Natural mixtures of algae and often of bacteria occur in globules of water bloom containing these organisms. More than one toxic substance occurs, some algal and some bacterial. More or less purified colonies have been isolated and cultures for study and extraction of toxic principles, one of which, the fast-death factor, is algal in origin and is believed to be a cyclic polypeptide. This molecule is heat stable, dialyzes slowly, and has moderate toxicity. The $LD_{50}$ (intraperitoneally in white mice) is 0.47 mg/kg. It is probable that some of the poisonings associated with algal blooms were caused by botulism (*Clostridium* spp. are common in such blooms). Fish may suffocate when blooms of algae deplete the oxygen in a natural body of water by means of respiration and/or decay. Most reports of algal poisoning agree in that symptoms occur within 15–45 minutes after ingestion of a toxic dose. Poisoning proceeds rapidly and is severe; death is common, occurring in less than 24 hours, often within 1 or 2 hours. Symptoms include nausea, vomition, abdominal pain, diarrhea, prostration, muscular tremors, dyspnea, cyanosis, general paralysis, convulsions, and death. Gastroenteritis occurs in varying degrees of severity and is occasionally absent. Pathological change may occur in gastrointestinal tract, liver, and kidney. Gastroenteritis increases in severity toward the caudal end of the tract and may be hemorrhagic. Acute cellular degenerative changes may be noted in liver and kidney. In animals poisoned by drinking toxic water blooms the liver is enlarged and mottled with yellowish patches; the kidney shows signs of toxic tubular nephritis. Warm, sunny weather favors growth of "blooms" rich in concentrated toxins often increased by prolonged gentle winds that carry the algae and bacteria to leeward shores. *Anabaena variabilis* is also toxic to fishes, causing erythropoietic disturbances in carp 2 years and older, but the effect occurs only with young Anabaena cultures developing under certain conditions (Gorchakova and Telitchenko, 1963).

## 7. *Red Tide*

Marine environments sometimes develop destructive "blooms "of "red tide" organisms such as *Gonyaulax catenella* and similar toxic dinoflagellates such as *Gymnodinium* sp. Galtsoff (1949) estimates that certain "blooms" of these dinoflagellates are able to kill between 100 and 200 million pounds of fish. While these toxins may be largely absorbed via the gills, Courville *et al.* (1963) state that fish become poisonous from ingesting certain marine algae. It is possible that shellfish poisoned by "red tide" or other poisonous algae and later ingested by mollusc-eating fish such as the wolf-eel (*Anarrhichthys ocellatus*) and the ratfish (*Hydrolagus colliei*), may in turn poison these fish. Shellfish poisoned by feeding on "red tide" organisms may in turn prove toxic to man if eaten, since cooking does not destroy the heat-stable toxins.

### 8. *Bacterial Contaminants*

The transmission of fish disease by feeding diseased salmon carcasses or other infected fish products had been suspected for some time when in the early 1960's attention was given to eradication from chinook and silver (coho) salmon of so-called "fish tuberculosis" (mycobacteriosis). Subsequently it was decided by various state and federal fishery personnel that all such fish products, especially salmon carcasses, should be pasteurized prior to their incorporation into fish feeds for salmon or trout hatcheries in western North America. Since pasteurization practices have been generally adopted, salmon "tuberculosis" has become a rarity in Pacific salmons. Affected fish often had dystrophic gonads, gray lesions scattered about in the kidney, liver, and spleen, and false membranes around various visceral organs (Parisot and Wood, 1959; Ross and Johnson, 1962). No doubt many forms of pathogenic bacteria, viruses, and parasites taken with the feed, result in diseased fish and a significant mortality increase. Much remains to be learned relative to this entire subject as it relates to various valuable fish species as well as to fish-borne infections that may be transmitted to man and other higher vertebrates and collectively grouped with the *zoonoses*.

### 9. *Detergents*

Bardach *et al.* (1965) reported damage to, and loss of sensibility of, taste buds on barbels of yellow bullheads (*Ictalurus natalis*) after exposure to 0.5 ppm of either "hard" or "soft" detergents. The morphology of the taste buds was altered by loss of the normal surface bulge and by progressive degeneration of its sensory and supporting cells. When detergent levels were increased to 4 or 5 ppm, histology revealed destruction of some bipolar cells in the taste buds. Control fish had none of these changes. In another study by Scheier and Cairns (1966) sunfish (*Lepomis gibbosus*) exposed for 24 hours to an 18 ppm alkyl benzene sulfonate (ABS) detergent suffered serious deterioration of the gills. Gill lamellae were distorted by clubbing and by epithelial hyperplasia with adherence of gill filaments. Efforts to restore the fish to normal by keeping them in clean "dilution" water failed. These authors did not discuss the condition of the tastebuds of sunfish in these experiments, and further work appears desirable in this connection inasmuch as taste is a function of the digestive system and taste impairment may lead directly or indirectly to inanition with consequent growth retardation.

## 10. *Saponins*

Saponins are glucosides found in various plants. Ebeling (1928) reported that wastes from potato starch factories carry sufficient saponin to be dangerous to fishes, and that consequently these wastes should be highly diluted. Ellis (1937) found 10 ppm of saponin in hard water produced marked distress in goldfish in 5 hours, while 100 ppm was rapidly fatal, killing goldfish in 7–24 hours. Histopathological changes were not reported. Dhekne and Bhide (1951) fed saponins extracted with alcohol from *Balanites roxburgii* seeds at 1 part to 60,000 parts fish feed. This dose was lethal to fish in these tests.

## 11. *Ichthyotoxism (Fish Poisoning)*

Ichthyotoxism is defined by a leading authority as a "nonspecific generic term covering intoxications caused by both oral and parenteral poisons originating from fishes—marine or freshwater" (Halstead, 1964). We are concerned here with only the oral forms of poisoning. Fish poisoning acquired by eating fish is known to affect man and various animals, but little is known as to whether piscivorous fish may be poisoned by feeding on other fish containing the poisons in question. However, inasmuch as many species of fish, particularly in the tropics, are known to have poisonous flesh, roes, or blood at least at certain seasons of the year, it appears likely that some species of piscivorous fish may become ill and possibly die after such a meal. To date, little is known about the chemical structure of the various fish poisons but Asano and Masao (1962) showed that the poison of a certain blenny, concentrated in its roes, was a lipoprotein rather than a toxalbumin as was formerly believed. This blenny (*Dinogunellus grigorjewi*) is widely used by Hokkaido natives who carefully avoid its roes; occasionally uninformed persons consume the roes and become violently ill. A man who ate the roes for supper and again for breakfast 10 hours later became acutely ill, comatose, and soon died according to Asano and Masao. Research is needed to throw light on the question as to whether or not piscivorous fish are similarly poisoned after the ingestion of poison fish or shellfish and whether syndromes may develop similar to those seen in man when poisoned.

## 12. *Antibiotics*

Antibiotics are sometimes employed as therapeutic agents in combating fish diseases. Many kinds of natural (mycotic) antibiotics such as penicillin, erythromycin, and chloramphenicol (Chloromycetin) have been used besides synthetic ones such as sulfamethazine, and many other sulfonamides are also commonly used. Currently there is disagreement as to the safety and the efficacy of many of these drugs in antibiotic therapeutics of hatchery fish.

Antimycin A was recently shown to be toxic to fish and has thus been tested and found useful in exterminating trash fish and for "sterilizing" ponds and reservoirs of their fish population. Loeb (1964) found that antimycin A produced rapid kills at concentrations of a few parts per billion, thereafter becoming nontoxic in a few days. Antimycin A was lethal to large carp when force fed at doses of less than 1 mg/kg body weight over a 2-day period at 65°F. Antimycin A dissolves slowly and brown trout (*Salmo trutta fario*), sunfish (*Lepomis gibbosus*), and golden shiners (*Notemagonus chrysoleucas*) were killed in 2 days by soaking impregnated baits in a 350-gallon aquarium containing test fish, even though the fish were unable to ingest the baits. Carp fry (*Cyprinus carpio*), small minnows, and yellow perch (*Perca flavescens*) all died in from 2 to 9 hours after an initial application of antimycin A. Some large carp survived even after 26 hours. Poisoned carp turned yellow only a short time before death. A few brown bullheads (*Ameiurus nebulosus*), newts, many frogs, and crayfish were not noticeably harmed by the poison. Antimycin A gives promise of becoming a valuable agent for the extermination of certain undesirable fish populations when fish rehabilitations are contemplated.

Erythromycin was fed at 4.5 gm/100 pounds of fish per day for 21 days as part of a feed mix composed of 50% meat and 50% dry meal. Brook trout (*Salvelinus fontinalis*) went off feed on the ninth day. Spasms, convulsions, and gasping movements occurred whenever fish became excited. Fish would sink, exhausted, to the bottom for several seconds up to 1 minute before swimming about again. The affected fish recovered in a few days after being returned to the regular hatchery diet. Autopsies of affected fish revealed inflamed ovaries and pustules on liver and kidneys. Control fish had none of these changes. Histological examination showed no marked pathology and kidney disease could not be identified in the treated fish (Piper, 1961).

### 13. Sulfonamides

Sulfonamides of many forms, employed as therapeutic agents against infectious diseases, vary widely in toxicity to fishes. Sulfonamides known to induce pathology after prolonged feeding at certain levels include sulfamerazine (SMA) as one of the most widely studied. Frequent SMA treatments of a female brook trout with furunculosis over a period of 2 years apparently caused sterility. Feeding SMA for 8 months resulted in massive kidney pathology, but the drug could be fed up to 13 weeks without damage to the kidneys (Wood *et al.*, 1955). Some sulfonamides fed over long periods tend to cause renal insufficiency. SMA was toxic to small coho salmon, 1 to 5 gm each, when reared in water at 9°–14°C and fed the drug 2 or more weeks at 6–12 gm daily per 100 pounds of fish. Adult brook trout fed SMA 2 years prophylactically had extensive tubular degeneration of kidneys. In sections stained with hematoxylin and eosin these tubules were opaque, very pale and had necrotic circular areas with all cellular details obliterated. When hemoglobin-specific stains were used, the necrotic areas together with surrounding congested or hemorrhagic hemapoietic tissues were found to be heavily impregnated with hemoglobin. In fish showing less advanced stages, degeneration of the kidneys, remains of red blood cells, and occasional entire red cells could be seen in the necrotic areas. No SMA crystals were observed but if present originally these may have been lost during processing for histology (Wood *et al.*, 1955) (Fig. 44). Other workers have reported various abnormalities from "sulfa" drugs fed to fishes. Snieszko and Wood (1955) reported growth retardation in brook trout and complete cessation of growth in brown trout. Johnson and Brice (1953) noted increased mortalities and Gutsell and Snieszko (1949) found growth retardation. These workers experimented on various trout and Pacific salmon species. After several experiments feeding sulfamethazine to young fall chinook salmon at levels up to 300 gm/100 pounds of fish to determine relative toxicity, Wood *et al.* (1957) found only minimal pathology in their experimental and production hatchery fish. The latter group had significant mortalities, and visceral arteries in these fish were damaged by necrotic lesions in the walls. Edema was also common among the visceral organs, particularly in the pancreas and extracaecal fat. Some of the fish had swollen stomachs and minor degenerative lesions were found in the livers. Production hatchery fish also had degenerative changes in kidney tubules but fish from the experimental hatchery had fewer lesions. Wood *et al.* (1957) emphasized the need for further study of the effects of various sulfonamides on hatchery-reared fish. Such studies should include histological and histochemical research whenever possible.

## 14. *Pesticides*

A crash program currently under way seeks to bioassay all known pesticides and to determine effects on the metabolic pathways of various species of animals. Fish are being used in part of the water quality control program. Pesticides may be ingested or absorbed through either gills or skin. In each instance these substances enter the blood and affect various

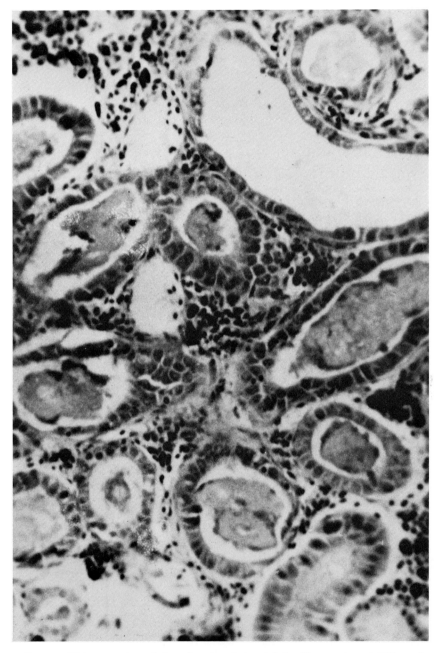

Fɪɢ. 44. Kidney section of fingerling brook trout fed sulfamerazine at 175 mg/kg body weight for 26 weeks. Note casts in renal tubules, pycnotic nuclei, and early degeneration of tubular epithelium. Tubular necrosis occurred in other areas of same kidney. H and E (×400).

tissues and organs in varying degrees. The young are most seriously affected and changes such as dysplasia or sterility of gonads, weakness, nervous disorders, gastrointestinal upsets, inappetance, and even death may occur. Since many chlorinated hydrocarbon pesticides induce varying degrees of similar pathology, discussion may be limited to DDT. Premdas and Anderson (1963) reported rapid absorption of DDT by young Atlantic salmon (*Salmo salar*) after only a 5 minute exposure to 1 ppm of DDT-$^{14}$C. Fish killed in these experiments had an average of 5.87 ppm DDT about one-third of which was adsorbed DDT. High concentrations of DDT were found in gills, spleen, heart, liver, kidneys, gonads, and swim bladder. Moderate amounts were in the stomach, intestine, spinal cord, and brain, while muscles, bones, and integument contained the least. King (1962) reported the effects of DDT on guppies (*Lebistes reticulatus*) and brown trout (*Salmo trutta fario*). The livers of young fish were severely vacuolated and more or less liver necrosis was reported. In some cases necrosis of connective tissue and vacuolation of muscle fibers also occurred. Fishes vary considerably in resistance to DDT as well as to most other pesticides, for example, progressing from most susceptible to least susceptible are rainbow trout (*Salmo gairdneri*), brown trout, guppy, bluegill (*Lepomis machrochirus*), and channel catfish (*Ictalurus punctatus*). The occurrence of several cases of toxic (hemorrhagic) gill disease in rainbow trout fry fed DDT in the daily ration at a level of 7.5 mg/100gm of dry diet has already been discussed (see Section IV,B,3).

Many authors have warned against using pesticides which may come in contact with fish. Such warnings are often ignored and fish are damaged either by direct contact with the poisons falling into feed or indirectly via drainage into the fish habitat. The histopathology of victims of pesticide intoxications may vary widely with the specific pesticide, the water chemistry, temperature, aeration, stream flow, density of other aquatic organisms, and with other factors. However, in general, these poisons tend to attack the brain and the ganglion cell cytoplasm (Kayser *et al.*, 1962). Cataract was experimentally induced at 90% incidence in rainbow trout fed 30 mg/100 gm dry diet of thioacetamide for 12 months (von Sallmann *et al.*, 1966) who found pathological proliferation of the anterior lens cortex with evidence of early neoplastic change in more advanced cases (Figs. 45 and 46).

There is need for extensive histopathological work on fish from well controlled pesticide experiments involving ingested, absorbed, and adsorbed toxins. A beginning has now been made but it is imperative that much more be done before fishery investigators can rest from their labors relative to this aspect of fish pesticide research.

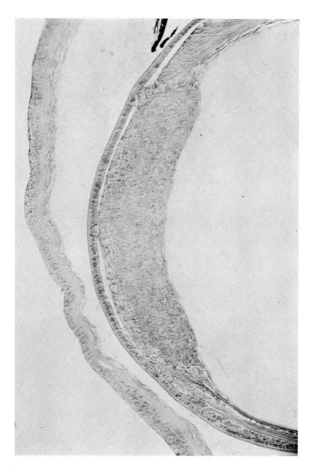

FIG. 45. Section of eye lens and cornea of rainbow trout fed 30 mg/100 gm dry diet of thioacetamide showing pathological proliferation of anterior lens cortex typical of cataract. H and E (×100). Courtesy of Dr. Ludwig Von Sallman, National Institute of Neurological Diseases and Blindness, Bethesda, Maryland.

## C. IRRADIATED FEEDS

Ionizing radiations ingested with irradiated foods by fishes do not appear to reach dangerous levels except under extraordinary circumstances (Nakatani and Miller, 1963; Nakatani and Liu, 1963). These authors worked with zinc ($^{65}$Zn) which proved to be one of the significant radionuclides found in irradiated fishes captured in the south Pacific Ocean after atomic bomb tests such as those at Eniwetok atoll. All radioactive

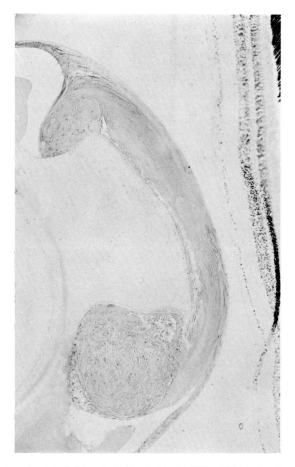

FIG. 46. Thioacetamide fed trout similar to that of Fig. 45 but showing proliferation of posterolateral lens cortex typical of cataract and suggesting neoplastic change. H and E (×100). Courtesy of Dr. Ludwig Von Sallman.

fish tested had levels too low to be hazardous to man. Morphological changes were not reported from these fish. Gong *et al.* (1957) noted that clams in Eniwetok atoll concentrated radioactivity to a level 2000 times that of the surrounding seawater. Davis and Foster (1958) observed that fish taken from the Columbia River below atomic reactors absorbed radio-active materials directly from reactor effluents up to only about 1.5% of the total radioactivity. They conclude that "sorption is of much less importance than ingestion in the uptake of radioactive materials by Co-lumbia River fish." Krumholtz (1956) found bluegills (*Lepomis machro-*

*chirus*) and black crappies (*Pomoxis nigromaculatus*) concentrated radio-strontium in amounts 20,000–30,000 times the amount in the aqueous environment. Under present world conditions fish in the natural environments are unlikely to concentrate sufficiently large amounts of ionizing radiations in the tissues to cause morphological change or even the symptoms of radiation sickness.

## V.  Malnutrition

Besides dietary imbalances, malnutrition implies dietary excesses, inadequacies, and starvation. Inadequate diets often result in lowered resistance to infection and to degenerative diseases. This synergism may result in greater damage to the organism than would result from the sum of uncombined infectious and degenerative disease (Scrimshaw, 1965).

### A.  IMPOVERISHED OR UNBALANCED DIETS

Impoverished diets, often deficient in more than one essential nutrient, result in greater susceptibility to disease, inanition, and, consequently, in greater losses from natural predation, and from increased mortalities in hatcheries. Unbalanced diets, on the other hand, may contain too much of certain nutrients and too little of others. Either of the above nutritional anomalies may contribute to fish losses but more research is needed regarding the effects of specific and nonspecific excesses, in particular, and regarding losses resulting from fish malnutrition, in general.

### 1.  *Pig Spleen and Horse Liver Diets*

Cataract (white blindness) in trout was reported by Hess (1937) and by Allison (1950). Hess noted bilateral cataract in most trout aged 6 months or more after feeding pig spleen exclusively. No evidence of contagion was detectable and a dietary deficiency was believed responsible. Similar fish fed concurrently a beef liver-beef heart ration never had cataract. Fish fed spleen–liver–heart diets were also free from the disease. Younger fish fed pig spleen only had 20% incidence of cataract. Exposure to light as a factor was ruled out and the incidence of cataract in hatchery-reared "wild" trout was even greater on the all pig spleen diet than in the case of domestic hatchery-reared trout. Although the obvious conclusion was that pig spleen alone did not provide a balanced diet, the missing essentials were not discovered. Allison's results show that hatchery brook trout fed 27% or more of horse products acquire a significant incidence of either peripheral or central cataract (Figs. 47 and 48). However, when

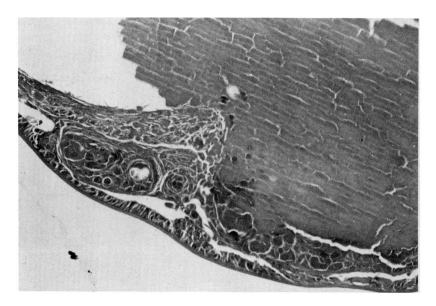

Fɪɢ. 47. Early proliferation of anterior lens cortex in brook trout fed 27% or more of horse meat which results in a significant incidence of cataract. H and E (×65). Courtesy of Leonard N. Allison, Michigan Department of Conservation, Grayling, Michigan.

fish are fed 90% horse liver there is 30% blindness among brook trout. Brown and rainbow trout are not affected. It is of interest to compare these two cases of cataract. The rainbow trout reported by Hess also had degeneration of fins, scales, and irides in older broodstock fish. Brook trout reported by Allison had pale coloration and the crystalline lens softened, became opaque, and acquired a milky hue as blindness occurred. Mortalities attributed to blindness in these fish were moderate and may be at least partially dependent upon emaciation owing to failure to find and consume adequate amounts of feed.

Various hatchery men have observed that certain commercial dry diets fed to brook trout fingerlings may induce "blue slime" disease, ragged fins, and increased mortalities but the addition of fresh meat to these diets prevents these anomalies.

### 2. *Unpalatable Feed*

Malnutrition amidst plenty may occur when feed is putrefied by bacteria (Besse, 1956) or is contaminated by various distasteful pollutants such as industrial wastes, pesticides, or other contaminants, because most fish will refuse such food. Complications normally following emaciation and starvation such as growth retardation, gonad dystrophy (Robertson, 1958), failure to spawn, infectious diseases, and predation may rapidly decimate a fish population under these conditions. Fish sickened by eating spoiled fish products may stop eating, suffer gastric "complaints" and exhibit various deficiency syndromes depending upon the specific contaminants involved.

Severe undernutrition retards growth in an abnormal ratio of muscle cells to connective tissue as determined by Dickerson and McCance (1960) in Rhode Island red cockerels. The deficient diet, in both younger (2–27 weeks) and in older (27–42 week) birds, increased amounts of water, chlorine, sodium, and the extracellular proteins per unit of weight of muscle and decreased those of potassium, phosphorus, and the intracellular proteins. Underfeeding appeared to result in excess hydration of the cells. Muscle tissues were almost completely restored to normal after 15

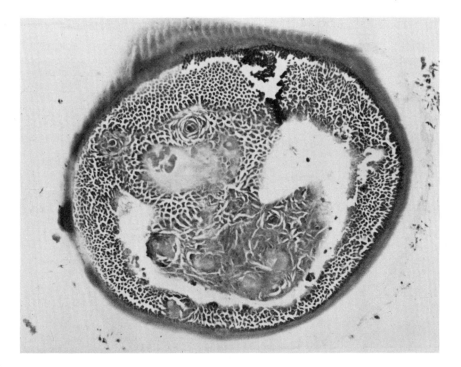

Fig. 48. Cataract in horse-meat fed brook trout showing proliferation of lens cortex through much of central portion of lens. H and E (×90). Courtesy of Leonard N. Allison.

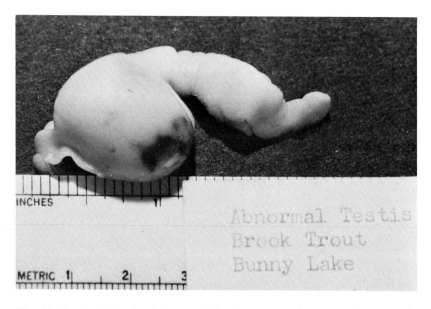

Fɪɢ. 49. Dystrophic testis of 14-year-old brook trout reared at more than 11,000 feet altitude in small lake in Sierra-Nevada Mountains of California. Growth was stunted in all fish planted at this site. Courtesy of Norman Reimers, Sierra Nevada Aquatic Research Laboratory, Bishop, California.

weeks on a recovery diet. Various observers have noted stunting of trout planted in oligotrophic, high mountain lakes. Although several years old, such fish often fail to spawn owing to anomalies of the gonads—testes were often misshapen and the swollen portions sometimes had internal hemorrhage with degenerated tissues while ovaries often contained atretic and dystrophic ova. Brook trout fry planted in a mountain lake near 11,000 ft. elevation suffered undernutrition and semistarvation but survived for more than 18 years as stunted fish, apparently unable to reproduce under the conditions imposed by the environment (Fig. 49). The water temperature ranged from 3° to 13°C. Histological study of most tissues in these trout revealed little histopathology except for ovaries and testes that were malformed and degenerated as above noted. Some of these trout were brought down to the hatchery at the 6000 ft. elevation, where they fed on fresh-frozen brine shrimp (*Artemia salina*), gained three to four times in weight in 1 year, and were artificially spawned but with very poor success—most ova and sperm being nonviable. These fish would not accept the regular hatchery rations (Reimers, 1958; N. Reimers and L. M. Ashley, 1969, unpublished data).

## B.  Starvation

### 1.  *Obstructions to Ingestion*

Starvation caused by inability to ingest food is rare among fish populations; but when one considers the many factors present in aqueous environments today—fallout, pollutants, pesticides, etc., many of which were formerly unknown—it is probable that a higher incidence of congenital malformities than formerly seen may now occur. Some of these anomalies may impair or prevent ingestion and deglutition of food thus leading to inanition or starvation, especially in fish fry and fingerlings. Once thriving salmon runs have been nearly or completely annihilated in many streams by pollution of various types. During such fish depletions many fish are likely to hatch malformed or appear as runts.

*a. Dystrophy of Jaws.* This may involve either lower, upper, or both jaws. These defects may so handicap a fish as to render it highly inefficient in capturing food (Fig. 50). Impaired growth, increased mortalities, and predation upon such fish are to be expected. Losses from these causes will vary with the incidence and severity of jaw anomalies in a given fish population and may only rarely reach significant proportions. While some of

Fig. 50. Dystrophy of jaws in chinook salmon fingerling reared on complete test diet under hatchery conditions. Western Fish Nutrition Laboratory, Cook, Washington.

these anomalies may be due to hereditary defects, it is highly probable that more are due to impurities in the water, the substrate, or both in the spawning and rearing areas. Consequently, exposure of fish eggs to toxins may result in a significant incidence of malformed jaws as well as of other forms of congenital anomalies.

*b. Dystrophy of the Tongue.* This anomaly may be more rare than is that of the jaws, but when it occurs affected fish may starve through inability to swallow or through inability to move food from mouth to gullet. Such fish usually die early from emaciation and may be counted as runts.

*c. Stenosis of the Gullet.* This is a stricture in either the outlet of the pharynx or in the esophagus. Such constrictions may constitute slight, severe, or even complete obstructions and are usually congenital but may at times be induced by traumata. Emaciation and early death are expected in these cases.

*d. Fishing Lures.* Lures lodged in mouth or gullet may interfere with feeding to the extent that emaciation, disease, and sometimes death may ensue. Migrating adult Columbia River chinook salmon are occasionally caught or seen at counting stations with five or six fishing lures impaled

FIG. 51. Effects of starvation shown in brown trout (lower) as compared with normally nourished rainbow trout (upper) both reared in mountain creek water. Courtesy of Norman Reimers, Sierra Nevada Aquatic Research Laboratory, Bishop, California.

in their mouths and jaws, but these migrant fish are little harmed in this way since they neither feed during the upstream spawning migration nor survive after spawning.

Prolonged starvation may result in an icterus of retention in carp and other pondfish during the period of "winter sleep." While food is not taken the liver continues to produce and to store bile. The gall bladder becomes distended with bile which may back up into the liver causing it to be a dark spinach green color (Schäperclaus, 1954).

### 2. *Lack of Food*

Starvation with emaciation or wasting of body tissues will result when food is absent over a prolonged period (several months), which varies with temperature and with amount of activity (Fig. 51).

## VI. Miscellaneous

### A. Slivers

Slivers and sharp fragments of metal, glass or rock are not infrequently ingested by fish that mistake them for something edible. If ingested, these objects may puncture the digestive tract and may even penetrate muscles and other more solid tissues resulting in more or less lasting damage or even death. Razor-sharp fragments may lacerate internal organs resulting in hemorrhage which, if extensive, will obviously result in anemia. Anemic fish may fall easy prey to more aggressive and cannabalistic peers or to various other predators.

### B. Fishing Lures

Most fishermen know the extent and kinds of damage commonly inflicted on food and game fish by barbed hooks. Fish often become badly hooked in jaws, gills, eyes, nostrils, throat, or even stomach. Some of these are thrown back mortally wounded while others, upon floundering about in a weakened condition, are eaten by predators. How many food and game fish have died of starvation while securely hooked and snagged in deep water with leader or line securely wrapped around a submerged deadhead or other object—the fisherman having retrieved only a portion of his line—can only be conjectured, but the number must be legion.

### C. Spines and Burrs

Fish are, at times found strangled or suffocated after having tried to swallow a catfish (Amieuridae, Ictaluridae), a bullhead (Cottidae), a stickleback (Gasterosteidae), or other kind of barbed fish whose recurved or extended and locked spines had become hopelessly snagged in the mouth or throat of its captor. Both traumatic and toxic tissue damage may occur following injury by various fish having venomous spines. Meehan (1964) described a juvenile coho salmon (*Oncorhynchus kisutch*) found with a large swelling on the left side, lateral to the stomach. Careful dissection in the laboratory disclosed a puncture wound in the side of the stomach, inflicted by the spine of a three-spined stickleback (*Gasterosteus aculeatus*). This lesion had caused infection of adjacent body wall tissues with incident swelling. The author stated that, "It appeared that the spine was gradually working its way through the muscle to the skin, and possibly might have been expelled without fatal results."

In addition to the many types of vertebrate spines which may become impaled in a fish's digestive anatomy are the occasionally dangerous barbed bristles of certain insects or of their larval (instar) stages. One such interesting case was reported by Wood and Yasutake (1956d) and consisted in myriads of barbed bristles from ingested larval instars of a small moth (*Halisodota argentata*) Packard. These authors found many wild silver salmon that had been traumatized after ingesting these larvae. The many spinose "hairs" had penetrated the stomach wall and lodged in the adjacent viscera. Some had even migrated into the brain, spinal cord, and eye, but heaviest damage was to such viscera as pyloric caeca, pancreas, and spleen. Gross pathology of heavily affected fish revealed many fine brownish to yellow lines scattered through the viscera. Some fish had many fine bristles radiating from the outer stomach wall and in the lumen were seen many bristles penetrating the mucosa to various depths. Hematoxylin and eosin stained sections showed the "hairs" as bright yellow refractile foreign bodies in the center of a small zone of chronic inflammation. Foreign body giant cells and monocytes predominated in the inflammatory areas. The bristles exhibited great size variation and their barbs angled away from the shaft in a base to apex direction necessitating a butt-end penetration of the tissues by each spiny "hair." Ten of seventy-five wild trout and salmon were found to be affected with *Halisodota* "hairs" (Fig. 52).

Plant spines and burrs sometimes become lodged in the mouth or throat of a fish with resulting damage. Trauma, inflammatory lesions, infections, or even death may ensue. Reimers and Bond (1966) reported a case of a chinook salmon parr injured by barbed spines of an achene of a beggartick (*Bidens* sp.) and pictured an inflammatory lesion in the roof of the mouth at the terminus of the spine. In addition, two redsided shiners (*Richardsonius balteatus*) were also found with similar spines in the snouts,

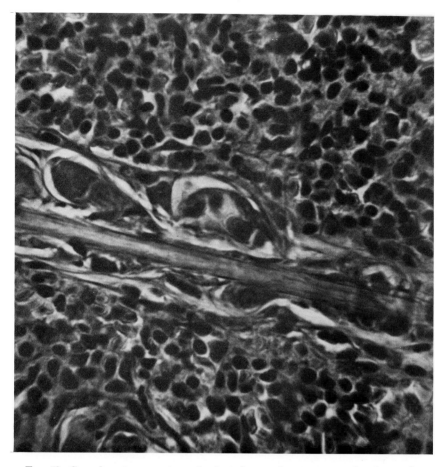

Fig. 52. Granulomatous response of coho salmon spleen to traumatism from minute bristled "hair" of ingested Lepidopteran larva. H and E (×450).

according to these authors. The present writer once found a shiner of this species with a beggar-tick achene lodged in its eye socket. Further investigation would doubtless disclose many instances where fish traumatized by plant spines, burrs, and fibers suffer inanition, lesions of the digestive tract, and even death.

### Acknowledgments

The assistance of Dr. Paul Yevich in translating foreign literature, of Mr. Charlie E. Smith for many of the photomicrographs, and of Dana Eshleman and Carlie Southard for microtechnical and other assistance is gratefully acknowledged.

## References

Allison, L. N. (1960). *Prog. Fish Cult.* **22**, 114.
Allison, L. N. (1950). *Prog. Fish Cult.* **12**, 52.
Ansbacher, S. (1941). *Science* **93**, 164.
Aoe, H. (1967). *Bull. Jap. Soc. Sci. Fish.* **33**, 681–685.
Aoe, H., and Masuda, I. (1967). *Bull. Jap. Soc. Sci. Fish.* **33**, 674–680.
Aoe, H., Masuda, I., Saito, T., and Komo, A. (1967). *Bull. Jap. Soc. Sci. Fish.* **33**, 970–974.
Arrington, L. R., Taylor, R. N., Jr., Ammerman, C. B., and Shirley, R. L. (1965). *J. Nutr.* **87**, 394.
Asano, M., and Masao, I. (1962). *Tohoku J. Agr. Res.* **13**, 151.
Ashburn, L. L. (1940). U.S. *Public Health Rep.* **55** (Pt. 2), 1337.
Ashley, L. M. (1967). *Bur. Sport Fish. Wildl. Res. Rep.* **70**.
Ashley, L. M., Halver, J. E., and Wogan, G. N. (1964). *Fed. Proc.* **23**, 105.
Ashley, L. M., Halver, J. E., Gardner, W. K., and Wogan, G. N. (1965). *Fed. Proc.* **24**, 2749.
Bardach, J. E., Fujiya, M., and Holl, A. (1965). *Science* **148**, 1605.
Bernhauer, K., Muller, O., and Wagner, F. (1964). *Advan. Enzymol.* **26**, 233.
Besse, P. (1956). *Ann. Sta. Centrale Hydrobiol. Appl.* **6**, 440.
Bessey, O. A., and Wolbach, S. B. (1939). *J. Exp. Med.* **69**, 1.
Boelter, M. D. D., and Greenberg, D. M. (1941). *J. Nutr.* **21**, 61.
Bowles, L. L., Hall, W. K., Sydenstricker, V. P., and Hock, C. W. (1949). *J. Nutr.* **37**, 9.
Buhler, D. R., and Halver, J. E. (1961). *J. Nutr.* **74**, 307.
Burrows, R. (1964). *U.S. Fish Wildl. Serv. Rep. No.* **66**, 1.
Burrows, R., Palmer, D. D., Newman, H. W., and Azevedo, R. L. (1952). *U.S. Fish Wildl. Serv. Spec. Sci. Rep.* **86**, 1.
Butler, W. H. (1965). *In* "Mycotoxins in Foodstuffs" (G. N. Wogan, ed.), pp. 175–186, M. I. T. Press, Cambridge, Massachusetts.
Calventi, I., and Nigrelli, R. F. (1961). *Amer. Zool.* **1**, 202.
Carson, B. W., and Bregesky, P. E. (1961). *Prog. Fish Cult.* **23**, 175.
Chick, H., El Sadr, M. N., and Worden, A. N. (1940). *Biochem. J.* **34**, 595.
Coates, J. A., and Halver, J. E. (1958). *U.S. Fish Wildl. Serv. Spec. Sci. Rep. Fish. No.* **281**, 1–9.
Coates, J. A., Potts, T. J., and Wilcke, H. L. (1967). *Bur. Sport. Fish. Wildl. Ser. Res. Rep.* **70**, 34–38.
Coburn, D. R., Metzler, D. W., and Treichler, R. (1951). *J. Wildl. Manage.* **15**, 186.
Cohan, S. Q. (1954). *Pediatrics* **13**, 556.
Cohen, J., Schwartz, R., and Wallace, W. M. (1952). *Arch. Pathol.* **54**, 119.
Cope, O. B. (1956). *U.S. Fish Wildl. Serv. Collected Reprints. Bur. Fish. Biol. Proc. 9th Annu. Meeting Utah Mosquito Abatement Ass.*
Courville, C. B., Courville, D. A., and Halstead, B. W. (1963). *Trans. Amer. Neurol. Ass.* **88**, 204.
Cowdry, E. V., and Scott, G. H. (1936). *Arch. Pathol.* **22**, 1.
Curran, G. L. (1965). *Pfizer Spectrum* (Spring, 1965).
Davis, H. S. (1953). "Culture and Diseases of Game Fishes." Univ. of Calif. Press, Berkeley, California.
Davis, H. S., and James, M. C. (1924). *Trans. Amer. Fish. Soc.* **54**, 77.
Davis, J. J., and Foster, R. F. (1958). *Ecology* **39**, 530.

DeLong, D. C., Halver, J. E., and Mertz, E. T. (1957). *Fed. Proc.* **16**, 384.
DeLong, D. C., Halver, J. E., and Yasutake, W. T. (1958). *Prog. Fish Cult.* **20**, 111.
Derse, P. H., and Strong, F. M. (1963). *Nature (London)* **200**, 600.
Deuel, H. J., and Reisser, R. (1955). *Vitamins Hormones* **13**, 30.
Dhekne, V. V., and Bhide, B. V. (1951). *Saponin* **28**, 588.
Dickerson, W. T., Jr., and McCance, R. A. (1960). *Brit. J. Nutr.* **14**, 75.
Doisy, E. A., Jr. (1961). *Fed. Proc.* **20**, 989.
Dubos, R. J., Jr. (1955). *J. Exp. Med.* **101**, 59.
Dukes, H. W. (1942). "The Physiology of Domestic Animals," p. 328. Comstock, New York.
Dunbar, C. E., and Herman, R. L. (1971). *J. Nutr.* **101**, 1445–1451.
Dunn, T. B., Morris, H. P., and Dubnick, C. S. (1947). *J. Nat. Cancer Inst.* **8**, 139.
Ebeling, G. (1928). *Mittheilungen des Fisherei-Vereins*, **32**, 521, Berlin.
Ellis, M. M. (1937). *U.S. Dep. Commerce Bur. Fish. Bull. No.* **22**, 48.
Ellis, M. M., Motley, H. L., Ellis, M. D., and Jones, R. O. (1937). *Proc. Soc. Exp. Biol. Med.* **36**, 519.
Emmel, V. M., and Bisett, T. C. (1965). *Amer. Ass. Anat. (Abstr.)* **151**, 451.
Emmel, V. M., and Mock, M. B. (1960). *Anat. Rec.* **136**, 313.
Engel, R. W., and Salmon, W. D. (1941). *J. Nutr.* **22**, 109.
Engel, R. W., Copeland, D. H., and Salmon, W. D. (1947). *Ann. N. Y. Acad. Sci.* **49**, 49.
Estremera, H. R., and Armstrong, W. D. (1948). *J. Nutr.* **35**, 611.
Faktorovich, K. A. (1956). Trans. from Rus. PST Cat. No. 630. *Tr. Soveschch. Fiziol. Ryb.* **237**.
Faktorovich, K. A. (1960). *Z. Fisherei* **9**, 95–99.
Faktorovich, K. A. (1963). *Biol. Abstr.* **44**, 1027 (Abstr. No. 13925).
Faktorovich, K. A. (1964). *Biol. Abstr.* **45**, 2180, (Abstr. No. 27224, transl. Russian.)
Ferm, V. H., Carpenter, S. J., and Faulkner, K. (1967). *Anat. Rec.* **157**, 358.
Finkelstein, M. H. (1932). *Proc. Soc. Exp. Biol. Med.* **29**, 969.
Follis, R. H., Jr. (1956). *Ciba Found. Bone Structure and Metabolism*, p. 249.
Follis, R. H., Jr. (1958). "Deficiency Disease." Thomas, Springfield, Illinois.
Follis, R. H., Jr., and Wintrobe, M. M. (1945). *J. Exp. Med.* **81**, 539.
Follis, R. H., Jr., Orent-Keiles, E., and McCollum, E. V. (1942b). *Arch. Pathol.* **33**, 504.
Follis, R. H., Jr., Orent-Keiles, E. and McCollum, E. V. (1942a). *Amer. J. Pathol.* **18**, 29.
Follis, R. H., Jr., Miller, M. H., Wintrobe, M. M., and Stein, H. J. (1943). *Amer. J. Pathol.* **19**, 341.
Frandsen, A. M., Becks, H., Nelson, M. M., and Evans, H. M. (1953). *J. Periodontol.* **24**, 135.
Fritz, J. C., Hooper, J. H., Halpin, J. L., and Moore, H. P. (1946). *J. Nutr.* **31**, 387.
Fromm, P. O., and Schiffman, R. H. (1958). *J. Wildl. Manage.* **22**, 40.
Galtsoff, P. S. (1949). *Sci. Mon.* **48**, 108.
Gaschott, O. (1929). *Allg Fishereiz.* (Cited by H. S. Davis, 1953.)
Gaylord, H. R., and Marsh, M. C. (1914). *Publ. State Inst. Study of Malignant Dis. Ser. No.* **99**, p. 363.
Gerking, S. D. (1961). *Publ. Amer. Inst. Biol. Sci.* **6**, 181.
Ghittino, P., and Ceretto, F. (1962). *NIH Rep. Nat. Cancer Inst. Pathol. Study Sess. Bethesda, Maryland*, pp. 62–68.
Gilbert, F. A. (1957). "Mineral Nutrition and the Balance of Life," p. 243. Univ. of Oklahoma Press, Norman, Oklahoma.
Gilderhus, P. (1964). *U.S. Fish Widl. Serv. Cir.* **199**, 31.
Gilderhus, P. A. (1966). *Trans. Amer. Fish Soc.* **95**, 289–296.

Glynn, L. E., Himsworth, H. P., and Neuberger, A. (1945). *Brit. J. Exp. Pathol.* **26,** 326.

Goettsch, M. (1949). *Arch. Biochem. Biophys.* **21,** 289.

Gong, J. K., Shipman, W. H., Weiss, H. V., and Cohn, S. H. (1957). *Proc. Soc. Exp. Biol. Med.* **95,** 451.

Gorchakova, R. I., and Telitchenko, M. M. (1963). *Byull. Mosk. Obshchest. Ispyt. Prir. Otd. Biol.* **68,** 132.

Gordeev, I. V. (1964). *Uch. Zap. Gor' K. Gos. Univ.* **64,** 16. (Ref. Zh. Biol. 151137, 1964.)

Gounelle, H. (1961). *Fed. Proc.* **20** (No. 1, Pt. Γ11, Suppl. No. 7), 389.

Graham, N. M. (1964). *Austr. J. Agr. Res.* **15,** 100.

Gunn, S. A., Gould, T. C., and Anderson, W. A. D. (1964). *Proc. Soc. Exp. Biol. Med.* **115,** 653.

Gutsell, J. S., and Snieszko, S. F. (1949). *Trans. Amer. Fish. Soc.* **77,** 93.

György, P., and Goldblatt, H. (1942). *J. Exp. Med.* **75,** 355.

Hall, W. K., Bowles, L. L., Sydenstricker, V. P., and Schmidt, H. L., Jr. (1948). *J. Nutr.* **36,** 277.

Halstead, B. (1964). *Clin. Pharmacol. Therap.* **5,** 615.

Halver, J. E. (1957). *J. Nutr.* **62,** 225.

Halver, J. E. (1965). *Fed. Proc.* **24,** Pt. 1, p. 169.

Halver, J. E. (1969). *In* "Aflatoxin" (Leo Goldblatt, ed.). 265–306. Academic Press, New York.

Halver, J. E., and Mitchell, I. (1967). *Bur. Sport Fish. Wildl. Pap., Res. Rep.* **70.**

Halver, J. E., and Shanks, W. E. (1960). *J. Nutr.* **72,** 340.

Halver, J. E., DeLong, D. C., and Mertz, E. T. (1957). *J. Nutr.* **63,** 95.

Halver, J. E., LaRoche, G., and Ashley, L. M. (1963). *Proc. 6th Int. Cong. Nutr. Edinburg,* p. 85.

Halver, J. E., Ashley, L. M., Smith, C. E., and Wogan, G. N. (1967). *Toxicol. Appl. Pharmacol.* **10,** 398.

Halver, J. E., Ashley, L. M., and Smith, C. E. (1968). *Proc. 23rd Annu. N. W. Region. Meeting Amer. Chem. Soc.,* Abstr. No. 32.

Halver, J. E., Ashley, L. M., and Smith, R. R. (1969). *Proc. 8th Int. Cong. Nutr. Prague, Czechoslovakia. 1969.*

Hands, A. R., Sutherland, N. S., and Bartley, W. (1965). *Biochem. J.* **94,** 279.

Helgebostad, A., and Martinsons, E. (1958). *Nature (London)* **181,** 1660.

Hess, W. N. (1935). *J. Exp. Zool.* **70,** 187.

Hess, W. N. (1937). *Proc. Soc. Exp. Biol. Med.* **37,** 306.

Higashi, H., Kaneko, T., Ishii, S., Ushiyama, M., and Sugihashi, T. J. (1966). *J. Vitaminol.* **12,** 74.

Holman, W. I. M., and McCance, R. A. (1956). *Brit. Med. Bull.* **12,** 27.

Hopkins, L. L., Jr., Pope, A. L., and Baumann, C. A. (1964). *J. Animal Sci.* **23,** 674.

Hove, E. L. and Herndon, J. F. (1955). *J. Nutr.* **55,** 363.

Hungate, R. E. (1950). *Bacteriol. Rev.* **14,** 1.

Hunt, C. E., and Carlton, W. W. (1965). *J. Nutr.* **87,** 385.

Hunter, H. A. (1950). *J. Dental Res.* **29,** 73.

Hurley, L. S., Volkert, N. E., and Eichner, J. T. (1965). *J. Nutr.* **86,** 201.

Iacobellis, M., Muntwyler, E., and Griffin, G. E. (1954). *Amer. J. Physiol.* **178,** 474.

Ikeda, S., and Sato, M. (1965). *Bull. Jap. Soc. Sci. Fish.* **31,** 814–817.

Jakowska, S. (1956). *Anat. Rec.* **125,** 655.

Johnson, H. E., and Brice, R. F. (1953). *Prog. Fish Cult.* **15,** 31.

Juhász, S., and Gréczi, E. (1964). *Nature (London)* **203**, 861.

Kayser, H., Ludemann, D., and Neumann, H. (1962). *Z. Angew. Zool.* **49**, 135. [Cited by H. Reichenbach-Klinke, and E. Elkan, (1965). *In* "The Principal Diseases of Lower Vertebrates." Academic Press, New York.]

Keenleyside, M. H. A. (1958). *Fish. Res. Bd Can. Prog. Rep. Atlantic Coast Sta.* **69**, 3.

King, S. F. (1962). *U.S. Fish Wildl. Serv. Spec. Sci. Rep. Fish. No.* **399**, 1–22.

Kingsbury, J. M. (1964). "Poisonous Plants of the United States and Canada," pp. 60–64. Prentice Hall, Englewood Cliffs, New Jersey.

Kitamura, S., Ohara, S., Suwa, T., and Nakagawa, K. (1965). *Bull. Jap. Soc. Sci. Fish.* **31**, 818–826.

Kraybill, H. F., and Shimkin, M. B. (1964). *Advan. Cancer Res.* **8**, 191.

Kramer, J., and Levine, V. E. (1953). *J. Nutr.* **50**, 149.

Krampitz, L. O., and Woolley, D. W. (1944). *J. Biol. Chem.* **152**, 9.

Krogh, A. (1939). "Osmotic Regulation in Aquatic Animals." Cambridge Univ. Press, London. (Cited by A. M. Phillips, H. A., Podoliak, and D. L. Livingston, *Fish. Res. Bull.* **24**.)

Krumholtz, L. A. (1956). *Bull. Amer. Mus. Nation. Hist.* **110**, 277–368. (Cited by Davis and Foster, 1958, *Ecology* **39**, 530–535.)

Kubo, A., Nakasato, M., Okamura, A., Furukawa, H., Ooka, Y., and Fukushima, M. (1961). (*Biol. Abstr.* **38**, 1735, Abstr. No. 22307.)

Lee, D. J., Wales, J. H., Sinnhuber, R. O., Ayres, J. L., and Roehm, J. N. (1966). *Fed. Proc.* **26**, 376.

Lippincott, S. W., and Morris, H. P. (1941). *J. Nat. Cancer Inst.* **2**, 39.

Loeb, H. A. (1964). *N. Y. Fish Game J.* **11**, 160.

Lucas, J., and Orten, J. M. (1954). *J. Nutr.* **52**, 89.

McCay, C. M., Bing, F. C., and Dilley, W. E. (1927). *Trans. Amer. Fish. Soc.* **57**, 240.

McHargue, J. S. (1925). *Amer. J. Physiol.* **72**, 583.

MacIntyre, I., and Davidson, D. (1958). *Biochem. J.* **70**, 456.

McLaren, B. A., Keller, E., O'Donnell, D. J., and Elvehjem, C. A. (1947). *Arch. Biochem. Biophys.* **15**, 169.

MacPherson, C. R., and Pearse, A. G. E. (1957). *Brit. Med. Bull.* **13**, 19.

Madden, S. C., Anderson, F. W., Donovan, J. C., and Whipple, G. H. (1945). *J. Exp. Med.* **82**, 77.

Marine, D., and Lenhart, C. H. (1910). *J. Exp. Med.* **12**, 311.

Martin, G. J. (1937). *Growth* **1**, 175.

Mathur, G. B. (1967). *Naturwissenschaften* **54**, 25.

Maynard, L. A., and Loosli, J. K. (1956). "Animal Nutrition," p. 45. McGraw-Hill, New York.

Meehan, W. R. (1964). *Prog. Fish Cult.* **26**, 142.

Meiklejohn, A.P. (1940). *New Engl. J. Med.* **223**, 265.

Mellanby, E. (1947). *J. Physiol.* **105**, 382.

Miller, J. A., and Miller, E. C. (1953). *Advan. Cancer Res.* **1**, 339–396. (Cited by Stewart and Snell, 1957. Extract from *Acta Int. Union Cancer* **13**, 769–803.)

Miller, L. L., Bly, C. G., Watson, M. L., and Bale, W. F. (1951). *J. Exp. Med.* **94**, 431.

Milne, M. D., Muehrcke, R. C., and Heard, B. E. (1957). *Brit. Med. Bull.* **13**, 15.

Moore, T., and Wang, Y. L. (1943). *Biochem. J.* **37**, (proc. viii).

Moore, T., and Wang, Y. L. (1945). *Biochem. J.* **39**, 222.

Nakatani, R. E., and Foster, R. F. (1963). *In* "Radioecology" (V. Shultz and A. W.

Klement, Jr., eds.). Reinhold, New York and Amer. Inst. Biol. Sci., Washington, D.C.

Nakatani, R. E., and Liu, D. H. W. (1963). *Hanford Biol. Res. Annu. Rep. 1963*, pp. 109–112. Richland, Washington.

Nakatani, R. E., and Miller, W. P. (1963). *Hanford Biol. Res. Annu. Rep. 1962*, pp. 109–114. Richland, Washington.

Nelson, M. M., and Evans, H. M. (1946). *J. Nutr.* **31**, 497.

Nelson, M. M., and Evans, H. M. (1953). *J. Nutr.* **51**, 71.

Nelson, M. M., Sulon, E., Becks, H., Wainwright, W. W., and Evans, H. M. (1950). *Proc. Soc. Exp. Biol. Med.* **73**, 31.

Nesheim, M. C., and Scott, M. L. (1961). *Fed. Proc.* **20**, 674.

Nicolaides, N., and Woodall, A. N. (1962). *J. Nutr.* **78**, 431.

O'Dell, B. L., Bird, D. W., Ruggles, D. L., and Savage, J. E. (1966). *J. Nutr.* **88**, 9.

Ogilvie, D. M., and Anderson, J. M. (1965). *J. Fish. Res. Bd. Can.* **22**, 503.

Ogino, C. (1965). *Bull. Jap. Soc. Sci. Fish.* **31**, 546–551.

Ogino, C. (1967). *Bull. Jap. Soc. Sci. Fish.* **33**, 351–354.

Parisot, T. J., and Wood, J. W. (1959). *U.S. Fish Wildl. Serv. Fish. Leafl.* **494**.

Parnell-King, J. (1964). *Anat. Rec.* **148**, 320.

Pfizer Spectrum, Spring (1965).

Phillips, A. M., Jr. (1959). *Trans. Amer. Fish. Soc.* **88**, 133.

Phillips, A. M., Jr. (1963). *Prog. Fish Cult.* **23**, 134.

Phillips, A. M., Jr., Brockway, D. R., Kolb, A. J. J., and Maxwell, J. M. (1951). *Fish. Res. Bull. No.* **14**.

Phillips, A. M., Jr., Lovelace, F. E., Podoliak, H. A., Brockway, D. R., and Balzer, G. C., Jr. (1956). *Fish. Res. Bull. No.* **19**.

Phillips, A. M., Jr., Podoliak, H. A., Dumas, R. F., and Thoesen, R. W. (1959). *Fish. Res. Bull. No.* **22**.

Phillips, A. M., Jr., Podoliak, H. A., Poston, H. A., Livingston, D. L., Booke, H. E., and Hammer, G. L. (1962). *Fish. Res. Bull. No.* **25**.

Phillips, A. M., Jr., Podoliak, H. A., Poston, H. A., Livingston, D. L., Booke, H. E., Pyle, E. A., and Hammer, G. L. (1964). *Fish. Res. Bull. No.* **27**, *Cortland Hatchery Rep. No.* **32**.

Piper, R. G. (1961). *Prog. Fish Cult.* **23**, 134.

Plehn, M. (1924). "Praktikum der Fischkrankheiten." E. Schweizerbart'sche Verlagsbuchhandlung. 179 pp. Stuttgart.

Pond, W. G. (1965). *N. Y. State J. Med.* **65**, 2369.

Poston, H. A. (1964). *Prog. Fish Cult.* **26**, 59.

Poston, H. A. (1967). *Fish. Res. Bull. No.* **30**.

Poston, H. A., Livingston, D. L., Pyle, E. A., and Phillips, A. M., Jr. (1966). *Fish. Res. Bull. No.* **29**, 20–24.

Premdas, F. H., and Anderson, J. M. (1963). *J. Fish. Res. Bd. Can.* **20**, 827.

Prickett, C. O. (1934). *Amer. J. Physiol.* **107**, 459.

Rachmilewitz, M., Izak, G., and Grossowicz, N. (1965). *Harefuah* **62**, 263.

Ralli, E. P., and Dumm, M. E. (1953). *Vitamins Hormones* **9**, 133.

Ramalingaswami, V., and Sinclair, H. M. (1953). *Brit. J. Dermatol.* **65**, 1.

Reid, M. E., and Martin, M. G. (1959). *J. Nutr.* **67**, 611.

Reimers, N. (1957). *Calif. Fish Game* **43**, 53.

Reimers, N. (1958). *Calif. Fish Game* **44**, 319.

Reimers, P. E., and Bond, C. E. (1966). *Prog. Fish Cult.* **28**, 62.

Reinhart, J. F., and Greenberg, L. D. (1949). *Amer. J. Pathol.* **25**, 481.
Reinhart, J. F., and Greenberg, L. D. (1956). *Amer. J. Clin. Nutr.* **4**, 318.
Roberts, H. (1963). *Prog. Fish Cult.* **25**, 216.
Robertson, O. H. (1958). *U.S. Fish Wildl. Serv. Fish Bull.* **58**, 9.
Rodahl, K., and Moore, T. (1943). *Biochem. J.* **37**, 166.
Rodahl, K., Issekutz, B., Jr., and Shumen, D. M. (1965). *J. Nutr.* **85**, 174–180.
Ross, A. J., and Johnson, H. E. (1962). *Prog. Fish Cult.* **24**, 147–149.
Sadkovskaya, O. D. (1957). *Proc. Conf. Fish Dis.* pp. 75–78. Leningrad.
Salmon, W. D., and Copeland, D. H. (1954). *Ann. N. Y. Acad. Sci.* **57**, 664.
Salmon, W. D., and Newberne, P. M. (1962). *Arch. Pathol.* **73**, 190.
Schaefer, A. E., McKibbin, J. M., and Elvehjem, C. A. (1942). *J. Biol. Chem.* **143**, 321.
Schäperclaus, W. (1954). "Fischkrankheiten," 3rd ed., pp. 128–130. Berlin.
Scheier, A., and Cairns, J., Jr. (1966). *Notulae Natur. Acad. Nat. Sci. Philadelphia,* **391**.
Schmidt, F. H. (1964). *Z. Aerztl. Fortbild.* **57**, 1315.
Schwartz, K. (1952). *Proc. Soc. Exp. Biol. Med.* **80**, 319.
Schwartz, K. (1961). *Fed. Proc.* **20** (No. 2, Pt. 1), 666.
Schwartz, K. (1965). *Fed. Proc.* **24**, 58.
Scott, E. B. (1960). *Arch. Pathol.* **69**, 390.
Scott, E. B. (1966). *Arch. Pathol.* **82**, 119.
Scrimshaw, N. S. (1965). *Borden Rev. Nutr. Res.* **26**, 17.
Sebrell, W. H., and McDaniel, E. G. (1952). *J. Nutr.* **47**, 477.
Seronde, J. J. (1964). *Fed. Proc.* **23**, 879.
Shanks, W. E., Gahimer, G. D., and Halver, J. E. (1962). *Prog. Fish Cult.* **24**, 72.
Sharma, G. L., Johnston, R. L., Leucke, R. W., Hoefer, J. A., Gray, M. L., and Thorp, F., Jr. (1952). *Amer. J. Vet. Res.* **13**, 298.
Sherman, H. C., and Lanford, C. S. (1957). "Essentials of Nutrition," p. 283. Macmillan, New York.
Sidransky, H., and Verney, E. (1965). *J. Nutr.* **86**, 73.
Simpson, C. F., and Harms, R. H. (1964). *Exp. Mol. Pathol.* **3**, 390.
Sinnhuber, R. O. (1969). *In* "Fish in Research" (O. W. Neuhaus and J. E. Halver, eds.), pp. 245–261. Academic Press, New York.
Sinnhuber, R. O., Wales, J. H., and Lee, D. J. (1966). *Fed. Proc.* **25**, 555.
Sinnhuber, R. O., Lee, D. J., Wales, J. H., and Ayres, J. L. (1968). *J. Nat. Cancer Inst.* **41**, 1293–1301.
Smith, C. E. (1968). *J. Fish. Res. Bd. Can.* **25**, 151–156.
Smith, S. E., and Medlicott, M. (1944). *Amer. J. Physiol.* **141**, 354.
Smith, S. G., Black-Schaffer, B., and Lasater, T. E. (1950). *Arch. Pathol.* **49**, 185.
Smith, H. A., and Jones, T. C. (1961). "Veterinary Pathology," pp. 1–1068. Lea and Febiger, Philadelphia, Pennsylvania.
Smith, W. O., Baxter, D. J., Lindner, A., and Ginn, H. E. (1962). *J. Lab. Clin. Med.* **59**, 211.
Snieszko, S. F., and Wood, E. M. (1955). *Trans. Amer. Fish. Soc.* **84**, 86.
Stothers, S. C., Schmidt, D. A., Johnston, R. L., Hoefer, J. A., and Leucke, R. W. (1955). *J. Nutr.* **57**, 47.
Sullivan, M., and Nicholls, J. (1942). *Arch. Dermatol. Syph.* **45**, 917.
Surber, E. W., and Meehan, O. L. (1931). *Trans. Amer. Fish. Soc.* **61**, 225.
Swan, K. C., and Salit, P. W. (1941). *Amer. J. Ophthalmol.* **24**, 611.
Sydenstricker, V. P., Hall, W. K., Bowles, L. L., and Schmidt, H. L., Jr. (1947). *J. Nutr.* **34**, 481.

Sykes, J. F., and Moore, L. A. (1942). *Arch. Pathol.* **33**, 467.

Szmigielski, S., and Litwin, J. (1964). *Pol. Arch. Med. Wewnetrznej.* **34**, 319.

Tannenbaum, A. (1953). *In* "The Physiology of Cancer," (F. Homburger and W. H. Fishman, eds.) pp. 392–437. Hoeber (Harper) New York.

Tannenbaum, A. (1959). "The Physiology of Cancer," 2nd edition. Hoeber (Harper), New York.

Thuman, M. E. (1940). *Z. Fischerei. Hilfswiss.* **38**, 659.

Titcomb, J. W., Cobb, E. W., Crowell, M. F., and McCay, C. M. (1929). *Trans. Amer. Fish. Soc.* **59**, 126.

Tomasch, J. (1960). *Anat. Rec.* **136**, 292.

Ullrey, D. E., Becker, D. E., Terrill, S. W., and Notzold, R. A. (1955). *J. Nutr.* **57**, 401.

Underwood, E. J. (1961). *Fed. Proc.* **20** (No. 1, Pt. 111, Suppl. No. 7), 284.

Vamos, R. (1963). *Acta Biol.* (*Szeged*) **9**, 291.

Vastesaeger, M. M., Gillot, P., and Vastesaeger, E. (1962). *Acta Cardiol.* **17**, 780.

Vohra, P., and Kratzer, F. H. (1956). *Science* **124**, 1145.

Von Sallmann, L., Halver, J. E., Collins, E., and Grimes, P. (1966). *Cancer Res.* **26**, 1819.

Wacker, W. E. C., and Vallee, B. L. (1961). *Borden's Rev. Nutr. Res.* **22**, 51.

Wainwright, W. W., and Nelson, M. M. (1945). *Amer. J. Orthodont. Oral Surg.* **31**, 406.

Wales, J. H. (1944). *Calif. Fish Game* **30**, 43.

Wales, J. H., and Sinnhuber, R. O. (1966). *Calif. Fish Game* **52**, 85.

Walker, A. R. P. (1965). *Amer. J. Clin. Nutr.* **16**, 327.

Werkman, C. H., Baldwin, F. M., and Nelson, V. E. (1924). *J. Infect. Dis.* **35**, 549.

West, E. S., and Todd, W. R. (1961). "Biochemistry," 3rd ed., p. 706. Macmillan, New York.

Whipple, G. H., and Robscheit-Robbins, F. S. (1940). *J. Exp. Med.* **71**, 569.

Wiebe, A. H. (1930). *Trans. Amer. Fish. Soc.* **60**, 270.

Williamson, R. (1941). *Biochem. J.* **35**, 1003.

Wilson, W. (1954). *Ann. N. Y. Acad. Sci.* **57**, 678.

Wintrobe, M. M., Mushatt, C., Miller, J. L., Jr., Kolb, L. C., Stein, H. J., and Lisco, H. (1942). *J. Clin. Invest.* **21**, 71.

Wintrobe, M. M., Follis, R. H., Jr., Alcayaga, R., Paulson, M., and Humphreys, S. (1943). *Bull. Johns Hopkins Hosp.* **73**, 313.

Wolbach, S. B. (1933). *Amer. J. Pathol. Suppl.* **9**, 689.

Wolbach, S. B., and Howe, P. R. (1926). *Arch. Path.* **1**, 1.

Wolf, H., and Jackson, E. W. (1963). *Science* **142**, 676.

Wolf, K. (1957). *Trans. Amer. Fish. Soc.* **86**, 61.

Wolf, L. E. (1945). *Fish. Res. Bull. No. 7.*

Wolf, L. E. (1951). *Prog. Fish Cult.* **13**, 17–24.

Wood, E. M., and Yasutake, W. T. (1950). *Parasitology* **42**, 544.

Wood, E. M., and Yasutake, W. T. (1956a). *Prog. Fish Cult.* **18**, 108.

Wood, E. M., and Yasutake, W. T. (1956b). *Amer. J. Pathol.* **32**, 591.

Wood, E. M., and Yasutake, W. T. (1956c). *Amer. J. Pathol.* **32**, 845.

Wood, E. M., and Yasutake, W. T. (1956d). *J. Parasitol.* **42**, 544–546.

Wood, E. M., Yasutake, W. T., and Lehman, W. L. (1955). *J. Infect. Dis.* **97**, 262.

Wood, E. M., and Yasutake, W. T. (1957). *Prog. Fish Cult.* **18**, 7.

Wood, E. M., Yasutake, W. T., Woodall, A. N., and Halver, J. E. (1957). *J. Nutr.* **61**, 465.

Woodall, A. N., and LaRoche, G. (1964). *J. Nutr.* **82**, 475.

Woodall, A. N., Ashley, L. M., Halver, J. E., Olcott, H. S., and Van Der Veen, J. (1964). *J. Nutr.* **84,** 125.
Woodbury, L. A. (1943). *Trans. Amer. Fish. Soc.* **72,** 30.
Zobairi, A. R. K. (1956). *Prog. Fish Cult.* **18,** 88.
Zucker, L. M., and Zucker, T. F. (1964). *Fed. Proc.* **23,** 881.

# 11

## THE DIET AND GENERAL FISH HUSBANDRY

*Pietro Ghittino*

## I. Introduction

An adequate diet for fish husbandry is obviously the foundation on which fish farming is built. Success or failure of the fish husbandry venture will be determined by the nutritional status of the fish reared. Yet, all too often availability of dietary ingredients, methods of storage and manufacture, and customs of the area alter the practices of general fish husbandry to conform to the diet used. Practical fish husbandry has been a necessity in many areas of the world to obtain protein for the population and supplement or provide total income for many people living around waters rich in nutrients and adequate to hold and rear fish. Unfortunately, much of the potential of many of these streams, ponds or impoundments has been lost from lack of application of knowledge known or which could be extended from research work completed in other areas of fish nutrition. Practical diets, supposedly adequate for rearing fish in these areas, were formulated originally from studies of natural food available to the fishes and from agricultural and slaughter house by-products not readily consumed as food by the populous of that area. Sometimes these diets worked fairly well; but often when fish population in the water increased to the point that growth had to come from the diet offered with only minor supplementation from natural foods endogenous to the system in which the fish were living, poor growth, nutritional diseases, and infestation with bacteria and parasites occurred. Even today, scientific knowledge on basic nutritional requirements and practical diets for feeding is restricted to a few species of fish; whereas, for many other kinds reared, empirical rules and practical methods are usually applied. Availability of dietary ingredients in a particular area, and means of preparation and storage of this material often determines many of the techniques of fish husbandry employed. Certain other fish feeding techniques, both natural and artificial, can develop fish with specific organoleptic characteristics, and basic economic aspects of fish husbandry are also involved because reared fish must constantly satisfy market demand. Hygienic aspects of rearing fish are also involved, since fish produced must be suitable for human consumption, organoleptically acceptable, and free from human pathogens or parasites.

General fish husbandry can be easily divided into two general types of fish production—that is, cold water fish husbandry and warm water fish production. Trout farming is a typical example of the first type. The nature of techniques involved, holding dense populations of fish in a temperate water environment between 5°–15°C, cause the diet for this husbandry to be the most important factor for economic production of trout for food or for planting for sport. Warm water fish culture can be best exemplified by traditional extensive carp culture with diet offered to increase growth and fish production from food available from aquatic plants and insects present in the impoundment. Much depends on metabolism differences between types of cultured fishes or rather on the different respiratory demands. Cold water fishes require large amounts of dissolved oxygen in water. This is only physically possible in cold water (5°–15°C). Warm water fish, on the other hand, are able to survive in water with low oxygen content, which is the case in water between 20°–40°C, where these fish are reared.

The growth rate of fish is directly proportional to the water temperature. In contrast, the amount of dissolved oxygen in the water is inversely proportional to the temperature. Therefore, since fish require oxygen to metabolize the food ingested, water temperature should be high enough to stimulate rapid growth but never beyond the degree to which fish reared would suffer oxygen deficiency for the population density involved and metabolism rate required by temperature and food offered.

Two distinct categories of fish may also be considered to determine husbandry techniques and diet used. Many of the cold and temperate water fishes have stomachs, are carnivores or omnivores, and can be reared easily on artificial diets. In contrast, warm water fish, like the carp are stomachless, have a long digestive tract, are omnivores or herbivores and require different diet formulation techniques and feeding practices for efficient fish husbandry. Since Salmonidae are carnivores, the diet must be high in protein and the economical food value for these fishes must be high, since the feeding costs represent the most important item in the budget of general cold water fish husbandry. Animal food manufacturers are interested in this type of fish husbandry and more basically applied nutrition and, in addition, general fish husbandry techniques, have been expended in this area since economical production is required for this expensive fish flesh for food or for sport. Warm water fish culture, as in pond culture of carp, focused efforts on methods to increase natural food in the pond. Artificial feeding is of secondary importance in consideration of pond density for good fish health, rapid growth, and husbandry techniques to handle the animals in these more labor- and time-consuming pond or impoundment growing areas. Natural food available in ponds is already high in protein and vitamin content, therefore, the supplementary diet has commonly been composed of vegetable compounds to increase starch and low cost nitrogen content. Therefore, it is easy to realize why artificial diets in warm water fish culture are not generally as important as other items like pond care, fertilization, pond sampling, fish grading, and final crop harvesting. Nevertheless, intensive effort is being expended by scientists and commercial companies in this area to perfect effective artificial diets for these fishes because of the tremendous acreage of water suitable for pond culture which must be devoted to warm water fish production to produce food, protein, and sport fishes for developing nations of the world which are located in tropical or semitropical areas. Somewhere between carp rearing and trout farming lies the recently developed intensive farming of catfish for food and for sport fishes. During the last 5 years, this industry has developed from experimental and private farm techniques into the most rapidly developing form of animal husbandry in agriculture in the United States, and promises to revolutionize low land use in semitropical areas of the world. These fish are omnivorous requiring less protein than the Salmonidae, but more than the Cyprinidae, supplementation of diet with aquatic forms present in the natural and artificial impoundments used, and minimal consideration of vitamin content and limiting amino acid content of the cheaper protein-containing diets used in this husbandry. The striking success and development of this industry has been recently thoroughly covered in Report to the fish farmers (1970).

## II.  Cold-Water Fish Husbandry (Salmonidae)

Trout production can be considered a classical example of salmonid husbandry. Scientific knowledge on basic nutritional requirements, practical diets, and husbandry techniques is more developed for trout, and especially for rainbow trout, than for any other species of fish reared. These data can also be generally applied and extended to other salmonids reared throughout temperate zones of the world for food and for sport fish planted in streams for the fisherman. Salmonidae husbandry is also extensively developed in the United States, Scandinavia, France, Italy, and Japan in production and maintenance of fish grazing the seas and oceans, coastal and off-shore waters, and sports fishery in estuaries and streams along the

TABLE I

YEARLY TROUT PRODUCTION (IN TONS) IN DIFFERENT COUNTRIES

| Country | 1961 | 1962 | 1963 | 1964 | 1965 | 1966 | References |
|---------|------|------|------|------|------|------|------------|
| United States | | | | | 13,000 | | Thompson, 1966 |
| | 3023 | | 3936 | | | | Fuhrmann, 1967 |
| Japan | | | | | 5,745 | | Nagayama, 1967 |
| | 7500 | | | | | | Christensen *et al.*, 1963 |
| Denmark | | | 9679 | | | | Bregnballe, 1963 |
| | | | | | 11,000 | | Rasmussen, 1966 |
| | | 2000 | | | | | Solacroup, 1963 |
| France | | | | | 10,000– | | |
| | | | | | 12,000 | | Tessier, 1967 |
| Italy | | | | | | 7000– | |
| | | | | | | 8000 | *Asso. Piscicolt. Ital.*, 1967 |
| West Germany | 1000 | | | | | | Mann, 1961 |
| Norway | | | | | 500 | | Jensen, 1966 |

coastline. This type of fish husbandry has been developing rapidly in the last 20 years and involves large-scale production of trout and salmon. Table I shows data on early trout production in some countries and points to the level that this kind of fish farming has reached.

Feeding methods in trout culture are based on high protein diets because trout are essentially carnivorous and digest and utilize protein well. Trout utilize only low quantities of digestible carbohydrates, many of which, though readily used by other animals, are excreted unhydrolyzed in the native state. Lipids and fats appear to be fairly well utilized and, in some species of fish such as salmon and lake trout, fat can be used as energy source to spare protein and carbohydrate up to 20% of the dry weight of the diet.

Methods of feeding trout have exhibited a remarkable development over the past 100 years. Today, one can distinguish old or traditional methods from modern methods and natural feeding is employed only in lakes or streams rich in natural food and only infrequently or sparingly harvested for the trout population. Original studies of natural foods form the basis for earliest methods of artificial feeding, however, and the original wet diets contain mostly fish and slaughter house by-products. These diets were traditionally employed both in Europe and America for many years with varying degrees of success. The nutrient content of the diet varied from batch to batch, and these diets had to be freshly prepared and refrigerated since the diet was subject to rapid oxidation and spoilage. Later, various high protein meals, both animal and vegetable, were added to increase the dietetic value, to utilize cheaper and more available products and to make up for the shortage of fresh products which had occurred during rapid development of trout hatcheries wherever good trout water was available. This problem was most manifest in the United States where not only trout but also salmon production relied upon supply of condemned beef liver, spleen, lungs, horse meat, tankage, and fish viscera. Several government laboratories focused attention on nutritional requirements of the trout and salmon and on a study of dietary ingredients to formulate dry meals and pellets for fish production. The Cortland Laboratory did much of the pioneering work and developed several formulas which could be used either alone or supplemented with wet trout diet mixtures to rear trout economically without producing severe deficiency symptoms. At the same time in Europe, an incalculable number of small industries for animal feeds were preparing trout pellets using their own private formulas. These formulas were obtained by modifying theoretically, as well as empirical, mixtures of diet ingredients for other animals. Some formulas suggested in early American literature on trout dry feeding were generally unacceptable for rearing trout for long growth periods. Therefore, the practice was to use these dry ingredients and then supplement with fresh food or wet trout diets once or twice a week to avoid undesirable mortality. Recently, several good dry rations for trout have become available in Europe and in the Orient. These allow production of trout to marketable size starting from swim-up fry. This is a tremendous improvement over previous diets available and, of course, revolutionized the husbandry techniques employed in the many hatcheries in Europe and Asia using these rations. Such dry diets are considered sustaining rations and it seems correct to predict that these may substitute for the traditional diets and improve feeding methods used in the developed countries in the temperate zones of the world.

Chronologically, the following diets have been used in trout culture:

    A. Natural Diets
    B. Artificial Diets
      1. Fresh wet diets
      2. Mixed diets
      3. Modern dry diets

## A. NATURAL DIETS

Natural feeding of trout generally starts with crustaceans, especially cladocera, copepoda, malacostraceans, isopoda, amphipoda, and water-insect larve, followed by adult insects, worms, molluscs, and other larger sized animals, such as, small fish, tadpoles, and frogs. Natural feeding has always been of secondary importance in trout husbandry except when fish are reared in large bodies of free-flowing or impounded water and the fish must forage for food. Obviously, only small populations of fish can be accommodated under these conditions, and it is not reasonable to rear more than three to fifteen trout fry per square surface meter of water without adding food (Schäperclaus, 1961). The production of market fish is not economically feasible and only a sport fishery with high access

TABLE II

Chemical Composition of Trout Diets[a]

| Type of Diet | Protein | Fat | Carbo-hydrate | Ash | Water | References |
|---|---|---|---|---|---|---|
| **Natural** | | | | | | |
| Invertebrates | 11.5 | 2.2 | — | 2.7 | 82.2 | Phillips *et al.*, 1956 |
| Phryganea | 12.78 | 7.08 | 8.17 | 0.75 | 70.42 | Schäperclaus, 1933 |
| Gammarus | 6.4 | 0.8 | — | 2.7 | 87.5 | Phillips *et al.*, 1956 |
| **Fresh or wet** | | | | | | |
| Beef liver | 20.2 | 3.1 | 2.5 | 1.3 | 72.3 | Phillips and Balzer, 1957 |
| Beef spleen | 18.0 | 2.3 | — | 1.4 | 75.2 | Phillips and Balzer, 1957 |
| Beef meat | 20.5 | 2.8 | — | 1.2 | 75.5 | Schäperclaus, 1933 |
| Lean seafish | 16.9 | 0.4 | — | 1.2 | 81.5 | Schäperclaus, 1933 |
| Fat seafish, mean | 10.6 | 4.05 | — | 1.15 | — | Leitritz, 1962 |
| Fresh fish, mixed | 12.5 | 6.3 | — | 2.0 | 72.0 | Phillips and Balzer, 1957 |
| **Dry meals** | | | | | | |
| Meat meal | 55.0 | 12.0 | 1.2 | 25.0 | 10.0 | Phillips and Balzer, 1957 |
| Fish meal | 61.2 | 8.6 | — | 18.0 | 11.6 | Nehring, 1957 |
| Soybean (expeller) | 49.9 | 6.2 | 26.4 | 5.4 | 10.0 | Phillips and Balzer, 1957 |
| Cottonseed | 38.0 | 8.0 | 39.9 | 6.4 | 10.0 | Phillips and Balzer, 1957 |
| Peanut meal | 44.8 | 10.2 | 33.6 | 4.8 | — | Leitritz, 1962 |
| Wheat meal | 12.3 | 1.9 | 70.0 | 1.8 | 12.0 | Nehring, 1957 |
| **Mixed** | | | | | | |
| 50% Fresh + 50% dry | 28.5 | 3.2 | 19.4 | 6.3 | 41.4 | Phillips *et al.*, 1956 |
| **Modern dry diets** | | | | | | |
| United States pellets | 43.0 | 8.0 | 28.0 | 16.0 | 9.0 | |
| Swedish pellets | 30.5 | 1.5 | 46.0 | 13.0 | 7.0 | |
| German pellets | 32.9 | 3.6 | 38.9 | 14.6 | 10.6 | |
| Holland pellets | 40.0 | 7–8 | 18–19 | 11–12 | 12–13 | |
| Italian pellets | 44.5 | 3.66 | 33.96 | 14.32 | 9.83 | |

[a] Values in percentage.

fees can support "wild" fish reared in a "natural" environment. This type of fish culture is still employed in some areas of the world where emphasis is placed upon the need for "wild" fish for stocking purposes and fish must be reared and sold at an exorbitant price for this inefficient use of the water area. In these situations, fertilization of a pond or lake waters is often employed to increase the nitrogen content of the biomass present on which these fish are foraging to satisfy their dietary requirements. It is interesting to point out that in the past attempts have been made to supplement the feed for trout with natural feed. This is done by installing lights over ponds to trap flying insects at night, and by suspending animal parts over the pond, which become infested with fly larvae, and then allowing the maggots to fall into the pond to supplement the natural diet material of the wild trout (Leitritz, 1962).

Chemical composition and conversion rates of certain natural trout diets are tabulated in Tables II and III. Many of these ingredients were used in preparing the original artificial trout diet. Other attempts to increase the natural ingredients of trout diets were accomplished by changing the pH of the water by liming and by general lake or pond fertilization with the missing nutrients. Culture of Daphnia was attempted in Sweden in plastic boxes (Fig. 1) and appeared suitable for experimental breeding of certain salmonids. Sometimes trout and salmon species which refused commercially prepared diets were taught to feed with Daphnia or with

TABLE III

CONVERSION RATE OF TROUT FOOD INTO TROUT FLESH

| Type of diet | Total conversion | References |
|---|---|---|
| Gammarus | 6.6 | Surber, 1935; Pyle, 1965 |
| Gammarus | 5.0 | Pentelow, 1939 |
| Gammarus | 3.9 | Cornelius, 1933 |
| Chironomus larvae | 4.4 | Cornelius, 1933 |
| Maggots | 7.1 | Phillips et al., 1956 |
| Freshwater fishes | 2.9 | Cornelius, 1933 |
| Seawater fishes | 5–7 | Bregnballe, 1963 |
| Beef liver | 2.9–3.3 | Phillips et al., 1956 |
| Spleen | 2.9 | Cornelius, 1933 |
| Fresh meat | 3.0 | Schäperclaus, 1961 |
| Mixed (wet 50% + dry 50%) | 3–4 | Deuel et al., 1952 |
| Oregon pellets | 2 | Hublou, 1963 |
| Standard Cortland pellet | 2.05 | Phillips et al., 1953 |
| Dry pellets | 1.80–2.10 | Phillips et al., 1964 |

Fig. 1. Daphnia culture in plastic boxes at Älvkarleö, Sweden.

brine shrimp larvae and then were converted as soon as possible to other natural food and then to artificial food. Traditionally, the development of diet for different species of fish has evolved from natural food with its problems of cost preparation, refrigeration, storage, and difficult feeding techniques, to wet flesh and glandular tissue diets, to meal meat mixes, and then finally conversion to dry meal or pellet artificial diet for economical rearing of that species.

## B. Artificial Diets

### 1. *Fresh Wet Diets*

This type of diet has long been used in salmonid culture and is still used today in some countries. It consists of animal slaughter by-products plus fish offal—fresh, refrigerated, or frozen. The slaughter house products consist of different by-products from several animals, such as beef, sheep, swine, poultry, and includes liver, spleen, heart, condemned meat, lung, kidney, testicles, ovaries, intestine, blood, brain, fat, and trimmings. These parts are often parasitized or infected with pathogens and therefore condemned by veterinary services; hence, these materials were cheap and not offered on the public market. Fish and fish products consisted chiefly of sea fish, brackish water fish, and freshwater trash fish. Sometimes crustacea, mollusks, and fish cannery scraps were used. These products all have different values for salmonid feeds and vary depending upon the nature and animal source used. Employing the traditional practical criteria, good feed value can be found in beef liver, spleen, heart, freshwater fish, lean sea fish, cod ovaries, crustacea, and poor value can be assigned to lung, kidney, trimmings, intestines, fat, offal, and ovaries. Fat sea fish tissues, although readily used by trout and salmon, are less suitable because these rapidly become rancid and are toxic to trout, causing liver lipoid degeneration (Ghittino, 1961). The best fresh products are generally employed for fry, fingerling, and brood stock diets, whereas those of poorer quality are utilized for table fish, especially during the finishing period. One can note the similarity between mink feeds and those fresh products used in trout culture. Therefore, competition exists for high value fresh products and, consequently, the market fluctuates in availability and price of these diet ingredients. Fresh feeding in trout culture still plays an important role in countries disposing of large amounts of suitable and cheap offal. In Denmark, for instance, traditional feeding of trout with fresh sea fishes forms the basis of most trout production and still is considered the most economical method there (Rasmussen, 1966). Chemical composition and conversion rates of several fish diets are recorded in literature and tabulated in Tables II and III.

## 2. *Mixed Diets*

Mixed diets, like fresh diets, represent a transitional feeding technique. These diets have gradually evolved from improvements on fresh diets. These mixtures can be considered as the first steps toward modern, dry diet feeding since this diet is composed of fresh products mixed with vegetable and animal dry meals. The dry meals used are roughly the same as those employed in feeding other animals. For trout feeding, high protein meals are selected. Among animal meals, fish, meat, blood, milk, liver, and silk worm pupae meals are included; among vegetable meals, soybean, peanut, cottonseed, and several cereal meals are used. The latter, particularly wheat meal and bran, are often used as a binder or roughage material. In addition, various levels of brewer's or torula yeasts are added to fresh diets to ensure a good content of water-soluble vitamins and to supplement the vegetable proteins. An example of a mixed traditional diet is the one referred to by Phillips *et al.* (1956) and is composed of 50% fresh feed and about 50% dry meal. The percentage of different feed ingredients may vary considerably according to the availability and quality of meals used. The addition of dry feeds to wet feeds produces an increase in nutritional value for hatchery use. Furthermore, the added meals absorb fluids which otherwise would be lost when the diet is dispersed in the water to feed the fish. Generally, such diets are made when the fresh diet ingredients are first ground or minced and mixed together. Thus, it is possible to obtain wet pellets by means of extruders of different size and, in some instances, these mixed diets are fed without cutting or pelleting. Today, one of these mixed diets is widely used in salmon culture. The Oregon "moist pellet" was developed in the state of Oregon and is composed of frozen, wet pellets made from 50% animal and vegetable dry meals and 50% fresh wet feeds with a supplementary supply of vitamins and other compounds. These pellets were tested in many Oregon and Washington hatcheries and are suitable for rearing trout and Pacific salmon. Oregon pellets were prepared on an industrial scale and are available on the United States market. This pellet is essentially a mixed diet but with several advantages as compared to the traditional mixed diet. The Oregon pellets, being industrially manufactured, are subject to close quality control and are more regularly purchased, more easily stored, and are more easily fed than the meal–wet feed diets prepared by the traditional method. Since several of the ingredients in the Oregon "moist pellet" are pasteurized, several diseases transmitted through wet fish viscera present in wet or mixed diet have been eliminated and a high conversion and low incidence of several diseases have been observed in fish reared on these rations (Hublou *et al.*, 1959; Sinnhuber *et al.*, 1961; Law *et al.*, 1961; McKee *et al.*, 1963; Hublou, 1963).

### 3. *Modern Dry Diets*

Pellet feeds for fish are based on formulations of dry concentrates. Dry pelleted diets for trout were prepared several years ago (Brockway, 1953), but best growth results were obtained when these were alternated with fresh feeds. Only recently, good sustaining dry feeds have appeared on the market. Today, one can grow trout, starting from the swim-up stage, exclusively on dry feed. Therefore, a large business is involved and almost all feed manufacturers in the world are preparing fish feeds in addition to the broad range of different animal feeds manufactured. The Eastern Fish Nutrition Laboratory, Cortland, New York, has been a leader in dry trout diet operations for the past 20 years. As a result of the work there, and at the Western Fish Nutrition Laboratory, Cook, Washington, the basic fundamental nutritional requirements of salmon have been investigated, and private firms have been able to manufacture and place on the market better fish feed.

Adaption of modern dry feeding methods varied greatly in fish culture in different countries. It is very likely that it was dependent upon the different degrees of availability of fresh products suitable for fish diets. This can be exemplified in Denmark where large amounts of fresh fish are available and still more dry diets are being employed for feeding of young fish. Fresh feed materials are added as these materials are available for finishing trout before marketing.

Detailed formulas for commercial pellets are often patented and are consequently not available, but the components are usually reported on the label accompanying the pellets. Several open formulas are listed in the appendix, but of the patented diets, dry meals of animal or vegetable origin are chiefly used. Fish meal, meat meal, blood meal, liver meal, soybean meal, peanut meal, cottonseed meal, wheat meal, kelp meal, distiller's solubles, brewer's yeast, torula yeast, salts, vitamin complex, antioxidants, binder, fish oil, or feeding oil is one example of a dry pellet mixture reported by Phillips *et al.* (1964): bone meal, 5.0%; fish meal, 24.0%; dried skim milk, 3.5%; cottonseed meal, 5.0%; wheat middlings, 7.0%; brewer's yeast, 10.0%; cellulose flour, 20.0%; vitamin mixture, 1.5%; A-D feeding oil, 3.0%. A comparison of the formulas listed in the appendix shows that the components of these dry diets may vary widely. Generally speaking, dry trout diets must be high in animal protein because this ensures a good level of essential amino acids and promotes the greatest growth response in fish in the water temperature used.

No particular problems are recorded concerning manufacturing techniques of dry diet in pelleted form suitable for large-scale fish feeding. Pellets are easily manufactured through normal extruders of different size, routinely employed in milling techniques for various animals. One technique used in Japan to increase food value and to minimize oxidation of fish oil is to add the oil after the pellet is formed and then tumble the pellets in a mixer. Certain trout pellets are slow in sinking and may be extruded with a small amount of steam in the die to gelatinize the starch and make a floating pellet. In contrast, dry feeds for small fish designated as starter feeds or crumble feeds must be carefully manufactured to obtain small uniformly sized particles and to avoid content of fine or dusty material which would be lost in the water. This preparation is rather difficult and has been developed industrially by several companies using their own techniques. As a consequence, a dry concentrate in fish feeding must be practically tested for the different starter sizes for the fish to be raised in the water temperature to be used. Conversion factors can be misleading for dry diets since these appear higher than those obtained with other feeding methods. One needs to compare the actual conversion factor of the dry ingredients in the diet rather than measure the conversion of the diet as fed since the amount of water in the ration varies from feed to feed. Today, the competition between various private companies is no longer based on the fact that the concentrates are complete, but is based on the higher conversion factor obtained when specific rations are used with different size trout or salmon under different feeding techniques in troughs, tanks, or ponds. Generally, the values tabulated by feed manufacturers are optimistic and cannot be realized in normal fish husbandry practice. Therefore, conversion factors in commercial dry diets are only indicative and range from 1.3–2.5 kg of diet/kilogram of wet trout reared.

Advantages from the use of dry pellets in trout feeding are evident when one considers the availability of different types and sizes, the reliability, the simplicity of feeding, and the ease of storage. Moreover, the use of dry diets has also allowed introduction of automatic feeding equipment and in western developed countries, the cost of labor often determines the degree of profit realized from the business.

Brood stock feeding requires the most careful selection of an adequate diet because the health of fish must be maintained and, in addition, adequate viable spawn must be produced to maintain the industry. Therefore, the use of dry concentrates is often supplemented with wet diet to assure adequate vitamin and other growth-promoting factors which may not be present or be lost in manufacture or storage of dry concentrates. Nevertheless, several studies have shown that certain lots of dry diets can be used to give viable eggs and additional knowledge on this subject is rapidly developing to assure the fish husbandman that adequate food will be available to maintain the brood stock with a great deal of reliability for maximum egg production when brood stock pellet feeds are used.

## C. Food Supply and Storage

Different types of fish diets require different arrangements for supply and storage. Fresh diets are rarely delivered to hatcheries in a regular routine manner. Fresh fish for diet manufacture are delivered directly to the hatcheries in only a few countries and delivery is generally restricted to areas not far from lakes or the sea. In many areas of Europe, iced or frozen fish are sent to central sites and from there are delivered from the distribution center to individual hatcheries in a particular area of the country. Refrigeration trucks are often used and for long-distance shipments, the product is generally frozen prior to transport and is not thawed until after delivery to the individual hatchery for incorporation into the diet. Slaughter house by-products are also sent fresh, refrigerated, or frozen to hatcheries. All these fresh materials require expensive refrigeration rooms to maintain the ingredients at subzero temperatures for even short-term storage. Most of the freezer rooms are divided into two compartments, one for sharp freezing and one for holding at subzero temperatures. Main-

FIG. 2. Silos for pellet storage at Snake River Trout Co., Hagerman, Idaho.

tenance and operation of the freezer is expensive but necessary for good preservation of fresh products to ensure adequate content of unoxidized fat and active vitamins in the ingredients when mixed into feed. These products are often only seasonally available and, therefore, often must be stored for periods up to 6 months for future needs. A typical example is the use of cod ovaries in Europe which are only available in early spring and which are used in many hatcheries to start fish feeding as a fry feed (Tack, 1963).

Generally speaking, good fresh products suitable for feeding are becoming less available. The shortage of fresh beef liver is a typical example. This material was used extensively as a fry feed and as an ingredient in other wet diets, but as numbers and size of trout hatcheries increased and competition for this product with other animal husbandry endeavors like mink feeding increased, less beef liver became available for fish hatchery diets.

Modern dry diets are industrially prepared and supplied periodically to distribution centers and to individual hatcheries. This material is packed in bags or delivered in bulk. Special trucks are required for transportation and farm storage bins, silos, and metal buildings have been adapted to hold this material until used. Storage of dry trout diets is therefore convenient and the material need only be protected from damp, warm conditions which promote mold growth and fat oxidation. Generally, fresh periodical delivery is advisable and material should not be stored more than 1 month to prevent loss of labile nutrients, such as vitamins, and to prevent rancidity of those compounds which might be oxidized. Large commercial hatchery silos are now employed for storage of pellets (Fig. 2) and some of these are equipped with conveyers or worm screws to move feed from area to area conveniently. Large silos must be equipped with collectors for dust which unavoidably accumulates from repeated storage of pellets. These dusty meals may be repelleted or fed mixed with fresh products for the fish. Pellets sold in bulk are slightly cheaper than those purchased in bags because of the cost savings in transportation and in material used. Some big commercial hatcheries are equipped for pellet manufacture at one central site and several others have rollers, crushers, and screens to prepare crumbles and specific pellet sized for different sized fish held in their impoundments.

### D. PRACTICAL FEEDING METHODS FOR TROUT AND SALMON HATCHERIES

Feeding trout and salmon must be accomplished with minimum waste and the least amount of labor. These postulates are satisfied in various degrees depending upon several factors such as type of diet, size of fish, water temperature, type of pond, design of hatchery, and equipment available. Each fish must have a daily ration of food to prevent irregular growth. Therefore, to avoid repeated grading of fish for size to promote rapid growth, it is necessary to feed fish carefully and accurately.

### 1. Hand Feeding

The oldest method of fish feeding is to spread the diet on the water with a spoon or hand ladle (Fig. 3). An experienced hatchery man can calculate the degree of hunger and satiety of fish by their actions during this process. Fish will feed avidly at the start and will tend to accumulate in the area in which food is offered. Soon the active feeding process subsides as the

FIG. 3. Trout hand feeding at Morgex, Aosta, Italy.

fish become satisfied and it is at this time that the hatcheryman must be careful not to overfeed and waste food, as well as pollute the water. He must take into account feeding charts for the particular type of diet used and estimate the approximate amount of food to be fed each feeding period. Practical examination of trout behavior during the feeding process is an art and is fraught with inaccuracies leading to inefficiency in fish husbandry. Hand feeding takes much time and therefore generally is employed only during start of the feeding process or on small trout farms where labor is not a major consideration.

### 2. *Semiautomatic Feeding*

A modified hand feeding method can be developed using mechanical feeders operated by a single worker. This type of equipment generally consists of food containers drawn by mechanical equipment and moving along or beside the raceway or pond. These devices spread food on and over the water. Some are equipped to broadcast wet diets (Fig. 4), and many types have been developed to spread or blow dry pelleted diets across great areas of the water surface (Fig. 5). Such methods are frequently employed in many commercial hatcheries. A single worker can feed many trout in a short time period moving along or between raceways. To operate with these devices a space of 3–4 m should be reserved between each pair of raceways (Fig. 6) to allow easy passage of mechanical equipment. Semiautomatic feeding must be planned by an experienced staff because it is important to feed fish according to body weight and water temperature or,

FIG. 4.  Semiautomatic trout feeding with a wet diet dispenser at Canizzano, Treviso, Italy.

Fig. 5. Semiautomatic trout feeding with a pellet blower at Snake River Trout Co., Hagerman, Idaho.

in other words, follow closely the feeding charts for best efficiency. Mechanical devices frequently have a tendency to overfeed and "feed the ponds rather than the fish" (Leitritz, 1962). Several inconvenient processes are involved in the use of this equipment although many trout farms use these devices to save labor and will waste some food to promote rapid growth in the stocks of fish (Fig. 7).

### 3. Automatic Feeding

Automatic feeding techniques in trout husbandry have been continuously studied and tested for many years. The advent of modern dry feeds has allowed development of numerous types of automatic feeders which are now available on the markets throughout the world. Automatic feeding has many practical advantages as the technique saves labor costs, gives better feed distribution, promotes rapid and regular growth of fish, providing that the diet is adequately balanced. Motionless automatic feeders are individually arranged at the head of raceways or along large circular trout tanks, (Figs. 8–10). Movable equipment usually is confined to rails between tanks or over rows of smaller tanks (Figs. 11 and 12). Some automatic feeders are operated by water flow (Gaver, 1964) (Fig. 13 and 14) but most are electrically powered. Many have rotating action dispensers and some are powered with compressed air (Fig. 15). The newest automatic feeders are equipped with devices which regulate feeding time and weight of food dispensed. These vary from very simple devices to highly elaborate start–stop operating systems operated from a central console (Carlin,

Fig. 6.   Spaces among trout raceways for passage of mechanical equipment at Cerano Novara, Italy.

1966). Some of the latest are equipped with photoelectric cells to activate and stop the feeding cycle. Regardless of what type of feed is used, fry and fingerling feeding is different from growing and adult fish feeding. Young salmonid should be frequently fed at least eight to ten times daily (Phillips, 1956). Frequent feeding prevents irregular growth and cannibalism and promotes the most rapid growth of the population.

Some hatcheries which do not have modern, automatic feeding devices attempt to feed fish by placing wet diets and finally ground materials on submerged screens or boards so fish in the container can feed continuously on demand. Most of these techniques have been abandoned and have changed to the use of finely powdered fry and fingerling feeds on the surface of the water, except in eel culture where use of starting wet diets and mash type diets are still used on submerged screens. Most modern fish hatcheries have adopted automatic feeding techniques and as new and better devices become available and better control of amount of food and frequency and duration of feeding become possible, more labor saving devices more efficient for sparing diets promoting growth, and minimizing water pollution will be adopted.

### 4. *Feeding Charts*

Fish should be fed according to body weight and water temperature. The amount of food can be calculated following the feeding chart originally developed by Deuel *et al.* (1952) prepared as a guide for feeding wet diets to trout. These data have been later modified for dry diets. The amount

Fig. 7.   Trout feeding with dry pellets delivered by mechanical equipment.

Fig. 8.   Motionless automatic pellet feeder in large round tanks at Bergeforsens, Sweden.

Fig. 9.  Motionless automatic pellet dispenser in trout raceway at Bellefonte, Pennsylvania.

suggested for dry diets should be about 40% of that used for wet diets (Phillips, 1956). Feeding charts were calculated according to the formula

$$\frac{\text{Average daily food fed}}{\text{Average weight of fish on hand}} \times 100$$

where average daily food fed = total weight food fed/number of days in month and the average weight of fish on hand = (weight at end + weight at start)/2.

The data tabulated in Table IV are for wet and dry feeding of rainbow trout. For feeding other trout species, amounts are slightly different. A review of the chart will show that for a given fish size the amount to feed increases with water temperature and for given water temperature, the amount decreases with increasing fish size. The feeding charts have been advantageous in promoting better diet utilization, optimum fish growth, and avoiding under- and overfeeding. Before the trout charts can be used, the weight of the trout in the ponds must be established. This can be done by obtaining a representative random sample of fish in the pond by count-ing the total population or estimating the number of fish in the pond and taking two or three representative samples from the pond or raceway. It is also possible to estimate fish size from trout length providing a standard condition factor is present, but inaccuracies soon occur when fish are ex-ceptionally fat or are lean or when different types of subspecies of fish

TABLE IV

RECOMMENDED AMOUNT OF FOOD TO FEED RAINBOW TROUT PER DAY[a,b]

| Water temperature (in °F) | No. Fish per pound | | | | | | | | | | | | | | | | | | | | | |
|---|---|---|---|---|---|---|---|---|---|---|---|---|---|---|---|---|---|---|---|---|---|---|
| | —2542 (—1)[c] | | 2542–304 (1–2) | | 304–88.3 (2–3) | | 88.3–37.8 (3–4) | | 37.8–19.7 (4–5) | | 19.7–11.6 (5–6) | | 11.6–7.35 (6–7) | | 7.35–4.94 (7–8) | | 4.94–3.47 (8–9) | | 3.47–2.53 (9–10) | | 2.53– (10–) | |
| | wet | dry | wet | dry | wet | dry | wet | dry | wet | dry | wet | dry | wet | dry | wet | dry | wet | dry | wet | dry | wet | dry |
| 36 | 5.3 | 2.7 | 4.4 | 2.2 | 3.5 | 1.7 | 2.6 | 1.3 | 2.0 | 1.0 | 1.6 | 0.8 | 1.3 | 0.7 | 1.1 | 0.6 | 1.0 | 0.5 | 0.9 | 0.5 | 0.8 | 0.4 |
| 37 | 5.5 | 2.7 | 4.6 | 2.3 | 3.7 | 1.8 | 2.8 | 1.4 | 2.1 | 1.1 | 1.7 | 0.9 | 1.4 | 0.7 | 1.2 | 0.6 | 1.0 | 0.5 | 0.9 | 0.5 | 0.8 | 0.4 |
| 38 | 5.8 | 2.9 | 4.8 | 2.4 | 3.9 | 2.0 | 2.9 | 1.5 | 2.2 | 1.2 | 1.7 | 0.9 | 1.4 | 0.8 | 1.2 | 0.7 | 1.1 | 0.6 | 1.0 | 0.5 | 0.9 | 0.5 |
| 39 | 6.0 | 3.0 | 5.0 | 2.5 | 4.0 | 2.2 | 3.0 | 1.7 | 2.3 | 1.3 | 1.8 | 0.9 | 1.5 | 0.8 | 1.3 | 0.7 | 1.1 | 0.6 | 1.0 | 0.6 | 0.9 | 0.5 |
| 40 | 6.3 | 3.2 | 5.2 | 2.6 | 4.2 | 2.2 | 3.1 | 1.7 | 2.4 | 1.3 | 1.9 | 1.0 | 1.6 | 0.9 | 1.4 | 0.8 | 1.2 | 0.7 | 1.0 | 0.6 | 1.0 | 0.5 |
| 41 | 6.6 | 3.3 | 5.5 | 2.8 | 4.4 | 2.2 | 3.3 | 1.8 | 2.5 | 1.4 | 2.0 | 1.1 | 1.7 | 0.9 | 1.4 | 0.8 | 1.2 | 0.7 | 1.1 | 0.6 | 1.0 | 0.5 |
| 42 | 6.9 | 3.5 | 5.7 | 2.8 | 4.6 | 2.4 | 3.5 | 1.8 | 2.6 | 1.4 | 2.1 | 1.2 | 1.7 | 0.9 | 1.5 | 0.8 | 1.3 | 0.7 | 1.1 | 0.6 | 1.0 | 0.5 |
| 43 | 7.2 | 3.6 | 6.0 | 3.0 | 4.8 | 2.5 | 3.6 | 1.9 | 2.7 | 1.4 | 2.2 | 1.2 | 1.8 | 1.0 | 1.5 | 0.9 | 1.4 | 0.8 | 1.2 | 0.7 | 1.1 | 0.6 |
| 44 | 7.5 | 3.8 | 6.2 | 3.1 | 5.0 | 2.5 | 3.8 | 2.0 | 2.8 | 1.5 | 2.3 | 1.3 | 1.9 | 1.0 | 1.6 | 0.9 | 1.4 | 0.8 | 1.3 | 0.8 | 1.1 | 0.6 |
| 45 | 7.9 | 4.0 | 6.5 | 3.3 | 5.3 | 2.7 | 4.0 | 2.1 | 3.0 | 1.6 | 2.4 | 1.3 | 2.0 | 1.1 | 1.7 | 1.0 | 1.5 | 0.9 | 1.3 | 0.8 | 1.2 | 0.7 |
| 46 | 8.2 | 4.1 | 6.7 | 3.4 | 5.5 | 2.8 | 4.1 | 2.2 | 3.1 | 1.7 | 2.5 | 1.4 | 2.1 | 1.2 | 1.8 | 1.0 | 1.5 | 0.9 | 1.4 | 0.8 | 1.2 | 0.7 |
| 47 | 8.6 | 4.3 | 7.1 | 3.6 | 5.8 | 3.0 | 4.3 | 2.3 | 3.2 | 1.7 | 2.6 | 1.4 | 2.2 | 1.2 | 1.8 | 1.0 | 1.6 | 0.9 | 1.4 | 0.8 | 1.3 | 0.7 |
| 48 | 9.0 | 4.5 | 7.5 | 3.8 | 6.0 | 3.0 | 4.5 | 2.4 | 3.4 | 1.8 | 2.7 | 1.5 | 2.3 | 1.3 | 1.9 | 1.1 | 1.7 | 1.0 | 1.5 | 0.9 | 1.3 | 0.8 |
| 49 | 9.4 | 4.7 | 7.8 | 3.9 | 6.3 | 3.2 | 4.7 | 2.5 | 3.5 | 1.9 | 2.8 | 1.5 | 2.4 | 1.3 | 2.0 | 1.1 | 1.8 | 1.0 | 1.5 | 0.9 | 1.4 | 0.8 |
| 50 | 9.9 | 5.2 | 8.1 | 4.3 | 6.5 | 3.4 | 4.9 | 2.7 | 3.7 | 2.0 | 2.9 | 1.7 | 2.5 | 1.4 | 2.1 | 1.2 | 1.9 | 1.1 | 1.6 | 1.0 | 1.5 | 0.9 |
| 51 | 10.3 | 5.4 | 8.5 | 4.5 | 6.8 | 3.5 | 5.1 | 2.8 | 3.8 | 2.1 | 3.1 | 1.7 | 2.6 | 1.5 | 2.2 | 1.3 | 1.9 | 1.1 | 1.7 | 1.0 | 1.5 | 0.9 |
| 52 | 10.7 | 5.4 | 8.9 | 4.5 | 7.1 | 3.6 | 5.3 | 2.8 | 4.0 | 2.1 | 3.2 | 1.7 | 2.7 | 1.5 | 2.3 | 1.3 | 2.0 | 1.1 | 1.8 | 1.0 | 1.6 | 0.9 |
| 53 | 11.2 | 5.6 | 9.3 | 4.7 | 7.5 | 3.8 | 5.6 | 2.9 | 4.2 | 2.2 | 3.4 | 1.8 | 2.8 | 1.5 | 2.4 | 1.3 | 2.1 | 1.1 | 1.9 | 1.1 | 1.7 | 1.0 |
| 54 | 11.6 | 5.8 | 9.7 | 4.9 | 7.8 | 3.9 | 5.8 | 3.0 | 4.4 | 2.3 | 3.5 | 1.9 | 2.9 | 1.6 | 2.5 | 1.4 | 2.2 | 1.3 | 1.9 | 1.1 | 1.8 | 1.0 |

TABLE IV (Continued)

| Water temperature (in °F) | −2542 (−1)ᶜ | | 2542–304 (1–2) | | 304–88.3 (2–3) | | 88.3–37.8 (3–4) | | 37.8–19.7 (4–5) | | 19.7–11.6 (5–6) | | 11.6–7.35 (6–7) | | 7.35–4.94 (7–8) | | 4.94–3.47 (8–9) | | 3.47–2.53 (9–10) | | 2.53– (10–) | |
|---|---|---|---|---|---|---|---|---|---|---|---|---|---|---|---|---|---|---|---|---|---|---|
| | wet | dry | wet | dry | wet | dry | wet | dry | wet | dry | wet | dry | wet | dry | wet | dry | wet | dry | wet | dry | wet | dry |
| 55 | 12.2 | 6.1 | 10.1 | 5.1 | 8.2 | 4.2 | 6.1 | 3.2 | 4.6 | 2.4 | 3.7 | 2.0 | 3.0 | 1.6 | 2.6 | 1.4 | 2.3 | 1.3 | 2.0 | 1.1 | 1.8 | 1.0 |
| 56 | 12.7 | 6.3 | 10.5 | 5.3 | 8.5 | 4.3 | 6.4 | 3.3 | 4.8 | 2.5 | 3.8 | 2.0 | 3.2 | 1.7 | 2.7 | 1.5 | 2.4 | 1.3 | 2.1 | 1.2 | 1.9 | 1.0 |
| 57 | 13.4 | 6.7 | 11.0 | 5.5 | 8.9 | 4.5 | 6.7 | 3.5 | 5.0 | 2.6 | 4.0 | 2.1 | 3.3 | 1.8 | 2.8 | 1.5 | 2.5 | 1.4 | 2.2 | 1.2 | 2.0 | 1.1 |
| 58 | 14.0 | 7.0 | 11.5 | 5.8 | 9.3 | 4.8 | 6.9 | 3.6 | 5.2 | 2.7 | 4.2 | 2.2 | 3.5 | 1.9 | 3.0 | 1.6 | 2.6 | 1.4 | 2.3 | 1.3 | 2.1 | 1.2 |
| 59 | 14.5 | 7.3 | 12.0 | 6.0 | 9.7 | 5.0 | 7.2 | 3.7 | 5.4 | 2.8 | 4.4 | 2.3 | 3.6 | 1.9 | 3.1 | 1.7 | 2.7 | 1.5 | 2.4 | 1.3 | 2.2 | 1.2 |
| 60 | 15.1 | 7.5 | 12.6 | 6.3 | 10.1 | 5.1 | 7.6 | 3.9 | 5.7 | 3.0 | 4.6 | 2.4 | 3.8 | 2.0 | 3.2 | 1.7 | 2.8 | 1.5 | 2.5 | 1.4 | 2.3 | 1.3 |

ᵃ From Deuel et al., 1952, and Leitritz, 1962.
ᵇ Values in percentage of body weight.
ᶜ Numbers in parenthesis are approximate size in inches.

TABLE V

Relationship between Total Lengths of Trout and Number of Trout per Pound[a,b]

| Brown, Brook, | | Rainbow trout | | Lake trout | | | |
|---|---|---|---|---|---|---|---|
| Size in inches | Number to pound | Range minimum–maximum | | Range minimum–maximum | | Number to pound | Size in inches |
| 0.75 | 5670 | 4106 | –Up | 5870 | –Up | 8250 | 0.75 |
| 1.00 | 2542 | 1920 | –4105 | 2654 | –5869 | 3492 | 1.00 |
| 1.25 | 1298 | 1019 | –1919 | 1435 | –2653 | 1815 | 1.25 |
| 1.50 | 740 | 608 | –1018 | 851 | –1434 | 1054 | 1.50 |
| 1.75 | 477 | 390 | – 607 | 542 | – 850 | 648 | 1.75 |
| 2.00 | 304 | 264 | – 389 | 374 | – 541 | 435 | 2.00 |
| 2.25 | 225 | 189 | – 263 | 270 | – 373 | 313 | 2.25 |
| 2.50 | 153 | 138 | – 188 | 202 | – 269 | 277 | 2.50 |
| 2.75 | 123 | 105.6 | – 137 | 155 | – 201 | 177 | 2.75 |
| 3.00 | 88.3 | 80.7 | – 105.5 | 119 | – 154 | 133 | 3.00 |
| 3.25 | 73.2 | 64.5 | – 80.6 | 96.1 | – 118 | 105 | 3.25 |
| 3.50 | 55.9 | 51.9 | – 64.4 | 78.0 | – 96.0 | 87.2 | 3.50 |
| 3.75 | 48.0 | 42.9 | – 51.8 | 62.8 | – 77.9 | 68.8 | 3.75 |
| 4.00 | 37.8 | 35.3 | – 42.8 | 51.95– | 62.7 | 56.7 | 4.00 |
| 4.25 | 32.9 | 29.9 | – 35.2 | 43.85– | 51.94 | 47.2 | 4.25 |
| 4.50 | 26.8 | 25.1 | – 29.8 | 37.05– | 43.84 | 40.5 | 4.50 |
| 4.75 | 23.4 | 21.6 | – 25.0 | 31.30– | 37.04 | 33.6 | 4.75 |
| 5.00 | 19.7 | 18.5 | – 21.5 | 27.00– | 31.29 | 29.0 | 5.00 |
| 5.25 | 17.3 | 16.1 | – 18.4 | 23.60– | 26.99 | 25.0 | 5.25 |
| 5.50 | 14.9 | 14.1 | – 16.0 | 20.45– | 23.59 | 21.8 | 5.50 |
| 5.75 | 13.3 | 12.5 | – 14.0 | 18.05– | 20.44 | 19.1 | 5.75 |
| 6.00 | 11.6 | 10.9 | – 12.4 | 15.80– | 18.04 | 17.0 | 6.00 |
| 6.25 | 10.2 | 9.68– | 10.8 | 13.95– | 15.79 | 14.6 | 6.25 |
| 6.50 | 8.15 | 8.63– | 9.67 | 12.60– | 13.94 | 13.3 | 6.50 |
| 6.75 | 8.10 | 7.73– | 8.62 | 11.20– | 12.59 | 11.9 | 6.75 |
| 7.00 | 7.35 | 6.93– | 7.72 | 9.98– | 11.19 | 10.5 | 7.00 |
| 7.25 | 6.50 | 6.25– | 6.92 | 9.09– | 9.97 | 9.45 | 7.25 |
| 7.50 | 5.99 | 5.70– | 6.24 | 8.27– | 9.08 | 8.72 | 7.50 |
| 7.75 | 5.40 | 5.17– | 5.69 | 7.46– | 8.26 | 7.82 | 7.75 |
| 8.00 | 4.94 | 4.70– | 5.16 | 6.79– | 7.45 | 7.09 | 8.00 |
| 8.25 | 4.45 | 4.29– | 4.69 | 6.22– | 6.78 | 6.48 | 8.25 |
| 8.50 | 4.12 | 3.94– | 4.28 | 5.68– | 6.21 | 5.96 | 8.50 |
| 8.75 | 3.75 | 3.61– | 3.93 | 5.17– | 5.67 | 5.40 | 8.75 |
| 9.00 | 3.47 | 3.30– | 3.60 | 4.74– | 5.16 | 4.94 | 9.00 |

[a] The average length for a group of fish which vary considerable in size will be somewhat less than the size given in the table. (From Deuel *et al.*, 1952.)

F ig. 10.  Electrical pellet dispenser settled in trout raceways at Hagerman National
Fish Hatchery, Hagerman, Idaho.

are raised, such as when lake trout are raised versus rainbow trout in a
similar environment (Table V).

Sometimes the amount of food should be increased during specific
conditions in the hatchery (Phillips, 1956). Sometimes the amount fed
must be decreased because of specific water conditions, external weather,
or predicted growth for the market. Finishing trout must be fed according
to market demand; thus, use of feeding charts will allow the producer to
market fish on the projected date at the desired size for most efficient
market considerations. In European countries, trout are sold seasonally
and often are sold alive. In these circumstances, forcing or controlling fish
growth may be important. This is not a usual condition in countries where
trout production is determined by availability of eggs and where the marketing of the trout is generally in the frozen state.

### 5. *Bottom and Surface Feeding Characteristic of Fish*

Bottom and surface feeding characteristics of hatchery salmonids differ
according to the species. Rainbow trout are typical surface feeders; whereas,
brown trout are bottom feeders. Undoubtedly, the former is more domesticated than the latter. However, the feeding characteristics of the fish
determine the feeding techniques to be employed. This is especially important in young fish. Older fish can be taught to feed by either method
and feeding techniques then become less particular problems. Fish at
swim-up stage and small fingerlings must be carefully fed otherwise irregular growth occurs, cannibalism occurs, high mortality may result from

disease, and a spread in size of fish soon occurs. Traditional feeding methods employ diets spread on the water which float or sink to the bottom. Pacific salmon hatcheries attempt to use floating diets since the young swim-up fry feed best at or slightly below the surface of the water. Dry complete diets for fry and fingerlings have a high oil content and the small size of the particle used and the surface tension of the water will suspend them. Hence, this type is suitable for rainbow trout feeding. Starter meals and crumbles, if gently placed near the water surface and dropped only a few centimeters, will float for a considerable length of time. After a few minutes, however, these break surfaced tension and slowly sink to the bottom. Frequently, it is advisable to employ devices illustrated in Fig. 16 which place the feed gently upon the water surface. With the general food and population densities used, this food will be quickly and completely consumed in a short period of time and food waste will be almost completely absent. Dry diets if fed to bottom feeding trout, such as brown trout, should be projected onto the water to break the surface tension and are often put at the water intake of the tank, pond, or raceway where the turbulence promotes rapid sinking. Water should be kept shallow, not more than 20–30 cm in depth, and a definite current should be established to move the food which facilitates consumption by the fish swimming at or near the bottom. Some food manufacturers maintain that red pigment in fry feed for brown trout and Atlantic salmon fry will promote consumption even though most tests have shown that fish are color blind. Sometimes, water is added to dry meal mixtures to form a cohesive mass which

FIG. 11. Automatic dry feeder moving on rails between trout tanks at Älvkarleö, Sweden.

Fig. 12. Bergeforsens salmon–trout hatchery. In this plant, fish feeding is fully automatic, computed, and controlled from the feed storage building in the foreground.

will rapidly sink to the bottom of troughs or tanks. Brown trout in hatchery environment tend to become domesticated and learn to see feed at or near the surface as they grow older but rarely do they develop the surface feeding characteristics dominant in rainbow trout. Some commercial pellets are extruded, expanded, and float. These are used to avoid wastage of food and are employed mostly with rainbow trout and other surface feeding salmonids. This process gelatinizes some of the carbohydrate components present and often fish feed for long time periods on these expanded floating pellets, becoming fatter than fish fed on other dry diets. Probably, a compromise in pellet consistency would be most desirable if a particular ration is to be fed to both brown and rainbow trout and a slowly sinking diet would probably be adequate to feed both types of fish after they have been started on fry feed and have begun to grow.

E. Handwork and Hatchery Techniques for Different Feeding Methods

1. *Preparation*

Traditional wet diets require careful preparation. These must be ground or thoroughly minced and stored under refrigeration until needed. Meat and fish offal may be easily ground when frozen and common food grinders have been employed for years at many hatcheries. Dry meals are often added into the grinder because these promote some dehydration with resultant better grinding and mixing of the wet foods. These traditional diets must be promptly utilized because degradation of nutritional constituents begins immediately and continues until the diet is consumed by the fish. Many diets employ whole small fish, fresh or frozen, for brood stock and Atlantic salmon feeding. Fresh herring, which is often used, contains thiaminase which hydrolyzes vitamin $B_1$ (thiamine) and, therefore, should be fed alone and not ground into wet diets because of the thiamine destroying characteristics of this diet ingredient. Clam necks and

Fig. 13 (Top) and 14 (Bottom). Automatic pellet feeder operated by water flow at Älvkarleö, Sweden.

Fig. 15. Automatic compressed-air operated dry feeder for trout fingerlings in the Danish Experimental Trout Farm at Bröns, Denmark.

Fig. 16. A method of dry feeding of rainbow trout fingerlings with hand blower. Crumbles dispensed close to the water surface will float.

several freshwater fish also contain much thiaminase and these diet constituents must be employed carefully. If ground into the wet diet, the diet must be fed promptly to prevent development of the fatal thiamine deficiency syndrome in the fish population. To compensate for the thiaminase content, several Danish fish hatcheries add a solution of synthetic vitamin $B_1$ mixed into the fish offal during the grinding process. A standard solution containing 1200 $\mu$g thiamine hydrochloride per milliliter is used at 2% of total food content (Rasmussen, 1966).

Workers involved in wet food preparation must employ protective techniques against human pathogen contact during the handling of meat scraps and fish offal. In certain countries, Germany, for example, slaughter house by-products must be cooked before utilized. Other countries, as for example, Italy, market disease condemned foods in the raw stage. Infection in hatchery workers may occur from common pathogens (*Erysipelothrix rhusiopathiae, Mycobacterium, Brucella*, etc.). Fish hatcherymen are also threatened by a variety of irritants which may cause several types of skin lesions. This subject was carefully discussed by Halstead (1962), and involves several dermatological disorders (wounds, secondary infections, strings, "red feed," and scombroid-dermatitis, skin cancer, allergy).

No problems have been recorded in preparation or use of modern dry pelleted diets in fish hatcheries which have been manufactured following standard industrial milling techniques.

## 2. Pond Cleaning

It is hardly necessary to point out that raceways and rearing ponds should be kept in good sanitary condition. Various methods of cleaning are suitable (Davis, 1961). Hatchery waters are generally polluted due to the presence of fish excrement and surplus food, both increasing oxygen demand. The nature of the diet often determines the extent of water pollution. Wet diets generally have a tendency to cause more pollution than dry diets. Meat and fish scraps, especially if not properly bound, lose soluble proteins in the water with an increase in organic water pollution, increased oxygen demand, reduced oxygen content, and increased disease and mortality in the population. Close examination of trout in a hatchery will show if the fish are fed meat scraps, because fish feces will show undigested connective tissue and fish which are swimming will have flags of stringy feces extruded from the vent. Feces tend to accumulate in ponds with poor circulation and release noxious compounds, clog the screen, and increase the labor for proper sanitation in the trout hatchery. Feeding trout with fish offal reduces these residues in the feces because offal is more completely digested. When fat sea fishes such as sardines and anchovy, are fed, an unpleasant film of fat and white foam will appear on the water surface.

Small lakes or settlement ponds can be prepared at the end of water flow from trout ponds to allow organic matter suspended in the water to settle or precipitate. Aerobic oxidation of these final settlement ponds will increase water sanitation and settled material can be removed to be used as fertilizer for nitrogen-deficient waters or soils.

## F. WATER QUALITY EFFECTS

### 1. *Temperature*

Fish are poikilothermic and water temperature plays a tremendous role in trout feeding. Feeding charts are regulated by water temperatures and temperature can condition fish digestion, growth, and general physiology and metabolism. As water temperature increases, fish metabolism increases up to a maximum tolerated temperature. Cold waters are not suitable for rapid, efficient fish growth. When water temperature used has a fluctuating temperature, which includes a low temperature in winter, it may take 2–2.5 years to produce table size trout. Constant temperature water, 13°–15°C, will produce trout to market weight within 1 year. Obviously, when the mean water temperature is lower, production costs are higher. Also, fish in warmer water demand a high maintenance food ratio. Trout in warm water become rapidly emaciated when starved and such phenomenon frequently appear when trout suffer an oxygen deficiency, when the population density is too great for the oxygen content of the water, or when fish are held in warm waters for several weeks to meet a particular demand. Experimental data need to be developed on differences in conversion rate of food between fish growing in warm and cold water.

### 2. *Salinity*

Salmon are euryhaline fish and can tolerate levels of water salinity. Like salmon, several trout migrate between sea- and freshwater and a percentage of the wild trout in a coastal stream still migrate between freshwater, brackish water, and the sea environment. These migrations are determined by fish size, water temperature, sea temperature, and salinity. Schäperclaus (1961) describes how trout can live and be reared in brackish waters. Experiments show that trout in seawater grow faster than those reared in freshwater (Canaga and Ratnam, 1959). Seawater trout culture is common in several countries in northern Europe and in the Orient. Norway, Sweden, Denmark and Japan all have estuary waters suitable for trout where the

FIG. 17. Floating bags of mesh nylon netting for seawater trout culture at Dalarö, Sweden. Note automatic dry feed dispensers over each bag.

temperature is not too high, an adequate amount of dissolved oxygen is present, and the salinity is not excessive.

Feeding methods used in these circumstances are very similar to those used in freshwater trout culture. Trout production in seawater in Norway was 500 tons in 1965 and the main food used was a wet diet composed of fish offal and shrimp waste. Food was offered in several places in huge ponds and rainbow trout reared learned promptly where and when to get food. The conversion rate with this diet was similar to the one used in freshwater and ranged from 1:5–1:6 (Jensen, 1966). In Sweden, dry pellets have been used to grow yearling rainbow trout confined in nylon bags floating in seawater (Fig. 17). The pellets were dispensed automatically and the conversion factor was about the same as those raised in freshwater (1:1.4). These rainbow trout were raised in the Baltic Sea where the salinity was less than that encountered in coastal areas bordering the major oceans.

Some years ago, saltwater trout culture was also started in Denmark using the same feeding methods as those used in freshwater trout culture. In Japan, rainbow trout are extensively raised in huge sea areas and are fed several types of diets with greater use of dry pellets as feeding devices become more automated. In at least one area, the pellets are automatically delivered by a dispenser at the same time an ultrasonic impulse is sounded under water to attract the trout to the area for feeding (Vouga, 1966).

Foods employed in saltwater trout culture are often supplemented with crustacean waste to produce fish with a bright salmon-colored flesh in many wild trout or salmon encountered in the same area.

The mineral content in freshwater may influence fish growth and food utilization. It is well known that fish sequester certain minerals through the gills and therefore a different growth rate and food conversion may exist in trout reared in waters with different mineral contents. Calcium in water has been reported to regulate trout metabolism (Phillips *et al.*, 1957a), and this mineral may be sequestered through the gills to maintain calcium reserves for the fish.

### 3. *Feeding and Production Costs*

Feeding techniques can directly influence production costs in trout farming. It is possible to calculate the price of a kilogram of trout based upon the conversion rate of diet employed. This value is influenced by other important variables—labor, growing time, capital, assets, mechanical equipment, disease treatment, storage costs, and market demand may be more important than the calculated major expenditure of the cost of the food to raise the fish.

Prices of modern dry complete diets are standardized throughout the whole world because the main components are purchased from only a few sources. Fish meal is a typical example. Peruvian fish meal determines price and availability of this ingredient on the world market. Wet diets, especially fresh fish offal, have different seasonal prices according to availability and transport distances in various countries. Labor costs also vary greatly from country to country and can be a major factor in production costs of the food ingredients or in the actual hatchery labor.

Rehbronn (1966) and Rasmussen (1966) have shown that use of dry pellet diets to feed trout will increase production costs because of the availability of the traditional wet diets. However, even here one must calculate important additional costs such as investing for food refrigeration and storage, food preparation equipment, pond cleaning, fish grading, water pollution, and sanitary appearance of the area, all of which are higher when these traditional fresh diets are employed. The adaption of modern dry feeds for feeding trout consistently allows higher trout production with less labor and lower food costs since traditional wet diet ingredients become less available and more expensive. Soon all efficient trout hatcheries in the world will be employing the majority of their food as complete dry feeds.

### G. ORGANOLEPTIC CHARACTERISTICS FROM FEEDING

Trout are very nutritive human food. The consumed fraction represents 66–78.2% of the body weight (Rohler-Metzner, 1932; Corti, 1949) with wet fat 4.2–6.8% in hatchery rainbow trout (Rohler-Metzner, 1932; Morawa, 1956) and about 2% in wild brown trout. Chemical comparisons of hatchery and wild brook trout showed that wild trout contained less water, more protein, more ash, and less fat than hatchery trout (Phillips *et al.*, 1957b). Similar data were not confirmed in wild and hatchery rainbow trout by Weiser and Otte (1964) where no significant differences in chemical composition of trout fed dry pellets and wild trout were found. Undoubtedly, the nature of diet used can greatly influence the organoleptic characteristics of the trout flesh. Trout fed dry complete diet has a flesh of firm consistency and of acceptable taste. The meat of trout fed the traditional wet diet is less consistent, higher in fat, and is softer. Often a disagreeable "hatchery taste" is present. Fresh sea fish are frequently responsible for the disagreeable strong taste in trout which is usually referred to as "sardine" taste by the industry. "Hatchery taste" can be furtherly determined by several other negative factors such as organic pollution in the water, poor water exchange, algae growth in ponds, and presence of other pollutants.

Particular mention should be made of "salmon color" of trout flesh, especially for the European market. It is well known that the typical red salmon color in trout is determined by assimilation of diet containing carotinoids which can be converted to astaxanthin-like compounds. This compound is present in most crustaceans. Waste from prawn, shrimp, and crustacea are currently employed to color trout during the finishing process. Salmon color is easily produced in large sized female trout, with undeveloped gonads, and in fat trout but is difficult to obtain in sexually mature trout and very lean and very young trout. Attempts have been made to reproduce the salmon color in trout fed dry complete diet by including carotinoids in the pellets. Few results have been obtained commercially by using carotinoids other than astaxanthin. Trout fed diets containing 2% of paprika with 400 mg of capsanthin/kg for several months, showed bright colored skin, red colored eggs, and pale orange flesh (Phillips *et al.*, 1946, 1947; Buss, 1958; Bitzer, 1963). Carotinoids used in poultry feeding to color chicken skin and egg yolk have also been employed in trout pellets. Deufel (1965) obtained a salmonlike color in rainbows fed pellets containing canthaxanthin at the rate of 40 mg/kg of pellet. Nevertheless, the salmonlike color contained in trout flesh with the pigment disappears rapidly during the cooking process. Therefore, the problem of conferring an effective artificial pigmentation in trout which is stable to cooking by adding colored compounds to the dry pellet is still not resolved.

## H. TROUT DIETS AND LIVE FISH TRANSPORTATION

Live trout can be satisfactorily transported only if healthy and starved. Disorders derived from feeding are frequently responsible for trouble in

Fig. 18.   Fish transport truck with bottle oxygen tanks.

respiration in transport. Some types of anemia connected with liver changes as in liver lipoid degeneration, prohibit transporting live trout for any distance without heavy losses. Other obscure pathological conditions can also influence live trout handling (Phillips *et al.*, 1958). Trout with sub-clinical stages of thiamine deficiency have impaired vitality, particularly during fish grading and transferring operations (Rasmussen, 1966). It is advisable to check trout blood for erythrocytes and hemoglobin content, particularly before transportation. When the hemoglobin level is lower than 8–9 gm % (Snieszko, 1960), an increase in the vitamin B complex of the trout diet is advisable for several weeks before moving the live fish any distance.

Starvation of fish is desirable and may be absolutely necessary before long-distance shipments. Trout should not be fed for at least 48 hours before transporting when previously actively feeding on wet or dry diets (Leitritz, 1962). It is well known that trout require more oxygen during digestion of food and more waste products are excreted in water during the stress of transport with resultant increased biological oxygen demand, excess ammonia production, and rapid toxicity and mortality in the transport container after a short time period. Today, many starved live fish are transported long distances to market using trucks and tanks equipped with bottled or liquid oxygen dispersing equipment (Fig. 18).

## I. Diet:Husbandry:Disease Relationships

Fish disease introduced by improper feeding techniques were a serious problem only a few years ago in many trout hatcheries. Careful research has disclosed several pathological conditions in trout which were introduced through the feed or by feeding.

Goiter in salmonids can regress and be prevented by adding iodine to the diet (Marine and Lenhart, 1910, 1911;Marine, 1914; Gaylord and Marsh, 1914). Unbalanced or spoiled fresh diets frequently affected the digestive tract of reared trout inducing gastroenteritis (Plehn, 1924; Schäperclaus, 1954). Liver lipoid degeneration occurred widely in trout fed fat sea fishes (Ghittino, 1961). Trout hepatoma seriously worried pathologists and the onset was connected with the presence of aflatoxin in the diet (Halver and Mitchell, 1967). Gill disease of young trout was recognized as induced by unbalanced or dusty feeds (Ghittino, 1967). Avitaminosis, hypervitaminosis, susceptibility to infection, and general malnutrition were carefully described by Halver (1953) and are reported in greater detail in Chapter 2 of this volume.

## III. Secondary Cold Water Fish Husbandry

Rearing cold water fish species to produce fry or fingerlings for stocking purposes may be considered a secondary type of cold water fish husbandry. Fish species such as grayling, cisco, hucho hucho, lake trout, pike, pink salmon, golden trout, and several other species are held in hatcheries only a short time after absorption of the yolk sac and little scientific data is available on artificial feeding. Therefore, only starting and natural feeds are normally employed. Only in a few instances are artificial diets used, and these mostly wet, traditional diets.

### A. GRAYLING

American grayling (*Thymallus signifer*) and European grayling (*T. thymallus*) are propagated, but only on a limited scale. Feeding swim-up grayling usually consists of natural living food like brine shrimp, tubifex, or plankton. Finely ground beef liver and beef heart is sometimes fed to grayling fry to supplement the natural food. These fish must be reared in temperature water because it is difficult to get the dry to feed in cold water (Davis, 1961).

European grayling are reared in ponds with a fast water flow and are fed natural liver diets composed of entomostracans and insect larvae (Svetina, 1956; Koch, 1960). Small fingerlings in the first month of feeding consumed 500–600 gm of live plankton a day for 15,000 fish. Later, the food was composed of crustaceans, fresh liver and spleen, minced gammarus, and dry meals (Vivier, 1958). In Bavaria, grayling are fed beef liver and trout dry diets in addition to natural feed. Fingerlings are sold when 9–12 cm long. The price determined by fish length is very high.

In Itally, minced freshwater fish flesh was occasionally employed in grayling feeding with varying degrees of success (Sommani, 1953).

Rearing grayling requires a highly specialized staff and access to lake or pond water in which plankton is produced and some catch-out fishing could be planned for better water use and to lower land and water costs.

## B. Cisco

Cisco (*Coregonus* sp.) have long been artificially propagated. Eggs are stripped from wild spawners and fertilized. The eggs are incubated in Zug jars and hatched fry are stocked in lakes after the yolk sac is absorbed. Cisco hatching may be delayed by using refrigerated water during the egg incubation period. The fry should be stocked in the lake when the temperature is not too cold or the fry will not eat and heavy losses will occur. At Bodensee (Germany) a hatchery is equipped with a water temperature control device which regulates the temperature in the incubation jars.

Cisco fry have been reared in concrete tanks (Fig. 19 and 20) to fingerling size a few centimeters long. These are fed exclusively on live plankton (entomostracans). This natural food can be caught in lakes with large plankton nets, or by pumping water from large lakes through a fine sieve. Sometimes fry are stocked in floating nets in lake water containing quantities of plankton (Schäperclaus, 1961; Huet, 1960; Koch, 1960).

Fig. 19.   Concrete circular pools for cisco fingerling rearing at Langenargen, Bodensee, West Germany.

Fig. 20. Circular pools for cisco fingerling rearing at Scharfling, Mondsee, Austria.

Fig. 21. Live "Moderlieschen" employed in feeding *Salmo hucho* in Bavaria, West Germany.

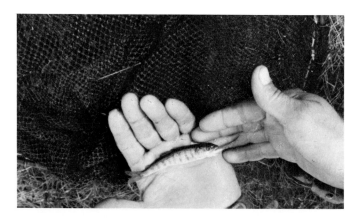

FIG. 22.  A *Salmo hucho* fingerling swallowing a "Moderliesche."

In one laboratory in the Soviet Union, Ropscha, *Brachionus moina*, were grown with *Chlorella* and the rotifers were used to feed cisco fry held in concrete tanks for 1 month (Schäperclaus, 1963).

### C. Hucho Hucho

*Salvelinus hucho hucho* is a well known salmonid fish which lives in some European rivers. This famous sport fish is very valuable and attempts have been made to propagate it artificially. Eggs and sperm from wild fish caught in the rivers and streams were incubated in trays and baskets as in standard trout culture. Fry are generally stocked in rivers after yolk sac absorption. Some are reared with great difficulty to 8–12 cm and planted as fingerlings (Koch, 1960). The feed used is generally a natural live food. At the start, fry are fed plankton until able to capture and swallow small live fish (Fig. 21 and 22). In one Bavarian hatchery, live "Moderlieschen" (*Leucaspius delineatus*) a small fish, was employed as the food for hucho hucho and the fish grew well.

### D. Ayu

Feeding ayu (*Plecoglossus altivelis*), a much appreciated salmonid fish in Japan, is now nearly completely based upon artificial feeding. The yearly production of ayu is about 1500 tons (Egusa, 1968). Earlier, feed for ayu consisted of mixed diets in paste form, but now special pellets suitable for this fish have been developed. During 1967 in Japan, 5100 tons of ayu pellets were produced (Nomura and Fuji, 1968).

## IV.  Warm Water Fish Husbandry

### A. DEFINITION

Warm water fishes are those which can tolerate high water temperatures (Doudoroff, 1957). Physiologically, these fish are also classified as eurythermal. Waters harboring trout and other members of the Salmonidae are commonly classified as thermally cold and waters intolerable to trout culture are arbitrarily classified as warm (Lagler *et al.*, 1962). Respiratory demands of the fish species is also related to the water temperature since the content of oxygen is inversely proportional to the temperature of the water.

Many warm water fish species are artificially cultivated in warm, fresh, brackish, or seawaters. The total production contributes tremendously to the world fish production. Usually such fishes are distinguished as principal or secondary cultivated species not only for the accumulative tonnage produced, but also for the knowledge of specific physiology and husbandry techniques used to support this cultivation. Thus common carp (*Cyprinus carpio*) is considered to be the principal warm water fish cultivated in the world. Carp culture is widespread throughout the world and total production of carp flesh is very high. Therefore, warm water pond fish culture is often identified with carp culture and other warm water fish culture is considered secondary but can still contribute large amounts of protein for the human population in various parts of the world. Recently, the advent of intensive catfish culture may displace carp culture as the most important warm water fish husbandry industry especially in certain parts of the world like the southern United States. This increase in warm water fish farming of channel catfish challenges, in tonnage at least, total weight of salmonids reared and nearly 100,000 acres of warm water fish ponds have been developed within the past 5 years to accommodate the explosive growth industry (Report to the fish farmers, 1970).

### B. NATURAL AND ARTIFICIAL FEEDING

Natural feed in ponds makes a substantial contribution to the food of warm water fish and much production is based upon increasing the natural feed concentration in the impoundment. Artificial feed is employed to a certain extent but not as much as in cold water fish culture and only in particular circumstances with certain fish species, size, age, water properties, and environmental factors. Scientific data on warm water fish nutrition are fragmentary although many studies are being performed by research groups in many countries of the world, at the present time, to define specific and general nutritional requirements for several of the warm water species reared. Effective artificial feeding of several warm water fishes is routine in several areas for carp, catfish, eel, yellowtail, milk fish, cultivated crustaceans, and tilapia. A review of history of warm water fish culture discloses several traditional methods for rearing carp and other species together with more modern methods for carp culture. Many of these methods depend upon the diets employed and artificial feeding of warm water fish is becoming more important each year as more knowledge is accumulated and more effective diets are formulated for these species in several environments.

## C. Carp Husbandry

Carp culture is the oldest type of fish culture as it was practiced in China thousands of years before Christ. Although it is the earliest and most traditional kind of fish farming, carp culture has gone through several periods of development. First, carp were kept for several years in ponds and only the largest fish were harvested. Later, during the 19th century, new rearing methods developed which involved separation of carp into various year classes and fish sizes. The more modern methods for production of table fish include holding carp in ponds which can be drained and managed, and also includes feeding and fattening carp in net cages floating in different lakes, streams, and ponds and feeding the confined fish with artificial feed.

Carp culture has recently become very important in many countries and contributes greatly to the total production of fish in the world market. Hickling (1962) estimated that 700,000 tons or 2% of the total world fish production was carp. Table VI reports data on carp production in several countries and points to the role that this type of fish culture represents in the supply of fresh protein for human consumption.

Common carp (*Cyprinus carpio*) is a typical warm water pond fish which requires little dissolved oxygen. It grows in waters at temperatures of 25°C or more and with oxygen content of 3–4 ppm (Schäperclaus, 1961). Latitude and altitude above sea level are important factors to consider in establishing carp culture, since water temperature in the summer must be at least 20°C to promote reasonable growth. Practically, growth of carp in ponds is dependent upon the length of the summer and the water temperature, because growth in winter is almost completely halted when water temperatures dip below 15°C. Therefore, carp pond culture is much more practical in countries where the summer is long and hot, but economical carp culture can still be found up to 60° north latitude in areas of Siberia.

Classical extensive carp pond culture in contrast to trout production

TABLE VI

CARP PRODUCTION IN SEVERAL COUNTRIES[a]

| Country | Year | Tons of carp produced | Surface in ha of carp farming | Kilogram of carp produced/ha | Observations | References |
|---|---|---|---|---|---|---|
| U.S.S.R. | 1957 | 113.000 | 440.000 | 375–2.000 | — | Steffens, 1958 |
| | — | 200.000 | 500.000 | 410 | — | Borgstrom, 1961 |
| | 1965 | 190.000 | — | 1.500 | — | Michler and Schäperclaus, 1963 |
| Poland | — | 1.500 | 70.000 | 400–2.000 | — | Mann, 1961 |
| | — | 11.000 | 70.000 | 100–600 | — | Kocylowski, 1963 |
| France | — | 9.000 | 110.000 | — | — | Solacroup, 1963 |
| Czechoslovakia | 1955 | — | 40–50.000 | 140–450 | — | Stroganov, 1959 |
| | 1959 | 5.500 | — | — | — | Tamura, 1961 |
| Hungary | 1953 | — | 52.000 | 170 | — | Schäperclaus, 1961 |
| Yugoslavia | — | 4.000 | 14.000 | — | — | Hickling, 1962 |
| | — | 4.000 | 7.500 | 350–1.700 | — | Mann, 1961 |
| | 1962 | 7.500 | 7.500 | — | — | Yashouv, 1966 |
| Germany | 1935 | 8.600 | 55.000 | — | — | Mann, 1961 |
| West Germany | 1957 | 1.500 | 14.300 | — | — | Mann, 1961 |
| East Germany | 1957 | 3.644 | 14.000 | — | — | Schäperclaus, 1961 |
| East Germany | 1963 | 3.669 | — | 434.6 | — | Menzel, 1967 |
| Israel | 1964 | 9.741 | — | 2.000–2.100 | — | Yashouv, 1966 |
| China | 1937 | 382.282 | 166.667 | — | Includes all fish culture | Shen, 1951 |
| | 1949 | 383.000 | 208.000 | — | Includes all fish culture | Lin, 1949 |
| | 1956 | 850.000 | — | — | Reared carp | Tamura, 1961 |

TABLE VI (Continued)

| Country | Year | Tons of carp produced | Surface in ha of carp farming | Kilogram of carp produced/ha | Observations | References |
|---------|------|------------------------|-------------------------------|------------------------------|--------------|------------|
| Japan | 1943 | 4.000 | — | 100–1.000 | Rice field carp farming | Hickling, 1962 |
| Thailand | 1957 | 10.100 | — | — | Seined carp | Tamura, 1961 |
| United States | 1955 | 16.500 | — | — | Seined carp | Tamura, 1961 |
| Mexico | 1964 | 9.000 | 12.650 | — | — | Miles, 1967 |

[a] From Ghittino, 1969.

Fig. 23.   Canal for water inlet to fill carp ponds during spring in a new Yugoslavian carp farm at Sumarija, Lipovljani.

requires a very large surface area but only a small replacement water supply (Fig. 23). The water supply must fill the pond and compensate only for losses induced by seepage into the earth and by evaporation into the atmosphere. Generally, a quantity of about 1 liter/sec/ha is suitable (Schäperclaus, 1933, 1961). The use of very large ponds is related to the feeding habit of carp (Fig. 24). This fish should have at its disposal a considerable amount of natural food like crustaceans, insect larvae, and worms (Fig. 25). According to Walter (1931), carp can neither digest nor economically utilize artificial food if the feed is not made up with at least 50% natural food. Classical carp culture, therefore, considers rearing fish in very large, shallow ponds and enhancing the biological fertility of the freshwater by fertilization. The physiology of digestion of this stomachless fish has been carefully studied. Schäperclaus (1961) reports a list of the various enzymes present in the carp digestive tract. According to his table, protein is digested by trypsin and erepsin, but not by pepsin, since the carp has no stomach; the lipids are hydrolyzed by lipase, the carbohydrates by amylase and maltase, and lichenase attacks fiberous carbohydrates. Yashouv (1956) reported that an experimental diet was improved by addition of a small amount of natural food consisting of insect larvae and crustaceans. He tested various vitamin supplements and concluded that vitamin B complex was also an important item in carp nutrition. Hickling (1962) emphasized the importance of this paper and suggested that in fish foods, as for other animals, vitamin $B_{12}$ was required. Jäncarik (1964) showed that various substances are digested in the intestinal tract of the carp through the action of endogenous and exogenous enzymes; the latter activated by the former. Starch was digested by enzymes present in the intestinal juices. In addition, crustaceans, worms, and insect larvae caused an amylolytic action. Therefore, better digestion of starch was observed in carp which had available a sufficient supply of natural food. Lipids were digested by enzymes present in the bile, pancreas, liver, and intestinal mucosa, but the addition of extracts of natural food enhanced the lipolytic activity of these enzymes. Proteins were digested like lipids, that is, split by endogenous enzymes activated by exogenous ones. Vegetable proteins (beans, peas, peanuts, soybeans, etc.) were better digested in the presence of crustaceans and worms, but the carp could readily digest animal protein in the feed. Jäncarik (1964) concluded that natural food present in the diet was able to improve the efficiency of food digestion and utilization.

The natural food of carp is very high in protein which is easily digested by the fish. About 50% of the dry weight of natural food was protein (Mann, 1961; Schäperclaus, 1962–1963). Traditional artificial feed for carp is composed of various grains. In Yugoslavia, for example, carp are fed only raw cereal grain. These products are high in carbohydrates and low in protein. When no artificial feed is available, part of the natural proteins are utilized as energy and the addition of supplementary feed composed of cereals, and hence, high in carbohydrates, increased the utilization of the natural proteins for growth instead of metabolism for energy and increases the fish yield in pond culture (Schäperclaus, 1963,

Fig. 24.   Very large ponds (350 ha each) in a carp farm in Yugoslavia.

Fig. 25.   Fertilizing pond in a Yugoslavian carp farm.

1964; Merla, 1963). The favorable effect of carbohydrates will continue as long as the amount of protein in the natural food is sufficient for fish growth (Schäperclaus, 1966).When the carp density in the pond is high, proteins may become growth limiting (Müller and Merla, 1964), and protein-rich supplementary feeds containing 28–30% crude protein will cause an increase in pond fish yield. In modern carp culture, the density of fish per unit pond area is high in comparison with traditional methods and hence more artificial feed is now employed (Hepher and Chervinski, 1965; Tal and Hepher, 1967).

Two kinds of carp culture exist in Japan (Lieder and Müller, 1965). The first type is similar to the methods traditionally employed in Europe and consists of rearing carp in large ponds (5 ha) in still water (Fig. 26). The second type is unusual in European countries, since carp are reared in deep ponds (2 m or more) with small surface areas (40 m²), and supplied with large amounts of running water (360 liter/sec). This latter method was introduced about 50 years ago by Tanaka (1929) (Fig. 27) who succeeded in rearing large quantities of carp in a very small pond by using substantial amounts of flowing water.(Kawamoto, 1957). One pond with a surface of 70 m² yielded 200 kg of carp/m² or 2000 ton/ha (Lieder and Müller, 1965) (Fig. 28). Both the Japanese methods, shallow and deep pond culture, use diets more complete than in traditional carp feeding (Tamura, 1961). These rations contain not only vegetable products like bran, oats, and wheat flour, but also animal products like silk worm pupae,

Fig. 26.   Carp rearing in a Japanese irrigating pond for rice fields.

fresh sardine, ox liver, powdered dry fish, and fish offal (Fig. 29, 30, and 31). Michler and Schäperclaus (1963) reported that high protein diets were employed in some Russian carp culture when carp were confined at high density in ponds.

Carp nutrition research in Israel is focused on finding supplements to the natural feed which apparently are insufficient at fish population densities used there for rapid growth in the warm water temperatures employed (Yashouv, 1965).

One other interesting type of carp culture involves confining the fish in floating net cages or in wooden cages in warm flowing streams (Hickling, 1962; Lieder and Müller, 1965; Kuronuma, 1968). Gribanov *et al.* (1968) reported that these new methods for carp rearing are one of the most important advances in fish culture in recent times. Fantastic fish densities were reported in Russian experiments with 100 kg of carp/m³ of water used in floating plastic bags. These carp were fed dry foods only and the water was warm, effluent from power stations at 23°–30°C.

### 1. *Natural Feeding of Carp*

Formerly, natural food for carp was believed to be composed of mud and water plants. Soon it was recognized, however, that the intestinal tract of this fish usually contained various amounts of microscopic animals.

Carp collect food slowly from the bottom of the ponds using sight, smell, and taste. The natural food of the carp is primarily protein represented by crustaceans, worms, insect larvae, small mollusks, etc., which are ingested. Carp fry primarily eat rotifers, but also microscopic algae, small crustaceans, and small insect larvae; older carp eat larger larvae and crustaceans according to the abundance in ponds during seasonal variations in type and concentration of biomass present. During the warm growing season, these foods rapidly develop and are more available than in the cold winter season.

Practically, one may assume that carp natural food is composed of freely floating animals like plankton and small animals living in close contact with the shore and bottom of ponds (benthos), plus vegetable matter which plays a secondary role (Wunder, 1949). Table VII reports the chemical composition of some of these natural carp foods.

FIG. 27. Mr. Tanaka feeding carp with pellets in a running water pond in the old farm of Annaka-shi, Gunma Prefecture, Japan.

FIG. 28.  Fantastic carp crowding in the Tanaka method of carp rearing in running water ponds.

FIG. 29.  A Japanese carp farmer feeding carp fingerlings with dry crumbles.

FIG. 30.  Silkworm pupae and pellets fed to carp reared in a still water pond in Japan.

FIG. 31.  Carp of a Japanese farm catching food at the water surface.

TABLE VII

CHEMICAL COMPOSITION OF NATURAL CARP FOODS

| Animal | Water (%) | Crude protein (%) | Pure protein (%) | Chitin (%) | Fat (%) | Carbo-hydrate (%) | Ash (%) | Reference |
|---|---|---|---|---|---|---|---|---|
| *Daphnia pulex* | 90.67 | 5.42 | 1.47 | 1.47 | 0.61 | 4.07 | 1.70 | Geng, 1925 |
| *Daphnia magna* | 91.60 | 3.53 | 2.98 | 0.78 | 0.62 | 2.63 | 1.62 | Mann, 1935 |
| *Chironomus gregarius* | 87.18 | 8.21 | 6.21 | 1.77 | 1.40 | 2.42 | 1.03 | Geng, 1925 |
| *Cloeon dipterum* | 77.32 | 13.05 | — | — | 5.96 | 1.87 | 1.80 | Geng, 1925 |
| *Tubifex* | 87.15 | 8.06 | 4.23 | 0.28 | 2.00 | 1.88 | 0.91 | Mann, 1935 |
| *Planorbis planorbis* | 73.00 | 10.58 | 7.10 | 0.66 | 0.65 | 8.72 | 6.95 | Mann, 1935 |
| *Anabolia* | 77.09 | 11.13 | 8.61 | 2.68 | 0.95 | 5.06 | 2.77 | Mann, 1935 |

A continuously increasing quantity of natural foods is most important in carp culture. This problem is generally solved by cultivating pond bottoms and by fertilization. The cultivation operation brings mineral and organic substances into solution which are able to supply the chain and the biological water cycle. The essential steps of which can be summarized as follows:

> minerals dissolved in water + sun light, heat, and chlorophyll → organic vegetable matter → small animal organisms → larger animal organisms → fishes → bacteria → mineralization of vegetable and animal waste

The problem of proper pond fertilization has been widely discussed in world literature. Since fertilization generally determines productivity in warm water fish culture, a tremendous number of papers are available on the subject. Major references on pond fertilization may be reviewed in the FAO World Symposium on Warm Water Pond Fish Culture held in Rome, Italy, 18–25 May 1966 (Hepher; Prowse; Gooch; Van Der Lingen; Wolny; Ling; Lessent; Fijan; Pujin; Banerjea and Banerjea; Rabanal; Lin and Chen; Satomi; Dobie).

Organic fertilization is the most common practice in carp farming to increase the natural food in ponds. Organic manure is immediately utilized by microscopic water animals to promote a luxuriant growth of submerged vegetation, and the colloidal humus of pond soil is generally improved (Fig. 32). Several organic fertilizers are used including dung from various animal sources (beef, swine, sheep, poultry), sewage waters from towns,

foodstuffs industry wastes, green manure, and animal by-products. Frequently, products suitable for fish feeding such as fish and meat offal and
vegetable by-products like cottonseed, peanuts, soybean meals, and rice
bran, are used depending upon availability as pond fertilizers.

A limiting factor to be considered in using organic fertilizers in fish ponds
is the possible toxicity to fish. The development of ammonia or severe
oxygen depletion can cause serious problems. Therefore, organic manure
must be added in repeated small amounts to avoid saturating and destroying the water environment. Inorganic fertilizers in pond fish culture have
been more recently employed. Calcium, phosphorus, and nitrogen play
particularly important roles in vegetable and animal growth, whereas
potassium is generally not as necessary since it is present in most ponds in
adequate amounts. Calcium is particularly important in acid ponds and
liming the ponds is a common practice. Phosphorus fertilizers are necessary
to stimulate growth and this mineral is generally lacking in most ponds.
Since phosphorus is an essential element in phyto- and zooplankton growth
and is also a binder of nitrogen through algae and bacteria (Schäperclaus,
1961), ponds should be tested periodically for phosphorus content during
the growing season. Various types of commercial fertilizers are usually
employed, such as superphosphate, urea, and nitrogen–potassium–phosphorus mixtures or carbon–nitrogen–phosphorus mixtures. Trace elements

Fig. 32. Liquid manure dispensed by motor boat in large carp pond in Poland (State
Fish Farm Grojec).

like manganese sometimes are used but should be administered only after careful testing of the natural elements present in the water (Hickling, 1962).

Pond soils play an important role in the production cycle of fish ponds. Originally productivity of ponds situated on fertile soils may be higher than others; however, the best advantage is generally found when carp farms are developed on poor, sandy, marshy soils on barren lands or on peat moss (Mints and Khairulina, 1968). These areas are generally not profitable for agriculture or forestry and carp culture, but if well managed, can produce a high yield (Schäperclaus, 1961; Huet, 1960; Hickling, 1962). The nature of the soil under the pond influences the chemistry of the water, which in turn is directly related to the productivity (Pasternak, 1958, 1965; Stangenberg, 1943; Wrobel, 1967; Matida, 1967; Sreenivasan, 1967; Golterman, 1967). Treatment of pond soil and temperate climate generally consists of a thorough annual winter draining, tilling the pond bottom, and allowing grass to begin to grow. This treatment increases nitrogen, decreases soil acidity, and partly sterilizes ponds from fish parasites (Wiesner, 1934; Danielewski, 1965; Wrobel, 1967).

Control of aquatic vegetation in fish ponds is another problem on increasing natural feed. An excessive growth of several aquatic plants is undesirable in pond culture. In fact, dense vegetation or aquatic weeds can seriously interfere with fish pond operations, restrict movements of fish, limit moving space, prevent proper water aeration, serve as ponds for fish pests, and increase the oxygen demand at night; thus, positive control over general aquatic vegetation in warm fish ponds is necessary and total eradication of certain unwanted plants, like the water hyacinth, is necessary for efficient and successful fish culture.

Several methods are employed in control or eradication of aquatic weeds. Traditional methods use mechanical elimination by cutting (Fig. 33), picking, beating, shading, or draining and freezing in winter. Other management methods are incorporated into general pond care and maintenance, such as, marginal shelf-deepening, burning marginal grasses, grazing, dikes, complete draining and drying, creating artificial water turbidity, and altering water pH. More modern methods of weed control employ several chemical compounds like arsenicals, copper, borates, chlorates, and commercial hormone weedicides. Some compounds have specific action on particular plant types and it is important to use those with a low toxicity to fish if weed control is needed when the ponds are stocked.

Several biological methods are also used. Herbivorous fishes, such as, *Ctenopharyngodon idella*, *Hypophthalmichthys molitrix*, the grass carps, common carp of large body size, and *Tilapia*, and rodents such as nutria

Fig. 33.   Mechanical weed cutter in warm water pond in Poland.

and muskrats, fowl such as geese and ducks, certain water beetles and their larvae all consume weeds. Often stocking densities in ponds will determine weed concentration and some control is effected by the type and density of the fish cultivated. Commercial fertilizers promote growth of phytoplankton, cause turbidity of water, and prevent growth of submerged vegetation. Therefore, proper balance of fertilization, fish density, and mechanical pond care techniques are needed to effect an efficient, economical maintenance of plant life in the impoundments. The control of aquatic weeds plays an important role in warm water fish culture. Several papers on this particular subject were included in the FAO World Symposium on Warm-Water Pond Fish Culture held in Rome, Italy, 1966. Major references on the subject are included in the papers by Schäperclaus (1961), Bennet (1962), Keiz (1964) Blackburn (1968), Philipose (1968), Van Der Lingen (1967), Timmermans (1968), Lawrence (1968), Ramachandran and Ramaprabhu (1968), and Avault *et al.* (1967a).

## 2. *Artificial Feeding of Carp*

Probably supplementary feeding is more correct than artificial feeding. In traditional carp farming in Europe, Schäperclaus (1961) lists the various grain products used to supplement natural feed available to carp in ponds. Barley, lupine, and corn are the most common grains used, but other agricultural products like rye, wheat, oat, beans, peas, vetch, millet, acorns,

TABLE VIII

CHEMICAL COMPOSITION OF SUPPLEMENTARY FOODS FOR CARP[a]

| Product | Dry matter (%) | Crude ash (%) | Crude protein (%) | Crude fat (%) | N-free extract (%) | Crude fiber (%) |
|---------|------|------|------|------|------|------|
| Wheat | 88.0 | 1.8 | 12.3 | 1.9 | 70.0 | 2.0 |
| Rye | 88.0 | 1.8 | 8.7 | 1.6 | 73.1 | 2.8 |
| Barley | 88.0 | 2.3 | 8.9 | 1.7 | 69.6 | 5.5 |
| Oats | 88.0 | 2.7 | 10.7 | 5.1 | 60.4 | 9.1 |
| Corn | 88.0 | 1.7 | 10.6 | 4.4 | 68.9 | 2.4 |
| Peas | 86.8 | 3.0 | 22.7 | 1.9 | 53.2 | 6.0 |
| Soybean | 90.0 | 4.7 | 33.2 | 17.5 | 30.2 | 4.4 |
| Sweet lupine | 90.0 | 4.2 | 34.2 | 8.2 | 34.9 | 8.5 |
| Vetch seed | 86.7 | 3.2 | 26.0 | 1.7 | 49.8 | 6.0 |
| Potatoes | 24.0 | 1.2 | 1.9 | 0.1 | 21.5 | 0.7 |
| Wheat bran | 85.2 | 6.0 | 14.9 | 4.7 | 50.7 | 8.9 |
| Rice bran | 90.0 | 10.3 | 12.5 | 14.3 | 44.5 | 8.4 |
| Meat meal | 91.5 | 12.5 | 66.0 | 10.5 | 2.5 | — |
| Fish meal | 88.4 | 18.0 | 61.8 | 8.6 | — | — |

[a] From Schäperclaus, 1961.

chestnuts, potatoes, soybean, rice bran, and grass seeds have been widely employed to increase the carbohydrate foods available. Some protein products are also employed, but since these are more expensive, traditional carp culture has not used large quantities of meat meals. Pond fish culture is exploited in undeveloped overpopulated countries during famine, war, and population explosion in the fight against hunger; therefore, the lowest carp carbohydrate products are used to supplement feed present in the ponds to obtain protein food from the carp for human consumption. Table VIII reports the chemical composition of the most common foods employed in traditional carp farming.

New concentrated, high density, high protein diets have been developed for intensive carp husbandry in Japan, Germany, the Soviet Union, and Israel. These rations are very similar to the dry fish feeds used in cold water fish husbandry but have slightly less protein concentration; the vitamin content is also lower. Older reports that carp will not grow if the food is not composed of at least 50% natural foods (Walter, 1931; Wunder, 1949; Schäperclaus, 1961) have not been substantiated when the diet formulated for the fish is adequately balanced with digestible protein, carbohydrates, fats, and vitamins. Wunder (1965) showed that carp held in aquariums and fed for 18 months on dry pellets, tripled body weight and appeared healthy. Detailed results were recently reported by Meske (1966) to obtain fantastic growth in carp held in 40-liter aquariums supplied with recirculating water at constant temperature (23°C). These carp fed commercial pellets grew from 140 gm to 7.5 kg in one experiment, and from 10 gm to 4 kg in another experiment over a 2-year period. He reported that carp grew from fry to 1.75 kg in 12 months when held in the constant-temperature aquariums and fed commercial pellets; whereas, the control carp held in ponds grew only to 40 gm in the same period.

Pellet feed for carp culture became available about 10 years ago in Europe. Mann (1958) reported that swine pellets were suitable for carp feeding when the fish were held in ponds and supplementary natural food was available. Additional references are included in the report by Steffens (1966).

Intensive carp husbandry employing modern feeding techniques and dry pellets in recirculating water ponds or in slow running water ponds appears very similar to trout feeding. The development of these techniques has been similar to that employed in the trout industry. Simple mixtures of dry and wet products have been improved until only mixtures of dehydrated material have been compounded into complete pellet rations. Schäperclaus (1961) points out that several agricultural by-products which formerly could not be used alone could be added to carp pellets to lower the manufacturing costs and still obtain good conversion from materials like broken grains, vetch seed, wheat screening, etc., into carp flesh.

Different areas use different ingredients (Michler and Schäperclaus, 1963). The carp feed employed in Russian experiments contained: oil cakes, 47–55%; vegetable products, 10–20% grains, 9–25%; wheat bran, 10–20% animal meals, 3–10%; and oyster shells, 1%. The chemical composition of this mixture was: protein, 23–28%, fat, 4–5%, and carbohydrate, 27–33%; and the conversion reported was 3.5 kg feed/kilogram carp. Other diets containing sunflower seeds, sunflower seed cake, fodder peas, corn, rye, wheat bran and benthonite, cottonseed meal, linseed oil meal, and rape seed oil cake were also used. In most of these diets, 10 gm of cobalt chloride and 1 gm of chloramphenicol were added per ton of feed to control infectious dropsy.

Extensive feeding experiments with dry diets were recently performed in Israel by Hepher and Chervinski (1965). The composition of the pellets used in these experiments included ground wheat, ground milcorn, ground corn, soybean oil meal, fish meal, wheat gluten, beet molasses, benthonite clay and gypsum. Crude protein varied from 26–30% and in two experimental diets, 20 kg of vitamin mix were added per ton of food. Each kilogram of the vitamin mix contained: vitamin A, 130,000 USP units; vitamin D, 130,000 USP units; riboflavin, 110 mg; pantothenic acid, 220 mg; niacin, 1100 mg; vitamin $B_{12}$, 0.44 mg; vitamin E, 55 mg; manganese, 4800 mg; iodine, 75 mg; copper, 190 mg; cobalt, 19 mg; zinc, 3800 mg; and iron, 1690 mg.

Steffens (1966) employed slightly different dry diets in experiments with carp held in aquariums. A simple diet consisting of fish meal 15.5%, oats 10.0%, corn 39.5%, rye 14.2%, and wheat 20.8% was used with a vitamin mix containing vitamin A 2,000,000 I.E., vitamin $D_3$ 300,000 I.E. vitamin C 20 gr, riboflavin 4 gr, paradoxine 5 gr, pantothenic acid 2 gr, and protein chloride 10 gr per ton, faired pretty well under the conditions used. A new commercial product, Carpi spezial, has been tested by Bank (1966a). The composition is listed in the appendix and the chemical analysis showed crude protein 25%, fat 3%, and fiber 6% in this diet.

Carp husbandry in floating bags has been conducted in Russia (Gribanov *et al.*, 1968) with diets containing mostly vegetable products. The formula included 35% sunflower seedcake, 35% soybean cake, 25% shorts, and 5% hydrolyzed yeast with fair growth results. Another formula contained grain waste 30–40%, sunflower seed meal 15–20%, peanut meal 15–20%, flax seed meal 10%,silk worm pupae 15%, fodder yeast 5%, and a paste prepared from aquatic plants of up to 20% wet weight was added to the other ingredients. This formula increased growth rate 14% above normal when used. Michler and Schäperclaus (1963) referred to other experiments in which 20% of the diet consisted of fresh aquatic plants (*Lemna*) added to broken grains to improve the vitamin content. An antibiotic, terramycin, at the rate of 5,000–10,000 units/kilogram of food was used to protect the carp contained in floating nets, and the report indicated action of the drug allowed increased growth of 10 to 17% over controlled groups.

The old belief that carp growth would be impossible on dry diets without added natural foods has been effectively altered to the conviction that intensive modern feeding of carp can be developed similar to the feeding of animals reared in agricultural animal husbandry. As new and more effective diets become available, the general carp husbandry technique will shift more into intensive fish farming where the water and land area will be used more effectively to utilize inexpensive carbohydrate agricultural materials supplemented with good protein and vitamins to produce tons of high quality carp for human food.

### 3. *Pond Crowding and Feeding*

Carp ponds can be more crowded than ever before, due to supplementary feeding. With higher carp density, the natural food present in the pond, formerly never completely eaten, is more thoroughly utilized. Production of pond waters is more complete when dry feeds are used because of the increase in carp excrement and uneaten food which stimulates the growth of other aquatic forms to minimize ultimate food loss. More dependence is placed on artificial foods because modern carp husbandry requires high fish yield per surface acre for the labor involved; the return to inefficient low productive, low density carp ponds is obsolete. The chief problem in intensive carp culture is to balance the supplementary feed with the natural feed available to minimize feed costs and still promote maximum growth. It is also essential to maintain optimum carp density for the condition of the pond. Practically, carp husbandry then consists of proper management to adjust fish density, pond fertilization, and balance of a supplementary feed for optimum utilization of the water volume and natural conditions present. Detailed rules on pond crowding in traditional carp farming are discussed by Schäperclaus (1961). The number of carp stocked depends on many variables such as pond class, fish age, previous fish yield per year, kind and rate of feeding employed, disease history, and replacement water flow. Schäperclaus indicates that in open ponds fish should grow to 25 gm after 1 year, 250 gm after 2 years, and 1.25 kg after 3 years. These growth rates are typical for northern European ponds. However, water temperature and availability of supplementary foods can triple these results with good management. Carp fry stock had a rate of 50,000–150,000/ha for first-year class ponds and 20,000–60,000 second-year class ponds. Carp fingerlings are stocked at 10,000–30,000/ha. One rule suggested by Schäperclaus is that number of fish equal total growth divided by individual growth plus the loss complement. The total growth is calculated based on production programs of the pond in previous years, and individual growth is expected fish weight of the fish during the growing season. Losses are estimated from the previous history of that particular pond. A practical example follows: A pond of 20 ha with a total productivity of 300 kg/ha should be stocked with 2-year-old carp of 250 gm. Fish loss of 5% is expected. The number of carp to be stocked is, therefore,

$$\frac{6000}{1\text{kg}} \text{ kg} + 300 = 6300 \text{ carp of 250 gm weight}$$

Today, more carp are held in ponds in the same pond size than in the past, and more intensive artificial feeding is employed, resulting in a more efficient and higher yield of finished carp. In Yugoslavia, carp yield has increased from 780 kg/ha in 1959 to 1500–1600 kg/ha at present (Livojevic, 1968). The average fish yield in Israel, reported by Tal and Hepher (1967), is 800–1000 kg/ha if fish are not fed and 2100 kg/ha when the carp are fed.

Hepher and Chervinski (1965) report that even higher fish density (4000 fish/ha) is possible when protein-rich pellets are employed, but that this fish density cannot be used when only high carbohydrates or grain diets are used. The author suggests two limiting factors in pond crowding may exist, that is, the total protein of the diet plus the pond and lysine limiting content of the supplementary diet. Bank (1966a) reported 1700 3-year-old 300 gm carp were stocked/ha and these grew 1.2–1.5 kg each. Similar yields were reported by Prokulevich (1941) for carp confined in a concrete tank when fed a complete diet. Probably the highest densities were used by the Japanese when they obtained a fish yield of 200 kg carp/m² of surface area (Lieder and Müller, 1965). In Russia, 100 kg/m² was obtained in the carp experiments in floating nets (Gribanov *et al.*, 1968).

### 4. *Feeding Methods*

Traditional carp culture feeding methods are simple, and consist in distributing feed along the shore or preferably by boat in well-defined places in the pond called feeding stations. These are generally marked with a small pile planted into the pond bottom or by floats, and the carp soon learn to accumulate at this site to feed at scheduled times each day (Fig. 34). It is important to establish a number of feeding places in the pond

Fig. 34.   Depression in bottom induced by carp in a feeding place of a drained Yugoslavian carp farm at Konchaniza.

since the carp must be fed uniformly to prevent irregular growth and loss of food. The carp feeder observes if food has been consumed since the last feeding period and some regulation of amount to be fed can be implemented with a trained staff. No advantage is obtained by using submerged feeding platforms because most of these are made of firm materials and the mouth of the carp is easily damaged (Schäperclaus, 1961). The Russian technique incorporates more frequent feeding places in ponds of 10–15 ha and carp feeding is accomplished with special designed boats which mechanically deliver a weighed amount of food at each station (Michler and Schäperclaus, 1963). Feeding frequency and quantity is dependent upon water temperature. Carp eat avidly only in warm waters. When the water drops below 13°C feeding ceases, except for maintenance requirements, and growth stops. Theoretically every 10°C rise in water temperature above 13°–15°C should warrant two to three times increase in food consumed (Schäperclaus, 1961). The exact amount varies with the condition of the pond and the presence of types of natural food available to the fish. Even in wintering ponds, some food must be offered, however, to ensure maintenance and health of the fish (Bank, 1966b). At 4°C about one-fourth of the fish are attracted to fish dispersal, but at 3°C no activity is observed (Krajuchin, 1955). Therefore, some winter feeding is necessary only at temperature above 3.5°C (Michler and Schäperclaus, 1963). Many of the aspects of the physiology of carp during hibernation have been described by Steffens (1964b).

Rajbanshi (1966) concluded that carp would not eat at water temperatures below 5°C and that food intake was only at the rate of 0.5% of the body weight per day at 6°C. Food intake increased to 2% of the body weight at 8°C but no weight gain could be measured. Thus, growth was registered when carp were able to consume more than 7% of the body weight of food.

The optimum temperature for growth of carp held in floating nets in running water ranged from 23°–30°C. At 22°C a decrease in growth rate was observed and at 20°C growth nearly ceased (Gribanov *et al.*, 1968). In Japan, however, water temperatures down to 15°C produced some growth and, of course, the rate of gain increased per unit time up to 30°C in running water ponds (Tamura, 1961).

The carp is a slow feeder in contrast to the actively feeding trout and salmon. Traditional grain supplementary rations are usually consumed by carp within 3 hours after application to the pond but some residue is present after even 5 hours of observation. Dry pellets are consumed more rapidly with almost all feed eaten within 30 minutes to 1 hour. This slow feeding characteristic presents a problem for carp pellet manufacture since the food must be stable in the water without disintegrating for at least 1

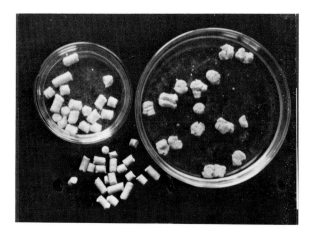

Fig. 35.   Pellets for control of infectious dropsy, containing 2–4% of chloramphenicol, resist destruction in water for 12-24 hours; *left bottom*, dry; *right*, after 24 hours.

hour. Experimental pellets have been processed wet and dry and often 50% wheat gluten has been added to minimize leaching. Pellets manufactured by the wet process appear stable in water for up to 1 day but exact measurements of loss of nutrients were not conducted (Hepher and Chervinski, 1965). Medicated pellets (Fig. 35) are now available in Yugoslavia and in other countries which resist disintegration in water for 12–24 hours. These pellets contained chloramphenicol and were used to control infectious dropsy (Fijan, 1969).

Evaluation of artificial diets in traditional carp culture is very difficult. Most diets should be calculated on the calorie content and the ultimate calorie requirement to produce a kilogram of fish. One technique used has been to establish a barley value equivalent of 100 in comparing other cereal grains with results from barley feeding. Thus, the barley value of any food would show how many kilograms of the test grain would be to 100 kg of barley. The chief problem in carp pond culture is, however, to balance the supplementary food with the natural food present in the pond and couple this with optimum carp density so that the total physiological utilization of the supplementary feeds and maximum use of the natural food is obtained (Schäperclaus, 1961).

Natural food in second and third summer ponds include chironomus larvae as a desirable species and common culture techniques involve supplementary feeding 2 kg corn or 8 kg potatoes/kilogram carp during the second and third summer. Some carp farmers assume that carp in the first summer eat 40 gm of barley, 1 kg in the second, and 2 kg in the third growing season.

Schäperclaus (1961) mentions three food quotients which must be considered· (1) physiological food quotient, which represents the amount of food that can produce one weight unit of growth; (2) relative food quotient which represents the quotient between the amount of food offered and total fish growth; and (3) absolute food quotient, which represents weight gain of carp produced by 1 kg of given food. Such quotients are used to calculate conversion of traditional carp feed when the carp were not reared, on artificial food alone. These three are being reduced through the physiological food quotient similar to the one used in trout husbandry to measure conversion of food to flesh in modern carp husbandry as more and more fish are being confined in less and less water and the contribution of natural food becomes less than a minor supplement for vitamins and unknown growth factors (Fig. 36).

Table IX reports conversion values for some artificial carp foods and

FIG. 36.   Carp growth checking by fling net.   (Photo Dr. H. Jähnichen, Inst. Binnenfischerei, Berlin-Friedrichshagen, DDR, 1968.)

TABLE IX

Food Quotient, or Conversion Factor, of Artificial Feeds Employed in Traditional and Modern Carp Culture

| Foods | Food quotient[a] | Experiment | Author |
|-------|------------------|------------|--------|
| Barley or lupine | 2.6–3.7 | In ponds | Schäperclaus, 1961 |
| Soybean | 5.0 | In ponds | Probst, 1937 |
| Corn | 4.8 | In ponds | Probst, 1937 |
| Wheat | 3.2–5.7 | In carp farm | Schäperclaus, 1962 |
| Oats | 2.6 | — | Tokuhisa, 1961 |
| Peas | 2.7–2.8 | — | Susta, 1961 |
| Potatoes | 33.9 | — | Schröder, 1961 |
| Dry silkworm pupae | 1.3–2.1 | — | Higurashi, 1961 |
| Fresh silkworm pupae | 5.0 | — | Tanaka, 1929 |
| Balanced diet | 2.5–3.0 | In aquariums | Yashouv, 1956 |
| Mixed dry diet | 3.2 | In carp farm | Michler and Schäperclaus, 1963 |
| Complex diet | 2.6 | In running water pond | Oren, 1963 |
| Complex diet | 5.4–6.5 | In floats | Gribanov *et al.*, 1968 |
| Commercial pellets | 3.9 | In small ponds | Keiz, 1965 |
| Commercial pellets | 2.5–3.9 | In aquariums | Steffens, 1966 |
| Commercial pellets | 6.44–6.45 | In aquariums | Rajbanshi, 1966 |
| Commercial trout pellets | 1.9 | In aquariums | Lühr, 1967 |

[a] Such food quotients are referable to the absolute food quotient reported by Schäperclaus.

indicates that in carp farming feed conversion varies from 1.6–3.0 on a dry weight of food to wet weight of fish basis.

5. *Organoleptic Characteristics in Carp from Feed*

Supplementary feeding can influence the organoleptic characteristics of reared carp and thus can condition the carp market value. Certain traditional foods improve the quality of the edible portions of carp and give the flesh a firm consistency and delicate flavor; other foods confer a disagreeable taste and make carp flesh of poor quality. Barley, rye, wheat, corn, soybean, and rice are considered good foods to improve carp but fish fed potatoes or bread have flesh with a wet and fatty consistency (Schäperclaus, 1961; Amlacher, 1961). The chemical composition of the diet also affect the carp flesh composition. Fish fed barley pellets had

63.5% moisture, 22% protein, 10% fat, and 2% ash; carp fed on milo had 17–18% fat in the flesh (Hepher and Chervinski, 1965). Grain feeding and fattening ponds improved the general appearance of carp and flavor; fish consuming only natural foods were more lean (Schäperclaus, 1963). Steffens (1966) compared the organoleptic characteristics of hatchery reared and wild carp and concluded that few differences occurred in carp taste if the fish were fed corn or consumed only natural food in ponds. He also mentioned some wild carp had a wild taste whereas flesh of fed carp was fatter and more delicate. Wunder (1935) stated that slowly grown carp had a good flavor but a strong taste and that carp from ponds lost a heavy and moldy taste only after 10 days of confinement in cleaner water and supplementary feed. The mud taste of carp was only slowly reduced after more than 10 days. Carp grown in polluted water and carp reared in fish farms supplied by sewage waters from towns frequently have a disagreeable phenol taste. Finishing these fish required long confinement in cleaner water, and supplementary feeding with corn or cereal grains promotes the disappearance of the off flavor. Recently in Israel, off flavors in carp from ponds containing *Oscillatoria tenuis* was improved by controlling the organism by applying copper sulfate at 100 mg/m² surface area (Aschner *et al.*, 1967).

Carp are caught in the fall in Europe by nets or by pond draining (Figs. 37 and 38) and then are moved to smaller wintering ponds. October and

Fig. 37. A scene of carp fishing in November in a Yugoslavian carp farm at Konchaniza.

Fig. 38. Carp-netting in a carp farm at Nasicka Breznica, Yugoslavia.

FIG. 39. After fall fishing, carp are transferred to wintering ponds.

November are months of intense fishing in eastern Europe with the fish caught marketed or held over until spring for another growing season (Fig. 39).

## D. Secondary Fishes in Carp Farming

Traditional carp farming performed in Europe includes other fishes in the ponds besides carp. Such fishes are referred to as secondary because these are stocked in addition to carp in ponds without noticeable change of the carp husbandry technique. Carp are the principal product produced but since carp do not fully utilize all the natural animal and plant foods present in ponds, cultivating secondary fishes with the carp increases the yield and at the same time increases efficiency of use of the water without dramatically changing the fish husbandry techniques. Sometimes several fish species enter carp ponds through the water supply and most of these are considered as noxious and undesirable food competitors with carp with little or no commercial value. To minimize these effects and gain additional revenue, some predator fishes are deliberately stocked in carp ponds or are allowed to enter with the river water to obtain utilization of such forage fish present. Balance of the fish population to minimize adverse effects on carp growth and to enhance the overall efficiency of fish production in the system is the main objective.

Tench (*Tinca tinca*) are the principal secondary fish in carp farming (Fig. 40). The physiological characteristics of this cyprinid are similar to

Fig. 40. Tench (*Tinca tinca*) represents the principal secondary fish in the European carp farms.

carp. It utilizes the same food and interferes with carp growth only if great numbers are present in the farm. The number of tench should be less than 10% of the carp present. Tench culture is more difficult than carp culture. Handling, harvesting, stocking density, growth characteristics, and disease control represent serious practical problems. The gross price of tench is generally higher than carp and a 5–10% tench population density of total fish in the pond is generally economically advantageous. Tench feed on natural food and some artificial or complementary utilization of dry food added is the marginal dividend desired. Knowledge of tench nutritional requirements and feeding techniques is fragmentary since less experimental work has been planned for tench compared with that of carp husbandry (Schäperclaus, 1961; Koch, 1960; Huet, 1960).

Many other fish species have been cultivated together with carp in European countries (Fig. 41). Many are used for stocking purposes in private or fee fishing waters. Some of these include *Idus melanotus* (in the yellow-red variety), *Carassius vulgaris, Carassius gibelio, Esox lucius, Lucioperca sandra, Eupomotis gibbosus, Ameiurus nebulosus, Silurus glanis, Salmo gairdneri* (Schäperclaus, 1961), *Gardonus rutilus, Scardinius ery-throphthalmus, Carassius carassius, Carassius auratus, Idus idus, Perca fluviatilis,* and *Anguilla vulgaris* (Huet, 1960).

Fig. 41.   A typical crop in mixed culture of a carp farm in German Democratic Republic.   (Photo Dr. H. Jähnichen, Inst. Binnenfischer., Berlin-Friedrichshagen, DDR, 1968.)

Woynarovich (1968) classifies three types of fish which are normally grown with carp: (1) predatory fishes: pike (*Esox lucius*), pike-perch (*Lucioperca sandra*), sheat fish (*Silurus glanis*), black bass (*Micropterus salmoides*), and rainbow trout (*Salmo gairdneri*); (2) competing fishes: tench (*Tinca tinca*), silver crucian carp (*Carassius auratus gibelio*), striped mullet (*Mugil cephalus*), and whitefish (*Coregonus peled*); and (3) herbivorous fishes: grass carp (*Ctenopharyngodon idella*), silver carp (*Hypophthalmichthys molitrix*), and bighead (*Aristichthys nobilis*).

Breeding nutria and rearing ducks in carp ponds increase the gross yield of marketable products in Europe. Some carp farms in Yugoslavia employ secondary crops of frogs and freshwater turtles suitable for human consumption that are planted or managed in large carp pond installations.

Tilapia (*Tilapia nilotica*) are cultivated as supplementary fish in carp ponds in Israel with a reasonable increase in total fish production (Sarig, 1955; Pruginin, 1962). Other references on mixed fish culture with carp include those by Lavrovsky (1968), Michler and Schäperclaus (1963), Huet and Timmermans (1966), Huet (1968), Anwand and Grohmann (1966), and Yashouv (1968). It is generally efficient to cultivate secondary fishes in carp culture when the ponds used contain large amounts of natural plant and animal feed, and intensive carp culture with large amounts of supplementary feeds are not employed. Consequently, all the feeding problems in mixed fish cultivation are generally limited to enhancing natural food production through pond fertilization and good pond management.

## E. Carp Culture in Rice Fields

The possibility of rearing carp as well as other species in flooded rice fields has been contemplated for many years (Piacco, 1955; Tonolli, 1955; Hickling, 1962) (Fig. 42). Rice grows in warm climates, and the water temperature in rice fields is very suitable for rapid growth of warm water fish. Furthermore, many rice fields contain abundant natural foods which will be employed by carp for rapid growth. In addition, the excrement from feeding carp will assist in fertilizing the rice growth. Carp do not interfere with the growth of rice and, in addition, eat several aquatic organisms which may damage the rice plant. Some aquatic worms and crustaceans like *Triops cancriformis* may occur in a tremendous number in rice fields and prevent optimum growth of the grain during the first stage of development.

Tonolli (1955) reports that superior rice yields were obtained from fields in which carp were reared. El Bolock and Labib (1967) reported about 200 kg of carp/ha could be raised in Egypt and the rice crop itself would

Fɪɢ. 42.  A simple screen to prevent carp escape from a rice field.

be increased by 5–7% over control fields in which no carp were reared. The growing season for carp coincides with the warm growing season for rice, and management techniques to introduce and retrieve carp from the fields during repeated draining and partial drying to increase the strength of the rice stock and for weed and algae control, and finally to allow heavy harvesting machinery, can be planned because the rice farms always have water reservoirs to which the growing fish may be returned. Significant results to improve rice yields or total production of rice and fish in India were not as successful as those employed in Japan (Bhimachar and Tripathy, 1967; Hickling, 1962). Today intensive modern systems of rice farming including use of more fertilizer, herbicides, algaecides, insecticides, and other agricultural chemicals, interfere with multiple use of the flooded fields for carp culture; but in several areas of the world, older methods of rice production in small farm lot areas lend themselves to multipurpose use of the land and water area for both cereal grain and fish flesh production. In Indonesia and countries where two rice crops are harvested each year and where rice fields are flooded even after rice is harvested, the abundance of water promotes carp culture not only for the subsistence of the farmer family but as a cash crop as well.

No supplementary feeding is generally offered in Europe to carp raised in rice fields, whereas, in Japan, silk worm pupae with or without bran, boiled wheat, dried mysis, shrimps, and other small crustaceans were added (Hickling, 1962). Kuronuma (1968) reported that the supplementary feeding of high protein materials was good economics. Harvesting and marketing the carp from rice fields present special problems in certain areas. The gross price of carp drops in Italy because the carp grown in rice fields are harvested within a few days and more carp is available than the market demands. Furthermore, small carp harvested must be kept in ponds over the winter and through the spring until growth begins again and they reach marketable size. During the winter months these fish suffer from serious parasites (*Ichthyophthirius, Trichodina, Gyrodactylus*), or infectious disease like infectious dropsy. Thus, many carp growers will sell their carp at a lower price, lowering the market further and inhibiting the true economic advantage that should be achieved from this multiple fish-grain carp farming.

### F.  Predacious Fish Culture

Rearing predacious fish in warm water ponds is quite similar to other pond fish culture methods and involves primarily natural feed for fish from fish and insects present or specifically reared for food. Bass (*Micropterus* spp.), pike (*Esox* spp.), pike-perch (*Luciopercà* spp.), and perch (*Perca* spp.) are artificially propagated only for stocking purposes. These are routinely grown in large ponds which contain many small forage fish which are cultivated by pond fertilization and water biomass management. Small animals, as entomostracans, shrimps, insect larvae, immature aquatic insects, and young and ova of forage fishes form part of the food supply. Larger fish prey on other fishes present. Pike-perch up to the age of 2 to 5 months are usually fed on invertebrates (*Crustacea, Chironomidae, Corethra, Cloeon*). This food is principally the same as that consumed by young carp in ponds. After 5 months pike-perch begin to feed on fish (Steffens, 1960). Woynarovich (1960) examined the stomach of small pike-perch fry and found the first food consisted of nauplius larvae of copepods; then, at the age of 20–25 days, the pike-perch turned predatory. Anwand and Grohmann (1966) and Anwand (1967) were able to hold yearling pike-perch in an aquarium on fish flesh, but the conversion factor of the food to flesh varied from 1:6 to 7.

Individual large-mouth bass fed with live fish showed a conversion rate from 2 to 7 (Prather, 1951). Bluegill sunfish (*Lepomis macrochirus*) and fathead minnow (*Pimephales promelas*) when used as live food for large-mouth bass gave an average food conversion of 6.9, whereas bluegill alone took 9.7 kg to yield 1 kg of bass (Snow, 1966). Over winter feeding of minnows suitable as bait for sport fishing or forage fish for bass showed fatter minnows could be raised successfully on dry fish feeds (Prather,

Fig. 43.   A pond for minnows in a large fish farm in Arkansas.

Fig. 44.   Large grading plant for minnows in the Anderson Minnow Farm, Lonoke, Arkansas.

Fig. 45.   Minnow transport truck equipped with liquid oxygen supplies.

1957, 1958). Bait fish culture is an important industry in the southern United States (Fig. 43 and 44). Bait minnows are raised in large ponds and fed ground meals blown over the water from a truck moving along the pond borders. When minnows reach market size, the fish are netted, graded, and moved long distances in special trucks equipped with liquid oxygen supplies (Fig. 45).

One important problem in predacious fish culture is the extreme cannibalism encountered. To limit cannibalistic tendencies, a very low stocking rate in ponds and dense vegetation with large numbers of forage fish is required. Therefore, commercial production of carnivorous, predacious fish for food is very inefficient; these fish are reared for minimum time periods with expensive natural food for sport fish stocking programs. As soon as dry artificial commercial rations become available, more effort will be expended in developing bass, pike, and perch farms, but probably most of the stock will be used for sport fishing programs rather than for food production. Only in the case of pike reared with carp to control forage fish densities is the husbandry of predacious fish warranted as a commercial venture.

### G. Catfish Husbandry

Many fish species commonly called catfishes are artificially propagated in many countries of the world for stocking waters for sport fishing. Recently, however, commercial catfish production in the southern United States has asymtotically exploded from a few thousand pounds of fish yearly to tons of catfish for human consumption. This catfish husbandry will have growing importance in the future as it becomes developed into efficient, economical, productive fish farming and will compete with the other major world carp and trout farming industries. New ponds are rapidly being constructed and the acreage increases monthly (Meyer *et al.*, 1967). Sneed (1966) reported that in Arkansas alone farmers sold 7000 metric tons of channel catfish for $6,000,000 plus fingerling catfish for stocking purposes worth at least another $1,000,000. The present status of warm water fish farming for catfish and some minnows is well covered in REPORT TO THE FISH FARMERS (1970). The most important species reared is the channel catfish (*Ictalurus punctatus*). It is considered an excellent game fish with excellent flavor (Davis, 1961). Several other species are cultivated to a lesser extent or on experimental basis and include the flathead catfish, the blue catfish, the white catfish, the brown bullhead, and the buffalo fishes (*Ictiobus cyprinella, I. bubalus, I. niger*) (Clemens, 1968). Buffalo fish were formerly raised by many fish farmers in the United States, but since 1960 this farming has been steadily replaced by channel catfish farming because the latter is more economical and easier to manage (Meyer *et al.*, 1967).

Catfish can be fed on natural or artificial feed (Fig. 46). Natural feed constitutes an important segment of the diet for the young fish and even under intensive catfish farming techniques natural food present in the ponds is relied upon to furnish some growth factors and vitamin components as well as supplementing the artificial diets used. Fresh and mixed diets were used at one time and consisted of beef liver, sheep liver, beef hearts, dried skimmilk, white fish meal, and shrimp waste (Davis, 1961). Ground goldfish and dried buttermilk (Morris, 1939), ground meat scraps (Toole, 1951), beef liver, beef spleen, egg yolk, cheese, canned dog food, canned salmon, and some cereal foods were also used (Sneed *et al.*, 1961). This type of diet is less prevalent today as modern complete dry feeds have been developed.

Red cat or speckled bullhead (*Ameiurus nebulosus marmoratus*) were grown in ponds where natural feed was supplemented with soybean cake, peanut meal, fish meal and distillers solubles. The Auburn No. 1 fish feed consists of 35% soybean meal, 35% peanut meal, 15% fish meal, and 15% distillers dried solubles. Efficient feed conversions and better survival of the stocked fish were obtained when this supplementary feed was used (Swingle, 1957a).

Swingle (1958) was able to grow channel catfish to marketable size in

Fig. 46.  Pellet feed for channel catfish. (Photo E. E. Prather, Auburn, Alabama, 1968.)

ponds supplemented with dry pelleted feeds, Auburn No. 2 fish feed, which contained 46% protein, 25% carbohydrate, and 5% fat, with conversion ranging from 2 to 3. This opened the door for the commercial channel catfish industry. Channel catfish were started with ground liver mixed with dry trout feed, and commercial trout pellets alone gave an excellent growth in larger fish held in ponds and reduced the cost per kilogram of fish produced (Snow, 1962). Better balanced channel catfish diets were soon developed, and studies were reported on major protein requirements (Nail, 1962), essential vitamins (Dupree, 1966), levels and balance of major nutrients in purified diets (Dupree and Sneed, 1966), on general diet processing and catering (Hastings, 1964), on formulation (Tiemeier *et al.*, 1967; Davis and Hughes, 1967), and on indispensable amino acid requirements (Dupree and Halver, 1970). The feeding methods and general fish husbandry techniques in catfish farming are similar to those used in trout and carp farming; since most of the catfish reared are held in ponds, more pond management techniques are used. Channel catfish are omnivorous and eat whatever animal and plant foods are available. The fish is a bottom feeder but can be trained to consume pellets thrown on the surface. Although the channel catfish consume food quicker than carp, the pellets still should remain intact for at least 10 minutes. It is desirable to feed the fish every day and in the same place, since the fish soon learn the feeding area. This feeding station should be carefully and periodically checked to make sure the feed is totally consumed and to check for mortality or diseased fish. For optimum growth catfish are fed at the rate of about 3% of the body weight per day up to 500 gm after which approximately 2% of the body weight per day is used. Catfish have a stomach and can digest efficiently many artificial diet ingredients, but the metabolism is still that of warm water fish. When the water temperature drops below 16°C, fish do not feed well, and when the water temperature falls between 13° and 15°C, the catfish do not eat. The demand for fingerling catfish for stocking ponds has greatly increased. Spawning behavior of this fish has been recently managed and today several catfish hatcheries have fingerlings available at low stocking costs. Data on the subject of inducing spawning and spawning techniques have been published by Clemens and Sneed (1957), Crawford (1958), Clemens (1968), and in the REPORT TO THE FISH FARMERS (1970).

The most profitable catfish size is about 1 kg (Fig. 47). Most fish are sold dressed, without viscera, head, and skin, and on ice or quick frozen.

Fig. 47. Channel catfish size ready to market.

Fig. 48. Channel catfish killed by electric shock.

Channel catfish dress out about 60–65% of the live weight, and dressed fish command a price two or three times as high as the price of live weight (Davis and Hughes, 1967). Catfish have recently been dressed in modern processing plants with innovative machinery. Fish are killed by electric shock, the head and fins removed, eviscerated, and skin pigments are removed with water jets. Scraps are processed for pet foods (Figs. 48–53).

Other more specific information on the details of the development of catfish farms, cost of production, and return to the farmer, together with many helpful recommendations on the care and management of the fish in this new industry, are included in the REPORT TO THE FISH FARMERS (1970).

Other fish species called catfish are cultivated in other countries of the world. Two species of catfish locally known as *Pladuk* that is, *Clarias macrocephalus* and *Clarias batrachus* are artificially cultivated in Thailand. Clarias can survive in many types of water and since these fish have accessory organs to breathe atmospheric air, oxygen content of the pond can become very low. Fish are grown with natural feed such as worms, insects, and shrimps, or with artificial feed like decayed protein food, meat and fish offal, and by-products of canning factories, boiled rice mixed with vegetable and peanut cake, fish meal, and silkworm pupae. Fingerlings for stocking can be harvested from natural waters, from broodstock held in ponds, or from broodstock held in small aquariums by using hormone in-

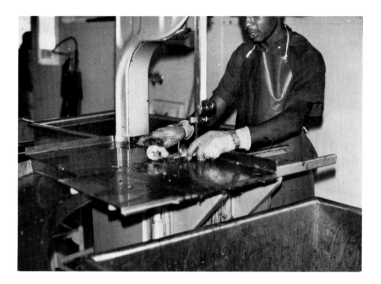

Fɪɢ. 49.  Fish head is removed with bandsaw.

Fɪɢ. 50.  Fish heads for pet animal foods.

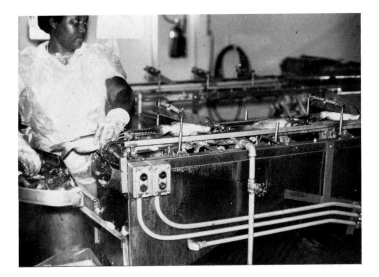

Fig. 51.  Fish are cleaned by mechanical processing equipment.

Fig. 52.  Packed cleaned fish are deep frozen.

Fig. 53. Fish cut in pieces frozen ready for market.

jections. The growth of these catfish is rapid and market size is reached in 4 or 5 months. Two to three crops of fish can be raised in 1 year in Thailand. Food conversion with the inexpensive diets used was about 6:1, and the cost to produce 1 kg of fish was 25¢ (U.S.), and the sale price varied from 40–50¢ per kilogram (Sidthimunka *et al.*, 1968). Ling (1967) reported fish intensively fed in small ponds of 400 m² with average depth 2 to 3 m. These ponds are stocked with 40,000 fingerlings (total weight 600 kg) and after 5 months, 4000–5000 kg of fish can be harvested. Fresh diets are generally used to supplement natural food. Fish and slaughter-house offal and oil bean cake are mixed with cooked broken rice. This food was offered at 6–8% of the body weight per day; the conversion rate was estimated between 6–8:1. Ling (1967) also reported that other catfish (*Pangasius* spp.) could be held in bamboo pens of different sizes and floated in rivers along the banks. These fish were fed with chopped trash fish, broken rice, rice bran, corn, and tender aquatic plants. The amount of food administered daily was about 6% of body weight, and the conversion ratio of these fish diets was 8–10:1.

In some European countries a highly appreciated catfish species is sheatfish (*Silurus glanis*). It is raised as a secondary fish in carp farming. Feed consists of several water organisms, fish included, and the fingerlings are fed on artificial food. The demand for this delicious fish is still increasing, and new methods to obtain artificial spawning are available in

Fig. 54.  Sheatfish, a secondary crop in carp farm in the Yugoslavian carp farm at Ribnjacarstvo Poljana.

Fig. 55.  A brood sheatfish of about 40 kg, reared in a carp farm of Yugoslavia at Ribnjacarstvo Poljana.

Hungary. Sheatfish reach a size of 500–100 gm the first summer, 1000–1400 gm the second, and 1500–2500 gm the third; brood fish are always older and larger (Figs. 54 and 55).

## H. Herbivorous Fish Culture

Great interest has been directed in recent years toward breeding several herbivorous fish, for the control of pond weeds and for simultaneous commercial fish production. These fish are typical warmwater fish and grow rapidly. Some species can tolerate cold water temperatures, whereas most do not survive water temperatures below 12°C.

There are four main species of cultivated fish reported as Chinese carps, i.e., the grass carp (*Ctenopharingodon idella*), the silver carp (*Hypophthalmichthys molitrix*), the bighead carp (*Aristichthys nobilis*), and the black carp (*Mylopharyngodon piceus*). Grass carp, silver carp, and bighead carp are intensively cultivated in Asia and in Europe as food fish (Fig. 56).

Grass carp are cultivated in ponds in many countries of southern Asia (Hora and Pillay, 1962) and recently have been introduced into Israel, Europe, and the United States (Hickling, 1962). In Russia, the fish is called the white Amur and is considered a valuable reservoir fish (Nikolski, 1957). The history of attempts to acclimate and breed carp from the Far

Fig. 56. A silver carp, or Tolstolobik (*Hypophthalmichthys molitrix*) reared as secondary fish in a Yugoslavian carp farm.

East in Russia was carefully described by Vinogradov (1968). Grass and silver carp were brought from the Amur River and from China and were bred in U.S.S.R. in 1961. Phytophagous carp were also introduced into France (Chimits, 1958), Germany (Schäperclaus, 1963; Scheer, 1964; Scheer and Jähnichen, 1967), Yugoslavia (Disalov, 1965), and the United States (Stevenson, 1965). Grass carp is used in western Germany for the control of aquatic vegetation in carp ponds, and the price of each yearling fish used to crop the aquatic vegetation is high.

The grass carp is native to the rivers in China and could be induced to reproduce by injection of pituitary compounds (Tang, 1960; Alikunhi *et al.*, 1963; Schäperclaus, 1963). Konradt (1968) was able to induce maturity and grass and silver carp spawned in ponds after pituitary injection. Some pituitary fractions were more effective than others in inducing spawning (Gerbilskii, 1959). Pituitary injections are widely used in Russia at all fish farms where grass and silver carp are cultivated (Aliev, 1961; Vinogradov, 1963), and thus artificial reproduction has made large-scale cultivation of these fishes possible. Bighead carp young were obtained for the first time in 1963 at the "Goryachy kluch" fish hatchery in Russia after repeated pituitary injections (Vinogradov, 1968). Good details of procedures employed for fertilization, incubation, and hatching of Chinese grass carp are described by Kuronuma (1968).

Fry have been imported from the Far East, China, and Russia to establish a colony of broodstock in many countries. Some new dangerous parasites have also been imported with these fry (Konradt, 1968; Szakolczai and Molnar, 1966; Mattheis, 1967). Therefore, it is important to assess the health and maintain sound sanitary standards of broodstock and to obtain fry from fish farms free from dangerous parasites.

The grass carp feeds on animal foods, mostly zooplankton, for the first few months of life. Fingerlings 3 cm or longer become phytophagous and live on aquatic plants, including soft submerged vegetation, grasses, and leaves. Grass carp also feed on filamentous algae. Silver carp also feed on aquatic plants and microscopic planktonic algae. These foods are filtered through the gill rakers and then ingested. Silver carp also become phytophagous only after fingerlings reach a length of 12–17 mm. Adult fish eat aquatic plants almost exclusively (Konradt, 1968). The bighead carp grows faster and reaches greater weight than silver carp in the water systems of China. It feeds partly on aquatic plants and partly on phyto- and zooplankton (Vinogradov, 1968).

Scheer (1964) reported that the grass carp has the most herbivorous feeding habits and that the silver carp feeds only on lower water plants (phytoplankton). Both the bighead and the silver carp select zooplankton when available, and the bighead carp will not tolerate water temperatures below 15°C. Both the grass and silver carp, however, can survive in water temperatures as low as 5°C and therefore are suitable for the water systems of temperate parts of the world.

The feeding habits of Chinese carp held in aquariums or in ponds have been investigated by several authors. Hora and Pillay (1962) reported that the grass carp is an omnivore which will eat several types of foods including chopped fish, silkworm pupae, refuse, and fecal matter, and will only subsist wholly on aquatic vegetation when other food supplies are absent. Stevenson (1965) investigated the feeding habits of grass carp to confirm the strict herbivore nature of the fish before its release in the water system of the United States. He showed that the grass carp would ignore vegetable matter in the water if other protein food was also available. Adult fish would consume some vegetation in ponds but preferred commercial fish feed whenever available. Prowse (1967) argued that grass carp are primarily herbivorous but would consume high protein food when available and that it would be used to control vegetation in carp ponds. A few adult grass carp were found to control several types of aquatic weeds in ponds or in pools within a few weeks after stocking (Avault, 1965). The plants regularly or occasionally consumed by fish were mostly surface plants and the fish rejected certain plants and vegetables while eating others (Jähnichen, 1967). Where no rooted vegetation is present and food is scarce, grass carp will leap out onto grass-covered banks to graze grass (Prowse, 1966). Penzes and Tölg (1966) listed twenty-two species of aquatic and land plants known to be consumed by grass carp held in aquariums. These authors indicate fish would not feed until the water temperatures exceeded 15°C.

No data on exact conversion factor of vegetable matter for grass carp is available. Ling (1967) reported value for some vegetables in the order of 40–50:1. Common carp and grass carp reared together showed an additional —1 ton more of fish per hectare on Russian pond farms. When grass carp were fed with ground vegetation, production of ponds could be increased an additional 3–4 tons/ha (Vinogradov, 1968). Russia produced 1200 tons in 1965 and projects 10,000 metric tons for 1970 (Jähnichen, 1968). Other fish such as the tawes (*Puntius javanicus*) in Indonesia or the gouramy (*Osphronemus goramy*) are also occasionally used for control of aquatic plants in pond culture in southeast Asia (Rabanal, 1968).

I. Tilapia Culture

Tilapia are considered another typical herbivorous cultivated fish which belong to the family Cichlidae, composed of hundreds of species and found mainly in tropical regions. Tilapia culture may be the oldest fish culture since it was practiced in Egypt about 2500 B.C. and has continued until today in small farm ponds. The first attempt to cultivate tilapia in Kenya, Africa, was recorded in 1924, followed by other trials in the Congo (1937), in Java (1938), in Indonesia (1939), in Zambia (1942), and in Rhodesia (1950). Tilapia cultivation is now encouraged in many countries to reduce protein deficiency in humans diets (Maar *et al.*, 1966; Swingle, 1960). Tilapia grow fast, reproduce rapidly, are easy to feed, easy to stock, of good food quality, and help control pond insects and weeds (Kelly, 1957). Tilapia have also been recently used to control aquatic vegetation in lakes and ponds in southern United States (Swingle, 1957b, 1960; Lahser, 1967). These fish will not survive cold water temperatures, and 12°–15°C appears fatal. Tilapia culture in tropical countries constitutes the most spectacular development in freshwater fisheries within the past quarter century. The inability to survive the cold winter temperatures of temperate countries, however, has restricted development of an active fish farming industry there, although certain fishery stations maintain tilapia indoors over the winter in troughs supplied with water maintained about 21°C by heating devices (Avault *et al.*, 1968b).

Three main species of tilapia are being widely cultivated: *T. mossambica, T. melanopleura* and *T. macrochir* (Huet 1960). Maar *et al.* (1966) report that *T. sparmanii, T. andersonii,* and *T. zillii* are important African cultivated fish. These tilapia species are easily identified by counting gill rakers.

Tilapia spawn in water above 22°C. Sexual maturity is reached at a few months and broodfish breed many times each year. When water temperature remains high, tilapia reproduction occurs, under pond conditions, every 5 to 7 weeks. Females lay from 100 to 6000 eggs per female, dependent upon species; repeated reproduction each year will account for 1000 to 40,000 fry per female per breeding year. Two different types of reproductive behavior have been recorded in tilapia. One group are mouthbreeders which hold the eggs in the mouth immediately after spawning and protect them during development of fry. *Tilapia mossambica* and *T. nilotica* are typical representatives of this group. The other group (*T. sparmanii*) are bottom spawners which lay eggs that adhere to the bottom of ponds and the broodstock guard the young until after hatching (Fishelson, 1966).

Male *T. nilotica* grow faster than females (Yashouv, 1958), and mechanical grading has been used to separate sexes in a fish pond population (Pruginin and Shell, 1962). Hybrids between *T. mossambica* and *T. nilotica* showed faster growth and better food conversion than the parent species, but over 90% of the young were male (Avault and Shell, 1967). Hybridization was adopted to produce monosexual culture using different tilapia species (Lessent, 1968; Pruginin, 1968; Semakula and Makoro, 1967). This technique may be valuable to prevent overcrowding of ponds with fishes of small size and low market value.

Most tilapia are omnivorous and readily consume both plant and animal matter. Huet (1960) claims tilapia utilize many different vegetable materials to the same degree that trout utilize animal materials. However, young tilapia up to 5 cm in length feed on small animals such as crustaceans, insect larvae, and other aquatic forms present in the pond and then gradually consume plant foods according to fish species and availability of food as the fish grow. When plant material and other food is lacking, fish will eat bottom detritus, muck, and decaying vegetation. Artificial feeds, therefore, consist mostly of vegetable by-products with some animal products to increase the nitrogen content of the diet. The diet not consumed fertilizes the pond increasing natural food present. Chopped grasses, water plants, algae, papaw, banana leaves, mill sweepings, bran, broken rice gains, and oil cake are usually used for tilapia feeding in several countries (Huet, 1960; Maar *et al.*, 1966; Ling, 1967). A list of food materials used in African tilapia culture is listed by Meschkat (1967) and includes all types of soft agricultural and household wastes. Some pellet feeding has been used with a formula similar to the one used for other warm water fishes (Kelley, 1957; Swingle, 1960).

Food conversion in tilapia varies according to food used and fish species. Little data are available but *T. mossambica* showed food conversion from 2.5 to 5.6, and *T. nilotica* from 2.8 to 6.0 on a diet of 80% Auburn No. 2 meal and 20% beef liver (Shell, 1967). Reports on African tilapia fish culture (Maar *et al.*, 1966) indicate that most cereals have a conversion of about 5, banana leaves only 25, cassava leaves 13, and napier grass 48. Meschkat (1967) indicates that food conversion of most leafy material must be in the order of 20:1 whereas more concentrated foods is about 6:1. Dry foods are fed in a form easily consumed by the fish, and grain fodder is soaked several hours before use. Vegetation is thrown into the ponds, often into rectangular floating feeding stations, and large leaves and coarse grass are usually coarsely chopped. Feeding frequency and ration may change from once a week to every day, depending upon the water temperature, fish density, and natural food present.

## J. Brackish Water and Sea Fish Culture

Several fish species are widely cultivated in brackish water areas in many countries. These are euryhaline fish which tolerate salinity change. This type of fish culture is generally performed in closed bays, lagoons, or

FIG. 57. A special boat, propelled by submerged jets, for lagoon bottom cultivation at Val Pisani, Cá Venier, Italy.

coastal lakes, where salinity can be regulated by introducing fresh- or saltwaters (Fig. 57). Installations employ several types of traps to allow young fish to enter from the sea, and to catch adult specimens returning to the sea. This form of fish culture is becoming more and more important in many areas of the world (Iversen, 1968).

Generally, young fish are caught by fishermen along the coast or near the river mouths and are sold alive to stock brackish water areas to increase the natural fish population present. Price of certain species is high because of the great demand and the low availability; in northern Italy, for example, gilthead fingerling have recently been priced at 20¢ each.

No pertinent data are available on the possibility of obtaining artificially spawned fry of important fish species cultivated in sea or brackish waters, although Swingle (1957c) reported that attempts had been made to strip and hatch eggs of practically all types of fresh- and saltwater fish. Almost all fingerlings used in this culture are collected from streams or along sandy beaches near the mouths of rivers or protected nursery areas.

Attempts have been made to induce mullet to breed by injection of hormone and then to raise the fry artificially. Preliminary attempts were made in India using *Mugil cephalus* and *Liza troschelii* brood fish collected from the sea near river mouths. Ovulation occurred when 8–16 mg of pituitary extract/kilogram body weight was used and the mullet could be stripped. These eggs developed only in seawater and on one occasion a *Mugil cephalus* egg hatched out only 48 hours at 23°C after fertilization. The sperm was found to be active for 10 minutes in seawater but died in freshwater. These results indicated that successful spawning may be achieved and commercial production of mullet fry made available when eggs are spawned and fertilized in seawater (Chaudhuri, 1968). Brood fish of *M. cephalus* were collected from the sea, held in boxes supplied with seawater, and injected with hormones in Taiwan (Tang, 1964). Mullet pituitary extract in combination with mammalian pituitary extract was used. Positive results were obtained only when two fish pituitaries were combined with forty rabbit units of Synahorin. The stripped eggs were artificially fertilized using the dry method and were hatched in aquariums with circulating seawater. The mullet eggs hatched but all the fry died within 4 days, indicating that the technique needed to be improved.

The potential was demonstrated, however, and undoubtedly the technique will be perfected shortly to provide mullet fry. Many countries have extensive fry collecting activities at the present time to obtain stock for ponds in northern Italy (Mann, 1961), in Tunisia (Meschkat, 1967), in Asia and the Far East (Tubb, 1967; Ling, 1967), and in Israel (Yashouv, 1966). In 1970 I assisted in a successful artificial propagation of *Mugil capito* at the Fish Culture Research Station, Dor, Israel.

Mullet feed on animal and vegetable matter and thus can be considered omnivorous. Several fertilizers have been employed in mullet culture to enhance the natural food content in fresh or brackish water ponds, with an increase in total fish yield (El-Zarka and Fahmy, 1968). *Mugil cephalus* and *M. capito* were reared in rectangular ponds of 3000–6000 m², supplied with brackish water. The ponds were fertilized with both commercial and organic fertilizers. Phosphate fertilizers gave better production than other compounds, organic fertilizers included. Fertilization increase mullet production by 160%. Mullet ponds in Israel were fertilized and were also supplementary fed. Superphosphate and chicken manure were employed to advantage (Yashouv, 1966). Ling (1967) reports that mullet ponds in Hong Kong and Taiwan were fertilized with organic manure and some supplementary feed was offered. Nitrate and phosphate fertilizer had no effect in Italian brackish water pond culture (Mann, 1961) because these brackish waters already had high natural organic content. A number of preliminary experiments in brackish water culture have been completed in the United States which indicate that this system is feasible on a commercial basis, when salinity can be easily controlled and water temperatures are within rapidly growing limits. Poor mullet production was observed, however, when inorganic fertilizer was used in ponds of high salinity (Fielding, 1968).

Several studies have been completed on the nutrition of mullet. Ling (1967) studied the natural feed which consisted of unicellular and filamentous algae, diatoms, benthic algae, detritus, and small pieces of soft vegetable matter. Recently Yashouv and Ben-Shachar (1967) have investigated the food for *M. cephalus* and *M. capito* in Israel. Fish on experiment were kept in aerated aquariums (7–10 liters) and in asbestos tanks of 675 liters. Fingerlings 3–6 cm in length were held in the aquariums and fish of 15–18 cm in the tanks. *Mugil capito* fry appeared to capture the food after visual contact. Animal food (larvae, ostracods, etc.) were apparently well digested whereas many of the algae ingested were not digested, and copepods appeared to have the greatest nutritional value for the small fish.

Supplementary feed for mullets varies from area to area. Small quantities of rice bran are generally used in India and in the Philippines, whereas in Hong Kong and Taiwan the feed is peanut meal and soybean cake (Ling, 1967). Other food employed in the supplementary feeding of carp and other warm water fishes was also used. Barley, wheat, other cereal grains, chicken offal, and animal offal were used (Yashouv, 1966), sorghum and pelleted foods mixed with wheat, fish meal, soya flour (Yashouv and Ben-Shachar, 1967), but no definite conclusions were made on rate of mullet growth and conversion rate. Commercial pellets have been offered on the Italian market by several companies for mullet feeding, but no reliable data are available on the suitability of these feeds and conversion rate for mullet reared in these ponds.

Mullet can also be reared with other fishes and Chinese carp, milkfish, sea perch (Rabanal, 1967), common pompano (*Trachinotus carolinus*), white shrimp (*Panaeus setiferus*) (Fielding, 1968), common carp and tilapia (Yashouv, 1966), tilapia hybrids (Fishelson and Popper, 1967), eels, and with other animals living in brackish water ponds.

One other important fish cultivated in brackish water is the milkfish (*Chanos chanos*). Culture of this fish was recently described in Taiwan by Tang and Chen (1967). The total area of milkfish ponds in Taiwan exceeds 18,000 ha, with average fish production of about 2000 kg of milkfish/ha. This culture of milkfish is well developed in the Philippines also (Rabanal, 1968) as well as in many other countries of Asia and the Far East (Ling, 1967).

Milkfish fry are collected from natural waters (Ling, 1967) but in the Philippines there are well-developed milkfish nursery ponds which secure the fry and raise them to fingerling stage to provide a continuing stock for fish ponds during the periods of the year in which no fry are available from marine spawning (Rabanal, 1968). The fry are first kept for a few days in boxes and are fed with mashed hard-boiled egg yolk, wheat starch, or rice bran, and are then transferred to ponds in which a rich growth of blue-green algae, diatoms, small invertebrate or vertebrate animals, and other insects has already started. The fry feed on natural food and on supplementary feeds such as rice bran, dried "lab-lab," and dried and ground submerged plants, which is fed once or twice a day (Ling, 1967).

Natural feed for milkfish consists of filamentous blue-green algae and diatoms growing in alluvional tidal flats or recent origin in salinity from 1 to 3%. Tang and Hwang (1967) measured the suitability of some brackish water pond algae as milkfish food. The digestion experiments were performed in brackish water concrete ponds of 6 × 4 × 0.5 m, and various groups of algae (green, blue-green, and phytoflagellatae) were used. The most nutritious feed for the fish appeared to be phytoflagellatae (mostly *Chlamydomonas* and *Chilodomonas*) which had a nutritive value (by Tang and Hwang's method of measurement) of 1:2.3. Diatoms and filamentous blue-green algae were also used with a nutritive ratio of 1:1.5 and 1:1.2, respectively, whereas fresh filamentous algae apparently was not digested and had a nutritive value of 1:33. Fresh filamentous blue-green algae and diatoms were preferred by the milkfish at any growing stage, including larval fish.

Since the production of milkfish from brackish water ponds is directly proportional to the growth of the algae pasture, the management of these ponds demands techniques for regulating the environmental conditions which favor the growth of desirable groups of algae (filamentous blue-green and diatoms). A constant supply of necessary plant nutrients is necessary and accomplished by fertilization and management of the bottom soil. The ponds are dried and flooded alternately to increase the supply of salt and other algae nutrients in the soil and to improve soil condition. The most common organic fertilizer used in milkfish farms is rice bran followed by compost manures. Rice bran is also used as a supplementary feed. Some chemical fertilizers have been used (Tang and Chen, 1967) and according to Ling (1967), the detritus of filamentous green algae becomes food for milkfish because the algae becomes softened by partial decomposition after death of the plant.

Silverside culture is common in South America in brackish water ponds (Conroy, 1967). Various representatives of the Aterinidae are found in South American brackish waters (*Odontesthes bonariensis*, *Austromenidia microlepidota*, *Odontesthes regia*), but the most important species for fish farming is *O. bonariensis*.

Fresh or slightly brackish waters prove excellent environments for this fish whenever the temperature is above 18°C. Two spawning periods occur each year, and mature brood silversides are caught in brackish waters and are stripped manually in the same manner as in trout husbandry. Fertilized eggs are incubated in MacDonald or Zug bottles. Alevins for the first 15 days are not fed and then are stocked into fertilized ponds in which natural foods are abundant (brine shrimp, Daphnia, Tubifex, etc.). After a few weeks small fingerlings are fed with wet diets containing liver, blood, and glandular tissue, and after 2 months various amounts of bran are offered. Silversides are cultivated in Argentina especially for stocking sport fishing waters. Some are raised for the meat market, and when better diets become available more will be used in fish farming.

## K. Eel Culture

Extensive eel culture is carried on in brackish waters very similar to mullet culture along the coastlines of the sea or ocean. In Italy, for example, near the Po delta brackish waters have been used for production of European eel (*Anguilla anguilla*) in "valli" (fenced-in ponds) for hundreds of years. Salinity can be regulated through sea gates and freshwater from adjacent streams or rivers. Small eels are allowed to migrate in from the sea or are caught along the coastal areas and transferred to the "valli" at the fingerling stage. No artificial feed was used for many years and the growth of the eel was very slow, covering several years to reach marketable size. Mature eels are caught in special traps which in the past were made with wood and cane but are now of concrete or aluminum rods. For several decades commercial plants have canned eel and other brackish water fishes such as the Mediterranean Aterinidae (*Atherina hepseptus*) to maintain the price of cultivated fishes because of seasonal variation in supply.

Recently artificial foods have been used with a protein content of 20–30% to augment natural foods present in these brackish water areas, but little attention has been placed on vitamin or fat supplements; and the eel farmers have relied upon natural food in the ponds to furnish these nutrients.

Several other brackish seawater fishes are cultivated along with the eel, such as gilthead (*Sparus auratus*), sea bass (*Dicentrarchus labrax*), mullets (*Mugil* spp.) Mullets and gilthead can be readily fed with trout diets but sea bass are more difficult to feed (Ghittino, 1969b). Yields of fish in unfertilized and unfed ponds become less and less profitable, going down from 150–200 to 50 kg/ha. When the yield in western developed countries is as low as 50 kg of fish/ha, many brackish water lands are converted into agricultural cultivation. Recently in Asia and in Europe, eel have been raised in freshwater ponds with excellent results.

Almost all of the eel (*Anguilla japonica*) served in Japan come from pond

F<small>IG</small>. 58.  A typical eel pond in Shizuoka Prefecture, Japan.  In the foreground, the
pumped water inlet in "rest channel;" in the pond middle, the working agitator.

operations (Fig. 58). These eels were fed a combination of mackerel and
silkworm chrysalids and were reared together with carp and mullet. This
trilogy of species has dominated Japanese commercial pond operations
for many years (Drews, 1961). Eel culture in Taiwan is also carried on in
running water ponds ranging from 800 to 2000 m² with an average depth
of 1–2 m. Eel fry averaging 0.2 gm are collected from lower estuaries of
the river, are cultured to fingerling size in nursery ponds, and are grown to
marketable size in the growing ponds (Figs. 59 and 60). The growth of eel
is slow compared to other fishes. In unfed ponds 1 year is necessary to grow
fry to young eel of 20 gm average weight and a second year is necessary to
reach marketable size of about 200 gm. Food used for the second growing
year consists of trash fish, small crabs and crustaceans, offal from slaughter
houses, fish markets, fish processing plants, beef blood, earthworms, aquatic
worms, and silkworm pupae. Some operations employ worms and cooked
trash fish to feed eel fingerlings. Food is placed in feeding baskets at or
under the surface and the daily ration varies from 5–10% of the body
weight of the fish according to the water temperature (Fig. 61). A conversion rate of food to fish flesh 10–15:1 was recorded (Ling, 1967). Kuronuma (1968) reported complementary culture of carp and eel in recirculating water in Japan, but the method was not readily accepted by
Japanese fish culturists (Fig. 62). A survey of Japanese pond culture of

Fig. 59. A feeding hut in a Japanese eel farm. See feeding basket (arrow).

Fig. 60. Astride two ponds, the feeding hut in a modern Japanese eel farm (Yaizu, Skizuoka Pref., Japan).

Fig. 61. Eels coming to feed in the feeding basket lowered into the water.

Fig. 62. A drained tank for eel rearing indoors with heated and recirculating water in Japan.

Fig. 63.  Mackerel skeletons left by eels in a Japanese eel farm.  (Photo Dr. C. J. Rasmussen, Exp. Trout Farm, Bröns, Denmark, 1969.)

eels was assembled by Koops (1966b) who found eel pond culture concentrated in the prefectures of Shizuoka, Aichi, and Mie in the southern part of Japan. Production in 1966 was about 8000 metric tons from nearly 2000 fish farms. These eels were fed chiefly with fish and fish cannery wastes supplemented with silkworm pupae, either raw or dried, fish meal, and liver. One common method for feeding pond eels was to string mackerel through the eyes on a wire, cook in boiling water for a few minutes, then immerse in the pond. The eels would consume the flesh, leaving only the skeletons (Fig. 63). Today, however, the fish are generally fed with paste foods. Dry food must be very finely ground, otherwise it is refused by the eels. Alfa potato starch is used to form a paste and when water and oil are added, a very sticky diet is formed (Figs. 64 and 65). Blocks of this paste are put into subsurface feeding baskets and eels run to it immediately, often passing through the mesh of the basket (Fig. 66), and feed out of water. Fish remain in the feeding basket until full, or for some minutes. In extreme cases, an eel can feed 15% of its body weight (Fig. 67). The composition of dry meals for eel is about 50% white fish meal plus other meals, vitamins, and minerals. The diet is diluted with 50–60% of water and 10–15% of fish oil just before feeding. Dry pellets and fresh fish are occasionally employed for larger eels.

Conversion for fresh fish in eel feeding ranges from 10–15:1 (Ling, 1967), 5–10:1 (Koops, 1966a, 1967), 7–8:1 (Meyer-Waarden and Koops, 1968). Modern Japanese dry foods have a conversion of 1.2–1.6:1, in paste form, and 1.0–1.6, in dry pellets (Ghittino, 1969a). Efforts are being made to

Fig. 64.   Eel paste hand mixing.

Fig. 65.   Eel paste ready to feed.

Fɪɢ. 66.  Voracious eels eating blocks of paste in the feeding basket.

Fɪɢ. 67.  A pond eel that had filled its stomach to 15% of body weight. (Photo Prof. S. Egusa, Dep. Fish., Fac. Agr., Tokyo, Japan, 1968.)

Fig. 68. Halver's synthetic diet used to study vitamin requirements of eel.

establish the vitamin requirements of eel and employ synthetic diets similar to the ones used by Halver for salmonids (Figs. 68 and 69).

Elvers are obtained in small ponds in Europe from adult migrating eel. Some are kept in aquariums and fed with natural foods like Daphnia, Enchyträe, Tubifex, Chironomus larvae until grown to elver size. Müller (1964) reported eels fed with minced freshwater fish grew 15–17 cm in the first year and 18–22 cm in the second year. Food was consumed both during daylight and night hours. Feeding experiments with eels of different sizes were completed in Germany by Koops (1965). Aquariums with a surface of 100 m² and a depth of 1 m were supplied with tap or well water and were stocked with eels of different year classes, i.e., elvers, yearling, and 2- year-old eels. The older fish were fed minced fresh fish, shrimp, and crab and the elvers were started on natural foods and then converted to beef and swine spleen plus minced fish. Food was offered in specific feeding places late in the afternoon. Large eels were kept in ponds at low density to eliminate the unpleasant phenol taste which occurred in eel from polluted rivers. Some groups were also fed with trout pellets, but the brand used rapidly disintegrated in the water and food was poorly used. Elvers were fed at 5–15% of the body weight and food conversion was recorded at 5–8:1. Yearling eels were fed at 10% of the body weight and showed a conversion of 7–8:1. Adult eels consumed 2% of the body weight/day but did not increase in size or length and did lose the unpleasant taste after several weeks in pond conditions. In other experiments, small eel (16 gm) were fed with minced coarse fish but the water temperature was higher than 15°C and food was fed at 10% of the body weight/day with poorer food conversion of 14:1. Nearly 25% of eels of the last experiment suffered cauliflower disease (Koops, 1966a). Later experiments showed that young elvers and eel fingerlings could be fed in ponds with minced fish, shrimp waste, and fresh meats with a conversion rate lower than 10:1, and he concluded that commercial pond feeding of eels would be feasible in Europe in freshwater or in brackish water ponds (Lauterbach, 1966).

The culture of ayu (*Plecoglossus altivelis*) is similar to eel culture although the ayu is a member of the salmon family which spawns at sea. This fish is reared in commercial quantities in ponds in Japan (Drews, 1961; Kuronuma, 1968; Egusa, 1968) from fry collected in streams, beaches, and estuaries during the spring months. These young fish are stocked in ponds and fed artificially with natural foods such as algae, rotifers, crustaceans, and then with supplementary artificial food. Fertilization and hatching of young is being practiced experimentally, and experiments have been planned to accumulate data and to develop a technique on a commercial basis. The first experiments used light to speed up sexual maturation and to stimulate fry to use natural foods more completely for longer feeding periods. Since ayu die after spawning, efforts were made to delay spawning to extend availability of young fish for extending rearing periods. Ayus

Fig. 69. During eel harvest in Japan, adjacent eel farms help each other.

Fig. 70.  A yellowtail rearing plant in floating net baskets in Kuchino, Numazu, shi, Shizuoka prefecture, Japan.

experimentally treated spawned about 2 months earlier than those in natural rivers, and adults would survive until spring months the following year without impaired reproductive activity. Further work, including endocrinology experiments, will be necessary to master this technique (Kuronuma, 1968).

Yellowtail (*Seriola quinqueradiata*) are reared in Japan in protected bays in nets and are fed fresh fish, food paste, or dry pellets (Figs. 70). Two years are required to produce 2-kg fish. Over 20,000 tons of yellowtail are reared annually in Japan (Egusa, 1968).

Many other euryhaline fish can be reared in brackish water in association with the above species. Generally any commercial brackish water pond culture system should be located in an area where a long warm growing season exists and supplies of larvae, fry, and trash fish for feeding are available at low cost. The ponds must be constructed on tight soil with good drainage and sources of both fresh- and seawater are necessary to control salinity (Fielding, 1968).

Small pompano (*Trachinotus carolinus*) can be collected along coastal areas and stocked in brackish water ponds for commercial production. These fish have been fed ground fish with an average conversion of about 6:1. Natural food content of the pond is generally enhanced with fertilizer before the pond is stocked with small pompano. Also spotted sea trout

(*Cynoscion nebulosus*) have been grown in similar areas and fed ground whole trash fish (Fielding, 1968). Multiple culture of complementary fish species in brackish water is common and often promotes more complete and efficient utilization of both natural food present and artificial food fed.

Obviously, many marine animals suitable for human consumption can be reared in brackish and saline water such as oysters, shrimp, crab, lobster, and prawn; when ponds are fertilized with organic and inorganic nutrients, an increase in the total yields can be expected. Some typical freshwater fish like the common carp can also be reared in certain brackish waters and research on acceptable salinity for carp is presently under way in Israel (Soller *et al.*, 1965).

## L. Other Cultured Fish of Commercial Importance

Indian major carps catla (*Catla catla*), rohu (*Labeo rohita*), mrigal (*Cirrhina mrigala*), and calbasu (*Labeo calbasu*), are grown extensively in well-developed industry throughout southeast Asia (Bhimachar and Tripathy, 1967). Fishermen collect spawn from flooded waters during monsoon months for stocking although recent work has shown the possibility of obtaining spawn from broodstock held in special ponds called bundhs. This ancient industry has been based on art and lacks scientific background, but the potential toward an efficient industry is present. Older empirical and traditional methods are currently followed although recent studies have been organized to induce these carps to breed. Heavy rains, partial or whole submersion in shallows, low alkalinity, and lunar periods were reported factors to stimulate spawning activity. The administration of pituitary gland extract was also employed for inducing ovulation in these fishes (Chaudhuri, 1968). Success of homoplastic pituitary injections to produce viable spawn indicates that Indian carp will probably be cultivated on a much larger scale in the future.

These carp feed not only on unicellular algae but also on zooplankton. Artificial fertilization including some micronutrients have been used. Control of predacious insects (*Anisopus* spp., *Laccoptephes* spp., *Ranatra* spp.) has been attempted by spreading vegetable oils slowly over the water surface. Supplementary feed includes rice bran and ground nut oil cake employed in finely powdered form; other studies have been conducted with dried powdered shrimp, notonectids, cereals, fat-free proteins, and supplemented with antibiotics and B complex vitamins (Bhimachar and Tripathy, 1967).

Food habits and survival of Indian carp fry were recently studied in aquariums (Das, 1967). These fish were fed live Daphnia and, in addition, the aquariums were fertilized with micronutrients including vitamin $B_{12}$, goat stomach extract, cobalt nitrate, water soluble vitamin complex, and dried brewer's yeast. Yeast at 15 gm/liter of water significantly increased growth and may be economical and easily administrated in large field crop cultivation.

Indian carp appear omnivorous but the major portion of the food consists of plant matter including algae and higher aquatic plants. Vegetable utilization is highest in *Cirrhina mrigala*, less in *Labeo rohita*, and least in *Catla catla;* animal foods are utilized in inverse order (Ranade and Kewalramani, 1967).

*Heterotis niloticus* has been cultivated in ponds in several African countries. This fast growing species, which utilized both natural and artificial feed and reaches large body weight, has been fed with peanut oil cake, crushed whole cottonseed, and rice bran (Lemasson and Bard, 1968). Conversion was measured at 50 for rice bran, 42 for cottonseed, and 27 for peanut cake. Sexual maturity was dependent upon fish growth and occurred 1 year before unfed controls when artificial feed was used (Reizer, 1967).

Several *Barbus* species (*Barbus grypus, B. xanthopterus, B. luteus,* and *B. sharpeyi*) have been cultured together with common carp in Iraq. Spawning was not observed in pond culture and therefore suitability of use of these four species of mixed pond culture must await techniques to induce replacement stock before the industry can develop (Al-Hamed, 1967).

Several indigenous fishes of temperate waters in South and Central America have been collected and reared on an experimental basis but no commercial industry has developed yet. Some were treated with pituitary extracts in Brazil and the fry obtained were stocked into reservoirs or used for large-scale fish farming. Successful breeding was induced in *Prochilodus, Leporinus, Curimata, Triportheus,* and *Trachycorystes*. Eight species of *Cichlasoma* are reared in Guatemala; in Brazil carnivorous fishes of the Cichlidae family, *Astronotus ocellatus, Chichla ocellaris,* and *C. Temensis,* and two carnivorous fishes, *Plagioscion surinamensis* and *P. squamosissimus,* have been bred on an experimental basis but have not been used in commercial fish farming. Fry of *Arapaima gigas* have been produced for fish culture in Peru and some species of pirana (*Serrasalmus*) have been reproduced in captivity under aquarium conditions in the United States (Menezes, 1968).

The government of several regions in India has established a program for the culture and distribution of larvicidal fish used for biological control of mosquito larvae which act as vector in the spread of various human diseases (*Lebistes reticulatus, Gambusia affinis, Etrophus suratensis, E. maculatus,* and *Horaichthys setnai*).

The loach (*Misgurnus anguillicaudatus*) is cultivated in Japanese ponds and is considered as equivalent in flavor to the eel. Several other fishes are reared also in pond culture including *Sarcocheilichthys variegatus,* the delicious pond smelt (*Hypomesus olidus*), and the wild form of the familiar goldfish (*Carassius auratus*). The general husbandry and the food used for this goldfish is virtually identical to that of carp pond culture, and this fish is considered in Japan to be an excellent food fish (Drews, 1961).

Ponds in Indonesia are stocked with combinations of indigenous and native species (kissing gouramy, *Helostoma temmincki;* tawes, *Puntius javanicus;* nilem, *Osteochilus hasselti;* gouramy, *Osphronemus goramy*) and introduced species like carp and tilapia (Rabanal, 1967). The kissing gouramy is a planktonic feeder while the tawes consumes coarse fish pond vegetation, playing the role of the grass carp in more temperate countries. The gouramy is an herbivore utilizing vegetable materials along the pond margins (Rabanal, 1968).

## M. STURGEON CULTURE

Russia has developed extensive sturgeon husbandry techniques. Spawn is obtained from both wild, ripe females and captured fish treated with pituitary extracts. These techniques and results to obtain replacement fry for sturgeon farming are well covered in a review by Pickford and Atz (1957).

Russian fish culturists found that not all members of a given species would enter freshwater at the same stage of sexual maturity. Consequently, various acipenserine fish could be separated into seasonal races. Sturgeons belonging to the same species enter the same river at different times of the year and spawn at different times. Berg (1934) identified two races in nearly all the species of migratory aciperserine fish in the U.S.S.R. Several biological groups were described for osetr (*Acipenser güldenstädti*), sevriuga (*A. stellatus*), sterlet (*A. ruthenus*), and beluga (*Huso huso*). Each group responded differently to pituitary treatment. Some, when injected shortly after capture, produced nonviable ova. Techniques were developed to hold and treat each sturgeon group differently for good production of young fish, and adequate numbers of young fry and fingerlings were obtained for stocking purposes. Most of the operations were directed toward replacing populations fishes for caviar production.

Rearing of Acipenseridae fry has been reviewed by several authors and illustrated by Liepolt and Weber (1964). Experiments were performed on

Danube River stations using sterlets, a fast-growing species with good flesh of fine quality. Spawn was obtained by pituitary injection from captured females. Fertilized eggs were incubated in troughs supplied with filtered Danube water at 16°C and fish hatched after about 1 week. At 10 days, fry were about 10–12 mm long and could be kept in wooden troughs supplied with water at 16°–17°C.

Sturgeon fry were fed nauplii of the crustacean *Artemia salina* and when over 10 cm long would feed at a low water temperature of 5°–6°C. *Artemia* eggs were incubated in salt water at 28°C and after the larvae had hatched were fed to the fry three times daily. Nauplii of artemia can survive in freshwater about 4–5 hours, then fall to the bottom where these were consumed by sturgeon fry. The abdomen of young sturgeon appeared distended and orange colored by the great number of crustacea larvae ingested. Dried crustacea was added to the food after 3–4 weeks and then the fish progressed to complete trimixtures made up of animal and vegetable meals and enriched with several vitamins. Fry food used to start fry feeding for intermediate sized fish were minced earthworms, tubifex, insect larvae, water fleas (Daphnia, Cyclops), brine shrimp (*Artemia salina*), and infusoria.

Extensive work has been completed on the metabolism and gross nutrient requirements of sturgeon by Winberg (1956/1960) and today results of these researches have been extended to develop the largest sturgeon farming ventures in the world throughout southern U.S.S.R. New complete dry mixtures consisting of fish and animal meals, brewer's yeast, distillers' solubles, oil seed meals, and vitamin supplements are used to accelerate growth of fish reared in lakes, ponds, raceways, and stream pens to be used as replacement stock in major rivers and lakes of this area.

Rearing of sturgeons with other species is feasible and often many fish farms employ several adult sturgeon to salvage extra food fed and consume mortalities which occur from other fish reared in the same fish farm.

## N. Crustacean Culture

Several species of crayfish (*Potamobius* spp., *Astacus* spp.) are found in European freshwaters, but only a few species are artificially cultivated. Koch (1960) reviews details on reproduction, molting, and feeding of crayfish cultivated in Germany. Several aquatic animals are used as natural feed for crayfish including snails, mussels, insect larvae, frogs, fish, and fish roe; under intensive culture crayfish will consume some vegetable matter as well as meat scraps, oil seed cake, and slaughter house by-products.

Crayfish culture is still performed in Italy where special breeding ponds are maintained to obtain larvae for stock into other ponds or into small streams where fishing is forbidden. After several months, young crayfish a few centimeters long are collected and put into rearing ponds alone or together with small rainbow trout. Crayfish are fed inexpensive sea fish anchovies, sardines, and with a soft, wet diet composed of cereal and animal meals. Market-sized crayfish are in great demand, and the diets used together with the simple husbandry can yield profitable margins on investment.

Giant freshwater prawn (*Macrobrachium rosenbergii*) have been used experimentally in pond culture (Sidthimunka and Choapaknam, 1968). This crustacean originates in Thailand and can grow to 500 gm in weight. Young prawns collected from ponds and streams were confined in growing ponds and fed boiled tilapia and chopped fresh waste carp flesh at about 5% of the body weight/day. A pile of bricks or dry branches is placed in the bottom of the pond to provide shelter during the molting period. Each pond is constructed with several feeding places on which artificial food is placed. Average food conversion was 6:1 in the first 3 months of rearing, but 13:1 during the last 3 months before marketing.

This brackish water crustacean has potential for intensive cultivation in several countries. It can be used as a secondary crop in many waters and efforts are directed toward development of more adequate artificial diets to promote increased production, since these animals are in great demand for gourmet human food.

The white shrimp (*Penaeus setiferus*) is another promising product for brackish water areas (Fielding, 1968). Propagation of white shrimp in captivity was accomplished in ponds. Shrimps spawn four times over a 2-year period in seawater with salinity ranging from 3 to 4%, but the water used in spawning tanks needed to be filtered to remove undesirable sea organisms. Food was introduced after the larvae entered the first feeding stage. Juvenile white shrimp grew at the rate of 1–2 mm/day for the first month. Various species of prawn (*Penaeus monodon, P. japonicus, P. indicus,* and *Metapenaeus ensis*) have been cultivated together with milkfish in brackish water ponds in the Orient. These prawns feed mainly on worms and insect larvae which are abundant in ponds and no supplementary feed was used (Ling, 1967). Shrimp have been raised in the Far East for over five centuries using tidal marshes and, in Japan, an extensive industry has developed both in marketing shrimp from fish farms and in breeder stations to develop larvae for stocking the growing areas (Borgstrom, 1962). This industry involves supplementary feeding of the shrimp in the impoundments with high protein food to exhilarate growth and increase the pond yield.

Larval and postlarval sand shrimp (*Crangon crangon*) collected in the North Sea have been reared in laboratory containers at a salinity of 3% in a constant temperature of 14°C. When the light was altered to simulate day and night conditions, larvae and postlarvae fed actively on nauplii of *Artemia salina* using the same methods described by Rollefesen (1939) for rearing of small seawater fish, and by Zein-Eldin (1962) for postlarval brown shrimp (*Penaeus aztecus*) rearing. Larger shrimp were fed juvenile or mature *Artemia* and the food supply was grown employing algae or a suspension of *Saccaromyces cerevisiae* (Meixner, 1966).

## O. Mollusk Culture

Many edible bivalve mollusks have been cultivated in brackish or seawater areas throughout the world. These shallow or tidal areas have different degrees of fertility dependent upon nutrients available, salinity, stable soil bed and, more recently, on pollutants occurring in the water. Organically rich seawater is most suitable for optimum growth of bivalves which filter and strain out nutrient particles from the water. Consequently, many strains of bacteria and yeast, some of which may be pathogenic to humans such as *Salmonella* spp., may become concentrated in the siphon or gills of the mollusks. The husbandry generally consists of physical maintenance of the rearing area, stocking and thinning, and sometimes fertilizing with inorganic fertilizers to increase the natural food on which the mollusks feed. Artificial spawning and fertilization has been accomplished in the American oyster (*Crassostrea virginica*) and in the Japanese oyster. The small bivalves have been reared in the laboratory and more recently commercially with natural food cultivated in adjacent tanks.

Brackish seawater pond fertilization enhances phytoplankton growth and within acceptable temperature limits mollusks can be grown to marketable size in 1 or 2 years less than in natural marginal food-containing environments (Fielding, 1968). Oysters can be reared together with marine species as long as food and salinity is properly maintained and predators or specific diseases are controlled. Several techniques for spawning egg cultivation, larval rearing, and farming of oysters have been reviewed by Loosanoff and Davis (1963) and by Sinderman (1970).

## V. Marine Fish Husbandry

The potential of marine fish farming has stimulated interest in fish husbandrymen from each country bounding the sea; with the exception of brackish water fish culture discussed previously, little concrete progress has been made because husbandry techniques, diet, and replacement stock have not been developed. Many marine fish begin life as tiny larvae which cannot ingest large food particles but only monocellular algae. Therefore, the preparation of micropulverized balanced stable rations for young larvae and fry has not yet been developed. A major effort to develop the techniques necessary for cultivation of valuable marine flat fish has been undertaken in Great Britain where developments in rearing techniques from metamorphosis of plaice (*Pleuronectes platessa*) were started in 1957. Five years later techniques for temperature, light, background, disease control, and tank design produced a tenfold increase in survival. Then in 1965 metamorphized sole (*Solea solea*) were reared successfully under hatchery conditions (Shelbourne, 1970). The food used in each case was brine shrimp nauplii for the young fry, then addition of small tubifex worms, and finally minced clam necks and ground sea fish flesh. These pioneer research experiments in sea fish husbandry encompassed spawning, hatching, initial rearing, feeding, marking, grading, fattening and processing plaice, sole, and turbot reared in many types of containers, floating or sunken in waters of different salinity, and in impoundments and nets along the shore line. Warm seawater was also used at the Hunterston Experimental Station where a nuclear powered electric generating station discharged warm seawater back into the estuary. An adequate review of the problems and progress of these efforts, plus a general discussion of problems of diet and husbandry techniques in sea fish culture, is included in the symposium on Marine Aquiculture (McNeil, 1970).

As soon as adequate diets for initial feeding fish, for fingerlings, and for growing fish have been developed, the potential of marine fish husbandry can be realized as more and more use of the sea environment is used to produce rich valuable protein for the ever hungry growing population of the world. Knowledge of basic nurtitional requirements is a necessary foundation for this work and several test diets are now available which will enable investigators to classify qualitative and quantitative requirements for vitamins, protein, and fat to enable the feed industry to formulate and manufacture balanced rations which will satisfy nutritional requirements of the species reared to convert inexpensive agricultural and animal waste products into expensive protein for human consumption. These diets and the husbandry to use them should be developed within the next decade.

## References

Al-Hamed, M. I. (1967). *FAO Fish. Rep.* 44(2), 135–142.
Aliev, D. S. (1961). *Vop. Ikhtiol.* 1(4), 650–568. (In Russian, quoted by A. G. Konradt, 1966.)

Alikunhi, K. H., Sukumaran, K. K., and Parameswaran, S. (1963). *Curr. Sci.* **32**, 103–106. (Quoted by D. Scheer, 1964, and by J. W. Avault, Jr., 1965.)

Amlacher, E. (1961). "Taschenbuch Der Fischkrankheiten." Veb G. Fischer V., Jena.

Anwand, K. (1967). *Z. Fisch. Hilfswiss.* **14**(3/4), 317–320.

Anwand, K., and Grohmann, G. (1966). *Z. Fisch. Hilfswiss.* **14**(5/6), 383–391.

Aschner, M., Laventer, C., and Chorin-Kirsch, I. (1967). *Bamidgeh* **19**(7), 23–25.

Associaz. Piscicolt. Ital., Via Indipendenza, 5, Treviso, Italy.

Avault, J. W., Jr. (1965). *Progr. Fish. Cult.* **27**(4), 207–209.

Avault, J. W., Jr., and Shell, E. W. (1967). *FAO Fish. Rep.* **44**(4), 237–242.

Avault, J. W., Jr., Shell, E. W., and Smitherman, R. O. (1967a). *FAO Fish. Rep.* **44**(5), 103–123. *Warm Water Pond Fish Cult.*, Rome, doc. FR:V/E-3, 2 pp.

Avault, J. W., Jr., Smitherman, R. O., and Shell, E. W. (1968b). *FAO Fish. Rep.* **44**(5), 109–122.

Banerjea, S. M., and Banerjee, S. C. (1967). *FAO Fish. Rep.* **44**(3), 132–152.

Bank, O. (1966a). *Oesterr. Fisch.* **19**(4), 56–59.

Bank, O. (1966b). *Der Fischbauer*, No. 215, 2 pp.

Bennet, G. W. (1962). "Management of Artificial Lakes and Ponds." Reinhold, New York.

Berg, L. S. (1934). Quoted by G. E. Pickford, and J. W. Atz, 1957, p. 252.

Bhimachar, B. S., and Tripathy, S. D. (1967) *FAO Fish. Rep.* **44** (2), 1-33.

Bitzer, R. R. (1963). *U. S. Trout News, July–August*, pp. 3.

Blackburn, R. D. (1968). *FAO Fish. Rep.* **44**(5), 7–17.

Borgstrom, G. (ed.). (1961). "Fish as Food," Vol. 1. Academic Press, New York.

Borgstrom, G. (1962). *In* "Fish as Food" (G. Borgstrom, ed.), Vol. II, p. 274. Academic Press, New York.

Bregnballe, F. (1963). *Progr. Fish. Cult.* **25**(3), 115–120.

Brockway, D. R. (1953). *Progr. Fish. Cult.* **15**, 92.

Brymer, J. H. P. (1954). "Water Life." Dorset House, London.

Buss, K. (1958). *Pennsylvania Angler*, Sept., 12–14.

Canaga, and Ratnam (1959). Quoted by Schäperclaus, 1961, pp. 439.

Carlin, B. (1966). *EIFAC, 4th Session, Belgrade, Yugoslavia*, May 9–14, 1966, 66/SC II-2.

Chaudhuri, H. (1968). *FAO Fish. Rep.* **44**(4), 30–66.

Chimits, P. (1958). *Bull. Fr. Piscicult.* **30**(188), 84–91.

Christensen, N. O., Jensen, M., and Rasmussen, C. J. (1963). *Bull. Office Int. Epizoot.* **59**(1–2), 21–29.

Clemens, H. W. (1968). *FAO Fish. Rep.* **44**(4), 67–80.

Clemens, H. P., and Sneed, K. E. (1957). *U.S. Dep. Int. Spec. Sci. Rep.* **61**, 30 pp.

Conroy, D. A. (1967). *Riv. Ital. Piscicult. Ittiopat.* **2**(3), 48–55.

Cornelius, W. O. (1933). *Z. Fisch. Hilfswiss.* **31**, 535–566.

Corti (1949). Quoted by W. Schäperclaus, 1961, pp. 504.

Crawford, B. (1958). *Proc. Southeast Ass. Game Comm.* **11**, 132–141.

Danielewski, S. (1965). *Rocz. Nauk Roln.* **86**(B-2), 341–359.

Das, B. C. (1967). *FAO Fish Rep.* **44**(3), 247–256.

Davis, H. S. (1947). *U. S. Gov. Printing Office Res. Rep.* 12.

Davis, H. S. (1961). "Culture and Diseases of Game Fish," Univ. Calif. Press, Berkeley and Los Angeles, California.

Davis, J. T., and Hughes, J. S. (1967). *Lo. Wildl. Fish Comm. Wildl. Educ. Bull.* **98**, 29 pp.

Denzer, H. W. (1968). *FAO Fish. Rep.* **44**(4), 357–366.

Deuel, C. R., Haskell, D. C., Brockway, D. R., and Kingsbury, O. R. (1952). *N. Y. Cons. Dep. Fish. Res. Bull.* (No. 3).

Deufel, J. (1965). *Arch. Fischereiwiss.* **16**(2), 125–132.

Disalov (1965). Quoted by A. Yashouv, 1966, pp. 4.

Dobie, J. (1966). *FAO Fish. Rep.* **44**(3), 274–284.

Doudoroff, P. (1957). *In* "The Physiology of Fishes" (M. E. Brown, ed.), Vol. II. Academic Press, New York.

Drews, R. A. (1961). *In* "Fish as Food" (G. Borgstrom, ed.), Vol. I., pp. 139–140. Academic Press, New York.

Dupree, H. K. (1966). *Tech. Pap. Bur. Sport Fish. Wildl.*, 12 pp.

Dupree, H. K., and Sneed, K. E. (1966). *Tech. Pap. Bur. Sport Fish. Wildl.*, 21 pp.

Dupree, H. K., and Halver, J. E. (1970). *Trans. Amer. Fish. Soc.* **99**, 90–92.

Egusa, S. (1968). *Bull. Office Int. Epizoot.* **69**(7–8), 1035–1044.

El Bolock, A. R., and Labib, W. (1967). *FAO Fish. Rep.* **44**(2), 165–174.

El Zarka, S. E., and Fahmy, F. K. (1968). *FAO Fish. Rep.* **44**(5), 255–266.

Fielding, J. R. (1968). *FAO Fish. Rep.* **44**(5), 143–161.

Fijan, N. (1967). *FAO Fish. Rep.* **44**(3), 114–123.

Fijan, N. (1969). Personal Communication.

Fishelson, L. (1966). *Bamidgeh* **18**(3–4), 67–80.

Fishelson, L., and Popper, D. (1967). *FAO Fish. Rep.* **44**(5), 244–245.

Fuhrmann, B. (1967). *Deut. Fisch. Ztg.* **14**(1), 26–30.

Gaver, F. E. (1964). *Progr. Fish. Cult.* **26**(1), 48.

Gaylord, H. R., and Marsh, C. (1914). *U. S. Bur. Fish. Bull.* **32** (1912), 157–220.

Geng (1925). Quoted by W. Schäperclaus, "Lehrbuch der Teichwirtschaft," 1961, p. 59.

Gerbilskii, N. L. (1959). *Acta Hydrobiol. Sin.* **4**, 489–509. (In Russian, quoted by A. G. Konradt, 1968.)

Ghittino, P. (1961). *Vet. Ital.* **12**, 3–16.

Ghittino, P. (1967). *Riv. Ital. Piscicolt. Ittiopat.* **2**(2), 24–29.

Ghittino, P. (1969a). "Piscicoltura e Ittiopatologia," Vol. I. Rivista Zootecnia, Milano, Italy.

Ghittino, P. (1969b). *Riv. Ital. Piscicolt. Ittiopat.* **4**(3), 61.

Golterman, H. L. (1967). *FAO Fish. Rep.* **44**(3), 27–42.

Gooch, B. C. (1967). *FAO Fish. Rep.* **44**(3), 13–26.

Greene, G. N. (1968). *FAO Fish. Rep.* **44**(4), 86–92.

Gribanov, L. V., Korneev, A. N., and Korneeva, L. A. (1968). *FAO Fish. Rep.* **44**(5), 218–226.

Gunjko, A. F., and Pleskachevskaya, T. G. (1962). *Probl. Ichthyol.* **2**(2), 371–374.

Halstead, B. W. (1962). *In* "Fish as Food" (G. Borgstrom, ed.), Vol. II,. pp. 534–535. Academic Press, New York.

Halver, J. E. (1953). *Trans. Amer. Fish. Soc.* **83**, 254–261.

Halver, J. E. and Mitchell, I. A. (1967). *Trout Hepatoma, Res. Conf. Pap., Res. Rep.* **70**, 199 pp. U. S. Govt. Print. Office, Washington, D. C.

Hastings, W. H. (1964). *Feedstuffs* **36**(21–23).

Hepher, B. (1967). *FAO Fish. Rep.* **44**(3), 1–6.

Hepher, B., and Chervinski, J. (1965). *Bamidgeh* **17**, 31–46.

Hickling, C. F. (1962). "Fish Culture." Faber and Faber, London.

Higurashi (1961). Quoted by T. Tamura, 1961.

Hora, S. L., and Pillay, T. V. R. (1962). *Proc. Indo-Pac. Fish Counc.*, 76 pp.

Hublou, W. F. (1963). *Progr. Fish. Cult.* **25**(4), 175–180.
Hublou, W. F., Wallis, J., McKee, T. B., Law, D. K., Sinnhuber, R. O., and Yu, T. C. (1959). *Oreg. Fish Comm. Res. Briefs* **7**(1), 28–56.
Huet, M. (1960). *In* "Traité de Pisciculture" (Ch. de Wyngaert, ed.). Bruxelles.
Huet, M. (1968). *FAO Fish. Rep.* **44**(4), 289–327.
Huet, M., and Timmermans, J. A. (1966). Trav. Ser. D., 38, Stat. Rech. Eaux Forêt Groenendaal-Hoeilaart, 68 pp.
Iversen, E. S. (1968). "Farming the Edge of the Sea." Fishing News, Books, Ltd., London.
Jähnichen, H. (1967). *Deut. Fisch. Ztg.* **14**(5), 147–151.
Jähnichen, H. (1968). *Deut. Fisch. Ztg.* **15**(4), 57–66.
Jäncarik, A. (1964). *Z. Fisch. Hilfswiss.* B**12**(8/9/10), 603–684.
Jensen, K. W. (1966). *EIFAC, 4th Session, Belgrade, Yugoslavia, May 9–14 1966,* 66/SC II-4.
Job, T. J. (1967). *FAO Fish. Rep.* **44**(2), 54–69.
Kawamoto, N. Y. (1957). *Progr. Fish. Cult.* **19**, 26–31.
Keiz, G. (1964). *Allg. Fischwirtschaftsztg.* **86**(1), 13–16.
Keiz, G. (1965). *Allg. Fischwirtschaftsztg.* **90**(18), 22–26.
Kelly, H. D. (1957). *Proc. Ann. Conf. S. E. Game Fish Comm.* **10**, 139–149.
Koch, W. (1960). "Fischzucht." Parey, Berlin and Hamburg.
Kocylowski, B. (1963). *Bull. Office Int. Epizoot.* **59**(1–2), 89–109.
Konradt, A. G. (1968). *FAO Fish. Rep.* **44**(4), 195–204.
Koops, H. (1965). *Arch. Fischereiwiss.* **16**(1), 33–38.
Koops, H. (1966a). *Arch. Fischereiwiss.* **17**(1), 36–44.
Koops, H. (1966b). *Arch. Fischereiwiss.* **17**(1), 44–50.
Koops, H. (1967). *FAO Fish. Rep.* **44**(3), 359–364.
Krajuchin (1955). Quoted by W. Schäperclaus, 1961, p. 408.
Kuronuma, K. (1968). *FAO Fish. Rep.* **44**(5), 123–142.
Lagler, K. R., Bardach, J. E., and Miller, R. R. (1962). "Ichthyology," Wiley, New York.
Lahser, C. W., Jr. (1967). *Progr. Fish. Cult.* **29**(1), 48–50.
Lauterbach, R. (1966). *Deut. Fisch. Ztg.* **13**, 276–280.
Lavrovsky, V. V. (1968). *FAO Fish. Rep.* **44**(5), 213–217.
Law, D. K., Sinnhuber, R. O., Yu, T. C., Hublou, W. F., and McKee, T. B. (1961). *Oreg. Fish Comm. Res. Briefs* **8**(1), 62–70.
Lawrence, J. M. (1968). *FAO Fish. Rep.* **44**(5), 76–91.
Leitritz, E. (1962). *Calif. Dep. Fish Game* (3rd Print.) *Fish Bull.* 107.
Lemasson, J., and Bard, J. (1968). *FAO Fish. Rep.* **44**(5), 182–195.
Lessent, P. (1967a). *FAO Fish. Rep.* **44**(3), 95–100.
Lessent, P. (1968b). *FAO Fish. Rep.* **44**(4), 148–159.
Liang, J. E. (1967). *FAO Fish. Rep.* **44**(3), 82–94.
Lieder, U., and Müller, W. (1965). *Deut. Fisch. Ztg.* **12**(6), 171–174.
Liepolt, R., and Weber, E. (1964). "Wasser und Abwasser," B. 1964 pp. 197–209.
Lin, S. Y. (1949). *UNESCO Conf., Warm Springs.* (Quoted by Hickling, 1962.)
Lin, S. Y., and Chen, T. P. (1967). *FAO Fish. Rep.* **44**(3), 210–225.
Ling, S. W. (1967). *FAO Fish. Rep.* **44**(3), 291–309.
Livojevic, Z. (1968). *FAO Fish. Rep.* **44**(4), 346–352.
Loosanoff, V. L., and Davis, H. C. (1963). *In* "Advances in Marine Biology" (F. S. Russel, ed.), Vol. I, pp. 2–130. Academic Press, New York.

Luhr, B. (1967). *Bund. Forsch. Fisch. Max-Planck-Inst., Hamburg,* pp. 47–58.

Maar, A., Mortimer, M. A. E., and Van Der Lingen, I. (1966). "Fish Culture in Central East Africa," FAO, Rome, 160 pp.

McKee, T. B., Wood, J. W., Sinnhuber, R. O., Law, D. K., and Yu, T. C. (1963). *Oreg. Fish Comm. Res. Briefs* **9**(1), 52–56.

McNeil, W. J. (1970). "Marine Aquiculture," 172 pp. Oregon State Univ. Press, Corvallis, Oregon.

Maloy, C. (1967). *FAO Fish. Rep.* **44**(2), 123–134.

Manea, G., and Mihai, M. (1957). Quoted by R. Liepolt and E. Weber, 1964.

Mann, H. (1935). *Z. Fisch. Hilfswiss.* **33**, 231–274.

Mann, H. (1958). *der Fischwirt* **8**(4), 106–107.

Mann, H. (1961). *In* "Fish as Food" (G. Borgstrom, ed.), Vol. I., pp. 77–102. Academic Press, New York.

Marine, D. (1914). *J. Exp. Med.* **19**, 79–88.

Marine, D., and Lenhart, C. H. (1910). *J. Exp. Med.* **12**, 311–337.

Marine, D., and Lenhart, C. H. (1911). *J. Exp. Med.* **13**, 445–475.

Matida, Y. (1967). *FAO Fish. Rep.* **44**(3), 54–63.

Mattheis, T. (1967). *Deut. Fisch. Ztg.* **14**(5), 151–157.

Meixner, R. (1966). *Arch. Fischereiwiss.* **17**(1), 1–4.

Menezes, R. S. (1968). *FAO Fish. Rep.* **44**(4), 81–85.

Merla, G. (1963). *Deut. Fisch. Ztg.* **10**(3), 77–82.

Meschkat, A. (1967). *FAO Fish. Rep.* **44**(2), 88–122.

Meske, C. (1966). *der Fischwirt* **12**, 303–316.

Meyer, F. P., Gray, D. L., Mathis, W. P., Martin, J. M., and Wells, B. R. (1967). *21st Ann. Conf. S. E. Ass. Game Fish Comm., New Orleans, Louisiana,* 9 pp.

Michler, G., and Schäperclaus, W. (1963). *Deut. Fisch. Ztg.* **10**(1), 21 pp.

Miles, C. (1967). *FAO Fish. Rep.* **44**(2), 34–44.

Mints, A. G., and Khairulina. (1968). *FAO Fish. Rep.* **44**(5), 233–243.

Morawa (1956). Quoted by W. Schäperclaus, 1961, pp. 504.

Morris, A. G. (1939). *Progr. Fish. Cult.* **44**, 23–27.

Müller, H. (1964). *Z. Fisch. Hilfswiss.* **12**(3/4/5), 295–306.

Müller, W., and Merla, G. (1964). *Deut. Fisch. Ztg.* **11**(9), 273–277.

Nagayama, F. (1967). Personal communication.

Nail, M. L. (1962). *Ann. Meet. South. Div. Amer. Fish. Soc. S. E. Ass. Game Fish Comm. Charleston, S. Carolina,* 20 pp.

Nehring (1957). Quoted by W. Schäperclaus, 1961, p. 60.

Nikolski, G. W. (1957). "Spezielle Fischkunde" (Transl. 2nd Ed., Moskwa, 1954), Berlin, VEB Deut. Verl. Wissensch.

Nomura, M., and Fuji, A. A. (1968). *FI/European Inland Fishery Advisory Commission,* 68/SC II–13, 23 pp.

Oren, O. H. (1963). *Minn. Agr., Dep. Fish. Haifa, Rep.* **1**, 30 pp..

Pasternak, K. (1958). *Biul. Zakl. Biol. Stawow* **7**, 27–60.

Pasternak, K. (1965). *Acta Hydrobiol* **7**(1), 1–26.

Pentalow, F. T. K. (1939). *J. Exp. Biol.* **16**, 446.

Penzes, B., and Tölg, J. (1966). *Z. Fisch. Hilfswiss.* **14**(1/2), 131–137.

Philipose, M. T. (1968). *FAO Fish. Rep.* **44**(5), 26–52.

Phillips, A. M., Jr. (1956). *Progr. Fish. Cult.* **18**(3), 113–118.

Phillips, A. M., Jr., and Balzer, G. C., Jr. (1957). *Progr. Fish. Cult.* **19**(4), 158–167.

Phillips, A. M., Jr., Brockway, D. R., Rodgers, E. O., Sullivan, M. W., Cook, B., and Chipman, J. R. (1946). *N. Y. Cons. Dep. Cortland Hatchery Rep.* **15**.

Phillips, A. M., Jr., Brockway, D. R., Rodgers, E. O., Robertson, R. L., Goodel, H., Thompson, J. A., and Willoughby, H. (1947). *N. Y. Cons. Dep. Cortland Hatchery Rep.* **16**.

Phillips, A. M., Jr., Lovelace, F. E., Brockway, D. R., Balzer, G. C., Ambrose, J. M. C., Mackinnon, D. F., French, T. E., and Camper, J. (1953). *N. Y. Cons. Dep. Cortland Hatchery Rep.* **22**.

Phillips, A. M., Jr., Lovelace, F. E., Podoliak, H. A., Brockway, D. R., Balzer, G. C., Chastain, T. R., Drake, G. A., Gernes, C. H., and Marchyshyn, M. J. (1956). *N. Y. Cons. Dep. Cortland Hatchery Rep.* **24**.

Phillips, A. M., Jr., Podoliak, H. A., Brockway, D. R., and Vaughn, R. R. (1957a). *N. Y. Cons. Dep. Cortland Hatchery Rep.* **26**.

Phillips, A. M., Jr., Brockway, D. R., Lovelace, F. E., and Podoliak, H. A. (1957b). *Progr. Fish. Cult.* **19**(1), 19–25.

Phillips, A. M., Jr., Podoliak, H. A., Dumas, R. E., and Thoesen, R. W. (1958). *N. Y. Cons. Dep. Cortland Hatchery Rep.* **27**.

Phillips, A. M., Jr., Podoliak, H. A., Poston, H. A., Livingston, D. L., Booke, H. E., Pyle, E. A., and Hammer, G. L. (1964). *N. Y. Cons. Dep. Cortland Hatchery Rep.* **32**.

Piacco, R. (1955). Cons. Génér. Pêches Méditerr., FAO, Rome, pp. 225–232.

Pickford, G. E., and Atz, J. W. (1957). *J. N. Y. Zool. Soc.*

Plehn, M. (1924). "Praktikum der Fischkrankheiten." Nägele, Stuttgart.

Popescu, C. P. (1965). Quoted by R. Liepolt and E. Weber, 1964.

Prather, E. E. (1951). *Trans. Amer. Fish. Soc.* **80**, 154–157.

Prather, E. E. (1957). *Proc. S. E. Ass. Game Fish Comm.* **10**, 249–253.

Prather, E. E. (1958). *Proc. 12th Ann. Conf. S. E. Ass. Game Fish Comm.* **12**, 176–178.

Prather, E. E. (1959). *13th Ann. Conf. S. E. Ass. Game Fish Comm.* **12**, 331–335.

Probst, E. (1937). *Allg. Fischwirtschaftsztg.* **40**, 315–404 (quoted by G. Keiz, 1965.)

Prokulevich, N. (1941). *Ryb. Khoz.* **1**, 1.

Prowse, G. A. (1966). *Progr. Fish. Cult.* **28**(2), 119–120.

Prowse, G. A. (1967). *FAO Fish. Rep.* **44**(3), 7–12.

Pruginin, J. (1962). *Bamidgeh* **14**(1), 16–18.

Pruginin, Y. (1968). *FAO Fish. Rep.* **44**(5), 18–25.

Pruginin, Y., and Shell, E. W. (1962). *Progr. Fish. Cult.* **24**(1), 37–40.

Pujin, V. (1967). *FAO Fish. Rep.* **44**(3), 124–131.

Pyle, E. A. (1965). *Fish. Res. Bull.* **28**, p. 44.

Rabanal, H. R. (1967). *FAO Fish. Rep.* **44**(3), 164–178.

Rabanal, H. R. (1968). *FAO Fish. Rep.* **44**(4), 274–288.

Rajbanshi, K. G. (1966). *der Fischwirt.* **4**, 99–102.

Ramachandran, V., and Ramaprabhu, T. (1968). *FAO Fish. Rep.* **44**(5), 92–108.

Ranade, S. S., and Kewalramani, H. G. (1967). *FAO Fish. Rep.* **44**(3), 349–358.

Rasmussen, C. J. (1966). *EIFAC, 4th Session, Belgrade, Yugoslavia,* May 9–14 66/SC II-9, 1966.

Rehbronn, E. (1966). *EIFAC, 4th Session, Belgrade, Yugoslavia,* May 9–14 1966, 66/SC II-10.

Reizer, C. (1967). *FAO Fish. Rep.* **44**(3), 326–348.

Report to the Fish Farmers. (1970). *Res. Rep. Bur. Sport. Fish. Wildl.* **83**, 124 pp.

Rohler-Metzner (1932). Quoted by W. Schäperclaus, 1961, pp. 504.

Rollefesen, G. (1939). *Rapp. Cons. Explor. Mer.* **109,** 133 (Quoted by Meixner, 1966.)

Sarig, S. (1955). *Bamidgeh* 7(3), 41–45.

Satomi, Y. (1967). *FAO Fish. Rep.* 44(3), 257–266.

Schäperclaus, W. (1933/1961). "Lehrbuch der Teichwirtschaft," 1st and 2nd. Ed. Parey, Berlin.

Schäperclaus, W. (1962–1963). *Z. Fisch. Hilfswiss.* 14(3/4), 265–300.

Schäperclaus, W. (1954). "Fischkrankheiten." Akad. Verl., Berlin.

Schäperclaus, W. (1963). *Deut. Fisch. Ztg.* **10,** 227–240.

Schäperclaus, W. (1964). *Deut. Fisch. Ztg.* **11,** 15–31.

Schäperclaus, W. (1966). *Z. Fisch. Hilfswiss.* 14(1/2), 71–100.

Scheer, D. (1964). *Z. Fisch. Hilfswiss.* 12(3/4/5), 327–339.

Scheer, D., and Jähnichen, H. (1967). *Deut. Fisch. Ztg.* 14(5), 129–141.

Schroder (1961). Quoted by T. Tamura, 1961.

Semakula, S. N., and Makoro, J. T. (1967). *FAO Fish. Rep.* 44(2), 161–164.

Shanks, W. E., Gahimer, G. D., and Halver, J. E. (1962). *Progr. Fish. Cult.* 24(2), 68–73.

Shelbourne, J. E. (1970). *In* "Marine Aquiculture" (W. J. McNeil, ed.), pp. 15–36. Oregon State Univ. Press, Corvallis, Oregon.

Shell, E. W. (1967). *FAO Fish. Rep.* 44(3), 310–325.

Shen, T. H. (1951). "Agricultural Resources of China." Cornell Univ. Press, Ithaca, New York.

Sidthimunka, A., and Choapaknam, B. (1968). *FAO Fish. Rep.* 44(5), 205–212.

Sidthimunka, A., Sanglert, J., and Pawapootanon, O. (1967). *FAO Fish. Rep.* 44(5), 196–205.

Sinderman, C. J. (1970). *In* "Marine Aquiculture" (W. J. McNeil, ed.), pp. 103–134. Oregon State Univ. Press, Corvallis, Oregon.

Sinnhuber, R. O., Law, D. K., Yu, T. C., McKee, T. B., Hublou, W. F., and Wood, J. W. (1961). *Oreg. Fish. Comm. Res. Brief* 8(1), 53–61.

Sneed, K. E. (1966). *Amer. Fish. U. S. Trout News* 11(4), 12–14.

Sneed, K. E., Dupree, H. K., and Green, O. L. (1961). *Proc. 15th Ann. Conf. S. E. Ass. Game Fish Comm. Atlanta, Ga.*, 6 pp.

Snieszko, S. F. (1960). *U. S. Fish Wildl. Serv. Spec. Sci. Rep. Fish* p. 341.

Snow, J. R. (1962). *Progr. Fish. Cult.* 24(3), 112–118.

Snow, J. R. (1966). *Bur. Sport Fish. Wildl., Marion, Ala. Annu. Rep.* 13 pp.

Solacroup, J. (1963). *Bull. Office Int. Epizoot.* 59(1–2), 51–58.

Soller, M., Shchori, Y., Moav, R., Wohlfarth, G., and Lahman, M. (1965). *Bamidgeh* 17(1), 16–23.

Sommani, E. (1953). *Boll. Pesca Piscicolt. Idrobiol.* 29(8), 16 pp.

Sreenivasan, A. (1967). *FAO Fish. Rep.* 44(3), 179–197.

Stangenberg, M. (1943). *Geol. Meere Binnengewass.* **6,** 1–64.

Steffens, W. (1958). "Der Karpfen." Ziemsen-Verl., Wittemberg.

Steffens, W. (1960). *Z. Fisch. Hilfswiss.* 9(3/4), 161–271.

Steffens, W. (1964a). *Z. Fisch. Hilfswiss.* 12(8/9/10), 725–800.

Steffens, W. (1964b). *Z. Fisch. Hilfswiss.* 12(1/2), 97–153.

Steffens, W. (1966). *Deut. Fisch. Ztg.* 13(10), 281–289.

Stevenson, J. H. (1965). *Progr. Fish. Cult.* 27(4), 203–206.

Stroganov, N. (1959). Quoted by H. Mann, 1961.

Surber, E. W. (1935). *Trans. Amer. Fish. Soc.* **65,** 300.

Susta (1961). Quoted by T. Tamura, 1961, p. 117.

Svetina, M. (1956). *FAO Cons. Gener. Pech. Mediterr. Istambul Doc. Tech.* **44.**

Swingle, H. S. (1957a). *Proc.* 10*th Ann. Conf. S. E. Ass. Game Fish Comm.* **10**, 156–160.
Swingle, H. S. (1957b). *Proc.* 10*th Ann. Meet. S. Weed Conf., August. Georgia,* pp. 11–17.
Swingle, H. S. (1957c). *Minutes Reg. Meet. Gulf States Mar. Fish. Comm.,* 4 pp.
Swingle, H. S. (1958). *Proc.* 11*th Ann. Conf. S. E. Game Fish Comm.,* 19 pp.
Swingle, H. S. (1960). *Trans. Amer. Fish. Soc.* **89**(2), 142–148.
Szakolczai, J., and Molnar, K. (1966). *Z. Fisch. Hilfswiss.* **14**(1/2), 139–152.
Tack, E. (1963). *Fischwirt.* **13**(2), 29–38.
Tal, S., and Hepher, B. (1967). *FAO Fish. Rep.* **44**(3), 285–290.
Tamura, T. (1961). *In* "Fish as Food" (G. Borgstorm, ed.), Vol. I., pp. 103–120.
Academic Press, New York.
Tanaka, T. (1929). "The Method of Tanaka's Intensive Carp Culture," 118 pp.
(In Japanese.)
Tang, Y. A. (1960). *Jap. J. Ichthyol.* **8**(1), 1–2.
Tang, Y. A. (1964). *Jap. J. Ichthyol.* **12**(1/2), 23–28.
Tang, Y. A., and Chen, S. H. (1967). *FAO Fish. Rep.* **44**(3), 198–209.
Tang, Y. A., and Hwang, T. L. (1967). *FAO Fish. Rep.* **44**(3), 365–372.
Therezein, Y. (1968). *FAO Fish. Rep.* **44**(4), 140–147.
Thompson, P. (1966). *Riv. Ital. Piscicolt. Ittiopat.* **1**(2). 49.
Tiemeier, O. W., Deyoe, C. W., and Wearden, S. (1967). *FAO Fish. Rep.* **44**(3), 388–399.
Timmermans, J. A. (1968). *FAO Fish. Rep.* **44**(5), 61–75.
Tokuhisa (1961). Quoted by T. Tamura, 1961.
Tonolli, V. (1955). *Proc. Tech. Pap. Gen. Fish. Counc. Mediterr. FAO, Rome, No. 3,*
151–159.
Toole, M. (1951). *Progr. Fish. Cult.* **13**, 3–10. (Quoted by H. S. Davis, 1961, pp. 161.)
Tubb, J. A. (1967). *FAO Fish. Rep.* **44**(2), 45–53.
Van Der Lingen, M. I. (1967). *FAO Fish. Rep.* **44**(3), 43–53.
Vinogradov, V. K. (1963). *Rybovod. Rybolov.* **6**, 9–13. (In Russian, quoted by A. G.
Konradt, 1966).
Vinogradov, V. K. (1968). *FAO Fish. Rep.* **44**(5), 227–232.
Vivier, P. (1958). *Bull. Fr. Piscicult.* **31**, 45–58.
Vouga, A. (1966). *La Piscicult. Fr.* **7**, 33–38.
Walter, G. (1931). Quoted by W. Schäperclaus, 1961.
Weiser, M., and Otte, E. (1964). *Wien. Tieraertzl. Monatsschr.* **51**(2), 98–106.
Wiesner, E. R. (1934). *Acta Hydrobiol.* **27**, 1.
Winberg, G. G. (1956/1960). *Trans. J. Fish. Res. Bd. Can.,* 194.
Wolny, P. (1967). *FAO Fish. Rep.* **44**(3), 64–81.
Woynarovich, E. (1960). *Z. Fisch. Hilfswiss.* **9**(1/2), 73–83.
Woynarovich, E. (1968). *FAO Fish. Rep.* **44**(5), 162–181.
Wrobel, S. (1967). *FAO Fish. Rep.* **44**(3), 153–163.
Wunder, W. (1935). *Fischer. Z. Neudamm* **38**, 618–619.
Wunder, W. (1949). "Fortschrittliche Karpfenteichwirtschaft." Stuttgart.
Wunder, W. (1965). *Der Fischwirt* **4**, 103.
Yashouv, A. (1956). *Bamidgeh* **8**(5), 79–87.
Yashouv, A. (1958). *Bamidgeh* **10**, 21–23. (Quoted by Y. Pruginin and E. W. Shell,
1962).
Yashouv, A. (1965). *Bamidgeh* **17**, 55–61.
Yashouv, A. (1966). *Bamidgeh* **18**(1), 3–13.
Yashouv, A. (1968). *FAO Fish. Rep.* **44**(4), 258–273.
Yashouv, A., and Ben-Shachar, A. (1967). *Bamidgeh* **19**(2–3), 50–66.
Zein-Eldin, Z. P. (1962). *U. S. Fish Wildl. Serv., Circ.* **183**, 65–67. (Quoted by R.
Meixner, 1966.)

# APPENDIX

Several typical diets for salmon, trout, and carp are listed. These formulas together with some constraints and specifications are included to serve as guides for type formula for fish diets. These formulas have been selected from many that are currently being fed to salmon, trout, carp, catfish, and several other important commercial species of fish, but these are not specific feed mixtures recommended by the authors or editor for any one specific type fish or environment. Dietary requirements for the different fish species vary with fish size, water temperature, water chemistry, fish activity, and final purpose of fish husbandry program. Therefore, it is recommended that appropriate rations be formulated from the more complete list of nutrients present in potential fish food ingredients included in the National Academy of Science, National Research Council bulletin, "Nutrient Requirements of Fish."

TABLE I

Typical Formula and Specifications for Moist
Salmon Pellets[a],[b]

| Ingredient | Percentage |
|---|---|
| Herring meal | 27 |
| Wheat middlings | 11.3 |
| Dried skim milk | 4 |
| Wheat germ meal | 5 |
| Corn distillers solubles | 5 |
| Brewer's yeast | 3 |
| Tuna viscera | 20 |
| Turbot | 10 |
| Beef liver | 10 |
| Crab solubles | 2 |
| Vitamin and antioxidant mix | 1 |
| Cod liver oil | 1 |
| Choline chloride | 0.7 |
|  | 100 |

[a] Detailed specifications for the processing of the Oregon Moist
Pellet are necessary for the manufacture of a satisfactory feed.
These are:

1. The dry meal ingredients should be passed through a 40-
mesh screen, 0.015 inch opening (0.42 mm).

2. The wet meat and fish ingredients should be ground
through a grinder plate with holes not larger than $5/64$ inch or
through a disintegrator providing that the particles are $5/64$
inch (2.0 mm) or smaller.

3. The wet ingredients are added to the dry ingredients in
a mixer and blended until homogenous and the desired degree
of plasticity necessary to extrude satisfactroy pellets is obtained.

4. The mix should not stand more than 4 hours before
pelleting.

5. Extruded pellets should be passed over a grader before
bagging to separate oversized particles and "fines." (23 kg).

6. Pellets should be packed in 50-pound (23 kg) net containers and within 1 hour placed in a freezer and quick frozen
at a temperature of at least −30°C.

7. Pellets may be transferred from the freezer to a storage
when they have reached a temperature of −9°C and will
not be received by a hatchery until they have reached a
temperature of −18°C.

[b] Frozen pellets, $1/8$ inch diameter," specified by Willard
National Fish Hatchery, Cook, Washington. (D. Cairns, personal
communication, 1965.)

TABLE II

SPECIAL HIGH PROTEIN DRY DIET FOR SALMON[a]

| | |
|---|---|
| Fish carcass meal (70% + protein, TBA-40) | 52.4% |
| Dried whey product (15% + protein) | 19.0% |
| Wheat germ meal (19% + protein, 8% lipid) | 19.0% |
| Wheat middlings | 6.6% |
| Soybean oil (fully refined + 0.01% BHA + BHT) | 2.0% |
| Vitamin mix | 1.0% |
|   Starter granule: 6% oil added | |
|   $\frac{2}{64}$-inch granule: 4% oil added | |

Abernathy vitamin mixture (95D):

| | |
|---|---|
| Thiamine mononitrate | 0.15 gm |
| Riboflavin | 0.69 gm |
| Pyridoxine hydrochloride | 0.30 gm |
| Niacin | 4.77 gm |
| D-Pantothenic acid | 0.68 gm |
| Inositol | 13.65 gm |
| Biotin | 0.03 gm |
| Folic acid | 0.10 gm |
| DL-$\alpha$-tocopherol acetate (10,500 IU) | 10.50 gm |
| Ascorbic acid | 25.50 gm |
| Wheat middlings | 397.23 gm |
| | 453.60 gm |

[a] Abernathy salmon diet 4a, 1971, courtesy of R. E. Burrows, personal communication, 1971.

TABLE III

TYPICAL FORMULA AND SPECIFICATIONS FOR TROUT PELLETS[a]

A. Formula SR-2[b]

| Ingredients | Percent (pounds) |
|---|---|
| 1. West coast Canadian or Alaskan herring meal, maximum fat 10.5%, minimum protein 70%, immediate past season. | 49.8 |
| (a) Lecithin (blended with fish meal). | 0.2 |
| 2. Corn gluten meal, 41% protein, 1% fat, 6% fiber. (Blend of 60% prime and 25% feed grade can be substituted.) | 5.0 |
| 3. Toasted, defatted soy flour, maximum fat 0.5%, minimum protein 50%. | 5.0 |
| 4. Steam dried brewer's yeast, minimum protein 40%, minimum fat 0.7%, maximum fiber 3.0%. | 4.0 |
| 5. A and D feeding oil, nonsynthetic, stabilized. | 6.0 |
| 6. Condensed fish solubles, dried on wheat middlings (equivalent to 100% condensed fish solubles). | 5.0 |
| 7. Soluble dried blood flour. | 2.0 |
| 8. Kelp meal. | 2.0 |
| 9. Wheat standard middlings. | 7.0 |
| 10. Dried skim milk. | 5.0 |
| 11. Unextracted liver meal. | 5.0 |
| 12. Vitamin premix 4-C. | 4.0 |

[a] National Fish Hatchery diet specifications for 1970–1971. Courtesy of Bureau Sport Fisheries and Wildlife, U.S. Dept.of Interior.

[b] Starter and No. 1 granule sizes only.

TABLE III   (Continued)

B. Vitamin Premix No. 4-C[a]

| Ingredients | Guaranteed potency per pound premix (mg) |
|---|---|
| Calcium D-pantothenate | 600.0 |
| Pyridoxine | 500.0 |
| Riboflavin | 1,750.0 |
| Niacin | 6,250.0 |
| Folic acid | 100.0 |
| Thiamine | 250.0 |
| Inositol | 6,250.0 |
| p-Amino benzoic acid | 250.0 |
| Biotin | 5.0 |
| Vitamin B$_{12}$ | 0.25 |
| Menadione sodium bisulfite | 125.0 |
| Vitamin E, from $\alpha$-tocopherol acetate ($d$ or $dl$) in beadlet form | 2.718.0 IU |
| Vitamin D$_3$ activity | 16.000.0 IU |
| Vitamin A activity (from Vitamin A palmitate in gelatin beadlets) | 75,000.0 USP |
| BHT antioxidant | 800.0 |
| Ferrous carbonate or ferrous oxide | 225.0 |
| Copper sulfate | 22.0 |
| Choline chloride[b] | 40.000.0 |
| Ascorbic acid[b] | 3.000.0 |

[a] One or more diet ingredients as carrier.

[b] These items will not be part of a packaged premix but shall be blended with one or more cereal ingredients and added to the mixture at the time of manufacture of feed.

TABLE III   (Continued)

C. Formula PR-2

| Ingredients | Percent (pounds) |
|---|---|
| 1. West coast Canadian or Alaskan herring meal, maximum fat 10.5%, minimum protein 70%, immediate past season. | 34.8 |
| (a) Lecithin (blended with fish meal). | 0.2 |
| 2. Corn gluten meal, 41% protein minimum, 1% fat, 6% maximum fiber. (Blend of 60% prime and 25% feed grade can be substituted.) | 18.0 |
| 3. Wheat standard middlings, 13% minimum protein, 9.5% maximum fiber. | 16.0 |
| 4. Soybean oil meal, solvent extracted, toasted, and dehulled, minimum protein 50%. | 10.0 |
| 5. Steam dried brew's yeast, minimum protein 40%, minimum fat 0.7%, maximum fiber 3.0%. | 4.0 |
| 6. Delactosed whey, minimum protein 16%, maximum sugar 50%. | 4.0 |
| 7. Dehydrated alfalfa meal, 17% protein, reground pellets. | 3.0 |
| 8. Trace mineralized salt. | 2.0 |
| 9. Vitamin Premix No. 14. | 4.0 |
| 10. A and D feeding oil, nonsynthetic, stabilized.[b] | 4.0 |

[a] No. 2 and larger granules and all pellet sizes.

[b] Contractor is authorized to use a lesser quantity of oil to control the total fat content of the finished product. Total calculated fat in the finished feed shall not be less than 7% or greater than 8%. Contractor will exercise such control by adjusting the amount of oil added during mixing operations.

TABLE III   (Continued)

D. Vitamin Premix No. 14

| Ingredients | Guaranteed potency per pound premix (mg) |
|---|---|
| Calcium D-pantothenate | 600.0 |
| Pyridoxine | 250.0 |
| Riboflavin | 1.750.0 |
| Niacin | 6.250.0 |
| Folic acid | 100.0 |
| Thiamine | 750.0 |
| Biotin | 5.0 |
| Vitamin B$_{12}$ | 0.25 |
| Menadione sodium bisulfite | 125.0 |
| BHT antioxidant | 250.0 |
| Vitamin E, from $\alpha$-tocopherol acetate (*d* or *dl*) in beadlet form | 675.0 IU |
| Vitamin D$_3$ activity | 8,000   IU |
| Vitamin A activity (from vitamin A palmitate in gelatin beadlets) | 40,000.0 USP |
| Choline chloride[b] | 12,500.0 |
| Ascorbic acid[b] | 3,000.0 |

[a] One or more diet ingredients as carrier.

[b] These items will not be part of a packaged premix but shall be blended with one or more cereal ingredients and added to the mixture at time of manufacture of feed.

TABLE IV

A. Pond Fish Formula[a,b,c]

| Ingredient | Amount per ton (pounds) |
|---|---|
| Fish meal, menhaden, minimum protein 60% | 240 |
|   or herring meal, Canadian or Alaskan, minimum protein 70% | 200 |
| Blood meal, minimum protein 80% | 100 |
| Feather meal, guaranteed digestibility 80% | 100 |
|   (Note: blood meal and feather meal may be used interchangeably) | |
| Soybean meal, solvent, toasted, dehulled, 50% protein | 400 |
| Dried distillers solubles or dried fermentation solubles | |
|   (a) If menhaden fish meal is used | 160 |
|   (b) If herring meal is used | 200 |
| Rice bran, 12% protein, 12% fat, 12% fiber or better | 700 |
| Rice mill dust or other organic dust passing a U.S. No. 80 mesh | 200 |
|   (Note: Wheat shorts, wheat middlings, cereal grains, vegetable oil or fish body oil and a pellet binder may be used for rice by-products) | |
| Dehydrated alfalfa, reground 17% protein pellets | 70 |
| Mineralized, iodized salt | 20 |
| Vitamin Premix (see additional specification for composition) | 10 |
| Total | 2000 |

[a] Guaranteed analysis of fish feed formula No. 1: Crude protein, more than 32.00%; animal protein, more than 15.00%; crude fiber, less than 12.00%; crude fat, more than 5.00%.

[b] Physical properties and processing specifications: Fry feed or fish starter meal—100% to pass through 595 $\mu$ opening or a U.S. No. 30 sieve; No. 2 pellet—$\frac{1}{8}$ inch diameter $\times$ $\frac{1}{8}$ inch long; No. 3 pellet—$\frac{1}{8}$ inch diameter $\times$ $\frac{1}{2}$–$\frac{3}{4}$ inch long; No. 4 pellet—$\frac{3}{16}$ inch diameter $\times$ $\frac{1}{4}$–$\frac{1}{2}$ inch long; No. 5 pellet—$\frac{1}{4}$ inch diameter $\times$ $\frac{1}{4}$–$\frac{1}{2}$ inch long.

Pelleted feed shall be retained on a $\frac{1}{8}$ inch mesh screen when immersed in water for 10 minutes, such that only 10% of the original weight is lost. This specification may be met by grinding the formula through a $\frac{1}{8}$ inch screen after mixing, using high pressure, high quality (dry) steam to condition soft feed before pelleting, cooling rapidly, and handling without undue breakage. No more than 4% fines should be present in bagged pellets.

[c] Courtesy, W. H. Hastings, personal communication, 1971.

TABLE IV (Continued)

### B. Pond Fish Vitamin Premix[d]

| (On finely ground soybean meal carrier) | Guaranteed potency per ton of feed |
|---|---|
| Vitamin A Activity (from palmitate in gelatin beadlets) | 5,000,000 IU |
| Vitamin $D_3$ Activity | 1.000.000 IU |
| $\alpha$-Tocopherol acetate (*d* or *dl* in beadlet form) | 20 gm |
| Menadione sodium bisulfite | 20 gm |
| Choline chloride | 1,000 gm |
| Niacin | 50 gm |
| Riboflavin | 10 gm |
| Pyridoxine | 5 gm |
| Thiamine | 5 gm |
| Calcium D-pantothenate | 20 gm |
| Biotin | 200 mg |
| Folic acid | 1,000 mg |
| Vitamin $B_{12}$ | 20 mg |
| BHT antioxidant | 10 gm |
| or Ethoxyquin | 136 gm |

[d] Premix on finely ground soybean meal carrier.

TABLE V

Essential Amino Acid (E. A. A.) Index and First Limiting
Amino Acid of Fish Feeds and Dietary Ingredients,
Based on Chinook Salmon Requirements[a]

| Diet and dietary ingredients | E. A. A. score | First limiting amino acid |
|---|---|---|
| Whole egg (Commercial) | 90.0 | Tryptophan |
| Salmon egg | 85.4 | Tryptophan |
| Casein | 81.7 | Arginine |
| Pasteurized salmon carcass | 77.7 | Tryptophan |
| Autolyzed salmon carcass | 77.6 | Tryptophan |
| Herring meal | 76.0 | Tryptophan |
| Commercial trout feed | 75.9 | Tryptophan |
| Commercial salmon feed | 75.5 | Tryptophan |
| Dried skim milk | 75.5 | Tryptophan |
| Drackett soybean protein | 75.2 | Methionine |
| Salmon viscera | 74.1 | Tryptophan |
| Commercial trout feed (imported) | 74.1 | Tryptophan |
| Experimental diet | 72.8 | Tryptophan |
| Fresh turbot | 71.9 | Tryptophan |
| Soybean meal | 71.0 | Methionine |
| Meat scraps | 70.8 | Tryptophan |
| Commercial trout feed | 68.9 | Tryptophan |
| Oregon moist pellet | 68.9 | Tryptophan |
| McNenny No. 31 feed | 68.3 | Tryptophan |
| Commercial trout feed | 67.5 | Tryptophan |
| Salmon meal | 67.4 | Isoleucine |
| Tuna viscera | 66.4 | Tryptophan |
| Sesame meal | 66.3 | Lysine |
| Brewer's yeast | 66.3 | Methionine |
| Wheat germ meal | 61.8 | Tryptophan |
| Distillers solubles | 59.3 | Tryptophan |
| Cottonseed meal | 59.1 | Tryptophan |
| Wheat middlings | 56.2 | Isoleucine |
| Shrimp meal | 50.4 | Tryptophan |
| Crab solubles | 43.8 | Tryptophan |

[a] Courtesy, W. E. Shanks, personal communication, 1964.

TABLE VI

<small>DIGESTION COEFFICIENTS OF FISH FEEDS</small>

| Ingredient | Test fish | Digestion coefficient | Reference |
|---|---|---|---|
| Crude protein | Carp | 69–92 | Knauthe (1898) |
| Raw beef heart | Brook trout | 95.7 | Morgulis (1918) |
| Cooked beef heart | Brook trout | 95.7 | Morgulis (1918) |
| Raw beef liver | Brook trout | 86.3 | Morgulis (1918) |
| Pork spleen | Brook trout | 92.5 | Tunison (1942) |
| Spleen : Skim milk-2 : 1 | Brook trout | 79.0 | Tunison (1942) |
| : Cottonseed meal-2 : 1 | Brook trout | 76.0 | Tunison (1942) |
| : Wheat middlings-1 : 1 | Brook trout | 76.0 | Tunison (1942) |
| Beef liver | Brook trout | 95.0 | Tunison (1942) |
| Pork spleen : Raw cornstarch-3 : 1 | Brook trout | 87.0 | Tunison (1942) |
| : Cooked cornstarch-3 : 1 | Brook trout | 80.0 | Tunison (1942) |
| : Sucrose-3 : 1 | Brook trout | 73.0 | Tunison (1942) |
| : Beef liver-1 : 1 | Brook trout | 96.0 | Tunison (1942) |
| Beef liver | Rainbow trout | 89.2–94 | Wood (1948) |
| Liver : spleen-1 : 1 | Rainbow trout | 86.3–91.7 | Wood (1948) |
| Pork spleen | Rainbow trout | 85.3–91.0 | Wood (1948) |
| Spleen : dry meal mixture-1 : 1 | Rainbow trout | 91.5–92.4 | Wood (1948) |
| Meal worms | Long ear sunfish | 94.0 | Gerking (1952) |
| Meal worms | Green sunfish | 92.3 | Wood (1952) |
| Potato starch : dry chlorella-4 : 1 | Goldfish | $25.9 \pm 8.7$ | Nose (1960)[a] |
| : dry chlorella-1 : 1 | Goldfish | $49.9 \pm 9.6$ | Nose (1960) |
| : dry chlorella-1 : 4 | Goldfish | 54.0–63.0 | Nose (1960) |
| Silk worm pupa 5 Wheat flour 4 Raw starch 1 | Goldfish | 80.0 | Nose (1960) |
| Silk worm pupa 5 Wheat flour 4 Raw starch 1 | Rainbow trout | 65–70 | Nose (1960) |
| Silk worm pupa | Rainbow trout | 80–88 | Nose (1960) |
| Red fish meal | Rainbow trout | 62–68 | Nose (1960) |
| Casein : gelatin-1 : 1 | Rainbow trout | 95.0 | Shanks (1964)[a] |
| Gelatin | Rainbow trout | 88.6 | Shanks (1964) |
| Casein | Rainbow trout | 79.0 | Shanks (1964) |
| Cottonseed meal No. 1 | Rainbow trout | 84.0 | Shanks (1964) |
| Cottonseed meal No. 2 | Rainbow trout | 72.7 | Shanks (1964) |
| Fish meal No. 1 | Rainbow trout | 72.7 | Shanks (1964) |
| Fish meal No. 2 | Rainbow trout | 75.6 | Shanks (1964) |
| Fish meal No. 3 | Rainbow trout | 93.0 | Shanks (1964) |

TABLE VI (Continued)

| Ingredient | Test fish | Digestion coefficient | Reference |
|---|---|---|---|
| Salmon meal | Rainbow trout | 80.0 | Shanks (1964) |
| Feather meal No. 1 | Rainbow trout | 52.4 | Shanks (1964) |
| Feather meal No. 2 | Rainbow trout | 70.5 | Shanks (1964) |
| Brewer's yeast | Rainbow trout | 80.5 | Shanks (1964)[a] |
| Skim milk | Rainbow trout | 94.7 | Shanks (1964) |
| Wheat middlings | Rainbow trout | 69.2 | Shanks (1964) |
| Whole soybeans | Channel catfish | 0 | Hastings (1965)[a] |
| Raw ground soybeans | Channel catfish | 31 | Hastings (1965) |
| Raw ground soybeans : rice hulls-4:1 | Channel catfish | 30 | Hastings (1965) |
| Soybean meal (50% protein) | Channel catfish | 56 | Hastings (1965) |
| Dehydrated alfalfa meal | Channel catfish | 12 | Hastings (1965) |
| Meat scraps (50% protein) | Channel catfish | 42 | Hastings (1965) |
| Fish meal (60% protein) | Channel catfish | 80 | Hastings (1965) |
| Dehydrated alfalfa meal | Goldfish | 66 | Hastings (1965) |

[a] Personal communications to authors, Chapter 7. References in Chapter 7.

TABLE VII

PROTEIN EFFICIENCY RATIO AND FEED CONVERSION FOR TROUT FED VARIABLE LEVELS OF NUTRIENTS[a]

| Protein (%) | Carbohydrate (%) | Fat (%) | Fiber (%) | P. E. R.[b] | Feed Conversion[c] |
|---|---|---|---|---|---|
| 25 | 10 | 15.6 | 35.4 | 0.80 | 0.061 |
| 25 | 22 | 10.0 | 29 | 1.17 | 0.140 |
| 25 | 34 | 4.4 | 22.6 | 0.09 | 0.108 |
| 32.5 | 10 | 15.6 | 35.4 | 1.25 | 0.113 |
| 32.5 | 22 | 10 | 29 | 1.57 | 0.142 |
| 32.5 | 34 | 4.4 | 22.6 | 1.78 | 0.161 |
| 40.0 | 10 | 15.6 | 35.4 | 1.49 | 0.153 |
| 40.0 | 22 | 10 | 29 | 1.60 | 0.164 |
| 40.0 | 34 | 4.4 | 22.6 | 1.42 | 0.145 |
| 47.5 | 10 | 15.6 | 35.4 | 1.62 | 0.182 |
| 47.5 | 22 | 10 | 29 | 1.59 | 0.178 |
| 47.5 | 34 | 4.4 | 22.6 | 1.58 | 0.155 |

[a] Courtesy, W. E. Shanks, personal communication, 1966.
[b] P. E. R. = grams gain/gram protein intake.
[c] Conversion = grams gain/calorie intake.

TABLE VIII

Analysis of Dried Powdered *Chlorella*[a]

| Nutrient | Percentage or concentration | |
|---|---|---|
| Protein (nitrogen $\times$ 6.25) | 55.5 | |
| Crude fat | 7.5 | |
| Carbohydrate (anthrone method) | 17.8 | |
| Ash | 8.25 | |
| Moisture | 7.00 | |
| Crude fiber | 3.1 | |
| Urea | 0.08 | |
| Chlorophyll | 2.68 | |
| Total calories | 5.2 | kcal/gm |
| Ascorbic acid | 14.6 | mg/100 gm |
| Pyridoxine | 3.0 | $\mu$g/gm |
| Thiamine | 7.7 | $\mu$g/gm |
| Pantothenic acid | 11.2 | $\mu$g/gm |
| $\beta$-Carotene | 50.2 | mg/100 gm |

[a] From Lubitz, 1963, reference in Chapter 7.
[b] Urea carried over from the growth medium.

TABLE IX

The Recommended Amount of Food to Feed Rainbow Trout per Day[a,b].

| Water temp. (F) | No. fish per pound | | | | | | | | | | |
|---|---|---|---|---|---|---|---|---|---|---|---|
| | -2542 (−1) | 2542-304[c] (1-2) | 304-88.3 (2-3) | 88.3-37.8 (3-4) | 37.8-19.7 (4-5) | 19.7-11.6 (5-6) | 11.6-7.35 (6-7) | 7.35-4.94 (7-8) | 4.94-3.47 (8-9) | 3.47-2.53 (9-10) | 2.53- (10-) |
| 36 | 5.3 | 4.4 | 3.5 | 2.6 | 2.0 | 1.6 | 1.3 | 1.1 | 1.0 | 0.9 | 0.8 |
| 37 | 5.5 | 4.6 | 3.7 | 2.8 | 2.1 | 1.7 | 1.4 | 1.2 | 1.0 | 0.9 | 0.8 |
| 38 | 5.8 | 4.8 | 3.9 | 2.9 | 2.2 | 1.7 | 1.4 | 1.2 | 1.1 | 1.0 | 0.9 |
| 39 | 6.0 | 5.0 | 4.0 | 3.0 | 2.3 | 1.8 | 1.5 | 1.3 | 1.1 | 1.0 | 0.9 |
| 40 | 6.3 | 5.2 | 4.2 | 3.1 | 2.4 | 1.9 | 1.6 | 1.4 | 1.2 | 1.0 | 1.0 |
| 41 | 6.6 | 5.5 | 4.4 | 3.3 | 2.5 | 2.0 | 1.7 | 1.4 | 1.2 | 1.1 | 1.0 |
| 42 | 6.9 | 5.7 | 4.6 | 3.5 | 2.6 | 2.1 | 1.7 | 1.5 | 1.3 | 1.1 | 1.0 |
| 43 | 7.2 | 6.0 | 4.8 | 3.6 | 2.7 | 2.2 | 1.8 | 1.5 | 1.4 | 1.2 | 1.1 |
| 44 | 7.5 | 6.2 | 5.0 | 3.8 | 2.8 | 2.3 | 1.9 | 1.6 | 1.4 | 1.3 | 1.1 |
| 45 | 7.9 | 6.5 | 5.3 | 4.0 | 3.0 | 2.4 | 2.0 | 1.7 | 1.5 | 1.3 | 1.2 |

| | | | | | | | | | | |
|---|---|---|---|---|---|---|---|---|---|---|
| 46 | 8.2 | 6.7 | 5.5 | 4.1 | 3.1 | 2.5 | 2.1 | 1.8 | 1.5 | 1.4 | 1.2 |
| 47 | 8.6 | 7.1 | 5.8 | 4.3 | 3.2 | 2.6 | 2.2 | 1.8 | 1.6 | 1.4 | 1.3 |
| 48 | 9.0 | 7.5 | 6.0 | 4.5 | 3.4 | 2.7 | 2.3 | 1.9 | 1.7 | 1.5 | 1.3 |
| 49 | 9.4 | 7.8 | 6.3 | 4.7 | 3.5 | 2.8 | 2.4 | 2.0 | 1.8 | 1.5 | 1.4 |
| 50 | 9.9 | 8.1 | 6.5 | 4.9 | 3.7 | 2.9 | 2.5 | 2.1 | 1.9 | 1.6 | 1.5 |
| 51 | 10.3 | 8.5 | 6.8 | 5.1 | 3.8 | 3.1 | 2.6 | 2.2 | 1.9 | 1.7 | 1.5 |
| 52 | 10.7 | 8.9 | 7.1 | 5.3 | 4.0 | 3.2 | 2.7 | 2.3 | 2.0 | 1.8 | 1.6 |
| 53 | 11.2 | 9.3 | 7.5 | 5.6 | 4.2 | 3.4 | 2.8 | 2.4 | 2.1 | 1.9 | 1.7 |
| 54 | 11.6 | 9.7 | 7.8 | 5.8 | 4.4 | 3.5 | 2.9 | 2.5 | 2.2 | 1.9 | 1.8 |
| 55 | 12.2 | 10.1 | 8.2 | 6.1 | 4.6 | 3.7 | 3.0 | 2.6 | 2.3 | 2.0 | 1.8 |
| 56 | 12.7 | 10.5 | 8.5 | 6.4 | 4.8 | 3.8 | 3.2 | 2.7 | 2.4 | 2.1 | 1.9 |
| 57 | 13.4 | 11.0 | 8.9 | 6.7 | 5.0 | 4.0 | 3.3 | 2.8 | 2.5 | 2.2 | 2.0 |
| 58 | 14.0 | 11.5 | 9.3 | 6.9 | 5.2 | 4.2 | 3.5 | 3.0 | 2.6 | 2.3 | 2.1 |
| 59 | 14.5 | 12.0 | 9.7 | 7.2 | 5.4 | 4.4 | 3.6 | 3.1 | 2.7 | 2.4 | 2.2 |
| 60 | 15.1 | 12.6 | 10.1 | 7.6 | 5.7 | 4.6 | 3.8 | 3.2 | 2.8 | 2.5 | 2.3 |

[a] Values in percentage of body weight for different size groups held in water of different temperatures.

[b] From Deuel *et al.* (1952) in references Chap. 1 and using moist diets.

[c] Values in parentheses indicate the approximate size in inches.

TABLE X

THE RECOMMENDED AMOUNT OF FOOD TO FEED BROOK TROUT PER DAY[a,b]

| Water temp. (F) | No. fish per pound | | | | | | | | | | |
|---|---|---|---|---|---|---|---|---|---|---|---|
| | $-2542$ $(-1)^c$ | $2542-$ $304$ $(1-2)$ | $304-$ $88.3$ $(2-3)$ | $88.3-$ $37.8$ $(3-4)$ | $37.8-$ $19.7$ $(4-5)$ | $19.7-$ $11.6$ $(5-6)$ | $11.6-$ $7.35$ $(6-7)$ | $7.35-$ $4.94$ $(7-8)$ | $4.94-$ $3.47$ $(8-9)$ | $3.47-$ $2.53$ $(9-10)$ | $2.53-$ $(10-)$ |
| 36 | 5.8 | 4.9 | 3.9 | 2.9 | 2.1 | 1.7 | 1.4 | 1.2 | 1.1 | 1.0 | 0.9 |
| 37 | 6.0 | 5.1 | 4.0 | 3.0 | 2.2 | 1.8 | 1.5 | 1.3 | 1.1 | 1.0 | 0.9 |
| 38 | 6.3 | 5.3 | 4.2 | 3.2 | 2.4 | 1.9 | 1.6 | 1.3 | 1.2 | 1.0 | 0.9 |
| 39 | 6.6 | 5.6 | 4.4 | 3.3 | 2.5 | 1.9 | 1.7 | 1.4 | 1.2 | 1.1 | 1.0 |
| 40 | 6.8 | 5.8 | 4.6 | 3.4 | 2.6 | 2.0 | 1.7 | 1.5 | 1.3 | 1.1 | 1.0 |
| 41 | 7.1 | 6.0 | 4.8 | 3.6 | 2.7 | 2.1 | 1.8 | 1.5 | 1.3 | 1.2 | 1.1 |
| 42 | 7.4 | 6.3 | 5.0 | 3.7 | 2.8 | 2.2 | 1.9 | 1.6 | 1.4 | 1.2 | 1.1 |
| 43 | 7.8 | 6.6 | 5.2 | 3.9 | 2.9 | 2.3 | 2.0 | 1.7 | 1.5 | 1.3 | 1.2 |
| 44 | 8.1 | 6.9 | 5.5 | 4.1 | 3.0 | 2.4 | 2.0 | 1.7 | 1.5 | 1.3 | 1.2 |
| 45 | 8.4 | 7.2 | 5.7 | 4.3 | 3.2 | 2.5 | 2.1 | 1.8 | 1.6 | 1.4 | 1.3 |

| | | | | | | | | | | |
|---|---|---|---|---|---|---|---|---|---|---|
| 46 | 8.8 | 7.5 | 6.0 | 4.4 | 3.3 | 2.6 | 2.2 | 1.9 | 1.7 | 1.5 | 1.3 |
| 47 | 9.2 | 7.8 | 6.2 | 4.6 | 3.5 | 2.7 | 2.3 | 2.0 | 1.7 | 1.5 | 1.4 |
| 48 | 9.6 | 8.2 | 6.5 | 4.9 | 3.6 | 2.9 | 2.4 | 2.1 | 1.8 | 1.6 | 1.4 |
| 49 | 10.0 | 8.5 | 6.8 | 5.1 | 3.8 | 3.0 | 2.5 | 2.1 | 1.9 | 1.7 | 1.5 |
| 50 | 10.5 | 8.9 | 7.1 | 5.3 | 3.9 | 3.1 | 2.6 | 2.2 | 2.0 | 1.8 | 1.6 |
| 51 | 11.0 | 9.3 | 7.4 | 5.5 | 4.1 | 3.2 | 2.7 | 2.3 | 2.0 | 1.8 | 1.6 |
| 52 | 11.4 | 9.7 | 7.7 | 5.8 | 4.2 | 3.4 | 2.8 | 2.4 | 2.1 | 1.9 | 1.7 |
| 53 | 11.8 | 10.1 | 8.0 | 6.0 | 4.4 | 3.5 | 3.0 | 2.5 | 2.2 | 2.0 | 1.8 |
| 54 | 12.3 | 10.5 | 8.4 | 6.3 | 4.6 | 3.7 | 3.1 | 2.6 | 2.3 | 2.1 | 1.8 |
| 55 | 12.9 | 10.9 | 8.7 | 6.5 | 4.8 | 3.8 | 3.2 | 2.7 | 2.4 | 2.1 | 1.9 |
| 56 | 13.5 | 11.4 | 9.1 | 6.8 | 5.0 | 4.0 | 3.4 | 2.9 | 2.5 | 2.2 | 2.0 |
| 57 | 14.1 | 11.9 | 9.5 | 7.1 | 5.2 | 4.2 | 3.5 | 3.0 | 2.6 | 2.3 | 2.1 |
| 58 | 14.7 | 12.5 | 9.9 | 7.4 | 5.5 | 4.4 | 3.7 | 3.1 | 2.7 | 2.4 | 2.2 |
| 59 | 15.3 | 13.0 | 10.3 | 7.7 | 5.7 | 4.6 | 3.8 | 3.2 | 2.8 | 2.5 | 2.3 |
| 60 | 16.0 | 13.6 | 10.8 | 8.1 | 6.0 | 4.8 | 4.0 | 3.4 | 3.0 | 2.6 | 2.4 |

[a] Values in percentage of body weight for different size groups held in different temperatures.
[b] From Deuel et al. (1952) in reference Chap. 1. and using moist diets.
[c] Values in parentheses indicate the approximate size in inches.

TABLE XI

THE RECOMMENDED AMOUNT OF FOOD TO FEED BROWN TROUT PER DAY[a,b,c]

| Water temp. (F) | No. fish per pound | | | | | | | | | | |
|---|---|---|---|---|---|---|---|---|---|---|---|
| | -2542 (-1)[d] | 2542-304 (1-2) | 304-88.3 (2-3) | 88.3-37.8 (3-4) | 37.8-19.7 (4-5) | 19.7-11.6 (5-6) | 11.6-7.35 (6-7) | 7.35-4.94 (7-8) | 4.94-3.47 (8-9) | 3.47-2.53 (9-10) | 2.53- (10-) |
| 36 | 4.9 | 4.1 | 3.3 | 2.4 | 1.8 | 1.5 | 1.2 | 1.0 | 0.9 | 0.8 | 0.7 |
| 37 | 5.0 | 4.2 | 3.4 | 2.5 | 1.9 | 1.5 | 1.3 | 1.1 | 1.0 | 0.9 | 0.8 |
| 38 | 5.2 | 4.4 | 3.5 | 2.6 | 2.0 | 1.6 | 1.3 | 1.1 | 1.0 | 0.9 | 0.8 |
| 39 | 5.4 | 4.5 | 3.7 | 2.7 | 2.0 | 1.6 | 1.4 | 1.2 | 1.0 | 0.9 | 0.8 |
| 40 | 5.6 | 4.7 | 3.8 | 2.8 | 2.1 | 1.7 | 1.4 | 1.2 | 1.1 | 1.0 | 0.9 |
| 41 | 5.8 | 4.9 | 3.9 | 2.9 | 2.2 | 1.8 | 1.5 | 1.3 | 1.1 | 1.0 | 0.9 |
| 42 | 6.0 | 5.1 | 4.1 | 3.0 | 2.3 | 1.8 | 1.5 | 1.3 | 1.1 | 1.0 | 0.9 |
| 43 | 6.3 | 5.3 | 4.2 | 3.2 | 2.4 | 1.9 | 1.6 | 1.4 | 1.2 | 1.1 | 1.0 |
| 44 | 6.5 | 5.5 | 4.4 | 3.3 | 2.5 | 2.0 | 1.6 | 1.4 | 1.2 | 1.1 | 1.0 |
| 45 | 6.8 | 5.7 | 4.6 | 3.4 | 2.5 | 2.0 | 1.7 | 1.5 | 1.3 | 1.1 | 1.0 |

| | | | | | | | | | | |
|---|---|---|---|---|---|---|---|---|---|---|
| 46 | 7.0 | 5.9 | 4.7 | 3.5 | 2.6 | 2.1 | 1.8 | 1.5 | 1.3 | 1.2 | 1.1 |
| 47 | 7.3 | 6.1 | 4.9 | 3.7 | 2.7 | 2.2 | 1.8 | 1.6 | 1.4 | 1.2 | 1.1 |
| 48 | 7.6 | 6.3 | 5.1 | 3.8 | 2.9 | 2.3 | 1.9 | 1.6 | 1.4 | 1.3 | 1.1 |
| 49 | 7.9 | 6.6 | 5.3 | 4.0 | 3.0 | 2.4 | 2.0 | 1.7 | 1.5 | 1.3 | 1.2 |
| 50 | 8.2 | 6.8 | 5.5 | 4.1 | 3.1 | 2.5 | 2.0 | 1.7 | 1.5 | 1.4 | 1.2 |
| 51 | 8.5 | 7.1 | 5.7 | 4.2 | 3.2 | 2.6 | 2.1 | 1.8 | 1.6 | 1.4 | 1.3 |
| 52 | 8.8 | 7.4 | 5.9 | 4.4 | 3.3 | 2.7 | 2.2 | 1.9 | 1.7 | 1.5 | 1.3 |
| 53 | 9.1 | 7.6 | 6.2 | 4.6 | 3.4 | 2.8 | 2.3 | 2.0 | 1.7 | 1.5 | 1.4 |
| 54 | 9.5 | 7.9 | 6.4 | 4.8 | 3.6 | 2.9 | 2.4 | 2.0 | 1.8 | 1.6 | 1.4 |
| 55 | 9.9 | 8.3 | 6.7 | 5.0 | 3.7 | 3.0 | 2.5 | 2.1 | 1.9 | 1.7 | 1.5 |
| 56 | 10.2 | 8.6 | 6.9 | 5.2 | 3.9 | 3.1 | 2.6 | 2.2 | 1.9 | 1.7 | 1.5 |
| 57 | 10.6 | 8.9 | 7.2 | 5.4 | 4.0 | 3.2 | 2.7 | 2.3 | 2.0 | 1.8 | 1.6 |
| 58 | 11.0 | 9.2 | 7.4 | 5.6 | 4.2 | 3.3 | 2.8 | 2.4 | 2.1 | 1.8 | 1.7 |
| 59 | 11.5 | 9.6 | 7.7 | 5.8 | 4.3 | 3.4 | 2.9 | 2.5 | 2.2 | 1.9 | 1.7 |
| 60 | 11.9 | 10.0 | 8.0 | 6.0 | 4.5 | 3.6 | 3.0 | 2.6 | 2.2 | 2.0 | 1.8 |

[a] Values in percentage of body weight for different size groups held in water of different temperatures.

[b] From Deuel *et al.*, (1952), Chapter 1 reference list.

[c] Using moist diets.

[d] Values in parentheses indicate approximate size in inches.

TABLE XII

FEEDING CHART FOR BLUEBACK SALMON EXPRESSED AS THE PERCENTAGE OF
THE BODY WEIGHT TO BE FED PER DAY[a,b]

| Average water temperature (°F) | Number of fish per pound | | | | | | |
|---|---|---|---|---|---|---|---|
| | Over 2500 | 2500–1400 | 1400–300 | 300–150 | 150–90 | 90–40 | 40–10 |
| 40 | 8.1 | 7.1 | 6.1 | 5.1 | 4.1 | 3.0 | 2.0 |
| 41 | 8.4 | 7.4 | 6.3 | 5.2 | 4.2 | 3.2 | 2.1 |
| 42 | 8.7 | 7.6 | 6.5 | 5.4 | 4.4 | 3.3 | 2.2 |
| 43 | 9.0 | 7.9 | 6.8 | 5.6 | 4.6 | 3.5 | 2.3 |
| 44 | 9.3 | 8.2 | 7.0 | 5.8 | 4.8 | 3.6 | 2.4 |
| 45 | 9.6 | 8.5 | 7.3 | 6.1 | 5.1 | 3.8 | 2.5 |
| 46 | 9.9 | 8.7 | 7.6 | 6.3 | 5.3 | 4.0 | 2.6 |
| 47 | 10.3 | 9.1 | 7.9 | 6.5 | 5.5 | 4.1 | 2.8 |
| 48 | 10.7 | 9.5 | 8.2 | 6.8 | 5.8 | 4.3 | 2.9 |
| 49 | 11.0 | 9.8 | 8.5 | 7.0 | 6.0 | 4.5 | 3.0 |
| 50 | 11.4 | 10.2 | 8.9 | 7.3 | 6.3 | 4.7 | 3.2 |
| 51 | 11.9 | 10.6 | 9.2 | 7.6 | 6.6 | 4.9 | 3.3 |
| 52 | 12.4 | 11.0 | 9.6 | 7.9 | 6.9 | 5.2 | 3.5 |
| 53 | 12.8 | 11.4 | 10.0 | 8.2 | 7.2 | 5.4 | 3.6 |
| 54 | 13.4 | 11.9 | 10.4 | 8.5 | 7.5 | 5.6 | 3.8 |
| 55 | 13.8 | 12.3 | 10.8 | 8.9 | 7.9 | 5.9 | 3.9 |
| 56 | 14.4 | 12.8 | 11.2 | 9.2 | 8.2 | 6.1 | 4.1 |
| 57 | 15.0 | 13.3 | 11.6 | 9.6 | 8.6 | 6.4 | 4.3 |
| 58 | 15.5 | 13.9 | 12.2 | 10.0 | 9.0 | 6.7 | 4.5 |
| 59 | 16.0 | 14.3 | 12.6 | 10.4 | 9.4 | 7.0 | 4.7 |
| 60 | 16.7 | 15.0 | 13.2 | 10.8 | 9.8 | 7.3 | 4.9 |
| 61 | 17.4 | 15.6 | 13.8 | 11.2 | 10.2 | 7.6 | 5.1 |
| 62 | 18.1 | 16.2 | 14.4 | 11.6 | 10.6 | 7.9 | 5.3 |

[a] From Burrows *et al.* (1951), Chapter 1 reference list.
[b] Using moist diets.

TABLE XIII

Some Typical Diets for Trout and Salmon[a]

| Mix weight | 1 (%) | 2 (%) | 3 (%) | 4 (%) | 5 (%) | 6 (%) | 7 (%) | 8 (%) | 9 (%) | 10 (%) |
|---|---|---|---|---|---|---|---|---|---|---|
| Fresh ingredients | | | | | | | | | | |
| Beef liver | 33.3 | 33.3 | 12.5 | 12.5 | 12.5 | 12.5 | 25 | 25 | — | 15 |
| Hog liver | 33.3 | 33.3 | — | — | — | — | — | — | — | — |
| Beef or pork spleen | — | 33.3 | 12.5 | 12.5 | 12.5 | 12.5 | 25 | 25 | — | 35 |
| Salmon viscera | 33.3 | — | — | — | — | — | — | — | — | — |
| Turbot | — | — | — | — | — | — | — | — | 20 | — |
| Tuna viscera | — | — | — | — | — | — | — | — | 20 | — |
| Dry ingredients | | | | | | | | | | |
| Cottonseed meal | — | — | 25 | 25 | 25 | — | 12 | 12 | 26.4 | 11 |
| Wheat middlings | — | — | — | — | — | — | 12 | 12 | — | 11 |
| Wheat germ meal | — | — | — | — | — | — | — | — | 3.6 | — |
| Crab solubles | — | — | — | — | — | — | — | — | 5.4 | — |
| Distillers solubles | — | — | — | — | — | — | — | 12 | 2.4 | 11 |
| Corn oil | — | — | — | — | — | — | — | — | 1.8 | — |
| Dried brewer's yeast | — | — | — | — | — | — | — | — | — | 2 |
| Cod liver oil | — | — | — | — | — | — | — | — | — | 2 |
| Fish meal | — | — | 25 | — | — | 25 | 12 | 12 | 18.0 | 11 |
| Salmon egg meal | — | — | — | 25 | — | 25 | — | — | — | — |
| Meat meal | — | — | — | — | 25 | — | — | — | — | — |
| Dried skim milk | — | — | 25 | 25 | 25 | 25 | 12 | — | — | — |
| Salt | 2 | 2 | — | — | — | — | 2 | 2 | — | 2 |
| Vitamins, etc. | — | — | — | — | — | — | — | — | 2.4 | — |

[a] Adapted from R. E. Burrows, personal communication, 1971, and W. E. Pearson, Unilever, Bedford, England, Tech. Rep., 1968.

TABLE XIV

SOME TYPICAL TROUT PELLET MIXTURES[a]

| Mix weight | 1 (%) | 2 (%) | 3 (%) | 4 (%) | 5 (%) | 6 (%) | 7 (%) | 8 (%) | 9 (%) | 10 (%) | 11 (%) | 12 (%) | 13 (%) | 14 (%) | 15 (%) | 16 (%) | 17 (%) | 18 (%) | 19 (%) | 20 (%) |
|---|---|---|---|---|---|---|---|---|---|---|---|---|---|---|---|---|---|---|---|---|
| Cottonseed meal | 15 | 23 | 20 | 15 | 15 | 5 |  | 16 | 15 | 24 | 23 | 23 | 19 | 24 | 10 | 10 |  |  |  |  |
| Soyabean meal |  |  |  |  |  |  | 10 |  |  |  |  |  | 19 |  |  |  | 5 | 8 | 5 | 4.5 |
| Groundnut meal | 20 | 24 | 20 | 22 | 19 | 7 | 20 | 16 | 25 | 24 | 24 | 24 |  | 24 | 10 |  | 5 | 8 | 5 | 14 |
| Wheat middlings |  |  |  |  |  |  |  |  |  |  |  |  |  |  |  |  |  |  |  |  |
| Wheat bran |  |  |  |  |  |  |  |  |  |  |  |  |  |  |  | 10 |  |  |  |  |
| Wheat pollards |  |  |  |  |  |  |  |  |  |  |  |  |  |  |  | 20 |  |  |  |  |
| Maize |  |  |  |  |  |  |  |  |  |  |  |  |  |  |  |  | 20 | 20 | 15 | 10 |
| Rye flour |  |  |  |  |  |  |  |  |  |  |  |  | 13 |  |  |  | 15 | 16 | 15 |  |
| Barley |  |  |  |  |  |  |  |  |  |  |  |  |  |  | 7 |  | 19.5 | 19.5 | 19.5 |  |
| Fish meal | 16 | 38 | 21 | 38 | 24 | 24 | 31 | 28 | 40 | 16 | 38 | 36 | 10 | 16 | 30 |  | 10 | 20 | 10 | 10 |
| Meat meal |  |  |  |  |  |  | 10 | 6 |  |  |  |  |  |  |  |  | 10 | 8 | 10 |  |
| Liver meal | 15 |  |  |  |  |  | 5 |  |  |  |  |  |  |  |  |  |  | 8 |  | 10 |
| Blood meal |  |  |  |  |  |  |  | 10 |  |  |  |  |  |  |  | 1.5 |  |  | 4 | 10 |
| Dried skim milk | 10 |  | 10 | 5.5 | 1.5 | 3.5 |  |  | 7 | 11 |  |  | 10 | 11 | 15 | 15 | 4 |  |  | 10 |
| Condensed fish solubles |  | 3 |  |  |  |  |  | 0.2 |  |  | 3 | 1.5 |  |  |  | 2 |  | 3 |  |  |
| Dried distillers solubles |  | 15 | 15 |  | 21 | 21 |  | 6 |  | 11 |  | 1.5 |  | 11 | 10 |  |  |  |  | 5 |
| Whey powder |  |  |  |  | 10 | 10 | 10 | 5 |  | 10 | 5 |  |  | 10 | 10 |  |  |  |  |  |
| Yeast | 10 | 5 | 8 | 10 | 10 | 10 | 5 | 5 | 10 | 10 | 5 | 7 | 15 |  |  |  | 4 | 3 | 4 |  |
| Alfalfa meal |  | 8 | 2 |  |  |  |  |  |  |  |  |  |  |  |  |  | 4 | 3 | 4 | 4 |
| Molasses |  |  | 2 |  |  |  |  |  |  |  |  |  |  |  |  |  |  |  |  | 6 |
| Wheat germ oil |  |  |  |  |  |  |  |  |  |  |  |  |  |  |  |  |  |  | 5 |  |
| Cod liver oil | 2 | 2 | 2 | 3 | 3 | 3 | 2 | 2 | 3 |  |  |  | 2 |  | 2 |  |  |  |  |  |
| Lard /animal fat |  |  |  |  |  |  |  |  |  |  |  |  | 6 |  | 2 |  |  |  |  |  |
| Seaweed meal |  |  |  |  |  |  |  | 3 |  |  |  |  |  |  |  |  |  |  |  | 4 |
| Beet pulp |  |  |  |  |  |  |  | 1.5 |  |  |  |  |  |  |  |  |  |  |  |  |
| Limestone flour |  |  |  |  |  |  |  |  |  |  |  |  |  |  |  | 2.5 | 1 | 1 | 1 |  |

| | | | | | | | | | | | |
|---|---|---|---|---|---|---|---|---|---|---|---|
| Bone meal | 2 | | 5 | 5 | 5 | | | + | | | 0.85 |
| Cellulose flour | 2 | | 5 | 5 | 5 | | | + | | 1 | 14 |
| Oat bran | | | | | 20 | | | | | | 7 |
| Shrimp meal | | | | | | | | | | | 0.5 |
| Salt | | | | | | 3.8 | 1 | | | | 3 |
| Gelatin | | | | | | | | 4 | 2 | | |
| Carboxymethyl cellulose | | | | | | | | | 2 | | |
| Vitamins | + | + | + | 1.5 | 1.5 | 0.2 | 0.5 | + | + | 1.5  1.5 | 5.15 |
| Dicalcium phosphate | | | | | | | | | + | 1 | 1 |
| Vitamins[b] | | | | | | | | | | | |
| Vitamin | | | | | | | | | | | |
| A (M.I.U.) | 1 | 1 | 1 | 1 | 1 | 0.002 | 0.005 | | | | 3.6 / 8 |
| D (M.I.U.) | 0.4 | 0.4 | 0.4 | | | 0.00036 | 0.0009 | | | | 0.36 / 1.6 |
| E (gm) | 1 | 1 | 150 | 150 | 150 | 60 | 150 | 150 | 150 | | 20 |
| K (gm) | 1 | 1 | 20 | 20 | 20 | | | 20 | 20 | | |
| B₁₂ (gm) | | | 0.04 | 0.04 | 0.04 | 0.02 | 0.05 | 0.04 | 0.04 | | |
| Thiamine (gm) | 20 | 20 | 20 | 20 | 20 | 90 | 225 | 20 | 20 | | 2 |
| Riboflavin (gm) | | | 66 | 66 | 66 | 90 | 225 | 66 | 66 | | 4.2 |
| Pantothenic acid (gm) | 32 | 32 | 110 | 110 | 110 | 50 | 125 | 110 | 110 | | 8 |
| Niacin (gm) | 90 | 90 | 300 | 300 | 300 | 100 | 250 | 300 | 300 | | 4 |
| Pyridoxine (gm) | 5.6 | 5.6 | 20 | 20 | 20 | 20 | 50 | 20 | 20 | | 2.3 |
| p-Aminobenzoic acid (gm) | | | 140 | 140 | 140 | | | 140 | 140 | | |
| Inositol (gm) | | | 500 | 500 | 500 | | | 500 | 500 | | |
| Choline (gm) | 100 | 100 | 3000 | 3000 | 3000 | 250 | 625 | 3000 | 3000 | | 145 |
| Folic acid (gm) | 5.6 | 5.6 | 5.6 | 5.6 | 5.6 | 3 | 7.5 | 5.6 | 5.6 | | |
| Biotin (gm) | 4 | 4 | 4 | 4 | 4 | 0.6 | 1.5 | 4 | 4 | | |
| Ascorbic acid (gm) | 340 | 340 | 340 | 340 | 340 | 200 | 500 | 340 | 340 | 1000 | 300 |

[a] Adapted from W. E. Pearson, Unilever, Bedford, Eng., Tech. Rep., 1968, and R. E. Burrows, personal communication, 1971.

[b] Vitamins added per ton of food.

# AUTHOR INDEX

Numbers in italics refer to the pages on which the complete references are listed.

# SUBJECT INDEX

## A

Acetylcholinesterase
  preparation and properties, 315–316
Activity
  oxygen requirements and, 379–380
Adenosinetriphosphatases
  activity and properties, 292-295
  myosin and, 293, 294–295
Adenosine triphosphate
  energy of, 3
Aflatoxins
  food contamination by, 221–226
  hepatoma from feeding, 221–226, 500–501
  toxic effects, 500–501
Agricultural chemical residues
  food contamination by, 216–217
Alcohol dehydrogenase
  properties of, 317
Aldolase
  preparation and properties of, 268
Algae
  nutritional value, 331
  toxic factors, 204–206
Alkaloids
  toxicity of, 194
Amino acid deficiencies
  syndromes of, 110–113, 135–137, 474–476
Amino acids, *see also* Essential amino acids
  degradation by muscle enzymes, 314–315
  plasma levels of, 139–141
  qualitative requirements, 106–113, 133–137
  quantitative requirements, 113–124
  test diets for, 106–109, 110–111, 113–117, 124
  toxicity of, 194–196

*p*–Aminobenzoic acid
  biological functions, 78
  chemistry, 77
Ammonia
  removal in reconditioning, 387
  toxic effects, 385, 498
Amylases
  post–mortem changes and, 274–275
Anemia
  causes of, 95–96
  cobalt deficiency and, 480–481
  copper deficiency and, 480–481
  diet development and, 31
  folic acid deficiency and, 57, 95, 419, 451
  iron deficiency and, 95, 480–481
  nutritional deficiencies and, 412
  thiamine deficiency and, 417
  visceral granuloma and, 428
  vitamin $B_{12}$ and, 62–63, 64–65, 95–96
  vitamin E deficiency and, 414–415
  vitamin K deficiency and, 415
Animal protein factors
  diets and, 93
Animals
  natural fish diets from, 331–333
Anserinase
  preparation and properties, 313–314
Antibiotics
  toxicity of, 515
Antibiotics in foods
  disease control by, 215–216
  growth promotion by, 214–215
  naturally occurring, 207–208
Antimycin A
  toxicity of, 515
Arginase
  activity in muscle, 315
Arginine
  dietary need, 112, 124
  protamine synthesis and, 310

Waxes
   composition of, 154
Weeds, *see* Vegetation
Weighing fish
   techniques for, 394–395
Weight of fish
   growth index as, 344–346

Winberg's method
   caloric requirement by, 17–19

## Z

Zinc
   deficiency of, 487
   toxic effect of, 499

B 7
C 8
D 9
E 0
F 1
G 2
H 3
I 4
J 5